ALTERNATIVE HEALTH ~e~ CARE ~e~

THE CANADIAN DIRECTORY

ALTERNATIVE HEALTH CARE

THE CANADIAN DIRECTORY

Bonni L. Harden, M.A., LL.B.
& Craig R. Harden, M.A.

Noble Ages Publishing Ltd.

Toronto

Published in 1997 by

Noble Ages Publishing Ltd.
1543 Bayview Ave, Unit 530
Toronto, Ontario
M4G 3B5

Canadian Cataloguing in Publication Data
Harden, Bonni L., 1956-
Alternative health care: the Canadian directory

ISBN 0-9681093-0-6

1. Alternative medicine - Canada - Directories
I. Harden, Craig R. (Craig Robert), 1958- II. Title.

R733.H37 1997   362.1'025'71   C96-900609-8

ISSN 1203-973X

 Publisher's Note
The pages in this book open easily and lie flat if you gently run your fingers down the spine, a result of the Otabind bookbinding process. Otabind combines advanced technology and a free-floating cover to achieve books that last longer and are bound to stay open.

 Cover and text pages are recyclable.

 All printing inks are manufactured from renewable vegetable base resources that replace traditional petroleum base inks. The text pages were printed on non-polluting coldset printing presses that do not emit hydrocarbons into the atmosphere.

Design: Steve Eby Production & Design

♾ Printed in Canada on acid-free paper.

Printed by Webcom Limited

✦ What Health Professionals are Saying about *Alternative Health Care: The Canadian Directory*

"...it's one of the best things to happen to complementary medicine in Canada. At last we have a frame of reference for information. It's like taking the blinders off the public - I don't know why it hasn't been done before. It's a splendid directory."

Keith Stelling, MA, MNIMH, Dip Phytotherapy, MCPP, Editor, *The Canadian Journal of Herbalism*

"...an accurate, straightforward and informative chapter on naturopathic medicine. They tell its history, benefits, training of naturopathic physicians, and how to find and evaluate a naturopathic doctor close to you. People interested in complementary medicine will find *Alternative Health Care: The Canadian Directory* a useful, definitive guide.

Paul Richard Saunders, PhD, ND, DHANP, Clinic Director, Canadian College of Naturopathic Medicine

"...this accurate information is extremely valuable not only to the practitioner but to the consumer. It's a case of buyer beware, and this is one of the few sources consumers can rely on to become educated and make informed decisions for their own health."

Crystal Hawk, Co-founder and Secretary of the Therapeutic Touch Network (Ontario); Life Member, Nurse Healers - Professional Associates Inc.

"It's important for the public to know how to find a practitioner who is competent and appropriate to their needs. The authors have been fair in telling...how to make an assessment of a practitioner's training, and explaining where practitioners are regulated and where they aren't. It's important to have a reference book like this. It's excellent."

Mary Sheila Watterson, Vancouver Traditional Acupuncture Clinic; Professional Member, College of Acupuncturists of B.C.

"It's vital information that has not been available before."

J. Mark Taylor, Master Herbalist, Editor, Citizens for Choice in Health Care *Self-Health* newsletter, Nova Scotia

"This book I highly recommend for all health care professionals, students of Chinese Medicine, and consumers to seek information for academic exchange, career and health services...valuable also as an introduction to the traditional Chinese medicine philosophical outlook...instructive, important, and innovative."

Cedric K.T. Cheung, President, Chinese Medicine and Acupuncture Association of Canada; Vice-President, World Federation of Acupuncture-Moxibustion Societies

"...your directory will prove to be a much needed educational tool for the public."

Marc Carpentier, President, Shiatsu Therapy Association (S.T.A.) of British Columbia

"A wonderful resource."

Susan James, past-President, Alberta Association of Midwives

"Extremely well researched and presented"

Ted Findlay, Doctor of Osteopathy, C.C.F.P., Calgary, Alberta

"...those who are seeking information regarding midwifery...whether as potential consumers, as students, or as applicants for registration will find this material an invaluable and comprehensive source of information."

Helen McDonald, RM, MHSc; Assistant Professor, McMaster University Midwifery Education Program

✦ Important Notice To Our Readers

This directory is intended as a resource guide only. It is the reader's responsibility to use this directory wisely in conjunction with the services of a family physician. If you have a medical problem, or are pregnant or nursing, it is recommended that you obtain appropriate medical advice before using any therapy. Many of the practices listed in this directory have not been investigated, approved by conventional medical authorities, or regulated by any level of government in Canada.

This directory is designed to help you check the qualifications of practitioners. Where credentials have been provided by associations, licensing or governing bodies, or practitioners, these have been noted. However, we have not verified these credentials, and urge you to use this directory to do so. The authors, publisher, and vendor make no representations or warranties regarding the qualifications of practitioners or teachers, or the quality of care or advice available from them. In jurisdictions where practitioners are required to be registered or licensed, the authors, publisher and vendor cannot and do not make representations or warranties that the practitioners listed are registered or licensed. The authors, publisher and vendor are not assuming any liability for claims or injury related to services of any practitioner or teacher, or for any claims or injury related to the use of any other information contained in this publication.

Inclusion of names of practitioners or others is not intended to imply an endorsement on their part of any material contained in this directory.

Laws are constantly changing. While every effort has been made to keep this publication current, it does not purport to comprise a complete account of the law in any jurisdiction. The reader should not rely on the authors or publisher for any professional advice. If legal advice is required, consult a lawyer qualified to practise in your jurisdiction.

NO FINANCIAL INTEREST

The authors and publisher of this directory have no financial interest or investment of any kind in any of the health practices mentioned in this book, nor in any health or health food products of any kind (apart from this or other Noble Ages Publishing Ltd. publications). Further, this publication contains no advertising, and no payment has been accepted for any listing.

IF WE MISSED YOUR PRACTITIONER OR ASSOCIATION...

We have collected the names, addresses and telephone numbers of practitioners, associations, governing bodies and educational institutes from across Canada. The information was gathered with the help of professional and consumer associations. While we have checked for accuracy, we cannot be responsible for errors or omissions. If we missed your association or a practitioner, or have made an error, please contact us so that we may include the information in our next edition. We also welcome your suggestions for future editions. You may reach us at:

Noble Ages Publishing Ltd.
1543 Bayview Avenue, Unit 530
Toronto, Ontario M4G 3B5

EXTRA COPIES OF *ALTERNATIVE HEALTH CARE: THE CANADIAN DIRECTORY*

For an extra copy of this directory, see the order form at the end of the book, or send a cheque or money order for $19.95 plus $3.50 for GST and shipping to the above address. Be sure to include your mailing address.

Contents

✦ Alternative Health Care: The Canadian Directory

Alternative Health Care: The Canadian Directory is your resource guide to finding qualified practitioners, educational programs, and information on the Canadian alternative health care scene.

There are many definitions of alternative, or complementary, health care. Common to most is the notion that the practitioner is treating the whole person, not the disease, and is stimulating the body's natural ability to heal itself. Symptoms of illness are considered signs of imbalance that must be corrected to help prevent disease and promote good health. Some practitioners prefer the title "Complementary Health Care," because they do not claim to replace conventional medical care, particularly in the case of injury or serious disease. If you have a medical problem, or are pregnant or nursing, consult with an appropriate physician before using any therapy.

In the pursuit of good health, we urge you to blend wisely the use of alternative health practices with conventional medicine. It is the philosophy of the authors that an informed public can make the best use of both worlds. We also believe that, ultimately, the conventional and alternative approaches to health care can co-exist in harmony and mutual respect, and it is in this spirit that this directory was compiled.

WHAT THIS DIRECTORY CAN DO FOR YOU

Alternative Health Care: The Canadian Directory is the first Canadian resource guide to help you:

✦ take responsibility for your health through a balanced approach, involving both alternative and conventional health care

✦ learn the basics of 20 types of alternative health care and how each may benefit you

✦ ask the right questions to find a qualified practitioner

✦ confirm that your practitioner has met educational standards and is registered with a governing body, where required by law

✦ contact professional associations for referrals and information

✦ check which practitioners are located near you, anywhere in Canada

✦ know which practitioners are covered by government health care funding in each province, and by how much

✦ choose a school or educational program if you are interested in pursuing a career in alternative health care

HOW TO USE THIS DIRECTORY

You will find chapters on the following 20 practices, arranged alphabetically:

Acupressure
Acupuncture
Alexander Technique
Aromatherapy
Ayurveda
Biofeedback
Chiropractic
Feldenkrais
Herbalism
Homeopathy

Massage Therapy
Midwifery
Naturopathic Medicine
Nutritional Counselling
Osteopathy
Reflexology
Rolfing
Shiatsu
Therapeutic Touch
Trager

In each chapter, you will find the following:

General Information

✦ The basics of the therapy or practice

✦ Its potential benefits

✦ Questions to ask to find a qualified practitioner

✦ A national overview of government regulation – which provinces have laws and governing bodies requiring practitioners to meet standards before practising

✦ A national overview of government or private health care coverage, where applicable

✦ National associations to contact for referrals

✦ Educational programs for those interested in pursuing a career

Information on Each Province

✦ Provincial Legislation Regulating Practitioners (where it exists)
  - procedures that your practitioner is permitted to perform under provincial law, where such laws exists
  - circumstances where the law requires you to consult with another medical professional

✦ Government Health Care Funding (where it exists)
  - details on the amount of coverage and eligibility in your province

✦ Provincial Governing Bodies (where they exist)
  - addresses and telephone numbers of governing bodies for you to call to check if your practitioner is registered and has therefore met professional standard
  - governing bodies are established under provincial legislation to regulate practitioners

✦ Provincial Associations (where they exist)
  - addresses and telephone numbers of provincial associations, which often provide referrals, or whose representatives may discuss with you the qualifications of your practitioner

✦ Listings of Practitioners
  - more than 8,000 practitioners, listed by therapy, province and city

Appendix - Government Regulation at a Glance

This table summarizes which practitioners are regulated across Canada. It lists the statutes regulating practitioners and their governing bodies, with page references.

Appendix - Other Organizations & Clinics

In this section you will find information on the following:

Chelation Therapy	Environmental Health
Consumer & Advocacy Organizations	Medical Doctors–Complementary Medical Associations
Dentistry - Alternative	Vancouver Hospital (Tzu Chi Institute)

✦ Major Developments in Alternative Health Care

The need for information on alternative health care has never been greater, in light of the growing use and acceptance of such therapies. Consider the following:

✦ 1 in 5 Canadian adults have visited alternative health care practitioners.
Source: Canada Health Monitor (1993) Price Waterhouse and Earl Berger, pp. 26-55.

✦ 1 in 3 American adults have used some form of non-conventional therapy.
Source: D.M. Eisenberg et al., "Unconventional Medicine in the United States: Prevalence, Costs and Patterns of Use" (1993) New England Journal of Medicine, pp. 246-252.

✦ In Canada, chiropractic is now one of the largest primary contact health professions after medicine (no referral necessary). The profession is regulated by legislation in all 10 provinces and the Yukon, with government health care funding available in Alberta, B.C., Manitoba, Ontario and Saskatchewan.
Sources: Chiropractic in Canada: A Directory of Facts (1992) Canadian Chiropractic Association, p.4, and Provincial Ministries of Health.

✦ Midwifery is now regulated or becoming regulated in Alberta, B.C., and Ontario, and several other provinces are considering similar legislation. A pilot project is under way in Québec.

✦ Demand for midwifery services in Ontario is more than double capacity. From January 1994 to March 1995, a total of 2,143 women gave birth with the help of midwives. However, over the same period, midwives were unavailable to an additional 2,336 pregnant women seeking their services.

Source: Lebel Midwifery Care, the Ontario government funding organization for midwifery services.

✦ Canada's first university bachelor's degree program in health sciences (midwifery) is now offered at Laurentian, McMaster and Ryerson Polytechnic Universities. The first class is graduating in 1996.

✦ Enrolment at the Canadian College of Naturopathic Medicine has increased by more than 100%, from 40 students in 1995/96 to 90 students in 1996/97.

Source: Paul Saunders, Clinic Director. This is the only Canadian college recognized by the profession's governing bodies in all four provinces that regulate naturopathic physicians (British Columbia, Manitoba, Ontario and Saskatchewan). The College moved to larger headquarters in 1996 to accommodate the demand.

✦ Acupuncture is now a regulated health profession in Alberta, Quebec, and, as of 1996, British Columbia.

✦ In 1996, Alberta passed legislation to protect physicians who practise alternative medicine from charges of unprofessional conduct. At the same time, physicians interested in complementary medicine are forming a new national complementary medical association, and a new provincial association in B.C.

Source: Bill 209, the Medical Profession Amendment Act. See appendix for association contacts.

✦ In 1996, Vancouver Hospital and Health Science Centre announced plans to open the Tzu Chi Institute for Complementary and Alternative Medicine, combining research, education and treatment.

Source: Vancouver Hospital. The Institute is a partnership between the Tzu Chi Buddhist Compassion Relief Foundation (a Taiwan organization founded in 1966) and Vancouver Hospital (a teaching and research hospital), with support from other hospitals and post-secondary educational institutions.

✦ In 1996, the Supreme Court of Nova Scotia described environmental medicine as a relatively new and developing discipline. The statement was made in deciding a Workers' Compensation Board case in favour of Ann Thompson, a nurse who turned to intravenous vitamin therapy to rid her body of toxins absorbed in her workplace. The court upheld an Appeal Board decision ordering WCB to pay for the treatment.

Source: Ann Thompson v. Workers' Compensation Board of Nova Scotia, Workers' Compensation Appeal Board and Camp Hill Medical Centre (1 February 1996), Halifax S.H. 121050 (N.S.S.C.).

✦ In 1993, Toronto East General and Orthopaedic Hospital became the first hospital in Canada to admit Therapeutic Touch into its policy and procedures manual, acknowledging that nurses could use the technique. Therapeutic Touch is a method of working with a person's energy flow as a means of inducing relaxation and speeding the healing process. It is rapidly becoming accepted at hospitals across Canada.

Source: Shirley Dalglish, Coordinator, Palliative Care, Toronto East General and Orthopaedic Hospital.

✦ Choice in Health Care & Protection of the Public

The flourishing of alternative health care brings with it many questions. What changes in law are required to keep pace with the changing landscape of medicine? How should public choice in health care be honoured, and what kind of balance should be struck with the need for public protection? The following outline of a few of the issues is offered with the hope that it may contribute to this public debate.

What is Meant by Government Regulation

In Canada, health care practitioners such as doctors, chiropractors, nurses and dentists are regulated by provincial governments. Regulation means that there is provincial legislation establishing a professional governing body. The governing body, usually called a "College," is given a duty in law to protect the public. Governing bodies are established to ensure that regulated practitioners meet specific standards before they practise, to investigate complaints, and to take disciplinary action against practitioners where appropriate.

There are two main types of regulation. The first is licensing, which gives the profession the exclusive right to provide a particular service to the public. This exclusive scope of practice makes it an offence for non-members to offer the service. The second type of regulation is 'protected title,' or a certification regime, which does not prohibit non-members from providing a service, but gives members of the profession the exclusive right to use a name or title. Both types of regimes are used by provincial governments in Canada.

Some Alternative Health Care Practitioners Now Regulated

As the demand for alternative health care has grown, several provincial governments have introduced legislation to regulate certain groups of practitioners. Highlights of such legislation appears in each chapter under the heading "Government Regulation." As well, the table at p. 240, *Government Regulation at a Glance*, shows which alternative health care practitioners are regulated in each province, with page references to the legislation and governing bodies.

Regulation is Costly

It is not necessarily appropriate that government regulation be introduced for each type of alternative health care. Establishment of a governing body is an expensive proposition for a profession, normally requiring full-time staff and the organization of several committees. A governing body includes members of the regulated profession, and there is normally a requirement for its governing council to include a percentage of public representatives. Not surprisingly, provincial governments usually have criteria to be met before a professional group may become regulated. For example, the Ontario government's criteria for regulation under the *Regulated Health Professions Act, 1991* includes the sufficiency of the membership size of the profession, willingness to contribute fees, and the existence of a substantial risk of physical, emotional or mental harm to patients or clients. Other criteria include the existence of a distinctive, systematic body of knowledge in assessing, treating or serving their patients or clients. Clearly, while some forms of alternative health care meet the criteria, others do not.

Other Ways of Protecting the Public

The Manitoba Law Reform Commission has recommended that regulation not be introduced unless its benefits (eg. public protection) outweigh its costs (Manitoba Law Reform Commission, *Regulating Professions and Occupations*, Winnipeg: Queen's Printer, October 1994). The report, which covers health care and other professions, notes that even where professions are regulated, there are no guarantees that a practitioner will perform in a competent and ethical manner. As well, the Commission notes that the power of self-government, especially in a licensing regime, can lead to restrictions on competition, reduced access to the service, higher prices, and increased power and financial benefits for members. These forms of regulation should therefore be considered only where harm results from incompetence or unethical behaviour. As well, the Commission recommends that at least one-third of the governing council of each self-governing body be public representatives rather than practitioners. Where government regulation is not appropriate, the Commission suggests that there may be other ways of protecting the public:

> Governments can engage in programs designed to educate the public or offer subsidies to organizations which provide information to consumers and thereby address a lack of consumer knowledge about the service; in some cases, this may prove even more effective than certification. In order to adequately address harm resulting from a lack of consumer information or from the effect of poor consumer choices on third parties, government could require that practitioners of a service obtain a minimum level of liability insurance, thereby enabling victims to recover for harm caused by practitioners. A government inspection system may also be effective in deterring practitioners from acting improperly (*Ibid.*, p.23).

Similarly, in its review of the regulation of alternative health care, the British Medical Association (BMA) distinguishes between those therapies which "at worst will have a placebo effect but may cause patients to delay seeking appropriate treatment, and those methods which in themselves could be harmful in the hands of an unskilled practitioner" (*Complementary Medicine: New Approaches to Good Practice*, Oxford: Oxford University Press, 1993, p.60). The BMA describes the professions of acupuncture, chiropractic, herbalism, homeopathy, and osteopathy as 'discrete, clinical disciplines', distinguishable from other forms of complementary therapy by having more established foundations of training, clinical practice and professional standards. These therapies are considered by the BMA as having "the potential for greatest use alongside orthodox medical care" (*Ibid.*, p.143). All these therapies use either physical manipulation or invasive techniques (eg. substances are swallowed, or needles are used). Clearly, the BMA notes, these are in another category from practitioners of, for example, Bach flower remedies, which carry virtually no risk of harm (see "Herbalism," p. 111). While the former types of practice require rigorous training, others, such as the flower remedies, may be adequately taught in shorter courses. Those therapies posing greater health risks to patients require legal regulation by statute to protect the public, according to the

BMA. "The present situation, in which anybody is free to practise, irrespective of their training or experience, is unacceptable" (*Ibid.*, p.143).

Whether one agrees with the Manitoba Law Reform Commission and the BMA on all points or not, the fact remains that different options may be appropriate for different types of alternative health care. The debate on regulation of these growing professions is an important one, in which the public should be involved.

Some Associations Fill the Gap

A degree of public protection is afforded by the growing number of associations of alternative health care practitioners. Some of these associations have set standards for professional membership, and require members to agree to a code of ethics. However, there are many types of associations. Not all of them screen their professional members and, of course, standards may vary among associations.

Medical Acts Restrict Alternative Health Care

The importance of public debate is underscored by the fact that restrictions currently exist on the practice of medicine in most provinces, with varying definitions of the 'practice of medicine.' These restrictions are contained in the legislation that regulates medical doctors, often entitled a 'Medical Act' or 'Medical Practitioners Act.' It is an offence under such legislation to practise medicine without a licence, with penalties that may include fines or jail. Where alternative health care practitioners are regulated, they are exempt from such provisions (eg. chiropractors are regulated in all provinces).

New Approaches in Ontario and Alberta

A different legislative approach has been taken in Ontario, where there is no general prohibition on the practice of medicine. Instead, a specific set of medical acts, such as diagnosis, are restricted to authorized practitioners under the *Regulated Health Professions Act, 1991*. There are 21 health professions regulated under the act, each with a defined scope of practice. This does not limit the rights of others, such as alternative practitioners, to provide similar services. However, such persons, as unregulated practitioners, may not treat or advise persons if it is reasonably forseeable that serious physical harm may result from the treatment or advice or from an omission from them. The maximum penalty for an offence is a $25,000 fine, a six-month prison term or both (section 40). Unauthorized practitioners may be prevented from performing controlled acts, but there is concern over the cumbersome enforcement procedures that must be followed.

Similarly, Alberta is in the process of drafting legislation that would restrict specific medical acts, based on the 1995 Final Report of the Health Workforce Rebalancing Committee, entitled *Principles and Recommendations for the Regulation of Health Professionals*. Among other recommendations, the report suggests that legislated exclusive scopes of practice be eliminated, and that public representation on each regulated profession's governing council be increased to 25 per cent.

These new approaches give the public the choice to use the services of alternative health care practitioners. Of course, it remains necessary to decide whether and how to regulate alternative health care practitioners. In the meantime, it is hoped that this directory will serve as a useful resource for making informed decisions.

Alberta has taken the lead in Canada on a related issue, the protection of medical doctors who practise alternative medicine (Bill 209, the *Medical Profession Amendment Act*). Roy Brassard, MLA, Olds-Didsbury, who sponsored the Bill, stated on April 24, 1996 that the change "makes it easier for Albertans to access as many health treatment options as possible" by removing the threat of charges of unprofessional conduct. Mr. Brassard added that patients are looking for new ways to heal themselves:

> They want to exhaust their less traumatic options before undergoing invasive surgeries, and many are turning to complementary medicines such as acupuncture, homeopathy, chiropractic or chelation therapy.

Similar laws to protect physicians and consumer choice are being sought in other provinces by Citizens for Choice groups (listed on p. 242). Alaska and several other U.S. states also have such legislation.

Alternative Health Care in Other Western Countries

There is a wide range of legislative approaches used to regulate alternative health care practitioners in other Western countries. At the open end of the spectrum, The Netherlands has passed a law lifting the current restrictions against the practice of alternative health care. *The Individual Health Care Professions Act* will come into effect in late 1997. The Netherlands Ministry of Health, in its 1994 fact sheet on the Act, states:

> The ban on the unauthorised practice of medicine had for quite some time been widely perceived as out of step with the times. Mature adults should as patients be able to consult the care provider they feel can

do them the most good, no matter whether he or she practices conventional or alternative medicine. Any restrictions on this freedom must be limited to those which are necessary in the interest of the patient.

According to Wyllï Storm, public affairs spokesperson with the Netherlands Ministry of Health, alternative health care practitioners will be free to practise whatever their level of education, with certain restrictions. For example, to prevent unacceptable health risks resulting from a lack of professional competence, certain procedures (eg. surgical procedures) are specifically excluded and may be performed only by authorized practitioners. In addition, there is a provision creating an offence to act in a way that is injurious to anyone's health. As well, there is a companion piece of legislation regarding quality of care, and a new system of protected titles which will also be introduced for certain professions, such as physicians and dentists.

In Denmark, alternative health care practitioners may practise legally, but their scope of practice may not include certain forms of treatment, such as surgery or the prescription of drugs. As well, there are provisions for sanctions against practitioners who harm patients.

In Britain, alternative health care practitioners are free to practise, whatever their level of training, provided that they do not imply they are a physician or other professional whose title is protected, and provided that they do not treat sexually transmitted diseases. The freedom to practise health care in Britain dates back to Henry VIII, who bowed to public pressure on the point, and persuaded Parliament to agree with him.

At the other end of the spectrum, in countries such as France, Belgium and Italy, and many states in the U.S., the practice of alternative health care by a person other than a physician is an offence, for which a person may be prosecuted. "The irony is that in these (European) countries the practice of non-conventional medicine is thriving and, for the most part, generally tolerated by the authorities." (*Complementary Medicine, supra,* p.26)

Complaints & Redress

Where practitioners are regulated, consumers may make complaints regarding competence or professional conduct to the profession's governing body, which has a duty to investigate and take appropriate disciplinary action (see *Government Regulation at a Glance,* at p.240). Disciplinary action may include cancellation or supension of a practitioner's registration or licence, and with it the right to practise. Where practitioners are not regulated, consumers may complain to a practitioner's association, but the process is usually less formal. While some associations register or 'certify' practitioners, the cancellation of such registration would not prohibit a practitioner from practising outside the association. However, such practitioners may be found in violation of provincial legislation, and subject to its penalty provisions.

Consumers are protected from incompetent or unskilled therapists, who cause injury in the course of professional services, through the common law of negligence. This provides for civil lawsuits based on a practitioner's duty of care. There are often limitation periods set out in the statutes that govern regulated practitioners, which means that the lawsuit for negligence or malpractice must be filed by the deadline. Increasingly, practitioners of alternative health care are obtaining professional liability or malpractice insurance. This is often a requirement for regulated practitioners. Some associations of unregulated practitioners also make this a requirement for membership. However, in the case of unregulated practitioners, it should be noted that such suits may be difficult to prove in the absence of clearly defined standards of practice for a profession.

Acupressure

WHAT IS ACUPRESSURE

Acupressure refers to the use of finger pressure on acupuncture points on the body to stimulate the flow of energy and promote the body's ability to heal itself. The theory is based on the same principles as acupuncture but no needles are used. Many practitioners of traditional Chinese medicine use acupressure, as part of tuina massage (see "Acupuncture and Traditional Chinese Medicine").

One of the best known forms of acupressure is Shiatsu. A separate chapter is devoted to this Oriental therapy (see "Shiatsu").

There are several other traditions and styles of acupressure. Jin Shin Jyutsu®, a physio-philosophy originating in Japan, was brought to the United States in the 1950s by Mary Burmeister. It is referred to as an art more than a technique and works with 26 'safety energy locks' to harmonize and restore energy flows. The practice can be applied as self-help or by a trained practitioner. Another form of acupressure is Jin Shin Do®, developed in 1972 by U.S. psychotherapist Iona Teeguarden as a combination of traditional Japanese acupressure, Chinese acupuncture theory, Taoist philosophy and Reichian segmental theory. Jin Shin Do combines deep finger pressure on acu-points with body focusing techniques to release tension.

BENEFITS OF ACUPRESSURE

Acupressure is said to restore balance in the body's energy and thereby release physical and emotional tension. Among the common problems it is said to alleviate are headaches, backaches, shoulder and neck tension, menstrual difficulties, respiratory congestion, insomnia, and joint problems. Its proponents generally do not describe it as a medical technique, and the Jin Shin Do Foundation suggests those with medical problems consult a physician.

QUESTIONS TO ASK

✦ Is your practitioner certified by an acupressure association? How many hours of training are required for certification? You may wish to contact the association to discuss the qualifications of your practitioner, or to obtain a referral (see below "Canadian & U.S. Associations & Schools" and "Acupressure in Your Province - Associations").

NOTE: Certified practitioners of the non-profit American Oriental Bodywork Therapy Association

(AOBTA) have a minimum of 500 hours of training. Beginner practitioners of Jin Shin Jyutsu and Jin Shin Do must have a minimum of 105 and 150 hours of training respectively.

✦ Is your practitioner trained in anatomy and physiology, CPR First Aid, and contra-indications (areas to avoid and health conditions requiring particular caution)?

✦ Is acupressure appropriate for you?

✦ How much experience does your practitioner have? Can your practitioner provide professional and client references?

NOTE: While reputable practitioners maintain client confidentiality, they may arrange for a client to contact you.

✦ Does your practitioner specialize in acupressure, or use it in combination with other alternative therapy techniques? What is your practitioner's background, and does it include training in these other techniques?

✦ How much will a session cost and how long will it last?

GOVERNMENT REGULATION

There is no government regulation of acupressure practitioners in Canada, meaning that there is no legislation establishing a governing body to register and discipline qualified practitioners. This also means that there are no minimum educational standards for those calling themselves acupressure practitioners. There are several organizations that certify practitioners after varying amounts of training, but this does not constitute registration or a licence such as that required in certain jurisdictions for practitioners such as massage therapists.

CANADIAN & U.S. ASSOCIATIONS & SCHOOLS

Listed here is a Canadian acupressure training insititute in B.C., and U.S. acupressure associations. The U.S. associations will provide referrals to their Canadian member practitioners, many of whom are also listed under each province below.

There is no national Canadian acupressure association. There is one provincial association, located in B.C. and a Maritime association in Nova Scotia, which includes Jin Shin Jyutsu practitioners among its members (see below, "Acupressure in Your Province").

Those wishing to become acupressure practitioners should further research the various forms of acupressure, and the standards required for certification by each organization. Some of the programs are listed below.

In choosing among schools, it is advisable to compare the qualifications of faculty (their education and professional experience), program content and length, admission requirements, and all fees and contract terms, including refund policies. It is also useful to speak with students and graduates of the various programs about their standards.

Most provinces have legislation requiring private vocational schools to meet certain minimum standards, often related to financial stability, for the protection of consumers. These requirements for registration vary from province to province, and certain alternative health care training programs are not always covered by such legislation. B.C. is the only province to require registration of all such training programs with its Private Post-Secondary Education Commission, a regulatory body established by the provincial government. Contact the Ministry of Education or Advanced Education in your province for more information on policies regarding registration of private vocational schools.

American Oriental Bodywork Therapy Association (AOBTA)
Ste 510, 1000 White Horse Rd
Voorhees, N.J. 08043
USA
Tel: 609-782-1616
Fax: 609-782-1653

This is a non-profit professional association of Oriental Bodywork Practitioners founded in 1990. Certified practitioners have completed a 500-hour program taught by an AOBTA certified instructor, or an equivalent program.

Certified instructors practising in Canada are identified by the notation "AOBTA" in the listings (see below, "Acupressure in Your Province"). The 500-hour program includes 160 hours of Oriental Bodywork Theory and Practice, 100 hours of Traditional Oriental Medical Theory, 70 hours of observed clinical practice, 100 hours of Western anatomy and physiology, and 70 hours of CPR First Aid, legal and ethical considerations, and the traditional Chinese therapeutic exercises of Tai Chi and Chi Gong.

Canadian Acupressure Institute
301-733 Johnson St
Victoria, B.C. V8W 3C7
Tel: 604-388-7475

The Institute, established in 1994, offers a 725-hour training program in Jin Shin Do acupressure. This program includes courses in counselling, anatomy, physiology, CPR First Aid, interpersonal skills, and the art of Jin Shin Do and its application to common conditions such as headaches, digestive disorders, and respiratory congestion. Minimum admission requirements include: Grade 12 graduation (mature students considered), minimum age of 18, fluency in written and spoken English, and good health. The Institute's Course Calendar contains details on the credentials of faculty members. The Institute also offers a 725-hour program in Shiatsu (see "Shiatsu - Education"). The Institute is registered, as required, with the Private Post-Secondary Education Commission of B.C.

High Touch®
4910 C Hannah Rd
Friday Harbor, Washington 98250
USA
Tel: 360-378-4901
Internet: http://www.hightouchnet.com

Practitioners certified by this organization have a minimum of about 40 hours of training. Certified instructors have about one additional week of training.

Jin Shin Do® Foundation
PO Box 1097
Felton, California 95018
USA
Tel: 408-338-9454
Fax: 408-338-3666

The Foundation was established as a trade organization in 1982 with the purpose of promoting the Jin Shin Do form of acupressure, and to serve as a network for authorized JSD teachers. Registered JSD practitioners have a minimum of 150 hours of training and 125 hours of experience. You will find registered practitioners in the listings below, identified by the notation 'JSD II'.

You may also find authorized teachers in the listings below, identified by the notation 'JSD I'. Teachers of the basic level must have an additional 100 hours of teacher training and at least 300 hours of experience. Authorized Jin Shin Do teachers are trademark licensees, who have agreed to maintain the organization's quality standards.

Jin Shin Jyutsu®, Inc.
8719 E. San Alberto
Scottsdale, Arizona 85258
USA
Tel: 602-998-9331
Fax: 602-998-9335

This organization will provide referrals to its qualified practitioners and instructors in Canada. Beginner practitioners receive a certificate after completing a minimum of about 105 hours of training. More in-depth training, called "Now Know Myself" is also available as an additional 35-hour course. Classes are held in Canada (eg. in 1996, classes were scheduled in Montréal and Halifax). Contact the organization for a schedule. There are eight instructors currently offering these classes. Instructors have a minimum of 10 years' experience as practitioners. The organization notes that the certificate does not constitute a licence such as that required by registered massage therapists in certain jurisdictions.

✦ Acupressure in Your Province

Each province is listed alphabetically below, with the following information:

Provincial Associations
✦ addresses and telephone numbers of the provincial acupressure associations in B.C. and Nova Scotia

Acupressure Practitioners
✦ names, addresses and telephone numbers of acupressure practitioners, listed alphabetically by city
✦ names listed below with the notation 'AOBTA' are instructors of the American Oriental Bodywork Association program in Canada. Practitioners listed below with the notation 'JSD II' are Jin Shin Do practitioners, with at least 150 hours of JSD training and 125 hours of experience. Practitioners with the notation 'JSD I' are Jin Shin Do teachers

✦ Alberta Acupressure Practitioners

NOTE: Check the credentials of your practitioner (see above, "Questions to Ask"). This publication cannot and does not certify or represent the qualifications of practitioners, or the quality of care available from them.

CALGARY

Oriental Medicine Acupuncture & Massage Clinic
433-131 9th Ave SW 403-233-0498

Yoon's Acupuncture & Acupressure Clinic
14-3510 27th St NE 403-291-2094

CAMROSE

Acupuncture Acupressure Clinic
6010 48th Ave 403-672-9360

EDMONTON

Vital Acupuncture Acupressure & Herbal Inc
10673-97th St 403-420-0775

✦ British Columbia

British Columbia Association

British Columbia Acupressure Therapists'
Association
718 Wallace Cr
Comox, B.C. V9M 3V8
Tel: 604-339-7830

This is a professional association of about 40 acupressure instructors, practitioners and students. The organization aims to increase public awareness and establish ethical standards. It also provides referrals.

✦ British Columbia Acupressure Practitioners

NOTE: Check the credentials of your practitioner (see above, "Questions to Ask"). This publication cannot and does not certify or represent the qualifications of practitioners, or the quality of care available from them.

BURNABY

Choi Acupressure
202-6916 Kingsway 604-540-9001

Lee's Acupressure
318-4501 North Rd 604-421-5050

CHEMAINUS

Nutt, Clare (JSD II)
9012 Chemainus Rd, RR 1 . .604-246-4270

COBBLE HILL

Richardson, Beryle (JSD II)
1265 Cherry Pt Rd 604-746-4086

COMOX

Thomas, Janella (JSD II)
718 Wallace Cr 604-339-7830

COOMBS

Bakstad, Doreen (JSD I)
2153 Pierpoint Rd 604-248-2793

COURTENAY

Holmes, Deborah (JSD II)
Site 288, C-23, RR 2 604-334-3428

Pankratx, Ron (JSD II)
By Appointment 604-338-1032

Petersen, Shelly (JSD II)
Site 686, C-1, RR 6 604-338-8898

CUMBERLAND

Purcell, Marie (JSD II)
By Appointment 604-336-8637

DUNCAN

Falch-Nielson, Beth (JSD II)
2424 Heather St 604-746-5640

GABRIOLA

Fahey, Gayle (JSD II)
S-52, C48, RR 1 604-247-7848

GIBSONS

Beynon, Ardith (JSD II)
S31, C7, RR 5 604-885-4503

HERIOT BAY

Richter, Leslie (JSD II)
By Appointment 604-284-2089

LADYSMITH

Hirt, Sharon (JSD I)
Athena Dr, RR 3 604-753-1509

Waller, Beverly (JSD II)
By Appointment 604-245-2364

LANTZVILLE

Therapeutic Bodywork
8-7234 Ware Rd 604-390-3267

LASQUETI ISLAND

Edwards, Dania (JSD II)
By Appointment 604-745-7501

Hildred, Rosalind (JSD II)
758-5810 Fletch Rd 604-333-8732

Jennings, Tolling (JSD I)
Main Rd 604-333-8868

Peterson, Tim (JSD II)
By Appointment 604-333-8834

Taylor, Noel (JSD I, AOBTA)
9 Teapot Rd 604-333-8878

MILL BAY

Diller, Jytte (JSD I)
3291 Kilipi Rd, RR 2 604-743-5835

MISSION

Lowinske, Bonni Ellen (JSD II)
10073 Wilkinson Ave, RR 3 .604-826-7947

NANAIMO

Hain, Maureen
304-235 Bastion St 604-753-4224

Moorman, Sharon
By Appointment 604-756-0130

PEACHLAND

Slater, Josephine (JSD II)
S. A-1, C-25, RR 1 604-979-6966

PORT HARDY

Nilsson, Carole (JSD II)
By Appointment 604-949-8303

PORT MACNEILL

Bartlett, Zaida (JSD II)
By Appointment 604-956-4354

POWELL RIVER

**Calvert, Fran (JSD II)/
Glen (JSD II)**
5918 Fraser St 604-483-4564

Dennie, Sharon (JSD II)
C-2 Southview Rd, RR 2 604-483-4924

Robson, Kathryn (JSD II)
Nassichuk Rd, RR 3 604-487-9956

Tanne, Miruh (JSD II)
4557 Harvie Ave 604-485-0077

QUALICUM BEACH

Jennings, Samantha (JSD I)
781 Canyon Crescent Rd 604-752-8968

QUATHIASKI COVE

Dempsey, Brenda (JSD II)
By Appointment 604-285-3054

Wolter, Marcia (JSD II)
By Appointment 604-285-3849

QUEEN CHARLOTTE CITY

Wiggins, Kathryn (JSD II)
By Appointment 604-559-4287

SAANICHTON

Greenwood, Gwen (JSD II)
8590 Alex Rd, RR 2 604-652-2876

SALT SPRING ISLAND

Free Spirit Acupressure
1125 North End Rd 604-537-5958

SIDNEY

Lines, Michael (JSD II)
1419 Hillgrove Rd, RR 3 604-656-6298

SOINTULA

Christensen, Mary Lee (JSD II) / Christensen, Peter (JSD II)
By Appointment 604-973-6003

VANCOUVER

Chinese Acupuncture, Acupressure & Qi Gong Clinic
402-1750 E 10th Ave 604-879-9686

Chinese Therapy & Acupressure Centre
3205 Fraser St 604-874-2186

Chinese Medicine & Health Care Centre
123 E Pender St 604-685-1871

Ki Kung Acupressure
2838 E. Hastings St. 604-255-6808

McMurty, Anne
By Appointment 604-734-8219

Michalik, Edward Acupuncture and Acupressure
320-1200 Burrard St 604-683-1505

Novotny, Patricia (JSD I)
1320 Dogwood Ave 604-261-2650

Thomas, Ted (AOBTA)
3261 Heather St 604-886-0701

VICTORIA

Borgerson, Bonnie (JSD I)
4470 Arsens Pl 604-477-3418

Bouchard, Nathalie (JSD II)
1819 Hillcrest Ave 604-472-8496

Canadian Acupressure Institute
301-733 Johnson St. 604-388-7475

DeBucy, Kathy (JSD I, AOBTA)
256 Linden Ave 604-388-7475

Caiden, R. (JSD I)
1122 Leonard St. 604-383-4162

Gilliand, Judith (JSD II)
1270 Johnson St, #102 604-384-4764

Harcos, Donna (JSD II)
170 Obed Ave 604-383-3367

Magee, Milt (JSD II)
45 Boyd St, #310 604-388-6697

Mol, Corinne (JSD II)
30 Pilot St 604-920-3704

Nielsen, Eileen (JSD II)
1161 Bute St 604-744-2174

Porter, Arnold (JSD I, AOBTA)
1270 Balmoral Rd 604-388-7475/360-0637

Rouleau, Paul (JSD II)
2526 Government St, #103 .604-383-2404

Walton, Merilee (JSD II)
#1-1140 Fort St 604-386-1311

Wiese, Maxine (JSD II)
4740 Eales Rd, RR 2 604-474-2350

WEST VANCOUVER

L'Estrange, Sarah (JSD I)
1836 Fulton Ave 604-925-4607

 # Manitoba Acupressure Practitioners

NOTE: Check the credentials of your practitioner (see above, "Questions to Ask"). This publication cannot and does not certify or represent the qualifications of practitioners, or the quality of care available from them.

WINNIPEG

McLellan, Steven (JSD II)
715 Cavalier Dr 204-896-0685

Newfoundland Acupressure Practitioners

NOTE: Check the credentials of your practitioner (see above, "Questions to Ask"). This publication cannot and does not certify or represent the qualifications of practitioners, or the quality of care available from them.

ST JOHN'S

The Acupressure Centre
98 Bonaventure Ave 709-738-4647

Nova Scotia

Nova Scotia Association

Massage Therapists & Bodyworker's Alliance of the Maritimes
2424 Herenow St
Halifax, NS B6T 3E5
Tel: 902-422-2222

This alliance includes practioners of Jin Shin Jyutsu.

 # Nova Scotia Acupressure Practitioners

NOTE: Check the credentials of your practitioner (see above, "Questions to Ask"). This publication cannot and does not certify or represent the qualifications of practitioners, or the quality of care available from them.

BEDFORD

Samon-Swiatoniowski, Bogda
By Appointment 902-835-4691

BERWICK

Connaughton, Jacqueline
By Appointment 902-538-8733

DARTMOUTH

Sutherland, Brian
By Appointment 902-462-4157

HALIFAX

Briggs, Victoria
By Appointment 902-492-4782

Conner, Loomis
By Appointment 902-422-3711

Forbes, Julie
By Appointment 902-492-8696

Fuller, Anne, R.N.
By Appointment 902-492-1933

Holden, Jane, R.N.
By Appointment 902-455-7402

KENTVILLE

Lockhart, Beverly
By Appointment 902-679-6451

Margeson, Cathy
By Appointment 902-678-6917

 # Ontario Acupressure Practitioners

NOTE: Check the credentials of your practitioner (see above, "Questions to Ask"). This publication cannot and does not certify or represent the qualifications of practitioners, or the quality of care available from them.

CUMBERLAND

Asselin, Jovette (JSD II)
1049 Moffatt Dr 613-746-4621

MISSISSAUGA

Erin Centre Physio & Acupressure Clinic
2555 Erin Centre Blvd 905-567-3630

NIAGARA FALLS

Acupuncture Acupressure & Chinese Herbal Clinic
6150 Valley Way 905-371-0775

OTTAWA

Nordin, Allaine
185 Augusta St 613-789-5912

TORONTO

Bendahan, Dora (JSD II)
422 College St 416-322-4138

Natural Health Centre
2221 Yonge St, Ste L11 416-932-9418

✦ Québec Acupressure Practitioners

NOTE: Check the credentials of your practitioner (see above, "Questions to Ask"). This publication cannot and does not certify or represent the qualifications of practitioners, or the quality of care available from them.

ANJOU

Chicoine, Louise (JSD II)
6945 David d'Angers 514-352-8027

BEACONSFIELD

Kralik, Theresa (JSD II)
194 Sherbrooke St 514-487-6522

BELOEIL

Michaud, Johanne (JSD II)
254, rue Lechasseur #5 514-446-2258

DOLLARD-DES-ORMEAUX

Macramallah, Marigo (JSD II)
315 W Acres Cr 514-686-6318

ESTCOURT

Laurence, Monique (JSD II)
1327 ch Guerette 418-859-3280

LASALLE

Pregent, Marie (JSD II)
2343 Gervais 514-364-0503

LEVIS

Faguy, Suzanne (JSD II)
8 A, rue St.-Felix 418-835-5969

LONGUEUIL

Millette, Ako (JSD II)
505, rue Alexandre #302 . . .514-679-2630

MATANE

Gagnon, Berangere (JSD II)
1578, Grand-Detour RR 2 . . .418-566-2081

MONT-JOLI

Sirois, Claudette (JSD II)
1164, av Sanatorium 418-775-5569

MONT SAINT-GREGOIRE

Rheaume, Lorraine (JSD II)
24 des Pins 514-347-6299

MONTREAL

Berlin, Sylvia (JSD I)
4432, rue De Bordeaux 514-597-0965

Dion, Andre (JSD II)
6060 Boul Gouin Est 514-327-8496

Doucet, Luc (JSD I)
4432, rue De Bordeaux 514-597-0965

Fortin, Lise (JSD II)
4391 Beaconsfield 514-484-6691

Funk, Gisele (JSD II)
2160, av Marcil 514-485-7871

Goris, Helena (JSD I)
6100, av Monkland 514-484-5423

La Belle, Marie Sylvie (JSD II)
1391, boul De Maisonneuve E.514-524-6097

Lavallée, Christiane (JSD II)
2495, boul Gouin Est 514-381-3354

Sevigny, Odile (JSD II)
3076, boul Edouard-Montpetit #1 514-738-9127

Vezina, Martine (JSD II)
1876, av William-David 514-257-7572

OUTREMONT

Lindeman, Yehudi (JSD II)
5354, rue Hutchison 514-277-8970

Ulrich, Freitag (JSD I)
5, rue Vincent D'Indy #101 .514-344-9570

QUEBEC

Levesque, Suzanne (JSD II)
137, rue Champlain Matane .418-566-2855

REPENTIGNY

Dube, Monique (JSD II)
892, rue Gatineau 514-581-1180

RIVIERE-DU-LOUP

Bouchard, Nancy (JSD II)
42, rue Sainte-Anne 418-862-2830

Savoie, Denise (JSD II)
31, rue Joly 418-862-4673

SAINT-HUBERT

Grimard, Claude (JSD II)
1585, rue Godin 514-676-0409

SAINTE-FOY

Voyer, Jacqueline (JSD II)
3320, rue de la Monnerie, #5 418-650-5411

ST-BASILE LE GRAND

Hebert, Luce (JSD II)
35, rue Savaria #6 514-441-2954

ST-VALERIEN

Bourdages, Louis (JSD I)
168, 4E Rang Est 418-736-4610

ST-ZENON

Paradis, Marie (JSD II)
481, Chemin du Lac
Saint-Louis Est 514-884-5953

TROIS-RIVIERES

Wheeler, Barbara (JSD I)
4965, boul des Cheneaux . . .819-691-3550

✦ Saskatchewan Acupressure Practitioners

NOTE: Check the credentials of your practitioner (see above, "Questions to Ask"). This publication cannot and does not certify or represent the qualifications of practitioners, or the quality of care available from them.

FORT SASKATCHEWAN

Acupuncture Acupressure Clinic
10101 100th Ave 403-998-2172

SASKATOON

Dixon, Janice (JSD II)
1034-5th St E 306-343-0696

Acupuncture
and Traditional Chinese Medicine

WHAT IS ACUPUNCTURE

Acupuncture originated several thousand years ago in China as part of a body of medicine which includes the use of herbs, tuina (Chinese massage), exercise and diet. Acupuncture itself refers to the insertion of very fine needles at different points on the body to stimulate the flow of energy, or Qi (or Chi, pronounced 'chee'). Acupuncture points are located along a network of 14 main meridian lines, or channels, through which the body's energy flows. Acupuncture is said to stimulate the body's natural healing abilities, relieve pain and restore internal regulation systems. Patients experience different sensations, but most feel minimal discomfort.

Two Approaches to Acupuncture

There are two main approaches to the practice of acupuncture: 'Traditional Chinese Medicine' and 'Medical Acupuncture.' Those whose primary practice is acupuncture often use it in conjunction with traditional Chinese medicine. Medical acupuncture usually refers to the practice of acupuncture as an adjunct, or additional service, offered by health professionals such as medical doctors, physiotherapists, and chiropractors. As well, acupuncture is practised by some naturopathic doctors.

1. Traditional Chinese Medicine

Traditional Chinese medicine is a holistic system of health care that aims to bring the body, mind and spirit into balance. The body is treated as an energetic and vibrating whole. It is also seen as a microcosm of the natural universe, governed by alternating forces of Yin (negative) and Yang (positive) and the five elements of fire, earth, metal, water and wood. Each of the elements represents different vibratory rates or stages in a cycle. Included in the framework is the Zang-Fu concept of the body's organs. Zang refers to the solid organs, such as the heart, and Fu refers to the hollow organs, such as the stomach. Also included in this framework are the Eight Principles (hot/cold; excess/deficiency; exterior/interior; Yin/Yang; pulse diagnosis; inspection/palpitation; auscultation/olfaction and inquiry).

In explaining the concept of acupuncture to Western minds, authors Peter Firebrace & Sandra Hill note in *A Guide to Acupuncture* (London: Constable and Company Ltd., 1994, p.69) that the close relationship between matter and energy, at the heart of traditional Chinese medicine, is reflected in Albert Einstein's Relativity Theory: "Matter is just vibrating energy, according to Einstein's formula ($E = mc^2$); by affecting that vibrating energy at key points (acupuncture points) you will affect matter."

Traditional Chinese medicine is said to bring the body's forces into balance through acupuncture, as well as through the following major disciples, often taught in three-year to five-year full-time programs:

Moxibustion

This is a traditional Chinese medical technique involving the application of heat, generated by burning dry moxa leaves (Artemisia Vulgaris) on or near an acupuncture point on the body. The purpose of this is to initiate the healing process. More than one method may be used. For example, moxa leaves may be mixed with certain other herbs before burning.

Chinese Herbology

In Chinese herbology, herbs are classified according to the five elements and their corresponding tastes of bitterness, sweetness, acridity (pungency), saltiness and sourness. Each category carries specific sets of healing properties. A prescription is often given for herbs to be purchased from a Chinese herb shop and brewed into a tea. Herbs are also prescribed in other forms, including powders, pills or salves.

Tuina

This refers to body massage of acupuncture points (acupressure) and manipulation, which can promote blood circulation and influence internal organs for the purpose of healing.

Nutritional Counselling

Nutritional advice relates less to calorie counts than to the balancing and energizing qualities of certain foods. Foods are categorized into the fives tastes, each nourishing a different organic system.

Therapeutic Exercises - Qi Gong and Tai Chi

Both Qi Gong and Tai Chi are widely recommended by traditional Chinese medicine practitioners for their therapeutic effects. Qi Gong consists of a series of exercises that emphasize correct posture and breathing to stimulate the flow of energy, calm the mind and reduce stress. Tai Chi is a series of flowing exercises through which a person seeks to harmonize Yin and Yang and increase the body's flexibility.

Courses in these exercises are widely available at community colleges.

Assessment by a traditional Chinese medicine practitioner usually involves an interview covering medical, history, diet, work and emotional states. The practitioner also conducts a visual examination and uses sophisticated techniques of wrist pulse-taking and tongue diagnosis. Signs and symptoms are classified according to principles of traditional Chinese medicine.

2. Medical Acupuncture

Acupuncture is also practised as an adjunct to other fields of medicine, in which case it is often referred to as "medical acupuncture" or "anatomical acupuncture." This form of acupuncture is performed by medical doctors as well as physiotherapists, and chiropractors. These health professionals often take courses in acupuncture over a series of weekends or months.

In Western terms, the benefits of acupuncture are sometimes explained in terms of the stimulation of the body's production of endorphins, pain-relieving chemicals. New technology, meanwhile, has been introduced to allow variations in acupuncture. One example is electro-acupuncture, the stimulation of inserted needles with mild electrical impulses. Low power laser is also used in place of needles in some instances. The Acupuncture Foundation of Canada (AFC), a non-profit organization representing medical practitioners who practise acupuncture, warns patients with pacemakers to avoid electrical stimulation unless their cardiologist approves. Caution is also advised for women in early pregnancy, as well as for haemophiliacs.

BENEFITS OF ACUPUNCTURE

Acupuncture is well known for providing relief from pain and stress, but it is also an integral part of a system of medicine. The following is a partial list of conditions that lend themselves to acupuncture treatment, as compiled in 1979 by the World Health Organization (WHO) Interregional Seminar held in Beijing, China. The World Health Organization is an international body with the aim of promoting health care. (There is no official WHO position on alternative medicine.) The list is based on experience, not on controlled clinical research. The inclusion of specific diseases is not meant to indicate the extent of acupuncture's effectiveness in treating them. For any condition requiring medical diagnosis and treatment, you should first consult a medical doctor.

Upper Respiratory Tract: Acute tonsillitis, acute sinusitis, acute rhinitis, common cold

Respiratory System: Acute bronchitis, bronchial asthma (with no complications)

Disorders of the Eye: Acute conjunctivitis, central retinitis, myopia (in children), cataract (with no complications)

Disorders of the Mouth: Toothache, post-extraction pain, gingivitis, acute and chronic pharyngitis

Gastro-Intestinal Disorders: Spasms of oesophagus and cardia, hiccup, gastroptosis, acute and chronic gastritis, gastric hyperacidity, chronic duodenal ulcer (with no complications; pain relief), acute and chronic colitis, acute bacillary dysentery, constipation, diarrhea, paralytic ileus

Neurological and Musculo-Skeletal Disorders: Headache, migraine, trigeminal neuralgia, facial palsy (early stage - within three to six months), pareses following a stroke, peripheral neuropathies, sequelae of poliomyelitis (early stage - within six months), Meniere's disease, neurogenic bladder dysfunction, noctural enuresis, intercostal neuralgia, cervicobrachial syndrome, "frozen shoulder", "tennis elbow", low back pain, osteoarthritis, sciatica

Before seeing an acupuncturist for any condition, you should be aware of regulations, where they exist, in your province (see below "Government Regulation" and "Acupuncture in your Province").

QUESTIONS TO ASK

✦ Is your acupuncturist registered? This question applies only if you live in a province where acupuncture is regulated (Alberta, B.C. and Québec). In Alberta, an acupuncturist may be registered, but this is not a requirement. In B.C. and Québec, however, acupuncturists must be registered to practise. You can check by contacting the governing body in your province (see addresses and telephone numbers below, "Acupuncture in Your Province - Governing Body").

NOTE: Be aware of the limitations on the practice of acupuncture under provincial law. For example, in Alberta, prior consultation with a physician or dentist is required. In B.C., no acupuncturist may treat active serious medical conditions without the patient having first consulted with a medical practitioner, dentist or naturopath, as appropriate (naturopathic doctors are regulated in B.C.).

✦ How much training in acupuncture has your practitioner received, and from which educational institute?

NOTE: As a benchmark, the Collège de Rosemont - the only Québec institute of acupuncture education recognized by the Québec government - has a three-year program (see below "Acupuncture Education"). This is also the U.S. standard for certified acupuncturists.

✦ Is your practitioner a member of an acupuncture association? You may wish to contact the association to discuss the qualifications of your acupuncturist, or to obtain a referral to an acupuncturist. (see below,

"National Associations" and "Acupuncture in Your Province - Associations").

NOTE: These associations are not governing bodies established under legislation to register and discipline practitioners. Associations do not necessarily check the qualifications of their members.

✦ How much experience does your practitioner have, and does it include treatment of your particular condition? What were the results? Can your practitioner provide professional references?

✦ Under what circumstances will your acupuncturist refer you to a physician or another regulated health professional? Is your practitioner trained to recognize conditions that require a physician's care?

✦ Does your practitioner specialize in acupuncture, or practise it as an adjunct to medicine, physiotherapy etc.?

✦ Is acupuncture an appropriate treatment for your condition? Would it affect other health problems that you may have?

✦ What is the estimated number of treatments required and at what cost? How long will each treatment take? Is it advisable to rest after treatment?

✦ What equipment sterilization methods and hygiene procedures are followed? Does the acupuncturist use pre-sterilized disposable needles?

NOTE: Disposable needles are mandatory under Alberta regulation, and are strongly recommended by public health inspectors in other jurisdictions. If permanent needles are used, they must be effectively sterilized. Under the B.C. Ministry of Health's "Guidelines for Personal Service Establishments," acupuncture needles are classed as critical items. They must be purchased as sterile and properly disposed of after a single use, or sterilized between each use according to specific methods, such as proper use of a steam autoclave. The boiling of needles is insufficient.

GOVERNMENT REGULATION
Provinces that Regulate Acupuncturists

In Canada, acupuncturists are currently regulated by the provincial governments of Alberta, B.C. and Québec. This means that governing bodies have been established, or are being established, under provincial legislation. These bodies are responsible for ensuring that registered practitioners meet certain standards before they practise, and for taking disciplinary action when appropriate. Alberta and B.C. are currently in the process of finalizing their educational standards.

In B.C. and Québec, only those registered with the governing body in the province will be permitted to practise acupuncture, subject to the rights of other health professionals. Alberta omitted this prohibition,

and reserves only the title, meaning that only those registered may use the title "acupuncturist."

In Québec, the practice of acupuncture is defined to include the stimulation of acupuncture points by means other than needles, including heat, pressure, electric current, or rays of light. In Alberta, acupuncture is defined to include acupressure, electro-acupuncture and moxibustion. The B.C. regulation defines acupuncture as an act of stimulation, by means of needles, of specific sites on the skin, mucous membranes or subcutaneous tissues of the human body to improve health or alleviate pain.

Note that acupuncturists face certain restrictions on their practice in each of these provinces. For example, acupuncturists in B.C. may not treat active serious medical conditions with disabling or life-threatening effects, which will not improve without intervention, unless the client has consulted with a medical doctor, naturopath or dentist, as appropriate.

For more information on the regulation of acupuncture in Alberta, B.C. and Québec, see below, "Acupuncture in Your Province - Legislation."

Provinces that Do Not Regulate Acupuncturists

Acupuncturists are not regulated as practitioners in Manitoba, New Brunswick, Newfoundland, Nova Scotia, Ontario, Prince Edward Island, Saskatchewan, the Yukon and the Northwest Territories. This means that no legislation exists in these jurisdictions to establish a governing body responsible for registering qualified acupuncturists and for disciplining them. This also means that no minimum educational standards exist for those calling themselves acupuncturists. This is a cause for concern for several acupuncture associations, which are in the process of applying for regulation in provinces such as Ontario.

With the exception of Ontario, every province and territory has legislation creating an offence to practise medicine without a licence, with varying definitions of what constitutes the practice of medicine. In Ontario, acupuncture is specifically permitted under Ontario law (see below, "Acupuncture in Your Province - Ontario"). In the Yukon, the Yukon Medical Council has issued a directive establishing guidelines limiting the practice of acupuncture to physicians and trained dentists.

If you live in a province where acupuncture is not regulated, you may wish to obtain referrals to practitioners and discuss their credentials with professional associations (see below, "National Associations" and "Acupuncture in Your Province").

GOVERNMENT HEALTH CARE FUNDING

None of the provinces allocates funding for acupuncture treatments. In Newfoundland only, the province's Medical Care Plan fully covers an initial visit to a licensed physician to determine if you are a candidate for acupuncture. The acupuncture treatments themselves are not covered.

PRIVATE HEALTH INSURANCE COVERAGE

Some private health insurance companies cover acupuncture treatment under their extended health care plans, but their policies are often subject to certain conditions, such as referral by a physician or membership in a particular association. Check your policy or speak with your agent.

WORKERS' COMPENSATION BOARDS

Contact the board in your province to determine if acupuncture treatment is covered and considered appropriate to your case. Check the conditions of coverage (eg. whether your practitioner must belong to a particular association).

NATIONAL ASSOCIATIONS

The following is a list of only national associations. For provincial associations see "Acupuncture in Your Province - Associations").

The Acupuncture Foundation of Canada
P.O. Box 93688
Shopper's World Postal Outlet
3003 Danforth Ave
Toronto, Ontario M4C 5R5
Tel: 416-752-3988
Fax: 416-752-4398

The Acupuncture Foundation of Canada (AFC), a non-profit charitable organization founded in 1974, provides referrals anywhere in Canada to a medical doctor, physiotherapist or dentist who has AFC certification. Such certification is obtained after passing a written and oral examination, following a minimum of three acupuncture courses, each consisting of a three-day weekend. The AFC has about 800 members across Canada. The foundation seeks to educate the public regarding acupuncture's "legitimate place in western medicine as a safe, effective complement to conventional medical treatment". The AFC recommends that its members use disposable needles. The Association is a member of the World Federation of Acupuncture Societies, a body endorsed by the World Health Organization. The AFC is recognized by most provincial medical colleges.

**The Chinese Medicine and Acupuncture
Association of Canada (CMAAC)**
154 Wellington St
London, Ontario N6B 2K8
Tel: 519-642-1970
Fax: 519-642-2932
President: Professor Cedric K.T. Cheung

This association provides referrals to 600 members across Canada. Incorporated in 1983, the association is a member of the World Federation of Acupuncture-Moxibustion Societies (WFAS), a body endorsed by the World Health Organization (WHO). The CMAAC notes that about 90% of its members have been trained in mainland China, some with a Doctor of Chinese Medicine Certificate (5-7 year program). The other 10% of members have a minimum of two years of university and three years of acupuncture training. The Association requires professional members to pass an examination. Professor Cheung is also vice-president of WFAS.

Canadian Council of Acupuncturists
599B Yonge St, Box 214
Toronto, Ontario M4Y 1Z4
Tel/Fax: 416-777-0585

This is a non-profit professional association. Many members are practitioners who use acupuncture as a complementary therapy to Western medicine.

New National Canadian Acupuncture Body
In January 1996, for the first time in Canada, representatives from 18 acupuncture organizations from across the country met in Richmond, B.C. to establish common goals, national standards and a national association. Developments will be noted in future editions of this directory.

U.S. ACCREDITATION BODIES & ASSOCIATIONS

Council of Colleges of Acupuncture and Oriental Medicine (CCAOM)
8403 Colesville Rd, Ste 370
Silver Spring, MD 20910
Tel: 301-608-9175
Fax: 301-608-9576

NAFTA Acupuncture Commission
14637 Starr Rd SE
Olalla, Washington 98359
Tel: 206-851-6895
Fax: 206-851-6883

The Commission is a group of private individuals, including educators, practitioners, acupuncturists, medical doctors and naturopaths, who exchange information regarding the practice of acupuncture in Mexico, Canada and the United States. The Commission developed from a meeting of practitioners from the three countries in Japan in 1993, and was formally established in 1994.

National Accreditation Commission for Schools and Colleges of Acupuncture and Oriental Medicine (NACSCAOM)
8403 Colesville Rd, Suite 370
Silver Spring, MD 20910
Tel: 301-608-9680
Fax: 301-608-9576

This is the specialized accreditation agency recognized by the U.S. Secretary of Education and by the Commission on Recognition of Postsecondary Accreditation (CORPA) for reviewing programs in this field. Accredited acupuncture schools must offer a minimum of three academic years, and accredited schools of Oriental medicine must offer a minimum of four years.

The National Acupuncture and Oriental Medicine Alliance
14637 Starr Rd SE
Olalla, WA 98359
Tel: 206-851-6896
Fax: 206-851-6883

This is the national professional membership association representing practitioners of acupuncture and Oriental medicine in the U.S..

National Acupuncture Detoxification Association (NADA)
c/o NADA Literature Clearinghouse
PO Box 1927
Vancouver, Washington 98668-1927
Tel/Fax: 360-260-8620
e-mail NADAclear@aol.com

National Association of Teachers of Acupuncture and Oriental Medicine
2525 South Madison
Denver, Colorado 80210
Tel: 303-329-6355

National Commission for the Certification of Acupuncturists (NCCA)
P.O. Box 97075
Washington, DC 20090-7075
Tel: 202-232-1404
Fax: 202-462-6157

This is the U.S. body whose examination is used as the basis for acupuncture licensure in most regulated states. As of early 1996, a total of 32 states, as well as the District of Columbia, allowed for the practice of acupuncture by non-physicians. Canadian members in the listing carry the notation 'NCCA.'

Society for Acupuncture Research
4733 Bethesda Ave, Ste 804
Bethesda, Maryland 20814
Fax: 202-363-3859

ACUPUNCTURE EDUCATION

For those seeking a career in acupuncture, there are a growing number of training programs and colleges opening across Canada. In choosing a training program, one may wish to compare the qualifications of faculty (their education and experience), student-teacher ratios, admission requirements, program content and length, number of clinical hours, and all fees

and contract terms, including refund policies. In addition, it is useful to speak with students and graduates of the various programs about their standards, and to consult with representatives of acupuncture associations. Ask the representatives if they are affiliated with a particular college.

So far, the only province to have set an educational standard for acupuncturists is Québec, and the only acupuncture training program recognized by it is offered by the Collège de Rosemont in Montréal (see description below). It is a full-time, three-year program. This is in keeping with the U.S. standard for certification, which is a three-year training program for acupuncture, and a four-year program for Oriental medicine (see above, "U.S. Accreditation Bodies & Associations").

In Alberta and B.C., the other two provinces where acupuncture practitioners are regulated, education standards have not yet been set.

Most provinces have legislation requiring private vocational schools to meet certain minimum standards, often related to financial stability, for the protection of consumers. These requirements for registration vary from province to province, and alternative health care education programs are not in all cases covered by such legislation. B.C. is the only province to require registration of all such training programs with its Private Post-Secondary Education Commission, a regulatory body established by the government. Contact the Ministry of Education or Advanced Education in your province for more information.

If you are seeking a career in acupuncture and live in a jurisdiction where acupuncture practitioners are not regulated (Manitoba, New Brunswick, Newfoundland, Nova Scotia, Ontario, Prince Edward Island, Saskatchewan, the Yukon and the Northwest Territories), you should be aware that each of these provinces has legislation restricting the practice of medicine or specific medical acts. Ontario is a special case as acupuncture practitioners are not regulated, but acupuncture is specifically permitted under law (see below "Acupuncture in Your Province").

Canadian College of Acupuncture and Oriental Medicine
855 Cormorant St
Victoria, B.C. V8W 1R2
Tel: 604-384-2942/385-6704

This college offers a three-year diploma program in traditional Chinese medicine. The curriculum includes Traditional Chinese acupuncture, herbology, acupressure and Western sciences.

Canadian College of Traditional Chinese Medicine
560 West Broadway, Ste 201
Vancouver, B.C. V5Z 1E9
Tel: 604-879-2365 or 876-2144
Fax: 604-877-0095

This college offers a 36-month diploma program as well as a three-month certificate course. Training is provided through classroom, laboratory and clinical training, with emphasis on acupuncture and herbalism. Students should have a minimum of one year post-secondary education or equivalent experience.

Collège de Rosemont
Department of Acupuncture
6400, 16e ave
Montréal, Québec H1X 2S9
Tel: 514-376-1620 ext 351

This three-year, 2550-hour program, taught in French, includes: 1,425 hours of acupuncture training; 465 hours of Western medical training, such as anatomy, physiology, microbiology, pharmacology, emergency care and pathology; 45 hours of patient relations; 45 hours of clinic administration; and 570 hours of basic college courses such as French, philosophy and physical education. The 1,425 hours of acupuncture training include 480 hours of supervised clinical experience and 51 hours of clinical observation. The Collège is in the process of increasing the number of hours of Western medical training. As this college is a CEGEP, the prerequisite for admission is completion of Grade 12, but competition for the 25 places is so high (more than 200 applications per year) that most successful applicants also have college or university degrees. This is the only college program in acupuncture in Québec recognized by the provincial government.

Institute of Chinese Medicine and Acupuncture, Canada
Director of Administration
Ms. Hsi Ping Lin
154 Wellington St
London, Ontario N6B 2K8
Tel: 519-642-1970
Fax: 519-642-2932

This Institute offers a full-time, four-year program. Upon completion, students may write examinations to qualify for membership in the Chinese Medicine and Acupuncture Association of Canada and the Professional Acupuncturists Association of Ontario. Applicants are required to have a three-year general science university degree with a B average. The degree must include courses in basic anatomy, physiology and microbiology. The curriculum includes courses in traditional Chinese medicine and acupuncture. Optional courses in Chinese languages and Tai Chi Chuan are available. Post-graduate studies may be arranged in China, if the student is interested. The Dean, Professor Cheung, is president of the Chinese Medicine and Acupuncture Association of Canada.

International College of Traditional Chinese Medicine
301-1847 W. Broadway
Vancouver, B.C.

V6J 1Y6
Tel: 604-731-2926
Fax: 604-731-2964

This college offers the following three-year programs: Traditional Chinese Medicine, including Chinese acupuncture and Chinese Herbology; Traditional Chinese Acupuncture; and Chinese Herbology. Admission requirements include a minimum of two years of college, or equivalent (such as work experience and vocational or professional training and education).

ACUPUNCTURE TRAINING FOR HEALTH PROFESSIONALS

The Acupuncture Foundation of Canada Institute
P.O. Box 93688
Shopper's World Postal Outlet
3003 Danforth Ave
Toronto, Ontario M4C 5R5
Tel: 416-752-3988
Fax: 416-752-4398

Courses and certification are offered only to physicians, physiotherapists and dentists. Courses are offered at locations across Canada. A minimum of three courses, each consisting of a three-day weekend, must be taken before the certification exam is written. The Foundation is recognized by several provincial colleges of physicians and surgeons.

Institute of Traditional Chinese Medicine
368 Dupont St
Toronto, Ontario M5R 1V9
Tel/Fax: 416-925-6752

The Institute offers a part-time two to three year program. Many students have a background in naturopathic medicine or chiropractic.

University of Alberta
Faculty of Extension
Certificate Program in Medical Acupuncture
93 University Campus NW
Edmonton, Alberta T6G 2T4
Tel: 403-492-3037
Fax: 403-492-1216

The Certificate Program in Medical Acupuncture is a postgraduate program for physicians, dentists, and other health care professionals. The 200-hour program aims to teach students medical acupuncture as a safe and reliable complementary therapeutic tool, used largely to manage pain. The CPMA is recognized by the colleges of physicians and surgeons in Alberta, B.C., Manitoba and Saskatchewan, along with the Yukon Medical Council. Students who successfully complete the four levels of the program are issued a certificate and are entitled to use the initials "CMAc" as part of their professional designation.

✦ Acupuncture in Your Province

Each province is listed alphabetically below, with the following information:

Provincial Legislation

✦ procedures that your acupuncturist is permitted to perform under provincial law, where such laws exists

✦ circumstances where the law requires you to consult with another medical professional

NOTE: The information given regarding legislation is by way of interest, and does not purport to offer legal advice or comprise a complete account of the legislation or regulations. If legal advice is required, consult a lawyer qualified to practise in your jurisdiction

Governing Bodies

✦ addresses and telephone numbers of governing bodies, where they exist

✦ these are the offices you may contact to make a complaint or to check if your acupuncturist is registered

Provincial Associations

✦ addresses and telephone numbers of provincial acupuncture associations, which often provide referrals, or whose representatives may discuss the qualifications of practitioners

Acupuncturists

✦ names, addresses and telephone numbers of acupuncturists, listed alphabetically by city

NOTE: Acupuncturists recognized by the U.S. Commission for the Certification of Acupuncturists carry the notation 'NCCA.' This is not a Canadian designation, or requirement. This publication cannot and does not certify or represent the qualifications of practitioners, or the quality of care available from them. In jurisdictions where practitioners are required to be registered, we cannot and do not confirm that those listed are registered as required by law.

✦ Alberta

Acupuncturists are regulated as practitioners in Alberta, meaning that there is legislation and a regulation establishing standards for registration and disciplinary procedures. There is no government health care funding.

Legislation

Acupuncture is one of 10 health care professions, or health "disciplines" governed under the *Health Disciplines Act*. Acupuncturists are also regulated under an Acupuncture Regulation made under the Act.

Right to Title

The legislation and regulation do not prohibit the practice of acupuncture by persons who are not registered. Rather this is so-called 'right to title' legislation under which only those registered are entitled to present themselves to the public as acupuncturists. In particular, the Act restricts the use of names of designated health professions (of which acupuncture is one) to registered members.

Education Requirements

As of printing, there was no provincial standard set for educational requirements. The Acupuncture Society of Alberta would like a minimum of 1,800 hours of training to ensure an adequate depth of knowledge. Others would like fewer hours to enable medical specialists, such as medical doctors and physiotherapists, to use acupuncture as an adjunct to their practice for pain relief. In the meantime, those now being registered must pass a provincial registration examination, but do not have to meet educational requirements.

Complaints

Complaint proceedings regarding conduct, skill, judgment or fitness to practise as a registered member are set out in Part 4 of the *Health Disciplines Act*. Complaints must be made in writing and accompanied by the complainant's mailing address. Contact the governing body listed below for details.

Scope of Practice

Under section 7 of the regulation, a registered acupuncturist may provide the services of acupuncture, "but in providing that service the only technical modes of practice that an acupuncturist may use are needle acupuncture, electro-acupuncture, moxibustion (defined in section 1 as the application of heat near an acupuncture point, generated by the burning of moxa wool), cupping (defined in section 1 as the stimulation of acupuncture points by the application of a small jar or cup within which a vacuum has been created) and acupressure (defined in section 1 as the stimulation of an acupuncture point by nominal pressure)."

Requirement to Consult Physician

A registered acupuncturist may not undertake the care and treatment of a person unless that person has already consulted with a physician or dentist about the condition, informs the acupuncturist that he or she has done so, and the acupuncturist completes a patient consultation form.

A registered acupuncturist may not inform a patient that acupuncture cures disease, nor advise a patient to discontinue any treatment prescribed by a physician or dentist.

Requirement for Pre-Sterilized Needles

A registered acupuncturist is required to use pre-sterilized disposable needles.

Requirement for Knowledge of English

Acupuncturists must provide satisfactory evidence of sufficient competence in the English language to practise as an acupuncturist in Alberta. As well, patient records must be kept in the English language. As a condition of practice, an acupuncturist must allow inspections during business hours to ensure that the requirements of regulation are met. This wording would appear to effectively exclude from registration highly trained Oriental practitioners who lack sufficient oral and written English skills. Alberta government officials recognize this issue and say that these types of provisions are applied with discretion.

Practice of Acupuncture by Medical Doctors

Medical doctors in Alberta wishing to practise acupuncture are required by the Alberta College of Physicians and Surgeons to hold a certificate from either the Acupuncture Foundation of Canada or the University of Alberta Program on Medical Acupuncture, and be accredited by the College.

Alberta Governing Body

Professional & Technical Services
Alberta Department of Labour
8th Fl, 10808-99th Ave.
Edmonton, Alberta T5K 0G5
Tel: 403-422-5685

Contact this office to check whether your acupuncturist is registered, to ask for a referral to a registered acupuncturist, or to make a complaint. To be registered, an acupuncturist must pass an examination. However, educational standards had not been set as of spring 1996. You may therefore wish to ask about your practitioner's training.

Alberta Associations

Acupuncture Society of Alberta
10665 Jasper Ave, Ste. 1210
Edmonton, Alberta T5J 3S9
Tel: 403-421-7766
Fax: 403-988-5592

Call this association for a referral to a member. The Society states that members have at least 1,800 hours of training. Members include practitioners of traditional Chinese medicine.

The Alberta Traditional Chinese Medical Science and Acupuncture Association
Room 101
805-9th St SW
Calgary, Alberta T2P 2Y6
Tel: 403-295-1375
Fax: 403-274-5077

Membership includes many traditional Chinese medicine practitioners. Call for a referral.

Canadian Medical Acupuncture Society
9904-106th St
Edmonton, Alberta T5K 1C4
Tel: 403-426-2760
Fax: 403-426-5650

The Society, incorporated in 1994, seeks to foster public recognition of medical acupuncture, as practised by qualified physicians.

The Chinese Medicine and Acupuncture Association of Canada (CMAAC)
Alberta Chapter
Ste 300, Plaza 124
10216-124 St
Edmonton, Alberta T5N 4A3
Tel: 403-482-6071

✦ Alberta Acupuncturists

NOTE: This list may include registered and unregistered practitioners. Call the governing body listed above to ensure that your practitioner is registered. Under Alberta law, a person does not have to be registered to practise acupuncture, but must be registered to use the title 'acupuncturist'. Check the credentials of your practitioner (see above, "Questions to Ask"). This publication does not and cannot certify or represent the qualifications of practitioners, or the quality of care available from them.

BANFF

Turning Point Acupuncture & Massage Clinic
111 Banff Ave 403-762-3818

CALGARY

Academy Place Physiotherapy
1609-1800 4th St SW 403-228-9230

Acupuncture Accredited Clinic
101-805 9th St SW 403-262-3213

Acupuncture Associates
110-519 17th Ave SW 403-228-3612

Acupuncture Services
1828-104th Ave SW 403-253-3103

Alternative Natural Therapies Ltd
420-131 9th Ave SW 403-237-0282

Asia Herbs & Acupuncture
121-4909 17th Ave SE 403-272-8667

Braecentre Medical Clinic
Cameron, Dr. Alison; Karim, Dr. Nasim
Nowak, Dr. Peter; Regehr, Dr. Sonya
11438 Braeside Dr SW 403-251-2535

Brown, Mark, D.C.
200-8180 Macleod Trail SE . .403-255-4461

Canada Esoteric Buddhist Yogachara Qigong Institute
899 Hunterston Rd NW 403-295-8868

Canton Acupuncture & Herbs Centre
201-1506 Centre St NE 403-230-4155

Chinese Herbs & Acupuncture Centre
2014 Centre St NE 403-277-6060

Chu, David
B2220 7th Ave NW 403-282-2223

Dong, Dr. Dennis
J100 3rd Ave SE 403-264-2150

Evergreen Acupuncture
B2220 7th Ave NW 403-282-2223

Galvez, Dr. Hugo
208-3509 17th Ave 403-272-4582

Great Wall Clinic
538-1011 1st SW 403-261-5975

Heritage Hill Natural Health Centre
Halowski, Allan, D.C.
200-8180 Macleod Tr SE . . .403-255-4461

Hoffman, Dr. Bruce
202-4411 16th Ave NW 403-286-7311

Jackson Huang Acupuncture & Herb Clinic
Bsmt 308 Centre St SE 403-269-9568

Kensington Physiotherapy
1167 Kensington Cres NW . .403-270-0053

Lehman Physiotherapy (Market Mall) Ltd
328-4935 40th Ave NW 403-286-5529

Oriental Acupuncture Clinic Ltd
7220 Fisher St SE 403-255-0133

Oriental Medicine Acupuncture & Massage Clinic
433-131 9th Ave SW 403-233-0498

Peking Acupuncture & Herbs Centre
2nd Fl 123 14th St NW 403-283-7052

Phuc Sinh Duong Herbs Acupuncture & Massage
4710 17th Ave SE 403-272-7697

Professional Acupuncture Clinic Ltd
7239d Flint Rd SE 403-253-1998

Rakhra, Dr. Raj-Inder
304-1235 17th Ave SW 403-244-4941

Rickhi, Dr. Badri
200-855 8th Ave SW 403-233-0917

Sanborn, G.Frank
110-519 17th Ave SW 403-228-3612

Seo-Am Hand Acupuncture Institute of Canada
370-7220 Fisher St SE 403-255-0133

Sincere Acupuncture - Herb Specialist
103-197 1st SW 403-234-9525

Sincere Acupuncture - Herb Specialist
105 Beddington Towne Centre403-295-1375

Skaken, Ross, N.D.
921 17th Ave SW 403-244-4920

Snyder, L.V.
401-817 5th St NE 403-277-9494

Stillpoint Clinics Ltd
110-159 17th Ave SW 403-228-3612

Vienna Clinics Health Services
921 17th Ave SW 403-244-4920

Wild Rose Wholistic Clinic Inc
302-1220 Kensington Rd NW 403-270-0891

Willow Park Physical Therapy Inc
101-816 Willowpark Dr SE . .403-278-1030

Yoon's Acupuncture & Acupressure Clinic
14-3510 27th St NE 403-291-2094

CAMROSE

Acupuncture Acupressure Clinic
6010 48th Ave 403-672-9360

Camrose Physical Therapy
1989-4825 51st St 403-672-3873

EDMONTON

Acupuncture Clinic
10648-101st St 403-425-1754

Alberta Acupuncture Institute
10155-120th St 403-488-6857

Alberta Chinese Acupuncture & Herbal Centre
10859-97th St 403-424-9133

Alta-Orthopaedic & Sports Physiotherapy Inc
7654-156th St 403-486-0200

Aung, Dr. S.,
9904-106th St 403-426-2760

Beverly Physiotherapy Ltd
4105 118th Ave NW 403-471-6161

Blue Quill Medical Clinic
374 Saddleback Rd 403-437-5914

Brown, Dr. Robert
206a-11010 101st St NW . . .403-421-4757

Calder Physiotherapy Clinic Ltd
210-11808 St Albert Trail NW403-454-0374

Canton Acupuncture Clinic
205-11109 95th St 403-474-9881

Chen, Dr. Grace
320-11808St Albert NW . . .403-452-4381

China Herbal & Acupuncture Centre
12211 107th Ave NW 403-482-2607

Chinese Acupuncture & Herbalist Clinic
101-9942 82nd Ave NW . . .403-433-9565

Chiu, Dr. Sy-Hua,
11503 100th Ave NW 403-488-3933

Dickson, Dr. Chris
439-10830 Jasper Ave 403-428-9333

Dujon, Dr. L.D.
360-8702 Meadowlark Rd . .403-484-8806

Fountain Of Life Clinic
103-10045 111th St 403-488-1060

Glenora Physio-Therapy Clinic Ltd
10155 120th St NW 403-488-8582

Huizing, A. M.
1106-10025 106th St 403-426-2322

Jeh, Dr. Jusli
374 Saddleback Rd 403-437-5914

Moe, Grace
10155 120th St NW 403-488-8582

New Life Clinic
2525-10155 102nd St 403-425-8181

Peking Acutherapy Clinic
3-10045 117th St NW 403-482-5232

Robinson, Barbara
7654-156th St 403-486-0200

Rydz, W. & Chiu, S., Drs.
11503-100th Ave NW 403-488-3933

Vital Acupuncture Acupressure & Herbal Inc
10673-97th St 403-420-0775

Yawrenko, David, N.D.
2525-10155 102nd St 403-425-8181

Zhang Ken
12211-107th Ave 403-482-2607

FORT SASKATCHEWAN

Acupuncture Acupressure Clinic
10101 100th Ave 403-998-2172

LETHBRIDGE

Meridian Therapy
801 3rd Ave S 403-327-0334

Goertz Eric Therapy Services
1222 3rd Ave S 403-328-1272

Peak Physical Therapy Ltd
Magrath, Dr. S
105-1410 Mayor 403-328-7325

MEDICINE HAT

Green Tree Better Health Centre
109-1899 Dunmore Rd SE .403-528-2299

Medical Arts Centre
770 6th St SW or
116 Carry Dr SE 403-527-2281

RED DEER

Roy-Poulsen Jytte
4702 50th Ave 403-347-1103

Natural Health Clinic
Box 116, 5018 47th Ave ...403-343-0051

Wu, Dr. Kenneth
4917 48th St 403-343-0355

ROCKY MOUNTAIN HOUSE

Altamed
5105 A 49th St 403-845-7223

Rocky Mountain House Physiotherapy Ltd
5105a 49th St 403-845-7222

SHERWOOD PARK

Health & Wellness Clinic
105-50 Brentwood Blvd 403-467-1420

STETTLER

Stettler Acupuncture Clinic
6600-50th Ave 403-742-3441

✦ British Columbia

Acupuncturists became regulated in B.C. in 1996 with the introduction of an *Acupuncturists Regulation* that designated acupuncture as a health profession under the *Health Professions Act*. In April 1996, a governing body, called the College of Acupuncturists of B.C., was established under this Act. The College is responsible for setting educational standards, qualifications for practitioners, and procedures for disciplining them. There is no coverage for acupuncture treatment under the province's government health care funding system, the Medical Services Plan.

Legislation

Under the *Acupuncturists Regulation*, acupuncture is defined as "an act of stimulation, by means of needles, of specific sites on the skin, mucous membranes or subcutaneous tissues of the human body to improve health or alleviate pain" (section 1).

Only Registered Acupuncturists May Practise

No person other than a registrant may use the title "acupuncturist," and only registrants may practise acupuncture. Subject to the rights of other health professionals and the provision of emergency assistance, only a registrant may insert acupuncture needles under the skin for the purposes of practising acupuncture (*Acupuncturists Regulation*, section 5, *Health Professions Act*, section 14).

Complaints

Complaints and investigation procedures are set out in Part 3 of the *Health Professions Act*. Section 31 requires a person who wishes to make a complaint against a registered practitioner to deliver the complaint in writing to the registrar. Contact the B.C. governing body listed below for details.

Scope of Practice

The scope of practice is set out in section 4 of the Regulation, which states that a registrant may practise acupuncture, based on the traditional Oriental method, including:

✦ the use of diagnostic techniques;

✦ the administration of manual, mechanical, thermal and electrical stimulation of acupuncture needles, and;

✦ the recommendation of dietary guidelines or therapeutic exercise.

Requirements for Consultation with Other Health Professionals

No acupuncturist may treat active serious medical conditions unless the client has consulted with a medical practitioner, naturopath or dentist, as appropriate (*Acupuncturists Regulation*, section 6(1)). "Active serious medical condition" is defined as a disease, disorder or dysfunction which has disabling or life-threatening effects which will not improve without intervention. An acupuncturist may administer acupuncture as a surgical anaesthesia only if a medical practitioner or dentist is physically present and observing the procedure.

An acupuncturist must advise the client to consult a medical practitioner, naturopath or dentist if there is no improvement in the condition for which the client is being treated within two months of receiving acupuncture treatment. If the client refuses, a registrant must discontinue treatment if there is no improvement after four months, if the condition worsens or if new symptoms develop.

B.C. Governing Body

The College of Acupuncturists of British Columbia
Mount St. Joseph's Hospital, Ste 216
3080 Prince Edward St.
Vancouver, B.C. V5T 3N4
Tel: 604-874-8421

As of July 1, 1997 acupuncturists must be registrants of the College. Call the College to ensure that your acupuncturist is registered and therefore meets its standards of practice and is subject to its disciplinary powers.

B.C. Associations

The Acupuncture Association of B.C.
1367 East 41st Ave
Vancouver, B.C. V5W 1R7
Tel/Fax: 604-261-8700
President: Daniel Cheng
Tel: 604-983-9754

Call for a referral to one of the association's 160 members in B.C. Members have a minimum of three years' training and have passed the association's examination. Many members practise Chinese herbology as well as acupuncture. The association states that it inspects clinics of members before they open for business. It has established a liaison with the Acupuncture Society of Alberta for membership in the World Federation of Acupuncture Societies.

Canadian Chinese Traditional Chinese Medicine & Acupuncturists Society
1160 Burrard St, Ste. 707
Vancouver, B.C. V6Z 2E8
Tel: 604-682-1268
Fax: 604-438-9922

Canadian Korean Acupuncturists of B.C.
1925 Kingsway
Vancouver, B.C. V5N 2T1
Tel/Fax: 604-873-8884

The Chinese Medicine and Acupuncture Association of Canada (CMAAC) B.C. Chapter
252 E Woodstock Ave
Vancouver, B.C. V5W 1N1
Tel: 604-325-9858

Traditional Chinese Medicine Association of B.C.
1200 Burrard St., Ste 801
Vancouver, B.C. V6Z 2C7
Tel: 604-602-9603

Second location
Box 8603
Victoria, B.C. V8W 3S2
Tel: 604-386-4181

Contact the association for a referral to one of about 50 member practitioners of traditional Chinese medicine in B.C. Many members practise acupuncture; others specialize in herbalism. To be eligible for membership, a practitioner must have three years of training. The association has applied for regulatory status, and is currently establishing qualification exams.

United Acupuncturists Association of B.C.
102A - 7031 Westminster Hwy.
Richmond, B.C. V6X 1A3
Tel: 604-821-1323

Call for a referral to one of 70 active members with a minimum of two years of college training.

Vancouver Chinese Acupuncture Association
1832 Valencia Pl
Victoria, B.C. V8N 5W1
Tel/Fax: 604-477-8197

✦ British Columbia Acupuncturists

Contact the newly formed College of Acupuncturists of British Columbia to ensure that your acupuncturist is registered. Under the new regulation, only registered acupuncturists are permitted to practise as of July 1977. Check the qualifications of your acupuncturist (see above, "Questions to Ask"). This publication cannot and does not certify or represent qualifications of practitioners, or the quality of care available from them.

ABBOTSFORD

Aquila Acupuncture Clinic
8-32700 Dahlstrom Ave 604-855-0688

BRENTWOOD BAY

Turner, Joe
7174b West Saanich Rd 604-652-8008

BURNABY

Beijing Acupuncture Clinic
312-4900 Kingsway 604-451-9002

Burnaby Wholistic Pain Relief Centre
201-3845 Hastings 604-473-4613

Can-Integrated Healing Centre
206-5481 Kingsway 604-438-9922

Lee's Acupuncture
4501 North Rd 604-421-5050

Magovern, Patrick
204-4603 Kingsway 604-432-1654

CAMPBELL RIVER

Campbell River Physical Therapy Clinic
991 Alder St 604-286-1046

Physiotherapy & Rehabilitation Clinic
Koeleman, Pieter
2315 S. Island Hwy 604-923-3773

COQUITLAM

Tri-City Acupuncture & Herb Clinic
208-3041 Anson Ave 604-944-6606

COMOX

Comox Physiotherapy Clinic
C-1822 Comox Ave 604-339-6221

COURTENAY

Cork, Gary
F-479-4th St 604-334-0388

Courtenay Healing Centre
519b-5th St 604-338-2866

DELTA

Ng, Dr. Douglas
7251-120th St 604-591-8911

DUNCAN

Ingram Physiotherapy Ltd
204-149 Ingram St 604-748-4818

Rose, Judy
28-127 Ingram St 604-748-2395

Turning Point Acupuncture
304-394 Duncan St 604-748-2060

FERNIE

Sparling East Medical Centre
402-2nd Ave 604-423-4442

KAMLOOPS

Kamloops Acupuncture Centre
Soo Hoo, Andy
476 Tranquille Rd 604-376-8878

KELOWNA

Harder, Rosalyn
649 Burne Ave 604-862-9003

Kelowna Physiotherapy Centre
2-1521 Sutherland Ave 604-860-4878

LADNER

Chen, Dr. Robert
102-4515 Harvest Dr 604-940-1224

LADYSMITH

Gauthier, Nicole
639 Maplewood Way 604-245-8544

Ladysmith Physiotherapy
411 1st Ave 604-245-3616

LANTZVILLE

Solutions Plus, John Parker
By Appointment 604-390-1984

MAPLE RIDGE

TCM Health Care Center
11924-223rd St 604-466-9938

MILL BAY

Mill Bay Acupuncture Clinic
19-850 Shawnigan-Mill Bay .604-743-2339

NAKUSP

Nu Beginnings
111-4th Ave NW 604-265-4126

NANAIMO

Alden Clinic Of Physiotherapy
150a Wallace St 604-753-7771

Burtney, C.
29 Gillespie St 604-753-2093

Gee, Rosa; Lim, Linna
303-235 Bastion St 604-753-4646

Farand, Patricia
Hill, Kathryn
103-55 Victoria Rd 604-753-1509

Nanaimo Acupuncture Clinic
27-55 Front St 604-755-1596

NANOOSE BAY

Eco Med Wellness Spa & Clinic
515 Pacific Shores
Nature Resort 604-468-7133

Red Gap Physiotherapy
3-2443 Collins Cr 604-468-5560

NELSON

Fischer, Dr. Warren
100-817 Vernon St 604-352-9952

NEW WESTMINSTER

Acupuncture & Chinese Health
Care Clinic
514-6th Ave 604-521-7288

Asher, John
414 Columbia St E 604-524-3145

Khare, Sidh
320-10th Ave 604-525-0647

NORTH VANCOUVER

Cheng's Acupuncture &
Health Center
Cheng, Daniel
102-1940 Lonsdale Ave . . .604-983-9754

Integrated Physiotherapy
4062 Violet St 604-929-3255

Natural Healing & Acupuncturist
Centre Ltd
755-333 Brooksbank Ave . .604-985-3005

North Shore Acupuncture Therapy
Webb, Craig
156 W 3rd St 604-984-9575

Woo, Dr. Y.K.
106-135 E 15th St 604-985-6613

PARKSVILLE

Oceanside Orthopaedic & Sports
Physiotherapy
Hepenstall, Janet
203-154 Memorial Ave . . .604-248-9666

Parksville Acupuncture Clinic
174 Morison Ave 604-248-2644

PENTICTON

Acupuncture Clinic
151 Nanaimo Ave W 604-493-6967

Pro-Physio Clinic
16-88 W Duncan Ave 604-490-8999

PORT HARDY

Serrano, Rick
9283 Carnarvon Rd 604-949-7681

QUALICUM BEACH

Elkes Natural Health &
Acupuncture Clinic
13-221 West 2nd Ave 604-752-5058

Jennings, Samantha; Thomas, D.
781 Canyon Cr 604-752-8968

RICHMOND

Acuhealth Chinese Therapy Clinic
Ltd
220-8055 Anderson Rd 604-273-3736

Ageless Traditional Chinese Health
Centre
110-3320 Jacombs Rd 604-606-6318

Cheung, Robert
6211 Lynas Lane 604-275-9805

Chinese Medicine &
Acupuncture Centre
740-4400 Hazelbridge Way .604-270-1818

Kiang, Lily
206-6411 Buswell St 604-273-2265

Natural Health Clinic
102A-7031
Westminster Hwy 604-821-1323

Poon, Dr. K.K.
211-8140 Cook Rd 604-270-2414

SAANICHTON

Medler, Linda and Sandy
6690 Welch Rd 604-652-8802

SALT SPRING ISLAND

Linklater, Ron
By Appointment 604-537-1195

SURREY

Liu, T.H.
211-9457-152nd St 604-583-3322

Yeh's Painless Acupuncture
204-13696-104th Ave 604-582-0823

Kwantlen Medical Clinic
Parikh, A.; Nelson, Urban; Sidhu, J.
1-12818-72nd Ave 604-572-8161

TERRACE

Physiotherapy & Acupuncture
Trappl, Elizabeth
4007 Eby St 604-635-4756

TRAIL

Kramer, Lisa Ann, NCCA
1138-A Cedar Ave 604-368-3325

TSAWWASSEN

Tsawwassen Acupuncture Clinic
5-5666-12th Ave 604-943-5411

VANCOUVER

Acupuncture Centre of Vancouver
102-283 E 11th 604-873-1166

Acupuncture Clinic
205-2525 Pine St 604-739-2828

B.C. Acupuncture & Herbal Centre
205-1852 W Broadway 604-736-3003
334-5740 Cambie St 604-321-6987

B.C. Natural Therapy
2-906 W Broadway 604-736-3003

Beijing Tang Acupuncture Centre
107-3195 Granville St 736-3868

Burrard Intergrated Health Clinic
604-1200 Burrard 604-687-0119

Caldwell Acupuncture Clinic &
Traditional Chininese Herbology
801-1200 Burrard 602-9603

Canadian College of Traditional
Chinese Medicine Clinic
202-560 West Broadway, . . .604-876-2144

Can-Integrated Healing Centre
707-1160 Burrard St 604-682-1268

Chan, Jim, N.D.
100-3380 Maquinna Dr 604-435-3786

Chinese Acupuncture, Acupressure
& Qi Gong
402-1750 E 10th Ave 604-879-9686

Chinese Therapy & Acupressure
Centre
3205 Fraser St 604-874-2186

Chinese Traditional Healing (Qi
Gong)
206 A-2525 Pine St 604-731-2202

Chu Chung Chang & Chu May Twin
Drs.
552 Kingsway 604-778-9117

Chung's Acupuncture Clinic
1084 Kingsway 604-879-5522

Demorest, Louise
By Appointment 604-641-0496

Dimonte, Vincent
201-2786 W 16th Ave 604-734-5655

East West Academy of Healing Arts (Qi Gong)
2678 W. Broadway 739-4284

Evergreen Acupuncture
203-560 W Broadway 604-876-2144

Fraser Acupuncture Centre
3278 Fraser St 604-873-9950

Glew, Tom, N.D.
207-2678 W Broadway 604-738-4085

Gong Yuan
107-3195 Granville St 604-736-3868

Ho, Laina
301-1847 W Broadway ...604-731-2926

Hou, Dr. Frank
315-888 W 8th 604-872-0305

Integral Chinese Therapy Centre
105-1956 W Broadway ...604-732-8968

Integrative Healing Arts Centre
Jiang, Ting Ting
201-958 8th Ave W 604-738-1012

International College of Traditional Chinese Medicine Clinic
301-1847 W Broadway ...604-731-2926

Jiang, Ding
106-2620 Commercial Dr. ..604-708-0889

Kong Tom Innovative Acupuncture
115-2838 E Hastings ST 604-255-6808

Kwak's Traditional Chinese Medicine Clinic
603 E Broadway 604-872-1227

Lakhani, Nafisa
260-2025 W 42nd Ave 604-261-6833

Lee, Sung Yong, NCCA
1155 Kingsway 604-879-2552

Louie, Laura Ann, NCCA
100-3380 Maguinna Dr 604-435-3786

Lu, Henry
301-1847 W Broadway 604-731-2926

Makhija, Dr. Jamuna Lal
5182 Victoria Dr 604-322-9224

Michalik, Edward
320-1200 Burrard St 604-683-1505

Murphy, Dr. E.
195 Granville St 604-731-1717

Ng, Dr. S.C.
201-2786 W 16th Ave 604-734-5655

Nixon, Dr. A.J.
207-2475 Bayswater St 604-734-2614

Oriental Acupuncture Clinic Centre
3-3439 Kingsway 604-438-9164

Pham Rang
104-830 E 7th Ave 604-876-1249

Skerritt, Lisa
312-2083 Alma St 604-222-2433

Sumimoto Oriental Theraputics
408-1541 W Broadway 604-734-7537

Takahashi, Hideo
200-1701 W Broadway ...604-736-2430

Traditional Chinese Medical Clinic
Farenholtz, Mary; Robinson, Bonnie
4-1854 W 1st Ave 604-731-1171

Tung Fong Hung Medicine Co.
Liping, Cai
536 Main St 604-688-0883

Vancouver Acupuncture & Chinese Herbology Clinic
404-1541 W Broadway ...604-739-8287

Vancouver Acupuncture
402-1750 E 10th Ave 604-879-9686

Vancouver Traditional Acupuncture Clinic
Watterson, Mary Sheila; Stan, John
5621 Dunbar St 604-261-8700

Wang, David, N.D.
604-1200 Burrard St 604-687-0119

Weiss, Sid, N.D.
207-2678 W Broadway ...604-738-4085

Wellness Connection
6272 E. Boulevard 604-266-4566

Wiseman, Carla
260-2025 W 42nd Ave 604-264-9921

Wong, Joe
1367 E 41st Ave 604-324-0445

Wu, Annie, David, Eunice & Joseph
105-1956 W Broadway ...604-732-8968

YCY Chinese Medicine & Health Care Centre
123 E Pender St 604-685-1871

Y.W. Chinese Herb & Acupuncture
3288 Cambie St 604-873-9682

Yam, Molino
640-943 W Broadway 604-734-1173

Yamaki, Kenzo
214-2211 W 4th Ave 604-730-1277

Yan Bin Ma's Natural Therapy
2-1734 W Broadway 604-733-1703

Zhen, Sophia
By Appointment 604-258-0269

VERNON

Mc Kinney, Neil, N.D.
206-2910 30th Ave 604-549-1400

Vernon Acupuncture Clinic
G-3105-31st Ave 604-542-0227

VICTORIA

Acumoxa & Herb Clinic
621-1207 Douglas St 604-388-0388

Akasha Health Clinic
Lindsay, Anne
1447 Jamaica Rd 604-472-0134

Albertson, Dr. David
4206 Cedarglen Rd 604-721-5017

April, Marie-Michele
152 Cambridge St 604-384-3553

Artemis Health Center
301-1005 Langley St 604-384-4350

Brown, Susan
29-610 Mc Kenzie Ave 604-479-5305

Buccoliero, Giuseppe
152 Cambridge St 604-384-3553

Caiden, Rosolynn
1122 Leonard St 604-383-4162

Chamberlain, Richard
1505 Fell St 604-592-3345

Chinese Acupuncture & Herbal Centre
108-1218 Wharf St 604-388-4266

Chu Chung Chang & Chu May Twin, Drs.
512-620 View St 604-383-0011

Cushing, Susan
226-733 Johnson St 604-388-3037

Dayman, Barry
104-1121 Yates St 604-382-5577

East West Medical Society
855 Cormorant St 604-385-6704

Fairfield Naturopathic & Acupuncture Clinic
1255 Fairfield Rd 604-384-9694

Giles, Dawn
300B-3060 Cedar Hill Rd ...604-592-1218

Greenspirit Holistic Health Centre
Lade, Arnie; Lade, Diane
208-26 Bastion Sq 604-383-1858

Kempling, Philip, N.D.
206-1175 Cook St 604-382-1223

Lam, Christopher
135-1555 McKenzie Ave ..250-472-3338

Lam, James
833 Cormorant St 604-388-2108

MacMillan, Sihoe C.
3928 Oakdale Pl 604-477-5387

McLean, Gail
203-1150 Hilda 604-385-5290

Ohalloran, Jane, N.D.
1255 Fairfield Rd 604-384-9694

Oriental Health Clinic
414-620 View St 604-381-6838

Pacific Acupuncture
625-1207 Douglas St 604-384-9866

Puhky, Ronald; Tucker, J.
1028 Fort St 604-389-0864

Rode, Albert, N.D.
206-1175 Cook St 604-382-1223

Rohon, Juan
1255 Fairfield Rd 604-384-9694

Sihoe, Chris
3928 Oakdale Pl 604-477-5387

Sim, Norman
1-1408 Broad St 604-383-3911

Sui Acupuncture Clinic
Issenman, N; Pritchard, J.
226-733 Johnson St 604-361-4606

TCM Clinic
323-645 Fort St 604-361-1616

Vickerd, Doug
301-1005 Langley St 604-384-4350

Victoria Naturopathic Clinic
206-1175 Cook St 604-382-1223

Yarrow Sports Injury & Orthopaedic Physiotherapy
330-645 Fort St 604-385-3151

Zhu, Hong Zhen
201-2722 Fifth St 604-361-1778

WEST VANCOUVER

West Vancouver Acupuncture Clinic
202-1865 Marine Dr 604-926-0238

West Bay Clinic
Scott, Susan; Shaw, Catherine
3396 Marine Dr 604-922-7242

WHISTLER

Whistler Therapeutic Centre
101-4208 Village Sq 604-938-4943

WHITE ROCK

Peace Arch Family Health Clinic
Levendusky, Paul, N.D.
202-15210 North Bluff Rd ..604-536-8600

White Rock Acupuncture Clinic
Tonskamper, Gudrun, N.D.
304-1493 Johnston Rd 604-536-1400

WINFIELD

Wagstaff, S. Craig, N.D.
11270 Robinson Rd 604-766-3633

Manitoba

Acupuncturists are not regulated as practitioners in Manitoba. This means that there is no governing body responsible for registering qualified acupuncturists and disciplining them. This also means that no minimum educational standards exist for those calling themselves acupuncturists.

Manitoba Association

The Chinese Medicine and Acupuncture Association of Canada (CMAAC)
Manitoba Chapter
858 McDermot Ave
Winnipeg, Manitoba R3E 0T7
Tel: 204-632-7966

✦ Manitoba Acupuncturists

NOTE: Check the credentials of your practitioner (see above, "Questions to Ask"). This publication cannot and does not certify or represent the qualifications of practitioners, or the quality of care available from them.

BRANDON

Naturopathic Physicians Clinic
Conyette, P.A.; Ge Yun Xia
708-A 10th St 204-727-3524

WINNIPEG

Back Consulting & Re-Education Services
1215-A Henderson Hwy 204-982-9191

Berzuk, Kelli
1204 Rothesay St 204-982-9195

Campbell, Lesa
Fitness Physiotherapy Clinic . .204-982-9600

Eastern Lights Life Centre
5-709 Corydon 204-452-0088

Fitness Physiotherapy Clinic
135 Roslyn Rd 204-982-9600

Gan, Dr. C
204-2265 Pembina 204-261-9236

Marcoux, Henri, D.C.
208 Marion St 204-237-0210

Massotherapy Clinic
286 Stradbrook Ave 204-284-0849

Medical Arts Building
Di Marco, Anna
215-233 Kennedy St 204-982-9176

Naturopathic Physicians Clinic
20-2727 Portage Ave 204-837-2042

Ness Acupuncture Clinic
Tokariwski, Julian
1700 Ness Ave 204-837-4115

Winnipeg Acupuncture & Reflexology Centre
204-309 Hargrave St 204-943-1120

Wong, Joe
1204 Rothesay St 204-982-9195

New Brunswick

Acupuncturists are not regulated as practitioners in New Brunswick. This means that there is no governing body responsible for registering qualified acupuncturists and disciplining them. This also means that no minimum educational standards exist for those calling themselves acupuncturists.

✦ New Brunswick Acupuncturists

NOTE: Check the credentials of your practitioner (see above, "Questions to Ask"). This publication cannot and does not certify or represent the qualifications of practitioners, or the quality of care available from them.

BATHURST

Fleurimond, Mathieu, N.D.
195 Main St 506-548-3898

BERESFORD

Roy, Jacques
1309 Principale 506-548-8732

CAMPBELLTON

Lambert, Steve A.
91 Roseberry St 506-753-4421

DALHOUSIE

Clinique Naturothérapeutique D'Acupuncture
Naturo-Therapeutic Acupuncture & Herbology Clinic
111 Brunswick 506-684-5144

FREDERICTON

Atlantic Chinese Acupuncture & Natural Medicine Clinic
386 Regent St 506-458-2211

Clavette, D./Brune, D.
34 Talmadge Ct. 506-450-6144

L-C Acupuncture & Natural Healing Clinic
785 McLaren Ave 506-457-0901

MONCTON

Acupuncture Clinic
Lee, Dr. H.
268 Mclaughlin Dr 506-856-7047

Clinique Acupuncture Alfred De Grace
250 Acadia Ave 506-855-6000

SAINT JOHN

Chinese Acupuncture & Herb Clinic
Che, Yi
289 Westmorland Rd 506-652-9729

Newfoundland

Acupuncturists are not regulated as practitioners in Newfoundland. This means that there is no governing body responsible for registering qualified acupuncturists and disciplining them. This also means that no minimum educational standards exist for those calling themselves acupuncturists. An initial visit to a licensed physician to determine if you are a candidate for acupuncture is fully covered under the province's Medical Care Plan (MCP), but not the acupuncture treatments themselves.

 # Newfoundland Acupuncturists

NOTE: Check the credentials of your practitioner (see above, "Questions to Ask"). This publication cannot and does not certify or represent the qualifications of practitioners, or the quality of care available from them.

ST JOHN'S

Delaney, John
98 Linegar Ave 709-753-4646

Melvin, Rose
10 Somerset Pl 709-753-2093

Chinese Therapy Centre
102 Lemarchant Rd 709-753-1150

Back To Health Inc.
724 Water St 709-738-0158

 # Nova Scotia

Acupuncturists are not regulated as practitioners in Nova Scotia. This means that there is no governing body responsible for registering qualified acupuncturists and disciplining them. This also means that no minimum educational standards exist for those calling themselves acupuncturists.

Nova Scotia Associations

The Chinese Medicine and Acupuncture Association (CMAAC)
Maritime Chapter
6156 Quinpool Road
Halifax, Nova Scotia B3L 1A3
Tel: 902-492-8839

Nova Scotia Association of Acupuncturists
c/o Eastwind Health Associates
2176 Windsor St
Halifax, Nova Scotia B3K 5B6
Tel: 902-420-9466

Call for a referral to a member acupuncturist. In 1996, the association stated that all members were certified by the U.S. certification body NCCA (see above "U.S. Accreditation Bodies & Associations"), with three years of training. The association, formed in 1989, will also handle complaints, and has adopted a code of ethics for its members.

✦ Nova Scotia Acupuncturists

NOTE: Check the credentials of your practitioner (see above, "Questions to Ask"). This publication cannot and does not certify or represent the qualifications of practitioners, or the quality of care available from them.

AMHERST

Amherst Physiotherapy Clinic
By Appointment 902-667-8188

DARTMOUTH

Ochterloney Medical Clinic
Kaminska, Dr. Irena;
Liszka, Dr. Bozenna; Campbell, Dr. Donald;
Sekula, Dr. Zygmunt;
Tereposky, Dr. Lynne
109 Ochterloney St 902-466-7530

KENTVILLE

West Park Wellness Centre
747 Park St 902-582-1305/679-5454

HALIFAX

Acupuncture & Healing Clinic
255 Lacewood Dr 902-443-5015

Atlantic Counselling and Consulting Associates
Roche, Derek
1649 Barrington St, 4th Fl ..902-422-3711

Eastwind Health Associates
Brosius, Cary, NCCA; Stick, Kermit, NCCA
2176 Windsor St 902-422-3760

Forden, Risa Anne, NCCA
5871 Spring Garden Rd 902-425-2406

L-C Acupuncture & Natural Therapy Clinic
Chen, Franklyn; Li, Diana
6165 Quinpool Rd 902-492-8839

Morningtide Traditional Acupuncture Clinic
Holden, Jane Louise, NCCA;
Speraw, Pamela A, NCCA
5523-B Young St 902-455-7402

Oriental Acupuncture & Natural Healing Clinic
2973 Oxford St 902-453-2392

Taussig, Frank E, NCCA
5871 Spring Garden Rd 902-420-9466

SYDNEY

Jessome, Phillip
54 Prince St/326
Champlain Ave 902-539-6262

✦ Ontario

In Ontario, acupuncturists are not regulated and there is no governing body responsible for setting educational standards, qualifications and disciplinary procedures. However, a coalition of acupuncture associations have applied to the provincial government for such regulation.

In the meantime, acupuncture is permitted under Ontario law. Specifically, section 27 of Ontario's *Regulated Health Professions Act, 1991* defines 13 medical acts, called controlled acts, which may be performed only by authorized persons. A regulation exempts acupuncture from this restriction for the purpose of performing a procedure on tissue below the dermis (skin) (Ontario Regulation 887/93, s. 1.1). There is no government health care funding.

Ontario Associations

Ontario Association of Acupuncture & Traditional Chinese Medicine
370 Dupont St
Toronto, Ontario M5R 1V9
Tel/Fax: 416-925-6752

This long-time association will give referrals to its 200 members, most of whom are graduates of the Institute of Traditional Chinese Medicine, affiliated with the association. Members must pass an examination and have their qualifications reviewed by the association.

Professional Acupuncturists' Association of Ontario (PAAO)
5213 Tiffany Court
Mississauga, Ontario L5M 5G9
Tel: 905-858-3630

Acupuncturists belonging to this association must pass an examination. PAAO suggests you call the Chinese Medical and Acupuncture Association of Canada for a referral. However, if you wish to discuss practitioner qualifications, contact Raymond Yeh, PAAO vice-president.

Supporters of Holistic Medicine and Acupuncture
57 Jena Cr
London, Ontario N5V 1L3
Tel: 519-451-8484

This volunteer consumer group lobbies government for the licensing of acupuncturists and raises public awareness as to the benefits of acupuncture. The group, established in the 1980's, is comprised of consumers who have had success with traditional Chinese medicine and acupuncture. The group recommends that those looking for referrals contact the Chinese Medicine and Acupuncture Association of Canada (CMAAC - see above, "National Associations").

✦ Ontario Acupuncturists

NOTE: Check the credentials of your practitioner (see above, "Questions to Ask"). This publication cannot and does not certify or represent the qualifications of practitioners, or the quality of care available from them.

ALLISTON

Alliston Chiropractic Centre
16 Victoria St E 705-435-6371

ANCASTER

Sloat, Dr. Barbara
124 Wilson St W 905-648-0661

Milroy, Pamela, N.D.
393 Wilson St E 905-648-5200

AJAX

Ajax Harwood Medical Clinic
Ajax Harwood Plaza 905-683-0690

Lee, Dr. E.
174 Harwood St 905-683-3572

AURORA

Khamissa Family Chiropractic Clinic
15483 Yonge St 905-727-0604

AZILDA

Magneto Therapy Acupuncture Clinic
339 Marier 705-983-0511

BARRIE

Allandale Physiotherapy Clinic
231 Bayview Dr 705-728-7676

Bell Farm Rehabilitation
125 Bell Farm Rd 705-722-7585

Bradley, Nancy
109 Bayfield St 705-721-9802

Cedar Pointe Physiotherapy
64 Cedar Pointe Dr 705-722-7585

Dixon, Liz
21-80 Bradford St 705-725-1831

Eastview Natural Therapy
123 St Vincent St 705-739-0025

Fieldstone Natural Health Centre
RR 6 705-436-2724

Makray, Dr. Leslie
Big Bay Pt Rd 705-722-8923

Perry, Margot
RR 6 705-436-2724

Quinn Rehab Services
2 Friesen Pl 705-726-2362

The Team Approach Self Care Centre
Symons, Peg; Hickling, Li; Romanic, G.
20 Bell Farm Rd 705-725-1831

BEAMSVILLE

Patel, Mukesh
5026 King St 905-563-5444

BELLE RIVER

Chiropractic Rehabilitation Group
419 Notre Dame 519-728-2711

BELLEVILLE

Chau, N.T.
213-A Front St 613-962-9429

Bayview Chiropractic Centre
218 College St W 613-968-9626

BINBROOK

Country Health Centre
4080 Hall 905-692-9300

BLACKSTOCK

Bowmanville Family Chiropractic Centre
43 Ontario 905-623-8388

BOBCAYGEON

Total Life Care
129 Main St 705-738-4451

BOLTON

Personal Best Rehabilitation
30 Martha St 905-857-9988

BRAMPTON

Accident Occupational Health
18 Kensington Rd 905-791-8048

Acupuncture & Laser Therapy
123 Queen St W 905-450-5445

Natural Health Services
123 Queen St W 905-450-5445

Springdale Chiropractic Clinic
40 Finchgate Blvd 905-791-8048

BRANTFORD

Brant Acupuncture Clinic
205 Brant Ave 519-752-7010

De Marchi Chiropractic Health Clinic
92 Elm St 519-756-8171

Hauk, Alfred
134 Charing Cross 519-751-3488

Wilson Physiotherapy
72 Brant Ave 519-759-1710

BROCKVILLE

Brockville Acupuncture Clinic
Liew, Kwong Kee
71 Windsor Dr 613-342-5961

BURLINGTON

Appleby Chiropractic & Acupuncture Clinic
Appleby Mall 905-639-7355

City Cope Physiotherapy
3027 Harvester Rd, 3rd Fl ..905-639-6332

Yamamoto, Dr. B.
Shin, Dr. Michael
2200 Fairview St 905-632-2542

CORNWALL

Lai, Shuikee
120-9th St E 613-936-2596

Nanji, Dr. Amir
240 Adolphus St 613-938-1721

Yu, Michael
614 E 2nd St 613-938-8643

DUNDAS

Dundas Naturopathic Centre
211 W King St 905-627-9434

GANANOQUE

Astley, Dr. Clair
140 Garden St 613-382-3330

Bergstrome, K.
280 Stone St S 613-382-7686

GODERICH

Palmer, Douglas, D.C.
73 Montreal St 519-524-4555

GUELPH

Chinese Health Clinic
173 Woolwich St 519-822-5555

Chinese Medicine & Acupuncture Clinic
206-33 Macdonell St 519-837-1010

Oriental Healing Arts & Health Institute
1-15 Surrey W 519-763-6340

Dronyk Clinic
2880 E King St 519-894-0024

HAMILTON

Acupuncture & Chinese Herbal
1264 E Main St 905-547-8839

Acupuncture Clinic
770 Mohawk Rd W 905-387-5557

Beer, Karen Inc
1461 Main St W 905-523-5161

Dunsmure Pain Clinic
59 Dunsmure Rd 905-547-5393

Hamilton Pain Clinic
1461 Main St W 905-523-5161

Hamsa Centre
245 King William St 905-577-6992

Holistic Centre
500 James St N 905-521-9664

Hopper, Elizabeth
444 Fennell Ave E 905-575-1615

Hutchison Chiropractic Clinic
214-350 King St E 905-528-8924

Naturotherapy Clinic
584 Concession 905-318-8518

Park, Anna H.
59 Dunsmure Rd 905-547-5393

Total Physiotherapy & Rehabilitation
631 Queenston Rd 905-578-1900

HARRISTON

Natural Health & Acupuncture
274 King St S 519-338-3104

HAWKESBURY

Acupuncture Clinic of Hawkesbury & District
151 Main St E 613-632-1315

HESPELER

Alternative Medicine Clinic
27 Cooper 519-658-9738

INGERSOLL

The Heath Centre
90 Charles W 519-485-3000

KANATA

Kakulu Physiotherapy & Sports Injury Clinic
203-99 Kakulu Rd 613-591-8832

KESWICK

Pike Chiropractic Health Centre
204 Simcoe Ave 905-476-6475

KINGSTON

Blasers Physiotherapy Clinic
202-321 Concession 613-542-3852

Kingston Acupuncture Clinic
654 Division St 613-545-0197

KITCHENER

Acupuncture by Nishi Kim
52 Bruce St 519-744-2132

Goodyear-Johnston, Sharon, D.C.
526 Frederick St 519-743-6339

Hwee, Dr. Peter
1221 Weber St E 519-894-8800

Stoll, A.
355 Veronica Dr 519-893-7997

LIMOGES

Limoges Acupuncture Clinic
1467 Route 300 613-443-9064

LINDSAY

Kent St Chiropractic Centre
245 Kent St W 705-324-8211

LONDON

Acupuncture & Natural Therapy Clinic
712 Oxford St E.........519-645-8038

Alternate Pain Management Clinic
897 Adelaide St N 519-642-2096

Cheung, Cedric, Professor K.T.
154 Wellington 642-1970

Clement, Dr. John S.
10 Hawthorne Rd 519-471-8273

Heilbrunn, Dr. David
499 Oxford St E.........519-673-3155

Holistic Therapy & Acupuncture
117 Grand Ave 519-439-0854

Institute Of Chinese Medicine
154 Wellington St 519-642-1970

Li, Suya
191 Base Line Rd W 519-434-5512

Natural Herbs & Acupuncture Centre
24 Holborn Ave 519-439-6773

Naturopathic Medicine & Health Clinic
208-746 Base Line E 519-433-3060

Polisak, James
712 Oxford St E 519-645-8038

Pond Mills Chinese Medicine & Acupuncture Clinic
Hosein, Sayeeda
1166 Commissioners Rd E...519-668-7891

MARKHAM

Markham Headache & Pain Treatment Centre
12 Main St N 905-471-9355

MEAFORD

Sager, Dr. R.E.
22 Nelson St 519-538-2821

MIDLAND

Huronia Medical Centre Physiotherapy
Hugel Ave &
Old Penetanguishene Rd 705-526-0174

MISSISSAUGA

Besik, Dr. Fred
2000 Credit Valley Rd 905-820-3694

Canadian Health & Acupuncture Clinic
5213 Tiffany Ct 905-858-3630

Credit Landing Medical Centre
244 Lakeshore Rd W 905-278-3868

Desouza, Joycelene, D.C.
2000 Credit Valley Rd ...905-607-8898

Erin Centre Physio & Acupressure Clinic
2555 Erin Centre Blvd 905-567-3630

European Acupuncture Inc
92 Lakeshore Rd E........905-891-3150

European Acupuncture Institute
3056 Southcreek Rd 416-622-2483

Franko, James, D.C.
3185 Cawthra Rd 905-276-2200

Goodman, Jess
224 Lakeshore Rd W 905-278-3868

Heinen, Shirley
224 Lakeshore Rd W 905-278-3868

Holden, Robert, D.C.
3185 Cawthra Rd 905-276-2200

Kaganovsky, Alexey
5805 Whittle Rd 905-890-4946

Lakeshore Chiropractic & Wellness Center
279 Lakeshore Rd E 905-274-1759

Meadow-West Family Practice
6855 Meadowvale Town Centre ...905-821-2114

Meridian Naturopathic Clinic
2087 Dundas E 905-238-9001

Shiatsu Acupuncture Centre
30 Eglinton Ave W 905-712-3706

Tai, Dr. Evelyn
6855 Meadowvale Town Centre ...905-821-2114

Traditional Acupuncture Clinic
3045 Southcreek Rd 905-629-8187

Ventures in Harmony
130 E Dundas St 905-897-8761

Wilson, Dr. Scott
3185 Cawthra Rd 905-276-2200

Wong, Dr. Clement
6855 Meadowvale Town Centre 905-821-2114

Wong, Mary
224 Lakeshore Rd W 905-278-3868

MOUNT FOREST

Mount Forest-Aletris Natural Health Clinic
Main & Birmingham E 519-323-1116

NEWMARKET

Newmarket Natural Health Centre
17817 Leslie St 905-853-0172

York Medical Acupuncture & Pain Clinic
Lai, Kenneth; Liedeman Mandy
Ye Yun; Yeung Clement
1100 Davis Dr 905-853-7107

Ruegg Chiropractic Clinic
109 Main St S 905-895-1299

NIAGARA FALLS

Acupuncture Acupressure & Chinese Herbal Clinic
6150 Valley Way 905-371-0775

Elliott Chiropractic Centre
5816 Main St 905-356-4484

Niagara Acupuncture Clinic
6453 Morrison St 905-356-4044

OAKVILLE

Meridian Naturopathic Clinic
113 Jones St 905-847-2470

Oakville Natural Health Clinic
77 Lakeshore Rd W 905-842-0226

Oakville Naturopathic Clinic
127 Trafalgar Rd 905-844-7718

Richman, Dr. J.
264 Elton Park Rd 905-845-9902

ORILLIA

Miller, Murray, D.C.
2-19 Albert St N 705-327-5400

Bryan Physical Therapy
210 Memorial Ave 705-327-7876

ORLEANS

Clinique D'acupuncture Et De Medicine Chinoise
Acupuncture & Chinese Medicine
862 Borland Dr 613-841-6814

Clinique Chiropratique Centrum Orleans Acupuncture Clinic
210 Centrum Blvd 613-830-4080

OSHAWA

Chuvalo, Antan Tony
By Appointment 905-434-8886

Central Health & Chiropractic
50 Richmond E 905-433-1500

OTTAWA

Acupuncture & Advanced Healing Centre
501-1525 Carling Ave 613-725-1100

Bayshore Physiotherapy & Sports Injury Clinic
200-2571 Carling Ave 613-596-0167

Britannia Chiropractic Clinic
S 11-1315 Richmond St Rd ..613-726-8830

Centrepointe Physiotherapy & Sports Clinic
1 Centrepointe Dr 613-723-6161

Chinese Acupuncture
Huang, D
1-13 Lebreton St N 613-232-0009

Chinese Acupuncture & Herbs
615 Somerset St W 613-235-9917

Chinese Acupuncture Clinic
501 Kent St 613-231-2363

Chinese Ditda-Tuila Healing Centre
1-1057 Somerset St W 613-722-2746

Chinese Medicine & Acupuncture
883 Somerset St W 613-233-1098

Chinese Traditional Acupuncture & Natural Medicine
867 Somerset St W 613-235-5504

Fournier, C.
460 Grebert 613-561-7771

Guo, Zhaoqi
152 Bayview Rd 613-729-6165

Kozlowski, Andrew/Christine
Upper 505-381 Kent St ...613-567-7607

Ortho-Sport Physiotherapy
Lower 476, Holland Ave 613-729-9079

Ottawa Chinese Medical Centre
89 Richmond Rd 613-729-9023

Reid, Michael, D.C.
S 11-1315 Richmond Rd 613-726-8830

Ridell, P.K.
1012-60 Cartier St 613-234-3767

Shis Chinese Medicine-Acupuncture & Massage Clinic
2-175 Preston St 613-234-3767

Sino Acupuncture Clinic
152 Bayview Rd 613-729-6165

Zhang Acupuncture Centre
237 Rochester St 613-230-1104

OWEN SOUND

Canadian Acupuncture & Pain Clinic
992 2nd Ave W 519-376-6033

Stress Reduction Centre
940 1st Ave W 519-372-0995

PELHAM

Taylor, Richard, D.C.
1512 Hwy 20 E 905-892-2683

PETERBOROUGH

Acupuncture Clinic
80 E Hunter St 705-742-0213

Millar, John
403 McDonnel St 705-743-2008

Peterborough Chiropractic Group
166 McDonnel St 705-748-6611

Thomson, Keith, D.C.
403 McDonnel St 705-743-5121

PICKERING

Pickering Family Physicians
1450 Kingston Rd 905-420-6025

POINT EDWARD

Acupuncture & Pain Clinic
Wan, D
704 Mara 519-332-5200

PORT HOPE

Port Hope Chiropractic
3 Dorset St 905-885-5111

PRESTON

A-1 Acupuncture Lai Tak Lin
995 E King St 519-653-3541

RICHMOND HILL

Richmond Hill Natural Therapies
Chuvalo, Antan Tony
By Appointment 905-883-9355

RUTHVEN

Acu-Clinic
RR 2 519-839-5387

SARNIA

Sarnia Chinese Medicine & Acupuncture Clinic
780 London Rd 519-337-3611

SAULT STE MARIE

Dipasquo Chiropractic Clinic
202-212 Queen St E 705-253-0253

ST. CATHARINES

Acupuncture & Chinese Herbal Medicine
Eles, Maria
209 Carlton St 905-984-5311

Athletes Clinic
290 Glendale Ave 905-680-2844

Orvitz, Edan, D.C.
278 Bunting 905-684-2225

Westlake Square Chiropractic Centre
353 Lake St 905-934-4357

ST GEORGE

Port Dover Accupuncture Clinic
627 St George 519-583-2880

SCHOMBERG

Acupuncture Centre
Makray, Susan
RR2, Kettleby 905-939-7053

SIMCOE

Downtown Chiropractic
1-111 N Colborne St 519-426-0944

STAYNER

Miller, Murray G.W.
25 Muskoka N 705-689-5400

STONEY CREEK

European Acupuncture Clinic
66 King St E 905-662-1992

Natural Therapies
72 Centennial Pkwy S 905-662-6566

STRATFORD

Perth Physiotherapy Clinic
282 Erie St 519-272-1939

Physiotherapy Associates of Stratford
413 Hibernia St 519-272-0122

SUDBURY

Baihui Acupuncture
174 Leslie St 705-673-0522

TECUMSEH

Chiropractic Rehabilitation Group
13300 Tecumseh Rd 519-979-4154

THORNHILL

Acupuncture Clinic of Thornhill
1118 Centre 905-881-5540

Dimerman, J, D.C.
300 John St 905-882-7688

Holistic Meridians & Qi Gong Research Centre
328 Hwy 7 E 905-886-8038

Shrott, Mark, D.C.
9184 Yonge St 905-881-4079

Steeles Chiropractic & Acupuncture Health Clinic
404 Steeles Ave W 905-886-6811

Thornhill Acupuncture Clinic
Olensky, David
1118 Centre St 905-881-5540

Thornhill Chiropractic
7690 Yonge St 905-886-9778

Usman, Abida
300 John St 905-764-5253

THUNDER BAY

Natural Health & Healing Centre
817 Victoria Ave E 807-622-4325

TILLSONBURG

Acupuncture Massage Clinic
264 Tillson Ave 519-688-0285

Ostrander Chinese Medicine & Acupuncture Clinic
RR 7 519-842-6840

TIMMINS

Ho, K.F.
Ste H-119 Pine St S 705-267-1515

TORONTO

A-1 Acupuncture
5140 Dundas St W 416-234-5502

Acupuncture Centre
717 Bloor St W 416-537-6164

Acupuncture Chiropractic & Naturopathic Medicine
778 Gerrard St E 416-469-2709

Acupuncture Clinic
717 Bloor St W 416-533-4106

Alternative Health Care Services
102-1 Gloucester St 416-967-6891

Argyropoulos, Nick
795 Pape Ave 416-469-1205

Begin, Marty
2-715 Bloor St W 416-533-2078

Borden Chiropractic Clinic
Kwong, Chiu
10 Borden St 416-961-5571

Canada Chi Kung Health Clinic
545 St Clair Ave W 416-653-4105

Carling, Anna, NCCA
7 Jackes Ave #208 416-963-9879

Castor Chiropractic Centre
174 Browns Line 416-251-4448

Chan, Raymond
6008 Yonge St 416-223-8666

Chinacare Wellness
1391 Yonge St 416-975-4539

Chinese Health & Healing Clinic
1130 Eglinton Ave W 781-8888

Chinese Herb & Health Clinic
276 Willard Ave 416-767-6266

Chinese Medicine & Acupuncture Clinic
3443 Finch Ave E 416-493-8447

Chiu Kowong Clinical Acupuncture
10 Borden St 416-961-5571

Classical Chinese Medicine Clinic
206-411 Parliament St 416-928-1335

Davey Wellness Clinic
57 Tilden Cr 241-7151

David Quang's Chinese Herbal Medicine
4186 Finch Ave E 416-321-8212

Deer Park Naturopathic Clinic
303-200 St Clair Ave W 416-921-3837

Downtown Natural Health Centre
86 Asquith Ave 416-922-6780

Dreu, Mark, NCCA
112A Yonge St 416-923-9576

Fung, Tom, NCCA
2656 Midland Ave 416-292-3641

Gao Acupuncture & Traditional Chinese Medicine Clinic
Gao, George
By Appointment/
House Calls 416-504-0939

Grant, Muriel, D.C.
2588-A Yonge St 416-485-3013

Health Reform Wellness Centre
102-2400 Midland Ave 416-291-5657

Holistic Aromatherapy Clinic
By Appointment 416-929-4451

Hui, Dr. Frederick
421 Bloor St E 416-920-4200

Hui John C., D.C.
4040 Finch Ave E 416-321-1701

Kent, Kate Blair, NCCA
55 Delma Dr 416-251-5710

Kokubos Acupuncture Clinic
208 Bloor St W 416-926-0466

Leca, Dr. R.
458 Eglinton Ave W 416-485-0600

Lee's Acupuncture & Herbalist Clinic
430 Dundas St W 416-591-7279

Linda Zhou's Acupuncture Clinic
500 Sheppard Ave E 416-512-6331

Ly's Acupuncture Clinic
1477 Queen St E 416-466-6157

Mah Acupuncture Clinic
464 Yonge St 416-920-3806

Melody Chiropractic & Acupuncture
885 Progress Ave 416-439-2672

Memrik, Dr. Edward
475 Dovercourt Rd 416-536-2888

Mezei, I., D.C.
1029-A St Clair Ave W 416-653-4273

Natural Health Centre
2221 Yonge St 416-932-9418

Naturopathic College Clinic
60 Berl Ave 416-251-7418

North York Acupuncture Clinic
345 Wilson Ave 416-631-6646

Olensky, David
345 Wilson Ave 416-631-6646

Pei, Paul
717 Bloor St W 416-533-4106

Rad, A.
2753 Eglinton Ave E 416-269-0151

Radojcic, Aleks
5 Carscadden Dr 416-636-8444

Rapson Pain Clinic
207-600 Sherbourne St 416-968-1366

Rice, Dr. Michael
22 Wellesley St W 416-920-2722

Robazza, Dr. Kelly
2212 Queen St E 416-698-5861

Rosedale Physiotherapy & Sports Injury Centre
421 Bloor St E 416-929-1995

S G Natural Herbs & Acupuncture Service
220 Duncan Mill Rd 416-510-0162

Shen, Pei Ying
586 Eglinton Ave E, # 711 . .416-932-3270

Shiatsu Acupuncture Clinic Tim Tanaka
80 Bloor St W 416-929-6958

Shiatsu Clinic West
3101 Bloor St W 416-236-2583

St Clair Acupuncture Clinic
1029-A St Clair Ave W 416-653-4273

Susie's Acupuncture
682 Euclid Ave 416-533-3814

Tokyo Shiatsu Clinic King St
214 King St W 416-595-8299

Toronto Health Centre
93 Harbord St W 416-929-5708

Toronto Natural Healing Centre
500 Sheppard Ave E 416-512-6331

Toronto Pain & Headache Clinic
9 Bloor St E, #206 416-925-2579

Toronto Wellness Centre
24 Wellesley St W 416-920-2722

Traditional Acupuncture & Healing
40 Pleasant Blvd 416-920-3056

Traditional Chinese Natural Therapy Specialists
3852 Finch Ave E, #407 416-298-3070

Wellness Counselling
170 St George St 416-925-7627

Wing Tai Hong Canada Enterprises Ltd
289 Spadina Ave 416-598-3030

Yan Oi Chinese Herbalist & Acupuncture
418 Dundas St W 416-591-6370

Yan-Yan Chinese Herbs Centre
25 Glen Watford Dr 416-292-8605

Yonge Wellesley Chiropractic & Acupuncture Centre
24 Wellesley St W 416-920-2722

Yorkville Chiropractic & Laser Acupuncture Centre
94 Cumberland St 416-928-0003

Zelsman, Marvin
4025 Yonge St 416-225-9530

Zheng, Jason
658 Danforth Ave 416-461-1312

UNIONVILLE

Fujimagari, Dr. John
4981 Hwy 7 905-470-2626

**Gillis, Susan, D.C.
Lawson, Gordon, D.C.**
2 Millstone Ct 905-475-8386

Markham Pain Clinic
4981 Hwy 7 905-470-2626

Quan, Terry
4981 Hwy 7 905-470-2626

Star Oriental Studio
1151 Denison St 905-474-5805

WATERDOWN

Flamborough Massage & Acupuncture Clinic
140 Mill St N 905-689-7175

WATERLOO

Anousaya, C.
22 Mcdougall Rd 519-885-3720

Bender, John
22 Mcdougall Rd 519-885-3720

Chinese Medicine & Acupuncture Clinic
Parkdale Plaza One 519-885-3902

Conestoga Natural Health Clinic
17 Waterloo St S 519-664-1665

Koegler Laboratories
22 Mcdougall Rd 519-885-3720

Tunstall, Richard
22 Mcdougall Rd 519-885-3720

Vital Health Therapies Inc
99 Northfield Dr 519-888-9000

WELLAND

Levay, Ronald, D.C.
57 Division St 905-735-9344

WHITBY

Chang, W.K.
220 Dundas St W 905-668-5871

WINDSOR

Acupuncture & Herbs Clinic
1210 Ouellette Pl 519-971-7762

Acupuncture Clinic
Kim, Peter
90 Erie St W 519-255-1699

Chinese Acupuncture Center
1163 Wyandotte St E 519-971-9021

Chinese Acupuncture Center Riverside
7735 Wyandotte E 519-974-7365

Genesis Health Centre
79 Giles Blvd E 519-258-5269

Goldstone Chinese Tai Chi & Acupuncture Centre
2115 Gladstone Ave 519-973-3967

Health Through Balance
654 Goyeau St 519-254-8872

Shuai, Songfang, NCCA
1210 Ouellette Ave 519-971-7762

WOODSTOCK

Olive Branch Natural Health Clinic
62 Wellington St S 519-539-7781

Quantum Health Centre
513 Admiral St 519-539-1992

✦ Prince Edward Island

There is no government regulation of acupuncture practitioners, meaning that there is no legislation establishing a governing body to register and discipline qualified practitioners. There is no government health care funding of acupuncture in Prince Edward Island.

✦ Prince Edward Island Acupuncturists

NOTE: Check the credentials of your practitioner (see above, "Questions to Ask"). This publication cannot and does not certify or represent the qualifications of practitioners, or the quality of care available from them.

CHARLOTTETOWN

Charlottetown Physiotherapy & Rehabilitation
28 Garfield St 902-566-2700/9990

 # Québec

In Québec, acupuncturists are regulated, meaning that there is legislation establishing a governing body responsible for setting educational standards, qualifications and disciplinary procedures. There is no government health care funding for acupuncture treatments.

Legislation

Acupuncturists are among the professions governed by Québec's *Professional Code*. Under section 32 of the Code, the title "acupuncturist" may be used only by members of the Ordre Professionnel des Acupuncteurs du Québec. Acupuncturists are further regulated by *An Act Respecting Acupuncture (Loi sur l'Acupuncture)*. Section 8 of the Act states that the "practice of acupuncture consists of any act of stimulation, by means of needles, of specific sites on the skin, mucous membranes or subcutaneous tissues of the human body to improve health or relieve pain." That definition is then broadened to include the clinical assessment, according to the traditional Oriental method, of a person's energetic state, the determination of appropriate treatment and the use of other means, such as heat, pressure, electric current, or rays of light, to improve health or relieve pain by stimulating specific sites on the skin, mucous membranes, or subcutaneous tissues of the human body.

Only Registered Acupuncturists may Practise

Subject to the rights granted by law to other professionals, no person other than an acupuncturist entered on the roll of the Order may perform needle acupuncture.

There are two sets of regulations, one covering the practice of acupuncture by non-physicians and the other covering the practice by physicians.

Regulation Covering Non-Physicians

This regulation requires non-physicians to meet professional standards before they may be registered as acupuncturists. A previous requirement that a client obtain a medical certificate before receiving acupuncture treatment has been revoked.

Requirement for Knowledge of French

A working knowledge of the official language is required in accordance with the linguistic standards prescribed in the Charter of the French language (R.S.Q., c.C-11) and its regulations. Contents of client records must be drafted in French or English.

Education

A person who wishes to practise acupuncture must hold a diploma of college studies in acupuncture awarded by a private institution recognized by the Ministry of Education. Only the Collège de Rosemont in Montréal has been recognized within Québec. Diplomas awarded outside Québec may be recognized if they represent equivalent training.

Examination

The competence of candidates in acupuncture and fundamental and clinical medical sciences is evaluated by a written examination and an oral examination.

Privacy

Acupuncturists must arrange their offices to ensure the privacy of patients.

Sterilization

Acupuncturists are required to follow proper sanitation and hygiene procedures, including effective equipment sterilization methods.

Regulation Covering Physicians

A regulation is in place respecting the training of physicians who wish to practise acupuncture, defined to include needles, heat, pressure, electric current or light. This regulation requires a minimum of 300 hours of theoretical and practical training.

Québec Governing Body

Ordre des Acupuncteurs du Québec
1600, Boul. Henri-Bourassa Ouest
Bureau 500, Montréal H3M 3E2
Tel: 514-331-8870

Call to ensure that your acupuncturist is registered and has therefore met the province's educational standard and passed the required examination. Contact the Ordre if you have a complaint.

Québec Associations

**L'Association de Medicine Chinoise et d'Acupuncture du Québec
The Chinese Medicine and Acupuncture Association of Québec**
68 Ouest, René-Levesque West
Montréal, Québec H2Z 1A2
Tel: 514-878-9933

Association Professionelle Acupuncteurs du Québec
4822 Christophe Colombe
Montréal, Québec H2J 3G9
Tel/Fax: 514-982-6567 or 525-2425

Association des Acupuncteurs du Québec
1251 Grand Pré
St. Lazare, Québec J0P 1V0
Tel: 514-424-0382

The Chinese Medicine and Acupuncture Association of Canada (CMAAC) Québec Chapter
310 Grand Cote
St-Eustache, Québec J7P 1E1
Tel: 514-491-0301

Syndicat Professional des Acupuncteurs et Acupunctrices du Québec
1601 De Lorimier
Montréal, Québec H2K 4M5
Tel: 514-738-6241
Fax: 514-598-2259

✦ Québec Acupuncturists

The following listings were obtained from the Ordre des Acupuncteurs du Québec. Contact the Ordre (see above, "Québec Governing Body") to ensure that your acupuncturist is registered, and to obtain the names of newly registered acupuncturists. Registrants living outside Québec are not listed below. Check the qualifications of your acupuncturist (see above, "Questions to Ask"). This publication cannot and does not certify or represent the qualifications of practitioners, or the quality of care available from them.

ALMA

Couture, Thérèse
340, rue Sacré-Coeur
Ouest 418-662-5254

Decoste, Marianne
509, rue d'Auvergne 418-668-4440

Grenier, Claudine
55, rue Rivest 418-668-8774

Lessard, Martine
531, rue Martel 418-662-6751

Nedelec, Giles
1120, rue Price Ouest, #3 .418-662-6463

AMOS

Billette, Louis
11, rue Louise 514-727-2111

Gauthier, Maurice
467, 1re rue Ouest,
#101 819-732-2976

Mireault, Luc
467, 1re rue Ouest 514-732-2976

ANCIENNE-LORETTE

Fortin-Gagnon, Jacqueline
1517, rue du Moulin 418-871-7182

Nadeau, Julie
1854, rue Damirno 418-877-8735

ANJOU

Granger, Alice
6153-A, boul.
Les Galeries d'Anjou 514-353-7682

BELOEIL

Deslauriers, Chantal
56, rue Jeannotte 514-467-1837

Filteau, Pierre
924, rue Richelieu 514-467-8788

L'Heureux, Françoise
301, rue Brodeur 514-446-8835

BEAUPORT

Belley, Sandra
500, boul.
Rochette, #200 418-660-3692

Camirand, Louise
161, rue Seigneuriale 418-666-7646

BLAINVILLE

Gilbert, Johanne
38, rue Yvan 514-434-9503

BOISBRIAND

Lefrançois, Nicole
188, Terrasse Guindon 514-435-7666

Nolin, François
206, Grande-Côte 514-437-1923

BOISCHATEL

Saint-Laurent, Micheline
112, rues des Grès 418-822-2984

BOIS-DES-FILION

Bergeron, Robert
345, rue Adolphe-
Chapleau 514-965-9847

Leblanc, Eveline
356, rue Pierre-Côté 514-965-1678

BOUCHERVILLE

Fontaine, André
109, rue De Mézy 514-449-1295

Pelchat, Sylvie
918, rue Charcot 514-449-7494

Rochefort, Madeleine
380, rue Samuel-de-
Champlain, #201 514-449-7461

Viau, Claudette
55, rue de Montbrun 514-655-6066

Vocelle, Louise
372, rue d'Avaugour 514-449-6863

BROSSARD

Bouré, Ginette
3740, rue Ovide 514-462-0896

Mai, Tam
8065, rue Niagara 514-445-6045

BROWNSBURG

Abran, Rose-Marie
516, rue Saint-Patrick 514-533-6376

CAP-CHAT

Blanchette, Lionel
71, place Delval 418-786-5361

CAP-ROUGE

Couture, Claude
4238, rue de la Rive 418-654-1829

Désaulniers, Sylvie
4614, rue Caroline Valin ...418-658-3820

Lacourt, Yolande
1368, rue
de Noirefontaine 418-652-3435

Morin, André
1100, boul. Chaudière,
C.P.5015 418-658-4358

CARIGNAN

Fontaine, Yves
3565, rue Lareau 514-658-5577

CARLETON

Desmanche, Marie-Pierre
101, rue
Penouil, C.P. 1125 418-364-6006

CHAMBLY

Guilmain, Guylaine
1101, rue
Brassard, #202 514-658-7809

Landry, Chantal
10, rue Dumain 514-447-7633

CHAMPLAIN

Gratton, Bernard
857, rue
Notre-Dame, C.P.103 819-295-3590

CHARLESBOURG

Boucher, Sonia
6780, 1ère Ave, #150 418-622-2309

Pelletier, Louise
1010, 80e Rue Est 418-622-2858

Pelletier, Micheline
1010, 80e Rue Est 418-622-2858

RUEL, Carol
5380, 1ère Ave 418-626-5180

Savard, Jacques
6780, 1ère ave, #150 418-622-9743

Zhou, Bending
905, rue
de Nemours, #218 418-624-3344

CHAMPLAIN

Poisson, Catherine
857, rue Notre-Dame 819-295-3590

CHATEAUGUAY

Blake-Drolet, Lise
155, rue Saint-Jean-
Baptiste, #2 514-698-2172

Thérien-B., Solange
407, rue Lafontaine 514-699-4535

CHESTERVILLE

Duceppe, Yvan
300, rue Boutin 819-382-2297

CHICOUTIMI

Gagnon, Alain
357, rue Malraux 418-696-3328

Joubert, Denis
551, rue
Jacques-Cartier Est 418-545-4062

Martel, Claude
216, rue de la Normandi ...418-545-2785

Prévost, Luce
5744, rue de l'Esplanade ...514-273-0633

CHISASIBI BAIE JAMES

Beloin, Claudette
E-2 3B, C.P. 635 819-855-3485

CONTRECOEUR

Boisvert, Patrick
660, rue Papin 514-587-5817

COOKSHIRE

Genest, Suzanne
160, rue Pope 819-875-5535

COWANSVILLE

Girard, Jean
413, rue Sud 514-263-7668

Grégoire, Diane
111, rue Rivière 514-263-8255

CRABTREE

Battisti, Claudio
321, 6e Rue 514-754-4522

Jackson, Shirley
71, 6e ave 514-754-4270

DEGELIS

Chamberland, Marie
454-A, rue Principale 418-853-9040

DRUMMONDVILLE

Côté, Monique
2170, rue Saint-Nicolas 819-474-5267

Kazazian, Nairy-Thérèse
2, rue des Châtaigniers 819-474-4148

Parent, Yves
150, rue Hériot 819-477-8081

GASPE

Brillant, Caroiline
C.P.1247 418-368-4240

GATINEAU

Fournier, Cécile
460, boul. Greber 819-561-7771

Paquin, Dominique, NCCA
210, rue Main 819-663-0219

GRANBY

Beaudoin, Désiré
133, rue Victoria 514-378-8999

GRAND-MERE

Quesnel, Sylvie
901, 15e Rue 819-538-7532

Saintonge, Michèle
1510, 15e ave 819-538-9743

GREENFIELD-PARK

Lafrenière, Louis
25, boul.
Taschereau, #03 514-466-7396

HULL

Benoit, Miriame
221, chemin
Freeman, #165 819-771-7532

Caron, Julie
350, rue de la Montagne,
#205 819-776-6199

Chhay, Sarith
195, rue Gamelin 819-770-5804

Roy-Beaudry, Rita
45, rue Desjardin 819-771-0083

ILE-AUX-COUDRES

Dufour, Michaelle
109, rue des Coudriers 418-438-2768

ILE-BIZARD

Beaudry, Magda Lena
982, rue Bellevue 514-696-5941

JOLIETTE

Hérard, Jacques
410, rue Melançon 514-436-7171

Rivest, Maryse
126, rue Saint-Paul 514-759-4773

JONQUIERE

D'Amour, Meldren
3529, rue Saint-Louis 418-542-1168

Trost, Monique
1807, boul. Mellon 418-548-9711

KIRKLAND

Trépanier, Gilles
41, rue Nelligan 514-695-9747

Viens, Claire
8, rue Edison 514-426-9771

LAC-ETCHEMIN

Morin, Hélène
125, ch Grande-Rivière 418-625-4321

LACHENAIE

Lamarche-M., Louise
845, rue du Gouffre 514-471-3133

Quintal, Mireille
2066, rue Florent 514-492-3441

LACHINE

Vu, Cong-Thuong
1155, rue
Notre-Dame, #105 514-537-4373

LACHUTE

Charlebois, Joanne
139, rue Béthanie 514-562-1113

LACOLLE

Deslauriers, Manon
62, Sude de l'Eglise,
C.P. 836 514-246-4226

LAFONTAINE

Thibault, Josée
190-A, rue Nicole 514-438-9828

LANORAIE

Plourde, Réjeanne
371-B, rue Notre-Dame 514-887-0233

Tremblay, Pascale
379, Notre-Dame,
C.P.151 514-887-0233

LANTIER

Raymond, France
2653, 10e rue R.R.1 819-326-3141

LA PLAINE

Loiselle, Magdeleine
783, rue Lizelle 514-968-0756

LA POCATIERE

Boucher, Yves
1208, 6e ave, C.P.517 418-856-3080

LA PRAIRIE

Tessier, Michel
60, boul. De la Mennais 514-659-9276

To, Tuyet Nga
285, rue des Pivoines 514-659-4209

LA PRESENTATION

Barbeau, Bernard
1130, Grand Rang 514-796-3211

LASALLE

LePham-Thi, Son-Tra
582, 90e ave, #204 514-365-2459

Lopez, Daniel
1550, boul. Dollard 514-366-3985

Pham-Thi, Dai-Doa
582, 90e Rue, #204 514-365-2459

Vincent, Johanne
7627, rue Centrale 514-367-1848

LA TUQUE

Vaillancourt, Emilienne
754, boul. Ducharme 819-528-8961

LAVAL

Beaumont, Claudette
3505, boul.
Saint-Martin Ouest, #203 . . .514-983-6019

Béland, Pierre
3841, boul.
De la Concorde Est 514-661-4102

Bourbonnais, Lyne
581, boul.
Des Laurentides, #1 514-891-1462

Bussières, Céline
1836, rue de Lunebourg 514-663-1334

Chicoine, Louise
101-F, boul.
De la Concorde Ouest 514-662-0999

Gariépy, Pierre
3030, boul.
Le Carrefour, #402 514-686-2516

Jobin, Diane
300, boul.
De la Concorde Est 514-667-5310

Landry, Geneviève
55, rue des Cèdres 514-665-3500

Lett, Marie-Andrée
143, ave Quintal 514-663-8165

McCarthy, Susie
3505, boul.
Saint-Martin Ouest, #203 . . .514-973-6019

Montemiglio, Louise
3550, boul.
De la Concorde 514-664-4212

Naccache, Marleine
4185, boul.
Saint-Martin Ouest, #411 . . .514-686-4728

Ouellet, Hélène
1957, 49e ave 514-627-7820

Parente, Carlos
3108, rue Glenn 514-628-7255

Pelletier, Hervé
3980, boul. Des Mille-Iles . . .514-666-3991

Philippon, Claude
3571, boul.
De la Concorde Est 514-664-0206

Roy, Adrienne
4194, rue de la Seine 514-681-9095

Roy-Rivard, Yvonne
784, rue Marsolais 514-661-3419

Saint-Laurent, Lise
4580, ch. Des Cageux 514-682-2920

Trudel, Gilles
4759, boul. Sainte-Rose 514-627-7538

LE GARDEUR

Gohier, Ghislain
516-B, boul. Lebourgneuf . . .514-939-6756

LEVIS

Blais, Louis
22, rue Sainte-Thérèse 418-833-8692

Dubois, Annie
4950, boul.
De la Rive-Sud, l. 108 418-834-2699

Germain, Normand
15, carré des Cascades 418-833-4747

Moreau, Lisette
4950, boul Rive-Sud, #108 . .418-833-5691

LONGUEUIL

Caron, Christine
153, rue
Saint-Laurent Est 514-677-9266

Comtois-Desf., Monique
66, rue
Saint-Laurent Ouest 514-677-3717

Gaignard, Yolande
2909, Terr. Bourgchemin . . .514-468-3244

Gervais, Gérard
17, rue Sainte-Catherine 514-651-0505

Mazzetti, Alain
441, rue
Sainte-Hélène, #1 514-463-0450

Mazzetti, Hélèe
441, rue
Sainte-Hélène, #1 514-463-0450

Ngo Thi, Kieu Mai
100, pl. Charles-
Lemoyne, #240 514-651-3010

Paré, Francine
441, rue Ste-Hélène, #1 514-463-0450

Toui-Kan, Evelyne
17, rue Sainte-Catherine 514-651-0505

Yang, Jai Hong
774, rue Maple 514-677-2515

LOUISEVILLE

Pagé, Gilles
45, rue Saint-Laurent 819-228-8177

MARIA

Poirier, Pierre
119, rue
Saint-Jules, C.P.1395 418-759-5969

MASCOUCHE

Ghirotto, Lisa
1316, croissant Louise 514-964-5246

MATANE

Gignac, Victor
368, rue Jacques-Cartier . . .418-562-6918

MCMASTERVILLE

Cardinal, Marie
714, rue Bernard-Pilon 514-446-4641

Jodoin, R. Michel
714, rue Bernard-Pilon 514-446-4641

Prévost, Laurent
718, rue Bernard-Pilon 514-464-8565

MONT-JOLI

Gagnon, Langis
1700, rue
Saint-Jean-Baptiste 418-775-4686

MONT-LAURIER

Perrier, Michel
477, rue Chapleau 819-623-2139

MONTREAL

Arragon, Georges R.
815 boul.
Henri-Bourassa Est 514-387-0010

Arsenault-L., Jeannine
2274, rue Marcil 514-486-5251

Arsianian, Abel-Claude
1405, boul. Henri-Bourassa
Ouest, #50 514-336-7434

Aubry, Josée
5870, rue Sherbrooke Est . . .514-899-0668

Bang-Hua, Thieu-Nga
6723, 25e ave 514-721-1291

Bardelli, Mireille
451, boul.
Saint-Joseph Est, #3 514-383-7762

Belzil, France
7081, 19e ave 514-376-2144

Bensimon, Abraham
6941, rue Lemieux 514-739-2670

Blain, Elaisne
583, rue Oak 514-466-7955

Bleau, Denise
6080, rue Mignault 514-256-5891

Boileau, Francine
10400, rue Saint-Denis 514-382-5564

Boissinot, Lynn
2100, boul.
Ed.-Montpetit, C.P.6128 . . .514-345-1741

Boissonnault, Robert
456, boul.
Saint-Joseph Est 514-284-1220

Bouillon, Isabelle
1695, boul.
St-Joseph Ests 514-522-9155

Bourque, Pierre
8021, rue de
Châteaubriand 514-279-1450

Chan, My-Hoa
4981, rue Dornal 514-733-7728

Chan, Sock-Laine
230, boul.
Henri-Bourassa Est, #230 . . .514-388-2282

Chang, Sie Shieng
3220, boul. Rosemont 514-727-8384

Chu, Nam Anh
6225, rue Clanranald 514-739-0076

Ciaralli, Laura
5010, rue Pierre-Bernard . . .514-493-6299

Clerk, Emmanual
30, boul. Saint-Joseph Est . . .514-499-1278

Côté, Bernard
1695, boul.
Saint-Joseph Est 514-522-9155

Couturier, Jacques-André
377-A, boul.
Saint-Joseph Est 514-278-4921

Cusson, Céline
464, boul.
Saint-Joseph Est, #2 514-845-4347

Daoust, André
4695, rue Saint-Denis 514-982-9046

De Montigny, Richard
30, boul.
Saint-Joseph Est, #1100 514-844-8563

di Villadorata, Massimo
1695, boul.
Saint-Joseph Est 514-522-8644

Douville, Ghyslaine
9206, 17e ave 514-322-8214

Drapeau, Colette
5658, rue Saint-Denis 514-272-4035

Dumais, Carole
4896, rue Henri-Julien 514-843-3912

Dupuis, Louise
974, rue Roy Est, #9 514-521-6433

Favreau, Denise
2150, boul.
Saint-Joseph Est, #2 514-521-2285

Fontaine, Anna-Louise
6303, rue Bordeaux 514-725-7646

Fortin, Sylvain
1374, rue Mont-Royal Est . . .514-421-5555

Fournier, Carl
3717, rue Coloniale 514-848-9633

Fournier, Hélène
1458, rue Cartier 514-526-1335

Fowler, Arthur
4876, rue Jean-Brillant 514-738-6241

Gagnon, Denis
415, boul.
Saint-Joseph Est 514-842-9458

Gagnon, Madeleine
6276, rue Saint-Denis 514-276-3372

Gauvreau, François
1603, rue Gilford 514-525-1222

Généreux, Hélène
4848, rue Cartier 514-522-8068

Germain, Chantal
6788, rue Saint-Denis 514-948-0434

Ghobril, Sami
6555, ch.de la Côte-des-
Neiges, #390 514-731-1186

Girard, Danielle
4432, rue Henri-Julien 514-286-1266

Girard, Diane
7488, rue
Chambord, #14 514-273-2103

Girard, Raymond
4434, rue Henri-Julien 514-286-1266

Giroux, Jacques
4310, boul. Gouin Ouest . . .514-338-1600

Gosselin, Louise
3460, rue
Jeanne d'Arc, #2 514-259-8251

Goulet, Dannie
8605, rue Saint-Denis 514-858-9485

Grimaux, Bernard
30, boul.
Saint-Joseph Est, #809 514-845-4139

Guévin, France
415, boul.
Saint-Joseph Est 514-286-0458

Hivon, Manon
1621, rue Beaudry, #9 514-596-1742

Ho-Viet, Minh
1337, rue Ontario Est 514-528-4908

Huynh, Anh-Triet
1330, rue Fleury Est 514-382-3221

Huynh, Hinh-Mieu
1330, rue Fleury Est 514-382-3221

Jacob, Lisette
4723, rue Berri 514-598-7307

Joannette, Michèle
8344, rue Saint-Denis 514-382-6550

Kim, Kwang Oh
765, rue Mont-Royal Est 514-597-1777

Lam, Dinh Co
6630, boul. Monk 514-768-5112

Lam, Phan Kok
6630, boul. Monk 514-768-5112

Langevin, Lucie
10185, rue Millen 514-384-7910

Lapierre, Elizabeth
310-A, boul.
Saint-Joseph Est 514-843-8603

Lapointe, Danielle
8898, 14e ave 514-955-9763

Lapointe, Michèle
7063, rue Sagard 514-729-3409

Latraverse, Sylvie
30, boul.
Saint-Joseph Est, #901 514-499-1278

Lebel, Denis
30, boul.
Saint-Joseph Est, #902 514-845-0778

Leduc, Louis-Philippe
945, rue Sherbrooke Est 514-529-8826

Lefebvre, Nicolas
500, boul.
Gouin Est, #303 514-387-1154

Lefrançois, Corinne
7513, rue Jacques-
Rousseau 514-494-9993

Legault, Alain
2760, rue Sherbrooke Est . .514-282-9197

Legault, Francine
1444, rue Fleury Est 514-388-3005

Legault, Richard
7538, rue St-Denis 514-278-2599

Léger, Claude-Louis
265, boul.
Saint-Joseph Ouest 514-273-7899

Lemelin, Céline
30, boul.
Saint-Joseph Est, #920 514-845-4926

Lemieux, Lorraine
281, rue Roy est 514-499-0986

Lévesque, Jean
4822, rue Christophe-
Colomb 514-525-2425

Lévesque, Marthe
415, boul.
Saint-Joseph Est 514-286-0458

Maranda, Monique
3437, rue St-Denis 514-849-2087

Matte, Sylvie
1695, boul. St-Joseph Est . .514-598-8882

Mouchahoir, Michel
1358, rue Sauvé Est 514-388-1997

Nguyen, Kim-Hoa
6431, rue de
Châteaubriand 514-270-3813

Nguyen, Van Chuong
6655, Côte-des-Neiges,
#235 514-735-9737

Nguyen, Vuong Hoang
2876, boul. Rosemont 514-727-8577

Pelletier, Claudette
10801, rue Laverdure 514-382-1565

Pham, Quang Bach
6455, rue Christophe-
Colomb, #207 514-271-2424

Pham, Thi-Nam Chieu
2876, boul. Rosemont 514-727-8577

Pimentel, Benjamin
6940, rue Louis-Dupire 514-252-0312

Poirier, Colette
8004, rue St-Denis 514-384-6060

Poulin, André
4950, ch. Queen Mary,
#350 514-340-9146

Poulin, Danielle
1900, rue Saint-
Catherine Est 514-525-4555

Poulin, Gilles
815, boul.
Henri-Bourassa Est, #12 514-388-3168

Pouliot, Alain
6773, rue Etienne-
Bouchard 514-254-9581

Prévost, Luce
5744, rue de'Esplanade 514-273-0633

Proulx, André
7310, 14e ave, #7 514-728-6514

Racette, Claude-Emile
370-A, boul.
Saint-Joseph Est 514-843-8606

Robert, Sylvie
2105, rue Van Horne 514-344-0843

Saint-Arnault, Monique
564, rue William-David 514-257-9429

Sermet, Michel
1052, rue Laurier Est 514-282-0279

Soucy, Jacinthe
310-A, boul.
Saint-Joseph Est 514-843-8603

Ta, Long
2557, boul. Rosemont 514-728-4629

Tang, Boon Sieng
12244, rue Pierre-
Blanchet 514-494-9662

Thomas, Philippe
8013, rue Saint-Denis 514-387-1204

Thu-Thon, Marc
6880, rue de Marseille 514-256-7820

Topakian, Maryse
1408, rue Jean-
Talon Est, #103 514-270-8438

Tougas, Danielle
7239, rue Henri-Julien 514-279-4668

Tremblay, Christine
5199, rue Drolet 514-272-4772

Truong, Phu-Quoc
5126, rue St-Denis 514-273-2664

Viens, Jasmine
4256, de Mentana 514-525-8351

Wexu, Mario
4970, ch. Queen
Mary, #29 514-735-1730

Wexu-Fowler, Amélie
4876, rue Jean-Brillant 514-738-6241

Yeh, Ching-Chuan
99, rue Viger
Ouest, #G02 514-879-1898

Yoo, Cécile
5180, ch. De la Reine-
Marie, #300 514-369-1924

Zhang, Aina
223, rue Mont-Royal
Ouest, #5 514-844-6730

MONTREAL NORD

Archambault, Michèle
12030, rue Ronald 514-329-0018

Castro, Curt
6892, boul. Gouin Est 514-324-7241

Jean-Gilles, Myrtho
6122, rue
Arthur-Chevrier 514-322-9264

Laplace, France
10755, rue Lamoureux 514-322-6393

Nguyen, Hoang-Thinh
3440, boul.
Henri-Bourassa Est, #12 514-327-8972

NAPIERVILLE

Gilbert, Pierre
462, rue Saint-Jacques 514-245-7774

NOTRE DAME DE BONSECOURS

Larochelle, Guyta
4, rue Leclair 514-347-2357

Pardiac, Antoinette
13, Montéee Daigneault 514-658-9862

NOTRE DAME DES PRAIRIES

Rail, Sylvain
100, boul.
Antonio-Barette 514-759-7615

Saint-Onge, Marc
100, boul.
Antonio-Barette 514-759-7615

OTTERBURN PARK

Dion, Claudette
301, rue Clifton 514-446-0278

NEUFCHATEL

Laroche, Diane
3360, rue Martineau 418-847-3902

OTTERBURN-PARK

Leigh, Viviane
301, rue Clifton 514-446-0278

OUTREMONT

Caron, François
1441, ave Van Horne 514-279-8403

L'Ecuyer, Danielle
735, rue Outremont 514-376-2519

Meloche, Pierre
17, ave Laviolette 514-273-5110

Pepin, François-Marie
735, ave Outremont 514-276-2712

PIERREFONDS

Larouche, Johanne
4940, rue Lalande 514-683-5296

Legault, Jean
4948, rue Perron 514-684-9857

Quérin, Marcel
4956, boul. Perron 514-684-1791

PINTENDRE

Lacroix, Chantal
835, rue des Ruisseaux 418-833-7414

POINTE-CLAIRE

Kang, Hui
506, boul. St-Jean, #200 ...514-694-6506

Shin, Sang Jin
189, boul. Hymus, #410 ...514-695-8275

PONT-ROUGE

Genois, Natacha
163, rue du Collège 418-873-3793

QUEBEC

Boisvert, Marcel
1105, rue Aiguebelle 418-522-8365

Boudreau, Madeleine
935, Sir Adolphe-
Routhier 418-681-7544

Carignan, Lorraine
2725, rue
Lafrance, #206 418-842-4750

Côté, Lise
1191, rue Cartier 418-522-1911

Couture, Johanne
370, 17e Rue 418-648-8582

Dion, Jeanine
1060, rue Raymond-
Casgrain, #307 418-688-3517

Dufresne, Réjane
233, rue Fraser 418-522-6891

Fortin, Johanne
1054, rue Lasarre, #102 ...418-649-7628

Gendreau, Jocelyne
1057, ave des Erables 418-648-8494

Guy, Thérèse
680, boul.
René-Lévesque Ouest 418-687-4969

Hotte, Lucie
1125, ch. Sainte-Foy 418-683-0867

Karakand, Yousri
675, rue Marguerite-
Bourgeoys 418-687-1165

Lemieux, Sophie
475, rue des
Franciscains 418-688-7655

Mainville, Lucie
831, boul.
René-Lévesque Ouest 418-687-2720

Martineau, Luc
1028, rue des Erables 418-687-1060

Nguyen, Huy
4103, rue Etape 418-872-2548

Noël, Marie
765, ch. Sainte-Foy, #6 418-683-6809

Ouellet, Christine
975, rue Joffre 418-687-4464

Paquin, Renée
1270, rue Maufils 418-664-1567

Paradis, Ginette
364, 10e Rue 418-529-2537

Paré, Anne
233, rue Fraser 418-648-1979

Pérusse, Claudette
999, ave de Bougainville . . .418-682-0306

Rouleau, Arlette
286, rue Dorchester 418-648-8370

Roussell, Robert
2780, boul. Masson, #40 . . .418-626-5180

Solinas, Henri
831, boul.
René-Lévesque Ouest 418-687-2720

Testaguzza, Sandra
1183, ch. Sainte-Foy 418-527-6810

Tremblay, Nicole
338, ch. Saint-Louis, #1 418-688-1711

Wang, Erh Zhi
220, Grande-Allée,
#1000 418-529-9691

REPENTIGNY

Arcand, Lise
72, rue Rodier 514-582-0169

Bérard-D., Pierrette
41, Plateau Norman 514-654-9881

Brochu, Isabelle
342, rue Notre-Dame 514-657-2004

Gratton-Noël, Monique
218, rue Plessis 514-582-0832

Lefebvre, Dora
117, rue Trudeau 514-582-7519

Raynault, Hélène
25, rue Beauchesne 514-654-2570

Roy, Andrée
258, boul. Brien 514-582-3938

RIMOUSKI

Cardinal, Sylvain
317, ave Parent Sud 418-723-8118

Gauthier, Carolle
317, ave Parent Sud 418-723-8118

Lévesque, Gisèle
317, rue Parent Sud 418-723-8221

RIVIERE-DU-LOUP

Bélanger, Fernand
126, rue Lafontaine 418-867-4828

ROUYN-NORANDA

Giasson, Louise
122, rue Richelieu 819-762-9710

SAINT-ANTOINE

Beauchamp, Gilles
1265 10e Rue 514-565-0871

Cyr, Christian
425, boul.
Des Laurentides 514-565-8787

Lépine, Diane
120, ch. des Phares 418-886-2602

SAINT-APOLLINAIRE

Drolet, Denise
856, rue de Pierriche 418-881-3839

ST. AUGUSTIN-DE-DES-MAURES

Allard-Breton, Nicole
109, de la Livarde 418-871-1083

ST-BENOIT-MIRABEL

Prince, Nicole
6841, rang Saint-Vincent . . .514-258-2568

SAINT-BLAISE

Caron, Nicole
1339, rue Principale 415-291-3172

SAINT-BRUNO

Chan, Hubert
1665, boul.
De Montarville 514-653-5403

Ferron, Rolande
1665, boul.
De Montarville 514-653-5403

Gingras-L., Diane
1534, boul.
Montarville, #102 514-461-0363

Lemire-Ouellet, Hélène
1597, rue de Bienville 514-653-0266

Rheault, Ginette
124, rue de zmési 514-441-9845

SAINT-CANUT

Desjardins, Diane
162, Montée Brisebois 514-258-2230

SAINT-CHARLES

Dupras, Suzanne
187, ch.des Patriotes 514-584-3475

SAINT-CHARLES-BORROMEE

Grégoire, Micheline
55, rue Rivest 514-759-1011

Leclerc, Anne-Marie
28, chemin du Golf 514-756-8482

ST-CHARLES-DRUM.

Letendre, Daniel
745, boul. Saint-Charles 819-478-3145

SAINT-DONAT

Léveillé, Gilles
429, ch. Lac de la
Montagne Noire 819-424-7609

SAINT-EUSTACHE

Ducharmé, Francine
596, rue Rivière Nord 514-491-2311

Girard, Marie-Claude
124, rue St.-Laurent 514-472-4619

Lai, Shuikee
77, rue Arthur-Sauvé 514-491-0301

ST-FELICIEN

Hogue, Sylvie
1035, rue Cartier 418-679-2303

ST-FELIX-DE-VALOIS

Bruneau, Nancy
132, chemin Barette 514-889-8810

Roy, Annie
132, ch. Barrette 514-889-8810

SAINT-GEORGES

Brochu, Michel
11875, 1ère ave 418-228-7711

SAINT-HILAIRE

Amann, Patrick
1122, rue d'Orly 514-464-8181

SAINT-HUBERT

Bachand, Sophie
1705, rue Soucy 514-676-7196

Bellemare, Lucie
5660, ch. Chambly, #202 . . .514-445-8724

Ducharme, Lucie
7072, rue Louis-Hébert 514-462-1495

Migneault, Alain
2450, montée
Saint-Hubert, #2 514-678-4072

Toutant, Christiane
5660, ch. Chambly, #202 . . .514-445-8724

SAINT-HYACINTHE

Gagnon-C., Marthe
1025, boul.
Casavant Ouest, #3 514-771-1551

Lesot, Alain B.
1775, rue des Cascades
Ouest 514-774-9855

Nguyen, Van Chuyen
2680, rue Bouchard 514-773-5018

Saint-Jean, Patrick
1375, rue Coulonge 514-778-3861

Saint-Ongé, René
2845, rue Notre-Dame 514-773-9221

SAINT-HYPPOLITE

Roy, Diane
28, rue Willie-Laroche 514-224-5214

Villemaire, Claudine
24, 390e ave 514-563-5249

SAINT-JEAN

Petiot, Jean-Claude
175, rue Laurier 514-346-5331

ST-JEAN-CHRYSOSTOME

Lessard, Caroline
848, rue Commerciale 418-834-2051

SAINT-JEROME

Hébert, Jacques
410, rue Melançon 514-436-7171

SAINT-JOSEPH-DE-SOREL

Lechasseur, Ginette
21, rue du Fleuve 514-743-2892

SAINT-JOVITE

Fecteau, Louise
911, rue Ouimet,
C.P.1449 819-425-9457

SAINT-LAMBERT

Ballard, Nicole
111, rue Green, #202 514-466-7026

Dionne-Simard, Pauline
4, rue d'Artois 514-671-5716

SAINT-LAURENT

Te, Suy-Huong
1250, boul. Poirier 514-747-0280

Zhang, Wen-Fang
1265, rue Crevier 514-747-3615

SAINT-LAZARE

Bourbonnais, Lise
1331, Pine Ridge 514-455-9127

Saint-Amant, Ann
1251, rue de Grandpré ...418-424-0382

SAINT-LEONARD

Chartier, Monique
8710, rue Marjoilaine 514-328-8984

Michard, Johanne
6302, rue de Beillefeulle ...514-251-5321

Vézina, Lise
5601, rue Bélanger 514-256-5011

ST.-LOUIS-DE-FRANCE

Adam, Sylvie
601, place Ouellet 819-379-3236

SAINT-LUC

Bertrand, Odette
25, rue Louise 514-349-2738

SAINT-MATHIAS

Côté, Francine
14, Place Adam 514-658-8610

SAINT-PASCAL

Dufour, Robert
625, rue Taché 418-492-9362

ST. PAUL-DE-JOLIETTE

Francoeur, Emmanuel
120, ch. Delangis 514-753-5055

Guilbeault, Guylaine
120, ch. Delangis 514-753-5055

SAINT-RAYMOND

Beaulieu, Huguette
743, rue des Sources 418-337-4468

SAINT-REDEMPTEUR

Fortin-Lamy, Raymonde
1236, rue de
law Chaudière 418-831-9939

SAINT-ROMUALD

Villeneuve, Lyne
1780, rue Albertine 418-839-6458

SAINT-SAUVEUR

Paquin, Nicolas
110, rue des Emeraudes 514-227-6530

Quesnel, Diane
Galeries des Bonts,
Block L-4 514-227-1864

Riopel, Claudia
110, rue des Emeraudes 514-227-6530

SAINT-SULPICE

Racine, Donald
1533, rue Notre-Dame 514-589-7519

Saint-Aubin, Jean
1507, rue Notre-Dame 514-589-2602

SAINT-THERESE

Marleau, Marie-Claude
25, rue St-Joseph,
bur.205 514-437-5557

Morissette, Diane
25, rue Saint-Joseph,
#205 514-437-5557

SAINT-ZEPHIRIN

Joubert, Diane
2200-A, rue Saint-Pierre ...514-564-2871

SAINTE-ADELE

Lasserre, Viviane
4520, rue des Cavaliers 514-229-5861

Mercier, Réjean
1332, boul.
Sainte-Adèle, #140 514-229-5948

SAINTE-AGATHE

Valiquette, Jean-Luc
26, rue Préfontaine Est 819-326-7271

ST-ANTOINE-DE-TILLY

Bergeron, Nicole
3854, ch. De Tilly 418-886-2407

SAINTE-CATHERINE

Archambault, Marielle
985, rue de la Frégate 514-635-3836

SAINTE-FOY

Bélanger, Sonia
2956, rue Gentilly 418-658-2684

Bernier, Marcel
3370, rue de la Pérade 418-654-0320

Bourret, Raymond
2900, ch. Des Quatre-
Bourgeois, #212 418-650-2228

Collin, Nancy
2750, chemin
Sainte-Foy, #250 418-658-3200

Delpech, Anne
2750, ch.
Sainte-Foy, #205 418-656-6022

Demers, Nicole
3019, rue Matapédia 418-656-6354

Guimont, Claude
1001, route
de 'Eglise, #407 418-659-3425

Jourdan, Philippe
1001, route de
l'Eglise, #506 418-659-2266

Lavoie, Lucie
3042, rue
Deschâtelets, #5 418-658-2666

Théberge, Charlotte
2750, ch.
Saint-Foy, #205 418-658-3200

Vermette, Lorraine
3220, ch. Es Quatre-
Bourgeois 418-654-9450

SAINTE-JULIE

Deschênes, Jean
1630-B, rue Principale 514-922-3636

SAINTE-PERPETUE

Cloutier, Sylvie
366, rue Principale 418-359-3176

SAINTE-ROSE

Leblanc, Estelle
125, rue Filion 514-628-0897

SHAWINIGAN-SUD

Doucet, Sylvie
555, 128e Rue 819-537-4848

Dupont, Danielle
88, rue Lacoursière 819-537-8753

SHERBROOKE

Comeau, Anita
2964, ch. Champigny 819-562-6814

Gendreau, Claude
1474, rue King Ouest 514-565-1955

Giguère, Suzanne
37, boul. Queen Nord 819-821-4163

Richard, Suzel
241, rue Wood 819-569-1872

Tran, Hy
99, rue Gorden 819-822-1153

Tran, Thi-Anh
1440, rue des Sables 819-823-0777

Wang, Zhanghong
2185, rue de Rouville 819-820-1828

SOREL

Bouchard, Christine
87-B Jacques-Cartier 514-746-1638

Casavant, Lorraine
369, boul. Fiset, #305 514-742-5147

Farley, Michelle
5, Côteau du Sable 514-742-6567

SUTTON

Ferron, Catherine
25-B, rue Maple,
C.P.1002 819-538-6371

TERREBONNE

Sohacki, Nikola
792, boul. Saint-Louis 514-471-4991

THETFORD-MINES

Lacroix, Lise
1178, rue Coleraine 418-338-8394

Massée, Lorraine
189, rue Dubé 418-338-1299

TROIS-RIVIERES

Bellerive, Jean-Claude
7355, rue
Hector-Héroux 819-378-0675

Dang, Jean Quoc-Dung
1066, rue Champflour 819-379-1525

Tousignant, Lise
1235, boul. Sain-Louis 819-379-8960

VAL D'OR

Adams, Yvon
575, rue de la Rivierère 819-825-1005

VALLEYFIELD

Lainey, Serge
510, Grande-Ile, #204 514-373-2332
Nguyen, Duy-Hoan
291, rue Bissonnette 514-371-0559

VARENNES

Aldama, Miguel
2341, rue
René-Gauthier 514-652-6483

Duclos, Jean
2341, rue René-Gaultier 514-652-6483

VERDUN

Brais, Françoise
3805, rue Verdun 514-769-9671

Côté, Lucie
4647, ave Verdun 514-765-3600

VILLAGE-HURON

Bastien, Louise-Hélène
81, boul. Bastien 418-843-1790

WESTMOUNT

Lee, Hi-Jae
345, rue Victoria, #201 514-489-9073

Saskatchewan

In Saskatchewan, there is no government regulation of acupuncture practitioners, meaning that there is no governing body responsible for setting educational standards, qualifications or disciplinary procedures. No government health care funding exists for acupuncture treatment.

Saskatchewan Association

The Chinese Medicine and Acupuncture Association of Canada (CMAAC)
Saskatchewan Chapter
3847 B Albert St S
Regina S4S 3R4
Tel: 306-757-2995

Saskatchewan Acupuncture Association
3-A, 1620 Idylwyld Dr N
Saskatoon S7L 6W6
Tel: 306-244-5328

Call for a referral to one of the association's 20 members, each of whom has an average of two years' experience. The association has set a minimum educational standard of three months of training. It has also recently established an entrance examination as a membership criterion for new members. Members are required to use disposable needles.

✦ Saskatchewan Acupuncturists

NOTE: Check the credentials of your practitioner (see above, "Questions to Ask"). This publication cannot and does not certify or represent the qualifications of practitioners, or the quality of care available from them.

PONTEIX

Ponteix Health Centre Doctors' Clinic
4th St W 306-625-3232

REGINA

Arcola Physiotherapy & Acupuncture Clinic
374 University Park Dr 306-789-2484

Northgate Medical Centre
Northgate Shopping Centre ..306-543-4566

The Meta-System Therapies Centre
3847b Albert St S 306-757-2995

Park Plaza Acu-Med Clinic
2022 Park St 306-757-0544

Regina Chinese Acupuncture Centre
1421 Albert St 306-525-5767

Yuen Tai Hong Chinese Herbal & Acupuncture Centre
3800 Dewdney Ave 306-522-3888

SASKATOON

Bao Kong Herbs Centre
2a-1540 Alberta Ave 306-653-2353

Chau, Peter
928b 8th St E 306-665-7300

Ma, H. F.
211-39 23rd St E 306-652-8705

Saskatoon Acupuncture Clinic
924 Northumberland Ave ...306-384-9222

Chinese Acupuncture
3a-1620 Idylwyld Dr N 306-244-5328

✦ Yukon Territory

The Yukon Medical Council, a body of physicians and lay members established under the Territory's *Medical Profession Act*, issued a directive on May 6, 1986 establishing guidelines respecting the use of acupuncture therapy in the Yukon.

The two-page guidelines define acupuncture as a "form of stimulation to and through the skin, muscles or nerves, by needles or by other means...to initiate changes in the locally treated tissues or peripheral, autonomic or central nervous system to bring about therapy of disease". The guidelines state that acupuncture is considered to have a valid role in the management of patients with selected pains and syndromes.

The guidelines deem acupuncture to be a medical procedure, regardless of the method used, and "as such should not be performed other than by members of the medical profession, or by dentists who have taken appropriate training and are knowledgeable in its use". It adds that the procedure is not without hazard, and aside from the obvious potential for infection and trauma to underlying viscera, it may produce cardiac difficulties, including cardiac arrest and death. The guidelines state that physicians wishing to administer acupuncture should have a special knowledge of the problems of chronic pain and an understanding of the principles of acupuncture as they pertain to anatomy and physiology. The physician should also be aware of and be able to deal with possible complications.

The guidelines further state the opinion that the procedure should not be delegated to other members of the profession such as physiotherapists except in an approved institutional setting. It recommends two training programs: a 200-hour course at Vancouver General Hospital, and a three-level course in acupuncture offered by the Acupuncture Foundation of Canada. The guidelines note that both programs have been accepted by the College of Physicians and Surgeons of B.C.

✦ Yukon Acupuncturists

NOTE: Check the credentials of your practitioner (see above, "Questions to Ask"). This publication cannot and does not certify or represent the qualifications of practitioners, or the quality of care available from them.

WHITEHORSE

Skinner, David, Dr.
101-3059 3rd Ave 403-633-2223

Alexander Technique

WHAT IS THE ALEXANDER TECHNIQUE

The Alexander technique teaches correct habits of body movement and posture. It is based on the theory that poor habits and self-created tension can lead to ill health. The technique is not offered as a health treatment, but as a form of instruction. In a typical session, a teacher assesses a person's manner of standing, sitting or moving. The teacher then uses gentle hand pressure to help the individual correct posture and improve coordination. The technique, taught worldwide, originated with Frederick M. Alexander (1869-1955), an actor who suffered from recurring loss of voice and could not find effective medical treatment. He recovered when he began noticing and changing his own habits, which included the unconscious tightening of his throat and neck muscles when he thought of speaking.

BENEFITS OF THE ALEXANDER TECHNIQUE

The Canadian Society of Teachers of the F.M. Alexander Technique (CANSTAT) notes that athletes and performing artists have found the technique useful for improving neuro-muscular coordination and posture. The technique is also said to be useful if you have subtle habits of movement or postural problems that interfere with your well-being, or contribute to chronic conditions such as arthritis, back pain, repetitive strain injury, stiff neck or shoulders. The technique is also considered potentially useful for tension-related speaking problems and tendonitis. The Alexander Technique is said to be ideally learned on an individual basis from a qualified teacher.

QUESTIONS TO ASK

✦ Is the Alexander Technique an appropriate approach for you, given what you hope to accomplish through it?

✦ Is your Alexander teacher certified by a school approved by the Canadian Society of Teachers of the F.M. Alexander Technique (CANSTAT), or one of its international affiliates? Confirm by contacting CANSTAT (see below, "Canadian Society").

  NOTE: There is only one approved school in Canada, with a second school in the approval process (see below, "Alexander Technique Education").

✦ How much experience does your Alexander teacher have? Does the experience include teaching a person with your condition? What were the results?

✦ Can your Alexander teacher provide professional references?

✦ Is your Alexander teacher trained in any other form of health care? If so, what is the extent of the training?

✦ What is the price of the lessons, and how many are there?

GOVERNMENT REGULATION

Teachers of the Alexander Technique in Canada are not regulated as practitioners by any provincial government. This means that there is no provincial legislation establishing a regulatory body responsible for registering qualified teachers.

However, as noted, there is a non-profit society, the Canadian Society of the F.M. Alexander Technique, which certifies teachers who meet its qualification requirements.

CANADIAN SOCIETY

Canadian Society of Teachers of the F.M. Alexander Technique (CANSTAT)
1472, boul St Joseph E
Montréal, Québec H2J 1M5
Tel: 514-522-9230

The Society, established as a non-profit corporation in Canada in the early 1980s, sets and maintains standards for the certification of teachers and teacher training courses. The Society approves training schools that meet its standards, and is affiliated with the Societies of Teachers of the Alexander Technique outside Canada.

ALEXANDER TECHNIQUE EDUCATION

There is one training course in Canada recognized by CANSTAT as meeting the requirements for teacher training as stipulated in the Society's by-laws. This is the Toronto School of the Alexander Technique, listed below. The requirements include 1,600 hours of training over a minimum three-year period, and a teacher-student ratio of 1:5. Students who satisfactorily complete course requirements are eligible for membership in CANSTAT. A second school, in Québec, is undergoing the approval process. For more information, contact Micheline Charron at 819-847-4397.

Toronto School of the Alexander Technique
Elaine Kopman, Director
465 Wilson Ave
North York, Ontario M3H 1T9
Tel: 416-631-8127

✦ Alexander Technique In Your Province

Provinces are listed alphabetically below, with the following information:

✦ names, addresses and telephone numbers of Alexander Technique teachers, listed alphabetically by city

NOTE: The names in this list were provided by the Canadian Society of Teachers of the F.M. Alexander Technique (CANSTAT). According to CANSTAT, as of 1996, all members have met requirements for certification and are qualified teachers of the Alexander technique. Contact CANSTAT for updated membership information.

✦ Alberta Alexander Technique Teachers

NOTE: Check the credentials of your practitioner (see above, "Questions to Ask"). This publication cannot and does not certify or represent the qualifications of Alexander Technique teachers, or the quality of care available from them.

CALGARY

Deib, Annette
1420-25th Ave NE 403-276-1987

✦ British Columbia Alexander Technique Teachers

NOTE: Check the credentials of your practitioner (see above, "Questions to Ask"). This publication cannot and does not certify or represent the qualifications of Alexander Technique teachers, or the quality of care available from them.

NORTH VANCOUVER

Maxwell, L.
485 Ventura Crescent 604-987-0252

SAANICHTON

Aylott, Boaz
PO Box 356 604-360-6186

VANCOUVER

Aikman, Marilyn
2107-1011 Beach Ave 604-689-9102

Hunter, Marta
302-590 W 12th Ave 604-874-3075

Minnes, Gabriella
Alexander Technique Centre
303-2515 Burrard St 604-737-2818

Mosmans, Wilma
11-1360 Burnaby St 604-683-0063

Owen, David
908-888 Hamilton St 604-684-8058

Shields, Aaron
101-1010 Salsbury Dr 604-255-4492

VICTORIA

The Body Learning Centre
Dobie, Gwen; Rizzo, Giancarlo
565 Toronto St 604-389-0611

✦ Manitoba Alexander Technique Teachers

NOTE: Check the credentials of your practitioner (see above, "Questions to Ask"). This publication cannot and does not certify or represent the qualifications of Alexander Technique teachers, or the quality of care available from them.

WINNIPEG

Daniels, Pat
348 Oakwood Ave 204-284-7289

Ontario Alexander Technique Teachers

NOTE: Check the credentials of your practitioner (see above, "Questions to Ask"). This publication cannot and does not certify or represent the qualifications of Alexander Technique teachers, or the quality of care available from them.

MISSISSAUGA

Van Weelden, Pamela
3218 Aubrey Rd 905-828-5694

OTTAWA

Albert, Richard;
Calvo-Albert, Elena
32-2939 Fairlea Cr 613-733-5119

Beaumont, Brenda
131 Ivy Cr 613-744-1636

Desbiens, Brigitte
By Appointment 613-364-0255

Quipp, Heather
c/o Norsama Academy
208-194 Main St 819-827-0486

TORONTO

Freeman, Boaz
732 Spadina Ave 416-929-9225

Johnson, Verna
530 Huron St 416-926-9544

Kopman, Elaine
Studio: 465 Wilson Ave 416-631-8127

Lambie, Doreen
By Appointment
(Bayview &
Sheppard area) 416-512-7449

Lucas, Kathy
By Appointment
(Pape & Danforth) 416-466-5263

McEvenue, Kelly
2-133 Ulster St 416-972-0575

McEvenue, Kevin
15 Dermott Pl 416-324-9676

Obljubek, Miriam
By Appointment 416-781-5044

Tomarelli, Ron
By Appointment 416-494-0107

Vasileski, Victoria
By Appointment 416-658-7798

✦ Québec Alexander Technique Teachers

NOTE: Check the credentials of your practitioner (see above, "Questions to Ask"). This publication cannot and does not certify or represent the qualifications of Alexander Technique teachers, or the quality of care available from them.

HULL

Albert, Richard;
Calvo-Albert, Elena
8, rue Wright 819-771-7745

MAGOG

Charron, Micheline
250, rue Bellevue Ouest 819-868-6956

MONTREAL

Ghiberti, Simon
5271 Hutchison St 514-270-1461
(Québec City) . . . . .418-649-5180)

Glassman, Steven
4412, Saint André 514-524-4703

Jacob, Suzanne
4617 rue de Bordeaux 514-598-9230

Morisette, François
4-1472, St Joseph Est 514-522-9230

Shach, Rehavia Ben
203, Terry Fox St Ile-des-Soeurs . .514-762-1284

OLD CHELSEA

Quipp, Heather
104 Kingsmere Rd, Box G.4 .819-827-0486

ST JEROME

Bissonnette, Luc
277, rue St Jovite 514-432-8077

SILLERY

Shneider Kropf, Amadea
2186, rue du Bois Joi 418-683-7166

Aromatherapy

WHAT IS AROMOTHERAPY

Aromatherapy is a branch of herbalism in which distilled essences of plants, called essential oils, are used for easing the symptoms of a wide variety of ailments. The essential oils are extracted from the bark, leaves, petals, resins, roots or stems of certain aromatic plants, and are used in massage, in bathing, or through inhalation. While aromatherapy was known in the ancient Egyptian and Asian cultures, the term was coined in the 1920s by French chemist René-Maurice Gattefossé, who discovered by accident the healing effect of lavender oil on a burn. Aromatherapy is also for skin beauty care and perfumes.

Essential Oils

The purity and quality of essential oils can vary dramatically, and labels apparently cannot always be trusted. It is therefore important to find reputable practitioners and suppliers. Essential oils are highly concentrated and are always diluted in a suitable carrier oil or water before use to prevent irritation.

Essential oils are sold in concentrated form. If they have been adulterated with vegetable or carrier oils, they should be labelled as such, and sold at a lesser price. Synthetic oils made from petroleum byproducts are not considered as desirable. "Perfume oils" and "nature identical" oils are not usually pure essential oils, but synthetics.

Risks

While aromatherapy is increasingly popular for home use, it is not without risk. Undiluted oils are never placed directly onto the skin, as this may be irritating or harmful. As well, some oils are more toxic than others, and must be combined with less toxic oils. Certain oils should not be used for certain health conditions, or should be avoided altogether. It is advisable to consult with a qualified aromatherapist aware of the properties of oils, the safest and most effective ways to use them, and the risks of certain oils for specific health conditions.

BENEFITS OF AROMATHERAPY

Aromatherapy is said to ease the symptoms of colds and flu, arthritic pain, muscle pain and post-traumatic stress, respiratory problems, scalp problems, fatigue, headache, insomnia, skin disorders, stress, menstrual cramps and pre-menstrual tensions. Jennine Stromkins

of the B.C. Association of Practising Aromatherapists also notes that some physicians and health practitioners work with aromatherapists to assist patients suffering post-traumatic stress after a car accident. Aromatherapy may also ease discomforts of pregnancy, but certain essential oils should not be used by pregnant women. As well, certain essential oils should not be used by those with asthma, epilepsy, high blood pressure or certain other health problems.

Aromatherapy is a supplement to medical care, and is not considered a replacement for qualified medical help. Aromatherapists are not qualified to diagnose medical problems.

QUESTIONS TO ASK

✦ Is your aromatherapist a certified member in good standing with an association?

✦ How much training has your aromatherapist received? Did the training include anatomy and physiology, as well as contra-indications for asthma, epilepsy, high blood pressure or early stages of pregnancy? A trained aromatherapist will ask whether you have any such conditions.

NOTE: The minimum amount of training for practitioners of aromatherapy is 160-500 hours, according to professional associations. This includes training in the properties and contra-indications of at least 20 essential aromatherapy oils, anatomy and physiology, as well as about five days (35 hours) of practical supervision (see below, "Aromatherapy Education").

✦ Does your aromatherapist have a valid CPR First Aid certificate?

✦ How does your aromatherapist maintain his or her skills? Many associations require professional members to spend two weekends a year upgrading their skills.

✦ Are there animal products or synthetic bases (eg. petroleum products such as methyl or propyl paraben) in the essential oils? Note that even if a label states that it is a "pure essential oil", this is not a guarantee. Aromatherapists warn that petroleum products in the base of an essential oil prevent proper absorption and render it ineffective.

✦ What is the fee for a consultation or treatment? How much are the essential oils?

GOVERNMENT REGULATION

Aromatherapists are not regulated as practitioners by any provincial government. This means that there is no provincial legislation establishing a governing body responsible for registering qualified practitioners. This also means that there are no minimum educational standards for those calling themselves aromatherapists. However, some associations set their own standards for professional membership. Every province has legislation restricting either the practice of medicine or the performance of specified medical acts.

NATIONAL ASSOCIATIONS

NOTE: Provincial associations are listed under each province (see below, "Aromatherapry in Your Province").

Canadian Federation of Aromatherapists (CFA)
868 Markham Rd, #109
Scarborough, Ontario M1H 2Y2
Tel: 416-439-1951
or 1-800-803-7668 (ask for extension CFA)
Fax: 416-439-4984

This voluntary non-profit organization, established in 1993, will provide referrals across Canada, and answer consumer questions. Professional aromatherapist members have been certified by an accredited training program, or passed a certification examination. The Federation has a code of ethics requiring members to refrain from overriding the opinions of the medical, naturopathic, chiropractic or registered massage therapist professions.

Canadian Society of Professional Aromatherapists
6-298 Grays Rd
Hamilton, Ontario L8E 1V5
Tel: 905-662-1350

This voluntary non-profit association, established in 1993, has a code of ethics for its members, and is affiliated with several provincial aromatherapy associations. It relies on its recognized schools to give referrals.

AROMATHERAPY EDUCATION

For those seeking a career in aromatherapy, there are a number of training schools in Canada. In choosing a training program, one may wish to compare the qualifications of the teachers (their education and experience), student-teacher ratios, program content and length, number of clinical hours, and all fees and contract terms, including refund policies. In addition, it is useful to speak with students and graduates of the various programs about their standards, and to consult with representatives of associations, including the national associations. Ask the representatives if they are affiliated with a particular college.

Basic aromatherapy education usually involves 160-500 hours, including classroom study, home study and supervised training. The Canadian Federation of Aromatherapists requires professional member training to include the following: at least 25 hours of home study of anatomy and physiology, 20 case studies (requiring at least two hours each), 80 hours of classroom time (including 36 hours of supervised practical training and 44 hours of theory). The Canadian Society of Professional Aromatherapists requires about 100 hours of class time, a five-day practicum and 10 home study assignments, as well as 25 case studies (requiring about two hours each).

Most provinces have legislation requiring private vocational schools to meet certain minimum standards, often related to financial stability, for the protection of consumers. These requirements vary from province to province, and certain health care training programs are not in all cases covered by such legislation. Contact the Ministry of Education or Advanced Education in your province for more information on their policies regarding registration of private vocational schools.

Listed below are schools recognized either by the Canadian Federation of Aromatherapists or the Canadian Society of Professional Aromatherapists. For complete course schedules and fees, please contact the schools.

Aroma Spa: The Aromatherapy & Reflexology Centre
868 Markham Rd, Ste 109
Scarborough, Ontario M1H 2Y2
(Other locations: Surrey, Vancouver & Salt Spring Island)
Tel: 416-439-4884 or 1-800-803-7668 (ext. Aroma)
Fax: 416-439-4984

This Centre offers certified courses in standard and advanced aromatherapy, including instructor level courses. The Centre is run by the vice-president of the CFA.

Canadian National School of Aromatherapy
3180 Ridgeway Dr #39
Mississauga, Ontario L5L 5S7
Tel: 905-607-0177
Fax: 905-569-9601
Contact: Bridget Le Chat

The Canadian National School, recognized by the CFA, offers standard and advanced level courses.

Centre of International Holistic Studies
Aromatherapy Reflexology Centre
6-298 Grays Rd
Hamilton, Ontario L8E 1V5
905-662-1350 or 662-7463

This school, affiliated with the Canadian Society of Professional Aromatherapists, offers a classroom diploma program, including a five-day practicum, training in anatomy, physiology and pathology, as well as contra-indications. There is an additional 50 hours of home study required to complete 25 case studies.

Aromatherapy Wholistic Centre
208-9054 51st Ave
Edmonton, Alberta T6E 5X4
Contact: Karim Kanjj
Tel: 403-463-6390

Recognized by the Canadian Society of Professional Aromatherapists.

Escential Footnotes
12 Coleen Ave
Barrie, Ontario L4M 2N1
Tel: 705-733-7777
Contact: Kym McOuat

Recognized by the CFA.

The Essential Path
65 Harris St.
Cambridge, Ontario NIR 3Y2
Tel: 519-624-1984
Contact: Carolyn Reid

Recognized by the Canadian Society of Professional Aromatherapists

Institute of Aromatherapy
300A Danforth Ave
Toronto, Ontario M4K 1N6
Tel: 416-465-3882
Contact: Jan Benham

Offers standard and advanced levels of training. Recognized by the CFA.

Institute of Classical Aromatherapy
544 Saville Cr
North Vancouver, B.C. V7N 3B1
Tel: 1-800-260-7401
Contact: Jade Shutes

This Institute, recognized by the CFA, offers correspondence courses combined with classroom study.

JoyEssence Aromatherapy Centre
689 Woolwich St, #306
Guelph, Ontario N1H 3Y8
Tel: 519-822-4205
Fax: 519-822-2379
Contact: Joy Johnston

Recognized by the CFA.

Kal Kotecha Academy of Aromatherapy
99 Northfield Drive E, Ste 106
Waterloo, Ontario N2K 3P9
519-885-6547
Contact: Kal Kotecha

The Academy offers correspondence courses combined with classroom study. Recognized by the CFA.

Muscles at Ease
3-267 Adams St
Fredericton, N.B. E3B 7C2
Tel: 506-458-1468

Recognized by the Canadian Society of Professional Aromatherapists.

Nuwave Aromatix
1112 Lasalle Blvd, #5
Sudbury, Ontario P3A 1Y4
Contact: Pina Castellani
Tel: 705-524-2068
Fax: 705-524-2068

Standard level courses available. Recognized by the CFA.

Prima Vera School of Aromatherapy
22 Howland Ave
Toronto, Ontario M5R 2B3
Tel: 416-536-5011
Contact: Layla Wilde

Complete aromatherapy training at advanced level. Private tutoring also available. Recognized by the CFA.

Scents of Comfort
421A-6th St
New Westminster, B.C. V3L 3B1
604-521-7670

This school follows the B.C. program of the Centre of International Holistic Studies, and is recognized by Canadian Society of Professional Aromatherapists. It includes a five-day practicum, training in anatomy, physiology and pathology, as well as contra-indications. In addition, 25 case studies must be completed.

Western Aromatheraphy Holistic Centre
9930-158A St.
Surrey, B.C. V4N 2A7
Tel: 604-930-2122
Contact: Launa Boire

Recognized by the Canadian Society of Professional Aromatherapists.

✦ Aromatherapy in Your Province

Provinces are listed alphabetically below, with the following information:

Provincial Associations

✦ addresses and telephone numbers of aromatherapy associations, where they exist; such associations often provide referrals

Aromatherapists

✦ names, addresses and telephone numbers of aromatherapists, listed alphabetically by city. The Canadian Federation of Aromatherapists supplied the names of its certified members, as of June, 1996, indicated by the notation (CFA).

✦ Alberta Aromatherapists

NOTE: Check the credentials of your practitioner (see above, "Questions to Ask"). This publication cannot and does not certify or represent the qualifications of practitioners, or the quality of care available from them.

CALGARY

Olson, Arlene, (CFA)
By Appointment 403-278-4286

✦ British Columbia

British Columbia Associations

B.C. Association of Practising Aromatherapists
421A 6th St
New Westminster, B.C. V3L 3B1
Tel: 604-521-7670

Founded in 1994, this association provides referrals to about 30 member aromatherapists who have received training in aromatherapy, as well as anatomy, physiology and contra-indications.

Pacific Coast Association of Aromatherapy
2015 Pauls Terrace
Victoria, B.C. V8N 2Z4
Tel: 604-472-8376
Tax: 604-472-8369
Contact: Beverley von Fuhrherr

This association, founded in 1996, requires its professional members to pass a written entrance examination. Call for a referral.

✦ British Columbia Aromatherapists

NOTE: Check the credentials of your practitioner (see above, "Questions to Ask"). This publication cannot and does not certify or represent the qualifications of practitioners, or the quality of care available from them.

CAMPBELL RIVER

Eikeland, Gabriela
1514 Stag Rd 604-923-1270

CASTLEGAR

Ward, Darlene (CFA)
By Appointment 604-365-1061

COURTENAY

Greenwood, Barb
By Appointment 604-334-2402

DELTA

Antoniak, Pat (CFA)
By Appointment 604-943-0300

DUNCAN

Earth's Essence - Nicole Paras
Appointment only 604-748-2225

LADYSMITH

Sole Therapy - Myrna Johnson
6-3560 Hallberg Rd,
RR #1 604-245-8951

NANOOSE BAY

Eco Med Wellness Spa & Clinic
515 Pacific Shores
Nature Resort 604-468-7133

NEW WESTMINSTER

Scents of Comfort
421A-6th St 604-521-7670

NORTH VANCOUVER

The Institute of Classical
Aromatherapy
544 Saville Cr 604-983-3401

SALT SPRING ISLAND

Essentially Yours
333 Stark Rd 604-537-9211

SURREY

Blindenbach, Brenda (CFA)
By Appointment 604-572-1136

Scents of Comfort (Sandcastle)
1938 152nd St 604-521-7670

VANCOUVER

Henderson, Lynda
By Appointment 604-731-3350

Lucia's Esthetics & Aromatherapy
203-2902 W Broadway 604-736-5460

Uncommon Scents Aromatherapy
By Appointment 604-921-8999

VICTORIA

Aromatherapy by Lynn
34 Camden Ave 604-479-0176

Escobar, Piedad (CFA)
By Appointment 604-361-1672

Essentially Yours
By Appointment 604-598-5881

Healing Scents Holistic Clinic
2071 Paul's Terrace 604-472-8376

Hill, Donna
By Appointment 604-727-7035

McPherson, Dana
By Appointment 604-388-3189

Neill, Fe
By Appointment 604-472-0704

Roberts, Elmarie
By Appointment 604-658-6265

Scents of Purpose Holistic Health
Centre
403-845 Burdett Ave 604-360-1092

Shaw, Ruth
2740 Avebury Ave 604-595-7191

✦ New Brunswick

New Brunswick Association

New Brunswick Association of Aromatherapists
267 Adam St, Unit 3
Fredericton, New Brunswick E3B 7C2
Tel: 506-458-1468

This newly formed association will start providing referrals to full member practitioners who meet the association's standards of training. This includes at least 300 hours of training, as well as five days of supervised practical work. The association office is also the office of the aromatherapy clinic, Muscles at Ease.

✦ New Brunswick Aromatherapists

NOTE: Check the credentials of your practitioner (see above, "Questions to Ask"). This publication cannot and does not certify or represent the qualifications of practitioners, or the quality of care available from them.

FREDERICTON

Muscles at Ease
Gillis, Monica
3-267 Adams St 506-458-1468

✦ Nova Scotia

Nova Scotia Association

Massage Therapist and Bodyworkers' Alliance of
the Maritimes
2424 Herenow St
Halifax, Nova Scotia B6T 3E5
Tel: 902-422-2222
Contact: Joseph V. Bloggs

This alliance includes practitioners of aromatherapy.

✦ Nova Scotia Aromatherapists

NOTE: Check the credentials of your practitioner (see above, "Questions to Ask"). This publication cannot and does not certify or represent the qualifications of practitioners, or the quality of care available from them.

HALIFAX

The Summit Aesthetic Spa
5657 Spring Garden Rd 902-423-3888

Ward, Linda
By Appointment 902-542-4700

✦ Ontario Aromatherapists

NOTE: Check the credentials of your practitioner (see above, "Questions to Ask"). This publication cannot and does not certify or represent the qualifications of practitioners, or the quality of care available from them.

BARRIE

McOuat, Kym
By Appointment 705-733-7777

ETOBICOKE

Davis, Linda M. (CFA)
By Appointment 416-622-2099

GUELPH

Johnston, Joy (CFA)
By Appointment 519-822-4205

KLEINBERG

Browne, Vicki Lynn (CFA)
By Appointment 905-893-0429

LONDON

Leverton, Connie (CFA)
By Appointment 519-439-5599

OAKVILLE

Aromatherapy Centre
467 Speers Rd 905-844-1916

ORONO

The Natural Nut Health Shop
5323 Main St 905-983-8162

OTTAWA

Hall, Patricia (CFA)
By Appointment 613-725-9226

PETERBOROUGH

Christopher, Karen
Karooch
PO Box 2465 705-749-1894

PORT HOPE

Wolff, Sigrid
144 Rose Glen Rd,
Apt 203 905-885-0912

SCARBOROUGH

Goodman, Victoria (CFA)
By Appointment 416-439-4884

Li, Jenny M. (CFA)
By Appointment 416-804-6868

ST. JACOBS

Yorysh, Eileen (CFA)
By Appointment 519-664-3648

STONEY CREEK

Aromatherapy & Reflexology Centre
298 Grays Rd 905-662-7463

TIMMINS

Wong, Fred C. (CFA)
By Appointment 705-264-2555

TORONTO

Aromatherapy-Osmosis Everyday
502 Queen St W 416-504-7673
or 1-800-474-7375

Aromatherapy Clinic
458 Eglinton Ave W 416-485-0600

Boulos, Laila (CFA)
By Appointment 416-362-1264

Cofell, Gilberte
By Appointment ....(416) 482-5584

Holistic Aromatherapy Clinic
By Appointment 416-929-4451

Institute of Aromatherapy
Benham, Jan
300A Danforth Ave 416-465-3882

Murphy, Deborah A., RMT
17 Ross Ave 416-754-4830

Patricia Miller Aromatherapy Clinic
458 Eglinton Ave W 416-485-0600

Thompson, Ivonie-Jean
By Appt 416-967-4399

Trimarchi, Ivana (CFA)
By Appointment 416-489-5922

WATERDOWN	WATERLOO	WINDSOR	ZEPHYR
Green, Trish (CFA)	**Kotecha, Kal (CFA)**	**May, Christine (CFA)**	**Daniel, Norma (CFA)**
By Appointment 905-689-3329	By Appointment 519-885-6457	By Appointment 519-255-1439	By Appointment 905-473-6132

Prince Edward Island

**Aromatherapy Massage Therapy Association of
Prince Edward Island**
22 Water St E
Summerside, PEI C1N 1A1
Tel: 902-436-4467

This association, formed in 1995, will refer callers to full members who meet the association's standards of training.

✦ Saskatchewan Aromatherapists

NOTE: Check the credentials of your practitioner (see above, "Questions to Ask"). This publication cannot and does not certify or represent the qualifications of practitioners, or the quality of care available from them.

SASKATOON

Stalwick, Allan (CFA)
By Appointment 306-242-9365

◆ Ayurveda

WHAT IS AYURVEDA

Ayurveda, or "science of life" in Sanskrit, is a health system from India dating back about 3,000 years. As in traditional Chinese medicine, Ayurvedic philosophy is a holistic one, based on restoring balance in an individual's energy systems. Ayurveda recognizes five categories of elements: ether (vibration), fire (heat, color), water (liquids), air (all gas-like substances) and earth (solids, such as bones), all of which are reflected in the human body.

The Ayurvedic practitioner begins by evaluating a person's health and physical makeup, and classifies the metabolic body type. Individuals are classified into three basic types, each with a set of distinguishing characteristics eg. vata (thin), pitta (medium build) and kapha (heavy set). Diagnostic techniques usually involve observation of the tongue, pulse, eyes and nails. Treatments can include remedies prepared from herbs, minerals and vegetables, as well as massage and exercise (such as hatha yoga). Ayurvedic practitioners also give advice on nutrition and diet.

In India, Ayurvedic medicine is taught at more than 100 colleges in five-year and six-year programs, and is widely practised. Ayurveda is also practised in other countries, including the U.S. and Britain. In Canada, there are a few Ayurvedic practitioners. As well, some medical doctors in Canada offer Ayurvedic medicine.

BENEFITS OF AYURVEDA

As a health system, Ayurvedic medicine is said to be beneficial for those suffering from a broad range of health problems, including heart disease and chronic illnesses, such as arthritis, rheumatism, asthma, allergies and liver problems. As well, Ayurveda is considered helpful for maintaining good health.

QUESTIONS TO ASK

✦ How much training has your Ayurvedic practitioner received, and from which institute or college?

NOTE: A practitioner fully trained as an Ayurvedic physician has a B.A.M.S. degree (Bachelor of Ayurvedic Medicine and Surgery), conferred on a graduate of a traditional Ayurvedic College in India (or its equivalent). Ayurvedic training at a recognized college in India is a five-year or six-year full-time program. According to the Ayurvedic Medical Association of Canada, anyone else practising Ayurveda should have a bachelor of science or medical degree, in addition to sufficient knowledge and training to understand symptomatology and to arrive at an appropriate ayurvedic diagnosis.

✦ Does your Ayurvedic practitioner have a working relationship with other health care professionals? Under what circumstances will your Ayurvedic practitioner refer you to a physician or other regulated health professional?

✦ How many years has your Ayurvedic practitioner been in practice, and has your practitioner had experience with someone with a similar condition? What were the results?

✦ Does your Ayurvedic practitioner have professional references?

✦ What is the cost of treatments, and how many would be required?

GOVERNMENT REGULATION

Ayurvedic practitioners are not regulated as practitioners in Canada. This means that there is no provincial legislation establishing a regulatory body responsible for registering qualified Ayurvedic practitioners and disciplining them. Nor are there minimum educational standards for those calling themselves Ayurvedic practitioners. Every province, however, has legislation restricting either the practice of medicine or certain medical acts, such as diagnosis.

NATIONAL ASSOCIATION

Ayurvedic Medical Association of Canada
1 Gloucester St, Ste 102
Toronto, Ontario M4Y 1L8
Tel: 416-922-2287

This association is an informal group of practitioners who donate their time to answer questions from the public about Ayurvedic medicine and discuss the qualifications of practitioners. The association does not run a formal referral service, but may be able to assist you in locating a practitioner. This is also the office of Bruce Ally and Dharmen Makwana.

AYURVEDIC EDUCATION

For those wishing to become practitioners, there are no college-level Ayurvedic medicine training programs in Canada equivalent to the five-year full-time programs offered in India. There are, however, general interest courses and programs offered in Canada. The Ayurvedic Medical Association of Canada cautions students who wish to practise Ayurvedic medicine to ensure that the program they choose will be awarded credit by a recognized college. There are more than 50 state and 70 private universities and colleges in India offering five-year programs. Colleges may also be found in Switzerland, and the U.S. Contact the Ayurvedic Medical Association of Canada for information. As noted, according to this association, anyone else practising Ayurveda should have a bachelor of science or medical degree, in addition to sufficient knowledge and training to understand symptomatology and to arrive at an appropriate ayurvedic diagnosis.

In choosing a training program, one may wish to compare the qualifications of faculty (their education and experience), student-teacher ratios, admission requirements, program content and length, number of clinical hours, and all fees and contract terms, including refund policies. In addition, it is useful to speak with students and graduates of the various programs about their standards, as well as practising professionals.

Most provinces have legislation requiring private vocational schools to meet certain minimum standards, often related to financial stability, for the protection of consumers. These requirements vary from province to province, and certain health care training programs are not in all cases covered by such legislation. Contact the Ministry of Education or Advanced Education in your province for more information on their policies regarding registration of private vocational schools.

If you are seeking a career in Ayurveda, you should also be aware that every province has legislation restricting either the practice of medicine generally or the practice of certain medical acts, such as diagnosis.

American School of Ayurvedic Sciences
10025 NE 4th St
Bellevue, Washington 98004
USA
Tel: 206-453-8022

This college provides training for health care practitioners as well as members of the public.

The Ayurvedic Institute
PO Box 23445
Albuquerque, New Mexico 87192-1445
USA
Tel: 505-291-9698

The Institute is a non-profit educational corporation which offers an eight-month introductory diploma classroom course in Ayurveda, with no academic admission requirements. The Institute has students sign a form agreeing that they may not work with clients solely on the basis of the course. The student also agrees not to offer services in the practice of Ayurveda until fully trained as an Ayurvedic Physician, having achieved the B.A.M.S. degree, (Bachelor of Ayurvedic Medicine and Surgery), conferred on a graduate of a traditional Ayurvedic College in India, or its equivalent. Advanced courses are also available

Canadian School of Eastern Medicine
394 Bloor St W, Ste 202
Toronto, Ontario M5S 1X4
Tel: 416-921-7610

This school offers a 350-hour certificate program in Ayurveda and a 546-hour diploma program.

Healing with Herbs
794 Fort St, PO Box 38056
Victoria, B.C. V8W 1H2
Tel: 604-598-8616
e-mail: healing @islandnet.com

This school offers a correspondence course entitled Healing Wisdom, which includes Ayurveda training.

Maharishi Ayur-Veda College
Centre of Natural Medicine and
Preventive Health Care
40 Cochrane Rd
Compton, Québec J0B 1L0
Tel: 1-800-575-5472

This College, founded in 1992, offers short courses and training programs in Ayurvedic medicine. Call for a referral to a medical doctor practising Ayurveda in your area, anywhere in Canada.

✦ Ayurveda in Your Province

Provinces are listed alphabetically below, with the following information:
✦ names, addresses and telephone numbers of Ayurvedic practitioners, listed within each province alphabetically by city

✦ Alberta Ayurvedic Practitioners

NOTE: Check the credentials of your practitioner (see above, "Questions to Ask"). This publication cannot and does not certify or represent the qualifications of practitioners, or the quality of care available from them.

CALGARY

Ayurved Naturopathic Clinic
Rakhra, Raj, N.D.
304-1235 17th Ave SW 403-244-4941

✦ British Columbia Ayurvedic Practitioners

NOTE: Check the credentials of your practitioner (see above, "Questions to Ask"). This publication cannot and does not certify or represent the qualifications of practitioners, or the quality of care available from them.

NANAIMO

Scotthorne, Roberta
Serenity Farm Retreat
RR4, SQ4, C23 604-245-2340

PARKSVILLE

Webber, Andrea
337 McKinnon St 604-954-1786

VANCOUVER

India Ayurvedic Homeopathic & Nutrition Clinic
Dhinsa, Balwant
201-6445 Fraser St 604-323-1400

VICTORIA

Houston, James G., Dr.
203-1711 Cook St 604-382-3456

✦ Ontario Ayurvedic Practitioners

NOTE: Check the credentials of your practitioner (see above, "Questions to Ask"). This publication cannot and does not certify or represent the qualifications of practitioners, or the quality of care available from them.

AMHERSTVIEW

Hajela, Raju, Dr.
PO Box 1873 613-634-4105

GUELPH

Quantum Ayurvedics & Healing Therapies
85 Norfolk St 519-766-0862

MITCHELL

Gall, Jim, MD
7 Frances St 519-348-8402

NORTH YORK

Maharishi Ayurveda
Parikh, M.
211-1448 Lawrence Ave E . .416-755-2285

TORONTO

Alternative Health Care Services
Ally, Bruce
Makwana, Dharmen
1 Gloucester, Ste 102 . . . . .416-922-2287/
967-6891

Modi, Ramesh N.
1410 Gerrard St E 416-778-9341

Renaissance Naturopathic Centre
394 Bloor St W 416-921-7610

Tripathi, S.
2558 Danforth Ave 416-691-6841

✦ Québec Ayurvedic Practitioners

NOTE: Check the credentials of your practitioner (see above, "Questions to Ask"). This publication cannot and does not certify or represent the qualifications of practitioners, or the quality of care available from them.

COMPTON

Maharishi Ayur-Veda College - Centre of Natural Medicine and Preventive Health Care Panchakarma (five action) Rejuvenation Treatments
40 Cochrane Rd 1-800-575-5472

SAINT PIERRE

Ayurvedic Technolgies
404 St Pierre 514-287-7171

✦ Saskatchewan Ayurvedic Practitioners

NOTE: Check the credentials of your practitioner (see above, "Questions to Ask"). This publication cannot and does not certify or represent the qualifications of practitioners, or the quality of care available from them.

SASKATOON

Pahwa, Ranvir
1527A Idylwyld Dr N 306-664-3873

✦ Biofeedback Training

WHAT IS BIOFEEDBACK

Biofeedback is a technique used to help individuals learn to relax and gain increased control over their heart, breathing and other body functions. This is done by allowing a person to monitor signals from his or her own body through a set of instruments, with sensors attached to the hands, head or other parts of the body. These instruments give continuous information - in the form of a metre, light, tone or computer display - on brainwaves, blood pressure or muscle tension. Biofeedback is premised on the idea that people may use their minds to influence the functioning of their bodies. Feedback of physical responses, for example, provides information to help patients recognize a relaxed state.

The U.S. National Institute of Mental Health, a research arm of the U.S. Department of Health and Human Services, notes that research on biofeedback has shown that it can help in the treatment of many diseases and painful conditions. As well, the research indicates that we have more control over so-called involuntary bodily functions than we once thought possible. However, it also states that such control does not appear to be unlimited, and it has not replaced conventional treatment for serious conditions.

The word biofeedback was coined in 1969 to describe laboratory procedures used to train experimental research subjects to alter their heart rates and other bodily functions not normally controlled voluntarily. Biofeedback is practised today by professionals in many disciplines, including psychology, medicine, nursing, and physical therapy. Psychologists use the technique to help clients learn to relax, while medical practitioners use it to help patients control high blood pressure. The Institute describes biofeedback as a tool that reminds physicians that behaviour, thoughts, and feelings profoundly influence physical health.

BENEFITS OF BIOFEEDBACK

The U.S. National Institute of Mental Health states that biofeedback is used to help patients control high or low blood pressure, sleep disorders, tension or migraine headaches, epilepsy, paralysis and other movement disorders, cardiac arrhythmias (abnormalities in heartbeat) and Raynaud's disease (a circulatory disorder that causes uncomfortably cold hands). The Institute notes that responsible biofeedback therapists will not treat you for headaches, hypertension, or most disorders until you have had a thorough physical examination. Some require neurological tests as well.

If you think you might benefit from biofeedback training, the Institute suggests that you discuss it with your physician or another health care professional, who may wish to conduct tests to make certain that your condition does not first require conventional medical treatment.

Instruments Used

An electromyograph (EMG) measures both brain waves and muscle tension. The EMG monitors brain wave activity from sensors placed on the scalp. Muscle tension feedback is provided by sensors placed on the skin over appropriate skeletal muscles. This is used for general relaxation training and is the primary means for treatment of tension headache, chronic pain, muscle spasm and partial paralysis or other muscular dysfunction. Physical rehabilitation through neuro-muscular re-education is another application.

As well, applications for EMG are being developed for epilepsy, hyperactivity and attention deficit disorder in children, addictive disorders, and traumatic brain injury.

Thermal feedback instruments measure blood flow in the skin, and feedback from the fingers is used in relaxation training. Blood flow feedback is also used in the treatment of specific vascular disorders, including migraine headaches.

Electrodermal feedback (EDR) measures skin conductivity from the fingers and palms. The EDR is sensitive to emotions in some people, and EDR feedback has been used to treat excessive perspiration (hyperdrosis) and related dermatological conditions, as well as for relaxation training.

Specialized biofeedback instruments have been developed to facilitate self-regulation in disorders such as heart arrhythmias, bedwetting, respiratory problems and irritable bowel syndrome.

QUESTIONS TO ASK

✦ Has your practitioner been certified by the Biofeedback Certification Institute of America (BCIA)? If your practitioner was certified more than four years ago, has he or she been recertified?

NOTE: The certification process of the non-profit Biofeedback Certification Institute of America (BCIA) includes a review of credentials, including education and experience. Confirm your practitioner's certification by contacting the Institute (see below, "Certification Body").

✦ How much training in biofeedback has your practitioner received and from which training institute? Is your practitioner trained in other forms of health care, apart from biofeedback? These questions are important if your practitioner is not certified by the Biofeedback Certification Institute of America.

NOTE: As a benchmark, practitioners certified by the BCIA must hold a bachelor's degree or higher from an accredited institution of higher education in one of the BCIA's approved health care fields, such as medicine, dentistry, nursing, sports medicine, chiropractic, psychology and speech pathology. At least 200 hours of formal biofeedback training, including supervised clinical experience, is also required (see below, "Biofeedback Education").

✦ Is biofeedback appropriate for your disorder?

✦ What are your practitioner's other professional competencies? What does your practitioner treat and not treat?

✦ How long has your practitioner been doing biofeedback? Does your practitioner have experience with your condition, and what were the results? How many patients has your practitioner seen using these techniques?

✦ Does your practitioner have professional references?

✦ What is the fee schedule, and what is the estimated length of the proposed treatment?

GOVERNMENT REGULATION

Biofeedback practitioners are not regulated by any provincial government. This means that there are no provincial laws establishing a governing body responsible for registering qualified biofeedback practitioners and disciplining them. This also means that there are no minimum educational standards. However, there is a U.S. certification body that sets standards for practitioners. Also, note that every province has legislation restricting either the practice of medicine, or the practice of a certain medical acts such as diagnosis.

CERTIFICATION BODY

There is no Canadian certification body. However, the U.S. certification body certifies Canadian practitioners.

Biofeedback Certification Institute of America (BCIA)
304-10200 44th Ave W
Wheat Ridge, CO 80033
Tel: 303-420-2902

The Institute was founded in 1981 as an independent non-profit organization to establish standards and provide certification for biofeedback practitioners. Call to check whether your practitioner is certified, and has recertified within the last four years.

U.S. ASSOCIATION

Association for Applied Psychophysiology and Biofeedback
304-10200 44th Avenue W
Wheat Ridge, Colorado 80033
Tel: 303-422-8436

This is the membership association for professionals using biofeedback. Membership does not indicate that a practitioner is certified.

BIOFEEDBACK EDUCATION

Those interested in a career in biofeedback should note that the certification process of the Biofeedback Certification Institute of America (BCIA) involves a review of credentials, including education and experience. You must hold a bachelor's degree or higher from an accredited institution of higher education in one of the BCIA's approved health care fields. These fields include medicine, dentistry, psychology, nursing, physical therapy, respiratory therapy, social work, counselling, rehabilitation, chiropractic, recreational therapy, dental hygiene, physician's assistant, exercise physiology, speech pathology, and sports medicine. A master's degree is required in the fields of music therapy, and counselling education. For the complete list, contact the BCIA. At least 200 hours of formal biofeedback training (including supervised clinical experience) from an accredited institutions is required. You must also pass a written examination and an assessment of practical skills. Contact the BCIA for a list of the accredited training programs in the United States. There is none in Canada.

Certification is granted for four years, and practitioners must therefore recertify every four years to ensure that they stay informed of new developments. Recertification requires continuing formal education and/or passing of a written examination.

✦ Biofeedback in Your Province

Provinces are listed alphabetically below, with the following information:

✦ names, addresses and telephone numbers of biofeedback practitioners, listed alphabetically by city

NOTE: The names in this list were provided by the Biofeedback Certification Institute of America (BCIA). Confirm the certification of your practitioner or obtain the names of newly certified practitioners in your area by contacting the BCIA (see above, "Certification Body").

✦ Alberta Biofeedback Practitioners

NOTE: Check the credentials of your practitioner (see above, "Questions to Ask"). This publication cannot and does not certify or represent the qualifications of practitioners, or the quality of care available from them.

CALGARY

Stanfield, F. Logan, M.D.
206-215 12th Ave 403-265-6171

Donaldson, Stuart C.
560-10655 Southport Rd SW 403-225-0900

✦ British Columbia Biofeedback Practitioners

NOTE: Check the credentials of your practitioner (see above, "Questions to Ask"). This publication cannot and does not certify or represent the qualifications of practitioners, or the quality of care available from them.

VANCOUVER

Trites, David
1460 Kamloops . . . . . . .St 604-254-5071

Pierce, Lorie
801-750 W Broadway 604-879-5017

Sequoia, Lundy
2922 W 3rd Ave 604-731-4441

Laye, Ronald
1904 Arbutus St 604-733-4321

✦ Ontario Biofeedback Practitioners

NOTE: Check the credentials of your practitioner (see above, "Questions to Ask"). This publication cannot and does not certify or represent the qualifications of practitioners, or the quality of care available from them.

AJAX

Cummings, Mark
38 Chatfield Dr 905-683-3283

SCARBOROUGH

Floyd, Carolina
10 Milner Business Ct 416-754-8459

Lau, Godwin
3443 Finch Ave E 416-502-1343

TORONTO

Wilson, Vietta Sue
4700 Keele St, 207
Winters College 416-736-5142

✦ Québec Biofeedback Practitioners

NOTE: Check the credentials of your practitioner (see above, "Questions to Ask"). This publication cannot and does not certify or represent the qualifications of practitioners, or the quality of care available from them.

DUVERNAY

Ligonde, Paultre
3195, rue Luzerne 514-661-4922

Chiropractic

WHAT IS CHIROPRACTIC

The word "chiropractic" is derived from Greek, and means treatment by hand ("cheir" meaning hand and "praktike" meaning practical science, or practice). The Canadian Chiropractic Association states in its Directory of Facts: "Chiropractors focus on the spine in relation to the body and specialize in the understanding and treatment of its component bone structures, muscles and nerves." The association also notes that chiropractors pioneered the holistic approach to health care in North America, in which a person's lifestyle, from eating to working habits, are taken into account. Chiropractors use neither drugs nor surgery. Their most commonly used therapy is manual adjustment, or manipulation, of the spine and extremities. Chiropractic was pioneered in 1895 by Daniel David Palmer of Port Perry, Ontario, who manipulated the spine of a man who had injured his back and neck.

Doctors of chiropractic may receive patients directly as primary contact practitioners, without the need for referral from medical doctors or other health practitioners. A chiropractor is trained to know when a patient requires treatment outside the scope of chiropractic, and to refer the patient accordingly. The practice of chiropractic, once controversial, is now well-established in Canada and the U.S. The Canadian Chiropractic Association estimates that there are about 4,500 licensed chiropractors in Canada, making chiropractic one of the largest primary contact health professions in the country (referrals are not necessary).

BENEFITS OF CHIROPRACTIC

Chiropractic may alleviate musculo-skeletal disorders, including headache, migraine, neck and back pain, and pain radiating to legs, shoulders and arms, as well as disorders caused by spinal dysfunction. Sports and work injuries, including joint injuries and hip problems, are also treated by chiropractic. Chiropractic may also bring relief for a variety of other conditions, such as insomnia, menstrual cramps and the symptoms of multiple sclerosis. Studies on the efficacy of chiropractic treatment have been published in medical journals. For more information contact the Canadian Chiropractic Association (see below, "National Association") or contact the Canadian Memorial Chiropractic College Library (see below, "Chiropractic Education").

QUESTIONS TO ASK

✦ Is your chiropractor registered, or licensed, to practise? This indicates that certain educational standards have been met. Contact the governing body in your province to check (see below, "Chiropractic in Your Province").

NOTE: If you live in the Northwest Territories, where there is no regulation or licensing of chiropractors, inquire as to the training and qualification of your chiropractor (see below, "Chiropractic in Your Province - Northwest Territories").

✦ Is chiropractic treatment appropriate for your condition? Under what circumstances will your chiropractor refer you to another health professional?

✦ Does your chiropractor treat particular types of problems, such as musculoskeletal disorders, occupational health problems and sports injuries? Does your chiropractor's practice emphasize certain types of patients, such as children or seniors?

NOTE: Some patients may wish to be directed to a chiropractor whose practice emphasizes a particular type of treatment.

✦ How much experience does your chiropractor have, and does it include treatment of your particular condition? What were the results?

✦ What is the fee schedule, and the estimated number of treatments required? Check if your provincial government health care funding plan covers part or all of the fee (see below, "Government Health Care Funding" and "Chiropractic in Your Province - Government Health Care Funding").

NOTE: If you live in B.C., ask if your chiropractor is "opted in" or "opted out" of the provincial health care funding program (the Medical Services Plan of B.C.). If the chiropractor is opted out, your share of the fee will be higher (see below, "Chiropractic in Your Province - B.C.").

GOVERNMENT REGULATION

Regulation means that there is provincial legislation establishing a professional governing body. This body, usually called a "College," is given a duty in law to protect the public. Governing bodies are established to ensure that regulated practitioners meet specific standards before they practise, to investigate complaints, and to take disciplinary action against practitioners where appropriate.

Chiropractic is recognized by legislation and chiropractors are regulated in all 10 provinces and the Yukon Territory. Some provinces limit chiropractic treatment to manipulation of the spine and extremities. In other jurisdictions, the legislation is silent or refers to a specific range of treatments, such as electrotherapy, thermotherapy and counselling in relation to exercise, nutritional supplements and diet. Methods of diagnosis, again depending upon the province, include X-ray, patient history, general examination, as well as neurological and orthopaedic tests. The Northwest Territories is the only jurisdiction in Canada where chiropractic is not recognized in law. For details regarding regulation of chiropractic, see below, "Chiropractic in Your Province."

GOVERNMENT HEALTH CARE FUNDING

Chiropractic services are partially or fully covered under provincial health care systems in Alberta, B.C., Manitoba, Ontario, and Saskatchewan (for details, see below, "Chiropractic in your Province").

WORKERS' COMPENSATION BOARDS

Chiropractic care is a part of Workers' Compensation Board coverage in all provinces if a claim is accepted. A medical referral may be necessary in some provinces.

HEALTH INSURANCE COVERAGE
Private Insurance

Most private insurance companies carry coverage for chiropractors under extended health care plans. Check the terms and conditions of your policy with your insurance agent.

Automobile Insurance

Coverage for chiropractic care is provided under many automobile insurance plans, including private plans and public plans such as the Manitoba Public Insurance Corporation, the Insurance Corporation of B.C. and the Saskatchewan public automobile insurance plan. Check the terms and conditions of your policy with your insurance agent.

Veteran Affairs Canada

Veterans with appropriate insurance coverage may have their chiropractic services paid by Veteran Affairs Canada through Blue Cross with a written referral from a medical doctor. Call Blue Cross at 1-800-387-0919 to determine if you are eligible and have coverage.

NATIONAL ASSOCIATION

The Canadian Chiropractic Association
1396 Eglinton Avenue West
Toronto, Ontario M6C 2E4
Tel: 416-781-5656
Fax: 416-781-7344

This is the national professional association for chiropractors. Contact the association if you would like information on chiropractic, or chiropractic education. This association does not provide a referral service.

CHIROPRACTIC EDUCATION
Education and Licensing

For those interested in a career in chiropractic, the Canadian Memorial Chiropractic College (listed below) is the only nationally accredited chiropractic educational institution in Canada. There is also a chiropractic educational program in French at the Université du Québec à Trois Rivières that leads to licensure in Québec only (see below).

Following their education, chiropractors must pass a national board examination as well as an examination in the province where they wish to practise. At that point, a chiropractor may be licensed upon payment of fees in accordance with provincial regulation. Chiropractors may apply for licensing in every jurisdiction in Canada except for the Northwest Territories. For more information, contact the Canadian Chiropractic Association (see above, "National Association").

The Canadian Memorial Chiropractic College (CMCC)
1900 Bayview Ave
Toronto, Ontario M4G 3E6
Tel: 416-482-2340 or Admissions 1-800-463-2923 (toll-free in Canada)

CMCC offers a four-year program, including clinical training and an internship. Studies focus on the biological sciences, including immunology, microbiology, pathology and nutrition, as well as diagnosis and radiology. Graduates are awarded a Doctor of Chiropractic Diploma (DC). Admission requirements include a minimum of 15 full courses (90 credit hours) of university study in Canada, or its equivalent. Applicants from Québec should have completed two years in the Colleges of General and Professional Education in the Health Sciences (CEGEP), supplemented by a minimum of 10 full courses (60 credit hours) of university study. Applicants require a minimum 2.25 GPA on a four scale to qualify for an interview, but should have a 'B' average to be competitive. It is recommended that applicants complete specific courses in the sciences and humanities.

Founded in 1945, CMCC is an independent, non-profit organization operating without government funding. The philosophy of chiropractic taught at CMCC holds that the human body has restorative processes to maintain its natural state of health. CMCC is fully accredited to international standards. It is therefore accredited by the Council on Chiropractic Education (Can.) Inc. Through a reciprocal agreement with CCE (USA) and the Austral-Asian Council on Chiropractic Education, graduates are eligible to apply for licensure in numerous other countries under their jurisdiction. A CMCC student who is a Canadian citizen or has Permanent Resident status (not a student visa) may apply to the Canada Student Loan Programme for financial assistance. There are also provincial student loan programs. Contact your provincial Student Loan Office or the CMCC Student Affairs office for details.

Université du Québec à Trois Rivières
C.P. 500
Trois-Rivières, Québec G9A 5H7
Tel: 819-376-5045

This program leads to a doctorate in chiropractic and the practice of chiropractic in Québec once the candidate passes the professional examinations set by the Ordre des Chiropracticiens du Québec. (see below, "Chiropractic in Your Province - Québec"). The university is seeking accreditation for the program from the Council on Chiropractic Education (Can.) and councils of other countries. The degree awarded is Doctor of Chiropractic (DC). Admission requirements include a diploma of collegial studies (D.E.C.) or equivalent, and completion of certain college level courses in sciences and mathematics. All applicants must be fluent in French, verified through a test. This new five-year program comprises 11 sessions. Enrolment is limited to 45 students per year.

✦ Chiropractic in Your Province

Each province is listed alphabetically below, with the following information:

Legislation

✦ procedures that your chiropractor is permitted to perform under law

NOTE: The information given regarding legislation is by way of interest, and does not purport to offer legal advice or comprise a complete account of the legislation or regulations. If legal advice is required, consult a lawyer qualified to practise in your jurisdiction.

Government Health Care Funding

✦ details on government health care funding, where it exists

Governing Bodies

✦ addresses and telephone numbers of governing bodies
✦ these are the offices you may contact to check if your chiropractor is registered or to lodge a complaint

Provincial Associations

✦ addresses and telephone numbers of provincial chiropractic professional associations, some of which provide referrals

Chiropractors

✦ names, addresses and telephone numbers of chiropractors, listed alphabetically by city
✦ the title 'Dr' or the initials 'DC' mean Doctor of Chiropractic.

✦ Alberta

Chiropractors are regulated in Alberta, meaning that there is legislation establishing a governing body responsible for registering and disciplining practitioners (see below, "Governing Body"). There is government health coverage under Alberta Health (see below, "Government Health Care Funding").

Legislation

Chiropractors are regulated under the *Chiropractic Profession Act* and regulation. Under the Act, "chiropractic" means the branch of the healing arts concerned with the restoration and maintenance of human health by the chiropractic adjustment or manipulation of the spinal column and other articulations of the body. Only those registered as chiropractors with the governing College are permitted to practise chiropractic, and to use the title "Chiropractor," "Doctor of Chiropractic" or any variation. No person registered under the Act may practise naturopathy.

Government Health Care Funding

Alberta Health covers a maximum of $12.66 per visit to a maximum of $200 a year for visits to chiropractors, with July 1 considered the start of the year. For information on Alberta Health coverage, call 403-427-0259 or toll-free 310-0000, and ask for Alberta Health.

Alberta Governing Body/Professional Association

College of Chiropractors of Alberta
1870 Manulife Place
10180-101 Street
Edmonton, Alberta T5J 3S4
Tel: 403-420-0932
Fax: 403-425-6583

This is the governing body and professional association for Alberta chiropractors. It does not provide a referral service, but will give the names of chiropractors in your area if you are having trouble locating one. Call the College to check if your chiropractor is licensed or to register a complaint.

✦ Alberta Chiropractors

NOTE: Check the credentials of your chiropractor (see above, "Questions to Ask"). This publication cannot and does not certify or represent the qualifications of practitioners, or the quality of care available from them. We cannot and do not confirm that those listed are registered as required by law.

AIRDRIE

Airdrie Chiropractic Office
Vance, Dr. M.J.
3-400 Main St 403-948-7171

Lees, Dr. Ryan
118 Main St N 403-948-4440

Swallow, Dr. John
1002 Allen St 403-948-3863

ATHABASCA

Deutscher, Dr. Kurt
Athabasca Centre 403-675-4030

Walter, Dr. Keith A.
101, 5402-50th Ave 403-675-2222

BANFF

Family Chiropractic Office
Biegel, Dr. Shawna
By Appointment 403-762-5555

BARRHEAD

Farnalls, Dr. Richard
5118-49a St 403-674-2577

Thompson, Dr. Wm. W.
5010-50th Ave 403-674-2861

BENTLEY

Chiropractic Health Centre
Giesbrecht, Dr. Roger
4941-50th Ave 403-748-4441

BLAIRMORE/ CROWSNEST PASS

Crowsnest Chiropractic
Morrish, Dr. Gordon
12825-20th Ave 403-562-2559

BONNYVILLE

Bonnyville Chiropractic Centre
Church, Dr. James R.
4906A-50th St 403-826-3396

BOW ISLAND

Holowiski, Dr. Clifford
604 Center St 403-545-6242

Layton, Dr. Robert K.
By Appointment 403-545-6242

BRAGG CREEK

Carrington, Dr. Natalie J.
Morris, Dr. Greg
17 White Ave 403-949-3953

McDougall, Dr. Roderick
By Appointment 403-246-6770

BRETON

Breton Chiropractic Clinic
Bergen, Dr. Barry L.
5012-50th Ave 403-696-2097

BROOKS

Brooks Chiropractic Office
Swanson, Dr. Donald R.
440 W 2nd St 403-362-2714

Krizsan, Dr. Victoria; McIver, Dr. Donald
715-2nd St W 403-362-5900

Liscombe, Dr. G.; Liscombe, Dr. T.
416-3 Ave W 403-362-3711

CALGARY

Advance Chiropractic Clinic
Hoetger, Dr. Rainer
182, 1440-52nd St NE 403-273-6537

Alto Chiropractic Centre
Alto, Dr. Alan
108-6449 Crowchild Trail S .403-249-1550

Amaolo Chiropractic Clinic
Amaolo, Dr. Glen; Amaolo, Dr. T.E.
Collins, Dr. J.D.; Harvey, Dr. Michael
Macleod, Dr. Norman; Manns, Dr. Ron
5004 Elbow Dr SW 403-243-8114

Armstrong, Dr. Ron; Jeffels, Dr. R. Allen
1005-16th Ave NW 403-282-1011/
284-2552

Austin, Dr. Sherri D.
11-5720 Silver Springs
Blvd NW 403-286-5557

Avenida Chiropractic Clinic
Mackay, Dr. Verna
509-12445 Lake
Fraser Dr SE 403-271-6611

Avenue Downtown Walk-In Chiropractic Care
Dean, Dr. John R.
Mn Fl, 734-8th Ave SW 403-262-3300

Awareness Chiropractic Clinic
Migliarese, Dr. Dan
1221 Canyon
Meadows Dr SE 403-225-1404

Baruta, Dr. John; Chambers, Dr. Patricia
385-10233 Elbow Dr SW . . .403-255-2020

Battershill, Dr. Doug
1519-19 St NW 403-284-2082

Beddington Chiropractic Clinic
Duce, Dr. Angela
Beddington Towne Centre . . .403-295-3008

Bow Bottom Chiropractic
Kawchuk, Dr. Greg
203-83 Deerpoint Rd SE 403-278-2077

Bow Valley Chiropractic
Menzies, Dr. Don
281 Bow Valley, Sq 4 403-262-2211

Bowness Chiropractic Office
Thompson, Dr. George
118-7930 Bowness Rd NW . .403-286-9319

Braecentre Chiropractic Clinic
Chlysta, Dr. Lisa
11432B Braeside Dr SW 403-251-0002

Brentwood Chiropractic Clinic
Marchand, Dr. Rolonde; Oliphant, Dr. Drew
232 J Brentwood
Village Mall 403-282-5557

Bridgeland Chiropractic Clinic
Materie, Dr. Corrie Ann
205, 1010-1st Ave NE 403-237-7686

Calgary Chiropractic Clinic
Goulet, Dr. Jeana; Lawson, Dr. David
740-10th St SW 403-262-1121

Calgary Chiropractic Clinic - South Branch
Lawson, Dr. Stephen; Murakami, Dr. Sheryl
8227 Elbow Dr SW 403-571-0965

Cameron Chiropractic Group
Cameron, Dr. David; Cameron, Dr. Jeff
6315-17th Ave SW 403-249-6678

Capitol Chiropractic Health Centre
Reid, Dr. Douglas; Wallace, Dr. Trevor
1432-19 Ave NW 403-284-4741

Carrington, Dr. Natalie; Shortreed, Dr. B.
1287 Sunridge Mall 403-293-5313

Carter, Dr. J. Ronald; Carter, Dr. Ryan
222 North Hill
Shopping Center 403-289-3768

Centre for Chiropractic Care
Labchuk, Dr. David
104, 240-4th Ave SW 403-237-5200

Centre for Health Inc./Taylor Physiotherapy Clinic
Chung, Dr. Wendy; Sali, Dr. Paul R.
102, 117-17th Ave NE 403-230-4191/7171

Chiropractic Associate Clinic
Nevison, Dr. Keath; Nevison, Dr. Kevin
206, 1609-14 St SW 403-244-2121

Chiropractic Care Centre
McDougall, Dr. Roderick
270-5255 Richmond Rd SW .403-246-6770

Chiropractic Family Care Centre
Breen, Dr. Michael; Dean, Dr. Trent
540, 255-17th Ave SW 403-299-0170

Chiropractic Health Care Centre
Hanus-Shephard, Dr. Jayson; Shaw, Dr. L.
200-1204 Kensington
Rd NW 403-270-7001

Chiropractic Spinal Care Centre
Peterson, Dr. David; Stewart, Dr. Michael
1761 S Chinook Centre 403-252-3316

Chiropractic Spinal Care Centre
Taylor, Dr. Robert G.
380 Scotia Center,
225-7th Ave SW 403-237-6000

Crowfoot Chirocentre
Morris, Dr. Greg; Ng, Dr. Hubert
610 Crowfoot Village
Shopping Centre 403-239-3000

Cumming, Dr. Robert; Lippitt, Dr. Gregory
Southcentre Mall 403-271-1081

D'Amico, Dr. Kevin K.
580-64th Ave NE 403-274-3000

Darroch, Dr. Lori
215, 510-5th St SW 403-266-2333

Desjardins, Dr. Dennis A.
11 Klamath Pl SW 403-253-0076

Duke, Dr. Gerald
Business Westhills Town Center403-242-4425

Edgemont Chiropractic
Abelson, Dr. Brian J.
Bay 5, 34 Edgedale
Dr NW 403-241-3772

Espaniola, Dr. Habib
107 Nottingham Rd NW 403-275-6159

Findlay, Dr. Donald R.
138, 3604-52nd Ave NW . . .403-282-4004

Fish Creek Chiropractic
Burchill, Dr. Keith
3215-380 Canyon
Meadows Dr SE 403-271-7224

Flanagan, Dr. Colleen; Kolanos, Dr. Richard
201 Canyon Meadows
Shopping Centre 403-281-7777

Flavin, Dr. Laurie; Radermacher, Dr. Margaret
3224A-28th St SW 403-240-4013

Fong, Dr. Kevin
125-2880 SE Glenmore Tr .403-279-0981

Forden, Dr. Jonathan M.
409, 1640-16th Ave NW . .403-284-1814

Forrester, Dr. Judy A.
216 Crowchild Square, 5403 Crowchild .403-247-2947

14th Street Chiropractic Clinic
Davidson, Dr. Les J.
100, 2004 NW 14th St 403-284-4743

Fujimoto, Dr. Teresa
568-64th Ave NE 403-275-8567

Graham, Dr. Ray; Palichuk, Dr. Ed
6130-1A St SW 403-255-4450

Gray, Dr. Hugh S.
1811 SW 4th St 403-228-4436

Halowski, Dr. Allan P.
200-8180 Macleod Tr S 403-255-4461

Harris, Dr. Stephen J.T.
107-5555 Elbow Dr SW 403-255-5378

Hartzell, Dr. Darrin
257 Westminister Dr SW 403-239-0007

Hasick, Dr. D. Gordon; Thomson, Dr. Gary
201-5005 Elbow Dr SW 403-243-0155

Haycock, Dr. Robert P.
692, 1414-8th St SW 403-571-1313

Heritage Chiropractic
Lyall, Dr. P.; Shah, Dr. Firoz M.
E7-8330 Macleod Tr S 403-255-7343

Heritage Hill Soft Tissue Pain Clinic
Brown, Dr. Mark D.
304-8180 Macleod Tr SE 403-640-4060

Hillhurst Chiropractic Office
McMorland, Dr. D. Gordon
405, 609-14th St NW 403-270-7252

Hogan, Dr. Debra L.
206-1228 Kensington Rd NW 403-283-3282

Hunter, Dr. John F.
4239 Bow Tr SW 403-686-3444

Kelly, Dr. J.R.
5012 NW 16th Ave 403-247-3231

Kensington Chiropractic Clinic
Tort, Dr. Tim W.
106, 213-19th St NW 403-270-7292

Kingsland Chiropractic Clinic
Bodell, Dr. Lonny D.
200-7720 Elbow Dr SW 403-253-3733

Klaudt, Dr. Gary; MacLellan, Dr. Catherine
Eau Claire Market 403-294-1999

Kricken, Dr. Michael D.
109-4616 Valinat Dr NW . . .403-286-2245

Ladell, Dr. D.K.; Ladell, Dr. Scott
216 Chinook
Professional Bldg 403-255-8161

Leung, Dr. Calvin
123, 233-16th Ave NW 403-230-9300

Liscombe, Dr. John R.
56-755 Lake Bonavista Dr SE 403-271-4322

London Town Square Chiropractic
Stannard, Dr. Daniel P.
225, 3545-32nd Ave NE 403-250-8383

Love, Dr. J.H.
11-1818 Centre St N 403-277-5381

Lutzer, Dr. Sharon; Mckay, Dr. Timothy
232 McKnight Blvd NE 403-275-3800

Macleod Trail Chiropractic Clinic
Hare, Dr. Lyle R.
Macleod Tr & 94 Ave SE 403-253-1555

Maier, Dr. Michael
10-113 Village Heights SW .403-242-3161

Major, Dr. Janet
200-4803 Centre St N 403-230-2559

Market Mall Chiropractic Clinic
Gainor, Dr. Ian
212 Market Mall
Professional Bldg 403-286-4341

Marlborough Chiropractic Centre
Conway, Dr. Philip; Jepp, Dr. H. Peter
Marlborough Mall 403-272-8800

Marlborough Chiropractic Office
McCulloch, Dr. Mark E.
560 Marlborough
Professional Bldg 403-248-4466

Mayfair Chiropractic Clinic
Cosman, Dr. Ernie; Cosman, Dr. L.
Farn, Dr. C. Glenn; Rosen, Dr. Murray A.
Mayfair Place, 209-6707
Elbow Dr SW 403-259-4443

Memorial Square Chiropractic Clinic
D'Amico, Dr. Ted L; Kraft, Dr. Shane B.
8-5268 Memorial Dr NE 403-248-3178

Midnapore Chiropractic Clinic
Jones, Dr. Stephen G.
107-239 Midpark Wy SE . . .403-254-9177

Minogue, Dr. W.M.
305-8180 Macleod Tr SE 403-252-8896

Monterey Square Chiropractic Clinic
Haaranen, Dr. Lynita
824, 2220-68th St NE 403-280-0945

Mount Royal Chiropractic Clinic
Lapointe, Dr. Larry; Politylo, Dr. Julian
1614-10th St SW 403-244-1600

Nakai, Dr. Tadashi
210, 3715 SW 51st St 403-242-1700

Northmount Wellness Clinic
Menzies, Dr. Greg
207, 3400-14th St NW 403-571-2475

Northside Chiropractic Office
Kucheran, Dr. Jack
136, 3350-34th St NE 403-291-0603

Northwest Chiropractic Office
McLelland, Dr. Dwight M.
4603 Varsity Dr NW 403-288-4733

Oakridge Chiropractic Centre
Laycraft, Dr. Kristi L.; Walcott, Dr. David
Oakridge Co-Op
Shopping Centre 403-281-2333

Oke, Dr. J. Douglas
215-11012 MacLeod Tr S .403-278-0833

On Centre Chiropractic
Pagenkopf, Dr. A.; Smith, Dr. Ian D.
405-1701 Centre St N 403-230-0066

Optimum Health Chiropractic
Robinson, Dr. Robert
115-150 Crowfoot Cr NW ...403-241-2225

Paterson, Dr. Stuart
3959-17th Ave SW 403-249-7731

Penny Lane Chiropractic Clinic
Watson, Dr. D.G.
214-513 SW 8th Ave 403-264-9621/
269-3115

Popham, Dr. Michael
6102 Bow Cr 403-288-0117

Properties Chiropractic Clinic
Gdanski, Dr. Gail; Parker, Dr. David A.
Russell, Dr. Allan
204-5401 Temple Dr NE 403-280-8992

Ranchlands Chiropractic Clinic
Chong, Dr. Alan M.; Lam, Dr. Linda K.
15-7750 Ranchview Dr NW ..403-239-2245

Riverbend Chiropractic Clinic
Gervais, Dr. Roland
8338-18th St SE,
Bay 412 ....403-279-2992/680-8866

Rowe, Dr. W.A.
5309 NE Rundlehorn Dr 403-285-6960

Samak, Dr. Dennis
16 Fl, 444-5th Ave SW 403-269-8077

Sawa, Dr. G. Jeffrey
117, 3411-20th St SW 403-240-2946

Schacter, Dr. Jeffrey
131-9th Ave SW,
102 Palliser Sq 403-263-7477

Shawnessy Village Chiropractic
McCulloch, Dr. Mark
124-70 Shawville Blvd SW .403-256-1377

Sloan, Dr. T.I.
203 Acadia Shopping Centre .403-255-1744

Smistad, Dr. Warren F.
134, 3604-52nd Ave NW ...403-282-9183

Smith, Ball, Lawson, McEwen & Bowman
Associates Chiropractors
1020 Centre St N 403-230-9003

Smith, Dr. Brian D.
306-4014 Macleod Tr S 403-243-8224

Southcentre Tower Chiropractic
Wagner, Dr. Dennis J.
215 Southcentre
Executive Tower 403-278-9333

Southland Chiropractic Centre
Sie, Dr. James H.
110-10655 Southport
Rd SW 403-271-7143

Southland Crossing Chiropractic
Uchacz, Dr. Greg
310-9737 Macleod Tr S 403-258-3858

Smith, Dr. Thomas C.
202-4625 Varsity Dr NW ...403-288-6551

Spring Hill Chiropractic
Osiowy, Dr. David
174-8060 Silver Springs
Blvd NW 403-288-4838

Strathcona Chiropractic Health Care
Morgan, Dr. Christopher J.
208-555 Strathcona
Blvd SW 403-686-3060

Third, Dr. John
115 Maunsell Close NE 403-277-4344

Westbrook Chiropractic Practice
Lee, Dr. Stan
204, 1610-37th St SW 403-249-3977

Westglen Medical Clinic
4550-17 Ave SW 403-240-2221

Westhills Chiropractic
Richmond Rd & Sarcee Tr SW 403-242-4425

Williamson, Dr. Judy
1409-2nd St NW 403-230-3181

Willow Park Chiropractic Office
Stoley, Dr. Ron
110-10655 Southport Rd SW 403-278-5350

Wilson, Dr. Frederick J.
122-7015 MacLeod Tr S 403-252-2869

Woo, Dr. Cindy C.
24, 3015-51st St SW 403-242-5667

Woodlands Chiropractic Clinic
Dahms, Dr. Janice; Dahms, Dr. Michael
24-523 Woodpark
Blvd SW 403-251-5050

Yoshida, Dr. T.
4-21C, 3012-7th Ave SE 403-272-6800

CAMROSE

Annis, Dr. Robert; Dielissen, Dr. L.
5003-49th St 403-672-8559

Camrose Chiropractic Clinic
Glambeck, Dr. Allan
102, 5015-50th Ave 403-679-2500

Jones, Dr. A. Campbell
4935-50th St 403-672-4578

Professional Building (Camrose) Ltd Chiropractors
Ladd, Dr. J.; Parsons, Dr. G.A.
4849-49th St 403-672-4408

CANMORE

Bow Corridor Chiropractic Clinic
Scriven, Dr. Bryan
207, 703-8th St 403-678-9393

Canmore Chiropractic Clinic
Weichel, Claude
820-8th St 403-678-2500

CARDSTON

Bridge, Dr. John
415 Main St 403-653-2666

Olsen, Dr. Shawn
93-2nd Ave W 403-653-2005

Southwest Chiropractic
Fox, Dr. Grant
80-2nd Ave W 403-653-4939

CAROLINE

Caroline Peak Chiropractic Centre
Larsen, Dr. Stacy
5039-49th Ave 403-722-7325

CASTOR

Castor Chiropractic Clinic
Larson, Dr. Craig
4902-50th Ave 403-882-2110

CLARESHOLM

Active Health Chiropractic
Jackson, Dr. Kathryn
107-50th Ave W 403-625-2523

Claresholm Chiropractic Clinic
Twiss, Dr. C. Michael
109-49th Ave W 403-625-2662

COALDALE

Gaulin, Dr. Pierre
1218B 21A Ave 403-345-2266

Harper, Dr. C. Brad; Harper, Dr. L.
1512-20th Ave 403-345-2266

COCHRANE

Koebisch, Dr. Peter B.
516-1st St W 403-932-3600

Kong, Dr. Eugene
115-4th Ave W 403-932-6222

CORONATION

Coronation Chiropractic Clinic
Sedun, Dr. Glenn
Coronation Mall 403-578-3316

DE WINTON

De Winton Chiropractic
Navratil, Dr. Darrel F.
By Appointment 403-630-6002

DEVON

Devon Chiropractic Office
Johnson, Dr. Grant; Johnson, Dr. Patricia
107 Devon Shopping Centre .403-987-2166

DIDSBURY

Didsbury Chiropractic Clinic
Phillips, Dr. J.D.; Phillips, Dr. K.
1704-20th St 403-335-4616

Mayor, Dr. Terry
By Appointment 403-335-4263

DRAYTON VALLEY

Ellis, Dr. Ray
5156-52nd Ave 403-542-5521

Wademan, Dr. Greg
5101-51st St 403-542-5690

DRUMHELLER

Drumheller Chiropractic Clinic
Sawa, Dr. Jeff
346-1st St E 403-823-4266

Gushaty, Dr. B.D.
150-3rd Ave W 403-823-3020

ECKVILLE

Eckville Chiropractic Clinic
Sedun, Dr. Glenn S.
5014- 50th St 403-746-2265

EDMONTON

Aaron Chiropractic Clinic
Colburn, Dr. Dennis; Pfaff, Dr. Juergen
Letourneau Centre
4624-99 St 403-433-6068

Advance Chiropractic Ltd
Komarnisky, Dr. Christopher L.
244 Mayfield Common 403-483-6275

Albrumac Chiropractic Center
Johnson, Dr. Landelin James
220, 8657-51th Ave 403-465-0050

Anderson, Dr. Anders A.
10660-156th St 403-486-2755

Associates Chiropractic Clinic
Sabo, Dr. Ellis; Sabo, Dr. Steven
10110-82nd Ave 403-433-9522

Avenue Chiropractic Clinic
Bortolotto, Dr. James; Hyderman, Dr. Stuart
Klesko, Dr. James
11737-83rd St 403-477-3611

Balwin Chiropractic Clinic
Daniel, Dr. Mike
13123-82nd St 403-475-8484

**Bayrock, Dr. R.G.;
Bayrock, Dr. V.A.**
9617-111th Ave 403-422-7656

Bergquist, Dr. K.A.
10140-113th St 403-426-6349

**Boyko, Dr. Percy; Cormier, Dr.
Michael**
4970-98th Ave 403-448-1444

**Brodeur, Dr. Robert; Fei, Dr.
Marie**
102, 8925-82th Ave 403-466-7111

**Broker, Dr. Lori; McDearmid, Dr.
Jane**
10534-124th St 403-482-2738

**Burns, Dr. Charles; Burns, Dr.
William**
104, 10160-116th St 403-482-3795

Burns, Dr. Gordon
206, 87045-51st Ave 403-448-9851

**Callingwood Family Chiropractic
Centre**
Semeniuk, Dr. Brad; Yarrow, Dr. Lori-Anne
6725-177th St 403-496-9980

Capilano Chiropractic Clinic
Miller, Dr. Lee; Redpath, Dr. J. Bryan
2, 9343-50th St 403-469-4881

Castledowns Chiropractic Clinic
Rogers, Dr. Renae; Rousselle, Dr. Damian
Schreiner, Dr. Deborah A.
2nd Floor, 12222-137th Ave .403-456-2221

Cook, Dr. Donald S.
317, 10310 Jasper Ave ...403-422-1225

Cook, Dr. G.W.
819 NW Saddleback Rd 403-438-4222

Cotter, Dr. G.J.
12304-107th Ave 403-452-4372

Creswell Chiropractic Centre
Creswell, Dr. Kevin
5710-19A Ave 403-450-1041

Delong, Dr. David
3917-106th St 403-462-6242

Edmonton Chiropractic Clinic
Bradley, Dr. Donald; Watson, Dr. Marcia
1407, 10104-103rd Ave ...403-422-1087

Family Chiropractic Centre
Fulford, Dr. J. Lorne; Fulford, Dr. Maggie
10121-151st St 403-448-7301

Forest Heights Chiropractic Centre
Buczynski, Dr. Paul; Moutran, Dr. Lorrie
10144-79th St 403-469-1561

Gajdos, Dr. L.J.
208-9074 NW 51st Ave 403-468-5172

Garrett, Dr. Vernon R.
501, 10053-111th St 403-482-5634

Gilbertson, Dr. Thor Edward
234, 6655-178th St 403-484-2288

Hurst, Dr. R.G.
1260, 10055-106th St 403-422-5477

Ibsen, Dr. Norman L.
350, 10123-99th St 403-429-2434

Inglewood Chiropractic Office
Latch, Dr. R.H.
12304-111th Ave 403-453-5751

Kingsway Chiropractic Centre
Elliott, Dr. David B.
310 Kingsway Garden Mall ..403-479-5353

Kuruliak Chiropractic Office
Kuruliak, Dr. M.; Kuruliak, Dr. Greg
11829 NW 127th St 403-454-3240

Lewis, Dr. Michael A.
2019-111th St 403-433-9920

Lifestyle Rejuvenation Clinic
Swanston, Dr. Randolph
11115-124th St 403-451-4600

Martin, Dr. N. Daniel
210-12220 Stoney Plain Rd .403-482-6644

**Mayfield Medical Soft Tissue Pain
Clinic**
Gelinas, Dr. Barry J.
11098-156th St 403-486-2225

McLeod Chiropractic Clinic
McLeod, Dr. Campbell A.
18123 NW 107th Ave 403-489-2222

McLeod, Dr. Curtiss A.
508, 10240-124th St 403-488-8156

McLeod, Dr. L.Douglas
202, 11813-123rd St 403-453-6646

Millwoods Chiropractic Centre
Ma, Dr. Seem
35 Millbourne
Shopping Centre 403-462-1456

Millwoods Mainstreet Chiropractic
Gallinger, Dr. Michael; Watson, Dr. Kevin
6542-28th Ave 403-496-9009

Morgan, Dr. Darrell J.
1503, 9740-106th St 403-992-0001

99th Street Chiropractic Office
Tripp, Dr. David
9009-99th St 403-433-0502

North Edmonton Chiropractic Clinic
Fitz, Dr. Bryan L.
12935-97th St 403-473-6441

**Petrolia Chiropractic Centre
Chiropractor**
Parish, Dr. Kevin A.
11404-40th Ave 403-434-0505

**Riverbend Family Chiropractic
Centre**
Berg, Dr. Todd A.
608 Riverbend Square 403-433-1450

Sears, Dr. T.H.
8227 NW 99th St 403-433-5364

Seung, Dr. Kyu S.
211, 3017-66th St 403-450-0060

Sharp Family Chiropractic Clinic
Sharp, Dr. Timothy J.
10204-112th St 403-425-1133

Smith, Dr. Darrell
14917-107th Ave 403-481-4903

So Chiropractic Clinic Chiropractors
McNiven-McKenna, Dr. Patrick;
So, Dr. David; Yee, Dr. Douglas
70, 4003-98th St 403-433-9399

Stiles, Dr. Gregory John
12504 NW 102nd Ave 403-453-3538

Sure-Back
Greer, Dr. Colleen
15307-96th Ave 403-484-2272

Tash Chiropractic Clinic
Tash, Dr. Kevin
Bsmt, 10313-82th Ave 403-433-6700

Terra Losa Chiropractic Clinic
Kole, Dr. David A.
9770-170th St 403-487-6161

Tin, Dr. Rodney K.
11818 NW St. Albert Tr ...403-453-3376

Tuck, Dr. P.
10824 A 82nd Ave 403-433-7791

Walsh, Dr. G. Brin
8806-92th St 403-448-1020

**Ward, Dr. J. Gary; Ward, Dr.
James**
10119 NW 123rd St 403-488-2151

West End Chiropractic Physicians
Beckhuson, Dr. Janet; Beckhuson, Dr. Murray
15614-95th Ave 403-489-8609

Westview Chiropractic Clinic
Fisher, Dr. Daniel; Galas, Dr. Brian
Labelle, Dr. Sydney B.
10126-149th St 403-489-7300

Williamson, Dr. R.L.
10455-84th Ave 403-439-4321

Witherbee, Dr. J. Ned
810-1 Thornton Crt 403-424-1733

Zimmerman, Dr. Carolyn A.
10203-121st St 403-482-7175

EDSON

Harrison Chiropractic Clinic
Harrison, Dr. Cameron; Harrison, Dr. Kenneth
524-50th St 403-723-4431

ELK POINT

Stewart, Dr. Alex
4906-50th St 403-724-3677

FAIRVIEW

**Adams, Dr. Jennifer; Hessel, Dr.
Brett**
By Appointment 403-835-5385

FORT MACLEOD

Fort Macleod Chiropractic
Poytress, Dr. Alan
2215-2nd Ave 403-553-4003

FORT MCMURRAY

Family Chiropractic Centre
Galenzoski, Dr. James; McBean, Dr. James
56 Fitzgerald Ave 403-743-1971

Fort McMurray Chiropractic Clinic
Laforest, Dr. Cheryl; Laforest, Dr. Tim
4-9908 Franklin Ave 403-743-8422

FORT SASKATCHEWAN

Fort Chiropractic Centre
Schneider, Dr. Murray
10404-99th Ave 403-992-7200

Fort Saskatchewan Chiropractic
Jones, Dr. Dorothea; Jones, Dr. Roger
10308-100th Ave 403-992-0001

Pinder, Dr. R.J.
10101-100th Ave 403-998-2211

Zimmerman Chiropractic Offices
Zimmerman, Dr. Robert
9821-108th St 403-998-2248

GRAND CACHE

Grande Cache Chiropractic Office
Bergquist, Dr. Ken
211 Pine Plaza 403-827-3111

GRAND CENTRE

**Bickert, Dr. John; Coleman, Dr.
James**
By Appointment 403-594-4547

GRAND PRAIRIE

Cheshire, Dr. Brian
102 Nordic Crt 403-532-2570

**Cooper, Dr. Thomas; Kary, Dr.
Louise**
9817-116th Ave 403-538-1422

**Harper, Dr. Keith G.; Strebohuk,
Dr. Garry**
102, 9803-101 Ave 403-532-1690

Shalagan, Dr. Wade
301, 9728 Montrose Ave ...403-539-4321

HANNA

Hanna Chiropractic Clinic
Kaster, Dr. John; Larson, Dr. Craig
609-2nd Ave W 403-854-2110

HIGH LEVEL

Bateson-Koch, Dr. Carolee; Koch, Dr. Helmut
By Appointment 403-926-4606

HIGH PRAIRIE

South Peace Chiropractic Centres
Penner, Dr. Derek R.
5001-49th St 403-523-4838

HIGH RIVER

Campbell, Dr. C. Dan
10 Pioneer Sq 403-652-7767

Corbett Chiropractic
Corbett, Dr. B. Jo-Anne; Corbett, Dr. Robert
1 Macleod Tr S 403-652-1020

Highwood Chiropractic
Wilson, Dr. Christopher C.
335 Macleod Tr 403-652-3803

HILL SPRING

Hill Spring Family Chiropractic
Schnoor, Dr. Kim
By Appointment 403-626-3899

HINTON

Hinton Chiropractic Clinic
Pleckaitis, Dr. Harold
Ogre Canyon
Professional Bldg 403-865-4706

Surmik, Dr. R.F.
566a Carmichael Lane 403-865-3970

INNISFAIL

Herman, Dr. G.R.
4919-52nd St 403-227-3433

Innisfail Chiropractic Clinic
Bystrom, Dr. L.C.
Co-op Mall 403-227-1777

Quartly, Dr. Loren
111, 4804-50th St 403-227-5721

KILLAM

Killam Chiropractic Clinic
Annis, Dr. Robert S.
5009-50th St 403-385-3734

LACOMBE

Haitsma, Dr. Clarence
4733-49B Ave 403-782-5858

Korsh Chiropractic Centre
Korsh, Dr. Thomas
By Appointment 403-782-3341

LEDUC

Cook, Dr. G.W.
4922-51st Ave 403-986-1101

Doren, Dr. Robert K.
22 Corinthia Park
Shopping Centre 403-986-8461

Tomich, Dr. Robert J.
5304-50th St 403-986-8488

LETHBRIDGE

Academy Chiropractic
Walcott, Dr. Ted
919-3rd Ave S 403-327-0345

Bridge, Dr. G.J.
501-7th St S 403-329-8266

Centre For Health & Wellbeing
Buchanan, Dr. Ian; Kane, Dr. Richard
1256-3rd Ave S 403-327-1118

Centre Site Chiropractic
Aldcorn, Dr. Leslie Lyn; Brosz, Dr. David
801-3 Ave S 403-329-1777

Chiropractic Associate Clinic
Anderson, Dr. Roy; Speelman, Dr. J.C.
Speelman, Dr. Lee C.
529-6th St S 403-327-2230

Cooper, Dr. Gary W.
229 N 13th St 403-320-1015

Corbett Chiropractic Lethbridge Office
111 Macleod Tr S 403-327-3130

Dudley, Dr. Alan; Dudley, Dr. Mark
Park Palace
Shopping Center 403-327-3203

Nemeth, Dr. Joe; Nemeth, Dr. Kevin
309 Woodward Tower 403-320-2778

Noji, Dr. Janice
416A Stafford Dr S 403-381-7766

Puhl Chiropractic
Hogue, Dr. Donald; Puhl, Dr. Bryon
118-8th St S 403-329-1300/0055

Purvis Chiropractic
Giacchetta, Dr. Rodney; Prince, Dr. James
Purvis, Dr. Julia
260,220-4th St S 403-329-6577/
                              380-3744

Skjonsberg, Dr. Norman; Skjonsberg, Dr. Pearl
1216-3rd Ave S 403-327-3130

Star Clinic
Sillito, Dr. R.W.
316-13th St S 403-328-7746

Tajiri, Dr. N.M.
104, 1201-3rd Ave S 403-327-1244

Takahashi, Dr. David
102, 1201-3rd Ave S 403-328-0412

Warren-Stroud Chiropractic
Stroud, Dr. David; Warren, Dr. Jeffrey
111-7th St S 403-320-8080

Westside Family Chiropractic Centre
Jackson, Dr. Don; Jackson, Dr. Kathryn
674 Columbia Blvd W 403-380-2611

LLOYDMINISTER

Hnatko, Dr. Thomas J.
106, 4402-52nd Ave 403-875-7707

Lloydminster Chiropractic Centre
Atkinson, Dr. Lee; Murray, Dr. F.R.
5013-48th St 403-875-3389

MAGRATH

Family Chiropractic
Murray, Dr. Harold R.
4S-1st St W 403-758-3118

MEDICINE HAT

Jackle, Dr. Chad L.
1377-22nd St SE 403-526-8300

Jans, Dr. Wallace; Powers, Dr. Rick
1007 Factory St SE 403-529-9069

Little, Dr. Lee; Marsh, Dr. D.G. Stiem, Dr. Ronald
360-2nd St SE . . .403-529-5177/526-4356

Smith McArthur & Bright Chiropractors
Bright, Dr. Kristine; McArthur, Dr. Ross
Smith, Dr. Donald F.
201, 533-2nd St SE 403-527-2200

Stannard, Dr. Dave
127 Carry Dr SE 403-526-8989

Werner, Dr. Derek B.
1-3151 Dunmore Rd SE 403-526-7233

MORINVILLE

Fromet, Dr. Serge
1049-101st St 403-939-3885

Morinville Chiropractic Clinic
Maloney, Dr. J. Allan
9707-100th St 403-939-3399

NANTON

Liscombe Chiropractic Clinic
Liscombe, Dr. G.M.
2121-18th St 403-646-3111

Wilson, Dr. Christopher
B 2019-20th Ave SE 403-646-2911

OKOTOKS

Foothills Chiropractic Centre
Samek, Dr. Dennis W.
30 Elm St W 403-938-8888

Okotoks Chiropractic Office
Sands, Dr. Edward W.A.
40 Elizabeth St 403-938-2065

OLDS

Chiropractic Health Centre
Herman, Dr. Edward
Mn Fl, 5112-50th Ave 403-556-3388

Olds Chiropractic Centre
Boyter, Dr. Tom
7, 4513-52nd Ave 403-556-6534

PEACE RIVER

Gingerich, Dr. Larry; Hall, Dr. Douglas
9813-98th Ave 403-624-2121

Grimble, Dr. Robert
10032-99th St 403-624-4434

PINCHER CREEK

Buchanan, Dr. R.I.
673 Main St 403-627-4357

Butler, Dr. Kenneth K.
686 Main St 403-627-3741

Creekside Family Chiropractic
Schnoor, Dr. Kim
1035 Hewetson Ave 403-627-5119

PONOKO

Bader, Dr. Dawn
By Appointment 403-783-3481

Chidlow, G.S.
4912-50th St 403-783-3481

Thomas, E.H.
5012-50th St 403-783-5022

RAYMOND

Bridge, Dr. G.
54 North Broadway 403-752-4042

RED DEER

Advanced Family Wellness
Waddell, Dr. Stephen
180, 5201-43rd St 403-342-7670

Associated Family Chiropractic
Didrikson, Garry I.
5415-49th Ave 403-342-2273

Bower Place Chiropractic
Lucci, Dr. Brian
1044A Bower Place
Shopping Centre 403-340-1133

Coates Chiropractic Clinic
Coates, Dr. Cheryl; Coates, Dr. David
Martens, Dr. Dianna J.
10-69 Dunlop St 403-343-7898

Demchuk, Dr. Edward L.
4922-53rd St 403-347-7100

Foord, Dr. W.B.
Mn Fl, 5010-43rd St 403-346-2744

Frenette, Dr. Brandy
By Appointment 403-347-5725

Hoffman Chiropractic Clinic
Hoffman, Dr. Norman; Hoffman, Dr. Teresa
4702-50th Ave 403-346-2297

Kristianson, Ivar J. (24 Hour Call)
6-88 Howarth St 403-346-1999

Peak Chiropractic Centre
Larsen, Dr. Stacy; Smethurst, Dr. Duane
Bay 128, Bower Plaza 403-343-7325

Pedersen Chiropractic Clinic
Pedersen, Dr. Donald
180-5201, 43rd St 403-347-3506

Smith, Dr. R. Lyle
105-4929 Ross St 403-346-4700

Snider, Dr. Brian M.
7 Sydney Close 403-341-4452

Village Chiropractic Clinic
Gellert, Dr. Greg; Newfield, Dr. Todd
Parker, Dr. Dean
Bay 18, Village Mall 403-340-1770

RIMBEY

Rimbey Chiropractic
Bergen, Dr. Barry L.
Co-op Shopping Centre 403-843-2626

ROCKY MOUNTAIN HOUSE

Gehrke, Dr. Richard; Gehrke, Dr. Tanis
5115-50th St 403-845-3536

Kariatsumari, Dr. Roy
4924-51st 403-845-2289

Rudkin, Dr. Bruce
4913-50th St 403-845-2111

ST. ALBERT

Albrumac Chiropractic Center
Johnson, Dr. L.J.
220, 8657-51st Ave 403-459-3165

Borley, Dr. J.M.; Rawlek, Dr. Anne
510 Grandin Park
Plaza Tower 403-458-5544/460-2200

Brodeur, Dr. Ray A.; Thomas, Dr. E.H.
60 Riel Dr 403-458-8200/459-8183

Cooper, Dr. Jon D.
Gateway Village Mall 403-460-9570

Froment, Dr. Colin
224, 2 Herbert Rd 403-460-4338

Hyderman, Dr. Stuart
14 Inglewood Dr 403-458-8180

McCurry, Dr. Reg F.
202-86th McKenney Ave ...403-458-0616

ST. PAUL

Lee, Dr. Edmund T.
4436-50th Ave 403-645-5793

Warchola, Dr. Randy S.
4913-50th Ave 403-645-3159

SHERWOOD PARK

Alton, Dr. Alan; McAuley, Dr. D. Court
214-80th Chippewa Rd 403-464-5220

Brentwood Chiropractic Clinic
Jones, Dr. Dorothea
15-99th Wye Rd 403-467-0892

Dunford, Dr. Daryl
305-101 Granada Blvd 403-464-3866

Sherwood Chiropractic
Fuller, Dr. Warren; McGinnis, Dr. Cameron
80 Athabascan Ave 403-467-8755

Sigurdson, Dr. P.M.
109-937 Fir St 403-467-3812

SLAVE LAKE

Slave Lake Chiropractic Clinic
Bergen, Dr. Barry; Chidlow, Dr. Glenn
Liebig, Dr. Todd
204-4th Ave NW 403-849-6821

Cotter, Dr. Brian
221-3rd Ave NW 403-849-2478

SPRING COULEE

Prince, Dr. James
By Appointment 403-732-4655

SPRUCE GROVE

Bamber, Dr. Lori
Friedenberg, Dr. Aubrey
215 Mcleod Ave 403-962-1567

Courteau, Dr. A.L.
Co-op Shopping Centre 403-962-3535

STETTLER

Becklund, Dr. Dennis
4214-62th St 403-742-0370

Lynes, Dr. E.
4719-49th St 403-742-5810

Nilsson, Dr. Doug B.
4928-50th Ave 403-742-2505

STONY PLAIN

Chiropractic Spinal Care Centre
Pyrozko, Dr. Jerry
4914-50th Ave 403-963-7090

Johnson, Dr. D.
By Appointment 403-963-6159

Shiloh Chiropractic Clinic
Mills, Dr. Clark R.
5105-48th St 403-963-3466

STRATHMORE

Maximum Wellness Health Centre
Whitaker, Dr. Mark
115-2nd Ave 403-934-5633

Procyshen, Dr. T.D.
118-2nd Ave 403-934-5175

SUNDRE

Watt, W.A.
105-4th St SW 403-638-4212

SYLVAN LAKE

Bierkos, Dr. R.
4938-50th Ave 403-887-3687

Sylvan Lake Chiropractic Clinic
Sedun, Dr. Glenn S.
2 Fl, Parkland Credit
Union Bldg 403-887-4242

TABER

Chipman, Dr. James D.
5208-48th Ave 403-223-3644

Holowiski, Dr. Clifford
5207-50th Ave 403-223-4419

Ripley, J.C.
4722-51st St 403-223-2062

Valgardson Chiropractic
Valgardsen, Dr. L. Blair
5217A-50th Ave 403-223-8044

THREE HILLS

Hall, Dr. Douglas
By Appointment 403-443-7999

Pedersen, Dr. B.W.
1041-2nd St N 403-443-5188

TROCHU

Trochu Chiropractic Clinic
Snider, Dr. Brian
205 Arena Ave 403-442-3111

VEGREVILLE

Fisher, Dr. Daniel
McKenzie, Dr. Kevin; McKenzie, Dr. Robert
4923-51st Ave 403-632-2181

VERMILION

Esak, Dr. Lloyd M.
5125-50th Ave 403-853-4585

Stewart, Dr. Alex J.
5031-50th Ave 403-853-6500

VULCAN

Liscombe Chiropractic Clinic
Liscombe, Dr. G.M.
209 Centre St 403-485-6005

Vulcan Chiropactic Clinic
Twiss, Dr. C. Michael
125 Centre St 403-485-2979

WEASKIWIN

Hewko, Dr. David
5004-51st St 403-352-0200

WAINRIGHT

Champion, Dr. Barry
1032-1st Ave 403-842-3301

WESTLOCK

Aspen Chiropractic Centre
Hrycaj, Dr. Sheila; Williams, Dr. Wayne
10419-100th Ave 403-349-3503

WETASKIWIN

Greenhorn, Dr. L.H.
5003-51st Ave 403-352-2101

Labelle, Dr. S.
102, 5108-50th Ave 403-352-3606

Sindelar, Dr. L.W.
5006-48th St 403-352-6411

WHITECOURT

Whitecourt Chiropractic Office
Kenlin, Dr. J.; Zierath, Dr. S.A.
5032-51st Ave 403-778-2674

✦ British Columbia

Chiropractors are regulated in B.C., meaning that there is legislation establishing a governing body responsible for registering and disciplining practitioners (see below, "Governing Body"). There is government health coverage under the B.C. Medical Services Plan (see below, "Government Health Care Funding").

Legislation

Chiropractors are regulated under the *Chiropractors Act*. Under this legislation, "chiropractic" means "the branch of healing arts that is concerned with the restoration and maintenance of health through adjustment by hand, or the use of devices directly related to the adjustment, of the articulations of the human body and that is involved primarily with the relationship of the spinal column to the nervous system" (section 1). It is an offence to practise chiropractic without being registered, or while registration has been cancelled or suspended.

Section 9(2) of the Act states that a registered chiropractor who has a certificate of competency from the Board of Chiropractors may use X-ray shadow photographs of the articulations of the human body. Section 10 states that nothing in the Act authorizes a chiropractor to prescribe or administer drugs or anaesthetics for any purpose.

Government Health Care Funding

User fees

There is a user fee for chiropractic services (set out below), unless you are a member of an exempt group, including those holding a native status card, persons receiving premium assistance, refugees, and those whose premiums are covered by the Ministry of Social Services and Housing. For medicare information, call 1-800-663-7100.

Maximum Number of Annual Visits

The maximum number of visits to a chiropractor, partially covered by the Medical Services Plan of B.C., is 12 per calendar year for those less than 65 years old, and 15 visits per calendar year for those 65 or over. An emergency visit (guidelines apply) is covered up to $34.85.

Chiropractors who have "Opted In" to the Medical Services Plan

First Office Visit:

Patient pays $7.50 user fee, and the Plan pays $14.77 for a total of $22.27. If the patient is exempt from user fees (see above), the government pays the entire $22.27.

Subsequent Office Visits:

Patient pays $7.50 user fee, with the Plan paying the balance of $9.85, for a total of $17.35. If the patient is exempt from user fees, medicare covers the entire $17.35.

Chiropractors who have "Opted Out" of the Medical Services Plan

First visit:

The chiropractor sets the fee, but no matter how high the bill, the government pays no more than $14.77. For example, on a bill of $35, the patient would pay $20.23, and the government $14.77. If the patient is exempt from user fees, the most the government will pay is $22.27, and the patient pays the balance.

Subsequent visits:

The government pays no more than $9.85, and the patient pays the balance. If the patient is exempt from user fees, the government would pay a maximum $17.35.

British Columbia Governing Body

British Columbia College of Chiropractors
130-10100 Shellbridge Way
Richmond, B.C. V6X 2W7
Tel: 604-270-1332

Call the College to check if your chiropractor is registered or to lodge a complaint. The College has the duty under the legislation to protect the public, govern chiropractic, enforce standards of professional ethics, and to require members to provide an individual with access to his or her health care records in appropriate circumstances.

British Columbia Professional Association

B.C. Chiropractic Association
2158 West Broadway
Vancouver, B.C. V6K 2C8
Tel: 604-737-1411

✦ British Columbia Chiropractors

NOTE: Check the credentials of your chiropractor (see above, "Questions to Ask"). This publication cannot and does not certify or represent the qualifications of practitioners, or the quality of care available from them. We cannot and do not confirm that those listed are registered as required by law.

100 MILE HOUSE

Chiropractic Associates
Mitchell, Dr. John
204-475 S Birch Ave 604-395-4833

Fairburn, Dr. Garth
108-475 S Birch Ave 604-395-4001

ABBOTSFORD

Abbotsford Chiropractic Center
Barwell, Dr. Richard G.; McCallum, Dr. Michael
Ward, Dr. Anthony D.; Ward, Dr. Jerry L.
101-2469 Pauline 604-852-5133

Clearbrook Chiropractor Clinic
Gueldner, Dr. Bradley; Gueldner, Dr. Dana
204-32555 Simon 604-852-1820

Enns Chiropractic
Abraham, Dr. Alden H.
107-2790 Gladwin 604-852-5070

Erickson, Dr. Dan
205-2580 Cedar Pk Pl 604-853-9898

Giesbrecht, Dr. Ron
2459 McCallum Rd 604-853-8121

Mayer, Dr. Richard
102-2306 McCallum Rd 604-853-4441

Raabe, Dr. Elmer E.
101-2306 McCallum Rd 604-853-4494

Sumas Mountain Chiropractic Center
Dietrich, Dr. Richard N.; Banman, Dr. Scott A.
102-34609 Delair 604-852-3930

Turner, Dr. Robert
32920 Ventura Ave 604-859-6781

AGASSIZ

Forde, Dr. Robert; Smith, Dr. Sophia-Anne
7054 Pioneer 604-796-3559

ALDERGROVE

Aldergrove Chiropractic
Meinzer, Dr. Fred K.
18-27514a Fraser Hwy 604-856-5299

Kilian, Dr. Gideon J.
27240-30th Ave 604-856-7781

Lacelle, Dr. Gabrielle
2905-272nd St 604-856-0333

ARMSTRONG

Ritchey, Dr. James
2510 Patterson Ave 604-546-6699

BOWEN ISLAND

Cates Hill Chiropractic Centre
Macdonald, Dr. Glenn
485 Mt Gardner 604-947-0102

BRENTWOOD BAY

Elder, Dr. Richard K.
7115 West Saanich 604-652-5211

BURNABY

Berti, Dr. Albert A.
3825 Sunset St 604-437-9949

Birzneck, Dr. Arthur R.
7527 Kingsway 604-526-9312

Burnaby Chiropractic
Cortese, Dr. D.
508-5050 Kingsway 604-434-5889

Central Park Chiropractic
Chiu, Dr. Leonard ; Johnson, Dr. Ted
Paterson, Dr. Gordon
4071 Kingsway 604-439-1230

Chan, Dr. Bill
6931 Kingsway 604-526-7255

Davis, Dr. John M.
201-1160 Douglas 604-294-2304

De Camillis, Dr. Richard A.
101a-3701 Hastings 604-291-1166

Dow, Dr. Steven R.
4322 Hastings 604-298-0525

Grant, Dr. Donald A.
7634-6th St 604-524-4959

Lee, Dr. Eugene; Maylin-Lee, Dr. Anne
4697 Kingsway 604-435-2283

McDiarmid, Dr. Frank; Sheard, Dr. Sid E.
101-4603 Kingsway 604-438-6106

Metrotown Chiropractic
Roberts, Dr. Tom
4923 Kingsway 604-434-6116

Rose, Dr. R.E. ; Dr. Turner, Mark
B-5593 Kingway 604-430-4324

Sauser, Dr. Barry
208-4603 Kingsway 604-432-1448

Shong, Dr. Kevan
E-7487 Edmonds 604-540-1551

CAMPBELL RIVER

Braun, Dr. J.C.
106-250 Dogwood 604-286-1614

Coulter, Dr. Murray
358 Cedar 604-286-6852

Cronk, Dr. Richard R.; Reynolds, Dr. L.
1180 Fir St 604-287-8487

Elmwood Chiropractic Clinic
Bradley, Dr. John; Fletcher, Dr. Bruce
1330 Elm St 604-287-7014

Grobman, Dr. Mark
610 Evergreen 604-286-6633

Koster, Dr. Michael
4-2380 S Island Hwy 604-923-2464

CASTLEGAR

M.C. Salmon Chiropractor Corp
Salmon, Dr. Margaret
A-1020 Columbia 604-365-3365

Williams, Dr. David S.
1406 Columbia 604-365-2106

CHASE

Martin, Dr. Paul F.
826 Thompson 604-679-3633

CHILLIWACK

Maier, Dr. A.; McConnell, Dr. G.W.
2-8330 Young St S 604-792-1388

Smith, Dr. David
9132 Mary St 604-792-9171

Wademan, Dr. Douglas A.
9365 Mary St 604-792-9133

CLEARBROOK

Fadden, Dr. Helen
203-2692 Clearbrook Rd ...604-852-4480

Munro, Dr. Darell
32920 Ventura Ave 604-853-3212

CLEARWATER

Hasler, Dr. Keith
50 Young 604-674-3366

COBBLE HILL

Holmes, Dr. R.M.
3720 Arbutus Dr N 604-743-9194

COMOX

Body Care Chiropractic
Titchener, Dr. Peter
2090 Comox 604-339-1148

Cameron, Dr. J. Blake
46-190 Port Augusta 604-339-3664

Comox Chiropractic Centre
Opitz, Dr.; Price, Dr. Douglas R.
1723 Comox Ave 604-339-4433

Gordon, Dr. John R.
262 Anderton 604-339-5538

COQUITLAM

Cariboo Health Centre
Johal, Dr. Shivraj; Meinzer, Dr. Fred K.
435 North Rd 604-939-1714

Davidson, Dr. Joan
201-1015 Austin 604-931-7797

Hayward, Dr. Bryan A.
1037 Ridgeway Ave 604-936-6577

Kapitza, Dr. Richard A.P.
114b-3030 Lincoln Ave 604-941-2332

Klein, Dr. Eric
210-403 North Rd 604-931-3044

Lepp Nero Chiropractic Group
Lepp, Dr. Jay; Nero, Dr. James
201-2773 Barnet Hwy 604-464-3424

Lougheed Chiropractic Centre
Morrison, Dr. D. Scott; Myers, Dr. Jordan A.
201-566 Lougheed Hwy ...604-931-7200

Mackenzie Chiropractic Associates
Hoskins, Dr. Heather
101-1108 Austin Ave 604-939-2201

McCann, Dr. Michael
1956 Como Lake 604-931-2225

Rogal, Dr. William
107-3020 Lincoln Ave 604-464-1325

Shepherd, Dr. Mark J.K.
901 Lougheed Hwy 604-931-7571

COURTENAY

Bozman, Dr. Gerard
355-6th St 604-334-2483

Cockwill, Dr. R.G.
102, 389-12th St 604-334-2262

Fenneman, Dr. D.A.; Koster, Dr. G.L.
951 Fitzgerald Ave 604-338-7351

Tenth Street Chiropractic Inc
Grant, Dr. Liza
580-10th St 604-338-9606

CRANBROOK

Harach, Dr. Michael
32 S 13th Ave 604-426-8792

Kemble, Dr. G.E.
6 S 10th Ave 604-426-7867

Mile, Dr. E.Z.
221 S 9th Ave 604-426-8398

Terai, Dr. Mark T.
824 Baker St 604-489-3200

CRESTON

Dobson, Dr. Richard
1008 Ibboston 604-428-4066

Mulligan, Dr. Mary Ann
2509 Erickson 604-428-7533

DAWSON CREEK

Gleadhill, Dr. A.O.
18, 1405-102nd Ave 604-782-9192

Irwin, Dr. David G.
1008-105th Ave 604-782-9360

South Peace Chiropractic
Mangel, Dr. Gerry
10200-8th St 604-782-7742

DELTA

Burkett, Dr. D.G.
1511-56th St 604-943-6626

Canil, Dr. Roy G.
208, 7313-120th St 604-594-0464

Coutts Chiropractic Clinic
Coutts, Dr. Susan; Coutts, Dr. Tom
1205-52nd St 604-943-8388

Douwes, Dr. Peter
11900-80th Ave 604-596-7355

Egan, Dr. David
8253-120th St 604-599-3997

Kennedy Heights Chiropractic Clinic
McCallum, Dr. Marshall B.; Smith, Dr. R.S.
11934-88th Ave 604-594-8144

Richmond, Dr. Robert W.J.
222, 1077-56th St 604-943-1164

Scottsdale Chiropractic Association
Siu, Dr. Hubert W.; Tanaka, Dr. Larry S.
7093-120th St 604-597-0542

DENMAN ISLAND

Titchener, Dr. Peter
1069 North West Rd 604-335-1182

DUNCAN

Boggs, Dr. Herbert W.; Hoshizaki, Dr. Donald S.
394 Duncan St 604-746-6171

Gregory, Dr. Ian R.
4-271 Ingram St 604-746-7422

Hicks, Dr. Geoffrey; Wynne-Smith, Dr. Julian
372 Coronation 604-746-7051

ENDERBY

Smith, Dr. Douglas R.
5-706 George St 604-838-6969

FORT ST. JOHN

Hendricks, Dr. Fred E.
1, 9730-101st Ave 604-787-9800

Kientz, Dr. L.D.
9936-102nd Ave 604-787-0380

North Peace Chiropractic Centre
De Camillis, Dr. R.; Mangel, Dr. G.
Zarchynski, Dr. Michael
9920-107th Ave 604-785-2830

GABRIOLA ISLAND

Wright, Dr. Douglas A.
5-590 North Rd 604-247-8780

GIBSONS

Simpson, Dr. Samuel
7-771 Hwy 101 604-886-3622

GOLD RIVER

Grobman, Dr. Mark
123-396 Nimpkish 604-283-7654

GOLDEN

Golden Chiropractic Clinic
Link, Dr. Alex
510 N 9th Ave 604-344-7337

GRAND FORKS

Kettle Valley Chiropractic
Campbell, Dr. P.G. 604-442-2883

Maskall, Dr. S.A.
7331-3rd St 604-442-3811

Naylor, Dr. L.I.
125 Market 604-442-2761

HOPE

Wademan, Dr. Douglas
835-6th Ave 604-869-2515

HOUSTON

Millar, Dr. Craig; Murdoch, Dr. Gary
2438 Poulton 604-845-7013

INVERMERE

Pepperdine, Dr. Ken
505b-7th Ave 604-342-9666

KAMLOOPS

Davidson, Dr. John V.; MacIntosh, Dr. D.
259-1320 W Trans
Canada Hwy 604-374-3226

Hasler, Dr. Keith
1-665 Tranquille Rd 604-554-7035

James, Dr. Michael V.
1540 Springhill Dr 604-372-7212

Kicia, Dr. Kenneth F.
789 Fortune 604-554-3446

Mcknight, Dr. Alan
512 Tranquille Rd 604-554-2355

Shea, Dr. Gerry M.
635 Victoria St 604-374-6938

Thomson, Dr. J.D.
220-1210 Summit 604-374-3522

Turner Chiropractic Associates
Turner, Dr. Kevin D.; Turner, Dr. W.D.
235-1st Ave 604-374-6223

KELOWNA

Active Care Chiropractic
Muzzin, Dr. Michael A.
11-605 KLO Rd 604-861-6151

Anderson, Dr. Robert E.
8-515 Harvey 604-860-9404

Back & Body Health Centre
Brummund, Dr. Mel A.
206-2365 Gordon 604-868-8578

Burtch Chiropractic
Sauve, Dr. Marc; Terai, Dr. Wayne
10-1470 Harvey 604-860-4518

Central Chiropractic Associates
Boruta, Dr. John; Lees-Taylor, Dr. Denise
Ritchey, Dr. Mervyn G.
1923 Kent Rd 604-860-6295

Cresswell, Dr. David L.
208-1980 Cooper 604-868-2225

Ferguson, Dr. William H.
505 Sutherland 604-762-5432

Forsythe, Dr.
225 S Rutland Rd 604-765-1466

James, Dr. Barbara
101-1823 Harvey 604-868-2951

Langedyk Chiropractic
Langedyk, Dr. C.; Langedyk, Dr. S.
430-2339 N Highway 97 ...604-763-8333

Marshall, Dr. Kenneth V.
101-1610 Bertram St 604-861-3251

Nairne, Dr. Roberta
210-1511 Sutherland 604-763-7757

Okanagan Chiropractic Centre
2640 Pandosy St 604-762-2888

Penner, Dr. Todd A.
104-1100 Lawrence 604-860-2212

Pereverzoff Chiropractic
Pereverzoff, Dr. J.
205-437 Glenmore Rd ...604-868-1167

Roy, Dr. Raymond J.
101-1470 St Paul 604-861-1332

Stirling Chiropractic Corp
Stirling, Dr. Glenn
2363 Hunter Rd 604-763-9355

KIMBERLEY

Murphy, Dr. Kathleen
3-495 Wallinger Ave 604-427-2281

KITIMAT

Good, Dr. Norman
101-180 Nechako Centre ...604-632-4773

LADYSMITH

Butcher, Dr. Marshall
225 High 604-245-7727

Carlson, Dr. Kevin A.
112 French 604-245-8778

Vogelzang, Dr. Henny
306b Rigby Pl 604-245-3831

LANGLEY

Brookswood Chiropractic
Noth, Dr. Chris
4041-200th St 604-530-6227

Grypma, Dr. Ronald
20765 Fraser Hwy 604-534-5121/
533-0911

Hopping-Geiger, Dr. Marie
20433 Douglas Cr 604-534-7451

Irving, Dr. Alan
104, 8843-204th St 604-888-1533/
3533

Mayer, Dr. Richard
23256-24th Ave 604-530-7432

Mikkelsen, Dr. Kenneth
4041-200th St 604-530-6227

Otterstrom, Dr. Erik
6-19950 Willowbrook Dr ...604-530-0530

Russell, Dr. K.W.
20103-50th Ave 604-534-9988

Short, Dr. Lawrence; Stork, Dr. Norman
203-5755 Glover ...604-533-9888/3033

Walnut Grove Chiropractic
Jones, Dr. Tamara
601-21183-88th Ave 604-888-1114

Warkman, Dr. Ronald
202-20609 Douglas Cr 604-533-8660

LANTZVILLE

Bunting, Dr. Frank
7175 Lantzville 604-390-4446

MAPLE RIDGE

Chiropractic Associates
Forest, Dr. Margaret; Kendall, Dr. James
Masse, Dr. Robert E.
22234 Selkirk Ave 604-467-6353

Hopper, Dr. M.J.; Passmore, Dr. David
22219 Dewdney
Trunk Rd 604-467-4222/3239

Maple Ridge Chiropractic
Gluckman, Dr. John
230-22529 Lougheed Hwy .604-463-9188

Meadowridge Chiropractic
Castro, Dr. Richard S.
11-20691 Lougheed Hwy ..604-465-4500

Westlake, Dr. Donald F.
11763 Fraser St 604-463-6313

MILL BAY

Cobble Hill Chiropractic
Smith, Dr. Donald G.
2583 Lodgepole 604-743-3264

Mill Bay Chiropractic
Lax, Dr. Michael
2670 Mill Bay Rd 604-743-2170

MISSION

Cedar Hills Chiropractic Center
Banman, Dr. Scott; Dietrich, Dr. Richard
32928-7th Ave 604-820-8811

Hand, Dr. Herbert
32094-7th Ave 604-826-5414

Mission Chiropractic Clinic
Perry, Dr. Grant
32162 Scott 604-826-1274

NAKUSP

Grove, Dr. Debra; Grove, Dr. Peter
By Appointment 604-265-2200

NANAIMO

Applecross Chiropractic Corp.
Austin, Dr. Randal
6441 Applecross 604-390-1123

Barons Road Chiropractic
Dyck, Dr. Terry
3188 Barons 604-758-0411

Gagnon, Dr. Robert
373 Franklyn St 604-753-3883

Ingram, Dr. C.D.
3955 Victoria Ave 604-758-1531

Lindsay, Dr. W.R. Rod
2224 Departure Bay Rd 604-758-6121

Long, Dr. Mary; Mattern, Dr. Karin; Quartly, Dr. Rod; Stochmal, Dr. Michael
2-1551 Estevan 604-753-4160/5351

Stefani, Dr. Ferenc H.
3-5148 Metral 604-751-2010

Thomson, Dr. Russell C.
150 Nicol St 604-754-5911

Williams, Dr. V.L.
3034 Ross Rd 604-756-9722

Woodgrove Pines Chiropractic
Scott, Dr. Stacey
A-6439 Portsmouth 604-390-2003

Wright, Dr. Douglas A.
1701 Kerrisdale 604-753-2226

NELSON

Hinton, Dr. Paul M.
384 Baker 604-352-5135

Michaux, Dr. Brian W.
805 Vernon 604-354-1606

Underwood, Dr. Kevin
626 Front St 604-354-4100

NEW WESTMINSTER

Bell Chiropractic
Bell, Dr. David J.
460 E Columbia St 604-522-3366

De Camillis, Dr. David J.
741-6th St 604-522-5225

New Westminster Chiropractic
Jakeman, Dr. Wayne P.
18-800 McBride Blvd 604-522-1622

Proskin Chiropractic
Carson, Dr. David
432-8th St 604-521-9531

NORTH VANCOUVER

Alderson, Dr. Chad; Alderson, Dr. Douglas
1372 Marine Dr 604-985-0461

Cameron, Dr. William Alexander
208-1200 Lynn Valley Rd .604-985-7485

Craver, Dr. Brian L.
101-135 E 15th 604-986-4900

Delbrook Plaza Chiropractic
Floyd, Dr. Brian
119-3721 Delbrook Ave ...604-987-7100

Lions Gate Chiropractic Clinic
Lonquist, Dr. Daniel; Verlaan, Dr. Paul
229-1433 Lonsdale 604-988-2460

Lonsdale Chiropractic Clinic
Holdsworth, Dr. Paul; Williams, Dr. Stephen
402-1124 Lonsdale ..604-987-7246/2225

Lynn Valley Chiropractic
Pereverzoff, Dr. John
3160 Mountain Hwy 604-988-2578

North Shore Chiropractic Clinic
Cosgrove, Dr. Lesley; Leigh, Dr. James
300-132 E 14th St 604-980-4538

Olson, Dr. David
101-3155 Highland Blvd ...604-986-5371

Parkgate Chiropractic Clinic
Outschoorn, Dr. Linda; Taher, Dr. Dina
208-3650 Mt Seymour Pkwy 604-924-0151

Potter, Dr. Brock A.
102a-1124 Lonsdale 604-986-7304

Quay Chiropractic
Johnson, Dr. Patrick G.
2-221 W Esplanade 604-988-2447

Robson, Dr. G.L.
166 E 15th 604-980-4215

Tanaka, Dr. Dale
106-133 W 15th 604-987-3436

Weller, Dr. Steven J.
130 E 14th 604-988-4810

Wiggins, Dr. Paul
461 N Dollarton Hwy 604-929-6633

Wong, Dr. William
2745 Mt Seymour Pkwy ...604-929-7222

OLIVER

Fleming, Dr. A. Owen
34841-97th St 604-498-6555

OSOYOOS

Deglan, Dr. R.E.
5606-63rd St, RR #1 604-495-6339

OYAMA

Binder, Dr. J.P.
17681 Crystal Waters Rd ...604-548-3340

PARKSVILLE

Brown, Dr. Richard A.
200-154 Memorial Ave ...604-248-5634

Knight, Dr. Terrence N.
660 Morison 604-248-4429

Smith, Dr. Larry
255a E Island Hwy 604-248-6333

Westcoast Chiropractic
Lunney, Dr. James
155 Weld 604-248-9414

PENTICTON

Berry, Dr. Condren R.; Garward, Dr. Russell E.
28 E Eckhardt Ave 604-492-7027

Cooper, Dr. James A.; Potter, Dr. N. Todd
3373 Skaha Lake Rd 604-492-2755

Hawthorne Jr., Dr. Richard T.
1348 Government ...604-492-7024/0175

Nutbrown, Dr. Dennis
3018 Skaha Lake Rd 604-493-5377

Souch, Dr. Wm.
225 Brunswick 604-493-8929

PITT MEADOWS

Giacometti, Dr. Nancy
19353 Hammond 604-460-0770

Meadow Vale Chiropractic
Kelsick, Dr. W.E.
107-19150 Lougheed Hwy .604-465-1711

PORT ALBERNI

Adelaide Chiropractic Clinic
Fletcher, Dr. Bruce
4528 Adelaide 604-724-0522

Alberni Chiropractic Services
Kozuback, Dr. Larry
4533 Gertrude 604-723-3933

Deelman, Dr. Paul
2, 3717-10th Ave 604-723-1400

Reynolds, Dr. G. Garnet
4330 China Creek Rd 604-723-3323

PORT COQUITLAM

Loh, Dr. John W.C.
201-3377 Coast Meridian ...604-941-0644

Longstaffe Chiropractic Associates
Longstaffe, Dr. Pia E.
Longstaffe, Dr. Wayne A.G.
340-2755 Lougheed Hwy ...604-942-1171

Olson, Dr. Eric
Warren, Dr. Daniel P.
130-1465
Salisbury 604-941-0496/5451

PORT HARDY

Braun, Dr. J.C.
8755 Granville 604-949-8233

PORT MCNEILL

Von Schilling, Dr. Ernie
3-1584 Broughton Blvd ...604-956-3443

PORT MOODY

Nairne, Dr. R.T.
3190 St Johns St 604-461-4021

Port Moody Chiropractic
Raggett, Dr. Gerald
1-86 Moody St 604-461-6666

POWELL RIVER

Gabelhouse, Dr. David
4454 Joyce Ave 604-485-2841

Richardson, Dr. Jack
4740 Joyce Ave 604-485-7907

PRINCE GEORGE

Madill, Dr. James A.
101, 1440-2nd Ave 604-562-2627

Merritt, Dr. Larry
1543-8th Ave 604-564-4202/1383

Mills, Dr. Randy
443 Carney 604-563-4563

Rigler, Dr. Dean R.
1653 Victoria 604-562-2225

Warawa, Dr. T.C.
1537 Victoria 604-562-2377/5318

PRINCE RUPERT

Lutz & Marshall Chiropractic Services
Lutz, Dr. R.
Marshall, Dr. Linda
133-9th St 604-624-4255

Fait, Dr. Karen
223-3rd St 604-627-1997

QUALICUM BEACH

Beach Road Chiropractor
Fletcher, Dr. Bruce
7-698 Beach Rd 604-752-1733

Olson, Dr. Lee
2-175 W 2nd Ave 604-752-2212

QUESNEL

Fox, Dr. Colin
355 Vaughan St 604-992-5110

Wheatcroft, Dr. David
2202 Valhalla 604-747-3686

Zradicka, Dr. George A.
441 Kinchant Ave 604-992-5825

REVELSTOKE

Hoshizaki, Dr. Ross
300 W 3rd St 604-837-2110

RICHMOND

Broadmoor Chiropractic
Klassen, Dr. A.G.
10020 No 3 Rd 604-271-6442

Chan, Dr. Adam
120-8151 Anderson 604-278-2928

Hong, Dr. H.P.
7480 Westminster Hwy 604-273-0862

**Kehoe, Dr. Brad A.;
Mcleod, Dr. Heather;
Nixdorf, Dr. Don**
440-6091 Gilbert Rd 604-270-1202/
278-3505

Richmond Chiropractic Centre
Lo, Dr. Tak-Yan; Lo, Dr. W.K.
5520-8181 Cambie 604-270-1007

Siu's Chiropractic Associates
Siu, Dr. Hubert W.; Tanaka, Dr. Larry S.
6860 No 3 Rd 604-270-2227/
273-9898

Steveston Chiropractic Office
Peters, Dr. Brett
160, 12000-1st Ave 604-275-9776

ROSSLAND

West Kootenay Chiropractic
Kutcher, Dr. Kurt
2029 Columbia 604-362-3338

SAANICHTON

**Marcus, Dr. Steve
Venchuk, Dr. Riesa**
By Appointment 604-652-4347

SALMON ARM

**Lee, Dr. Gordon; Pilias, Dr. Tom
Raymant, Dr. David**
360 Ross St NE 604-832-4186

Martin, Dr. Lyle A.
81 Hudson Ave NE 604-832-9279

Picadilly Chiropractic Clinic
Martin, Dr. Paul F.
53, 712-10th St SW 604-832-3857

SALT SPRING ISLAND

Barlow, K.E. Libby
3-323 Lower Ganges Rd 604-537-4142

Blanes, Alda M.
102 Douglas Rd 604-537-4977

**Dares, Dr. Danny;
Richardson, Ross J.**
198 Salt Spring Way 604-537-9399

SARDIS

**Clark, Dr. William;
Giesbrecht, Dr. Ron**
7447 Vedder 604-858-9467

Maier, A.V.
46226 Greenwood Dr 604-858-7656

SECHELT

Bishop, Dr. Graham
5666 Cowrie 604-885-2333

SIDNEY

Laidley, Dr. Sean
E-2412 Beacon 604-655-6643

**Marcus, Dr. Stan; Venchuk, Dr.
Riesa**
1975 Bazan Bay 604-655-3717

**Repsch, Dr. Harry R.; Roper, Dr.
Robert W.**
9837-7th St ..604-656-6733/4611/5011

Rowe, Dr. Robert
9743 West Saanich 604-655-1233

SMITHERS

**Bulkley Valley Chiropractic
Millar, Dr. Craig;
Murdoch, Dr. Gary**
1322 Main 604-847-4468

SOOKE

Sooke Chiropractic
Grove, Dr. Peter; Lambert, Dr. Rick M.;
Pistak, Dr. Kevin
6545 Sooke 604-642-5929

SPARWOOD

Elk Valley Chiropractic Offices
Malone, Dr. Robert
2-127 Centennial Sq 604-425-0097

SQUAMISH

Dawydiak, Dr. Myron T.
38112 Second Ave 604-892-5233

Martin, Dr. Frank
38155 Second Ave 604-892-3064

SUMMERLAND

Simmons, Dr. Joseph C.
11305 Ward 604-494-8561

**Summerland Chiropractic &
Massage Therapy Centre**
White, Dr. Leslie
13008 S Victoria 604-494-7000

Zagrodney, Dr. Ken
13219 N Victoria 604-494-0050

SURREY

Brown, Dr. David A.
12084-96th Ave 604-585-3444

Fong, Dr. Ho-Cheung
106, 8232-120th St 604-543-6392

**Grant, Dr. James P.;
Massier, Dr. Robert**
104, 10340-134th A St 604-588-6505

Guildford Chiropractic
Nielsen, Dr. Robert G.
203, 15135-101st Ave 604-581-0232

**Hatch, Dr. Paul C.; Maxwell, Dr.
D.J.**
102, 10340-134A St 604-584-7464

Johal, Dr. Shivraj
103, 8318-120th St 604-591-9211

Kliem, Dr. Wolfgang
3344 King George Hwy 604-535-3357

MacMillan, Clive S.
6235b-136th St 604-594-6670

McRae, Dr. G. Cam
105, 13771-72a Ave 604-594-8555

Munro, Dr. Gary D.
106-6840 King George Hwy 604-594-7774

Newton Chiropractic Centre
O'Neill, Dr. Grant; Zayonc, Dr. D
5, 13791-72nd Ave 604-599-1777

North Surrey Chiropractic Clinic
Gordon, Dr. Linda; Konanz, Dr. Adam
Wasylynko, Dr. David
101, 10340-134th A St 604-585-1588

Stuart, Dr. David C
10311-150th St 604-581-3411

**Titchener & Associates
Chiropractic Clinic**
Titchener, Dr. Michael J.
4, 9965-152nd St 604-589-4555

Williams, Dr. Wm. M.
5766-175th St 604-576-2449

Wong, Dr. Leong C.
8926-152nd St 604-951-8959

TERRACE

Greenwood, Dr. R.D.
1-4623 Park Ave 604-638-8165

TRAIL

Brandvold, Dr. D.G.
1214 Pine 604-368-5528

Gallo, Dr. Jerry J.R.
1628-2nd Ave 604-368-8111

Lemoel Brian
108-8100 Highway 3b 604-364-1322

VANCOUVER

Akerley, Brenda
204-3077 Granville 604-732-3422

**Alderson, Dr. Blake; Schneider, Dr.
Norman**
6685 Fraser St 604-327-9204

Armitage & Associates Chiropractic Group
Armitage, Dr. Robert
101-2880 W 4th Ave 604-731-6679

Bayside Chiropractic
May, Dr. Richard
600-1200 Burrard St 604-689-9308

Beaton, Dr. Keith
1397 Commercial Dr 604-253-2515

**Blower, Dr. Brian;
Read, Dr. Steven;
Sheikh, Dr. Gohar**
1775 Nanaimo St 604-253-0004

Bourke Chiropractic Clinic
Croxall, Dr. Daryl
605-1200 Burrard St 604-687-5712

Burrard Chiropractic Clinic
Didyk, Dr. William
605-1200 Burrard 604-687-1457

Cambie Chiropractic Centre
Fedder, Dr. Pauline; Quon, Dr. Jeffrey
7293 Cambie 604-322-7600

Campbell, Dr. Charles; Quinn, Dr. Wayne
211-2678
W Broadway ..604-734-2900/736-5157

Chan, Dr. Kenny
936 W King Edward 604-739-2118

Chen, Dr. Edward Y.C.; Underhill, Dr. Frank D.
5885 Victoria Dr 604-324-3212

Chiu, Dr. Leonard
501 E Hastings 604-255-0633

Cho, Richard
#B13-525 W Broadway 604-872-4476

City Square Chiropractic
Numerow, Dr. David
164-555 W 12th 604-871-9100

Com El Chiropractic Clinic
Ma, Dr. Hilda; Yee, Dr. Bradley
206-2620 Commercial Dr ..604-876-4988

Crossroads Chiropractic
Greenwood, Dr. Dean M.; Hunter, Dr. Richard Lo, Dr. Gary, C.P.
13b-525
W Broadway ..604-873-6535/6029/8033

Downtown Chiropractic
Lee, Dr. David
105-736 Granville 604-685-9444

Dudek-Larsen Health Services Inc
3077 Granville St, #204 ...604-732-4077

Ewert, Dr. David R.
301-2083 Alma St 604-224-1886

Follis, Dr. Malcolm R.
5203 Victoria Dr 604-324-6411

Fong, Dr. Ho Cheung
4570 Main St 604-876-3368

**Foran, Dr. G. Patrick;
Foran, Michael J.**
8041 Granville St 604-266-1461

**Forbes, Dr. Diane;
Kehoe, Dr. Brad A.**
104-2220
W Broadway 604-738-0990/1021

Fraser Chiropractic Group
Brown, Dr. Julian; Dueck, Dr. Cheryl;
Zindler, Dr. Randall;
Zindler, Dr. Rainier
6154 Fraser 604-321-6704

Gertz, Gordon
1065 Cambie St 604-687-2900

Gordon, Dr. William
430-744 W Hastings St 604-681-7937

Hargreaves, Dr. Richard O.
310a-595 Burrard 604-683-3811

**Hasegawa, Dr. Robert
Lopes, Dr. Arthur**
101-2786 W 16th 604-734-2258

Hastings Chiropractic Clinic
Hartwick, Dr. W.G.
2721 E Hastings 604-255-8123

Ho, Dr. George
4007 Knight St 604-872-6686

Hoy, Dr. Aaron K.
2231 Granville St 604-738-2503

Integrative Healing Arts Centre
Meinzer, Dr. Fred K.; Panet, Dr. John E
958 W 8th Ave 604-738-1012

Kanwischer, Dr. Philip F.
8041 Granville St 604-266-2304

Karse, Dr. Bradley M.
18u-601 W Broadway 604-874-9779

Kerrisdale Chiropractic
Arthur, Dr. Brian E.
232-2025 W 42nd 604-261-1540

**Khan, Dr. Aslam;
Viken, Dr. Paul M.**
2027 W 42nd 604-266-8349

Kvalheim, Dr. David
302-1001 W Broadway 604-732-9007

Lai, Chester Ho Kon
2705 Lynbrook Dr 604-325-3493

Lee, Dr. Herbert
204-950 W Broadway 604-731-6135

Little, Donna M.
3446 W Broadway 604-731-6773

Macdonald, Dr. Glenn
100-1727 W Broadway 604-737-4305

Madahar & Associates Family Chiropractors
Csabai, Dr. Joe
Madahar, Jaswinder Singh
1315 Kingsway 604-876-0220

Marpole Chiropractic Centre
Chan, Dr. Frederick
8301 Granville 604-266-4323

**Matsubara, Dr. Ken H.;
Wright, Dr. Jerry W.;
McCallum, D**
2158 W Broadway ..604-737-0706/1411

McNeil, C. Duncan
4154 Musqueam Dr 604-266-2985

Meindersma, Dr. Ernest
2557 E Hastings St 604-253-6930

Morgan, Wilf
4228 Staulo Cr 604-261-0740

Moore & Cho Chiropractors
Moore, Dr. Steven D.; O'Neil, Dr. Peggy
13b-525 W Broadway 604-872-4476

Mulyk, Dr. Peter W.
803 Denman St 604-685-9416

Murphy, Sean
600-1200 Burrard St 604-689-9308

Nellis, Dr. Richard
833 Bidwell St 604-685-1684

Oakridge Plaza Chiropractic
Kang, Dr. Russell M.
225-5780 Cambie 604-322-2828

Reimann, Dr. Lyall V.
4340 Main St 604-876-3738

Richmond, Dr. Robert W.J.
1709-650 W Georgia 604-682-6637

Royal Centre Chiropractic
Mallory, Dr. David S.
1055 W Georgia 604-688-0077

Sabados, Wade
3011-42nd Ave W 604-263-8594

Sam, Dr. Victor
1929 Commercial Dr 604-251-6878

South Granville Chiropractic Group
Berry, Dr. J.; Dudek, Dr. F.J.;
Larsen, Dr. E.H.; Rivera, Dr. G.
204-3077 Granville St 604-732-3422

South Slope Chiropractic
Dickson, Dr. Bradley; Roxborough, Dr. R.
5756 Fraser St 604-321-8027

Spence, Dr. Andrew K.
300-2245 W Broadway 604-732-0664

St. Denis, Dr. E.M.
825 Granville St 604-681-4912

Vipond McCallum Chiropractic Associates
Vipond, Dr. Michael J.
215-2902 W Broadway 604-737-7161

Wooden, Dr. Gary E.
301-3680 E Hastings 604-299-0821

Yaletown Chiropractic
Gaston, Dr. Stephanie
310-1090 Homer 604-688-1500

Young, Dr. Keith
5862 Cambie 604-321-0755

VERNON

Allcare Chiropractic Clinics
Roze, Dr. M.B.
3107-34th Ave 604-542-2386

Farnsworth, Dr. R.D.
176 Mt Fosthall Rd 604-542-2705

Kievit, Dr. Murray
3, 2901-27th St 604-558-0688

Main, Dr. Corinne
3006-34th St 604-545-8334

Shannon, Dr. William Darcy
3212-31st Ave 604-545-7545

Shikaze, Dr. Thomas
3109-34th Ave 604-542-7878

Smith, Dr. D.R.
3105-34th Ave 604-545-6061/7277

Valley Chiropractic
Kinakin, Dr. Larry T.
3502-31st St 604-549-4535

Wickstrom, Dr. James B.
3002-33rd St 604-545-5566

Woodliffe, Dr. William J.
3609-32nd St 604-545-9111

VICTORIA

Allen, Dr. James C.
2602 Quadra St 604-386-8887

Aramenko, Dr. Merv
308-645 Fort 604-382-1000

Beale, Dr. W. Charles
176-2945 Jacklin 604-474-2828

Beesley, Dr. J. Thomas
885 McAdam Pl 604-388-3911

Berna, Dr. Cindy; Berna, Dr. Michael
4092 Shelburne St 604-721-4656

Broadmead Chiropractic Inc.
Upton, Dr. John
350-777 Royal Oak Dr 604-744-2882

Buna, Dr. Michael; Lloyd, Dr. Jeff
560-3147 Douglas 604-384-2412

Cabrita, Dr. Anna; Chin, Dr. Jack
125-3066 Shelbourne 604-592-2521

Colwood Family Chiropractic Centre
Correlje, Dr. Bob; Gusta, Dr. Dave
Hunter, Dr. Paul; Vari, Dr. Rob
385 Lagoon 604-478-4734

Commandeur, Dr. Ruby
1205 Deeks Pl 604-472-0004

Curran, Dr. Barry J.
206-1581 Hillside 604-592-6230

Douglas Chiropratic Clinic
202-2950 Douglas St 604-385-2212

Edgar, Dr. Garth
415-1900 Richmond Ave ...604-595-0706

Elder, Dr. Donald J.; Elder, Dr. James K.
1116 Blanshard St 604-384-9615

Frackson, Dr. Ted; Walker, Dr. Wayne
401-3939 Quadra St 604-727-2790

Gainor, Dr. Grant R.
223-3930 Shelbourne 604-477-5776

Gordon Head Chiropractic
Tangri, Dr. Sheel
4086 Shelbourne St 604-477-6666

Graas, Dr. David
1383 Hillside Ave 604-381-3622

Grove, Dr. Debra; Grove, Dr. Peter; Johnson, Dr. Pauline
337a Cook St 604-361-9311

Harwijne, Dr. Dawn
104-1020 McKenzie Ave ..604-727-2004

Holmes, Dr. R.M.
103-2610 Douglas 604-384-3555

Kristianson, Dr. Richard A.
206-3994 Shelbourne St ..604-477-4702

Lambert, Dr. Richard
4468b West Saanich 604-727-9495

Littlejohn, Dr. Brian D.
2008 Douglas 604-385-6932

Mack, Dr. Sandra L.
514-1207 Douglas 604-384-6767

Manson, Dr. Brent
204-2951 Tillicum 604-381-1124

Martin, Dr. Chris L.
104-3561 Shelbourne 604-598-0666

Morash, Dr. Ralph E.
370 Hector 604-727-3113

Murray, Dr. Michael; Wensley, Dr.Mark
220-2950 Douglas 604-385-2212

Parker, Dr. Grant E.
202-821 Burdett Ave 604-383-3002

Pennimpede, Dr. Irene
3473 Cedar Hill 604-598-2199

Pirie, Dr. Alastair S.
4640 Cordova Bay Rd 604-658-2321

Quinn, Dr. Karen; Quinn, Dr. Peter
313-3995 Quadra 604-727-7773

Robson Chiropractic Health Care
Robson, Dr. Mark P.
217-2187 Oak Bay 604-592-6464

Russell, B.J.
4502 Cottontree Lane 604-658-0667

Shamess, Dr. Fiona P.
996 Lucas Ave 604-727-9501

Smerdon, Dr. Peter
1744 Richmond Ave 604-592-1254

Tancock, Dr. Jeffrey; Tancock, Dr. John; Williams, Dr. Natalie A.
105-920 Hillside 604-383-6013

Victoria Chiropractic X-Ray Clinic
302-2994 Douglas 604-388-3949

Victoria Family Chiropractic
Macleod, Dr. Gordon W.
203-3200 Shelbourne 604-592-5553

Ward, Dr. Thomas S.
8-310 Goldstream 604-478-4057

Wheatcroft, Dr. David
110-1811 Victoria 604-561-1916

Wyllie, Dr. Steven P.
1977 Carrick 604-592-7556

WEST VANCOUVER

Ambleside Chiropractic Clinic
Laurillard, Dr. Derek; Strongitharm, Dr. M.
102-1590 Bellevue ..604-922-8421/2556

WESTBANK

Westbank Chiropractic
Kellerman, Dr. Todd; Manns, Dr. David
2447 Main 604-768-5114

Boruta, John
3570 McIver Rd 604-768-1165

WHISTLER

Martin, Dr. Frank
4208 Village Sq 604-938-0105

Schmidt, Dr. Ralph D.
6301 Lorimer 604-932-3106

Whistler Chiropractic
Hasegawa, Dr. Robert
206-4433 Sundial Pl 604-932-1922

WHITE ROCK

Anderson, Dr. Gregg C.
3091-1656 Martin 604-531-6446

Burge, Dr. Thomas
108, 2055-152nd St 604-535-7373

Butcher, Dr. R. Frederick
301-1493 Johnston Rd ...604-531-3322

Deslauriers Chiropractic Group Inc
1219 Johnston 604-535-2500

McLaughlin, Brian J.
202-1493 Johnston Rd ...604-531-5078

Whitehead, Dr. Brian S.
1635-128th St 604-536-8116

Wiese, Dr. Henning
205, 1959-152nd St 604-535-1242

Wyner Chiropractic Care
7-1381 George 604-531-3066

WILLIAMS LAKE

Cariboo Chiropractic Centre
Mortenson, Dr. Matt
350 Borland St 604-392-7717

Carson, Dr. Kelly
118G N 1st Ave 604-392-1077

Chiropractic Associates
Mitchell, Dr. John C.
37 S 4th Ave 604-392-6544/8288

Erickson, Dr. Dan
29a S 3rd Ave 604-392-5711

Fairburn, Dr. Garth
306-35 S 2nd Ave 604-398-5707

WINFIELD

Kobayashi, Dr. Randy A.
21-3121 Hill 604-766-3155

✦ Manitoba

Chiropractors are regulated in Manitoba, meaning that there is legislation establishing a governing body responsible for registering practitioners who meet its educational standards (see below, "Governing Body"). Partial government health care funding is available (see below "Public Health Care Funding - Manitoba Health").

Legislation

Chiropractors are regulated under *The Chiropractic Act* and Regulation. Under section 1 of the Act, "practice of chiropractic" means

(a) any professional service usually performed by a chiropractor, including the examination and treatment, principally by hand and without use of drugs or surgery, of the spinal column, pelvis and extremities and associated soft tissues; and

(b) such other services as may be approved by the regulations.

Only licensed chiropractors are entitled to practise chiropractic. Chiropractors are authorized to use X-rays for diagnostic purposes. Requirements regarding patient records and professional misconduct are set out in the regulation.

The legislation also establishes the Manitoba Chiropractors Association as the governing body (see below) responsible for licensing and disciplining chiropractors.

Public Health Care Funding - Manitoba Health

Chiropractors are partially covered under Manitoba Health. The plan pays $11.56 to the chiropractor for hand manipulation treatments only - not machine therapy or X-rays. The patient pays the balance. The coverage extends to a maximum of 15 visits per calendar year. For information, contact Manitoba Health at 1-800-407-5551.

Manitoba Governing Body/Professional Association

Manitoba Chiropractors Association
2706-83 Garry Street
Winnipeg, Manitoba R3C 4J9
Tel: 204-942-3000

Contact the office to ensure that your chiropractor is licensed, or if you have a complaint. An attempt is first made to resolve complaints informally. If this fails, the matter is formally investigated and penalties may include revocation or suspension of the licence to practise.

✦ Manitoba Chiropractors

NOTE: Check the credentials of your chiropractor (see above, "Questions to Ask"). This publication cannot and does not certify or represent the qualifications of practitioners, or the quality of care available from them. We cannot and do not confirm that those listed are registered as required by law.

ALTONA

Altona Chiropractic Centre
Redhead, Dr. G. Dan
86-2nd St NE 204-324-5325

ASHERN

Palaschuk, Dr. Greg
Hospital Ave 204-768-3319

BEAUSEJOUR

Duprat, Dr. D.R.
8-31 1st St 204-268-1876

Kobelka, Dr. John D.
39-3rd St S 204-268-3533

BRANDON

Pavillion Chiropractic Centre
Weston, Dr. Guy M.
845-18th St 204-725-2209

Stitt Chiropractic Centre
Stitt, Dr. Gerald; Tessier, Dr. Kathryn
302-10th St 204-726-1283

Westman Chiropractic Centre
Martin, Dr. Allan; Rust, Dr Gordon;
Webb, Dr. B.L.
801-B 10th St 204-727-2735

CARMAN

Carman Chiropractic Office
Ledger, Dr. Ian
12 S Main St 204-745-3521

DAUPHIN

Dauphin Chiropractic Centre
Allen, Dr. Donald; Symchych, Dr. Mark
21-2nd Av NE 204-638-6642

Sorlie, Dr. P.I.
214 Main St N 204-638-5343

FLIN FLON

Flin Flon Chiropractic Centre
Klitsas, Dr. Vassilios
49 Main St 204-687-4909

GIMLI

Gimli Chiropractic Centre
Pethrick, Dr. Timothy
H2-41 Centre St 204-642-5397

KILLARNEY

Klassen, Dr. Leonard P.
230 Broadway 204-523-7792

LAC DU BONNET

Duprat, Dr. D.R.
Government Rd 204-345-6195

LOCKPORT

Lockport Chiropractic Centre
Mclachlan, Dr. W. Al
By Appointment 204-757-2287

LORETTE

Lorette Chiropractic Center
Pelissier, Dr. Rosalie; Rempel, Dr. Jacqueline
5-411 Dawson Rd 204-878-3554

MINNEDOSA

Remillard, Dr. Tracey
131 Main St 204-867-5290

MORDEN

Morden Chiropractic Centre
Kolt, Dr. Alain; Oliviero, Dr. Irene
515 Stephen St 204-822-5403

MORRIS

Morris Chiropractic Office
Gurvey, Dr. Martin
156 W Boyne Ave 204-746-2867

NEEPAWA

Neepawa Chiropractic Centre
Dunn, Dr. G.N.
487 Mountain Ave 204-476-3984

NIVERVILLE

Lecker, Dr. Brian E.
1-227 Main St 204-388-6195

OAKBANK

Oakbank Chiropractic Centre
Daien, Dr. Alan; Ledger, Dr. Ian
B-662 Main St 204-444-2111

PORTAGE LA PRAIRIE

Graham, Dr. Brian G.
612 Saskatchewan Av E 204-857-5051

Hewett, Dr. W. John
19-1st St SW 204-239-6078

Mitchell, Dr. Keith
39 Royal Rd N 204-857-4777

Narvey, Dr. E. Bruce
1200 Saskatchewan Ave W ..204-857-9452

POWERVIEW

Esser Chiropractic Health Centre
Esser, Dr. Clinron; Esser, Dr. Nicole
By Appointment 204-367-4858

RUSSELL

Russell Chiropractic Centre
Kaminski, Dr. Robert
203 N Shell River Ave 204-773-2223

ST. PIERRE JOLYS

St. Pierre Chiropractic Centre
Rosenberg, Dr. Herbert; Rosenberg, Dr. Richard
539 E Jolys Ave 204-433-7256

STE. ROSE DU LAC

Symchych, Dr. Mark A.
612 Central Ave 204-447-3206

SELKIRK

Colmer, Dr. L.H.
255 Main St 204-482-6116

Jenkinson, Dr. D.G.
208 Main St 204-482-4464

Red River Chiropractic Centre
Podaima, Dr. Clark
357 Main St 204-482-4144

STEINBACH

Gatten Chiropractic Clinic
Blatz, Dr. Corneil; Gatten, Dr. A.D.;
Swenarchuk, Dr. G.B.
325 Henry St 204-326-3817

Hector, Dr. Darren
By Appointment 204-346-0560

Kehler Chiropractic Clinic
Kehler, Dr. Terry
6 Hwy 12 N 204-326-4854

Loewen Chiropractic Clinic
Petrilli, Dr. Lori Ann
B 4 Loewen Blvd 204-326-3400

Steinbach Chiropractic Clinic
Duerksen, Dr. Ken; Winzoski, Dr. Trevor
6 Hwy 12 N 204-326-1103

STONEWALL

Stonewall Chiropractic Centre
Zurbyk, Dr. Robert J.
389 Main St 204-467-5523

SWAN RIVER

Dahl Family Chiropractic
Dahl, Dr. Cheryl
524 Main St E 204-734-3300

Klack, Dr. Sam
520 Main St E 204-734-3011

Swan Valley Chiropractic Centre
Watkins, Dr. Neal
705 Main St 204-734-3013/9236

TEULON

Teulon (Interlake) Chiropractic
White, Dr. Vaughn P.
48 Main St 204-886-2356

THE PAS

The Pas Regional Chiropractic Office
Marsh, Dr. Gary
229 Fischer Ave 204-623-2924

THOMPSON

Thompson Chiropractic Clinic
Pritchard, Dr. R. Paul
3 Station Rd 204-677-4912

TREHERNE

Narvey, Dr. Bruce E.
187 Broadway St 204-723-2610

VIRDEN

Renaissance Chiropractic Centre
Stitt, Dr. Robert L.
281 Nelson St W 204-748-1492

Westman Chiropractic Centre - Virden Office
Rust, Dr. Gordon
264 Nelson St W 204-748-1044

VITA

Vita Chiropractic Centre
Palaschuk, Dr. Robert
217-1st Ave 204-425-3026

WINKLER

Winkler Chiropractic Office
Corbett, Dr. R.P.
200-561 Main St 204-325-9604

WINNIPEG

Aberdeen Chiropractic Office
Specht, Dr. Garry C.
1080 Main St 204-586-8424

Academy Chiropractic Centre
Desaulniers, Dr. Mike
525 Academy 204-253-7896

Active Chiropractic
Thompson, Dr. R.A.
130-115 Vermillion 204-256-2273

Alverstone Walk-In Chiropractic Office
Leslie, Dr. Howard
831 Sargent 204-774-6485

Arlington Chiropractic Office
Rothman, Dr. W.
8-794 Sargent 204-783-8474

Assiniboine Chiropractic Centre
Gustavson, Dr. Krisjan M.
1763 Portage Ave 204-888-1202

Atlas Chiropractic Center
Mestdagh, Dr. Laurie Robert
558 Selkirk 204-586-9771

Avenue Chiropractic Centre
Schledewitz, Dr. Lawrence
306-428 Portage 204-942-8666

Baizley, Dr. Brian
723 St. Mary's Rd 204-257-0453

Baron, Dr. Russell; McRitchie, Dr. Neil
1700 Ness 204-837-4115

Birchwood Chiropractic Centre
Walterson, Dr. K.F.
2523 Portage Ave 204-885-5407

Bohemier Chiropractic Centre
Bohemier, Dr. Gerald; Bohemier, Dr. Gilbert
154 Provencher 204-233-3060

Broadway Chiropractic Office
Hamin, Dr. Tracey
103-555 Broadway 204-775-4539

Cathedral Chiropractic Office
Gurvey, Dr. Martin B.
1360 Main 204-586-7518

Central Chiropractic X-Ray Service
Collett, Dr. R.H.
303-171 Donald 204-942-7659

Charleswood Chiropractic Office
Minik, Dr. Darrell E.
3404 Roblin 204-888-0675

College Ave Chiropractic
Wilson, Dr. Daniel H.
980 Mc Phillips St 204-582-2381

Corydon Chiropractic Center
Lodewyks, Dr. G.
104-897 Corydon 204-284-9218

Crescentwood Massage/Chiropractic Centre
Naccarato, Dr. C.A.
671 Stafford 204-453-1699

Dakota Chiropractic Office
Raizman, Dr. A.
1056 St. Mary's Rd 204-257-7685

Downtown Chiropractic Centre
Daien, Dr. Alan; Ledger, Dr. Ian
401-171 Donald St 204-942-8940

Du Charme, Dr. Pierre L.
3-150 Goulet St 204-233-7820

Ellice Chiropractic Centre
Partridge, Dr. Gordon; Thiessen, Dr. Richard
724 Ellice 204-772-7700

Elmwood Chiropractic Centre
Lecker, Dr. D. Brian; Wiens, Dr. A. John
178 Henderson Hwy 204-669-6967

Feasey, Dr. Darin W.
7-208 Marion St 204-237-0210

Fermor Crossing Family Chiropractic
Ainley, Dr. Andrew
4-172 St. Anne's 204-253-6553

Fort Garry Chiropractic Centre
Lohrenz, Dr. Brad
6-1235 Pembina 204-287-8383

Fort Richmond Chiropractic Center
Chenier, Dr. Jacqueline
I-2750 Pembina 204-261-0043

Fox, Dr. Hartley C.
C-1510 St. Mary's Rd 204-257-3757

Gainor, Dr. B.G.
104-1695 Henderson 204-338-5252

Gall, Dr. Steven J.
1287 Jefferson Ave 204-632-4080

Garden City Chiropractic Office
Johnson, Dr. A. Wray
2140 McPhillips 204-697-0928

Garden Oaks
Kurtas, Dr. Ted K.
2136 McPhillips 204-694-9493

Gelley Chiropractic Office
Gelley, Dr. Geoffrey M.
12-845 Dakota 204-254-0130

Gilbert, Dr. Steven C.
915 Ellice Ave 204-775-0536

Grant Park Chiropractic Office
Chalaturnyk, Dr. Robert J.
225-1120 Grant 204-453-8822

Henderson Chiropractic Office
Jensen, Dr. Bruce
1723 Henderson Hwy 204-339-8781

Island Lakes Chiropractic Centre
Malenchak, Dr. Gary D.
5-20 Island Shore 204-253-3666

Jefferson Chiropractic Walk-In Centre
Tavares, Dr. Carlos A.P.
3-2055 McPhillips 204-334-6303

Keewatin Park Chiropractic
Kowal, Dr. S.A.
11-1030 Keewatin 204-632-0386

Kelvin Professional Centre
Hawkins, Dr, E. Allan
NW Henderson & Carmen ...204-667-8331

Kildonan Crossing Chiropractic Clinic
White, Dr. Vaughn P.
645-1615 Regent W 204-654-1175

Kildonan Park Chiropractic Centre
Pops, Dr. Henry
1926 Main 204-339-1635

Kingswood Chiropractic Centre
Miron, Dr. Ernest P.
8-741 St. Mary's Rd 204-254-0055

Kos Chiropractic Centre
Kos, Dr. Gregory; Kos, Dr. John
2033 Portage Ave 204-831-8000

Kowall, Dr. P.W.
340 Stafford 204-453-2987

Leader, Dr. Eric M.
611 Roberta Ave 204-669-2493

Lindenwoods Chiropractic Centre
Bohemier, Dr. Roland
9-1080 Waverley 204-474-1159

Markham Chiropractic Centre
Bourdon, Dr. Gary J.
2255 Pembina 204-269-0445

McGregor Chiropractic Centre
Palaschuk, Dr. Greg; Palaschuk, Dr. P.J.;
Palaschuk, Dr. Robert
135 McGregor 204-582-2303

McPhillips Chiropractic Office
Douglas, Dr. F.P.
P-2211 McPhillips 204-339-1959

Meadowwood Family Chiropractic Centre
Champagne, Dr. Robert; Remillard, Dr. Tracey
1549 St. Marys Rd 204-255-6666

Mestdagh Chiropractic Clinic
Desmarais, Dr. Paulette;
Desmarais, Dr. Gerald P.;
Eng, Dr. Garry; Mestdagh, Dr. Brian;
Mestdagh, Dr. Robert
11-1530 Rengent W 204-661-6595

Morin, Dr. Guy A.
281 Tache Ave 204-237-7153

Nassau Chiropractic X-Ray Service
Bailey, Dr. Glenn; Chester, Dr. D.;
Harpley, Dr. Tom; Kremer, Dr. G.F
301 N Nassau St 204-453-0042

North Kildonan Family Chiropractic
Carter, Dr. Brett J.
1185 Henderson 204-334-8383

Osborne Chiropractic Office
Stuart, Dr. Tim
757 Osborne St 204-475-9188

Pembina Chiropractic Office
Fogel, Dr. Richard B.
1096 Pembina 204-452-6946

Polo Park Chiropractic Centre
Cohn, Dr. Arnold
Polo Park Shopping Centre ..204-774-9066

Portage & Dominion Chiropractic Office
Michalyshyn, Dr. T.
1062 Portage 204-774-5521

Portage Avenue Chiropractic Office
Stedman, Dr. Neil
1137 Portage Ave 204-896-5717

Regent Chiropractic Center
Possia, Dr. Curtis M.
705 Regent W 204-222-1571

River East Chiropractic
Kisil, Dr. Douglas; Scott-Herridge, Dr. Gerard
3-1110 Henderson 204-334-3334

River Park South
Toth, Dr. Audrey; Toth, Dr. J.M.
1921 St. Mary's Rd 204-253-6995

Riverton Family Chiropractic
Rutherford, Dr. Peter
3236-A Portage Ave 204-888-8515

Roblin Chiropractic Centre
Plueschow, Dr. Michael G.
210-4910 Roblin Blvd 204-885-6640

Rosenberg Chiropractic Centre
Rosenberg, Dr. Herbert;
Rosenberg, Dr. Richard
1600 Regent W 204-837-8878

Rossmere Chiropractic Centre
Nachtigall, Dr. Harold; Zink, Dr. Richard
899 Henderson 204-669-7689

Roslyn Road Chiropractic Centre
Di Bernardo, Dr. Maria
36 Roslyn Rd 204-284-9175

St. Anne's Road Chiropractic Office
Stewart, Dr. Greg; Wilson, Dr. Kenneth
308 St. Anne's 204-255-0296

St. Boniface Chiropractic Centre
Du Charme, Dr. Hubert R.
292 Goulet St 204-237-3591

St. Vital Chiropractic Office
Allen, Dr. Donald E.
547 St. Mary's Rd 204-233-0682

Seven Oaks Chiropractic Centre
Chlysta, Dr. Walter; Laurencelle, Dr. Rick
1817 Main 204-338-7057

Shupena, Dr. Ray E.
2573 Portage Ave 204-885-5516

Southdale Chiropractic Centre
Tole, Dr. Gerald D.
120-40 Lakewood 204-253-1900

South Winnipeg Chiropractic Walk-In Clinic
Lambos, Dr. Steven
7-580 Pembina Hwy 204-474-0252

Southwood Chiropractic Office
Schaeffer, Dr. Daniel A.
1875 Pembina 204-269-6866

Stradbrook Chiropractic Centre
McWhirter, Dr. Brian
439 Stradbrook 204-477-5734

Sturgeon Creek Chiropractic Centre
Starodub, Dr. Douglas C.
101-2565 Portage 204-831-1122

Sun Chiropractic Centre
Capitano, Dr. Eugenio; Castle, Dr. Kim
5-3421 Portage 204-885-4842

Taylor Chiropractic Office
Taylor, Dr. Perry D.
1919 Henderson 204-339-1631

Therrien, Dr. Daniel
1104-40 Dalhousie 204-261-6088

Transcona Chiropractic Centre
Moorhead, Dr. Lloyd; Moorhead, Dr. Richard
501 W Regent Ave 204-222-2969

Tuxedo Family Chiropractic Centre
Alevizos, Dr. John
128-2025 Corydon 204-488-4174

Warrack, B.P.
387 Cordova St 204-489-5978

Watkins, Dr. T.A.
207-1700 Corydon 204-489-1061

Westwood Chiropractic Centre
Kucheravy, Dr. Michael
3278 Portage 204-888-1234

Windsor Park Chiropractic Centre (24 Hour Emergency)
De Jong, Dr. Michael
690 Elizabeth Rd .204-256-8741/255-3767

Yurkiw, Dr. Cary
42 Laurel Bay 204-228-1704

Zink Family Chiropractic Centre
Zink, Dr. Richard P.
2983 Pembina 204-261-7367

✦ New Brunswick

Chiropractiors are regulated in New Brunswick, meaning that there is legislation establishing a governing body responsible for registering and disciplining practitioners (see below, "Governing Body"). There is no government health care funding.

Legislation

The New Brunswick legislation dates back to 1958, and is currently being revamped. As it now stands, *The Chiropractic Act* defines chiropractic as "that part of the philosophy, science and art of things natural consisting of a system of adjusting, by hand only, the articulations or segments of the human spinal column and other articulations incidental thereto, for the purpose of removing nerve interference, without the use of drugs or surgery" (section 2(c)). The Act states that it does not authorize the prescription of drugs or anaesthetic, or the practice of surgery.

The legislation also establishes the New Brunswick Chiropractors Association as the governing body, and provides for the board to make regulations regarding registration and discipline of chiropractors. Only members of the New Brunswick Chiropractors Association are entitled to practise chiropractic. Under the Constitution and bylaws of the Association, members using X-rays must pay higher dues, and all members must observe the ethical standards, which include moderation in charges for professional services. The same section notes that the minimum fee for an adjustment or office call is $3 - a reflection of the vintage of the legislation.

New Brunswick Governing Body

New Brunswick Chiropractors Association
PO Box 21046
Oromocto, N.B. E2V 2R9
Tel: 506-357-8803

This is the governing body. Call to ensure that your chiropractor is licensed, or to make a complaint.

✦ New Brunswick Chiropractors

NOTE: Check the credentials of your chiropractor (see above, "Questions to Ask"). This publication cannot and does not certify or represent the qualifications of practitioners, or the quality of care available from them. We cannot and do not confirm that those listed are registered as required by law.

BATHURST

Blanchette, Dr. Michel
102 St George 506-548-9595

Hache, Dr. Denis
275 Main Harbourview Place 506-548-3238

CAMPBELLTON

Gagnon, Dr. J. Hermile;
Racine, Dr. Marie France
10 Water St 506-753-6369

DIEPPE

Centre Chiropratique Dieppe
Gautreau, Dr. Paul E.
421 Acadia Ave ..506-389-9529/532-4884

Cormier, Dr. Maurice
133 Champlain 506-857-0566

EDMUNDSTON

Clinique Chiropratique Cote
Cote, Dr. Renaud
18 Thirty-Ninth Ave 506-735-5424

Lavoie, Dr. Madeleine
264 Victoria 506-739-8711

Ouellette, Dr. Anne-Marie
600 St-Francois 506-739-6660

FREDERICTON

Allaby, Dr. Robert M.
763 Regent 506-454-2225

Johnston Chiropractic Office
Johnson, Dr. Glenn; Leve, Dr. Carolyn
312 Main 506-457-1704

Pollack, Dr. Martin C.
371 Brunswick 506-450-7979

Redstone, Dr. J. Wayne
864 Smythe 506-454-2202

GRAND FALLS

Poitras, Dr. Guildor
131 Evangeline 506-473-1777

MONCTON

Clinique Chiropratique
Levesque, Dr. Pierre;
Robichaud, Dr.Marie-Josee
234 Church 506-857-0095

Leblanc, Dr. Michel
233 Archibald 506-855-6636

Moncton Chiropractic Center
Randall, Dr. Robert
126 Steadman St 506-853-8110

Robichaud, Dr. Langis J.
372 Lutz 506-857-4080

NEWCASTLE

Luke, Dr. Benjamin J.
261 King George Hwy 506-622-1358

OROMOCTO

Levere, Dr. Carolyn J.
83 Broad Rd 506-357-8803

REXTON

Bitting, Dr. Bruce
By Appointment 506-523-9075

Kenney, Dr. Mark
By Appointment 506-523-7243

ROTHESAY

Rothesay Chiropractic Center
Forgie, Dr. David; Forgie, Dr. Elizabeth
Rothesay Corner 506-847-7263

ST. GEORGE

Magee, Dr. Peter G.
21 Main 506-755-1122

SAINT JOHN

Hayhoe, Dr. B.A
3 Peters St 506-652-1778

Magee, Dr. Peter G.
1 North Market 506-648-9922

ST-QUENTIN

Lebel, Dr. Daniel
168 Canada 506-235-1189

ST. STEPHEN

Boeckman, Dr. John
4 Watson 506-466-1569

SHEDIAC

Clinique Chiropratique Shediac
Chiropratic Clinic
Robichaud, Dr. Yves-Martin
Centreville Mall 506-532-1114

SUSSEX CORNER

Sussex Chiropractic Centre
Hache, Dr. Rene
79 Broad 506-433-4711

TRACADIE-SHEILA

Dufour, Dr. Ghislain
By Appointment .506-395-2560/727-2536

WOODSTOCK

Clark, Dr. Rex; Clark, Dr. Simon
779 Main 506-328-2194

✦ Newfoundland

Chiropractors are regulated in Newfoundland, meaning that there is legislation establishing a governing body responsible for registering and disciplining practitioners (see below, "Governing Body"). There is no government health care funding.

Legislation

Chiropractors are regulated under the *Chiropractors Act* and regulation. Under section 2 of the Act, "chiropractic" means "a professional service usually performed by a chiropractor directed towards the diagnosis, examination and treatment, principally by hand, and without the use of drugs or surgery, of the spinal column, pelvis, extremities and associated tissues." The Act states that a chiropractor may employ as an aid to treatment electrotherapy, thermotherapy and counselling in relation to exercise, nutritional supplements and diet.

Only registered and licensed chiropractors are entitled to practise chiropractic. The Act also establishes the governing body and its functions and duties, which include hearing complaints against chiropractors and administering disciplinary procedures.

Chiropractors are prohibited from prescribing a laboratory test or having use of hospital or laboratory services. They may not use or prescribe the use of an anaesthetic for any purpose or give treatment for dislocations or fractures. A chiropractor may provide X-ray services to patients by prescription, to be carried out at a chiropractic clinic or hospital or other health care facility.

Newfoundland and Labrador Governing Body

Newfoundland and Labrador Chiropractic Board
PO Box 8243, Station A
St. John's, Newfoundland A1B 3N4
Tel: 709-747-4976
Fax: 709-747-4545

This is the governing body. Call to ensure that your chiropractor is licensed, or to register a complaint.

Newfoundland and Labrador Professional Association

Newfoundland and Labrador Chiropractic Association
Box 1081, Station C
St. John's, Newfoundland A1C 5M5
Tel: 709-726-4076

✦ Newfoundland Chiropractors

NOTE: The following names were provided by the Newfoundland & Labrador Chiropractic Board. However, this publication cannot and does not certify or represent the qualifications of practitioners, or the quality of care available from them. We cannot and do not confirm that those listed are registered as required by law.

CLARENVILLE

Dr. Roland Bryans Chiropractic Clinic
328 Memorial Dr 709-466-3200

CORNERBROOK

Provincial Chiropractic Clinic
Joyce, Stephen, DC
44 Main St 709-634-1477

West Coast Chiropractic Clinic
Andrews, John, DC; Lee, Jene, DC
19-21 West St 709-639-2225

GRAND FALLS

Chiropractic Clinic
Woolfrey, Paul Gregory, DC
5 Cartwright 709-489-4998

Chiropractic Office
Browne, Philip T., DC
60 Carmelite Rd 709-489-5554

MARYSTOWN

Burin Peninsula Chiropractic Clinic
Slaney, Paul, DC
McGettigan Centre,
PO Box 1178 709-279-4401

PORT AUX BASQUES

Gateway Family Chiropractic Clinic
Spicer, Deanna, DC
11 Midway Rd 709-695-3870

ST. JOHN'S

Avalon Chiropractic Clinic
MacAllister, Lee, DC
1st Fl, 20 Crosbie Pl 709-579-5900

Chiropractic Associates
Eustace, Carl, DC; Ryan, Rowena, DC
92 LeMarchant Rd 709-753-3300

Chiropractic Health & Wellness
Burton, Robert, DC
570 Newfoundland Dr,
Ste 102 709-726-2225

Family Chiropractic Centre Inc.
Vance, Donald, DC
251 Empire Ave 709-579-0008

Mallett, Douglas V., DC
220 LeMarchant Rd 709-579-5721

Topsail Rd Chiropractic Clinic
Hynes, Sharon, DC
Sobey's Sq,
760 Topsail Rd 709-747-4976

Water St Chiropractic Clinic Ltd
Beatty, K.C., ND; Goyeche, Laurie, ND
724 Water 709-726-4076

STEPHENVILLE

Bay St. George Chiropractic Clinic
Brake-Patten, Dr. Deborah
90 Main St 709-643-3111

WABUSH (LABRADOR)

Burn, Monty, DC
PO Box 316 709-944-6050

Heinen-Burn, Jan, DC
PO Box 310 709-944-6050

✦ Northwest Territories

There is no government regulation of chiropractors. There is therefore no governing body to register chiropractors who meet minimum educational standards.

If you wish to see a chiropractor in the Northwest Territories, you should therefore check the practitioner's qualifications. For example, ask where the practitioner was educated. Note that the Canadian Memorial Chiropractic College is the only nationally accredited institution in Canada. In addition, in all provinces, chiropractors are required to pass both national and provincial exams before they are licensed to practise. You may therefore wish to ask whether your chiropractor has ever taken and passed the Canadian Chiropractic Examining Board exam. You may also wish to ask if he or she has ever attempted to become qualified at a provincial level.

If you wish to verify that a chiropractor passed the Canadian Chiropractic Examining Board exam, obtain a signed consent from the chiropractor and send it to the board with your request. The address is:

Canadian Chiropractic Examining Board
Chairman
1020 Centre St. N
Calgary, Alberta T2E 2PN
Tel: 403-230-9003
Fax: 403-277-8162

✦ Northwest Territories Chiropractors

NOTE: Check the credentials of your chiropractor (see above, "Questions to Ask"). This publication cannot and does not certify or represent the qualifications of practitioners, or the quality of care available from them.

HAY RIVER

Tordoff, Rod
103-62 Woodland Dr
PO Box 4203 . . . . . . .403-874-3763/6502

Zondag, David
204-31 Capital Dr 403-874-3434

✦ Nova Scotia

Chiropractors are regulated in Nova Scotia, meaning that there is legislation establishing a governing body responsible for registering and disciplining practitioners (see below, "Governing Body"). There is no government health care funding for chiropractic treatment.

Legislation

Chiropractors are governed under the *Chiropractic Act* and regulation. Under the Act, chiropractic is defined as the system of treatment to relieve interference with the normal functioning of the nervous system of the body by the adjustment and manipulation of the articulations and the tissues, especially those of the spinal column. When necessary, treatment includes the aid of exercise, light, thermotherapy, hydrotherapy or electrotherapy.

No person other than a registered chiropractor may engage in the practice of chiropractic or use any title to imply that the person is engaged in the practice of chiropractic.

The Act states that nothing in it or the regulations authorizes a person to prescribe or administer drugs for use internally or externally, or to use or direct or prescribe the use of anaesthetics for any purpose, or to practise surgery or midwifery.

Nova Scotia Governing Body

Nova Scotia Board of Chiropractors
950 Bedford Highway, #204
Bedford, Nova Scotia B4A 4B5
Tel: 902-835-7878

This is the governing body. Call to ensure that your chiropractor is registered or to make a complaint. This is also the office of Wanda Lee MacPhee, D.C.

Nova Scotia Association

Nova Scotia Chiropractic Association
Box 1041
Port Hawkesbury, Nova Scotia B0E 2V0
Tel: 902-625-0005

Nova Scotia Chiropractors

NOTE: Check the credentials of your chiropractor (see above, "Questions to Ask"). This publication cannot and does not certify or represent the qualifications of practitioners, or the quality of care available from them. We cannot and do not confirm that those listed are registered as required by law.

AMHERST

Rainbow Chiropractic Office
Parker, Dr. Mary-Irene
65 Willow St 902-667-1236

Robichaud, Dr. Adrien J.
165 Victoria 902-667-9734

ANTIGONISH

Stephenson, Dr. Bruce B.
48 Hawthorne 902-863-6924

BEDFORD

Bedford Chiropratic Clinic
Bodner, Dr. Mark
1475 Bedford Hwy 902-835-6865

Hammond Chiropractic Health Centre
Macphee, Dr. Wanda
950 Bedford Hwy 902-835-7878

Yuen, Dr. Benjamin
206-15 Dartmouth Rd 902-835-6699

BRIDGEWATER

Anctil Chiropractic Clinic
Anctil, Dr. Robert O.
83 Churchill St 902-543-2131

Cowie, Dr. Laurel J.
110 Dufferin St 902-543-1660

CLEVELAND (PORT HAWKESBURY)

MacNeil, Dr. M. Douglas
301 Pitt 902-625-0005

DARTMOUTH

Helson Chiropractic Health Centre
Helson, Dr. Eric
590 Portland, Unit #8 902-434-8816

Ibsen, Dr. George F.
77 Woodlawn Rd 902-434-9227

DIGBY

La Pierre, Dr. Philip L.
By Appointment 902-245-5225

HALIFAX

Clayton Park Chiropractic Centre
Penrose, Dr. Douglas J.
287 Lacewood Dr 902-443-5669

Fenwick Chiropractic Clinic
Tharp, Dr. G. Robert
5595 Fenwick St 902-421-7501

Halifax Chiropractic Clinic
Seaman, Dr. Brian S.
6112 Willow St 902-423-9223

Spring Garden Chiropractic
Milroy, Dr. Patrick C.
460 Halifax
Professional Centre 902-429-3443

KENTVILLE

Back School of Nova Scotia
La Pierre, Dr. Philip L.
521 Main 902-678-1500

Eaton, Dr. Leslie J.
252 Park 902-678-4524

West Park Wellness Centre
Cere, Dr. G.P.
747 Park 902-678-1475

LOWER SACKVILLE

Kitt, Dr. Kevin
512 Sackville Dr 902-864-4411

LUNENBURG

Nelson Chiropractic Clinic
Nelson, Dr. M. Jean
169 Pelham 902-634-3600

MIDDLETON

Howlett, Dr. Sandra J.
239 Marshall 902-825-2323

NEW GLASGOW

Short, Dr. Albert L.
346 Abercrombie Rd 902-752-0811

SACKVILLE

Thompson, Dr. Rodney M.
100-179 Sackville Dr 902-865-6593

ST. MARGARET'S

Kleinknecht, Dr. Andrew
St. Margaret's Bay
Shopping Plaza 902-826-1088

SYDNEY

Sydney Chiropractic Back Care & Health Centre
Dunn, Dr. David; Dunn, Dr. Frances
262 Kings Rd 902-562-1407

TRURO

Carter Chiropractic Clinic
Carter, Dr. Sharon
73 Dominion 902-893-7477

Gillam Chiropractic Clinic
Gillam, Dr. Garry B.
36 Harris Ave 902-895-8881

Truro Chiropractic Clinic
Christianson, Dr. Joanna
800 Prince 902-895-4334

WOLFVILLE

Wolfville Chiropractic Centre
Macdonald, Dr. Ward
98 Front 902-542-5380

YARMOUTH

Daniels, Dr. Charles
By Appointment 902-742-9419

✦ Ontario

Chiropractors are regulated in Ontario, meaning that there is legislation establishing a governing body responsible for registering and disciplining practitioners (see below, "Governing Body"). There is government health care funding under the Ontario Health Insurance Plan (see below, "Government Health Care Funding").

Legislation

Chiropractors are a self-governing health profession under the *Regulated Health Professions Act, 1991*. The Act sets out the duties of the governing body (see below) in governing the practice of the profession and protecting the public interest. This includes procedures for investigating complaints and disciplining members. Chiropractors are also covered by the *Chiropractic Act, 1991* and regulations made under this Act.

Section 3 of the *Chiropractic Act, 1991* states that the "practice of chiropractic is the assessment of conditions related to the spine, nervous system and joints and the diagnosis, prevention and treatment, primarily by adjustment, of:

(a) dysfunctions or disorders arising from the structures or functions of the spine and the effects of those dysfunctions or disorders on the nervous system and

(b) dysfunctions or disorders arising from the structures or functions of the joints."

Section 4 states that a chiropractor, subject to any conditions imposed on his or her certificate or registration, is authorized to perform the following:

1. Communicating a diagnosis identifying as the cause of a person's symptoms,

    (i) a disorder arising from the structures or functions of the spine and their effects on the nervous system, or

    (ii) a disorder arising from the structures or functions of joints of the extremities.

2. Moving the joints of the spine beyond a person's usual physiological range of motion using a fast, low amplitude thrust.

3. Putting a finger beyond the anal verge for the purpose of manipulating the tailbone.

Government Health Care Funding - Ontario Health Insurance Plan (OHIP)

Coverage is provided as follows: a maximum of $11.75 toward the fee for an initial visit, and a maximum of $9.65 for subsequent visits, up to $220 per year. This includes a maximum $40 for radiographic (X-ray) services. For OHIP information, in Toronto call 416-482-1111; in Ottawa, call 613-783-4400; in Mississauga call 905-275-2730; for other areas, check your telephone book blue pages under Health.

Ontario Governing Body

College of Chiropractors of Ontario
130 Bloor St W, Ste 702
Toronto, Ontario M5S 1N5
Tel: 416-922-6355
Fax: 416-925-9610

This is the governing body. Call to ensure your chiropractor is registered or to make a complaint.

Ontario Professional Association

Ontario Chiropractic Association
5160 Explorer Dr, Unit 30
Mississauga, Ontario L4W 4T7
Tel: 905-629-8211
REFERRALS 1-800-558-5031

This is the professional association for chiropractors. Call the referral number for listings of a maximum of three chiropractors in your area (you will be asked for your postal code and telephone number).

✦ Ontario Chiropractors

NOTE: Check the credentials of your chiropractor (see above, "Questions to Ask"). This publication cannot and does not certify or represent the qualifications of practitioners, or the quality of care available from them. We cannot and do not confirm that those listed are registered as required by law.

ACTON

Telford, Dr. Richard
65 Mill E 519-853-2483

AJAX

Ajax Chiropractic & Sports Medicine Centre
Thomas, Dr. Linda
33 Church S 905-619-2193

Ajax North Chiropractic Centre
Arbour, Gerard
596 Kingston Rd W 905-427-9912

Delmonte Chiropractic Office
676 Monarch 905-427-3869

Discovery Bay Chiropractic Clinic
Mcgarrie, Dr. Ronald; Pilkington, Dr. Richard
487 Westney Rd S 905-683-1814

Ellis, Dr. Barbara
59 Westney Rd S 905-434-7524

Macleod, Dr. Norman
172 Harwood S 905-683-8695

Rusinek, Dr. Jacques
92 Church S 905-427-1226

Westney Heights Chiropractic Clinic
Martindale-Sliz, Dr. Karen
15 Westney N 905-428-2984

ALLISTON

Alexander, Catherine
Lowe, Dr. David E.
118 Victoria W 705-435-5122

Alliston Chiropractic Centre
Burgess, Dr. G.S.
16 Victoria E 705-435-6371

ALMONTE

Almonte Chiropractic Centre
118 Water 613-256-2813

AMHERSTBURG

Pietrangelo, Dr. Donato
197 S Sandwich St 519-736-7379

ANCASTER

Ancaster Chiropractic Clinic
Barnard, Dr. L.E.
73 Wilson W 905-648-6653

Malpass, Dr. Sandra
352 Wilson E 905-648-9991

Sloat, Dr. Barbara
124 W Wilson St 905-648-0661

ANGUS

Angus Chiropractic Centre
Debeer, Dr. Frank
56 River Dr 705-424-1666

ARNPRIOR

Hayes, Dr. J.R.; Wheeler, Dr. G.B.
74 Madawaska 613-623-2912

AURORA

Armata, Dr. Sterling; Armata, Dr. Steven
15242 Yonge St 905-727-9401

Aurora Family Health Clinic
Heavener, Dr. Cynthia; Janowicz, Dr. Frank
2 Orchardheights Blvd 905-727-0119

Moore Chiropractic Group
267 Edward 905-727-1817

AYLMER WEST

Aylmer Chiropractic Office
Warnock, Dr. Robert S.
210 Talbot E 519-773-9276

Oswell Chiropractic Centre
8-420 Talbot W 519-765-2565

BANCROFT

Bancroft Chiropractic Clinic
Wyard-Scott, Dr. Tricia
113 N Hastings 613-332-4554

BARRIE

Anderson Chiropractic Clinic
Andeson-Peacock, Dr. Elizabeth
274 Burton 705-734-9520

Armitage, Dr. Diana
79 Mary 705-722-9955

Barrie Health Group
Jongsma, Dr. David M.
151 Essa Rd 705-739-9585

Barrie South Chiropractic Centre
Teschl, Dr. Hans G.
190 Minet S Point Rd 705-728-9909

Bell Farm Chiropractic
Dell'Oso, Dr. Claudio
59 Bell Farm Rd 705-721-4404

Boyes, Dr. R.H.
20 Bell Farm Rd 705-722-3131

Brownhill, Dr.
130 Penetang 705-726-4331

Dyck, Dr. V. Gary
27 Gowan 705-726-9292

High St Chiropractic Office
Willson, Dr. Robert
79 High St 705-721-1611

Shaw, Dr. Susan
48 Ellen 705-725-8632

Tuck, Dr. O.H.
21 Essa Rd 705-728-3070

Veitch Chiropractic Clinic
Veitch, Dr. Marcia; Veitch, Dr. Peter
119 Bayfield 705-728-2538

BEAMSVILLE

Gadsby Chiropractic Offices
5026 King W 905-563-8558

BELLE RIVER

Chiropractic Rehabilitation Group
St. Louis, Dr. G.
419 Notre Dame 519-728-2711

BELLEVILLE

Bayview Chiropractic Centre
Valchar, Dr. Jan S.
218 College W 613-968-9626

Chambers, Dr. Dennis
125 Foster Ave 613-968-4144

Clements, Dr. Susan D.
156 Victoria Ave 613-969-8200

Dundas Chiropractic Group
Girduckis, Dr. Michele; Girduckis, Dr. Sean
59 Dundas E 613-962-7619

Kerr Chiropractic Clinic
Dinsmore, Dr. F. Kevin; Kerr, Dr. R.J.; Kerr, Dr. T.F.
34 Bridge W 613-967-8307

BELMONT

Easterbrook, Dr. Kevin J.
240 Main 519-644-1299

BLENHEIM

Mclauchlin, Dr. R. Murray
110 Talbot W 519-676-3311

BLIND RIVER

McLean, Dr. M.E.
By Appointment 705-356-7372

BOBCAYGEON

Bobcaygeon Chiropractic Centre
Bjornson, Dr. Grant; Bjornson, Dr. Julie
182 East S 705-738-3573

Village Chiropractic
Hoski, Dr. Robert; Iamarino, Dr. J.
Hwy 36 S 705-738-5600

BOLTON

Bolton Chiropractic Centre
Shore, Dr. Michael H.
53 W King St 905-857-0858

Caledon Chiropractic Centre
Brubacher, Dr. Eric
15 Allen 905-857-5622

Johnston, Dr. R.J.
Queen S 905-857-1313

Mensch, Dr. D.
18 King E 905-951-2081

BOWMANVILLE

Herron Family Chiropractic
98 King W 905-623-5509

Optimal Health Chiropractic Centre
Lott, Dr. Dianne; Wood-Bastedo, Dr. Katherine
152 Church 905-697-0355

BRACEBRIDGE

Bracebridge Chiropractic Centre
Kilpatrick, Dr. Grant
163 Baysville Rd 705-645-9544

Harper, Dr. R.W.
1 Westvale Dr 705-645-5792

Kimberley Ave Chiropractors Association
Dunlop, Dr. Kevin; Moore, Dr. Don
82 Kimberley 705-645-9954

Miksza, Dr. Jason
14 Ontario 705-645-8221

Ruttle, Dr. David
95 Manitoba 705-645-3283

BRADFORD

Bradford Chiropractic Office
Gordon, Dr. Robert
157 Hollande 905-775-4848

Town & Country Chiropractic
Hull, Dr. Sharon E.
75 Frederick 905-775-9027

BRAMPTON

Abbott Chiropractic Clinic
Pope, Gordon B.
550 Queen W . . .905-454-1400/453-0032

Allen, Dr. L.A.; Beals, Dr. Simon J.
169 Queen E 905-453-1806

Bramalea Chiropractic Clinic
Keogh, Dr. Patrick
18 Kensington Rd 905-791-7011

Buss, Dr. Timothy E.
20 Nelson W 905-451-3963

Courtwood Chiropractic Clinic
Naylor, Dr. Tom
200 County Court Bl 905-454-8080

Heart Lake Chiropractic Clinic
Glatter, Dr. Arnie
10425 N Kennedy Rd 905-840-1330

Henderson Chiropractic Clinic
Henderson, Dr. Maureen
188 Main S 905-453-3385

Hill, Dr. Ron
389 N Main 905-451-7157

McLaughlin Chiropractic
Roberts, Dr. G.
2 Brookview Rd 905-452-0499

Schinbein, Dr. Stewart
36 Vodden E 905-451-7160

Thicke, Dr. Joanne
157 Queen E 905-454-0800

Wexford Chiropractic Centre
Finewax, Dr. Jeffrey; Guttman, Dr. Allen
1 Wexford Rd 905-840-1880

BRANTFORD

Academy Chiropractic Office
Pikula, Dr. Edward T.
94 St George St 519-752-5512

Avenue Chiropractic Office
Frame, Dr. Edward
215 Brant Ave 519-753-7732

Brantford Chiropractic Associates
Barker, Dr. Stephen; Dailey, Dr. Darrell;
Langlois, Dr. Ann
124 Charing Cross 519-756-1303

De Marchi Chiropractic Health Clinic
De Marchi, Dr. Ivone
92 Elm St 519-756-8171

Erie Ave Chiropractic
Elkin, Dr. Colin D.
183 Erie 519-751-1154

Hill, Dr. J. Jay
30 William St 519-759-0330

Hughes, Dr. Janice
330 West 519-753-9596

BRIGHTON

McQuoid, Dr. C.G.
RR #3 613-475-1764

BROCKVILLE

Basiren, Dr. Stephen L.
1275 Kensington Pkwy 613-498-2249

Carson, Dr. Robert Charles
131 Pearl W 613-342-9278

Pickett, Dr. D.S.
779 Chelsea 613-342-5544

Sykes, Dr. Allan K.
15 Parkview 613-342-3065

BROOKLIN

Brooklin Family Health Centre
Du Quesnay, Dr. Katharine
4945 Baldwin S 905-655-5767

BURK'S FALLS

Gooch, Dr. Katherine
By Appointment 705-382-3438

BURLINGTON

Back On Track Chiropractic and Wellness Centre
Heidary, Dr. William
2025 Guelph Line 905-319-6606

Brown, Dr. Jeremy
666 Appleby Line 905-639-0073

Cornale-Smith, Dr. Caroline
280 Plains W 905-527-5573

Duller, Dr. H.
S 101-2201 Brant 905-335-0536

Embree, Dr. B.E.
602-2319 Fairview 905-632-7797

Gates, Dr. Reginald
454 Maple Ave 905-634-1024

Headon Chiropractic Clinic
Jasek, Dr. Derek
1450 Headon 905-332-7758

Higgins, Dr. D.R.
2421 New 905-634-2581

Lakeshore Chiropractic Clinic
Norman, Dr. Heather
2159 Lakeshore 905-333-1104

**Lee, Dr. Scott;
Patrick, Dr. Colleen**
720 Guelph Line 905-681-2521

Life Chiropractic Centre
Ivanchuk, Dr. Brad; Shewchuk, Dr. Lynne
8-3030 Carncastle 905-335-5433

Malstrom, Dr. Gary
783 Brant St 905-681-3342

Millrose Chiropractic Clinic
Kirk, Dr. Rod; St. Clair, Dr. Steven
2025 William Oconnell Bl . . .905-319-2222

Ricottone, Dr. Sal
246 W Plains Rd 905-528-4024

Wellum Chiropractic Clinic
Wellum Jr., Dr. Colin; Wellum Sr., Dr. Colin
276 E Plains Rd 905-634-9535

Wingfield, Dr. Robert
464 Locust 905-637-0212

Zarins, Dr. S.M.
934 King Rd 905-637-0361

CALEDON EAST

Caledon East Chiropractic Office
Mensch, Dr. Dieter
15771 N Airport 905-584-2250

CALEDONIA

Aldridge, Dr. James
RR #3 905-765-4025

CALLANDER

Hegyi, Dr. Imre
299 Main N 705-752-4572

CAMPBELLFORD

Austring, Dr. John
39 Doxsee Ave N 705-653-2674

CARLETON PLACE

Hewitt, Dr. Neil E.
9 Emily 613-257-4098

Mississippi Chiropractic Health Centre
Earle, Dr. Robert
89 Beckwith 613-253-8345

CARP

Carp Chiropractic Clinic
Tucker, Dr. Michael
By Appointment 613-839-5316

CHAPLEAU

Mione, Dr. Angelo
75 Birch E 705-864-1372

CHATHAM

Chatham-Kent Chiropractic Centre
Merritt, Dr. Mark
555 Richmond 519-352-4180

Clement Chiropractic Centre
Aerssen, Dr. Donald; Bedard, Dr. Michael;
Zavitz, Dr. Stephen
152 Thames 519-354-4074/354-5555

Lemak, Dr. James J.
230 St Clair 519-354-5475

CHELMSFORD

Centre Chiropractic
Beauchamp, Dr. Annette
338 Errington Ave N 705-855-9054

CLARKSBURG

Luck, Dr. Richard
By Appointment 519-599-2421

CLINTON

Clinton Chiropractic Centre
Colquhoun, Dr. K.L.; Wood, Dr. C.
160 Huron 519-482-3481

COBOURG

Bradford Chiropractic Clinic
Bradford, Stephen
386 Division 905-372-2946

Chiropractic Care Clinic
Woodland, Dr. W.; Vanderham, Dr. B.
541 William 905-372-0060

Cobourg Chiropractic Centre
Kryluk, Dr. V.C.
471 Division 905-372-0166

Hubbel, Dr. M.J.
197 Third 905-372-1885

COCHRANE

Bourassa, Dr. Claude; Bulgar, Dr. Sharon
142-5 Ave 705-272-6718

COLDWATER

Coldwater Chiropractic Office
Town, Dr. David F.
19 Coldwater Rd 705-686-7000

COLLINGWOOD

Collingwood Chiropractic Clinic
Coghlan, Dr. Wayne
516 Hurontario St 705-445-5401

Cruise, Dr. Michael
450 Hume St 705-444-1202

Stackhouse Chiropractic Clinic
Stackhouse, Dr. Jeffrey
243 Hurontario 705-444-1515

CORNWALL

Beaumont, Dr. Robert
123 Amelia 613-933-3083

DORCHESTER

Colquhoun, Dr. C.B.
4035 Hamilton Rd 519-268-8616

DRYDEN

Dryden Chiropractic Clinic
Zmiyiwsky, Dr. O.P.
101 Duke St

Jeans, Dr. A.
34a King St 807-223-3121

DUNDAS

Churchill, Dr. David A.
20 Sydenham 905-628-8112

Dundas Chiropractic Office
Macrae, Dr. John E.; Prosia, Dr. Lou
50 Park W 905-628-3600/8771

Lilja Chiropractic Clinic
Lilja, Dr. R.
182 King W 905-628-2225

DUNNVILLE

Inch, Dr. Ronald B.
104 Lock E 905-774-5645

Wingfield, Dr. John C.
126 Queen 905-774-7774

DURHAM

Durham Chiropractic
Woods, Dr. Doug
293 Elgin North 519-369-5511

ELLIOT LAKE

Balsam Chiropractic Office
Johnston, Dr. Michael D.
18 Balsam Pl 705-848-7745/6919

Chiropractic Health Office
Sprague, Dr. Donald
34 Ottawa 705-848-1811

ELMIRA

Brubacher Chiropractic Office
Brubacher, Dr. Mark
10 Hampton St 519-669-1621

Hutson Chiropractic
Hutson, Dr. W.
1-63 Arthur S 519-669-3840

Kleinknecht, Dr. B.W.
2 E Park Ave 519-669-5571

ELORA

Dubler, Dr. Richard
43 Henderson 519-846-0230

ERIN

Erin Chiropractic Centre
Thomas, Dr. G.K.
162 Main 519-833-9379

Sherrington Chiropractic Clinic
Sherrington, Dr. David
Boland Dr 519-833-2946

ESPANOLA

Espanola Chiropractic Office
Laurenti, Dr. Dario
Highway 6 705-869-2737

ESSEX

Pascoe, Dr. Richard
106 S Talbot St 519-776-5151

EXETER

Exeter Chiropractic Centre
Hann, Dr. David
105 Main S 519-235-1535

Webb, Dr. G.A.
438 Main S 519-235-1680

FENELON FALLS

Scott Chiropractic Offices
Scott, Dr. Robert
205 Francise 705-887-9701

FERGUS

Armstrong, Dr. E.
200 Tower S 519-843-1581

Eveleigh, Dr. Lois A.
400 N St David St 519-843-1850

Gatten, Dr. Jon C.
195 S St David St 519-843-1490

FLESHERTON

Lakeview Chiropractic
Seim, Dr. George M.
Eugenia 519-924-2272

FONTHILL

Fonthill Chiropractic Clinic
Payson, Dr. Ron W.
1512 Pelham Rd 905-892-8920

FOREST

Delugt Chiropractic Centre
Delugt, Dr. G.
68 E King 519-786-2500

Forest Chiropractic Centre
Baker, Dr. M.
11 N James 519-786-2862

FORT ERIE

Brown, Dr. Samuel D.
509 Niagara 905-871-3354

Drost Chiropractic Clinic
Drost, Dr. Edwardine
1226 Garrison 905-871-0776

Ogilvie Chiropractic Clinic
Ogilvie, Dr. David; Ogilvie, Dr. Ted
170 Central Ave 905-871-2193

FORT FRANCES

Chiropractic Centre-Fort Frances
Curtis, Dr. A. Mark
255 Scott St 807-274-2545

Chiropractic Clinic-Rainy Lake
Jeans, Dr. Barbara
517 Mowat Ave 807-274-4414

GEORGETOWN

Beaton, Dr. Robert L.
9 Wesleyan 905-877-7333

Chiropractic & Sports Injuries Centre
Jones, Dr. Robert M.
211 Guelph 905-877-9996

Georgetown Chiropractic Clinic
Madarasz, Dr. Gabor
80 Guelph 905-873-1871

Hassard, Dr. Mark
108 Main S 905-873-7743

GLOUCESTER

Beacon Hill Chiropractic Clinic
Bordeleau, Dr. Sylvie; Vandervoort, Dr. Daniel
2200 Ch Montreal 613-747-0444

Blackburn Hamlet Chiropractic Office
Cyr, Dr. Denis
110 Bearbrook Rd 613-837-6690

GODERICH

Huron Chiropractic Centre
Gianoulis, Dr. Helen; Norsworthy, Dr. Douglas
107 South 519-524-9661

Palmer, Dr. Douglas B.
73 Montreal 519-524-4555

GRAVENHURST

Adair, Dr. Grant K.
Elder St 705-687-2012

Taylor, Dr. Gary
161 Brock 705-687-5592

GRIMSBY

Belford, Dr. Christine; Saigeon, Dr. Brent
87 E Main St 905-945-7676

Cruise, Dr. Brian; West, Dr. David
17 Ontario 905-945-3731/3981

Gardiner, Dr. Amber
208-155 Main E 905-945-6768

GUELPH

Chiropractic Care Centre
Dukelow, Dr. W.
186 Norfolk St 519-822-7721

Church Lane Chiropractic/Norfolk Chiropractic Centre
Nolet, Dr. Paul S.
8 Church Ln 519-763-2436

Fera Chiropractic Office
Fera, Dr. Peter
93 W Speedvale Ave 519-836-3372

Guelph Chiropractic Health Cen
Grabowski, Dr. Russell; Scinbein, Dr. Stewart
150 Woolwich St 519-763-4561

Guthrie, Dr. Frank Q.
291 Victoria N 519-837-3100

Huffman, Dr. Dennis
363 Woolwich 519-836-4861

Keys-Riley, Dr. Bonnie
101-511 Edinburgh S 519-837-9711

Munro Chiropractic Health Centre
Munro, Dr. Christie C.
55 Queen 519-821-0645

Stoneroad Mall Chiropractic & Health Clinic
Grape, Dr. M.A.
214-435 Stone Rd Mall 519-837-0411

University Square Chiropractic Centre
Mahoney, Dr. Kevin G.
987 Gordon 519-837-1234

Walton Chiropractic Centre
Walton, Dr. J.B.
7-45 Speedvale E 519-766-1250

Wellington Chiropractic Group
Kinat, Dr. Kim Carl; Whiteny-Douglas, Dr. R.C.
12 Waterloo Ave 519-822-4205

HAGERSVILLE

Werner, Dr. Wm.C.
12 Alma S 905-768-1721/5834

HALIBURTON

Hill, Dr. Robert
By Appointment 705-457-9895

HAMILTON

Advantage Chiropractic Health Centre
Millett, Dr. John
3-66 Mall 905-574-1181

Cattafi, Dr. Arthur J.
7-588 Barton E 905-529-4844

Centennial Chiropractic Office
Swaby, Dr. Trevor
160 Centennial Pkwy N 905-573-7337

Cooke, Dr. Catherine
1300 Garth 905-574-3274

Crews, Dr. J.
565 Sanitarium Rd 905-383-6433

Dunsmure Pain Clinic
Kolios, Dr. Dorothy; Park, Dr. Anna
59 Dunsmure Rd 905-547-5393

Fennell Chiropractic Clinic
Mayall, Dr. Roger; Meikle, Dr. David
1011 Fennel E 905-388-2665

Huehn, Dr. S.D.; Jenkins, Dr. G.D.; Pernfuss, Dr. M. W.
136 Young 905-528-6426

James South Chiropractic Clinic
Matteson, Dr. Brian E.
2 Young St 905-525-5959

Koch Chiropractic Clinic
Aceti, Dr. Iva;
Koch, Dr. Roberta
866 Main E 905-544-5688

Manzuk, Dr. T.M.
1378 Barton E 905-547-6677

Mason Shaler Chiropractic
Mason, Dr. Bruce; Shaler, Dr. Mark
196 George 905-523-5010

Mountain Chiropractic Office
Tartaglia, Dr. Anthony
682 Upper James 905-574-6511

Persi, Dr. Adriano
118 George 905-572-7141

Pringle, Dr. James
444 Fennell E 905-575-1444

Rosedale Chiropractic Clinic
Lamontagne, Dr. James A.
230 Graham S 905-545-5570

Shaw Chiropractic Clinic
Shaw, Dr. Ian H.
676 Upper James 905-389-5029

Smith, Dr. Thomas J.
263 Mohawk Rd W 905-388-1851

Stevenson Chiropractic Offices
Stevenson, Dr. David; Stevenson, Dr. Judith;
Stevenson, Dr. Scott
843 Main E 905-544-5787

Stonechurch Chiropractic Centre
Hockridge, Dr. M.J.; Jerome, Dr. Wayne
549 Stone Church E 905-575-0300

Thurlow Chiropractic Office
Thurlow, Dr. R.
970 W Main St 905-527-6250

Waxman, Dr. Earl
67 Bond St S 905-570-2739

Wellington Medical Centre
Misale, Dr. John P.
293 Wellington N, Suite 122 .905-529-5221

Westdale Chiropractic Clinic
Stevenson, Dr. Daniel D.
775 King W 905-525-5052

Wright, Dr. Catherine N.
419 Concession 905-385-3338

HANMER

Hanmer Chiropractic Centre
Landry, Dr.Ghislaine; Welsh, Dr. David
Hanmer Valley
Shopping Centre 705-969-4475

HANOVER

Kucan Chiropractic Office
Kucan, Dr. J.
285-12th St 519-364-3020

HASTINGS

Hastings Chiropractic Clinic
Vanderham, Dr. Bert
196 Bridge 705-696-1285

HAWKESBURY

St-Jean, Dr. Denis
130 Principale W 613-632-0953

HEARST

Dalcourt, Dr. Pierre P.
1425 Front St 705-362-4425

HOLLAND LANDING

Curphey-Hardman, Dr. Elda
19 Sunrise 905-853-9630

HUNTSVILLE

Anderson, Dr. Wm. J.
76 King William 705-789-7577

Hough, Dr. I.C.
21 Herman 705-789-4781

Neudorf, Dr. Douglas; Watson, Dr. Todd
367 Muskoka Rd 3 N 705-789-7600

INGERSOLL

Hunt, Dr. B.R.
238 Thames S 519-485-1750

IROQUOIS

Summers, Dr. Dean A.
5 Plaza Dr 613-652-2177

IROQUOIS FALLS

Van Baker, Dr. Teresa
By Appointment 519-653-2036

KANATA

Family Chiropractic Centre
Fefferman, Dr. Andrea; Lovsin, Dr. David;
Mahoney, Dr. Keith
214-99 Kakulu Rd 613-592-7660

Kanata Holistic Chiropractic Centre
Brunelle, Dr. Tony;
Forget-Brunelle, Dr. Marcelle
208-2 Beaverbrook Rd 613-592-8100

KAPUSKASING

Chiropractic Centre
Oldaker, Dr. Ken
3 Queen St 705-335-8551

Kowalski, Dr. Z.
2 Brunetville Rd 705-335-4244

Martin Chiropractic Clinic
Martin, Dr. Peter
18 Byng Ave 705-337-1900

KEMPTVILLE

Hadden, Dr. G. Reid
30 Clothier W 613-258-3480

Kemptville Chiropractic Clinic
Crook, Dr. Parnell
RR #4 613-258-5911

KENORA

Causyn Chiropractic Centre
Causyn, Dr. Michael
201 S 5th Ave 807-468-9876

Norton, Dr. W.E.
685 Lakeview Drive 807-468-9563

KESWICK

Keswick Chiropractic Centre
Bar, Dr. Kevin
183 Simcoe Ave 905-476-9229

Pike Chiropractic Health Centre
204 Simcoe Ave 905-476-6475

KINCARDINE

Rapley, Dr. Karen E.
264 Lambton 519-396-4552

Willis, Dr. John C.
996 Queen 519-396-9515

KING CITY

Houlton, Dr. Timothy J.
1229 King Rd 905-773-5122

KINGSTON

Cataraqui Chiropractic Clinic
Mills, Dr. Brent J.
911 Purdymills Rd 613-544-0591

Chiropractic Associates
Collins, Dr. Martha; Weber, Dr. C.M.
182 Nelson St 613-549-7977

Gibson, Dr. George H.
730 Milford Dr 613-384-6797

Houde, Dr. Marie; Shulman, Dr. Lorne
296 Princess 613-545-9553

Medora, Dr. Richard P.
1101 Lombardy 613-384-2563

Mills-Murphy Chiropractic Clinic
Murphy, Dr. Carol; Mills, Dr. David
295 Brock St 613-549-7376

Wright, Dr. Thomas S.
811 Blackburn Mews 613-384-7432

KINGSVILLE

Kingsville Chiropractic Clinic
Crawford, Dr. Barry; Staddon, Dr. Caroline
7 King St 519-733-3732

Main Street Chiropractic
Cooper, Dr. Walter
243 Main E 519-733-8111

KIRKLAND LAKE

Burns Chiropractic Clinic
Burns, Dr. Paul
14 Government Rd E 705-568-8313

KITCHENER

Belmont Chiropractic Clinic
Riddell, Dr. W.R.
665 W Belmont Ave 519-579-1360

Caruk, Andrew
267 Tagge Cr 519-570-9053

Christopher, Dr. Paul
15 Hazelglen 519-571-8321

Cochrane, J.G.
339 Highland W 519-578-7840

Country Hills Chiropractic Centre
Georgopoulos, Dr. Paul
700 Strasburg Rd 519-744-7234

Dronyk Clinic
Dronyk, Dr. W.
2880 E King St 519-894-0024

Fairway Chiropractic Centre
Murdoch, Dr. S.P.
5 Manitou Dr 519-748-5535

Frey Chiropractic Office
Frey, L.W.
242 S Queen St 519-578-3920

Goodyear-Johnston, Dr. Sharon
526 Frederick 519-743-6339

Highland Chiropractors
Gilmore, Dr. P.C.
73 W Highland Rd 519-576-7340

Johannes Chiropractic Office
Johannes, Dr. C.
1454 E King St 519-744-3582

Lutzer, Dr. Klaus
1005 Ottawa N 519-893-8800

Meyer, Dr. Paul
2-510 Frederick 519-745-3231

Miller, Dr. Robert
1058 Queens Bl 519-741-8787

Owers Chiropractic Office
Owers, Dr. Bruce A.
1454 E King St 519-744-3091

Peever Chiropractic Office
Peever, Dr. J.
1454 E King St 519-576-4422

Reinhart Chiropractic Offices
Reinhart, Dr. D.
84 W Weber St 519-742-1211

Rockway Chiropractic Clinic
Lichti, Dr. Janice; Near, Dr. Tammy
589 Charles E 519-744-4745

Smith Chiropractic Clinic
Smith, Dr. K.L.; Smith Sr., Dr. K.W.; Smith, Dr. Sharon
227 Dumfries Ave 519-742-4471

Straus, Dr. Catherine
322 Lawrence 519-579-2430

Vander Beek, Dr. Ron
123 Pioneer Dr 519-895-0765

Victoria-Westmount Chiropractic Centre
Mackay, Dr. Tim
101 Hazelglen Dr 519-570-3300

Westheights Chiropractic Clinic
Kniess, Dr. Robert
950 Highland W 519-744-9904

Westmount Chiropractic Office
Ambos, Dr. Peter
400 W Westmount Rd 519-743-4838

KLEINBURG

Pragnell, Dr. N. Richard
855 Nashville Rd 905-893-2771

LASALLE

Lasalle Chiropractic
Masse, Dr. Mark
805 Front 519-978-3160

Nautical Mile Chiropractic Centre
Cerchie, Dr. A.N.
995 Front 519-978-3305

LAKEFIELD

Owens, Dr. Catherine
36 Bridge 705-652-8009/6741

LAMBETH

Lambeth Chiropractic Clinic
Oates, Dr. Greg
38 Main E 519-652-5597

LEAMINGTON

Renaissance Chiropractic
Reimer, Dr. Henry
91 Erie St S 519-326-0675

LEVACK

Larochelle, Dr. Marc
Onaping Falls Medical Centre 705-966-3425

LINDSAY

Kent Street Chiropractic Centre
Croutch, Dr. Philip; Hay, Dr. Ronald
245 Kent W 705-324-2556/8211

Lindsay Chiropractic Centre
Wetzel, Dr. F.G.
128 Angeline N 705-324-1667

Rahn Chiropractic Centre
Rahn Dr. A. Warren
216 Lindsay S 705-324-6201

Scott Chiropractic Offices
Staples, Dr. Mary Anne
206 Lindsay S 705-328-3834

LION'S HEAD

Lions Head Chiropractic Clinic
Logan, Dr. Kenneth C.
2 Helen St 519-793-3092

LISTOWEL

Hemingway Chiropractic Office
Hemingway, Dr. P.
290 Main E 519-291-3640

Listowel Chiropractic Centre
Mason, Dr. James
102 Main W 519-291-4030

LIVELY

Walden Chiropractic Centre
Mahonen, Dr. Mark A.
Phinehill Plaza 705-692-3646

LONDON

Adelaide Chiropractic Care Clinic
Shulman, Dr. L.
604 Oxford E 519-660-6377

Adelaide Chiropractic Centre
Connor, Patrick J. ; Latta, Dr. David G.
1061 Adelaide N 519-642-2579

Alternative Health Clinic (London)
Bruce, Dr. A. Raymond
954 Richmond St 519-433-1003

Bauman, Dr. Craig
540 Queens Ave 519-432-5752

Bell, Dr. Diane
229 Clarke Rd 519-452-3030

Bellwood Chiropractic Centre
Harvey, Dr. N.J.
900 E Oxford St 519-455-3312

Burden, Dr. Neil A.
514 Oxford E . . .519-673-1666/858-4257

Byron Village Chiropractic Centre
Somers, Dr. Matthew
1240 W Commissioners Rd . .519-657-3567

Cherryhill Chiropractic
Watson, Dr. David
203-101 Cherryhill Bl 519-433-7281

Colborne Chiropractic Office
Millar, Dr. Donald
423 Colborne St 519-663-1166

Dalgity, Dr. Carolyn
90 Riverside Dr 519-673-6666

Dryburgh, Dr. Dean
202 Wharncliffe Rd S 519-663-9759

Folkard, Dr. Robert
994 Oxford E 519-659-7220

Gdanski, Dr. A.J. Ted
994 Oxford E 519-451-4010

Gdanski, Dr. John S.
1719 Dundas 519-659-2225

Gdanski, Dr. Sharon Lee
343 Hamilton Rd 519-438-9342

Gregory, Dr. Janice M.
Sutherland, Dr. C. Scott
167 Oxford W 519-433-1714

Hardick Chiropractic Centre
Hardick, Dr. Clifford; Hardick, Dr. Robert
331 Queens Ave 519-673-1132

Huron & Highbury Chiropractic Center
Atchison, Dr. J. Byron
1315 Highbury Ave 519-451-4000

Jones, Dr. Mark E.
1849 Jalna Blvd 519-686-9000

Judge, Dr. Ian A.
By Appointment 519-472-5000

London Chiropractic Clinic
Deshane, Dr. P; Langford, Dr. Don
423 Colborne 519-434-4493

London Chiropractic Health Center
Eidt, Dr. Robert; Eidt, Dr. T. Tyler; Morrison, Dr. Kevin
204 Oxford W 519-661-0285

London West Health Centre
Dronyk, Dr. Robert J.
307 Commissioners Rd W . . .519-471-1917

Masonville Chiropractic Centre
Valente, Dr. Danny; Valente, Dr. Robin
101 Franshawe Park Rd E . . .519-645-2444

Mathies, Dr. Robert J.
666 Wonderland Rd N 519-474-7200

Moss, Dr. George; Scott, Dr. Stephen
232 Oxford W 519-672-3322

Neely, Dr. Calvin
354 Boler 519-472-8700

Neely, Dr. James
275 Belfield 519-642-7800

Orenchuk, Dr. Dennis
1-25 Base Line W 519-672-2214

Overton, Dr. R.B.
994 Oxford E 519-659-1578

Oxford & Wharncliffe Chiropractic Offices
Meiklejohn, Dr. Walter R,
81 Oxford W 519-679-8901

Pond Mills Chiropractic Service
Wilson, Dr. David
1166 Commissioners Rd E . . .519-681-0026

South London Chiropractic Office
Jansenberger, Dr. William
142 Wortley 519-672-4776

Stewart, Dr. Scott
90 Riverside Dr 519-432-7775

Stover, Dr. Richard
401-1151 Florence 519-457-3844

Wellington Chiropractic
Coleman-Kay, Dr. Victoria; Steckel, Dr. Cheryl; Steckel, Dr. Mark
332 Wellington Rd 519-675-1030

Westmount Chiropractic Offices
Hildebrandt, Dr. Frank; Todorovich, Dr. Radmila
844 Wonderland Rd S 519-472-5000

LUCAN

Biddulph Chiropractic Office
Pugh, Dr. Ruth
280 Main 519-227-1363

MADOC

Burtt, Dr. R.S.
Medical Centre 613-473-2383

MANITOUWADGE

Manitouwadge Chiropractic Clinic
70 Huron Walk 807-826-4211

MANOTICK

Manotick Chiropractic Centre
Hardtke, Dr. Dieter; Pratt, Dr. Mary-Lee
5482 Main 613-692-2561

MAPLE

Maple Professional Centre
Ammendolia, Dr. Carlo
2301 Major Mackenzie Dr . .905-832-8880

MARKDALE

Markdale Chiropractic Clinic
Viljakainen, Dr. Stephen
65 Main W 519-986-2311

MARKHAM

Chiropractic Centre
Boehnke, Dr. H.W.
134 Main Street
Markham N 905-294-1400

**Definney Chiropractic and Sports
Injuries Clinc**
Definney, Dr. John
5871 Hwy 7 905-294-0454

Garrity, Dr. Christine
22 Wootten Way N 905-471-2225

Market Village Chiropractic
Traitses, Dr. George I.
4394 E Steeles Ave 905-940-8778

Markham Chiropractic Centre
Baird, Dr. John; Baird, Dr. Wm.S.
369 Main St N 905-294-6000

**Markham-Unionville Chiropractic
Clinic**
Robbins, Dr. Michael G.
9704 McCowan 905-471-6711/6696

Newton-Leo, Dr. Linda
5811 Hwy 7 905-294-0454

Poblete, Dr. Cecilia
9275 Markham Rd 905-471-8810

White Chiropractic Centre
White, Dr. Eleanor; White, Dr. Paul
8-A Centre St 905-294-7000

MEAFORD

Family Chiropractic Centre
Fascinato, Dr. Frank; Thompson, Dr. James
51 Sykes N 519-538-3747

**Hooper Chiropractic Sports Injury
Center**
Hooper, Dr. K.A.
364 Sykes S 519-538-5420

Meaford Chiropractic Centre
Miller, Dr. Ian M.
47 Nelson W 519-538-3700

MIDLAND

Cornerstone Chiropractic
Shewfelt, Dr. John; Weber, Dr. James
336 First 705-526-5850

Edwards, Dr. Wm. R.
By Appointment 705-527-9021

Mavrou Chiropractic Clinic
Mavrou, Dr. D.; Mavrou, Dr. L.
229 First 705-526-6401

Midland Chiropractic Clinic
Nicholson, Dr. W.; Watson, Dr. Colleen
1a-578 King 705-526-6221

MILFORD BAY

Kinsman, Dr. Robert
By Appointment 705-764-0022

MILTON

Barrow, Dr. James R.
180 Ontario S 905-878-8127

Koeth, Dr. Angelika P.
106 Wakefield Rd 905-878-5165

Milton Mall Chiropractic Clinic
Houston, Dr. James D.
Milton Mall 905-878-8131

Phillips, Dr. David L.
310 Main E 905-878-5656

Turner, Dr. Marlene
95 E Main St 905-876-1888

MINDEMOYA

Manitoulin Chiropractic Office
Simon, Dr. H.F.
By Appointment 705-377-5290

MINDEN

Minden Chiropractic Clinic
Guthy, Dr. Janis
Heritage Plaza 705-286-6645

MISSISSAUGA

Applewood Hill Chiropractic Office
Lach, Dr. Stanley
1092 Bloor St E 905-277-3411

Bork, Dr. I.H.
4272 Dixie 905-238-1600

Burns Chiropractic Centre
Burns, Dr. Ronald
2563 Hurontario St 905-275-2102

Chiropractic Care Centre
Lanoue, Dr. Serge
Mississauga Square One 905-848-8900

City Centre Chiropractic
Fong, Dr. Victor W.
900 W Rathburn Rd 905-897-5005

Clarkson Turtle Creek Chiropractic
Bracchetti, Dr. Gloria
1801 Lakeshore Rd W 905-855-7370

Credit Valley Chiropractic Centre
Cohen, Dr. Robert
1250 Eglinton W 905-819-9000

Demborynsky, Morris H.
3460 Cawthra Rd 905-270-9621

Desouza, Dr. Joycelene
2000 Credit Valley Rd 905-607-8898

Di Carolei, Dr. Oliver
4237 Tomken 905-897-7114

Dunwin Chiropractic Centre
Thiessen, Dr. Stephen
2285 Dunwin Dr 905-828-0236

Edmark, Dr. Monica
332 Queen S 905-567-0019

Erindale Chiropractic Clinic
Andersen, Dr. Emily; Cote, Dr. Micheline J.
3173 Erindale Stn 905-848-1990

Fairview Chiropractic Centre
Stants, Dr. Carlan; Dos Santos, Dr. David
3355 Hurontario St 905-566-5300

Fligg, Dr. D. Burce
3461 Dixie Rd 905-624-0233

Glen Erin Chiropractic Centre
Amlinger, Dr. Peter J
3476 Glen Erin Dr 905-569-9060

Holden, Dr. Robert D.
3185 Cawthra Rd 905-276-2200

Holmes, Dr. J. Merton
1609 Truscott Dr 905-855-1655

Hurontario Chiropractic Office
Sabucco, Dr. Roberto P.
101 Queensway W 905-566-0889

**Kingsbridge Family Chiropractic &
Sports Injury**
Trim, Dr. Astrid
20 Kingsbridge Garden 905-712-1939

Lakeshore Chiropractic Office
Banks, Dr. Bryan W.
279 E Lakeshore Rd 905-274-1759

Levine, Dr. Howard
5780 Timberlea 905-625-1528

Mayers, Dr. Henry
377 Burnhamthorpe E 905-276-4343

**Meadowvale Centre Chiropractic
Clinic**
Goldman, Dr. Charles E.
6855 Meadowvale
Town Centre 905-826-3153

Moore, Dr. Terence W.
2155 Leanne Blvd 905-822-5656

Ridgeway Chiropractic
Hewitt, Dr. P.F.
3100 Ridgeway Dr 905-820-4620

Robinson, Dr. Donald D.
1368 Rometown Dr 905-274-3091

Sawa, Dr. Thomas M.
2087 Dundas E 905-238-3233

Streetsville Chiropractic Clinic
Sinclair, Dr. Vincent K.
206-B Queens S 905-826-0900

Sturino, Dr. F.
1077 North Service 905-277-2161

**Swyszcz, Dr. Orysia; Swyszcz, Dr.
Oryst**
1385 Hurontario 905-891-9197

Titus, Dr. G.W.
1494 Southdown 905-822-8606

**Tomlin, Dr. Denise; Tomlin, Dr.
Mark**
3058 Loyalist & The Collegeway . .905-820-
5660

Uchikata, Dr. Paul
3197 Dixie 905-624-4123

MITCHELL

Cartwright Chiropractic
Cartwright, Dr. Dean
26 Ontario Rd 519-348-4690

MOUNT FOREST

**Mount Forest Chiropractic Health
Centre**
Gohn, Dr. David W.
146 Main S 519-323-2960

NAPANEE

Hawley Chiropractic Offices
Hawley, Dr. P.
51 Kingston Rd 613-354-4646

NEPEAN

Barrhaven Chiropractic Associates
Lindsay, Dr. Thomas W.
204-900 Greenbank Rd 613-825-1814

**Barrhaven Chiropractic Health
Centre**
Lafreniere, Dr. Joanne; Pickett, Dr. Donald
3500 Fallowfield Rd 613-825-7773

Bells Corners Chiropractic Office
Burman, Dr. Ronald T.
138 Robertson Rd 613-829-3580

Centrepointe Chiropractic
Tullock, Dr. Mark
100 Centrepointe Dr 613-723-5000

Johnston, Dr. Bruce
1435 Woodroffe Ave 613-224-8543

Merivale Chiropractic Clinic
Thulien, Dr. Jann
1547 Merivale Rd 613-226-8142

Panetta, Dr. Lino
250-B Greenbank Rd 613-596-0646

NEW DUNDEE

Pigott-Kowalski, Dr. Marilyn
549 Bridge 519-696-2499

NEW HAMBURG

New Hamburg Natural Health Care Center
Kinakin, Dr. Ken
3 Waterloo 519-662-2123

Rhem, Dr. Stuart R.
111 Waterloo 519-662-1885

NEW LISKEARD

Reilly, Dr. James
234 Whitewood 705-647-6120

Riverfront Chiropractic Health Centre
Kramp, Dr. Kelly
51 Murray St 705-647-6363

Timiskaming Chiropractic Health Clinic
Giuliano, Dr. Dominic
221 Whitewood 705-647-7333

NEWCASTLE

Newcastle Chiropractic Centre
Baarbe, Dr. Johannes
29 King W 905-987-4600

NEWMARKET

Anderson, Dr. David
531 Davis Dr 905-853-0755

Leslie Davis Chiropractic Centre
Ramsay, Dr. Kelly; Wright, Dr. Dean
1065 Davis Dr 905-853-4900

Mulock Chiropractic
Dies-Keys, Dr. June G.
140 Mulock Dr 905-853-9685

Newmarket Chiropractic Clinic
Hunt, Dr. Edwin J.
31 Lundys Ln 905-898-1230

Ruegg Chiropractic Clinic
Delgrande, Dr. Anne
109 Mains 905-895-1299

Sieber, Dr. Brian I.
18025 Yonge 905-836-4200

Stewart Chiropractic Health Centre
Stewart, Dr. Murray J.
17817 Leslie 905-853-3603

Timothy Street Chiropractic
Sleeth, Dr. Pamela
543 Timothy 905-836-4325

NIAGARA FALLS

Cabin Chiropractic Clinic
Orr, Dr. R.C.
4735 Ontario Ave 905-356-8674

Ciolfi, Dr. Michael
4300 Drummond 905-374-0981

Elliott Chiropractic Centre
Scappaticci, Dr. M.
5816 Main St ..905-356-4484/227-5606

Giallonardo Chiropractic Center
Giallonardo, Dr. A.
7116 McLeod 905-357-9755

Graham Chiropractic Clinic
Graham, Dr. Donald
6246 Glengate St 905-357-4144/356-9107

McKinley-Molodynia, Dr. Joanne
4750 Valley Way 905-357-2060

Newman, Dr. Charles E.
4079 Drummond 905-354-1431

Niagara Chiropractic (Health) Centre
Wetherup, Dr. D.J.
4444 Drummond 905-356-3989

Niagara Falls Chiropractic Clinic
Vaccaro, Dr. Nick
3950 Portage Rd 905-357-5566

Pihack, Dr. Brian George
4245 Portage 905-356-1212

NIAGARA-ON-THE-LAKE

Haigh, Dr. N.J.
519 Mississauga 905-468-2442

NOBLETON

Jones, Dr. Christopher
12510 Hwy 27 905-859-4417

NORTH BAY

Body Back In Motion
Bowness, Dr. N. Anne; Nori, Dr. Susan
400 Main W 705-840-2502

Cassells Chiropractic Centre
Swain, Dr. Mark; Wolfe, Dr. Bryan
1138 Cassells 705-840-2360/2255

Lakeshore Chiropractic Centre
Yeates, Dr. Noreen
108 Lakeshore Dr 705-476-1122

Laycock, Dr. P.A.
124 Main E 705-472-1890

Mackenzie, Dr. David W.
348 McIntyre W 705-474-4454

Macleod Chiropractic Centre
McLeod, Dr. M.E.
91 Charnplain 705-495-1168

Nipissing Chiropractic Clinic
Paju, Dr. L.T.; Tetrault, Dr. E.R.
240 W 1st Ave 705-476-1978/2700

O'Connor Chiropractic Centre
O'Connor, Dr. Greg
391 E Main St 705-476-4335

Total Health Centre
Shepherd, Dr. Kristin
91 Champlain ..705-476-7366/494-9421

Turner Wellness & Learning Interference Centre
Turner, Dr. Roger L.
128 Mcintyre St W 705-497-9355

NORTH GOWER

Hunter, David
6387 Third Line Rd S 613-489-2678

NORVAL

Butwell, Dr. Garry
518 Guelph 905-877-9159

OAKVILLE

Arishenkoff, Dr. Michele; Macdougall, Dr. Lloyd
145 Trafalgar 905-338-1548

Bronte Chiropractic Office
Allman, Dr. Joyce
2368 W Lakeshore Rd 905-827-1633

Chiropractic Health And Wellness Care Centre
Grolmus, Dr. R.
2169 Sixth Line 905-338-5558

Halton Chiropractic Clinic
Laughlin, Dr. L.; Stackhouse, Dr. Wm.
250 Wyecroft ...905-844-9117/825-1011

Hassard Chiropractic Clinic
Hassard, Dr. M.R.
2361 W Lakeshore Rd 905-847-2225

Maple Grove Chiropractic Clinic
Wilson, Dr. James; Zak, Dr. Patrick
511 Maple Grove Dr 905-338-3732

McPhail Chiropractic Centre
McAlister, Dr. Ron; McPhail, Dr. Murray
1500 Heritage Way 905-825-1992

Moore Chiropractic Centre
Meyer, Dr. Dianne; Moore, Dr. Brett; Moore, Dr. Donald
220 Randall 905-845-4541/842-5560

Nottinghill Place Chiropractic
Simpson, Dr. H.S.
1131 Nottinghill Gate 905-827-4197

Oakville Chiropractic Centre
Fenn, Dr. Richard; Roper, Dr. Arnold
145 Dunn 905-845-2291

Oakwest Chiropractic Clinic
Hammond, Dr. Donald J.
635-4th Line 905-845-9777

Shaw Chiropractic Pain Relief & Wellness Centre
Shaw, Dr. Greg
586 Argus 905-842-5489

ORANGEVILLE

Crawford, Dr. John P.
39 First 519-942-0084

Ferguson, Dr. Brian R.
26 First 519-941-1570

Kennedy, Dr. J. Gary
1-3rd Ave 519-941-1986

Somerville Chiropractic Clinic
Somerville, Dr. Keith
2-279 Broadway 519-942-1810

Sudden Comfort
Gaw, Dr. Thomas E.A.
26 Fead St 519-941-2311

ORILLIA

Albert St Chiropractic Clinic
Munro, Dr. Donald
36 Albert N 705-326-7458

Bell Chiropractic Clinic
Bell, Dr. Lawrence; Nichols, Dr. Jim
390 Laclie St 705-326-2200

Corriveau, Dr. P.J.
63 Matchedash N 705-325-2086

Family Chiropractic Centre
Rosen, Dr. Glenda
137 Colborne W 705-325-2225

Ingard, Dr. R. Anton
West N 705-325-7311

Mississaga Street Chiropractic Clinic
Sinclair, Dr. Susan; Lafrance, Dr. Lawrence
138 W Mississaga 705-325-5152

Wainman Chiropractic Centre
Wainman, Dr. Greg
233 West N 705-325-3168

ORLEANS

Centrum Chiropractic Clinic
De Haas, Dr. Kenneth; Bruneau, Dr. Evelyne
210 Centrum Blvd 613-830-4080

Family Chiropractic & Health Centre
Banks, Dr. Brad
3025 St. Joseph Bl 613-837-7463

Orleans Chiropractic Clinic
Chagnon, Dr. Jean; Lalonde, Dr. Nicole
2543 St. Joseph Blvd 613-824-1988

OSHAWA

Advantage Chiropractic
Simpson, Dr. David
631 Montrave 905-404-2688

Brownlee, Dr. Lee D.
86 Park S 905-723-7443

Dormon Chiropractic Clinic
Dormon, Dr. Thomas M.
1400 Ritson N 905-436-7277

Down, Dr. Larry; Koss, Dr. Ted
356 Simcoe S 905-725-4331

Kniznik, Dr. Zev
18 Gibbons 905-728-5512

Krantz, Dr. Leo L.
47 Prince 905-723-2634

Martin, Dr. Chiropractic Clinic
Martin, Dr. Greg; Martin, Dr. Scott
204-247 Simcoe N 905-725-4020

McAllister, Dr. Kevin I.
17 Ontario 905-433-4131

Northern Chiropractic Centre
Smith, Dr. Phil; Richter, Dr. Marty
4-133 Taunton W 905-436-6666

Shlapak, Dr. Sally P.
702 King W 905-723-7573

Simcoe Chiropractic Centre
Lysyk, Dr. Antony G.
848 Simcoe S 905-436-7255

OTTAWA

Alta Vista Chiropractic Clinic
Laquerre, Dr. Jacques; Spratt, Dr. Patricia
1690 Bank St 613-731-5775

**Andrews, Dr. Ginger; Degruchy,
Dr. Mark; Payne, Dr. Greg**
164 Metcalfe St . .613-594-2853/567-4156

Back To Health Chiropractic Center
Rodwin, Dr. B.; Schneider, Dr. T.D.
240 Catherine 613-237-3306

Barrigar, Dr. Matthew
304-168 Charlotte 613-789-0140

Bayfield, Dr. D.G.
180 Metcalfe St 613-594-3117

Beaton, Dr. Michael L.
2-1889 Baseline Rd 613-224-8582

Bedard Chiropractic Clinic
Bedard, Dr. J.
415 Mcarthur Ave 613-746-5467

Britannia Chiropractic Clinic
Dick, Dr. Ken; Reid, Dr. Michael
S 11-1315 Richmond Rd 613-726-8830

**Carling Chiropractic & Sports
Injury Clinic**
Emmett, Dr. James; Henderson, Dr. John;
Mallory, Dr. Robin; Ripley, Dr. Robert
2565 Carling Ave 613-828-1494

Carson, Dr. W.E.
430 Maclaren St 613-237-1416

Cox, Dr. Gerard P.
36 Monk 613-233-7800

Faloon, Dr. Patrick
480 Somerset W 613-230-3028

Fisher Heights Chiropractic Clinic
Smith, Dr. Duane
780 Baseline Rd 613-723-5555

**Gauthier, Dr. Jean-Francois;
Gauthier, Dr. Jean-Robert**
445 Cumberland 613-241-3434

Glebe Chiropractic Clinic
Brough, Dr. Ken
99 Fifth Ave 613-237-9000

Holistic Chiropractic Clinic
Balon, Dr. J.W.; Norton, Dr. J. Todd
1125 Bank 613-730-8794

Hunt Club Chiropractic Clinic
Chewpa, Dr. Yurij; Geschwandtner, Dr. Marie
1179 Hunt Club Rd 613-739-9474

Keenan Chiropractic Clinic
Keenan, Dr. D.W.; Keenan, Dr. H.W.
303 S Harmer Ave 613-728-9414

**McCooey, Dr. D. Dale;
McCooey, Dr. Nancy**
1755 Carling Ave 613-729-6405

Ottawa Chiropractic Centre
Komesch, Dr. Daniel
200 Metcalfe St 613-234-1333

Ottawa South Chiropractic Clinic
Fortin, Dr. Normand; Gorka, Dr. Suzanne
204-2430 Bank 613-738-1882

**Rothwell Chiropractic & Sports
Injury Clinic**
Henderson, Dr. John C.; Mallory, Dr. Robin
1657 Montreal Rd 613-748-1199

Southbank Chiropractic Centre
Mankal, Dr. Kahlid
1883-B Bank 613-731-3000

Surko, Dr. George J.
430 Maclaren St 613-235-6449

Wellness House
Hall, Dr. John; Jackson, Dr. Eric
148 Richmond Rd 613-722-7799

OWEN SOUND

Georgian Chiropractic Centre
Montgomery, Dr. Lynda; Yurkiw, Dr. Dennis
274-10th St W 519-376-1266

Miller Chiropractic Clinic
1161-2nd Ave E 519-371-5334

Owen Sound Chiropractic Centre
Miller, Dr. Ian; Miller, Dr. W. Murray
898-2nd Ave W 519-376-3700

Smyth, Dr. M.A.
695-2nd Ave E 519-376-6587

Vail-Renfrew Chiropractic Clinic
Renfrew, Dr. Sheila; Vail, Dr. Donald E.
329-10th St W 519-371-1851

PALMERSTON

**Palmerston Chiropractic &
Naturopathic Office**
Hutson, Dr. Wayne; Maclachlan, Dr. D.J.
336 Main W 519-343-2264

PARIS

Dix Chiropractic Office
Dix, Dr. G.
120 Grand River N 519-442-2237

Paris Chiropractic Centre
McCutcheon, Dr. M.W.
36 Mechanic 519-442-7100

PARKHILL

Wagner, Ron L.R.
260 Union 519-294-6946

PARRY SOUND

Buck, Dr. Martin
72 Church 705-746-7655

Michael, Dr. Tom
21 William 705-746-9416

Parry Sound Chiropractic Office
Davidson, Dr. Alan
By Appointment 705-746-2901

PEFFERLAW

Family Health Centre of Pefferlaw
Bebbington, Dr. Robert
By Appointment 705-437-2057

PELHAM

Bosilac, Dr. Mark A.
10 Hwy 20 E 905-892-3003

PEMBROKE

Ewart, Dr. John H.C.
377 Nelson 613-732-8512

PENETANGUISHINE

Dowling, Dr. Vic
36 Robert St E 705-549-3200

PERTH

Chiropractic Care Center
Wickens, Dr. Kathy
55 North 613-264-0616

PETERBOROUGH

**Cruikshank, Dr. Ian; Penner, Dr.
Tammay**
1113 Clonsilla 705-743-1587

Drysdale, Dr. Heather
340 Charlotte 705-740-9693

Humphrey, Dr. Peter G.
181 Simcoe 705-741-6171

Kawartha Chiropractic Centre
Kinsey, Dr. Barry
Brookdale Plaza 705-743-1223

**Lustig, Dr. Jeffrey; Thomson, Dr.
Keith**
403 Mcdonnel 705-743-5121/1661

Peterborough Chiropractic Group
Balson, Dr. Chris; Leeson, Dr. James;
Rae, Dr. James M.; Slobodian, Dr. Daniel;
Smith, Dr. Lawrence
166 Mcdonnel 705-748-6611

Westside Chiropractic Clinic
Denis, Dr. Helene; Storey, Dr. Mike
1840 Lansdowne W 705-741-2225

Zurawel Chiropractic Office
Zurawel, Dr. D.
885 Clonsilla Ave 705-743-8555

PETROLIA

Lambton Chiropractic Centre
Storozuk, Dr. K.
4108 Petrolia 519-882-1880

PICKERING

Amberlea Chiropractic Clinic
Isaacs, Dr. T.E.; Tibbles, Dr. A.C.
1885 Glenanna 905-831-3939

**Bay Ridges-Pickering Chiropractic
Clinic**
Sasse, Dr. R.; Thackeray, Dr. C.
1420 Bayly 905-839-4723

Brock Bayly Chiropractic Clinic
Kleinberg, Dr. Ira
1016 Brock 905-831-4444

Cornerstone Chiropractor
Town, Dr. Ian
924 Kingston Rd 905-831-3578

PICTON

Floros, Dr. Ruth
16 Centre 613-476-6223

Smith, Dr. G.W.
49 Mary 613-476-6800

Williams, Dr. William L.
42 Main 613-476-3644

POINT EDWARD

Clubb, Dr. Johnny
704 Mara 519-332-1847

PORT COLBORNE

**Chiropractic Associates of Port
Colborne**
Salanki, Dr. David G.
258 Killaly W 905-835-1303

PORT ELGIN

**Hartwell Chiropractic Family Care
Clinic**
Hartwell, Dr. Gary
578 Goderich 519-832-2225

Port Elgin Chiropractic Clinic
Fryday, Dr. Douglas
544 Goderich St 519-832-9088

PORT HOPE

McIntosh, Dr. A.J.
40 Martha 905-885-4282

Northumberland Chiropractic Care
Whale, Dr. Robin
249 Ontario 905-885-7460

Port Hope Chiropractic
Carmichael, Dr. C.M.
3 Dorest E 905-885-5111

PORT PERRY

Bathie, Dr. Reva; Peel, Dr. Helen
186 Casimir 905-985-3702

PORT ROWAN

Port Rowan Chiropractic Office
Rodger, Dr. R. Bruce
6 Erie 519-586-3529

PORT STANLEY

Port Stanley Chiropractic Centre
Handford, Dr. Gerald
285 Bridge 519-782-4771

PRESCOTT

Fort Town Chiropractic
King, Dr. Steven
303 King W 613-925-0653

Prescott Chiropractic Centre
Shankar, Dr. Gauri
114 W King 613-925-3436

RENFREW

Fletcher, Dr. R.J.
313 Raglan S 613-432-5041

RICHMOND

Lindsay, Dr. Donald A.
6212 Perth 613-838-3160

RICHMOND HILL

All About Health
Tenenbaum, Dr. Stanley B.
9325 Yonge 905-884-0666

Doctors Office, The
Nusbaum, Dr. Ron
9625 Yonge St 905-508-4114

Horowitz, Dr. Allan; Levy, Dr. Sandra
9640 Bayview Ave 905-737-9090

Makos, Dr. B.K.; Viscomi, Dr. S.V.
10039 Yonge 905-737-2333

New Directions In Health
Meschino, Dr. Paul J.
9955 Yonge St 905-737-0810

Silver, Dr. Eve
420 E Hwy 7 Hwy 905-889-8865

Snider, Dr. Judith
11 Headdon Gate 905-770-5131

Wasser, Dr. Howard
10815 Bathurst 905-737-7463

Wiltshire Chiropractic Clinic
Wiltshire, Dr. Les
139 O'Connor Cr 905-883-0106

Yonge-Elgin Chiropractic Centre
Bornstein, Dr. Richard
57 W Elgin Mills Rd 905-883-5900

RIDGETOWN

Kay, Dr. Scott
15 Youke 519-674-2081

ROCKLAND

Chiropractic Clinic of Rockland
Dance, Dr. Barbara; Vandervoot, Dr. Dan
661 Laviolette 613-446-4088

ST. CATHARINES

Chiropractic Emergency Service
Diakow, Dr. P.; Leprich, Dr. D.
By Appointment .905-682-8484/685-6571

Court Street Chiropractors
Diakow, Dr. P.R.P.
10 Court 905-682-8484

Drynan, Dr. Tracy
3 Geneva St 905-641-3000

Fast, Dr. Ronald
33 Lakeshore 905-935-1400

Glendale Chiropractic Clinic
Ottaviano, Dr. T.
290 Glendale Ave 905-227-4411

Grantham Chiropractic
Fiorucci, Dr. Gino
408 Niagara 905-646-2631

Haig, Dr. Robert D.
236 Glenridge 905-688-4949

Lake Street Chiropractic Centre
Cowherd, Dr. Geron P.
116 Lake 905-641-0400

Langdon Chiropractic Clinic
Langdon, Dr. S.
260 Lakeshore Rd 905-646-2722

Ley Chiropractic Offices
327 Scott St 905-937-5042

Loon Chiropractic Centre
Knof, Dr. Jens E.
310 Lake 905-646-5101/2888

Luck Chiropractic Clinic
Luck, Dr. L.
140 Church St 905-687-4181

Midtown Chiropractic
Devries, Dr. William P.
83 Welland 905-684-1104

Mizel Chiropractic Clinic
320 Vine 905-934-7776

Nazar, Dr. G.P.
123 Niagara 905-688-5150

Orvitz, Dr. Edan
278 Bunting 905-684-2225

Queenston-Hartzel Chiropractic Clinic
Roberts, Dr. Thomas E.
345 Queenston 905-685-0733

Reinhart, Robert W.
101 Lakeport 905-646-3232

Scales, Dr. Albert M.
126 Lakeshore 905-935-3355

Welland Avenue Chiropractic
Leprich, Dr. David J.
278 Welland 905-685-6571

Westlake Square Chiropractic Centre
Nagel, Dr. Michael; Torigian, Dr. Michael
353 Lake St 905-934-4357

ST. GEORGE

Stubal, Dr. Rodney
By Appointment 519-448-4418

ST. MARY'S

Berry, Dr. Donald
RR #1 519-229-8227

Omel, Dr. Richard
158 Queen E 519-284-4200

ST. THOMAS

Noad Chiropractic Clinic
Noad, Dr. D.
42 Churchill Cr 519-633-6623

Perry, Dr. Steven; Pooley, Dr. Douglas
18 Metcalfe 519-633-1444

St. Thomas Chiropractic Clinic
Murray, Dr. James
2 Princess Ave 519-633-2840

Steele, Dr. E.T.
24 Hincks 519-631-2283

SARNIA

Brad, Dr. J.A.
325 Wellington 519-337-2221

Butler, Dr. E.B.
217 George 519-344-6671

Hare Chiropractic Centre
Hare, Dr. G.G.
859 Exmouth 519-332-4222

Harper, Dr. Jeff
500 Christina N 519-344-8258

Matheson Chiropractic Clinic
Matheson, Dr. D.
230 N Vidal St 519-332-8133

Matheson, Dr. Kevin
307 Wellington 519-383-6655

Schwab, Dr. Stephen T.
112 Russell N 519-344-2642

Vargo, Dr. John W.
500 Christina St N 519-344-5665

SAULT STE. MARIE

Campana, Dr. E.N.; Campana, Dr. K.A.; Campana, Dr. R.D.
525 Wellington E 705-256-8112

Dipasquo Chiropractic Clinic
202-212 Queen E 705-253-0253

Great Northern Chiropratic
Pszeniczny, Dr. Marty
143 Great Northern Rd ...705-945-0555

Jarrett, Dr. Lorne E.
15 Great Northern Rd 705-759-2303

Levy, Dr. David J.
Mn Flr, 402 Albert E 705-946-3043

Love, Dr. Dean
15-123 March 705-942-1882

Luck Chiropractic Clinic
343 Trunk Rd 705-256-1909

Maclean, Dr. Todd
391 Pim 705-759-1353

Mazzuca, Dr. Dino
275 Second Line W 705-256-2225

Myers, Dr. Rodney L.
153 Great Northern Rd ...705-759-1075

Nenonen, Dr. Michael
373 Mcnabb 705-759-5941

Orosy, Dr. S.G.
1729 Queen St E 705-945-7005

Simpson, Dr. Ann Liz
27 Great Northern Rd 705-759-3944

West, Dr. Stephen E.
66 March 705-254-4831

Yates, Dr. R. Glenn
27 Great Northern Rd 705-946-2947

SEAFORTH

Devereaux, Dr. T.J.
77 Main S 519-527-1242

SHELBURNE

Weinper, Dr. Robert A.
215-1 Ave E 519-925-3400

SIMCOE

Brunarski Chiropractic Office
354 Norfolk N 519-426-8656

Downtown Chiropractic
Kinsinger, Dr. Stuart F.
1-111 N Colborne St 519-426-0944

Santo, Dr. Margaret
101 Union 519-426-0190

Simcoe Chiropractic Centre
Beck, Dr. R.W.
228 John 519-426-7272

Veltri Chiropractic Clinic
191 W Queensway St 519-426-7300

SMITH'S FALLS

Chiropractic Health Centre
Hagan, Dr. W.J.
RR #3 613-283-7085

Farrell Chiropractic Centre
34 James St 613-283-3369

Smiths Fall's Chiropractic Centre
Collis, Dr. Dennis
22 William W 613-283-4100

SOUTH PORCUPINE

Jarvensivu, Dr. Richard
103 Bruce 705-235-3386

SOUTHAMPTON

Huron-Bruce Chiropractic Health Centre
Goertzen, Dr. R.
290 Rankin 519-797-3238

Southampton Chiropractic Clinic
Campbell, Dr. Patricia
65 Albert N 519-797-5112

STAYNER

McNabb Chiropractic Centre
McNabb, Dr. J.W.
222-A Gideon 705-428-3409

STITTSVILLE

Stittsville Chiropractic Clinic
Blenkarn, Dr. Steven G.
1339 Main St 613-836-1711

STONEY CREEK

Actin Chiropractic Centre
Ouellette, Dr. Victor J.
181 Millen Rd 905-664-9540

Bodden Daniel
Oswald, Dr. Ronald A.
102 King E 905-662-8358

Crowther, Dr. Edward R.
19 King W 905-664-2125

East Stoney Creek Chiropractic
Rocci, Dr. Claudio; Rocci, Dr. Paul
360 Hwy 8 905-662-5604

Frisina, Dr. Angelo A.
181 Hwy 8 905-664-1660

Paramount Family Chiropractic
Jeffrey, Dr. Mary Anne; Morris, Dr. Jerry
1050 Paramount Dr 905-573-6468

Ramelli, Dr. Frank D.
38 King W 905-664-2225

Stoney Creek Chiropractic Clinic
Boynton, Dr. David; Till, Dr. Roy
70 King E 905-662-1637

Watson, Dr. William A.
23 Lake Av Dr 905-662-5511

STOUFFVILLE

Stouffville Chiropractic
Turner, Dr. Allen R.
6219 Main St 905-640-4440

Stouffville Chiropractic Center
Croft, Dr. Brian B.
6096 Main St 905-640-3562

STRATFORD

Chiropractic Centre
Reed, Dr. W. Peter
162 Huron St 519-271-7721

Chiropractic Health Centre
Carey, Dr. Paul F.
89 Waterloo S 519-273-0500

Huggins Chiropractic
296 Ontario 519-273-4404

Malott, Dr. W.L.
40 Delamere 519-271-2562

Vail, Dr. Norman W.
227 Erie 519-271-9951

Walden, Dr. Tom
155 Erie St 519-271-5511

STRATHROY

Roder Chiropractic Office
301 Caradoc S 519-245-1272

Thyret, Dr. John M.
117 Thomas 519-245-2580

STROUD

Stroud Chiropractic Clinic
Hull, Dr. James D.
217 Yonge N 705-436-5361

STURGEON FALLS

Nipissing Chiropractic Clinic
Paju, Dr. L.T.
202 E Main St 705-753-3100

SUDBURY

Adams, Dr. James D.
43 Elm St 705-675-8450

Cedar Chiropractic Centre
Brosseau, Dr. Michel
205-124 Cedar St 705-673-0493

Colwell Chiropractic Clinic
Colwell, C.G.
767 Barrydowne Rd 705-566-0723

Dumencu, Dr. Alan P.
1893 Regent S 705-522-7780

Fantin, Dr. J.V.
1708 Lasalle 705-560-4090

Fera, Dr. Robert
208 Loachs Rd 705-522-7678

Kahkonen, Dr. Sonja
195 Pine St 705-673-7367

Lockerby Chiropractic Clinic
Veitch, Dr. J.T.
1503 Paris St 705-522-2136

Michlowski, Dr. Clark
586 Lasalle Blvd 705-566-0205

Staffen, Dr. Michael
586 Lasalle Blvd 705-525-5655

SUNDERLAND

Sunderland Chiropractic Centre
Schlag, Dr. P.H.
26 Church 705-357-3139

SUNDRIDGE

Kreps Chiropractic Centres
161 Main E 705-384-7123

SUTTON

Sutton West Chiropractic Clinic
Beleutz, Dr. Jeff
By Appointment 905-722-6704

SYDENHAM

Sydenham Chiropractic Clinic
Berry, Dr. D.; Tucker, Dr. T.A.
By Appointment 613-376-3439

TECUMSEH

Community Chiropractic Centre
Anderi, Dr. Susanne; West, Dr. Neil
11811 E Tecumseh
Rd 519-735-7555/1939

Nantais Chiropractic
U3-1614 Lesperance 519-979-2273

THAMESVILLE

McDiarmid, Dr. G.
14 Victoria 519-692-3337

THORNHILL

Bennett, Dr. Joanne
7330 Yonge 905-881-6922

Bornstein, Dr. Ronald; Grossman, Dr. Mark
180 Steeles W 905-886-0116

Gotlib, Dr. Allan C.
288 Greenln 905-889-6415

Ho, Dr. David
8185 Yonge 905-889-5297

Laufer Chiropractic Clinic
Laufer, Dr. Linda
150 E Steeles Ave 905-731-7075

Laufer, Dr. Stephen
#504-800 Bathurst St 416-535-2211

Leesai Chiropractic Centre
Lee, Dr. Joseph
209-2900 Steeles E 905-881-8991

Rennicks, Dr. J.D.
218 Steeles E 905-889-3781

Schiable, Dr. Imke
420 E Hwy 7 905-889-8865

Zuck, Dr. Elaine
78 Binscarth Cr 905-881-3722

THOROLD

Pelino, Dr. Joseph
3350 Merrittville Hwy 905-682-0999

Thorold Chiropractic Centre
Szczurko, Dr. Bob
35 Albert W 905-227-5751

THUNDER BAY

Algoma St Chiropractic Clinic
McCallum, Dr. William M.
153 Algoma St S 807-345-6680

Brimmell, Dr. Stuart
Petrus, Dr. H.D.
562 Red River Rd 807-345-6700

City North Chiropractic
Holmes, Dr. J. Andrew; Smith, Dr. Allen
565 Red River Rd 807-344-7568

Gleeson Clinic Of Chiropractic
Gleeson, Dr. Dana; Gleeson, Dr. Daniel;
Klymenko, Dr. Lisa
1304 Victoria Ave E 807-623-5531

Gleeson, Dr. Rodman L.
777 Red River Rd 807-767-4423

Grandview Chiropractic Clinic
Bryan, Dr. Charles; Robson, Dr. Richard
Grandview Mall,640 River St 807-345-1351

Jessiman Chiropractic Clinic
2813 Arthur St E 807-623-6500

Dr. Patrick Manduca Chiropractor Clinic
Manduca, Dr. Patrick
220 Archibald St N 807-623-4237

Natural Health & Healing Centre
Schroeder, Dr. Brian
817 Victoria Ave E 807-622-4325

Northwood Chiropractic Clinic
Gleeson, Dr. Daniel M.
2833 Redwood Ave 807-768-1512

Pustina Chiropractic Centre
RR #12, 1091 Dawson Rd ...807-767-7000

Trevisan, Dr. Robert J.
Mn Fl, 1820 Victoria Ave E .807-623-6118

Westfort Chiropractic Clinic
Macdonald, Dr. Peter; Tester, Dr. George
143-145 Frederica St W 807-475-5339

TIMMINS

Columbus Chiropractic Clinic
Litt, Dr. James O.
87 Pine Sts 705-268-4211/264-9300

Columbus, Dr. M.J.
700 Murray St 705-264-7681

Geddes, Dr. C.C.
255 Algonquin Blvd E 705-268-9711

Lamarche, Dr. Gilles
665 Pine St N 705-268-5082

Martin Chiropractic Clinic
404-690 River Park Rd 705-268-1328

Russell, Dr. D.K.
Suite C-119, Pine S 705-267-5856/
268-8719

TORONTO

A&C Chiropractic Clinic
Liang, Dr. C.R.
6087 Yonge St 416-221-3601

A-T Chiropractic Clinics
Lee, Dr. Henry
2950 Birchmount Rd 416-498-0688

Abbey Lane Chiropractic Office
Robichaud, Dr. R.
91 Rylander 416-283-3666

Academy Chiropractic Clinics
Hardy, Dr. John; Zamick, Dr. Howard
752 Broadview 416-465-8737

Adio Chiropractic Centre
Lebrun, Dr. Pierre; Mak, Dr. Dennis; Malet, Dr. Barry
2 Carlton St 416-598-3433

Adler, Dr. Judy; Bellis, Dr. Shirley
3 Irwin 416-967-0365

Agincourt Chiropractic Association
Fermanian, Dr. Sylvia; Lemasurier, Dr. P.R.
100 Cowdray Ct 416-293-0044

Agincourt Chiropractic Centre
Szaraz, Dr. Zoltan
100 Cowdray Crt 416-291-1235

Albion-Humber Valley Chiropractic Centre
Kroft, Dr. Joseph
2630 Kipling Ave 416-743-5315

Amodeo, Frank
105 Granby St 416-340-1973

Ashfield, Nicholas
#8-717 Bloor St W 416-536-3836

Athabaska Chiropractic Centre
Damecour, Dr. E.
6464 Yonge St 416-221-5575

Athletic Therapy & Chiropractic Clinic
Laws, Dr. James
11 Yorkville Ave 416-961-5400

Augustatos, Dr. C.G.
745 Danforth Ave 416-463-2933

Barnes, Dr. Frederick N.
3293 Lake Shore Bl W 416-251-9327

Barnett, Dr. David
3164 Yonge St 416-484-6161

Barrett, Dr. Bruce
160 Armour 416-633-0600

Bathurst & Eglinton Chiropractic & Shiatsu Centre
Fillion, Dr. Edward
2020 Bathurst 416-783-2333

Bathurst Chiropractic Clinic
Pisarek, Dr, Irving S.
4430 Bathurst 416-633-3000

Bathurst-Steeles Chiropractic Centre
Frydman, Dr. Larry; Taca-Silbermann, Dr. Ester
6257 Bathurst St 416-222-7900

Bathurst-Wilson Chiropractic Clinic
Shane, Dr. Edward H.
333 Wilson Ave 416-633-3144

Bay-Wellesley Chiropractic Clinic
Rice, Dr. Michael
22 Wellesley W 416-920-2722

Beaches Chiropractic Centre
Robazza, Dr. Kelly
2212 Queen E 416-698-5861

Beaches Wellness Centre
Gable, Dr. Helen
2276 Queen E 416-698-7070

Begley, Dr. Meaghan K.
483 Renforth Dr 416-621-8119

Bekeschus, Dr. Jenny M.
123 Edward 416-979-3022

Bellamy North Chiropractic Centre
Innes, Dr. Keith
1920 Ellesmere 416-439-9542

Ben-Israel, Dr.Yaacov
145 Strathearn Rd 416-638-6265

Birchmount Chiropractic
Locke, Charlton
Birchmount Rd 416-694-9688

Bjarnason, John
1906 E Queen St 416-694-2868

Bloom, Dr. Darryl
4716 Jane 416-661-0004

Bloor-Dundas Chiropractic Clinic
Munk, Dr. Peter
1552 W Bloor St 416-533-0005

Bloor-High Park Chiropractic Clinic
Byskosz, Dr. Irena
2100 Bloor W 416-767-3593

Boggio, Dr. Glenn
5740 Yonge St 416-222-0598

Bovay, Dr. Sherilynn D.
468 Queen St E, 5th Fl 416-861-1173

Borden Chiropractic Clinic
Chiu, Dr. Kwong; Simonsen, Dr. Inger
10 Borden St 416-961-5571

Broadview-Danforth Chiropractic Clinic
Waalen, Dr. David P.
741 Broadview Ave 416-469-2411

Broadview-Pottery Health Clinic
Lee, Dr. Henry
1042 Broadview Ave 416-467-1969

Broadway Chiropractic Clinic
Cott, Dr. Jerry
2357 Yonge St 416-489-2357

Brown, Dr. D.M.
2191 Victorzia Park 416-447-9001

Brown's Chiropractic Office
Brown, Dr. Suzanne L.
2161 Yonge 416-322-3619

Bulman, Dr. R.J.
414 Sutherland Dr 416-425-6551

Cabbagetown Chiropractic Health Centre
Berinati, Dr. William; Bluck, Dr. Cathie
214 Carlton 416-922-3020

Campese, Dr. M.
1743 W Lawrence Ave 416-247-1314

Canadian Memorial Chiropractic College
- Herbert K. Lee Outpatient Clinic
1900 Bayview Ave 416-482-2340

Cannon, Dr. Robert; Erwin, Dr. Mark; Grisdale, Dr. Robert
400-1407 Yonge 416-924-0777

Carlton Chiropractic Centre
Nelson, Dr. Brian J.; Dilawri, Dr. Nitin
120 Carlton St 416-964-1318

Castor Chiropractic Centre
Dadoun, Dr. G
174 Browns Line 416-251-4448

Cedar Heights Chiropractic Clinic
Gammie, Dr. Jill D.
695 Markham Rd 416-439-2001

Central Chiropractic Clinic
McLachlan, Dr. David T.
2200 Yonge 416-481-4184

Central Queensway Chiropractic
Cotoia, Dr. Alfonso
773-N The Queens Way 416-252-7111

Chambul Chiropractic Group
Chambul, Dr. Borys M.
2300 Yonge 416-322-7155

Chan, Dr. Julie
2873 St Clair Ave E 416-755-3220

Charlton, Dr. Paul D.; Hardy, Dr. John A.
206-1719 E Lawrence Ave .416-752-5390

Chiaravalloti, Dr. George
2978 Islington 416-745-1081

Chiropractic Acute Emergency Services 416-222-7900

Chiropractic at Keele Medical Clinic
Kobrossi, Dr. Toffy
2830 Keele St 416-635-6028

Chiropractic Emergency Services
Keshavjee, Dr. Ameen
5 Fairview Mall Dr 416-497-2358

Chiropractic Wellness Centre
Mere, Dr. Andrew
223 Sheppard Ave W 416-223-1433

Ciulini, Dr.Francesco
1848 Bloor St W 416-769-2259

Cliffcrest Chiropractic Centre
Kinnersly, Dr. Jeffrey; Schlag, Dr. Peter
3013 Kingston Rd 416-269-5249

Corbo, Dr. Sebastien
714-1280 Finch W 416-661-7850

Cumberland Chiropractic Office
Tchoryk, Dr. Roman
50 Cumberland 416-926-0258

Dales, Dr. Shannon; Fitz-Ritson, Donovan
#605-99 Avenue Rd 416-968-0484

Danforth-Greenwood Chiropractic Centre
Lacaria, Dr. B.
1154 Danforth Ave 416-462-0235

Danwood Chiropractic Clinic
Truelove, Dr. Paul
1985-A Danforth Ave 416-694-4100

D'Arcy, Dr. Janet
1986 Queen E 416-690-6257

Davisville-Yonge Chiropractic Clinic
Reux, Dr. Marcel; Ricciardi, Dr. Vincent; Russell, Dr. Marg
1849 Yonge St 416-481-6100

Deer Park Chiropractic Clinic
Huska, Dr. Oksana; Wons, Dr. Peter
6 Alcorn 416-960-3400

Dembe, Dr. Elaine
200 St Clair W 416-960-5353

Detzler, Dr.Dale
101 Southvale Dr 416-423-8399

Dippolito, Dr. Joseph
328 Kingston Rd 416-698-4699

Don Mills Chiropractic Office
Gleeson, Dr. Gary M.
1090 Don Mills Rd 416-445-2079

Don Mills-Lawrence Chiropractic Therapy Clinic
Azzopardi, Dr. Dawn; Mallan, Dr. Joseph
1262 Don Mills Rd 416-444-0944

Douglas, Dr. Robin
5353 Dundas W 416-231-5656

Downsview Chiropractic
Brickman, Dr. Michael
552 W Sheppard Ave 416-635-1818

Downtown Chiropractic Centre
Robinson, Paul W.
84 Adelaide 416-364-2072

Doyle, Dr. William, A.
35 Halford 416-769-9341

Dundas Chiropractic Office
Kunashko, Dr. D.N.
#203-3416 Dundas W 416-767-2225

Dundas-Dufferin Chiropractic Clinic
Moreira, Dr. Michael; Rodrigues, Dr. Manuel
1458 W Dundas St 416-536-5700

Dundas-Spadina Chiropractic Centre
Wong, Dr. Jackson
283 Spadina Ave 416-593-0425

Dundas-University Chiropractic Clinic
Graham, Dr. Patrick; McBean, Dr. Scott
438 University 416-598-4999

Dunk, Dr. Kenneth R.
1042 Coxwell Ave 416-423-5996

East Side Chiropractic & Wellness Centre
Janelle, Dr. Lise
880 Broadview 416-463-6363

Eastview Chiropractic Clinic
Kang, Dr. Stephen; Li, Dr. Samson
10 Milner Business Crt 416-292-8200

Eglinton-Bellamy Chiropractic
Jones, Dr. Robert; Schut, Dr. Brian
358 Trudelle St 416-439-6166

Eglinton-Birchmount Chiropractic-Medical Office
Rivietz, Dr. Zechariah
2296 Eglinton E 416-755-9258

Eglinton Chiropractic Clinic
Slater, Dr. Joy
2221 Yonge St 416-488-3660

Elenbaas, Dr. J.
3269-A Bloor W 416-231-5327

Ellesmere Chiropractic Centre
Hardman, Dr. Leonard A.
54 Saratoga Dr 416-438-9777

Enersis-Forest Hill Centre
Rice, Dr. Michael R.
1218 Eglinton W 416-785-5433

Fera, Dr. Mark
#1109-200 Elm St 416-603-9009

First Chiropractic Care Centre
Perry, Dr. Ernest
700 Lawrence Ave W 416-787-1127

First Chiropractic Care Centres - East Beaches
Sheppard, Dr. Donald
848 Kingston Rd 416-699-6333

Franko, Dr. M.A.
316 Dupont 416-961-3069

Fruitman, Dr. B
#218-3089 Bathurst 416-789-7059

Gaibisels, Dr. Peter J
7 Indian Grove 416-766-7188

Garbutt, Dr. Mark T
2277 Queen E 416-691-2289

Gayah, Dr. Gerald F.
567 Bathurst St 416-964-8572

Gitelman, Dr. R.
1 Valentine Dr 416-447-7600

Glen Park Chiropractic Clinic
Fisher, Dr. Howard
103 Shelborne 416-785-1211

Gold, Dr. Paul
4800 Leslie 416-492-0012

Greco, Dr. Richard
660 Eglinton Ave E 416-485-9907

Grittani, Dr. Norman; Grittani, Dr. Paul
1710 Dufferin 416-652-1849

Grod, Dr. Jaroslaw; Steiman, Dr. Igor
#702-130 Bloor St W 416-922-6355

Guerriero Chiropractic Clinic
Guerriero, Dr. Rocco
2040 Sheppard Ave E 416-497-7100

Guildwood Chiropractic Centre
Le Brun, Dr. Pierre
Malet, Dr. Barry
81 Livingston Rd 416-266-7723

Haase, James A.
4235 E Sheppard Ave 416-299-7606

Hardy, Dr. John A
798 Broadview Ave 416-465-8737

Harper, Dr. David
555 Burnhamthorp Rd 416-620-9998

Hartlieb, Dr. James B.
#306-30 Gloucester St 416-966-3245

Harvey, Dr. Kym
#245-3219 Yonge St 416-631-3988

Hayes, Dr. Edward
807 Bloor St 416-588-1855

Hayman, Dr. E.K.
730 Yonge St 416-968-6986

Henriksen, Dr. Niels
365 Bloor E 416-944-3117

Herman, Dr. Leonard
1011 Pape Ave 416-422-2222

Hewitt, Dr. Jina
2175 Danforth Ave 416-698-3060

High Park Chiropractic Clinic
Miekus, Dr. Andrew; Zubkewych, Dr. Morris
2184-D W Bloor St 416-762-7591

Ho, Dr. Mary
301-2347 Kennedy 416-754-2922

Hogg-Kopp, Dr. Joan
82 Marilake Dr 416-298-4433

Horowitz, Dr. Leslie
#215-640 Roselawn Ave 416402-5955

Horseman, Dr. Ian
2150 W Bloor St 416-769-1163

Hudon, Dr. Katherine Y.
#3-88 Madison Ave 416-963-9042

Hui, Dr. John C.
4040 Finch E 416-321-1701

Humber Family Chiropractic Centre
Gryfe, Dr. David
100 Humber College 416-744-7900

Hunter, Dr. Amy
3-B Wendover 416-236-9919

Injeyan, Dr. H. Stephen
2297 Weston 416-247-2361

Injuries Assessment & Rehabilitation Centre
Au, Dr. F.
4631 Steeles E 416-297-0800

Isenberg, Dr. J.
701 Evans Ave 416-695-0702

Islington Chiropractic Clinic
Rosenberg, Dr. Leo; Rosenberg, Dr. Paul
4202 Dundas W 416-231-2487

Islington-Rathburn Chiropractic Clinic
Henderson, Dr. Donald; Henderson, Dr. Maureen
1494 Islington 416-231-9502

Ivey, Dr. David
68 Shaughnessy 416-494-7337

Jethalal, Dr. Gita
3443 Finch E 416-490-9400

Jinnah Chiropractic Care
Jinnah, Dr. Sheleena; Graham, Dr. Patrick
#200-2171 Queen St E 416-690-9777

Johnson, Dr. G.E.
East York Town Centre 416-421-5300

Keele-Densley Chiropractic Centre
Crescenzi, Dr. John
5 Densley 416-614-7011

Keele Finch Chiropractic Centr
Awenus, Dr. G.C.
1315 W Finch Ave 416-636-2300

Kennedy-Sheppard Chiropractic Centre
Blau, Dr. Mark
2235 Kennedy 416-291-0070

Kim, Dr. Peter
#203-726 Bloor St W 416-532-3397

Kinakin, Dr. Ken W.
250 Consumers 416-499-1330

Kingston Rd Chiropractic Centre
Arbour, Dr. Gerard T.
2236 Kingston 416-261-2890

Kipling Chiropractic Group
Ng, Dr. Peter K.
2141 Kipling Ave 416-745-1974

Kulhay Wellness Centre
Kulhay, Dr. Katrina; Proctor, Dr. Karen
#607-2 St Clair W 416-961-1900

Kunkel, Dr. T.H.
1250 Victoria Park 416-757-5620

Kushnir, Dr. Leon
578 St Clair Ave W 416-654-4542

Labelle Chiropractic Clinic
261 Davenport 416-964-1200

Lakeshore Chiropractic Centre
Soloduka, Dr. Steven
2970 W Lake Shore Blvd . . .416-252-3327

Lawrence Chiropractic Clinic
2083 Lawrence Ave W 416-248-4222

Lawrence-Kingston Rd Chiropractic
Lyons, Dr. D.W.S.
4125 Lawrence Ave E 416-284-6800

Lawson, Dr. Gordon E.
22 Bartley Dr 416-288-0666

Leaside Chiropractic Clinic
Douglas, Dr. Lesley
586 E Eglinton Ave 416-487-1942

Leck, Dr. Donald R.
10 Gateway 416-424-1995

Lee, Dr. Sandra
340 College St 416-922-8154

Lee(Life), Dr. Herbert
101 McRae Dr 416-482-2340

Lewis, Dr. Blair J.
65 Front E 416-366-5660

Li, Dr. Samson
192 Dupont St 416-967-1909

Life Chiropractic Health Centre
Butz, Dr. Eric; Pike, Dr. Robert
98 Symington 416-534-7927

Listro Chiropractic Clinic
111 Redpath Ave 416-481-3378

Lockhart Health Clinics
2300 Finch W 416-746-1558

Love, Daria P.
14 Prince Arthur Ave 416-961-0208

Lubberdink, Dr. Ed
Bayview Village
Shopping Centre 416-221-7724

MacGillivray, Charles J.
4986 W Dundas St 416-233-5673

Mahoney Chiropractic Health Clinic
1409 Yonge St 416-967-1234

Malvern Chiropractic Office
Hunter, Dr. Amy; Robichaud, Dr. Rhea; Wiles,
Dr. Michael
1333 Neilson Rd 416-281-0640

Manias, Dr. O.
790 College St 416-536-0934

Maple Leaf Chiropractic Clinic
Campo, Dr. Vincent
1740-A Jane 416-241-2781

Marzec, H.T.
2331 W Dundas St 416-532-1397

McCarthy, Lawrence J.
2428 Islington Ave 416-747-6678

McLean, John F.
2477 W Bloor St 416-767-9245

Memrik, Dr. Edward
475 Dovercourt Rd 416-536-2888

Meschino, Dr. James P.
Stillo Andrew Dr
960 Lawrence Ave W 416-787-1249

Mid-Scarborough Chiropractic Clinic
Liberty, Dr. Michelle
2401 Eglinton E 416-755-7017

Milner Chiropractic & Sports Injury Clinic
Schoales, Dr. Donna; Thomas, Dr. Linda
1530 Markham Rd 416-299-5455

Mimico Chiropractic Center
Ettenson, Dr. A.S.; Jaskot, Dr. John
2362 Lake Shore Blvd W ..416-255-2231

Morito, Dr. Roger
13 Lapsley 416-754-3454

Morton, Dr. David
3187-A Yonge 416-487-9095

Mount Pleasant Chiropractic Clinic
Kuretzky, Dr. M.
542 Mount Pleasant Rd 416-484-1645

Muir Park Chiropractic Offices
Dewolfe, Dr. Susan; Merali, Dr. Shahroze
2926 Yonge St 416-486-6567

Naiman, Dr. J.
3333 Bayview Ave 416-733-4339

Nathanson, Dr. J.A.
344 Bloor W 416-929-4488

North Toronto Chiropractic Clinic
Collis, Dr. Richard S.
151 Eglinton W 416-482-1332

North-West Chiropractic Clinic
Ross, Dr. Marshall
1977 W Finch Ave 416-743-8641

North York Chiropractic Clinic
Varadi, Dr. A.
3383 Bathurst St 416-781-4809

Oakdale Chiropractic Clinic
Ferrari, Dr. Joe; Pulinec, Dr. Andrew
2065 Finch W 416-749-7533

Oolo Chiropractic & Rehab Clinic
3420 Finch E 416-498-9355

Oswald Chiropractic Offices
Bardwell, Dr. Christopher
200 W St Clair 416-972-6279

Overlea Chiropractic Centre
Kennedy, Dr. G.E.; Kennedy, Dr. P.A.
65 Overlea Bl 416-467-5748

Parkway Forest Chiropractic Office
Mannington, Dr. J.; Ross, Dr. J. Kim
103 Parkway Forest Dr 416-756-0178

Parkwood Athletic Injury & Chiropractic Clinic
Rosenberg Ben-Israel, Dr. Judith
300 W St Clair Ave 416-964-2056

Patterson, Dr. Thos.
1835 W Eglinton Ave 416-782-1532

Petelka, Dr. Donn-Ivan; Veiledal, Dr. T.B.
900 Dufferin 416-588-2663

Pharmacy Chiropractic Clinic
Boylan, Dr. J.A.; Campbell, Dr. D.R.; Shatilla,
Dr. K.L.
1857 E Lawrence Ave E ..416-755-6324

Prendergast, Dr. Michael J.
1450 Midland Ave 416-288-9993

Price, Dr. James A.
605 McCowan 416-439-5538

Progress Place Chiropractic Clinic
Salituro, Dr. Peter
885 Progress Ave 416-431-5489

Raffi, Dr. Nader
500 Sheppard Ave E 416-221-7177

The Rehabilitation Clinic (WCB/Insurance Claims)
1900 Bayview Ave 416-480-2820

Rennicks Chiropractic Offices
Rennicks, Dr. J.D.; Rennicks, Dr. John V.
84 Adelaide E 416-364-1040

Rexdale Plaza Chiropractic Centre
Bachir, Dr. Ziad H.
2267 Islington 416-740-1060

Reynolds, Dr. Frederick H.
4190 E Finch Ave 416-298-4847

Robinson, Paul W.
1368 Rometown Dr 416-364-2072

Rosedale Chiropractic Centre
Mesaros, Dr. Luke
421 Bloor E 416-928-1652

Royal Health Care Centre
Greenberg, Dr. Stephen
200 Bay 416-361-6142

Ryan, Dr. D.L.
3107 Bloor W 416-239-2526

Sanders, Dr. G.A.
363 Jane St 416-769-8072

Sarman, Dr. Sheila
103-2560 Gerrard St E ..416-699-0368

Scarborough Chiropractic Clinic
Rissis, Dr. Peter
2931 Lawrence E 416-267-1146

Scarborough Consillium Chiropractic Centre
McCord, Dr. P.
100 Consilium Pl 416-290-5100

Scheer, Dr. Jacob
2100 Finch W 416-739-7766

Shahidi, Dr. F.
501-1110 Sheppard Ave E ..416-250-0289

Shapiro, Dr. Barry P.
27 Belmont 416-923-3030

Shedletzky, Dr. Marvin
578 W St Clair Ave 416-654-4542

Shrubb, Dr. Eric F.
816 Kennedy 416-751-6998

Silverthorn Medical Centre
Salituro, Dr. Peter
1707 W St Clair Ave 416-656-1944

Singh, Dr. Rudy
1646 Victoria Park 416-757-6756

Smolders, Dr. J.
700-208 Bloor W 416-920-3231

Soloduka, Dr. Frederick
1615 Kingston Rd 416-698-4111

Spadina Chiropractic Centre
Lee, Dr. Rick
732 Spadina Ave 416-928-1124

Sport & Injury Rehabilitation
Gushaty, Dr. B.R.
105 Gordon Baker 416-492-6565

Sports Injury And Rehabilitation
Gringmuth, Dr. Robert H.
2780 Jane 416-745-2162

St. Clair Chiropractic Clinic
Kutsukake, Dr. Dennis
1029-A St Clair W 416-653-4273

St. Clair Chiropractic Health Centre
Smith, Dr. Barbara; Ganstal, Dr. Angela
201-15 St Clair Ave W 416-944-1600

Tchoryk, Jerry
201 Lloyd Manor Rd 416-234-5417

Thomson, Dr. D. Verne
3367 W Bloor St 416-239-0403

Tomac, Jasminka A.
2443 W Dundas St 416-534-2494

Toronto Healing Arts Centre
Ashfield, Dr. Nicholas
717 Bloor W 416-535-8777

Toronto Health Centre
Mah, Dr. John F.
93 Harbord 416-961-2225

Toronto Pain & Headache Clinic Chiropractors
Ho, Dr. Michael; Ho, Dr. Paul
9 Bloor St E 416-925-2579

Toronto West Chiropractic Clinic
Posa, Dr. Anthony
1017 Wilson Ave 416-638-2225

Toth, Dr. Leslie Andrew
41 Longhope Pl 416-493-1734

Trull, Dr. Douglas L.
673 Brimorton Dr 416-439-6900

University Chiropractic Center
Budish, Dr. David C.
700 University Ave 416-596-1771

Van Nieuwenhove, Roger
210 Empress Ave 416-221-7717

Vavougios, Dr. Joanne
1473 Danforth Ave 416-463-8372

Victoria Park Chiropractic Centre
Cirone, Dr. Samuel A.
3100 Danforth Ave 416-691-8717

Viggiani, Dr. Donald H.
120 Carlton St 416-960-9388

Village Chiropractic Clinic
Mrozek, Dr. John P.
1646 Victoria Park Ave 416-757-6756

Visalpatara, Dr. Ekchai
1500 Royal York Rd 416-244-3879

Vitko Chiropractic Clinic
Vitko, Dr. Bojan
19 Yorkville 416-960-9355

Warden-Ellesmere Chiropractic Office
Porter, Dr. Janet L.
204 Ellesmere 416-447-3550

West Rouge Chiropractic Centre
Kiely, Dr. Roy C.
102 Conference Blvd 416-282-6750

Weston Chiropractic Centre
Grice, Dr. Adrian; Grice, Dr. Kevin; Grice, Dr.
Leslie
2297 Weston 416-247-0653

Westown Chiropractic Centre
Gillies, Campbell
235 Dixon Rd 416-241-7890

Woburn Chiropractic Clinic
Charlton, Dr. W.
836 Markham Rd 416-439-3710

Yip, Dr. Elaine
74 Lawrence Ave W 416-486-0083

Yonge-Gerrard Chiropractic Physiotherapy Clinic
Russell, Dr. Marg E.
415 Yonge 416-585-2322

Yonge-Sheppard Chiropractic Clinic
Bellis, Dr. Shirley
23 Florence Ave 416-226-4478

Yonge-Steeles Chiropractic Centre
Stevenson, Dr. Gary W.
177 Steeles E 416-225-3987

Yonge-Wellesley Chiropractic & Acupuncture Centre
Bardekjian, Dr. Berj K.
22 Wellesley W 416-920-2722

York Central Chiropractic
Smaye, Dr. S.D.R.
629 W St Clair Ave 416-656-3431

Yorkdale Chiropractic Clinic
Di Biase, Dr. R.S.
Yorkdale Shopping Centre ..416-782-1700

Yorkview Chiropractic Centre
Heaps, Dr. Glen W.
2784 Keele St 416-633-7376

Young, Dr. R. Goddard
4891 Dundas St W 416-231-3911

Your Total Health Centre
Finewax, Dr. Jeff; Guttman, Dr. Allen; Vernon, Dr. Howard
240 Alton Rowers Cir 416-298-1303

Zielonka, Dr. J.
Centerpoint 416-226-9499

Zwarick, Dr. W.E.
636 Scarlett 416-244-4269

Zylich, Dr. S.A.
447 Church 416-925-1868

TOTTENHAM

Guild Chiropractic Clinic
Guild, Dr. Sunyatta
58 Walkem 905-936-6544

Tottenham Chiropractic Centre
Pollock, Dr. R.T.
19-B Queen S 905-936-4257

TRENTON

Clements, Dr. David; Maybin, Dr. Donald
455 Dundas W 613-392-6663/4008

Waunch, Dr. Paul R.
1-7 Metcalfe 613-394-4823

UNIONVILLE

Gillis, Dr. Susan A.
2 Millstone Ct 905-475-8386

Houle, Dr. Normand
1 Hollingham Rd 905-470-0770

West Chiropractic Clinic
West, Dr. James L.
4747 Hwy 7 905-477-5557

UXBRIDGE

Begg Chiropractic Centre
290 Hwy 47 905-852-9700

Chiropractic Centre
Winder, Dr. V.G.
26 Brock E 905-852-7704/6241

VAL CARON

Family Wellness Chiropractic Center
Nelson, Dr. H.B.
3133 Hwy 69 N 705-897-6711

VANIER

Aime, Dr. M.J.
Grd 101-150 Montreal Rd ..613-748-7757

Lindsay, Dr. R.D.
406-261 Montreal Rd 613-749-4647

Vanier Chiropractic Centre
Lemieux, Dr. Roger
397 Montreal Rd 613-745-7766

WALKERTON

Chiropractic Team
Batte, Dr. Ronald
1200 Yonge S 519-881-3441

WALLACE

Currier Chiropractic Clinic
632 Wellington St 519-627-4311

Duke, Dr. Ronald L.
222 Nelson 519-627-5261

WATERLOO

Beechwood Chiropractic Clinic
Higginson, Dr. D.S.; Keil, Dr. C.J.
450 W Erb St 519-888-6030

Bricker, Dr. John B.
35 Union E 519-742-9341

Bridgeport Chiropractic
Fleming, Dr. J.B.; Winchester, Dr. Jeffrey
48 Bridgeport E 519-886-4210

Chiropractic Associates
Mullins, Dr. D. Kenneth; Pamer, Dr. William C.
175-100 Regina S 519-747-1650

Dewit Chiropractic Centre
Moses, Dr. Greg
425 Albert St 519-885-5290

Gall, Dr. T.M.
15 Westmount S 519-885-3210

Hickson, Dr. George S.
228 King S 519-743-5215

Hollingsworth Chiropractic Office
Fancy, Dr. Jane
125 Park St 519-743-5711/576-7930

Martin, Dr. J. Scott
57 Albert 519-886-2570

Moeller, Dr. W. Gunter ; Orchard, Dr. David
366 King N 519-725-1300

Paisley, Dr. Harold
99 Northfield Dr 519-886-3191

Wand, Dr. B.E.
27 University E 519-885-4930

Waterloo North Chiropractic
Heick, Dr. Jennifer
554 Weber N 519-746-3838

WAWA

Sanders, Dr. Norma
1st Flr, 14 Ganley 705-856-7167

WELLAND

Adams, Dr. J.W.
75 Lincoln 905-735-0248

Bovine, Dr. Gary
233 Division 905-735-3098

Marando, Dr. Paul
Lincoln Centre 905-735-4840

Simunic, Dr. J.E.
Welland Plaza 905-735-7100

Sundy & Swick Chiropractic Clinic
140 Thorold Rd 905-732-4464

Taylor Chiropractic Offices
250 Division St 905-734-4515

Zavitz, Dr. Craig D.
340 Thorold Rd 905-735-8422

WHITBY

Carrie, Dr. Colin; Enns, Dr. Rudy; Wysotski, Dr. Peter
1631 Dundas E 905-579-9180/
436-3333

Durham Chiropractic and Rehabilitation Centre
Adams, Dr. Gary L.
420 Crawforth 905-430-0830

Jakym, Dr. Orest J.
304 Brock N 905-666-2322

Karam, Dr. Roger
208-3000 Garden 905-430-1341

McConnell, Dr. Gregory C.
Peacock, Dr. Matthew D.
519 Dundas E 905-430-1750

Rossland Chiropractic Associates
Macaskill, Dr. David C.
701 Rossland E 905-430-6787

Whitby Chiropractic Centre
Knight, Dr. John
117 Byron N 905-668-7153

Whitby Chiropractic Group
Garfinkel, Dr. Louis; Goldhawk, Dr. Mary Ann
420 Green 905-668-2888

WIARTON

Fenwick, Kenneth G.
699 Berford 519-534-1991

Wiarton Family Chiropractic Centre
Silk, Dr. Steven J.
417 Brown 519-534-1330

WINDSOR

Baker, Dr. Wm. Joseph
1716 Mercer 519-977-2225

Bell, Dr. A.J.
3798 Howard 519-966-3074

Bray Chiropractic
3200 Deziel Dr 519-945-9229

Cooper, Dr. G.
458-1720 Howard 519-258-9833

Genesis Health Centre
Gemel, Dr. Erwin
79 E Giles Blvd 519-258-5269

Harrison, Dr. Margaret J.
B-2819 Alexandra 519-969-4414

Hawthorne Chiropractic Centre
Oozeer, Dr. Riaz
6720 Hawthorne Dr 519-974-2211

Hollinger, Dr. Todd
1608 Tecumseh Rd W 519-258-9962

Lauzon Parkway Chiropractic Clinic
Jones, Dr. Douglas; Jones, Dr. Ronald
2825 Lauzon Pkwy 519-948-9022

Ottawa Mall Chiropractic
Crnec, Dr. Madeline
870 Ottawa St 519-977-5928

Oza Chiropractic Clinics
841 Ouellette Ave 519-258-0841

South Windsor Chiropratic Clinic
Miller, Dr. Todd; Miller, Dr. Herbert
1490 W Cabana Rd 519-969-2920

Stover, Dr. Daniel D.
205-7651 E Tecumseh Rd ...519-944-0160

Walkerville Chiropractic
Hammerschmidt, Dr. Katie
1275 Walker 519-258-7979

Walls Chiropractic Centre
1307 Pelissier St 519-258-8881

Wellman, Dr. John C.
6215 Wyandotte St 519-944-6232

Windsor Chiropractic Centre
Kempe, Dr. John; Shwery, Dr. Kenneth
458-1720 Howard 519-258-9833

Wyandotte Chiropractic Centre
Lebenbaum, Dr. J.; Smolen, Dr. Richard
4758 E Wyandotte St 519-948-7434

WINGHAM

Wingham Chiropractic Centre
Anderson, Dr. Stewart
334 Josephine 519-357-1224

WOODBRIDGE

Ariko, Dr. B.
740 Kipling 905-851-3212

Chiropractic Health Care Centre
Brooksbank, Dr. John C.
7845 Kipling 905-851-6848

Duperrouzel, Dr. Paul
450 Jevlan Dr 905-851-0284

Pecora, Dr. Cosma G.
Terenzi, Dr. Mauro
8077 Islington 905-851-6814

Pine Valley & 7 Chiropractic Clinic
Gagliardi, Dr. Maria G.
7700 Pinevalley Dr 905-856-1611

Scott, Dr. R.D. Wayne
5220 Hwy 7 W 905-851-2216

WOODSTOCK

Barnes, Dr. G.
540 Peel St 519-537-6471

Cantelon, Dr. Wm.R.
54 Vansittart Ave 519-537-3922/2182

Krushel, Dr. M.
Meyers, Dr. Donna E.
554 Princess 519-539-7221

✦ Prince Edward Island

Chiropractors are regulated by law, but there is no provincial medicare coverage of chiropractors in P.E.I.

Legislation

Chiropractors are regulated under the *Chiropractic Act*. Under the Act, "chiropractic" means that system of therapeutics based on the science and art of adjusting the articulations or segments of the body, especially those of the spinal column, for the purpose of removing nerve interference, without the use of drugs or surgery.

Chiropractors may not prescribe or administer drugs or perform surgery or give treatment for dislocations or the reduction of fractures. They may not administer physiotherapy except as a secondary adjunctive therapy. Chiropractors may use diagnostic procedures, including laboratory work, and may use the additional therapies of exercise, nutritional supplements, diet, electrotherapy and thermotherapy.

The Act also establishes the governing body (see below) and its purpose of protecting the public from untrained and unqualified practitioners.

Prince Edward Island Governing Body/Professional Body

Prince Edward Island Chiropractic Association
41 Pine Dr
Sherwood, P.E.I. C1A 6R6
Tel: 902-892-6432

This is the governing body for chiropractors in Prince Edward Island. Call to ensure that your chiropractor is registered or to make a complaint.

✦ Prince Edward Island Chiropractors

NOTE: Check the credentials of your chiropractor (see above, "Questions to Ask"). This publication cannot and does not certify or represent the qualifications of practitioners, or the quality of care available from them. We cannot and do not confirm that those listed are registered as required by law.

CHARLOTTETOWN

Belyea, Dr. Roderick
41 Pine Dr 902-892-6432

Sider, Dr. Michael D.
565 N River Rd 902-892-3494

SUMMERSIDE

Adams, Dr. Vincent
266 Read Dr 902-436-7183

✦ Québec

Chiropractors are regulated in Québec, meaning that there is legislation establishing a governing body responsible for registering and disciplining practitioners (see below, "Governing Body"). There is no government health care funding.

Legislation

Chiropractors are regulated under Québec legislation, the *Professional Code*, and the *Chiropractic Act*. Under section 32 of the Code, the title "chiropractor" may be used only by members of the Ordre Professional des Chiropracticiens du Québec.

Under the *Chiropractic Act*, "Every act the object of which is to make corrections of the spinal column, pelvic bones or other joints of the human body, by use of the hands, constitutes the practice of chiropractic" (section 6). Chiropractors may determine by clinical and radiological examination of the spinal column, pelvic bones and other joints of the human body, the chiropractic treatment indicated. However, they may not make radiological examinations unless they hold a radiology permit issued in accordance with the *Professional Code*.

Québec Governing Body

Ordre Professional des Chiropracticiens du Québec
7950, boul Metropolitain est
Ville d'Anjou, Québec H1K 1A1
Tel: 514-355-8540
Fax: 514-355-2290

This is the governing body. Call to ensure that your chiropractor is registered or to file a complaint.

Québec Professional Association

Association des Chiropracticiens du Québec
7960, boul Metropolitain est
Ville d'Anjou, PQ H1K 1A1
Tel: 514-355-0557

This is the professional body for chiropractors in Québec.

✦ Québec Chiropractors

NOTE: Check the credentials of your chiropractor (see above, "Questions to Ask"). This publication cannot and does not certify or represent the qualifications of practitioners, or the quality of care available from them. We cannot and do not confirm that those listed are registered as required by law.

ACTON VALE

Chiro-Clinique
Seyer, Sophie
202-975, Boulay 514-546-3663

ALMA

Centre Chiropratique
660, boul Dequen N 418-668-3021

Centre Chiropratique D'alma
Paille, Dr. Louis
205, rue Collard O 418-662-2422

AMQUI

Clinique Chiropratique
Parent, Dr. Richard
66, St-Benoit 418-629-2606

AMOS

Clinique Chiropratique Amos
Guarnaccia, Dr. Sebastiano
727, av 1e O 819-727-9307

ANGLIERS

Bourbeau, Dr. Robert
204, ch des Rgs 5-6 819-949-2143

ANJOU

Centre Chiro-Sante Gelinas
7077, Beaubien 514-354-2029

Centre Chiropratique Charest
7405, Beaubien 514-351-0428

Chiropratique Sante Plus
7050, Jean Talon 514-351-1716

Marcil, Dr. Raymond
8646, Chaumont 514-493-4314

ARTHABASKA

Grondin, Dr. Yvon
554, boul Bois-Francs S 819-357-8238

ASBESTOS

Clinique Chiropratique Lessard Marcel
Lessard, Dr. Marcel
330, av 1ere 819-879-2626

ASCOT CORNER

Carrefour Chiropratique Ascot Corner
Alarie, Dr. Sylvain
5828, Rte 112 819-564-5011

AUTEUIL

Clinique Chiropratique Renaissance
Dupuy, Dr. Guy
15, rue Boismou 514-625-2511

AYLMER

Amyotte, Dr. Jean R.
138, av Frank Robinson 819-682-0100

Chiropratic Clinic
24, Principale 819-684-3555

Chiropratique Glenwood (Clinique)
Rioux, Dr. D.
U 201-24, rue Principale . . .819-684-3555

Paris, Dr. Denis R.
106, Principale 819-684-4488

BAIE COMEAU

Healey, Dr. Bruno;
108 boul Lasalle 418-296-4630

Henry, Dr. Denis;
Levesque, Dr. Eric;
Martel, Dr. Guy
815, rue Parefondeval 418-589-5890

BEACONSFIELD

Centre Chiropratique Beaconsfield
Dahlager, Dr. Brad
101, Amherst 514-426-0042

BEAUHARNOIS

Denis, Dr. Jerome
52, St-Laurent 514-429-6177

BEAUPORT

Centre Chiropratique de l'Avenue Royale
Bendle, Dr. Roger; Genest-Boudreau, Dr. S.
698, av Royale 418-660-0141

Cote, Dr. Ghislain
2128, av Royale 418-661-6750

Dufresne, Dr. Marc
1020, Royale 418-661-1225

BERTHIERVILLE

Cloutier, Dr. Real
30, pl du Marche 514-836-4966

BLAINVILLE

Clinique Chiropratique Blainville
Belanger, Dr. Rene
615, boul Cure Labelle, Loc. 1514-434-4324

Levesque, Dr. Vincent
846, Cure Labelle 514-434-2428

BOIS-DES-FILIONS

Cardinal, Dr. Remi
492, ch Adolphe Chapleau ..514-621-9537

BOISBRIAND

Cardinal, Dr. Leo
189, ch Grande-Cote 514-434-1819

BOUCHERVILLE

Boisvert, Dr. Michel
#204-150,
boul de Montarville 514-449-4468

Gatien, Dr. Jean-Provost
800, rue Pierre Viger 514-655-8374

**Menard, Dr. Jean;
Menard, Dr. Raymond**
100, boul de Montarville 514-641-4808/655-5555

BREAKEYVILLE

Clinique Chiropratique Breakeyville
Davy, Dr. Jean
21, rue des Sapins 418-832-8163

BROMONT

A.R.P. Clinique Chiropratique
Parrot, Dr. Alain R.
5, des Verrieres 514-534-4808

Centre Chiropratique Bromont
Brunelle, Dr. Gilles D.
103, de Bromont 514-534-2533

BROSSARD

Bergeron, Dr. Marcel
5405, Grande Allee 514-676-1002

Centre Chiropratique
Bienvenue, Dr. Charles; Desmarais, Dr. Pierre
6975, Taschereau 514-676-5955

Clinique Chiropratique L.F.R.
5811, Taschereau 514-656-0723

Desmarais, Dr. Jacinthe
7900-D, Taschereau 514-923-8899

BUCKINGHAM

Rondeau, Dr. Patrick
605, Principale 819-986-5252

Lamothe, Dr. France
634 Main St 819-986-7272

CABANO

Beaulieu, Dr. Paul
186, Commerciale 418-854-2496/859-3460

CACOUNA

Clinique Chiropratique de Cacouna
Hudon, Dr. Julie
502, Principale O 418-862-6540

CAP-AUX-MEULES

Hudon, Dr. Danielle
55, ch Principal 418-986-2223

CAP-DE-LA-MADELEINE

Bouille, Dr. Rene E.
512, rue Notre-Dame 819-379-1293

Clinique Chiropratique Chateaudun
Parent, Dr. Rene
821, rue Thibeau 819-373-1685

Clinique Chiropratique des Estacades Enr
Rocheleau, Dr. Guy
525, rue Vachon 819-375-5577

Clinique Chiropratique Cap-de-la-Madeleine
Houle, Dr. Jean-Jacques
195, rue Fusey 819-375-2795

Hains, Dr. Jean
293, boul Ste-Madeleine 819-374-9965

CARLETON

St- Laurent, Dr. Guy
440, boul Perron 418-364-7714

CHAMBLY

Centre Chiropratique de Chambly
Potvin, Dr. Marc
1315, rue Bourgogne 514-658-2821

Clinique Chiropratique Chambly
Roy, Dr. Yves P.
729, St-Pierre 514-658-3636

CHARLESBOURG

Centre Chiropratique Duranleau
Duranleau, Dr. Mireille; Plaisance, Dr. Lucie
8875, boul
Henri-Bourassa 418-622-0236

Centre Chiropratique Jacob
Jacob, Dr. Denis
525, rue 80 E 418-628-3827

Clinique Chiropratique Charlesbourg
Saint-Denis, Dr. Roger P.
6590, av Isaac Bedard 418-628-1242

Clinique Chiropratique Marcel Perron
Perron, Dr. Denis; Perron, Dr. Marcel
6640, 3 Ave O 418-628-2234

Clinique Chiropratique Notre Dame des Laurentien
Foucault, Dr. Paule; St-Hilaire, Dr. Claude
1360, av Notre Dame 418-841-4321

Clinique Chiropratique Richard
Richard, Dr. Yves
4545, av 3 O 418-622-1234

Verreault, Dr. Jacques
120, rue 45 E 418-627-5032

CHATEAUGUAY

Cloutier, Dr. Pierre
132, boul St-Jean Baptiste ..514-699-1102

Julien, Dr. Roland
130-B, boul St-Joseph 514-691-4890

Lemieux, Dr. Pierre
19, boul Vanier 514-692-0598

CHICOUTIMI

**Anctil, Dr. Caroline;
Thibault, Dr. Marc**
515, rue E Jacques-Cartier ..418-549-8412

**Audet, Dr. Johanne;
Bilodeau, Dr. Richard;
Garant, Dr. Raymond**
940, boul Saguenay E 418-543-4942

Clinique Chiropratique Lebel
Lebel, Dr. Denis
477, rue Plamondon 418-545-9266

Glidden, Dr. Danny
1646, av des Engoulevents .418-696-4900

CHOMEDEY

Blain, Dr. Andre
394, Laurier 514-686-2808

Caron, Dr. Gilbert
3860, Notre Dame 514-681-9441

Chiropratique St-Martin
315, St-Martin O 514-662-0100

Clinique Chiropratique Laval
Lachaine, Dr. Claude; Valiquette, Dr. V.
3001, Levesque O 514-681-5986

Clinique Chiropratique le Corbusier
Parent, Dr. Roch
1800, boul
le Corbusier 514-687-0109/681-3239

Clinique Chiropratique Samson 7 Jours
Dube, Dr. Guy
4005, boul Samson 514-681-4022

Complexe Chiropratique St-Maxime
St-Louis, Dr. Jacques
3820, boul Levesque O 514-681-6487

Vidas, Dr. Giovanni
1130, Cure Labelle 514-682-7987

COATICOOK

Bureau, Dr. Martine
38, rue Child 819-849-4871

Lajeunesse, Dr. Jacques B.
712, rue Child 819-849-2224

COTEAU DU LAC

Brodeur, Dr. Gerard
362, ch du Fleuve 514-763-0910

COWANSVILLE

Centre Chiropratique Cowansville
Leduc, Dr. Jean-Paul
445, Bachand 514-263-4881

Clinique Chiropratique de Cowansville
Girard, Dr. Jean
413, du Sud 514-263-7668

DEGELIS

Clinique Chiropratique Degelis
Ringuette, Dr. Luc
454, av Principale 418-853-3877

Clinique Chiropratique Optimale
Keenan, Dr. Timothy
455-A, av Principale.......418-853-3584

DOLBEAU

Clinique Chiropratique Jean Gagne
Gagne, Dr. Jean Clinique
397, boul Wallberg 418-276-9066

DOLLARD-DES-ORMEAUX

Scott, Dr. W.A.
4309-C, boul St-Johns 514-626-1999

DORION

Clinique Chiropratique Dorion
#4-100, boul Harwood 514-455-1910

DORVAL

Centre Chiropratique Scrase
Scrase, Dr. Christopher
185, av Dorval 514-636-8725

Clinique Chiropratique Dorval
267, av Dorval 514-631-3352

Hains, Dr. Francois
#120-1405, S Rte
Transcanadienne 514-683-3360

DRUMMONDVILLE

Chiro-Clinique
Trudel, Dr. Pierre
310, Marchand 819-477-3331

Choiniere, Dr. Bruno
533, rue St-Pierre 819-478-0014

Claveau, Dr. Maurice
182, rue Heriot 819-478-2882

Clinique Chiropratique
Martin, Dr. Andre; Roberge, Dr. Luc
410, rue St-Georges 819-472-7008

Deshaies, Dr. Rene
405-235, rue Heriot 819-478-0324

DUVERNAY

Genois, Dr. Guy
2255, de la Concorde 514-668-6325

FABREVILLE

Alguire, Dr. Normand
3051, Dagenais O 514-622-7505

FLEURIMONT

Chiropratic Clinic Lajeunesse
Lajeunesse, Dr. Gerard-M
1800, rue Des Pelerins 819-569-3838

GASPE

Clinique Chiropratique Henry
Henry, Dr. Louiselle
26, de Sandy-Beach 418-368-4838

GATINEAU

Centre Chiropratique La Gappe
Marcotte, Dr. Denis
675, boul La Gappe 819-243-7574

Centre de Chiropratique Sportive
Laplante, Dr. Andre; Breton, Dr. J.D.
193-B, ch de la Savane ...819-568-3313

Chouinard, Dr. D.M.
370, boul Greber 819-246-2424

Clinique Chiropratique St-Rene
Veillette, Dr. Edith
210, boul St-Rene O. 819-669-9676

Malouin, Dr. Pierre
225, boul La Gappe 819-568-2224

GRANBY

Brouillard, Dr. Leon
326, Robinson S. 514-378-3789

Centre Chiropratique de Granby
Larochelle, Dr. Eric
#4-398, rue Principale 514-777-3600

Centre de Sante
Dumas, Dr. Paul
380, rue Principale 514-372-1366

Chiro Clinique Denicourt
459, rue Principale 514-378-1110

Choiniere, Dr. Jean-Pierre
630, rue Guillette 514-372-8100

Clinique Chiropratique Bouchard
Bouchard, Dr. Luc R.
58, rue St-Antoine N 514-378-2432

Clinique Chiropratique de Granby
Quintal, Dr. Richard
52, rue St-Louis 514-378-5590

Clinique Chiropratique Gingras
Gingras, Dr. Sylvain
315, rue Robinson S 514-378-2227

Enright, Dr. Michael
232, Deragon 514-372-9995

Lafleur, Dr. Andre; Lafleur, Dr. Herve
14, rue Court ...514-372-4436/375-7293

Rainville, Dr. Gysele
344, Pare St 514-372-4224

GRAND'MERE

Clinique Chiropratique Bellerive
Bellerive, Dr. Claude
1197, av 6e 819-538-1761

Clinique Chiropratique Boisvert & Therrien
Boisvert, Dr. Daniel; Therrien, Dr. Lise
859, av 6 819-538-0295

Metivier, Dr. J. Noel
496, av 6 819-538-5250

GREENFIELD PARK

Guertin, Dr. Rene
121, boul Churchill 514-466-0634

HUDSON

Centre Chiropratique Hudson
438, Main Rd 514-458-1991

HULL

Centre Chiro Specifique Ayers & Chevallier
Ayers, Dr. Isabelle; Chevallier, Dr. Jean-Louis
26, boul St-Raymond 819-777-6735

Clinique Chiropratique de Hull
Perodeau, Dr. France
48, Promenade du Portage ..819-778-6217

Clinique Chiropratique Gamelin
Poelman, Dr. Hans
73 Gamelin 819-595-1319

Clinique Chiropratique St-Joseph
Bernier, Dr. Pierre; Bourque, Dr. Christine
673, boul St-Joseph 819-777-0577

Delorme, Dr. Pierre
137, rue Notre-Dame 819-771-1447

HUNTINGDON

Centre Chiropratique Huntingdon
Vance, Dr. Peter
10, rue Henderson 514-264-6153

ILE-BIZARD

Houle, Dr. Diane
#102-560, boul
Jacques Bizard 514-620-1000

ILE PERROT

Centre Chiropratique Roxboro Ile-Perrot
Flipo, Dr. Jean-Luc
559, boul Grand 514-453-0001

Clinique Chiropratique de Lile Perrot
Poirier, Dr. Mario
565, boul Grand 514-425-1611

JOLIETTE

Maille, Dr. Alain
812, Camille Bonin 514-756-1323

Verreault, Dr. Richard
357, rue Papineau 514-759-1611

JONQUIERE

Clinique Chiropratique Cox
Cox, Dr. David
3670, rue Royaume 418-695-3307

Clinique Chiropratique Jonquiere
O'Malley, Dr. Joan; Poupart, Dr. Pierre
2309, rue St-Dominique ...418-542-3111

Glidden, Dr. Larry
2872, rue Davis 418-548-7689

Laroche, Dr. Jacques
434, rue St-Dominique 418-542-3211

KIRKLAND

Beauchamp, Dr. G.
100, rue du Barry 514-426-5500

Cloutier, Dr. Pierre J.
3608, boul St-Charles 514-694-0085

KNOWLTON

Cote, Dr. G.H.
15, Rock Hill 514-243-0480

Dandenault, Dr. Suzanne
4-483, ch Knowlton 514-242-1463

Muir, Dr. Vivien
44 Victoria St 514-242-2299

L'ASSOMPTION

Massicotte, Dr. Carole; Massicotte, Dr. Jean
636, boul L'Ange-Gardien ...514-589-6413

LA BAIE

Clinique Chiropratique
Lavoie, Dr. Patrice; Simard, Dr. Jacquelin
750, boul de la Grande Baie N ...418-544-8641

LA PLAINE

Centre Chiropratique La Plaine
Louis, Dr. Felix
#100-1264, rue Rodrigue ...514-477-4570

LA POCATIERE

Centre Chiropratique Kamouraska
Lilley, Judith
1200, av 6 418-856-4120

Clinique Chiropratique La Poca
Villemure, Dr. Jean
803, av 4e 418-856-1123

LA PRAIRIE

Bonvouloir, Dr. Maurice
545, av Godin 514-659-5511

LA SARRE

Bourbeau, Dr. Robert
23, av 8 O 819-333-2825

Clinique Chiropratique Belanger
671, rue 2 E 819-333-4500

Clinique Chiropratique Mercier
Mercier, Dr. Richard
655-A, rue 2 E 819-339-5333

LA TUQUE

Gagne, Dr. Normand
380, rue Tessier 819-523-6930

Sirois, Dr. Diane
569, St-Louis 819-523-2150

LAC MEGANTIC

Plamondon, Dr. Yvan
4728, rue Laval 819-583-3187

LACHENAIE

Clinique Chiropratique des Moulins
Desroches, Dr. Jean
940, Montee Masson 514-471-0156

LACHUTE

Centre Chiropratique Chevrefils
Chevrefils, Dr. Jean
244, rue Georges 514-562-3563

LANORAIE

Arcand, Dr. Yves
329, rue Aqueduc 514-887-2954

LAVAL

Alguire, Dr. Normand
3051, boul Dagenais O. .514-622-7505

Bessette, Dr. Nathalie
#103-1800, boul
Le Crosbusier 514-687-0109

Bezeau, Dr. Martin
184, boul Ste-Rose 514-628-8500

Deslauriers, Dr. Pierre
2000, boul Concorde E. ...514-667-3020

Dube, Dr. Guy
4005, boul Samson 514-681-4022

Giroux, Dr. Claude
#202-3360, boul Concorde .514-663-4511

Lachance, Dr. Daniel
425, boul Des Prairies 514-978-9009

Marcotte, Dr. Justin; Martin, Dr. Denise
#200-315, boul St. Martin O. 514-662-0100

Pare, Dr. Bernard
3680, boul St. Martin O....514-686-9801

Philippon, Dr. Claude
3571, Concorde E. 514-664-0206

Theroux, Dr. Jean
101-C, Concorde O. 514-668-1220

Tomassini, Dr. Bruno
2315, boul Concorde 514-662-1595

LAVAL- DES- RAPIDES

Centre Chiropratique Laval
Thoret, Dr. Guy
48, Bord Du Lac 514-694-2211

LE GARDEUR

Chiro Clinique Legardeur
Coutu, Dr. Sophie
266, rue Bonnard 514-581-0991

Clinique Chiropratique le Gardeur
Jolicoeur, Dr. Sylvain
#202-535, rue
Notre Dame 514-657-1896

LEVIS

Charland, Dr. Come
115, rue St-Augustin 418-837-5567

Clinique Chiropratique Canuel Levis
Canuel, Dr. Bertrand; Thibault, Dr. Gaston
16, Camire 418-837-7073/833-2023

Clinique Chiropratique Couture
Couture, Dr. Jean; Couture, Dr. Johanne
#102-104, rue Kennedy 418-833-4248

Clinique Chiropratique Gelinas
Gelinas, Dr. Claude
5411, boul De La Rive S 418-835-6064

Clinique Chiropratique Levis
Gervais, Dr. Jean; Nadeau, Dr. Normand
5600, rue St-Georges 418-837-9745

Clinique Chiropratique Paquet
Paquet, Dr. Mario
2122, ch du Fleuve 418-839-7364

LONGUEUIL

Centre Chiropratique Chemin de Chambly
2044, ch de Chambly 514-670-1820

Centre Chiropratique Dussault & Assoc
Dussault, Dr. Richard P.
550, ch de Chambly 514-646-2677

Centre Chiropratique Lemieux
Lemieux, Dr. Gontran
1128, rue St-Laurent O ...514-677-8181

Chiro Clinique Desormeaux
Grenon, Dr. Claude
3065, ch de
Chambly Chem 514-442-2162

Chiro Clinique Rive-Sud
Vigeant, Dr. Jacques
425, rue St-Charles O 514-670-8861

Clinique Chiropratique L'Optimum
2020, Marie Victorin 514-442-1148

Clinique Marc Bernard
#100-24, rue De Gentilly O .514-677-8363

Raymond, Dr. Jean A.
1203, rue Emma 514-677-7411

LORETTEVILLE

Clinique Chiropratique Lebel
Lebel, Dr. Gabriel
157, boul Valcartier 418-843-4381

LOUISEVILLE

Clinique Chiropratique de Louiseville
Drouin, Dr. M. Robert
1, rue Notre-Dame S 819-228-5221

Clinique Chiropratique Lessard Guylaine
Lessard, Dr. Guylaine
255, av St-Laurent 819-228-3005

MAGOG

Clinique Chiropratique St-Patrice
Lefebvre, Dr. Michel
280, rue St-Patrice 819-847-3455

Page, Dr. B.J.
74, rue Laurier 819-843-4523

MANIWAKI

Gagnon, Dr. Jean-Pierre
S 102-208, rue
Commerciale 819-449-5680

MARIEVILLE

Clinique Chiropratique Marieville
Lecuyer, Dr. Jacques
427, rue Ste-Marie 514-460-3207

MASCOUCHE

Bellavance, Dr. Yves
210, ch Des Anglais 514-477-5025

Clinique Chiropratique Mascouche
Paiement, Dr. Michel
2694, ch Ste-Marie 514-474-4103

MATANE

Jean, Dr. M.; Donaldson, Dr. R.
750, av Du Phare O 418-562-6665

MERCIER

Clinique Chiropratique de Mercier
Poirier, Dr. Gilles
771, boul St-Jean Baptiste ..514-692-1692

MIRABEL

Desjardins, Dr. Serge
8300, St-Jacques 514-475-8788

MISTASSINI

Clinique Chiropratique de Mistassini Inc
Marchand, Dr. Carl
260, av Louis-Hemon 418-276-2892

MONT-JOLI

Clinique Chiropratique Roussel
Roussel, Dr. C. Marcel
159, Sanatorium 418-775-3320

MONT-LAURIER

Centre de Sante Dr Jacques Lemieux Chiropratic
Lemieux, Dr. Jacques
1400, boul Albiny Paquette .819-623-6099

Gagnon, Dr. Jean-Pierre
401, rue Du Pont 819-623-1336

MONT-ST-HILAIRE

Clinique Medicale Mont St-Hilaire
Bolduc, Dr. Marie France
261, boul Laurier 514-464-5151

MONTREAL

Alternative Chiropratique
Rioux, Dr. Ghyslaine
757, boul St-Joseph E 514-277-7823

Arsenault Chiro-Clinique
Arsenault, Dr. Daniel
7642, rue Centrale 514-363-2223

Azoulay, Dr. David; Labrosse, Dr. Rene
6756, rue St-Denis 514-274-5880

Blanchette, Dr. Bernard
934, boul St-Joseph E 514-527-5651

Bois, Dr. Dominique Yan, Dr. Ronald K.
5015, rue Belanger E 514-729-2505

Bourdon, Dr. Annette
#205-2360, rue
Notre-Dame O 514-931-6342

Brouillet, Dr. Francois
6500, av Louis-Hebert 514-722-0277

Centre Chiropratique Familial Morisset
Morisset, Dr. Jean-Pierre
2260, boul Pie IX 514-255-4121

Centre Chiropratique Fleury Ouest
Doucet, Dr. Chantal
#1-212, rue Fleury O 514-385-5100

Centre Chiropratique Henri Bourassa
Calixte, Dr. Arthur; Charles, Dr. Voltaire
3300, boul Henri Bourassa E 514-326-0594

Centre Chiropratique Ville-Emard
Makohniuk, Dr. Joy
6032, boul Monk 514-766-1577

Centre de Sante Chiropratique Specifique
Corps, Dr. Alain; Marcoux, Dr. Jean-Philppe
300, Marcel Laurin 514-744-0499

Centre Sante Chiropratique des Ormeaux
Masse, Dr. Michel
2306, rue Des Ormeaux ...514-355-8222

Chenier, Dr. Leo; Picard, Dr. Lyne
2403, rue Centre 514-932-2885

Chevrefils, Dr. Lucille
7965, rue St-Denis 514-385-3224

Chevrefils, Dr. Roger
7965, rue St-Denis 514-387-6440

Chiro Clinique
Audet, Dr. Andre; Fournier, Dr. Yves;
Robidoux, Dr. Andre
3611, rue St-Denis 514-842-0842

Chiro Clinique St-Hubert
Brossard, Dr. Andre
2070, rue St-Hubert 514-982-6111

Chiropratic Clinic St-Joseph
Luckhurst, Dr. Neil
400, boul St-Joseph E 514-288-5998

Chiropratique Familiale St-Joseph
Gendron, Dr. Isabelle
2250, boul St-Joseph E ...514-525-4563

Choiniere, Dr. Jean-Pierre
485-A, boul St-Josephe E .514-287-1147

Clinique B C Chiropratique
Boisvert, Dr. Laurent
4146, rue Belanger E 514-725-9588

Clinique Chiro-Energie
Marchand, Dr. Claude
1311, boul St-Joseph E ...514-529-0930

Clinique Chiro-Sante Rosemont
Gelinas, Dr. Luc
2160, boul Rosemont 514-270-1517

Clinique Chiropratique
Lalonde, Dr. Carole
119-A, boul
Henri Bourassa O 514-331-5877

Clinique Chiropratique
Laperriere, Dr. Andre
3500, boul Industriel 514-326-1064

Clinique Chiropratique Beaubie
Leo, Dr. Raymond
4470, rue Beaubien E 514-374-1830

Clinique Chiropratique Bois de Boulogne
Rafie, Dr. Paul
1600, boul Henri Bourassa O 514-335-4040

Clinique Chiropratique Cherrie
Verissimo, Dr. Nelson
546, rue Cherrier 514-849-5186

Clinique Chiropratique du Plat
501, rue St-Joseph E 514-987-1155

Clinique Chiropratique G.E.M.I.
Paradis, Dr. J. Paul J.
7454, rue St-Denis 514-271-3963

Clinique Chiropratique Gonthier Moisan
Gonthier, Dr. Andre-Marie;
Laflamme, Dr. Sylvie; Moisan, Dr. Dany
2409, rue Fleury E 514-388-0202

Clinique Chiropratique Guy
Biancardi, Dr. Paul; Cote, Dr. Georges;
Gehl, Dr. Terry; Felteau, Dr. Chantal
2100, av Guy 514-933-2657

Clinique Chiropratique Hochela
David, Dr. Robert; Fournier, Dr. Monique;
Giguere, Dr. Richard
7707, rue Hochelaga 514-355-3375

Clinique Chiropratique L'Acordaire
5803, rue Sherbrooke E ..514-256-3380

Clinique Chiropratique Montreal
1260, rue Jarry E 514-727-9944

Clinique Chiropratique Outremont Dr
1577, av Vanhorne 514-273-8820

Clinique Chiropratique Sante
Bouffard, Dr. Raymond; Lapointe, Dr. Marcel
2024, rue Peel 514-287-7111

Clinique Chiropratique Snowdon
Shadowitz, Dr. Robert
4950, rue Queen Mary ...514-344-5005

Clinique Chiropratique Sportive du Quebec
6872, rue St-Denis 514-271-8118

Clinique Chiropratique Viau
Valente, Dr. Riccardo
8715, rue Viau 514-329-5111

Constant, Dr. Daniel
#104-4980, boul
Henri Bourassa E 514-322-2404

Cormier, Dr. Conrad
7252, rue St-Denis 514-272-0320

Cyr, Dr. Richard
7454, rue St-Denis 514-271-3963

Daigneault, Dr. Francois
#101-5694, rue
Laurendeau 514-769-1532

Des Ruisseaux, Dr. Pierre
461, boul St-Joseph E 514-849-9732

Deschamps, Dr. France
4083, boul Decarie 514-481-6570

Dumoulin, Dr. Regent
4415, rue Belanger E 514-721-1701

Gagliardi, Dr. Frank
8776, rue Esplanade 514-389-1971

Gauthier, Dr. Martin; Genest-Boudreau, Dr. C.
501, boul St-Joseph E 514-845-2977

Gravel, Dr. Pierre
1804, rue Rachel E 514-521-6197

Julien, Dr. Roland
1683, boul St-Joseph E ...514-528-1960

Karout, Dr. Hani
1951, rue Sherbrooke E ...514-522-9787

Kudo Gerald & Ronald Clinique Chiropratique
4083, boul Decarie 514-488-8961

Lafleur, Dr. Jean-Francois
6867, rue St-Denis 514-279-1711

Lapointe, Dr. Marcel
1430, rue Belanger E 514-272-5454

Leblanc, Dr. Marie Sylvie
1652, rue Fleury E 514-382-4950

Lefrancois, Dr. Robert
5968, rue Hochelaga 514-254-4124

Mayer, Dr. Serge
7968, rue St-Denis 514-383-4229

Montagne, Dr. Eric
750, boul Henri-Bourassa E .514-384-5577

Morin, Dr. Bernard
10655, rue St-Denis 514-387-0628

Nathaniel, Dr. Charles
#139-175 rue, Stillview ...514-694-6332

Picard, Dr. Raoul
2823, boul Rosemont 514-722-7576

Pitre, Dr. Jasmin R.
7229, rue St-Denis 514-274-2415

Roy, Dr. Richard
#205-7655, boul
Newman 514-364-1756

Tasse, Dr. Gabriel
#11-2033, rue
De Salaberry 514-332-1517

Therrien, Dr. Henri
6060, boul
Maurice-Duplessis 514-323-6321

Tourigny, Dr. Carmelle
6553, rue Lacordaire 514-254-2077

Vidas, Dr. Giovanni
6287, Sherbrooke E 514-252-4444

MONTREAL NORTH

Centre Chiropratique Diagnostic Plus
Daneault, Dr. Line; Danis, Dr. Normand
5946, boul Leger 514-328-7723

Centre Chiropratique Leger Enr
Desrosiers, Dr. Nicole
#206-5835, boul Leger 514-328-1677

NAPIERVILLE

Marcil, Dr. Raymond J.
429, St-Jacques 514-245-0162

NEUFCHATEL

Guillot, Dr. Pierre
#107-4100, boul
de L'Auvergne 418-845-1234

NEW RICHMOND

Clinique Chiropratique Lebel
Godbout, Dr. Nathalie; Lebel, Dr. Jean-Louis
115, boul Perron O 418-392-4439

NICOLET

Clinique Chiropratique du Dr. Denise Lemire
Lemire, Dr. Denise
91, Pl du 21-Mars 819-293-6383

ORMSTOWN

Brodeur, Dr. Gerard
64, rue Bridge 514-829-2352

ORSAINVILLE

Clinique Chiropratique Orsainville
Morissette, Dr. Maurice
5014, boul du Jardin 418-627-3151

PIERREFONDS

Chiropractic Clinic Gaylard
Gaylard, Dr. John L.W.
13141, rue Ancourt 514-696-0760

PINCOURT

Cardinal, Dr. Raynald
116, boul Cardinal Leger ...514-453-2631

PLESSISVILLE

Clinique Chiropratique Marcel Veilleux
Malenfant, Dr. Johanne; Veilleux, Dr. Marcel
2222, rue De La
Cooperative 819-362-6161

POINTE-AUX-TREMBLES

Centre Chiropratique P.A.T.
Langlois, Dr. Stephan; Paille, Dr. Claude
13080, rue Sherbrooke E ...514-642-2002

Chiro Clinique Ricard
Ricard, Dr. Guy
#200-12085, rue
Rene-Levesque E 514-645-2231

Lacoursiere, Dr. Jacques
3365, av 40 514-642-0258

Ratthe, Dr. Denise
#101-503-8e ave 514-645-2602

POINTE CLAIRE

Centre Chiropratique Pointe Claire
Theoret, Dr. Guy
48, Bord Du Lac 514-694-2211

Nathaniel, Dr. Charles
#139-175, rue Stillview ...514-694-6332

QUEBEC CITY

Auger & Auger Chiropraticiens
Auger, Dr. Jacques; Auger, Dr. Yhann C.
2755, boul Pere Lelievre ..418-683-2545

Bell, Dr. Richard
7-1750, rue Vitre 418-522-5666

Centre Chiropratique
Gosselin, Dr. Guy; Wang, Dr. Philippe
1393, rue Jean Devin 418-877-4440/
872-6934

Centre Chiropratique Ancienne-Lorette
Guillemette, Dr. Denis; St-Laurent, Dr. Nicole
2035, rue
St-Jean-Baptiste 418-872-3755

Centre Chiropratique Limoilou
Cossette, Dr. Jacques; Gendron, Dr. Claire
1307, -4e av 418-523-9933

Centre Chiropratique Moore
Moore, Dr. David
543, Grande Allee E 418-529-4862

Centre Medical Laennec-Centre Urgence Chiropratique
By Appointment 418-684-8030

Clinique Chiropratique Bourlamaque
Langdeau, Dr. Jean-Bruno
989, av Bourlamaque 418-647-3600

Clinique Chiropratique Pere Lelievre
Nolet, Dr. Michel
2985, boul Pere-Lelievre ...418-681-8686

Clinique Chiropratique St-Sacrement
Boulianne, Dr. Gabriel
780, av Pere-Pelletier 418-683-1393

Clinique de Sante Chiropratique
Montreuil, Dr. Gaetan; Trottier, Dr. Renee
1295, boul St-Joseph 418-622-5871

Clinique Dr Robert Coulombe
Coulombe, Dr. Robert
1465, rue
De L'Islet (Mesnil) 418-626-3112

Morency, Dr. Richard
#400-580, Grande Allee E ..418-647-3976

Rivard, Dr. Jean G.
347, boul
Rene Levesque O 418-683-8241

RAWDON

Centre Chiropratique Rawdon
Croisetiere, Dr. Yves
3580, rue Queen 514-834-4338

REPENTIGNY

Centre Chiropratique Carignan
Carignan, Dr. Denis A.
45, boul Industriel 514-585-1121

Centre Chiropratique Comeau
Comeau, Dr. Benoit
522, rue Notre-Dame 514-581-2299

Centre Chiropratique Dr. G.F. Giroux
579-A, rue Notre Dame 514-657-2748

Centre Chiropratique Fillion
Fillion, Dr. J.P.
300, boul Iberville 514-581-4940

Filion, Dr. Christine
#102-735, rue Notre Dame .514-654-8446

Meunier, Dr. Diane
1277, rue Notre Dame 514-581-1878

Tremblay, Dr. Jacques
513, Bl L'Assomption 514-654-9506

Vendittoli, Dr. Robert
86, rue Cherrier 514-581-9292

RIGAUD

Gauvreau, Dr. Francois
30A St-Jean Baptiste O 514-451-4925

RIMOUSKI

Centre de Sante Chiropratique
Richard, Dr. Claude
125, Rene-Lepage E 418-723-4808

Clinique Chiropratique Bahan
Bahan, Dr. Arthur
193, rue St-Pierre 418-723-4671

Clinique Chiropratique Dr Jean Guay
Guay, Dr. Jean-M
174, rue Lavoie 418-723-3655

Clinique Chiropratique Familiale
Szoke, Dr. Laszlo
95, av Rouleau 418-722-8081

Clinique Chiropratique St-Pierre & Associes
Dandurand, Dr. Michel; St-Pierre, Dr. Gilles
143, boul St-Germain E 418-723-4733

Demalsy, Dr. Michel
208, av de la Cathedrale ..418-723-4522

Malenfant, Dr. Laurent
183, av Rouleau 418-723-7528

Morissette, Dr. Georges
57, rue de L'Eveche O 418-724-7636

Viel, Dr. Andre
5, rue 2e O 418-722-6491

RIVIERE-DU-LOUP

Beaulieu, Dr. Claude
24, rue Frontenac 418-867-2773

Centre Chiropratique de Rivière-du-Loup
Pelletier, Dr. Andre
35, rue Delage 418-862-7225

Clinique Chiro Frontenac
Martin, Dr. Gilles
34, rue Frontenac 418-862-0661

Raymond, Dr. Jean-Pierre
169, de la Seigneurie
(St-Roch des Aulnaie) 418-856-5133

ROBERVAL

Clinique Chiropratique de Roberval
Martel, Dr. Michel
437, rue Bourgoing 418-275-0395

ROCK FOREST

Clinique Chiropratique des Haut-Bois Ltee
Veilleux, Dr. Bertrand
938, rue Haut-Bois 819-564-1011

ROSEMERE

Centre Chiropratique Specifique Rosemere
132, boul Labelle 514-433-2145

Clinique Chiropratique Rosemere
Filiatrault, Dr. Luc; O'Meara, Dr. Deborah
233, Grande Cote 514-437-8711

Leclerc, Dr. Andre
464, boul Roland Durand ...514-965-6980

ROUYN-NORANDA

Centre de Sante Chiropratique
Plourde, Dr. Richard
66, rue Monseigneur-Tessier O 819-797-2325

Clinique Chiropratique du Cuivre
40, rue 19 819-762-2130

Clinique Chiropratique Matte Lemay & Dallaire
Dallaire, Dr. Nathalie; Lemay, Dr. Jacques;
Matte, Dr. Claude
33, av Horne 819-762-1222

ROXBORO

Centre Chiropratique Roxboro Pincourt
10400-A, boul Gouin O 514-683-3476

ST-ALPHONSE DE GRANBY

Chiropractique Clinique Sante
Lapointe, Dr. Marcel
108, Rte 139 514-375-4592

ST-ANDRE AVELLIN

Denis, Dr. Fournelle
186, Principale 819-983-2213

ST-AUGUSTIN

Centre Chiropratique St-Augustin
314, Rte 138 418-878-2525

ST-BASILE-LE-GRAND

Marcoux, Dr. Bertrand
14, rue Robert 514-441-4888

ST-BRUNO

Centre de Chiropractie Mont St-Bruno
380, de Mesy 514-441-1679

Labarre, Dr. Adrien
1534, rue Montarville 514-461-0361

ST-CESAIRE

Leduc, Dr. Marcel
1301, rue Notre Dame 514-469-3222

ST-CHARLES-BORROMEE

Dube, Dr. Yvan
28, ch du Golf 514-759-2626

Pangakis, Dr. Dimitri
#103-127, Visitation 514-755-5576

ST-CHARLES DE BELLECHASSE

Clinique Chiropratique St-Charles
Laflamme, Dr. Jean-Guy
2675, Royale O 418-887-3214

ST-CONSTANT

Clinique Chiropratique Dargis
255, ch Ste-Catherine 514-635-1125

Clinique Chiropratique de St-Constant
35, rue St-Pierre 514-635-0221

ST-CYPRIEN

Clinique Chiropratique Optimale
April, Dr. Nathaly; Keenan, Dr. Timothy
106, Leblanc 418-963-3060

ST-EMILE

Clinique Chiropratique Philippe Wang
Wang, Dr. Philippe
202-6476, des Erables 418-843-4444

ST-ESPRIT

Desbiens, Dr. Claude
96, Principale 514-839-3725

ST-ETIENNE-DE LAUZON

Clinique Chiropratique St-Etienne
987, Rte Lagueux 418-831-8503

ST-EUSTACHE

Chevrefils, Dr. Marc; Desaulniers, Dr. Denis
197, rue Hemond 514-472-2098/
473-5375

Cifola, Dr. Roberto Sesto
468, Grande Cote 514-491-0140

Clinique Chiropratique Grande Cote
O'Neill, Dr. Russell
365, Grande Cote 514-623-4418

Clinique Chiropratique Kingsbury
Kingsbury, Dr. Robert
50, boul Arthur Sauve 514-472-9758

Clinique Chiropratique St-Eustache
Rose, Dr. Denis
134, rue St-Laurent 514-472-5462

Couture, Dr. Joanne
136, rue St-Louis 514-623-8828

O'Leary, Dr. Gilles
208, rue Louise 514-473-5250

Tasse, Dr. Gabriel
65, rue St-Laurent 514-472-1233

ST-FELICIEN

Centre Chiropratique de St-Felicien
Guay, Dr. Bruno
821, boul Sacre Coeur 418-679-4233

ST-FELIX DE VALOIS

Lacroix, Dr. J. Andre
6365, ch St-Jean 514-889-4406

ST-GABRIEL-DE-BRANDON

Clinique Chiropratique Brandon
Fisette, Dr. Angele
350, Beauvilliers 514-835-2203

ST-GREGOIRE

Masse, Dr. Gilles
106-4825, av Bouvet 819-233-4334

ST-HONORE-DE-TEMISCOUATA

Clinique Chiropratique St-Honore
Bourdeau, Dr. J-Andre; Bourdeau, Dr. Serge
157, rue Principale 418-497-2361

ST-HUBERT-DE-TEMISCOUATA

Bigaouette, Dr. Guy
#102-5100, boul
Cousineau 514-445-5454

Centre Chiropratique Desmarais
Desmarais, Dr. Francois;
Hamel, Dr. Patrick
2355, Montee St-Hubert ...514-462-2025

Clinique Chiropratique
Beaudoin, Dr. Claude
10304, St-Hubert 514-384-5210

**Clinique Chiropratique
Grande Allee**
4008, boul Grande Allee ...514-462-4220

ST-HYACINTHE

Boisseau, Dr. Eric
1275, rue Blanchette 514-774-2131

**Clinique Chiropratique
Centre Ville**
Morier, Dr. Serge
2035, rue Girouard O 514-778-1166

**Clinique Chiropratique
Martin Lessard**
Lessard, Dr. Martin
5440, boul Laurier 514-778-2922

**Clinique Chiropratique
St-Hyacinthe**
Remy, Dr. Martine ; Roux, Dr. Serge
2965, boul Laframboise ...514-774-7065

**Clinique Chiropratique
Touchette Belisle**
15305, av St-Louis 514-778-0101

Pilon, Dr. Claude
5730, boul Laurier 514-774-3071

Roussel, Dr. J. Pierre
1295, Sacre-Coeur E 514-773-6724

ST-JACQUES

Maille, Dr. Luc
2, rue Paul Masse 514-839-2497

ST-JEAN SUR-RICHELIEU

**Clinique Chiropratique Bienvenue
Charles**
950, du Seminaire N 514-349-6700

Clinique Chiropratique Corps
Corps, Dr. Alain
120, rue Champlain 514-347-4812

Clinique Chiropratique Ouimet
Ouimet, Dr. Jocelyn
659, boul Dorchester 514-348-5155

Clinique Chropratique Trudeau
Trudeau, Dr. Michel
525, Jacques-Cartier S 514-346-5145

Lafleur, Dr. Raoul
234, rue Champlain 514-347-3488

ST-JEAN-CHRYSOSTOME-DE-LEVIS

**Clinique Chiropratique
Beaudoin Gilles**
Beaudoin, Dr. Gilles
793, ch Vanier 418-839-7676

Clinique Chiropratique St-Jean
Labrecque, Dr. Charles
848, rue Commerciale 418-834-1126

ST-JEROME

Centre Chiropratique de St-Jerome
Dionne, Dr. Jean-Claude
611, rue St-Georges 514-438-4007

Centre Sante Chiro-Plus
Chartrand, Dr. Maryse;
Desjardins, Dr. Martine
145, rue De Martigny O 514-565-1525

Clinique Chiropratique St-Antoine
Karout, Dr. Michel S.
593, boul St-Antoine 514-438-5522

Fournelle, Dr. Denis
138, rue Labelle 514-565-5550

Numainville, Dr. Louis-Rene
129, rue De Martigny O 514-438-1004

Trudel, Dr. Joseph A.
681, rue St-Georges 514-436-2627

ST-JOVITE

**Centre Chiropratique Martine
St-Germain**
St-Germain, Dr. Martine
443, rue Leonard 819-425-8877

Chiropraticien Moreau
Moreau, Dr. Pierre
1260, rue Ouimet 819-425-5269

ST-LAMBERT

Briand, Dr. Guy
652, Victoria 514-466-8535

**Clinique Chiropratique
Normand Voisard D.C.**
219, Green ave 514-923-3515

Clinique Chiropratique Victoria Inc.
Matte, Dr. Stephane A.
61, Aberdeen 514-671-6841

Lavigueur, Dr. Luc
7, Edison St 514-465-9863

Clinique Chiropratique Laflamme
Laflamme, Dr. Yves
739, Des Erables 418-889-0544

ST-LAURENT

Fregeau, Dr. Carl
#9-1179, boul Decarie 514-747-5772

ST-LEONARD

Couture, Dr. Daniele
#210-5960, rue
Jean-Talon E 514-253-9244

Ippolito, Dr. Giovanni
5167, Jean Talon E 514-593-4777

Scalia, Dr. Giovanni
#200-4830, rue Jarrey E ...514-322-1980

ST-MATHIEU DE BELOEIL

Bernard, Dr. Luc
#312-535, boul Laurier ...514-467-9992

Bouthillette, Dr. Sylvie
81, ch Des Vingt 514-446-6211

Cabana, Dr. Wilfrid
46, boul Cartier 514-464-4834

Centre Chiropratique de Beloeil
de Vigne, Drs. J. & F.
#100-545, boul Laurier ...514-467-5151

**Centre de Sante et Harmonie
Richelieu Inc.**
Charbonneau, Dr. Donald;
Levesque, Dr. Yves
924, rue Richelieu 514-467-8788

Gerard, Dr. Alain
400, rue Des Tilleuls 514-467-0443

Marcoux, Dr. Jean Claude
642, ch Des Patriotes N ...514-467-1666

ST-NICEPHORE

Centre Chiropratique St-Nicephore
Vallancourt, Dr. Alain
4565, boul St-Joseph 819-472-7294

ST-NICOLAS

**Clinique Chiropratique Boutet
Helene D.C.**
Boutet, Dr. Helene
1400, rue Marie Victorin ...418-836-5234

**Clinique Chiropratique de la Rive
Sud**
Vigeant, Dr. Bernard
203, rue Marie Victorin 418-831-9421

**Gagne, Dr. Nathalie; Gagne,
Dr. Robert L.**
890, rue Marie Victorin ...418-831-1457

ST-PASCAL

Clinique Chiropratique St-Pascal
Levesque, Dr. Patrick
563, boul Hebert 418-492-2068

ST-PIE

Boisseau, Dr. Eric
221, ch St-Dominique 514-772-2325

ST-PIERRE-LES-BECQUETS

**Clinique Chiropratique
St-Pierre-Les-Becquets**
Beaudet, Dr. Sylvie
A-418, rue Marie-Victorin ...819-263-2546

ST-THERESE

**Blanke, Dr. Janice; Tasse, Dr.
Louis**
31, rue Turgeon 514-435-3231

Brisson, Dr. J.
17, rue St-Charles 514-434-4004

Desjardins Clinique Chiropratique
Desjardins, Dr. Ivan; Desjardins, Dr. Stephane
1, rue Tasse 514-435-9455

Labelle, Dr. Guy
151, rue Turgeon 514-434-4114

Laprade, Dr. G.R.
95, rue Turgeon 514-435-5111

STE-AGATHE-DES-MONTS

Chiro-Centre Arguin & Charland
Arguin, Dr. Gaston; Charland, Dr. Louise
33, rue Ste-Agathe 819-326-1666

Complexe Sante Chiropratique
Binette, Dr. Francois
38, St-Vincent 819-326-4311

STE-ANNE DE BEAUPRE

Thibeault, Dr. Jean
10624, boul Ste-Anne 418-827-4794

STE-ANNE-DE-BELLEVUE

Harvey, Dr. Robert W.
17A, rue St-Paul 514-457-3311

STE-ANNE DE LA PERAD

Clinique Chiropratique la Perade
321, de Lanaudiere 418-325-2715

STE-ANNE DES PLAINES

Chiro-Sante Ste-Anne
Hogue, Dr. Fernand
104, boul Ste-Anne 514-478-5476

STE-CATHERINE

Chatelois, Dr. Rejean
1110, rue Union 514-638-1244

Clinique Chiropratique de la Jacques Cartier
4753, Rte de Fossambault . .418-875-1090

STE-DOROTHEE

Centre Chiropratique Ste-Dorothee
645, pl Publique 514-689-1144

Morin, Dr. Mark
641, boul Samson 514-689-7361

STE-FOY

Baker, Dr. Aylmer
2080, boul
Rene Levesque O 418-688-8424

Beaudoin, Dr. Jacques
By Appointment 418-682-5750

Centre Chiropratique Lacoursiere Yves
Lacoursiere, Dr. Yves
3730, ch St-Louis 418-654-1788

Centre Chiropratique Specifique(Le)
Belanger, Dr. Yves; Bureau, Dr. Marc;
Eglin, Dr. Elaine; Lajoie, Dr. Daniel
210-2480, ch Ste-Foy 418-652-8181

Clinique Chiropratique Canuel
Canuel, Dr. Bertrand
3801, Francois Borel 418-871-5202

Clinique Chiropratique de Ste-Foy
Paille, Dr. Pierre
955, de Bourgogne 418-658-8838

Clinique Chiropratique Dominique Dufour
Dufour, Dr. Dominique
102, 1000 Ch 418-687-5372

Clinique Chiropratique Duplessis
Beland, Dr. Guylain; Lavoie, Dr. Pierre;
Tranchemontagne, Dr. Pierre
3340, de la Perade 418-653-7493

Clinique Chiropratique Tremblay
3700, rue du Campanile . .418-652-1234

Cote, Dr. Robert
3260, boul Neilson 418-652-0962

Jalbert, Dr. Michel
969, Rte De l'Eglise 418-659-1417

Tremblay, Dr. Danielle
3653, rue du Campanile . . .418-652-1234

STE-JULIE

Centre Chiropratique Familial Hamel
1410, rue Principale 514-922-4424

Clinique Chiropratique Ste-Julie
Boisvert, Dr. Sylvain
1593, ch du Fer A Cheval . . .514-649-1411

STE-MARTHE SUR LE LAC

Clinique Chiropratique Ste-Marthe-Sur-le Lac
2951, ch D'Oka 514-491-5885

STE-ROSE

Centre Chiropratique du Village
Bezeau, Dr. Martin
184, boul Ste-Rose 514-628-8500

Clinique Chiropratique Dr Riccardo Cifola
Cifola, Dr. Riccardo
550, Cure Labelle 514-628-7014

Clinique Chiropratique Ste-Rose
Bernatchez, Dr. Michele; Valade, Dr. Richard
190, boul Ste-Rose 514-963-1367

Dupuy, Dr. Guy A.
15, Boismou Auteuil 514-625-2511

SALABERRY DE VALLEYFIELD

Centre Chiropratique Familial
McCarthy, Dr. Richard
55, rue du Marche 514-373-7171

Chiro Clinique Valleyfield
Houle, Dr. Andre
412, boul du Havre 514-371-0321

Julien, Dr. Roland
111, St-Thomas 514-377-1889

SEPT-ILES

Clinique Chiroppatique Cote-Nord
Jean, Dr. Denis
891, Arnaud 418-968-8848

Clinique Chiropratique de Sante
Henry, Dr. J.M.
626, Gamache 418-962-1007

Clinique Chiropratique de Sept-Iles
Christian, Dr. Allard
205, Comeau 418-962-3738

Clinique Chiropratique Poirier
Poirier, Dr. Jacques
631, Franquelin 418-962-1552

SHAWINIGAN

Bouchard, Dr. Serge
755, rue 5 819-537-9273

SHAWINIGAN SUD

Clinique Chiropratique de Shawinigan-Sud
Hayes, Dr. David
1100, av 5e 819-537-0958

Clinique Chiropratique des Cascades
Paquin, Dr. Pierre; Boisclair, Dr. Suzanne
550, rue 119e 819-537-1885

SHERBROOKE

Centre Chiropratique Specifique de Lestrie
Gelinas, Dr. Mariel; Roy, Dr. Michel
234, Dufferin 819-820-2242

Clinique Chiropratique Dionne
Dionne, Dr. Sylvie
128, rue Jean Talon 819-566-8448

Clinique Chiropratique Goulet J-M
Goulet, Dr. J-M
1191, rue O King 819-562-1210

Clinique Chiropratique Montreal
Pomerleau, Dr. Luc
395, rue Montreal 819-564-0112

Gagnon, Dr. Helene
35, boul Queen N 819-564-2131

Gobeil & Bolduc Chiropraticiens
Bolduc, Dr. Francois; Gobeil, Dr. Michel
359, rue King E 819-564-8815

La Place Chiropratique de Sherbrooke
Lebreux, Dr. Denis; Renaud, Dr. Christine;
St-Pierre, Dr. D.; Wallis, Dr. Alan R.
1871, rue Galt O 819-566-2565

SILLERY

Clinique Chiropratique de Sillery
Morin, Dr. Louis-Philippe; Morin, Dr. Sonia
2255, boul Laurier 418-683-1505

Clinique Chiropratique des Erables Enr
Pouliot, Dr. Guy
1030, des Gouverneurs 418-527-3458

Clinique Chiropratique des Gouverneurs
Hamel, Dr. Marcel; Houle, Dr. Suzanne
1325, des Gouverneurs 418-684-0004

Clinique Chiropratique Dr Guy Savoie
Savole, Dr. Guy
1917, boul Rene Levesque O 418-527-6123

SOREL

Centre Chiropratique Dargis
Bouchard, Dr. Stephane
48-B, Augusta 514-743-5040

Rinfret, Dr. Sylvie
137, boul Fiset 514-742-1306

STANSTEAD

Clinique Chiropratique de Stanstead
25-B, Dufferin 819-876-2374

TEMISCAMING

Temiscaming Chiropractic Centre
321, Kipawa Rd 819-627-8181

TERREBONNE

Centre Chiropratique des Seigneurs
Dubouilh, Dr. Pascal
#107-500, boul Des Seigneurs 514-492-1212

Clinique Chiropratique Terrebonne
Lachaine, Dr. Claude
987, rue Moody 514-471-3511

Deraiche, Dr. Pierre
654, rue St-Pierre 514-471-2983

Gagnon, Dr. Luc J.
761, rue Lachapelle 514-471-9190

Maille, Dr. Luc
1620, Gascon 514-961-0311

Ouellette, Dr. Alain
933, rue St-Michel 514-492-4600

THETFORD MINES

Centre Chiropratique de Thetford Mines
Laverriere, Dr. John
420, Notre-Dame N 418-338-8285

Centre de Sante Chiropratique
Labrecque, Dr. Jimmy
733, boul Smith S 418-334-0233

Fortier, Dr. Roger
81, boul Smith S 418-338-5500

Hamel, Dr. Raymond
236, rue Notre-Dame S 418-338-4634

Vaillancourt, Dr. Jean
130, rue Gagne 418-335-7159

TRACY

Clinique Chiropratique de Tracy
St-Amand, Dr. Roger; Veilleux, Dr. Jacques
4575, Rte Marie-Victorin ...514-743-6268

TROIS PISTOLES

Beaulieu, Dr. Pierre
449, Chanoine Cote 418-851-1621

Clinique Chiropratique Optimale
April, Dr. Nathaly; Keenan, Dr. Timothy
582, rue Gobelet 418-851-4050

TROIS RIVIERES

Cabinet de Chiropratique du Dr Jean-Paul Herou
Heroux, Dr. Jean-Paul
1305, rue Laviolette 819-374-3363

Centre Chiropratique Dr Yves Heroux
Heroux, Dr. Yves; Martin, Dr. Andre
3930, boul Rigaud 819-373-8392

Centre Chiropratique Les Boule
Vezina, Dr. Michel
4870, boul des Forges 819-375-8070

Centre Chiropratique Paquette
Paquette, Dr. Lynda
2010, boul Des Chenaux ...819-376-2212

Centre Chiropratique Specifique de Trois-Rivière
Letendre, Dr. Louise
2121, boul des Forges 819-370-1950

Clinique Chiropratique
Diamond, Dr. Jacques; Parr, Dr. Jean-Guy
1640, rue 6e 819-375-1322

Clinique Chiropratique du Dr Roch Parent
Parent, Dr. Roch
3100, boul des Forges 819-373-2224

Clinique Chiropratique du Dr Perigny Robert
Bourdon, Dr. Louis; Perigny, Dr. Robert
1020, boul
des Recollets 819-373-7222/375-8511

Dober, Dr. Richard W.
1351, rue Jean-Nicolet 819-375-1444

Marchand, Dr. Jean-Denis
2675, boul De Varennes 819-378-1313

TROIS RIVIERES OUEST

A La Clinique Chiropratique Dr David Leclerc
Leclerc, Dr. David
3290, rue Normandie 819-373-2241

A La Place Chiropratique Trois-Rivieres-Ouest
Dober, Dr. Maitland M.
3085, Ct Rosemont 819-373-2777

Centre Chiropratique Cote Richelieu
Hains, Dr. Guy
2930, cote Richelieu 819-375-5600

Clinique Chiropatique Dr Helene Gervais
Gervais, Dr. Helene
2930, Cote Richelieu 819-374-1234

VAL D'OR

Clinique Chiropratique Familiale Val D'Or
Guarnaccia, Dr. Rocco;
Guarnaccia, Dr. Sebastien
Parent, Dr. Pierre
199, av Lasalle 819-824-6592

Clinique Chiropratique Roy
Roy, Dr. Roger
153, rue Perreault 819-825-5002

VARENNES

Clinique Chiropratique Familiale de Varennes
1417, Rene Gaultier 514-652-7444

VAUDREUIL

Centre Chiropratique St-Lazare
Poitras, Dr. Jean-Pierre
1537, ch Ste-Angelique 514-424-9288

Sirois, Dr. J.P.
412, boul Roche 514-455-4731

VERCHERES

Clinique Chiropratique de Vercheres
630, rue Duvernay 514-583-6226

VERDUN

Chiro-Centre de Verdun
Berube, Dr. Gerard M.
176, av De L'Eglise 514-766-0176

VICTORIAVILLE

Carignan, Dr. Rejean
367, rue Notre-Dame E 819-752-6823

Centre Chiropratique Place St-Georges
Masse, Dr. Louis
184, boul des
Bois Francs N 819-758-1200

Clinique Chiropratique Chartier
Chartier, Dr. Lyne
367, rue Notre-Dame E 819-751-2212

Clinique Chiropratique des Boulevards
Veilleux, Dr. Marcel
193, boul des
Bois-Francs S 819-752-5999

Place Chiropratique Victoriaville
Moreau, Dr. Simon G.;
Poisson, Dr. Peguy
261, rue Notre Dame O 819-758-5036

VILLE-DES-LAURENTIDES

Lacoursiere, Dr. Jacques
232, boul Laurier 514-439-3160

VILLE MARIE

Chartier, Dr. Michel
14, Notre-Dame S 819-622-0155

VIMONT

Centre Chiropratique Vimont
1711, boul des
Laurentides 514-967-0779

Sylvain, Dr. Lauzon
2102, boul des Laurentides .514-967-1656

WAKEFIELD

Chicoine, Dr. Ed
191, ch Riverside 819-459-2318

WESTMOUNT

Clinique de Sante Chiropratique Westmount
245, Victoria 514-932-0180

Centre Chiropratique Westmount
Hollender, Dr. Annick
324, av Victoria 514-486-7737

WINDSOR

Duguay, Dr. Yvan
75, rue De l'Eglise 819-845-7885

YAMACHICHE

Clinique Chiropratique du Dr Lamy, Dr. Raymond
1511, Principale
(St-Thomas de Caxton) 819-296-2200

✦ Saskatchewan

Chiropractors are regulated in Saskatchewan, meaning that there is legislation establishing a governing body responsible for registering and disciplining practitioners (see below, "Governing Body"). There is government health coverage under the Saskatchewan's Medical Care Insurance Branch (see below, "Government Health Care Funding").

Legislation

Chiropractors are regulated under *The Chiropractic Act, 1994.* The Act defines "chiropractic" as including the following points as they relate to disease or disability where the treatment or diagnosis is taught in an accredited College of Chiropractic:

(i)   the science and art of treatment, by methods of adjustment, by hand, of one or more of the several articulations of the human body;

(ii) diagnosis, including all diagnostic methods, and spinal analysis; and

(iii) the provision of direction and advice, written or otherwise.

Only a member of the Chiropractors' Association of Saskatchewan is entitled to practise chiropractic, unless assistance is being offered in an emergency.

Section 25(1) states that nothing in the Act or bylaws (made by the governing body) authorizes chiropractors to prescribe or administer prescription drugs, practise medicine, surgery or midwifery, or use any method other than chiropractic in the treatment of disease. Section 25(2) states that, subject to bylaws, a chiropractor may use X-rays and produce plain film radiographs. The legislation also sets out the responsibilities of the governing body (see below), which registers chiropractors and issues an annual licence to practise. Disciplinary procedures and procedures for investigating complaints are set out in sections 26-45.

Government Health Care Funding

Chiropractors are covered under Saskatchewan's Medical Care Insurance Branch. On the initial visit, the patient pays $15 and the Health Plan pays $13. On subsequent visits, the patient pays $10 and the Health Plan pays $10. Certain groups do not have to pay the patient fee: seniors over 65 receiving the Saskatchewan Income Plan Supplement (SIP); those on the Family Income Plan (FIP); and those on the Social Assistance plan. To inquire about the Saskatchewan Income Plan, call 1-800-667-7161. Chiropractors call 1-800-667-7533 to verify that a person is on the Plan. For medicare information, call 306-787-3475.

Saskatchewan Governing Body/Professional Association

The Chiropractors' Association of Saskatchewan
3420-A Hill Ave
Regina, Saskatchewan S4S 0W9
Tel: 306-585-1411

This is both the governing (regulatory) and professional body. Call to ensure that your chiropractor is licensed, or to register a complaint.

✦ Saskatchewan Chiropractors

NOTE: Check the credentials of your chiropractor (see above, "Questions to Ask"). This publication cannot and does not certify or represent the qualifications of practitioners, or the quality of care available from them. We cannot and do not confirm that those listed are registered as required by law.

ALLAN

Clark, Dr. John
216 Main St
ASSINIBOIA 306-257-4247

Community Chiropractic
Vallee, Dr. D.M.
131-3rd Ave W 306-642-4199

BIGGAR

Meszaros Chiropractic Office
Meszaros, Dr. Keith B.
113-3rd Ave E 306-948-5044

CANORA

Canora Chiropractic Centre
Rostotski, Dr. Ivan;
Rostotski Sr., Dr. Michael;
Rostotski Jr., Dr. Michael
706 Norway Rd S 306-563-5090

DAVIDSON

Davidson Chiropractic Clinic
Paull, Dr. Heather
605 CN Tower 306-653-1325

ESTERHAZY

Nischuk, Dr. L.J.
420 Main St 306-745-6676

ESTEVAN

Royal Heights Chiropractic Centre
Armstrong, Dr. G. Hugh;
Kitchen, Dr. R.G.
130-1175
Nicholson Rd 306-634-2918

FORT QU'APPELLE

Fritz, Dr. Douglas J.;
Strudwick, Dr. Arden
241b Broadway E 306-332-4522

HAGUE

Papish, Dr. Rory
309 West Railway St 306-225-2240

HUMBOLDT

Chiropractic Associates
Martinuk, Dr. David; Martinuk, Dr. Edward
Martinuk, Dr. Karen
716 Main St 306-682-2440

INDIAN HEAD

Ziolkowski, Dr. Barbara
610 Grand Ave 306-695-2260

KAMSACK

Strukoff Chiropractic Clinic
Strukoff, Dr. Fred; Strukoff, Dr. Wayne
423-3rd Ave S 306-542-2353

KENASTON

Delaire, Dr. Ronald
1411-100th St 306-445-9391

KINDERSLEY

Kindersley Chiropractic Office
Teichroeb, Dr. Reuben
109-1st Ave W 306-463-2046

LA RONGE

La Ronge Chiropractic Clinic
McKee, Dr. James G.
215 La Ronge Ave 306-425-3342

LUMSDEN

Goldie, Dr. J. Kenneth
400 James St N 306-731-2587

MARTENSVILLE

Wallace, Dr. N.G.
61 Centennial Dr 306-242-3633

MEADOW LAKE

Meadowlands Chiropractic
McKee, Dr. James G.
321 Centre St 306-236-1970

MELFORT

Mindiuk, Dr. John
By Appointment 306-752-6363

Schulte, Dr. A.H.
210 Main St 306-752-3215

MELVILLE

Stechishin, Dr. Dale
317 Main St 306-728-5929

MOOSE JAW

Beleshinski, Dr. R .
3a-54 Stadacona St W 306-692-3113

Glenn Chiropractic Clinic
Glenn, Dr. Gale Thomas
24 Athabasca E 306-692-5944

Heritage Chiropractic Clinic
Heidinger, Dr. Steven; Majeran, Dr. Christine
351 Main St N 306-691-4040

**Kloczko, Dr. Rhonda J.;
McMaster, Dr. Graeme**
1-245 E Fairford St 306-692-0488

Reihl, Dr. Jeffrey
24 Athabasca St E 306-692-6403

MOOSOMIN

Grassick, Dr. Brian G.
906 Main St 306-435-4250

NIPAWIN

Jurgens, Dr. Blair A.
344-1st Ave E 306-862-3129

NORTH BATTLEFORD

Dean, Dr. William; Delaire, Dr. Ronald T.
1411-100th St 416-445-9391

Garrett & Runge Chiropractic Office
Garrett, Dr. Kenneth Allan; Runge, Dr. Rodney
1662-100th St 306-445-8322

Palmer, Gordon S.
1491-100th St 306-445-4766

OUTLOOK

Mah, Dr. Edward
116 Saskatchewan Ave W ...306-867-9695

PRINCE ALBERT

Boden, Dr. Mark; Broker, Dr. Blaine
587-28th St W 306-922-7028

Buettner, Dr. David; Mindiuk, Dr. John
585 W 28th St 306-764-6115

Martsinkiw, Dr. Reginald J.
589 W 28th St 306-763-7343

South Hill Chiropractic Clinic
Henbid, Dr. Kevin; Lovell, Dr. Alan
3, 150-32nd St W 306-922-5772

REGINA

Albert North Chiropractic Office
Joyce, Dr. Robert
315 Albert St 306-775-2115

Albert Park Chiropractic Clinic
Brady, Dr. Ron; Gillis, Dr. Pala;
MacNeill, Dr. Shannon
4303 Albert St 306-585-3696

Albert St Chiropractic Clinic
Johnston, Dr. R.J.; Johnston, Dr. W.A.
2155 Albert St 306-522-4738

Ashcroft, Dr. R.E.A.
2120 College Ave 306-522-4224

Avord Chiropractic
Dowhaniuk, Dr. M.J.; Millar, Dr. D.P.; White, Dr. S.G.
2300 McIntyre St 306-525-3388

Bramham, Dr. D.T.; Kraft, Dr. Jason
670, 2220-12th Ave 306-522-7097

Broad St Chiropractic Centre
Chadwick, Dr. Gordon; Chadwick Sr., Dr. R.G.;
Greenman, Dr. Gary A.; Scraper, Dr. Darren J.
1858 Broad St 306-359-3060

Cathedral Chiropractic Group
Nelson, Dr. D.W.D.
3500-13th Ave 306-757-3500

Chiropractic Arts Clinic
Flash, Dr. J.E.; Moffatt, Dr. M.I.
2524-11th Ave 306-525-6151

Chiropractic Associates Clinic
Donbrook, Dr. B.M.; Donbrook, Dr. Douglas;
Hamilton, Dr. Robert; Kelm, Dr. J. Donald;
Ottenbreit, Dr. Kerry Ann
1540 Albert St 306-359-3333

Collins, Dr. Dean
44 Willoughby Cr 306-949-8664

Maplebrook Chiropractic Office
Leskun, Dr. Jim
143 Albert St N 306-543-6644

McIntyre Street Chiropractors
Barber, Dr. Sharon; Rodgers, Dr. Gregory
1840 McIntyre St 306-565-8500

Regina East Chiropractic Office
Goertzen, Dr. Dale; Laplante, Dr. Garth
233 Victoria Ave E 306-757-5212

South Albert Chiropractic Clinic
Kloczko, Dr. Brent; Kloczko, Dr. Rhonda
4040 Albert St 306-585-3949

Transcona Medical Clinic
Fritz, Dr. Douglas J.
4936-4th Ave 306-775-2688

Ziolkowski, Dr. Barbara
3414 Clover Pl 306-757-4060

Ziolkowski, Dr. Lorna
2010 Wascana Greens 306-359-3060

ROSETOWN

Meszaros Chiropractic Office
Meszaros, Dr. Keith
201 Main St 306-882-4040

SASKATOON

Andronyk, Dr. A.
607 Cn Towers 306-664-3936

Bedford Square Chiropractic Clinic
Lemire, Dr. Joe; Skjaveland, Dr. Terri
5, 3110-8th St E 306-373-0337

Canarama Chiropractic Clinic
Bay 9-7 Assiniboine Dr ...306-665-8008

Cassidy, Dr. John David
By Appointment 306-966-8198

Centre City Chiropractic Office
Wallace, Dr. N.G
237-20th St E 306-664-3244

Circle Centre Chiropractic Clinic
Foster, Dr. K.D.; Pankiw, Dr. J.K.;
Sand, Dr. J.B.; Simpson, Dr. R.A.
105, 3301-8th St E 306-955-5005

Clark, Dr. Gary W.
215 N 5th Ave 306-244-5358

Clark, Dr. Randy L
106 Cumberland Ave N 306-653-4933

8th Street Chiropractic Health & Wellness Clinic
Barber, Dr. N.C.; Harder, Dr. S; Majeran, Dr. M.
1269-8th St E 306-955-1561

Fairhaven Chiropractic Centre
Yeomans, Dr. G.G.
205 Fairmont Dr 306-384-6363

Fourth Avenue Chiropractic Clinic
Cote, Dr. Pierre; Mierau, Dr. Dale
9, 119-4th Ave S 306-242-5300

Kays, Dr. Bernard
1105-8th Ave 306-931-2225

Lakeview Chiropractic Clinic
3-1945 Mckercher Dr 306-955-5888

Lenore Chiropractic Clinic
Fenrich, Dr. K; Nykoliation, Dr. Jim;
Papish, Dr. R.
6-123 Lenore Dr 306-934-6066

Levesques' Chiropractic Clinic
Graham, Dr. Christopher; Levesques, Dr.
Constant; Levesques, Dr. Jean (John)
200-102 Wall St 306-652-4070

Mah, Dr. E.K.
116 Saskatchewan Ave W ...306-244-7004

Market Mall Chiropractic Clinic
Grabowski, Dr. John; Lewchuk, Dr. Stan
125-2325 Preston Ave 306-955-5900

Mount Royal Chiropractic Clinic
5, 1640-33rd St W 306-382-9299

Palisades Chiropractic Clinic
Balchen, Dr. Kendall; Grabowski, Dr. John R.;
Jenssen, Dr. Mark; Jurgens, Dr. Richard
111, 514-23rd St E 306-934-1012

Paull, Dr. Heather
605 Cn Towers 306-653-1325

Pleasant Hill Chiropractic Clinic
Burns, Dr. Steven; Schuster, Dr. Rachel;
Sheppard, Dr. Scott W.
4, 1615-20th St W 306-384-5344

Queen Street Chiropractic Group
Clark, Dr. J.T.; Fyfe, Dr. Ryan;
Grier, Dr. A.R.; Zeman, Dr. Don
200-514 Queen St 306-665-6840

Second Avenue Family Chiropractic Centre
Brandt, Dr. Julie; Labrecque, Dr. Mark G.; Mah, Dr. Edward; Mintzler, Dr. Daryn; Wilkinson, Dr. Timothy
724-2nd Ave N 306-244-7004

Stern, Dr. Paula
91 Campus Dr, U of SK 306-966-5768

Sutherland Chiropractic Clinic
Hornick, Dr. Michael; Marcotte, Dr. D.D.; Pochylko, Dr. Duane
2-705 Central Ave 306-374-4390/
955-5900

Thompson, Dr. Brian
135 Whiteswan Dr 306-665-8008

Westgate Chiropractic Clinic
21, 2410-22nd St W 306-384-7800

Wirth, Dr. G.I.
1028d-8th St E 306-343-1659

SHAUNAVON

Chiropractic Clinic
Shadbolt, Dr. M.
420 Centre 306-297-2838

STRASBOURG

Goldie, Dr. J. Kenneth
Health Centre 306-725-4887

SWIFT CURRENT

Chiropractic Clinic
Smith, Dr. William M.
102-12 Cheadle St W 306-773-3144

Chiropractic Office
Bolton, Dr. Stacy; New, Dr. Travis
2, 244-1st Ave NE 306-778-6464

Foss, Dr. Elwood
1445 Winnie St 306-773-5155

TISDALE

Flonder, Dr. P.A.
507a 100a St 306-873-2828

UNITY

Clark, Dr. D.L.
309 Main 306-228-2525

WEYBURN

**Corrigan, Dr. John R.;
Roundy, Dr. Cheryl L.**
20-4th St NE 306-842-3131

Waddell, Brad M.
112 Railway Ave 306-842-3323

WYNYARD

MacNeill, Dr. Shannon
220 Main St 306-554-3886

YORKTON

Cymbalisty, Dr. E.
520 W Broadway St 306-783-4486

Howlett, Dr. James D.
41 W Broadway St 306-783-3722

Nischuk, Dr. L.J.
318 W Broadway St 306-783-3366

 # Yukon Territory

Chiropractors are regulated in the Yukon, with legislation establishing a register of qualified chiropractors, their scope of practice and a means of discipline. Instead of a self-governing body, as found in the provinces, the Territory government handles these functions. (see below, "Licensing Body"). There is no government health care funding.

Legislation

Yukon chiropractors are regulated under the *Chiropractors Act*. Under the Act, "chiropractic" means "the method of treating human beings for disease and the causes of disease by means of adjustment by hand and the articulations of the spinal column and other adjustments by hand incidental thereto" (section 1). Chiropractors may use X-ray shadow photographs, and may use X-ray equipment if they file a certificate of competency pursuant to the regulations (section 10). Chiropractors are prohibited from prescribing or administering drugs, treating communicable diseases,

performing surgery, and prescribing anaesthetic. It is an offence to practise chiropractic without a licence. In case of complaint, the Commissioner in Executive Council may appoint a board of inquiry, which may recommend penalties ranging from fines to cancellation of a licence to practise.

Licensing Body

There is no governing body. However, you may ensure that your chiropractor is licensed, or make inquires regarding initiating a complaint, by calling the following government office:

Consumer Services
Department of Justice
Yukon Government
Box 2703
Whitehorse, Yukon Territory Y1A 2C6
Tel: 403-667-5940

 # Yukon Chiropractors

NOTE: Check the credentials of your chiropractor (see above, "Questions to Ask"). This publication cannot and does not certify or represent the qualifications of practitioners, or the quality of care available from them. We cannot and do not confirm that those listed are registered as required by law.

WHITEHORSE

Chiropractic Clinic
Holway-McIntyre, Dr. Rhonda; Lelek, Dr. David
306 Hoge St 403-667-7308

✦ Feldenkrais

WHAT IS FELDENKRAIS

The Feldenkrais Method® is a system of retraining the body to improve its movement and reduce pain from disease or injury. Russian-born Israeli physicist Moshe Feldenkrais developed the technique in the 1940s as an alternative to surgery to deal with an old knee injury that was bothering him. By researching human movement, anatomy, biochemistry, physiology, and learning theories, he taught himself to use the knee correctly and to walk without pain. The method relies on the interaction between the sensory pathways of the central nervous system carrying information to the brain, and the motor network carrying messages from the brain to the muscles. Feldenkrais believed that the brain adopts motion that strains the body the least. His method is meant to communicate with the nervous system by physically showing the body a more effective way of moving, allowing the brain to cancel the old distorted pattern. The method, presented as a form of instruction rather than as a health treatment, is often compared to the technique developed by Frederick Alexander (see "Alexander Technique").

Group and Individual Lessons

The Feldenkrais Method may be taught in group classes, known as Awareness Through Movement® or in private classes, called Functional Integration®. In the group classes, the practitioner verbally guides you through a sequence of movements while you sit, stand, or lie on the floor. Students are taught to discover how they move and to abandon habitual patterns that are detrimental to the body. In the private classes, a movement lesson is custom-tailored to the student, and movements are communicated though slow, gentle touch. The student, wearing comfortable clothing, lies or sits on a low padded table, or may stand, walk or sit in a chair. The practitioner guides the student though a series of precise movements to alter habitual patterns and provide new learning for the neuromuscular system.

BENEFITS OF FELDENKRAIS

The Feldenkrais Guild® does not claim to treat or eliminate disease, but it may help make body movements easier. The method attracts accident victims, and those with back problems, cerebral palsy or multiple sclerosis. It also attracts musicians, athletes and others whose careers may benefit from improved body movement. The individual classes are considered especially useful for those wishing to deal with limitations brought on by stress, accident or illness.

QUESTIONS TO ASK

✦ Is your practitioner certified by the Feldenkrais Guild? Confirm by contacting the Guild (see below ("Guild").

NOTE: Such certification means that the practitioner has met the standards set by the non-profit Guild, but this does not constitute a licence, such as that obtained by health practitioners regulated under provincial law.

✦ How much experience does your practitioner have? Has your practitioner helped a person with your condition, and what were the results? Does your practitioner specialize in a particular area?

✦ What is your practitioner's background, and is he or she trained in other forms of health care?

✦ Is the Feldenkrais Method an appropriate technique for what you hope to achieve? If so, are group or individual lessons more appropriate?

✦ How much do the lessons cost and what is the estimated number required?

GOVERNMENT REGULATION

There is no government regulation of the practitioners of the Feldenkrais Method in Canada, meaning that there is no legislation establishing regulatory bodies to register and discipline qualified practitioners. However, the Feldenkrais Guild, listed below, has registered the name "Feldenkrais" for use only by those practitioners certified by the Guild. The Guild certifies practitioners who meet its standards.

GUILD

Feldenkrais Guild®
524 Ellsworth St
PO Box 489
Albany, Oregon 97321
Tel: 1-800-775-2118 or 503-926-0981
Fax: 503-926-0572
Contact: Michael Purcell, President

This non-profit membership organization, founded by Dr. Moshe Feldenkrais in 1977, is the professional organization for the Feldenkrais Method. Only those trained by Dr. Feldenkrais or graduates of Guild accredited training programs are eligible to become members and to use the Registered Service Marks of the Feldenkrais Guild. The Guild offers referrals to a network of practitioners and establishes curriculum requirements for certification of practitioners. The Guild also sells self-help books and audio tapes.

FELDENKRAIS EDUCATION

Those interested in becoming a certified practitioner of the Feldenkrais Method should seek programs accredited by the Feldenkrais Guild. The Guild's training programs consist of 800 hours of training over a period of four years. Once certified, the practitioner must meet yearly requirements to retain certification. These requirements, as of June 1996, include at least 100 hours of practice in the Feldenkrais Method every year and 20 hours of class study every year. Training programs are held in the U.S., Canada, several European countries, Israel and Australia. Knowledge and experience from a variety of professional and occupational fields is encouraged, but no specific academic background is required for the training program. The Québec Institute listed below offers training in French, and a training program is in progress in Vancouver, B.C. Contact the Feldenkrais Guild, listed above, for more information.

Feldenkrais® Institute of Somatic Education, Inc.
PO Box 363 Stn Delorimier
Montréal, Québec H2H 2N7
Tel: 514-521-2418

This Institute is affiliated with the Feldenkrais Guild. It offers certification training in French.

✦ Feldenkrais in Your Province

Provinces are listed alphabetically below, with the following information:

✦ address and telephone number of the one provincial association in Québec

✦ names, addresses and telephone numbers of Feldenkrais practitioners, listed alphabetically by city

NOTE: The names in this list were provided by the Feldenkrais Guild. According to the Guild, all these practitioners were certified as meeting its standards as of March. Confirm the certification of your practitioner or obtain the names of newly certified practitioners in your area by contacting the Feldenkrais Guild, located in Albany, Oregon (see above, "Guild"). The initials 'ATM' mean Awareness Through Movement®.

✦ Alberta Feldenkrais Practitioners

NOTE: Check the credentials of your practitioner (see above, "Questions to Ask"). This publication cannot and does not certify or represent the qualifications of practitioners, or the quality of care available from them.

CALGARY

Black, Robert
#13, 4940-39th Ave, SW 403-240-3425/242-2909

EDMONTON

Heayn, Arnie
9211 Ottewell Rd 403-473-1681/469-7170

Ogg, Jacqueline
c/o Top to Toe Inc.
6627 128th St 403-435-1691

Oliva, Margherita (ATM teacher only)
#71 2703 79th St 403-490-0974

Stanley, Joan
7127 Saskatchewan Dr 403-435-0818

✦ British Columbia Feldenkrais Practitioners

NOTE: Check the credentials of your practitioner (see above, "Questions to Ask"). This publication cannot and does not certify or represent the qualifications of practitioners, or the quality of care available from them.

GALIANO ISLAND

Lemoine, Louise
398 Morgan Rd
COMP 4, Site 22 604-539-2445

NORTH VANCOUVER

Clark, Dianne (ATM Teacher Only)
546 E 5th St 604-988-1286

Williams, Jane
224 W 19th St 604-988-5221

PENDER ISLAND

Adam-Smith, Brenda
3422 S Otter Bay Rd 604-629-3322

SALT SPRING ISLAND

Feldenkrais Works
Haltrecht, Anna
104 Langs Rd 604-254-2534

Friedman, Alice
325 Mountain Rd 604-537-2343/653-4332

SOOKE

Moore, Warren
6775 Pascoe Rd, RR 2 604-642-4732

SURREY

Moving into Life
McNally, Louise
#2 6601-138th St 604-599-7003

VANCOUVER

Balas, Marty
2081 Napier St 604-253-1189

Purkis, Helen
801-2370 W 2nd Ave 604-731-3029

Stanley, Mary Lou
801-750 W Broadway 604-879-5017

Willson, Janet
2570 Yale St 604-255-6376

VICTORIA

Hammond, Vanessa
(Physiotherapist)
4706 Eales Rd, RR 2 604-478-4981

Lynn, Brian
2114 Oregon St 604-598-8992

McLynn, Margaret
303 Gorge Rd W 604-386-1618

WEST VANCOUVER

Ezzy, Suzanne R.
1881 22nd St 604-922-9664

✦ Manitoba Feldenkrais Practitioners

NOTE: Check the credentials of your practitioner (see above, "Questions to Ask"). This publication cannot and does not certify or represent the qualifications of practitioners, or the quality of care available from them.

BRANDON

Universal Stress & Therapy Clinic
Derkson, Roxanne
242-11th St 204-726-8851

WINNIPEG

Fitness Physiotherapy Services
Pianosi, Marina
135 Roslyn Rd 204-982-9600

✦ Newfoundland Feldenkrais Practitioners

NOTE: Check the credentials of your practitioner (see above, "Questions to Ask"). This publication cannot and does not certify or represent the qualifications of practitioners, or the quality of care available from them.

ST. JOHN'S

Winsor, Beverley
81 Penetanguishene Rd 709-576-7003

✦ Nova Scotia Feldenkrais Practitioners

NOTE: Check the credentials of your practitioner (see above, "Questions to Ask"). This publication cannot and does not certify or represent the qualifications of practitioners, or the quality of care available from them.

HALIFAX

Beale, Kelly
5871 Spring Garden Rd 902-477-8569

✦ Ontario Feldenkrais Practitioners

NOTE: Check the credentials of your practitioner (see above, "Questions to Ask"). This publication cannot and does not certify or represent the qualifications of practitioners, or the quality of care available from them.

CRYSTAL BEACH

Rubin, Sally
PO Box 667 905-894-0517

GLOUCESTER

Beggs, Nicole
6141 Larivière Cr 613-834-3439

Morrow, Sally
2172 Bickerton Ave 613-747-3925

HAMILTON

Tausch, Harold
By Appointment 905-521-9664

OTTAWA

Kadlec, Mirko
1517 Morisset Ave 613-234-9348

Murnaghan, Rosa
1401-1171 Ambleside Dr ...613-820-2546

Nichols, Patricia
PO Box 4795, Stn E 613-231-7545

Parker, Nancy
349 MacKay St 613-744-5671

Woolnough, Lisa
143 Rideau Terrace 613-744-0868

SCARBOROUGH

Alexander, Janet
131 Newlands Ave 416-265-0735

TORONTO

Duke, Shelley
190 St George St 416-961-8123

The Feldenkrais Centre
Harris, Marion
390 Dupont St, Ste 201 416-928-3505

The Feldenkrais Method
Dack, Judith
390 Dupont, Ste 201 416-964-2532

Holland, Margo
50 Thursfield Cr 416-467-7153

Jenkins, Peter, BA
2238 Dundas St W #303 ...416-588-9773

Nitefor, Olena, M Ed
493 Broadview Ave 416-466-6143

Pos, Alberta Eveline
44 Jackes Ave #810 416-963-4995

Tank, Paul
40 High Park Ave #1401 ...416-763-4652

Tausch, Harold
259 Withrow Ave 416-463-3846

Voss, Frauke
16 Oriole Rd 416-929-0394

Williams, Betty
505-25 George St 416-777-1914

Zimmerman, Maya
Swimming Education Specialist
720 Spadina Ave, #1610 ...416-920-4172

WILLOWDALE

Sigesmund, Eunice, BSc
26 Danville Dr 416-223-2662

WINDSOR

Motion-Wise
Kellerman, Sara Sandra, BScN
2549 Academy Dr 519-969-5683

✦ Québec

Québec Association

Association Québécoise
c/o Institut Feldenkrais d'Education Somatique
CP 363, Succursale Delorimier
Montréal, Québec H2H 2N7
Tel/Fax: 514-529-5966
Contact: Yvan Joly, President

This is the only association in Canada affiliated with the Feldenkrais Guild®.

✦ Québec Feldenkrais Practitioners

NOTE: Check the credentials of your practitioners(see above, "Questions to Ask"). This publication cannot and does not certify or represent the qualifications of practitioners, or the quality of care available from them.

MONTREAL

Charbonneau, Suzanne
4684 Garnier 514-521-2418

Joly, Yvan
PO Box 363, Stn Delorimier .514-529-5966

Leblond, Philippe
5165 Sherbrooke St W #206 514-273-9621

Montreal Dance Exchange
Hébert, Michaël
5464 Rue Chabot 514-526-5092

QUEBEC

Berube, Marie-Lorraine
640 Chemin St Louis, Apt. #3 418-527-8232

Herbalism

WHAT IS HERBALISM

Herbalism refers to the use of plants for healing and preventive medicine. Herbal products are derived from roots, stems or leaves and are frequently sold in liquid extract, pill form, or as teas. The practice of herbalism, also known as phytotherapy, traces its origins to the earliest forms of medicine. Some herbalists are trained exclusively in herbalism, and receive their training from institutes grounded in Western scientific medicine. Others consider themselves part of the native, Wise Woman or other traditions. Herbs also form part of the treatment techniques of Traditional Chinese Medicine (see "Acupuncture and Traditional Chinese Medicine"), Ayurvedic medicine (see "Ayurveda") and naturopathic medicine (see "Naturopathic Medicine").

Physicians and Herbalism

Herbal remedies are not commonly prescribed by Canadian physicians. However, they are frequently prescribed by physicians in Britain and Germany. In these countries, herbs are a more integral part of conventional health care than in North America, according to the Institute for Clinical Evaluative Sciences in Ontario (ICES), an independent non-profit research body. In Britain, the *British Herbal Pharmacopoeia* is often used as a reference by physicians, and a similar publication is used in Germany. The practice of herbalism is considered by the British Medical Association as one of the forms of alternative health care with established foundations of training and "the potential for greatest use alongside orthodox medical care" (*Complementary Medicine: New Approaches to Good Practice*, Oxford: Oxford University Press, 1993, p.143).

Herbal medicine is beginning to receive notice from conventional medical circles in North America. As the *Canadian Journal of Herbalism* reported (Winter, 1995, Vol XVI, No.2), Canada's first international conference on phytotherapy in October 1995, at Mohawk College in Hamilton was hailed as a breakthrough for herbalism in this country. The conference included a presentation on Evening Primrose Oil by Dr. Fargas-Babjac, teaching professor at McMaster University's Medical school.

Differences Between Pharmaceutical Drugs and Herbs

The healing properties of many herbs are widely recognized within both alternative and conventional health care circles. In fact, herbs form the basis of an estimated 25-30% of pharmaceutical drugs (eg. foxglove is the origin of the heart disease drug, digoxin). In many cases, these drugs have been derived by extracting a single active constituent from a plant (the part of the plant with a particular therapeutic value) and synthesizing it in a chemical compound. Herbalists take a different approach. They generally prefer to use remedies extracted from a part of the whole plant, with all its bio-chemical constituents. Britain's National Institute of Medical Herbalists, the oldest body of practising medical herbalists in the world, notes that herbalists believe that the active constituents are naturally balanced within the plant. For example, the Institute notes that synthetic diuretics (drugs that increase the flow of urine) seriously reduce the potassium level in the body. To restore the loss, potassium supplements are required. By contrast, the herbalist uses dandelion leaves, which are a potent diuretic, but which contain potassium to naturally replace that which is lost.

There are other differences between drugs and herbs. According to information published for medical practitioners by the Institute for Clinical Evaluative Studies (ICES), a body jointly sponsored by the Ontario Ministry of Health and the Ontario Medical Association, herbal medicines are generally not as pharmacologically active as drugs, and drug/herbal medicine interactions do not pose nearly as much danger as drug/drug interactions ("Getting Acquainted with Herbs", *informed*, March 1996, Vol.2, No.2). However, the article notes that information in this area is still limited, and that the subtle actions of herbal medicines can result in serious interactions with certain drugs. The British School of Phytotherapy states that herbal medicines do not have the aggressive and invasive action of modern drugs, and instead support the body's own natural tendency to heal itself. Many of the uses of herbs are based on traditional methods with long histories, and without the backing of scientific research. However, research is now being published in international and botanical journals on the beneficial and adverse properties of various herbs.

Quality of Herbal Products

Herbalists such as Hein Zeylstra, founder of the English School of Phytotherapy, have called for better quality controls in the production of herbal products, and for the standardization of the amount of the active constituent so that herbalists may give the exact optimum dosage. Consumers should be aware that the quality standards among herbal products vary dramatically. As well, products that appear similar often have different amounts of the active constituent (i.e. different strength). There are also reports of poor quality substitutions being made for ingredients printed on labels, particularly in the case of Chinese herbal remedies. The need to find reputable suppliers and qualified herbalists is underscored by the above. Some herbalists hand-craft their own herbal products to ensure quality control.

BENEFITS OF HERBALISM

Herbalists use herbs to strengthen the body and assist its natural ability to heal itself. However, herbalists are not replacements for physicians, and many herbalists suggest that you consult a qualified health practitioner for a diagnosis before deciding on a course of treatment, especially for serious illnesses. Herbalists suggest that herbs represent one means of helping the body to function well, and make it less susceptible to conditions such as the following:

Skin Problems: Psoriasis, acne and eczema

Digestive disorders: Peptic ulcers, colitis, irritable bowel syndrome and indigestion

Heart and circulation problems: Angina, high blood pressure, varicose veins, varicose ulcers

Gynaecological disorders: Premenstrual syndrome and menopause

Allergic responses: Hayfever and asthma

Other: Arthritis, liver problems, insomnia, stress, moods, migraine, headaches, tonsillitis, influenza, side effects of conventional cancer therapy, and problems affecting older adults

Herbs provide a gentle, low cost form of medication for older adults, according to Keith Stelling, editor of *The Canadian Journal of Herbalism*. Modern herbalism "offers non-toxic, gentle solutions to many critical areas of geriatric pathology including digestive problems, anxiety and depression, circulatory stagnation and hypertension, skin irritations and support in countering the side effects of many drugs" (*The Canadian Journal of Herbalism*, Spring, 1996, Vol. XVII, No.1, p.22). Mr. Stelling noted in an interview with *Alternative Health Care: The Canadian Directory* that trained herbalists can work effectively with physicians to assist patients of all ages in dealing with a wide variety of health issues, but not structural problems.

Herbalists generally place a great emphasis on dealing with underlying causes more than symptoms. Anthony Godfrey, the president of the Ontario Herbalists Association stated in *The Canadian Journal of Herbalism* (Spring, 1996, Vol. XVII, No.1, p.42): "The true herbalist is one who has reverence for the natural order and works to learn how to participate in its restoration." He added: "This is how healing will occur."

Bach Flower Remedies

Moods and emotions are also said to be soothed with certain herbs, and the Bach Flower Remedies in particular are devoted to this theory. British physician and homeopath Dr. Edward Bach concluded that many of his patients' ills were related to negative states of mind. He classified 38 emotional states and developed herbal remedies from flowers. He tested the remedies to eliminate those that produced side effects - using himself as the research subject for much of his work. Some herbalists specialize in Bach flower remedies, and self-help booklets are also available.

QUESTIONS TO ASK

✦ What is the nature of your herbalist's training and how extensive is it? If your herbalist was formally trained in botanical medicine, did this include clinical training, as well as training in anatomy, physiology, and pathology? If your herbalist was trained in a tradition, such as Wise Woman, how extensive was this training and is this person known in the community as a reputable herbalist? (see below, "Herbalism Education"). If your herbalist is trained in Ayurvedic medicine or traditional Chinese medicine, has your practitioner received a thorough grounding in the tradition? (see "Ayurveda" and "Acupuncture and Traditional Chinese Medicine")

NOTE: A "Master" herbalist or other designation may signify different amounts of training at different schools. The benchmark for the clinical herbalist is a full-time three-year or four-year program. Associations differ in the standards set for consultant herbalists, a loose category of practitioners considered qualified by some to set up practice, and by others to give advice in health food stores. The minimum amount of training for consultant herbalists is often cited as one to two years. Many associations suggest that practitioners should supplement correspondence training with supervised practical training. While it is important to find a practitioner with adequate training, it is also important to avoid shrouding herbalism in a mystique of professionalism, notes Mark Taylor, a Master Herbalist from Yarmouth County, Nova Scotia. "Everybody is capable of managing their own health, and an herbalist can help you sort through all the available information."

✦ Does your practitioner's training, conventional or otherwise, include contra-indications (symptoms or conditions indicating against the advisability of a particular remedy) for pregnancy, breast-feeding, children, other health conditions and illnesses?

✦ How much experience does your herbalist have, and does it include experience with your condition? What were the results? Can your herbalist provide professional references?

✦ Does your practitioner have a working relationship with other health care professionals? Under what circumstances will your practitioner refer you to a physician or other regulated health professional? Is your practitioner trained to recognize conditions that require a physician's care?

NOTE: Herbalists do not claim to replace physicians. It is important to obtain a diagnosis for health problems from a qualified physician or regulated health practitioner. Dominion College in B.C., among other schools, advocates that its graduates develop close working relationships with other health care professionals.

✦ Is your herbalist a member of a professional association? You may wish to contact the association to discuss the qualifications of your herbalist, or to obtain a referral (see below, "National and International Associations" and "Herbalism in Your Province") .

NOTE: Bear in mind that associations do not necessarily check out the qualifications of their members. Also note that most professional associations are not regulatory bodies established by legislation to register or license practitioners.

✦ Does your practitioner practise primarily as an herbalist, or does he or she practise herbalism as an adjunct to the practice of conventional medicine, physiotherapy, etc.? How much experience does your practitioner have as an herbalist? Does your practitioner specialize in particular types of care?

✦ How does your practitioner stay informed of the numerous research developments on the benefits and adverse effects of herbs? (eg. Does your practitioner subscribe to research journals and review the research reports in professional newsletters?)

✦ How does your practitioner obtain herbal remedies, and ensure that the supplier is reputable?

NOTE: This is a critical issue, given the labelling problems with some herbal remedies. Some herbalists avoid the problem by hand-crafting their own tinctures (liquid extracts).

✦ What are your practitioner's fees and prices for the herbs? While rates vary, $60 is a standard maximum charged by highly qualified herbalists for an initial consultation in Ontario, with subsequent visits costing about $40.

✦ Is the practitioner aware of possible interactions between herbal remedies and other conventional medications that you may be taking?

NOTE: If you are taking medication, find an herbalist who knows of the research on which herbs to avoid with different medications.

GOVERNMENT REGULATION
Regulation of Practitioners

Canadian herbalists (also called phytotherapists) are not regulated as practitioners by any provincial government, except insofar as practitioners such as naturopathic doctors trained in botanical medicine are regulated in some provinces (see "Naturopathic Medicine, Government Regulation"). This means that there are no provincial laws establishing a governing body responsible for registering qualified herbalists and disciplining them. This also means that there are no minimum educational standards for those calling themselves herbalists. However, several herbalist associations set standards for membership or registration.

Every province has legislation restricting either the practice of medicine, or the practice of a certain medical acts, such as diagnosis.

Regulation of Herbal Products

The federal government regulates herbal products and homeopathic remedies through the *Food and Drugs Act* and regulations. Herbal products demonstrated to be safe and effective for various ailments are assigned Drug Identification Numbers (DINs). There is controversy over the government requirement for herbal remedies to undergo extensive testing before they may be issued a DIN, and be legally sold in Canada.

There are federal government restrictions on claims that may be made in advertising to the general public and on product labels. The Act prohibits claims as to the product being a treatment, preventative or cure of any of the diseases, disorders or abnormal physical states listed in Schedule A to the Act.

Health Protection Branch Review

The regulation of herbal products has undergone more than a decade of review by the Health Protection Branch of Health Canada, with reports published by an Expert Advisory Committee in 1986 and 1993. The second report concluded that herbs sold for medicinal purposes should not be regulated as foods. Rather, the report pointed to a need for an herbal monograph system to specify ingredients in herbal products appropriate for use as non-prescriptive drugs, and to list the cautions that should be exercised. These monographs are now being developed. This approach may speed the process of assigning a Drug Identification Number (DIN) to herbs which have shown evidence of safety and efficacy. The monographs may be found at the federal government's Internet home page: http://www.hwc.ca.8300

NATIONAL AND INTERNATIONAL ASSOCIATIONS

Following are the national and British herbalist associations. Provincial associations are listed under each province. Several provincial associations, particularly those in Ontario, have members across Canada (see below, "Herbalism in Your Province").

The Canadian Association of Herbal Practitioners
#400 - 1228 Kensington Rd NW
Calgary, Alberta T2N 4P9
Tel: 403-270-0936
Fax: 403-283-0799

This professional association was founded by a group of herbalists and naturopaths in 1964. Call for referrals to about 100 professional members, who are located mainly in western Canada. Active professional members must hold a certificate from an approved herbal college and provide letters of reference. Professional members must have three years of full-time study, including a 500-hour practicum, at a recognized college, such as Coastal Mountain College of Healing Arts in Vancouver, B.C. The association is establishing standards for herbalists with less training. Terry Willard, president of the CAHP, is also the founder of the Wild Rose College of Natural Healing in Calgary, Alberta.

National Institute of Medical Herbalists
56 Longbrook St
Exeter, Devon
England EX4 6AH
Tel: 01392-426022
Fax: 01392-498963

This British association, established in 1864, is the oldest body of practising medical herbalists in the world and sets the highest standards for membership. All members have passed a membership examination following four years of full-time training, including a minimum of 500 hours of supervised clinical training. They adhere to a code of ethics, and have the letters MNIMH or FNIMH, signifying that they are members or fellows of this Institute. Many are graduates of Britain's School of Phytotherapy (Herbal Medicine) or Middlesex University in England. There are six Canadian members listed in the 1996/97 register: Chanchal Cabrera (Vancouver, B.C.); Amanda Howe (Courtenay, B.C.), H. Mattu (Vancouver, B.C.); J. Mattu (Vancouver, B.C.); Keith Stelling (Stoney Creek, Ontario); and Bernice Toews (Virden, Manitoba). Rowan Hamilton, a U.K. member, is now Director of of the Department of Herbal Studies at Coastal Mountain College of Healing Arts in B.C. Their addresses and telephone numbers are noted below (see "Herbalism in Your Province"). For details or to obtain the full register of qualified members, write to the above address. The Institute publishes the *European Journal of Herbal Medicine*, and liaises with the British Parliamentary Group for Complementary and Alternative Medicine.

HERBALISM EDUCATION

If you wish to become a practitioner, it is advisable to contact several colleges and associations before making a choice on a particular program. Some of the well-known colleges and programs are listed below. Compare the qualifications of faculty (their education and professional experience), program content and length, admission requirements, number of clinical hours, and all fees and contract terms, including refund policies. In addition, it is useful to speak with students and graduates of the various programs about their standards, and to consult with representatives of herbalist associations. Ask the representatives if they are affiliated with a particular college. If you do not wish to become a practitioner, but wish to study herbalism, many of the colleges and programs noted below offer home-study courses.

The schools recognized by the Canadian Herbalist Association of B.C. for professional membership as a Registered Herbal Practitioner are: Coastal Mountain College, Dominion Herbal College, Emerson College, Nature's Way Herbal Health, and the School of Phytotherapy in England (see telephone numbers and addresses below). Contact the association for details regarding the course requirements at these schools, as well as other requirements, for professional membership as a Clinical Herbal Therapist or Consultant Herbal Therapist. In other provinces, the amount of training that an herbalist should receive before practising has been subject to recent review within several herbalist associations. Training programs based on the orthodox Western model vary dramatically in length and content, as do the requirements of different institutes for diplomas and designations such as "Master Herbalist". The lack of standardization makes it difficult to compare practitioners' qualifications, and to set standards. Some programs are measured in hours, others by years of part-time or full-time study.

A distinction is sometimes drawn between a consultant herbalist and a clinical herbalist. The consultant usually has the lesser amount of training, often about one year. Depending upon the association, the consultant is considered qualified to give advice in health food stores or to establish a practice. Clinical herbalists often have three years of full-time training, including medical sciences courses, and are considered qualified to set up a practice, consult clients and hand-craft herbal products. For example, the Coastal Mountain College of Healing Arts, Inc. (formerly Wild Rose) in Vancouver, B.C. offers a three-year, full-time program. The School of Phytotherapy (Herbal Medicine) has a full-time, four year program. Traditional Chinese herbalists have often received five years of full-time training in Traditional Chinese Medicine in China, followed by a period of apprenticeship. Naturopathic doctors normally receive training in botanical medicine in at least two courses dedicated to the subject in a four-year, full-time program that also includes related courses, such as bio-chemistry.

Training is different in the folk traditions, such as the native Indian and Wise Woman traditions, where knowledge of the healing properties of plants is passed down through the generations. Helen Bakazias, a practitioner in the Wise Woman tradition from Singhamptom, Ontario, told *Alternative Health Care: The Canadian Directory* that some practitioners take formal Western training, but the key to their practice comes from wisdom passed down through the centuries. This is acquired through time spent working in the field with locally grown plants, without letters of qualification. She noted that the emphasis in the Wise Woman tradition is on nourishing rather than cleansing the body. There are no formal associations, and practitioners must be sought out by word of mouth.

If you are seeking a career in herbalism, you should be aware that herbalists are not regulated in any province, and that every province has legislation restricting the practice of medicine or specific medical acts, such as diagnosis (see above "Government Regulation").

Most provinces have legislation requiring private vocational schools to meet certain minimum standards, often related to financial stability, for the protection of consumers. These requirements for registration vary from province to province, and alternative health care training programs are not in all cases covered by such legislation. B.C. is the only province to require registration of all such training programs with its Private Post-Secondary Education Commission, a regulatory body established by the government. Contact the Ministry of Education in your province for more information.

L'Académie de Phytothérapie du Québec
3805, rue Bélair
Montréal, Québec H2A 2C1
Tél: 514-725-1712
Fax: 514-722-5164

The Academy is a private school offering a program leading to a diploma in phytotherapy. The Quebec Association of Phytotherapists (see below, "Québec - Association") grants the title "Phytothérapeute® diplôme." The phytotherapist may then use the letters Phy. D. To obtain the diploma, the student must first be a member of the association and agree to abide by its rules and code of ethics. The 1000-hour program is divided equally between theory and practical experience. Applicants must be at least 18 years old, with a college-level diploma or proof of relevant experience.

alive Academy of Nutrition
7436 Fraser Park Dr
Burnaby, B.C. V5J 5B9
Tel: 604-435-1919
Fax: 604-435-4888

This Academy offers a home study course in Herbs and Healing, taught in eight comprehensive lessons with practical 'hands-on' assignments and self-testing questions. A final test will be provided for certification.

Artemesia Institute
General Delivery
Jackson's Point, Ontario L0E 1L0

The Institute offers a correspondence course.

Balance Life Gardens
RR3
Lambeth, Ontario N0L 1S0
Tel: 519-645-6733

This school offers an 8-month apprenticeship course in therapeutic herbalism, as well as lectures and workshops.

The Botanic Institute
Unit 5, 180 Southgate Dr
Guelph, Ontario N1G 4P5
Tel: 519-824-9980 or 519-824-4280

This institute, associated with the Central Canadian Herbal Practitioners Association, began offering a consultant herbalist diploma program in 1995 in conjunction with Wild Rose College in Alberta (see below). Courses are offered one weekend per month. The 725-hour two-year program is comprised of 500 hours of classroom time, 75 hours on a thesis, and 150 hours of apprenticeship time. It leads to a diploma as consultant herbalist.

Coastal Mountain College of Healing Arts, Inc.
1745 West 4th Ave
Vancouver, B.C. V6J 1H2
Tel: 604-734-4596
Fax: 604-734-4597
E-mail: cmc@infoserve.net
http://www.coastal.bc.ca/cmc.holistic.college/

Formerly the Wild Rose College of Natural Healing (B.C.) Inc., Coastal Mountain College offers the most extensive herbal training programs in Canada. The three-year, full-time Clinical Herbalist Diploma Program includes courses in biochemistry, physiology, pathology, anatomy and botany, as well as 400 hours of supervised clinical work. The College, founded in 1989, is in the process of affiliating itself with Middlesex University in England, which offers a B.Sc. (hons.) in Herbal Medicine. Middlesex University graduates are eligible to apply for membership in the National Institute of Medical Herbalists (see above, "National and International Associations"). Applicants must meet course prerequisites. There is also an eight-month certificate Practical Herbalist program for those interested in becoming growers, distributors, wholesalers or retailers, with emphasis on job training. Other continuing education programs are offered.

Dominion Herbal College
7527 Kingsway
Burnaby, B.C. V3N 3C1
Tel: 604-521-5822
Fax: 604-526-1561
Email: herbal@uniserve.com

Second Location:
200 St. Clair Ave W, Ste 303
Toronto, Ontario M4V 1R1
Tel: 416-964-3377

This college, founded in 1926, offers a range of herbal study programs, as well as courses for physicians and pharmacists. For example, the college offers a home study Chartered Herbalist course, which takes six months to one year, and includes lessons on anatomy and physiology. Upon completion of the Chartered Herbalist program, students may apply to the Master Herbalist program. The college also offers a three-year, part-time Clinical Herbal Therapist Diploma course in West Vancouver and in Toronto consisting of monthly 4-day weekend sets of classes, with 15-20 hours home study per week. The total number of course hours is about 3,747, including 500 clinical hours and home study. As well, the college offers a four-year home study (15-25 hours per week) in clinical phytotherapy, with 500 hours of supervised clinical training.

East-West Course in Herbology - Michael Tierra

P.O. Box 712
Santa Cruz, California 95061
USA
Tel: 408-429-8066

This is a correspondence course in Western and Eastern Herbalism

Emerson College of Herbology Ltd
582 Cummer Ave
Willowdale, Ontario M2K 2M4

The College offers diploma and master's correspondence courses.

Healing with Herbs
794 Fort St, P.O. Box 38056
Victoria, B.C. V8W 1H2
Tel: 604-598-8616
e-mail: healing@islandnet.com

This school offers a 9-month part-time classroom certificate course, including clinical work. The course is conducted on weekends. There is also a correspondence course entitled Healing Wisdom, which includes Ayurveda training.

Heritage Holistic Health and Environmental Institute
1527A Idylwyld Dr N
Saskatoon S7L 1A9
Tel: 306-664-3873

A correspondence course is available through this Institute.

Living Harmony
33 Aziel St
Toronto, Ontario M6P 2N8
Tel: 416-604-1811

Weekend or evening classes and workshops in basic herbalism are offered by Michael Vertolli, a Toronto herbalist.

Mohawk College
Program in Phytotherapy (Herbal Medicine)
Continuing Education - Health Sciences Department
PO Box 2034
Hamilton, Ontario L8N 3T2
Tel: 905-575-2520
Contact: Betsy Mercuri - 905-575-2503

Mohawk College offers a part-time diploma program in herbal medicine to the standards required to write membership exams with the National Institute of Medical Herbalists of Great Britain. The program is based on the syllabus of Britain's School of Phytotheapy.

Nature's Way Herbal Health Institute
RR2, S18A, C-4
Lumby, B.C. V0E 2G0
Tel: 604-547-2281
Fax: 604-547-8911

This Institute offers a one-year combination classroom and home study Consultant Herbal Therapist course. Students attend class one weekend a month, and complete the balance of their studies at home. The school is run by Kathy Deane, a registered herbalist practitioner with the Canadian Herbalist Association of B.C. Ms. Deane is on the Association's Examining Board and is Secretary-Treasurer. She also runs an herbal practice in Lumby.

The Packard School of Nutrition
586 Alexander St
Sudbury, Ontario P3A 1R3
Tel: 705-560-5275

This schools offers correspondence courses in herbology, as well as nutrition. The herbology course is 270 hours.

The School of Natural Health Care
St. Clements, Ontario N0B 2M0
Tel: 1-800-665-2175

The School offers classroom and correspondence courses.

The School of Phytotherapy (Herbal Medicine)
Bucksteep Manor
Bodle Street Green
Hailsham, E. Sussex
England BN27 4RJ

Tel: Hailsham (01323) 833812/4
Fax: Hailsham (01323) 833869

This British school offers a four-year, full-time degree program leading to a Bachelor of Science (Hons). The program, formerly a diploma program, includes courses in biochemistry, physiology, anatomy, pathology, clinical diagnosis and nutrition. Students must also complete 500 hours of clinical training. Entrance requirements include academic training, but equivalent qualifications are acceptable, and consideration is given to mature individuals who do not satisfy the requirements, but who are motivated. Graduates are eligible to apply for membership in the National Institute of Medical Herbalists (see above, "Associations"). There is also a 12-month certificate home-study course available, but the school notes this does not qualify a person to practise professionally.

Sutton Institute
Main St S
Exeter, Ontario M0M 1S1
Tel: 519-235-4014

This Institute offers classroom courses in herbology, iridology, and nutrition.

Therapeutic Herbalism - David Hoffman
2068 Ludwig Ave
Santa Rosa, California 95407
Tel: 707-544-7210;
Fax: 415-753-1169

David Hoffman is a prominent figure in herbalism, as well as a clinician, educator, member of the National Institute of Medical Herbalists and author of six books.

While the one-year certificate course is a home study program, it is widely accepted as laying an excellent foundation for future practitioners, who may supplement the course with clinical work. The course is intended for both the professional health care practitioner and the student of holistic medicine. The course includes ten lessons, covering 800 pages of text. Completion of homework lessons requires thorough responses. Lessons are corrected by Mr. Hoffman.

Wild Rose College of Natural Healing
#400-1228 Kensington Rd NW
Calgary, Alberta T2N 4P9
Tel: 403-270-0936
Fax: 403-283-0799
e-mail: wrc@cia.com
http://www.infoserve.net/netquest/wildrose/index.html

Wild Rose College, founded in 1975 by Terry Willard, offers a Wholistic Therapist Diploma program by correspondence. The estimated length of study is three years of part-time study, or one and one-half years of full-time study. It includes courses in areas such as nutrition, herbology and related sciences.

Wise Woman Tradition
Herbs and Healing Workshops
Helen Bakazias, R.N.
PO Box 77
Singhampton, Ontario N0C 1M0
705-445-7565

Helen Bakazia offers Herbs & Healing workshops in the Wise Woman tradition, both for those wishing to learn about local herbs as backyard herbalists.

✦ Herbalism in Your Province

Each province is listed alphabetically below, with the following information:

Provincial Associations

✦ addresses and telephone numbers of provincial herbalist associations, where they exist; such associations often provide referrals

NOTE: national associations also provide referrals (see above "National Associations)"

Herbalists

✦ names, addresses and telephone numbers of herbalists, listed alphabetically by city

NOTE: Where known, the following initials appear after a practitioner's name: CH (Chartered Herbalist); Cl H (Clinical Herbalist); CHT (Clinical Herbal Therapist); Dip Phytotherapy (Diploma Phytotherapy); MH (Master Herbalist); MNIMH (Member, National Institute of Medical Herbalists); RHP (Registered Herbal Practitioner). Also, recall that nautropathic physicians, acupuncturists and ayurvedic practitioners practise herbalism.

✦ Alberta Herbalists

Check the credentials of your practitioner (see above, "Questions to Ask"). This publication cannot and does not certify or represent the qualifications of practitioners, or the quality of care available from them.

CALGARY

van Heerden, Merv, MA, BEd, CHT
By Appointment 403-218-0334

Wild Rose Clinic
Bishop, Dorothy, MH
Bossert, Annette, MH
Willard, Terry, PhD, Cl H
400-1228 Kensington
Rd NW 403-270-0891

EDMONTON

Byo Balance Ltd.
Carpenter, Brian
101-17409-107th Ave 403-484-9936

Kieler's Health & Herbal
Geertz, Rainer, MH; Weigl, Cathy, MH
6803-170th St 403-487-7995

Le, Ben
10105-82nd Ave 403-433-8380

Rogers, Robert D., MH
10326-81 Ave 403-433-7882

LEDUC

Bossert, Annette, MH
By Appointment 403-986-1075

ROCKY MOUNTAIN HOUSE

Eagle's Nest Holistic Centre Ltd
Lawrence, George W., MH . . . .
4923 50th St 403-845-6625

ST. ALBERT

Grandin Health & Healing Centre
Coughlan, Lorraine, MH, CR
367 Rivercrest Plaza 403-459-7796

✦ British Columbia

British Columbia Association

Canadian Herbalist Association of B.C.
RR 2, S18A, C-4
Lumby, B.C. V0E 2G0
Tel: 604-547-2281
Fax: 604-547-8911

This non-profit association, incorporated in 1973, has more than 50 professional active members. Members are licensed by the association after graduating from a recognized herbal course and passing an entry exami-

nation. The public may contact Secretary-Treasurer Kathy Deane for the name of a Registered Herbal Practitioner (RHP) in their area. The Registered Herbal Practitioners include both Clinical Herbal Therapists with three years of training and Consultant Herbal Therapists with about one year of training. This training includes supervised practical training, anatomy, physiology, and pathology. The association has established standards of practice and a code of ethics for members.

✦ British Columbia Herbalists

Check the credentials of your practitioner (see above, "Questions to Ask"). This publication cannot and does not certify or represent the qualifications of practitioners, or the quality of care available from them.

ANMORE

Blazek, Hanna
By Appointment 604-469-7002

BURNABY

Dominion Herbal College Student Clinic
7527 Kingsway 604-521-5822

COQUITLAM

Tri-City Acupuncture & Herb Clinic
208-3041 Anson Ave 604-944-6606

COURTENAY

Howe, Amanda, MNIMH
460A 6th St 604-338-2992

Circles - The Total Health Connection
Meredith, Mary-Ann, RHP
477-5th St 403-897-0055

ERRINGTON

Ross, Daphne
By Appointment 604-248-4181

LUMBY

Country Friendly
Deane, Kathy, RHP
RR 2, S-18A, C-4 604-547-2281

MAPLE RIDGE

Bennett, Judy
By Appointment 604-463-1295

VANCOUVER

The Gaia Garden Herbal Apothecary
Cabrera, Chanchal, MNIMH
Cameron, Christine, CHT
Hamilton, Rowan, MNIMH, Dip Phytotherapy, MSCS, ACIM
McCandless, Bob, MH, CHT
2672 W Broadway 604-734-4372

Mattu, H., MNIMH
871 54th St E 604-325-5924

Mattu, J., MNIMH
2672 W Broadway 604-734-4372

Ren Gee Tong Herbal Store
5310 Victoria Dr 604-322-6066

Vancouver Acupuncture & Chinese Herbology Clinic
404-1541 W Broadway 604-739-8287

Wellness Connection
6272 E Boulevard 604-266-4566

Wui King Herbal Co Ltd
5837 Victoria Dr 604-323-1283

Yue Wah Enterprises Ltd
279E Pender St 604-662-8885

Wiseman, Carla
260-2025 W 42nd Ave 604-264-9921

Zhen, Sophia
(Traditional Chinese Medicine)
By Appointment 604-258-0269

VERNON

Herbs Learning Institute
Sontag, Sonia
3705-27th St 604-549-2545

✦ Manitoba Herbalists

Check the credentials of your practitioner (see above, "Questions to Ask"). This publication cannot and does not certify or represent the quaifications of practitioners, or the quality of care available from them.

WINNIPEG

Bailey, Allan
1177 Fife St 204-694-1342

VIRDEN

Toews, Bernice, MNIMH
708-11th Ave S 204-748-1042

✦ Nova Scotia Herbalists

Check the credentials of your practitioner (see above, "Questions to Ask"). This publication cannot and does not certify or represent the qualifications of practitioners, or the quality of care available from them.

HALIFAX

Speraw, Pamela
By Appointment 902-455-7402

YARMOUTH COUNTY

Taylor, J. Mark, MH
R.R. #4, Box 7360 902-648-3445

✦ Ontario

Ontario Associations

Central Canadian Herbal Practitioners Association
6022 Yonge St N
Willowdale, Ontario M2M 3V9
Tel: 1-800-267-3802 or 416-221-9818

Formerly the Ontario Herbal Practitioners' Association, the association was formed in 1995 to represent herbalists in dealings with government, to carry out training programs and to establish education standards. Membership is open to all practising herbalists, as well as students, growers, manufacturers and distributors. The association seeks to attract traditional herbalists, including those who practise Oriental, Ayurvedic, native and traditional North American forms of herbalism. The association is affiliated with the Botanic Institute, which offers a program in conjunction with the Wild Rose College of Natural Healing in Alberta.

The Ontario Herbalists Association
11 Winthrop Place
Stoney Creek, Ontario L8G 3M3
Tel: 416-536-1509

This is an 18-year-old non-profit association of almost 1,000 members from across Canada. The Association, which pioneered the establishment of qualification standards for practitioners, is now tailoring these standards for those trained in different herbal traditions, such as native, Wise Woman, Ayurvedic, and Oriental. The OHA provides referrals to a small core of professional members. As well, the OHA frequently schedules public lectures, herb walks and field trips. It also organizes an annual Herbal Fair in Toronto, which draws thousands of people. The Association and its broad lay membership has played a significant role in providing information to the provincial and federal levels of government regarding the regulation of herbs. The OHA publishes *The Canadian Journal of Herbalism*, a quarterly journal featuring research news, legislative developments, feature articles and a calendar of events.

✦ Ontario Herbalists

Check the credentials of your practitioner (see above, "Questions to Ask"). This publication cannot and does not certify or represent the qualifications of practitioners, or the quality of care available from them.

ELORA

Elora Holistic Health Centre
29 Church W 519-846-2579

GUELPH

The Herb Works
DeSylva, Richard, MH
Unit 5, 180 Southgate Dr . . .519-824-4280

HAGERSVILLE

Longboat, Janice, OHA
Oshweken Six Nations Reservation
RR #6 519-445-2442

KIRKFIELD

Sacred Sisters Moonlodge
Stephens, Maureen
RR4 705-438-1170

KINGSTON

Kingston Natural Nutrition
1201 Division St 613-544-8535

LONDON

Kacera, Walter, CH, PhD, OHA
Grandwood Park Health Centre
81A Grand Ave 519-645-6733

MISSISSAUGA

China City Herbs Co.
888 Dundas St E 905-566-8711

OWEN SOUND

Aiken, Betty, MH, OHA
833 5th Ave W 376-8647

SCARBOROUGH

Suleiman, Habib, MH, OHA
80 Nashdene Rd,
Unit 19 416-299-1354

SINGHAMPTON

Bakazias, Helen, RN
By appointment 705-445-7565

STONEY CREEK

Stelling, Keith, MA, MNIMH, Dip Phytotherapy, MCPP
11 Winthrop Pl 905-664-6715

TORONTO

Chinese Herb & Health Clinic
276 Willard Ave 416-767-6266

Dominion Herbal College
Clinical Herbal Therapy Student Clinic
303-200 St. Clair Ave W 416-964-3377

Godfrey, Anthony, ND, PhD
2826 Dundas St W 416-763-3211

Great China Herb Centre
405 Dundas St W 416-977-8858

Health Service Centre
971 Bloor St W 416-535-9562
1660 Jane 416-249-4631

Herbalist & Acupuncture Office
753 E Gerrard St 416-465-7249

International Herbs Co
55 Kinsington Ave 416-593-5238

Laker, Peter, CH
6022 Yonge St N 416-221-1662

Lee's Acupuncture & Herbalist Clinic
430 Dundas St W 416-591-7279

Naturopathic College Clinic
2300 Yonge St, 18th Fl . . .416-486-8260

Neighbourhood Herbal Remedies
2222 Dundas St W 416-535-5513

Ottway Herbalist
300 Danforth Ave 416-463-5125

Pimental, Manuel, MH, OHA
7 Alpine Ave 416-536-3835

Pui Woon Chinese Herbal Healthy Centre
11-A Glen Watford Dr 416-609-2838

Remmer, Kelly L., MH
341 Friendship Ave 416-282-7305

Thuna Herbals
298 Danforth Ave 416-465-3366

Vertolli, Michael - Clear Stream Natural Health Clinic
980 Bathurst St -
By Appointment 416-530-6959

Viriditas Herbal Products - John Redden
By Appointment 416-767-5885

Wayne Chinese Herbs Consultants Services Co Ltd.
3601 Victoria Park Ave 416-502-3969

Xiang Yu Tang Chinese Herbs
665 Gerrard St E 416-778-8399

Yan-Yan Chinese Herbs Centre
25 Glen Watford Dr 416-292-8605

✦ Québec

Québec Association - Referrals

L'Association Québécoise des Phytothérapeutes™ Inc.
3805 rue Bélair
Montréal, Québec H2A 2C1
Tel: 514-722-8888 or 1-800-268-5878
Fax: 514-722-5164

Contact the Quebec Association of Phytotherapists for referrals to herbalists in Québec. The Association represents more than 1,000 Québec phytotherapists and phytotherapy students. It was founded in 1969, and in 1982 it became a non-profit association. The association aims to protect the public, maintain professional standards and uphold a code of ethics. It publishes the journal *Phytothérapie* four times a year.

✦ Saskatchewan Herbalists

Check the credentials of your practitioner (see above, "Questions to Ask"). This publication cannot and does not certify or represent the qualifications of practitioners, or the quality of care available from them.

HUMBOLDT

Laville, Flo
By Appointment 306-682-5144

OSLER

Dyck, Tina
By Appointment 306-239-4600

SASKATOON

Laville, Flo
143 Crean Cr 306-477-1643

Natural Healing Centre
3a-1620 Idylwyld Dr N 306-244-5328

Yao, Michelle
901 W 22nd St 306-652-1118

SPEERS

Farmer, Carell, CH
Box 60 306-246-4712

✦ Homeopathy

WHAT IS HOMEOPATHY

Homeopathy refers to the use of highly diluted traces of botanical, mineral and other natural substances to stimulate the body's self-healing abilities. Developed in the 18th century by German physician Samuel Hahnemann, the word homeopathy is derived from the Greek: "homoios" meaning similar, and "pathos" suffering. It is based on the principle that a person should be treated with something that produces an effect similar to the suffering - or "let likes be cured by likes." That is, a substance that would create symptoms of disease in a healthy person is said to trigger the immune system of the ill person. The homeopathic practitioner's skill lies in matching a person's symptoms and body type correctly with the hundreds of remedies available. This involves compiling a detailed medical history and record of symptoms. Remedies are taken in liquid or milk sugar pellet form.

One advantage of homeopathy, as with other forms of alternative health care, is said to be its ability to deal with symptoms for which no medical reason can yet be found (eg. the person feels ill but a medical diagnosis presents a clean bill of health). In homeopathy, pain and discomfort are considered the body's signal of a pending problem. In fact, advanced diseases are considered more difficult to manage with homeopathy.

But the practice of homeopathy is not without controversy, due largely to the lack of an accepted scientific explanation for any results produced. Homeopathic practitioners acknowledge that the results cannot be rationalized according to the laws of physics and biology known today. But they point to practical research on the effects of homeopathic remedies on thousands of individuals, compiled in vast compendia used by practitioners. Through Dr. Hahnemann's research on himself and colleagues, he found that the more he diluted a homeopathic solution to ensure its safety, the more potent it became, particularly when the medicine was shaken with each dilution.

Who Practises Homeopathy

Homeopathy is practised in Canada by practitioners specializing in homeopathy, as well as by naturopathic physicians (see "Naturopathic Medicine") and some chiropractors. It is rarely practised by medical physicians in Canada. In France, on the other hand, an estimated 10,000 physicians regularly prescribe homeopathic medicines, and in Britain about 250 physicians are practising members of the Faculty of Homeopathy,

a post-graduate and professional body established in 1844 for doctors practising homeopathic medicine (British Medical Association, *Complementary Medicine: New Approaches to Good Practice*, Oxford: Oxford University Press, 1993, pp. 26, 41). Britain's Royal Family have received homeopathic care since the 1800s, and there are six National Health Service homeopathic hospitals in the United Kingdom. The practice of homeopathy is considered by the British Medical Association as one of the forms of alternative health care with established foundations of training, and with "the potential for greatest use alongside orthodox medical care" (*Ibid.*, p. 143). However, the BMA recommends that homeopathic practitioners be regulated to ensure that practitoners conform to minimum standards.

Research and Safety Issues

According to information published for medical practitioners by the Institute for Clinical Evaluative Sciences in Ontario (ICES), homeopathic remedies are "extremely dilute solutions that contain only minute traces of substances and virtually no chemically discernible ingredients (except perhaps the alcohol or lactose used as a dispensing vehicle). Consequently, they have little substantiated pharmacological activity and no adverse effects" (Getting Acquainted with Herbs, *informed*, March 1996, Vol.2,No.2). ICES is an independent, non-profit research body jointly sponsored by the Ontario Ministry of Health and the Ontario Medical Association.

On the same issue, the Ontario Homeopathic Association states: "When the correct remedy is recommended by a qualified professional, homeopathy is gentle and effective. Contrary to popular belief, however, homeopathy is not always free of side effects; the wrong remedy can cause unnecessary aggravation, further complicate a condition and may ultimately cause more harm than good. So, before booking a consultation, please inquire about a homeopath's qualifications and investigate the standards of the organization by which he or she is accredited" (*Health and Homeopathy*, Vol.1, No.1, Fall, 1995).

Classical Homeopathy and Combination Remedies

Classical homeopathy refers to the use of a remedy that most closely matches a person's combination of symptoms. One medicine is taken at a time in the healing process. Combination remedies include more than one homeopathic medicine. There are varying opinions on the advisability of combination remedies. Unlike the single remedies, many combination remedies have not undergone extensive research on their effects.

Early Established Medicine in Canada

Homeopathic practitioners were once a self-regulating profession in Canada. As early as 1845, homeopathic doctors began practising in Québec and shortly after that in Toronto. Homeopathic doctors became regulated under legislation in Upper Canada and Montréal in 1859 and 1865 respectively. They were also represented in the College of Physicians and Surgeons of Ontario from 1869 to 1960. In B.C., legislation regulating homeopathic practitioners was passed in 1889.

A homeopathic hospital opened in Montréal in 1894, and a homeopathic dispensary opened in Toronto in 1888. This was followed in 1890 by the opening of the Toronto Homeopathic Hospital.

The legislation regulating homeopathic practitioners was eventually superseded. Reasons for homeopathy's decline may include the rise in popularity of antibiotics. A more complete history of homeopathy in Canada may be found in an article by naturopathic doctor and homeopath Fernando Ania ("Homeopathy in Canada: A Synopsis," *Health and Homeopathy*, Vol.1, No.1, Fall, 1995, pp 4-10).

BENEFITS OF HOMEOPATHY

Homeopathy is said to assist the body's process of healing, particularly in the case of chronic conditions such as asthma, as well, symptoms of the common cold and flu. As well, homeopathy is said to alleviate certain emotional disorders and injuries, as well as insomnia, rheumatoid arthritis, hay fever, PMS, gout, constipation, headache and migraines, and children's colic or ear ache. Homeopathic remedies may also assist bleeding and receding gums. However, homeopathy is not a replacement for professional dental care.

Note that homeopathy does not treat structural problems. If your headache, for example, is related to a structural problem, homeopathy would not assist.

Homeopaths are not replacements for physicians, and they generally suggest that patients seek a diagnosis from a physician.

QUESTIONS TO ASK

✦ Where was your practitioner trained, and what was the length of training?

NOTE: There are different opinions as to the amount of training required for practitioners of homeopathy. The highest Canadian standard for a fully qualified homeopathic practitioner is three years of full-time training, including medical sciences and a clinical internship, required by the Canadian Association of Homeopathic Physicians and the Ontario Homeopathic Association. Naturopathic doctors educated at recognized colleges of naturopathic medicine are taught homeopathy as part of a four-year full-time training program.

✦ Under what circumstances will your practitioner refer you to a physician or other regulated health professional? Recall that homeopaths are not regulated health practitioners, and are not qualified to give a medical diagnosis.

✦ Is your practitioner a member of a professional association? Contact the association to ask about the educational standards required for membership.

NOTE: Several homeopathy associations are affiliated with particular educational institutes, and have adopted their standards for training.

✦ Does your practitioner practise primarily as an homeopath, or as an adjunct to another form of medicine? What is the extent of your practitioner's training in other forms of health care?

✦ Does your homeopathic practitioner have professional references?

✦ How much experience does your practitioner have with homeopathy and does it include treatment of people with your condition? What were the results?

✦ Is homeopathy appropriate for you? Will your condition likely worsen before improving? What products or ingredients should be avoided while on homeopathic medication? How should you adjust the remedy in case of a change in symptoms, and how can you reach the practitioner after-hours?

NOTE: Homeopathic remedies are said to lose their effectiveness if taken with certain substances, such as coffee, camphor, cortesone, aspirin, raw onion, raw ginger, or mint. Check with your practitioner.

✦ What is the cost of the homeopathic remedies, and how many will be required over what period of time? Is there a separate charge for consultation?

GOVERNMENT REGULATION

Regulation of Practitioners

Once regulated in B.C., Québec and Ontario, homeopaths are no longer regulated as practitioners by any provincial government, except insofar as practitioners such as naturopathic physicians trained in homeopathic medicine are regulated in certain provinces (see "Naturopathic Medicine, Regulation"). This means that there is no provincial legislation establishing a regulatory body responsible for registering qualified homeopaths and disciplining them. This also means that there are no minimum educational standards for those calling themselves homeopaths. However, some associations set professional standards for membership.

Every province has legislation restricting medical practice or the performance of specific medical acts, such as diagnosis. In the Northwest Territories, the *Medical Profession Act*, 1988, C. M-9 creates an offence to practise medicine without a licence, but also states that "medicine" does not include homeopathy (sections 1,48). According to a policy analyst with the Northwest Territories government, this provision means that, while homeopathy is not a regulated profession, it may be practised without contravening the Act.

Regulation of Products

The federal government regulates products such as homeopathic remedies through the *Food and Drugs Act* and regulations. Homeopathic products bearing Drug Identification Numbers (DINs) are considered safe. Because homeopathic remedies are tailored to the individual, federal policy requires product labels to note that the remedy should be taken on the advice of a health practitioner, and the label may not refer to the conditions treated. This policy is currently under review.

Subsections 3 (1) and (2) of the *Food and Drugs Act* prohibit the advertising or the sale of any food, drug, cosmetic or device labelled or advertised to the general public as a treatment, preventative or cure for any of the diseases, disorders or abnormal physical states referred to in Schedule A to the Act.

CANADIAN, BRITISH & U.S. ASSOCIATIONS

NOTE: Provincial associations are located in B.C., Manitoba, Ontario, and Québec (see below "Homeopathy in Your Province").

British Homeopathic Association
27a Devonshire St
London, England WC1N 1RJ
Tel: 071-935-2163

A list of physicians who practise homeopathy in Britain is available from this association.

Canadian Association of Homeopathic Physicians
10240A 152nd St
Surrey, B.C. V3R 6N7
Tel: 604-951-9987
Fax: 604-951-9920
Contact: Harjot Sidhu

Alternate Location:
4624 99th St
Edmonton, Alberta T6E 5H5
Contact: S.S. Sandhu

This association, started in 1995, provides referrals to about 25 members across Canada, all of whom have a minimum of three years' full-time training. The association has a code of ethics.

National Centre for Homeophathy
306-801 N. Fairfax St
Alexandria, VA
22314 USA
Tel: 703-548-7790

This centre has a directory of homeopaths.

National United Professional Association of Trained Homeopaths (NUPATH)
194 Main St, Ste 208
Ottawa, Ontario K1S 1C2
Tel: 613-830-4759
Fax: 613-830-9174
President: Rudi Verspoor

This professional association, formed in 1994, welcomes as members all those who practise homeopathy, with various levels of training. The association, which currently has 150-200 members, is in the process of producing a register of qualified professional members.

North American Society of Homeopaths (NASH)
10700 Old County Rd 15
Plymouth, Minnesota 55441
Tel: 503-345-9815

This society of professional non-medical homeopaths was founded in 1990, and currently has 50-60 members. Professional members must have 500 hours of education, six months' clinical training, and one year of experience in full-time practice. A NASH spokesman said that the Society is independent, not affiliated with other societies, and does not have a list of recognized schools.

Society of Homeopaths
2 Artizan Rd
Northampton, England NN1 4HV
Tel: 0604-21400

This is the professional body for non-medically qualified Homeopaths. This body sets standards for members and for training institutes.

United Kingdom Homoeopathic Medical Association
6 Livingstone Road
Gravesend
Kent, England DA12 5DZ
Tel: 011-44-1-474-560336

This is an association of professional homeopaths, whose members have passed a qualifying examination at an approved college.

HOMEOPATHIC EDUCATION

If you wish to become a practitioner, it is advisable to contact several colleges and associations before choosing a program. Some of the colleges and programs are listed below. Compare the qualifications of faculty (their education and professional experience), program content and length, admission requirements, number of clinical hours, and all fees and contract terms, including refund policies. In addition, it is useful to speak with students and graduates of the various programs about their standards, and to consult with representatives of homeopathy associations. Ask the representatives if they are affiliated with a particular college. If you do not wish to become a practitioner, but wish to study homoepathy, many of the colleges and programs noted below offer home-study courses.

Most provinces have legislation requiring private vocational schools to meet certain minimum standards, often related to financial stability, for the protection of consumers. These requirements vary from province to province, and certain health care training programs are not in all cases covered by such legislation. Contact the Ministry of Education or Advanced Education in your province for more information on their policies regarding registration of private vocational schools.

If you are seeking a career, you should be aware that homeopaths are not regulated in any province, and that every province has legislation restricting the practice of medicine or specific medical acts, such as diagnosis (see above "Government Regulation"). Homeopathy is specifically exempt from the definition of "practice of medicine" in the Northwest Territories (see above, "Government Regulation").

alive Academy of Nutrition

7436 Fraser Park Dr
Burnaby, B.C. V5J 5B9
Tel: 604-435-1919
Fax: 604-435-4888

This Academy offers a home study course on homeopathy and first aid, based on materials from Steven R. Olsen, N.D., a faculty member at Bastyr University. The Academy also offers a course on homeopathy and acute ailments, including ear aches and infections.

The British Institute of Homeopathy (Canada)

194 Main St, Ste. 208
Ottawa, Ontario K1S 1C2
Tel: 613-830-4759 or 1-800-475-HEAL
Fax: 613-830-9174
Director: Rudi Verspoor

This Institute offers basic, practitioner and homeopathic pharmacy diplomas by correspondence. Clinical work is arranged with a homeopath in the student's area. The Director is also president of the National United Professional Association of Trained Homeopaths (NUPATH).

Centre de Techniques Homéopathique

910, rue Bélanger
Montreal, PQ H2S 3P4
Tel: 514-277-1007
Fax: 514-277-5927

This 10-year-old school offers a 1,500-hour professional program, including 250 hours of clinical training. The program is offered in French, and as of October 1996, also in English.

Hahnemann College of Homeopathy

Ste 607, 170 St George St
Toronto, Ontario M5R 2M8
Tel: 1-800-563-1613

This college offers a part-time, three-year diploma program in homeopathy. Students attend two weekends a month, and receive clinical training in the third year. Classes are held at Ryerson College in Toronto. There is also an accelerated part-time, one-year course on weekends for health professionals. The College is recognized by the U.K. Homeopathic Medical Association.

Homeopathic College of Canada & Humber College

3255 Yonge St
Toronto, Ontario M4N 2L5
Tel: 416-481-8816 or toll-free 1-888-374-6636
Internet Address: http://www.inforamp.net/~homeo-col/homepage.html
e-mail: homeocol@inforamp.net
President: Fernando Ania

Formerly the International Academy of Homeopathy, the non-profit Homeopathic College of Canada has established a partnership with Humber College to implement a new full-time, three-year program. This new 3,045-hour program includes a clinical internship, and training in conventional medical sciences. This is the most extensive training program in homeopathy in Canada. The College is associated with the Ontario Homeopathic Association, the newly formed Pacific Homeopathic Association of B.C., the Manitoba Homeopathic Association and the Canadian Association of Homeopathic Physicians. The Homeopathic College of Canada also runs a program for physicians and naturopathic doctors, as well as a 14-week diploma course for those seeking positions in health food stores, or distributors and manufacturers of natural health products.

Toronto School of Homeopathic Medicine

717 Bloor St W
Toronto, Ontario M6G 1L5
Tel: 416-532-8706
Fax: 416-532-1394

This school, opened in 1995, offers a part-time, three-year training program. The school has established the Ontario Society of Homeopaths, primarily as a local Toronto number to call for information on the North American Society of Homeopaths (NASH) (see above, "Canadian, British and U.S. Associations").

✦ Homeopathy in Your Province

Provinces are listed alphabetically below, with the following information:

Homeopathy Associations

✦ addresses and telephone numbers of provincial homeopathy associations, where they exist; such associations often provide referrals

Homeopathic Practitioners

✦ names, addresses and telephone numbers of homeopathic practitioners, listed alphabetically by city

NOTE: Recall that naturopathic physicians also practise homeopathy

✦ Alberta Homeopathic Practitioners

NOTE: Check the credentials of your practitioner (see above, "Questions to Ask"). This publication cannot and does not certify or represent the qualifications of practitioners, or the quality of care available from them.

CALGARY

Ayurved Naturopathic Clinic
Rakhra, Raj, ND
304-1235 17th Ave SW 403-244-4941

Healthy Alternatives
By Appointment 403-281-6301

Taylor, A.
RR 12 PO Box 16, Ste 27 . . .403-686-2808

EDMONTON

Sandhu, S.S.
4624 99th St 403-438-4465

✦ British Columbia

British Columbia Association

Pacific Homeopathic Association of B.C.
c/o Burrard Integrated Health Clinic
604-1200 Burrard St
Vancouver, BC V6Z 2C7
Tel: 604-687-0119

This association will provide referrals to homeopathic practitioners with 3-4 years of training. This is also the office of the Burrard Integrated Health Clinic.

✦ British Columbia Homeopathic Practitioners

NOTE: Check the credentials of your practitioner (see above, "Questions to Ask"). This publication cannot and does not certify or represent the qualifications of practitioners, or the quality of care available from them.

COQUITLAM

Olsen, S., ND
211-3030 Lincoln Ave 604-942-9925

DUNCAN

Dodd, Cam
109 Kenneth St 604-746-9509

NANAIMO

The Metacine Centre
Van de Water, M., DHMS
427-C Fitzwilliam St 604-741-8489

SALT SPRING ISLAND

Coleman, Phyllis, RN
By Appointment 604-537-2378

SURREY

Homeopathy Services
Sidhu, Dr. Harjot
10240A 152nd St 604-951-9987

Homeopathic Practitioners Homeopathic Clinic
205-7028 120th St 604-572-7765

VANCOUVER

Burrard Integrated Health Clinic
500-1200 Burrard 604-687-0119

India Ayurvedic Homeopathic & Nutrition Clinic
201-6445 Fraser St 604-323-1400

Vancouver Centre for Homeopathy
2246 Spruce St 604-732-7276

VICTORIA

Chapman, E.
141 Turner St S 604-383-0454

Malthouse, Dr. S.
141 Turner St S 604-383-0454

WHITE ROCK

Oceanside Homeopathic Healing Centre
15727 Marine 604-536-1500

✦ Manitoba

Manitoba Association

Manitoba Homoeopathic Association
101-912 Portage Ave
Winnipeg, Manitoba R3G 0P5
Tel: 204-774-2616

This association includes about 80 professionals and members of the public who support the practice of homeopathy in Manitoba. The Association is establishing a medical college of homeopathy. This is also the office of Leelama Nielsen, a homeopathic practitioner.

✦ Manitoba Homeopathic Practitioners

NOTE: Check the credentials of your practitioner (see above, "Questions to Ask"). This publication cannot and does not certify or represent the qualifications of practitioners, or the quality of care available from them.

WINNIPEG

Nielsen's Homoeopathic Clinic
Nielsen, Leelamma
101-912 Portage Ave 204-774-2616

✦ Ontario

Ontario Association

Ontario Homeopathic Association
P.O. Box 852, Station P
Toronto, Ontario M5S 2Z2
Tel: 416-488-9685

This association, founded in 1992, will provide referrals to members who have satisfied the association's standards for training. This includes three years of full-time training, with university-level medical science courses and clinical training. The Association is recommending that these standards be adopted for the regulation of homeopathic practitioners in Ontario.

✦ Ontario Homeopathic Practitioners

NOTE: Check the credentials of your practitioner (see above, "Questions to Ask"). This publication cannot and does not certify or represent the qualifications of practitioners, or the quality of care available from them.

HUNTSVILLE

Baker, Deborah
4-59 Main St E 705-789-9636

Murphy, Angela
By Appointment 705-789-3737

KITCHENER

Meissner, Julek
174 Victoria St S 519-570-1942

MARKHAM

Hardy, Gary
5762 Hwy #7, Ste 212A 905-472-2186

MISSISSAUGA

Bio-Health Balancing Centre
895 Rangeview 905-271-3009

Covino, Salvatore
206-5805 Whittle Rd 905-453-6336

Homeopathy Plus
Namdar, Aamer
720 Burnamthorpe Rd W ...905-279-0330

Sharda Homeopathy Centre
7071 Airport Rd, Unit 3 905-677-8796

NEWMARKET

Zimmerman, Anke
431 Timothy St 905-895-8285

OAKVILLE

Hassard, Murray
2361 Lakeshore Rd W 905-847-2225

OSHAWA

Kellerstein, Joseph
111 Simcoe St 905-433-8666

OTTAWA

Verspoor, Rudolf
208-194 Main St 613-569-7154

PERTH

MacNeil, J.
RR 4 613-267-7470

STURGEON FALLS

Aubry, Jean
By Appointment 705-753-2300

TORONTO

Cawston,Reid
607 Medical Arts Building
170 St. George St 416-254-5684

Centre for Classical Homeopathy
Tulbert, D., DC
50 St Clair Ave E 416-927-9988

Chopra Homeopathy Centre
1395 Gerrard St E 416-778-7334

Complementary Health Associates
Medical Arts Building
607-170 St. George St 416-254-5684

Devgan, Ravi MD
42 Redpath Ave 416-687-0882

Eldridge, Thomas
3 Graham Gardens 416-653-2274

Homeopathic College of Canada Clinic
Ania, Fernando, ND
3255 Yonge St ....416-481-8816 or
888-374-6636

Homeopathy Centre
1391 Gerrard St E 416-778-7334

Jaconello, Paul
201-751 Pape Ave 416-463-2911

Kellerstein, Joseph ND, FCAH
70 Davisville 416-484-1673

McFarland, Robert
75 Eastdale 416-690-3807

Nichol, D.J., DHMS
By Appointment 416-534-7024

Radionics Institute & Homeopathic Clinic
75 Eastdale 416-690-3807

School of Homeopathic Medicine Clinic
717 Bloor St W 416-532-8706/
800-572-6001

Shannon, L., DHMS
By Appointment 416-533-3371

Thompson's Homeopathic Supplies Ltd.
844 Yonge St 416-922-2300

Toronto Homeopathic Centre
2042-3080 Yonge 416-489-1236

Vital Force Homeopathic Clinic
Elekes, A., DHMS
880 Broadview Ave 416-574-0575

Your Good Health Naturally
Jardine, J.
152 Carlton 416-929-5551

Zubkewych, Morris
2184D Bloor St 416-762-7591

✦ Québec

Québec Asssociation
Syndicat Professionnel Des Homéopathes Du Québec
1222 Mackay
Montreal, PQ H3G 2H4
Tel: 514-525-2037 or 1-800-465-5788
Fax: 514-525-1299

This non-profit organization represents about 360 professional homeopathic practitioners in Québec, and is committed to persuading the provincial government to recognize and regulate the profession.

✦ Québec Homeopathic Practitioners

NOTE: Check the credentials of your practitioner (see above, "Questions to Ask"). This publication cannot and does not certify or represent the qualifications of practitioners, or the quality of care available from them.

CAP DE LA MADELEINE

Homeopathie De La Mauricie
17, Fusey 819-691-3337

CHICOUTIMI

**Clinique De Medecine
Homeopathique Du Saguenay**
216, ch des Bois-de-Boulogne 418-545-4131

HULL

**Homeopathie, Lemaire, Marie
Sylvie**
109, rue Ste Marie 819-770-8069

Homeopathie
 Morisette, Michel
145, rue Gamelin 819-777-9099

MONTREAL

Haskell, A; Javanmardi, M.
1550 Pine Ave W 514-989-9067

**Herbier Du Midi Centre
Homeopathique**
5032, av Du Parc 514-271-1494

Homeopathie Montréal
7216, av Des Erables 514-374-4663

TROIS RIVIERES-OUEST

Centre D'homeopathie 2000 Inc
2930, Côte Richelieu 819-378-7656

Lessard Francois Homeopathe
133, rue Bonaventure 819-378-0466

✦ Saskatchewan

NOTE: Check the credentials of your practitioner (see above, "Questions to Ask"). This publication cannot and does not certify or represent the qualifications of practitioners, or the quality of care available from them.

SASKATOON

Pahwa, Ranvir
1527A Idylwyld Dr N 306-664-3873

Massage Therapy

WHAT IS MASSAGE THERAPY

Massage therapy is a hands-on manipulation of the soft tissues of the body, including muscles, connective tissue, tendons, ligaments and joints. The therapy is used to develop or rehabilitate the body and relieve pain by acting directly on the muscular, nervous and circulatory systems. According to the governing body of Ontario massage therapists, modern massage therapy originated in the late 1700s in Sweden when Henrik Ling developed Swedish Massage, the first systematic method of therapeutic massage based on physiology. This approach is the basis for much of massage therapy practised in Canada today.

The practice of massage therapy begins with the assessment of the soft tissues and joints of the body, and the testing of a person's muscles and range of motion. Treatment may include soft tissue manipulation, as well as hydrotherapy and remedial exercise programs.

Massage therapists may be found in private practice, as well as in clinics, spas and health clubs, sports clinics, nursing homes, hospitals, and in practice with physicians or chiropractors. Depending on the treatment and the comfort of the client, pieces of clothing are removed, and the massage therapists may use oil or lotion.

A distinction is often drawn between a masseur and a massage therapist. The latter usually have more training in the therapeutic aspects of massage.

BENEFITS OF MASSAGE THERAPY

Massage therapists treat stress and muscular weakness resulting from disease or injury. Massage therapy is also said to alleviate conditions such as: migraine, post-injury rehabilitation, whiplash, respiratory problems, arthritis, circulatory problems, frozen shoulder, neuritis/neuralgia, tendinitis/bursitis, neck and shoulder tension, low back pain, digestive/lower bowel problems, muscle spasm, and leg aches.

Massage therapy is said to benefit people of all ages, including those in chronic care and those who need palliative consideration.

QUESTIONS TO ASK

✦ Is your massage therapist registered? This question applies only if you live in B.C. or Ontario, the two provinces where massage therapists are regulated. You can check by contacting the governing body in your province (see addresses and telephone numbers below, "Massage Therapy in Your Province - Governing Body").

✦ How much training in massage therapy has your practitioner received, and from which educational institute? Did the training include clinical experience, as well as courses in anatomy, physiology, pathology, kinesiology, hydrotherapy, remedial exercises and treatment of medically related conditions? This question is important if you live in the following jurisdictions, where massage therapists are not regulated, and there is no governing body to establish educational standards: Alberta, Manitoba, New Brunswick, Newfoundland, Northwest Territories, Nova Scotia, Prince Edward Island, Québec, Saskatchewan and the Yukon.

NOTE: Training requirements vary for practitioners. In Alberta, the Massage Therapists Association of Alberta requires massage therapists to have at least 500 hours of training. In B.C., the amount of training required for registered massage therapists is being increased from 2,200 to 3,000 hours (from two to three years). In Ontario, the minimum amount of training required for registered massage therapists is 2,200 hours (two years). In Québec, La Fédération Québécoise des Masseurs et Massothérapeutes requires its masseurs to have at least 400 hours of training. The Fédération's massage therapists, more highly trained in the therapeutic aspects of massage, must have at least 1,000 hours.

✦ Is your practitioner a member of a massage therapists' association? You may wish to contact the association to discuss the qualifications of your massage therapist, or to locate a therapist (see below, "Massage Therapy in Your Province - Association").

NOTE: Bear in mind that associations do not necessarily check out the qualifications of their members. Also note that these associations are not governing bodies established by legislation to register and discipline practitioners.

✦ How much experience does your practitioner have, and does it include treatment of your particular condition? What were the results?

✦ Does your massage therapist have a working relationship with other health care professionals? Under what circumstances will your massage therapist refer you to a physician or other regulated health professional? Can your practitioner provide professional references?

✦ Is your massage therapist trained in other forms of health care? If so, what is the extent of the training?

✦What is the estimated number of treatments required and at what cost? How long will each treatment take?

NOTE: See below "Government Health Care Funding" and "Private Health Insurance".

GOVERNMENT REGULATION

Regulation means that there is provincial legislation establishing a professional governing body. This body, usually called a "College," is given a duty in law to protect the public. Governing bodies are established to ensure that regulated practitioners meet specific standards before they practise, to investigate complaints, and to take disciplinary action against practitioners where appropriate.

Provinces that Regulate Massage Therapists

Massage therapists are regulated by the provincial governments of British Columbia and Ontario, with governing bodies established to register qualified practitioners. For more information, see below, "Massage Therapy in Your Province - Legislation."

Provinces that Do Not Regulate Massage Therapists

Massage therapists are not regulated in Alberta, Manitoba, New Brunswick, Newfoundland, Nova Scotia, Northwest Territories, Prince Edward Island, Québec, Saskatchewan and the Yukon Territory. This means that no minimum educational standards exist for those calling themselves massage therapists. If you live in a province where massage therapists are unregulated, you may wish to obtain referrals to practitioners and discuss their credentials with professional associations (see below, "Massage Therapy in Your Province"). Each of these jurisdictions has laws restricting the practice of medicine, with varying definitions of what constitutes the practice of medicine.

GOVERNMENT HEALTH CARE FUNDING

British Columbia is the only province to provide partial government health care funding. If you live in B.C., ask if your therapist is 'opted in.' If not, your share of the fee is higher (for details, see below, "Massage Therapy in Your Province - British Columbia").

PRIVATE HEALTH INSURANCE

Many private insurance companies cover massage therapy under their extended health care plans. Consult your policy or speak with your insurance agent.

WORKERS' COMPENSATION BOARDS

Contact the board in your province to determine if massage therapy is covered and considered appropriate to your case. Check the conditions of coverage (eg. whether a physician referral is required).

NATIONAL ASSOCIATION

Canadian Massage Therapists Alliance (CMTA)
365 Bloor St E, Ste 1807
Toronto M4W 3L4
Tel: 416-968-2149
Fax: 416-968-6818

This association is an alliance of the professional associations of massage therapy in Canada. It is located in the office of the Ontario Massage Therapist Association.

MASSAGE THERAPY EDUCATION

For those seeking a career in massage therapy, there are many training programs in Canada. In choosing a training program, one may wish to compare the qualifications of faculty (their education and experience), student-teacher ratios, admission requirements, program content and length, number of clinical hours, and all fees and contract terms, including refund policies. In addition, it is useful to speak with students and graduates of the various programs about their standards. Admission requirements often include a minimum high school graduation, along with certain Grade 12 subjects, such as English, as well as Biology or Chemistry. The curriculum usually includes anatomy, physiology and pathology, kinesiology, C.P.R., and clinical practice. Many colleges include courses on hydrotherapy, the physiological effects of warm and cool water on the body, in the form of steam, mud packs, or contrast baths.

In B.C. and Ontario, the two provinces where massage therapists are regulated under provincial law, students must complete training at a recognized school and write a qualifying examination before they may be registered with the governing bodies as practitioners. In Ontario, students must complete 2,200 hours (two years) of study. In B.C., that standard has been raised, effective September 1996, from two to three years of full-time study. The last sitting of examinations for the two-year program is in August 1997. In provinces where massage therapists are not regulated, there is no minimum educational standard.

The governing body in B.C., the College Of Massage Therapists of British Columbia, recognizes the two B.C. schools listed below (West Coast College of Massage Therapy and Okanagan Valley College of

Massage Therapy). The governing body in Ontario, the College of Massage Therapists of Ontario, recognizes the Ontario schools listed below, as well as those in B.C. and the school listed below in Michigan (Health Enrichment Centre).

For information on massage therapy schools in other provinces, contact the provincial associations (see below, "Massage Therapy in Your Province - Association").

Most provinces have legislation requiring private vocational schools to meet certain minimum standards, often related to financial stability, for the protection of consumers. These requirements vary from province to province, and certain health care training programs are not covered by such legislation. Contact the Ministry of Education or Advanced Education in your province for more information on their policies regarding registration of private vocational schools.

Canadian College of Massage and Hydrotherapy

North York Campus
5160 Yonge St
North York, Ontario M2N 6L8
Tel: 416-250-8690
Fax: 416-222-9424

Sutton Campus
85 Fairbank Ave
Sutton West, Ontario L0E 1R0
Tel: 905-722-3162
Fax: 905-722-3106

The college is recognized by the governing body of Ontario massage therapists.

D'Arcy Lane Institute
627 Maitland St
London, Ontario N5Y 2V7
Tel: 519-673-4420
Fax: 519-673-0645

The Institute is recognized by the governing body of Ontario massage therapists.

Health Enrichment Centre
1820 Lapeer Rd N
Lapeer, Michigan
Tel: 810-667-9453
Fax: 810-667-4095

The college is recognized by the governing body of Ontario massage therapists.

Kikkawa College
3 Riverview Gardens
Toronto, Ontario M6S 4E4
Tel: 416-762-4857
Fax: 416-762-5733

Founded in 1981, Kikkawa was the first school in Ontario to offer the 2,200-hour curriculum. The college is recognized by the governing body of massage therapists of Ontario.

Okanagan Valley College of Massage Therapy
3317-30th Ave
Vernon, B.C. V1T 2C9
Tel: 604-558-3718
Fax: 604-558-3748

This college is recognized by the governing bodies of massage therapists in B.C. and Ontario. It is increasing the length of its program to 3,000 hours, to allow students to meet the new standards established by the governing body in B.C.

Sault College of Applied Arts and Technology
School of Health Sciences
PO Box 60, Northern Ave
Sault Ste Marie, Ontario P6A 5L3
Tel: 705-759-6774
Fax: 705-759-1319

The college is recognized by the governing body of Ontario massage therapists.

Sir Sanford Fleming College
Lakeshore Campus
1005 William St
Cobourg, Ontario K9A 5J4
Tel: 905-372-6865
Fax: 905-372-8570

The college is recognized by the governing body of Ontario massage therapists.

Sutherland-Chan School
330 Dupont St
Toronto, Ontario M5V 1V9
Tel: 416-924-1107
Fax: 416-924-9413

The college is recognized by the governing body of Ontario massage therapists.

West Coast College of Massage Therapy
6th Fl, Spencer Building, Harbour Centre
Box 12110, 555 W Hastings St
Vancouver, B.C. V6B 4N6
Tel: 604-689-3854
Fax: 604-689-9730

The college is recognized by the governing bodies of massage therapists in both B.C. and Ontario. It is extending its training to a 3,000-hour, three-year, full-time program to meet the new standards in B.C.

✦ Massage Therapy in Your Province

Each province is listed alphabetically below, with the following information:

Legislation

✦ procedures that your massage therapist is permitted to perform under law, where such laws exists

NOTE: The information given regarding legislation is by way of interest, and does not purport to offer legal advice or comprise a complete account of the legislation or regulations. If legal advice is required, consult a lawyer qualified to practise in your jurisdiction.

Government Health Care Funding

✦ details on government funding available in B.C., the only province to provide such funding

Governing Bodies

✦ addresses and telephone numbers of the governing bodies established under provincial law in B.C. and Ontario, the two provinces where massage therapists are regulated

✦ these are the bodies to contact to make a complaint or to check if your massage therapist is registered

Provincial Associations

✦ addresses and telephone numbers of massage therapy associations, which often provide referrals, or with whom you may discuss the qualifications of practitioners

Massage Therapists

✦ names, addresses and telephone numbers of massage therapists, listed alphabetically by city

NOTE: Many of the massage therapists listed below are members of the College of Massage Therapists of Ontario. In B.C. and Ontario, the initials 'RMT' signify Registered Massage Therapist. Confirm the registration of your therapist by contacting the College (the governing body).

Alberta

In Alberta, massage therapists are not regulated, meaning that there is no legislation establishing a governing body to register and discipline qualified massage therapists.

Alberta Association

Massage Therapists Association of Alberta
Box 24031, RPO, Plaza Centre
Red Deer, Alberta T4N 6X6
Tel: 403-340-1913
Fax 403-346-2269

This 43-year-old association offers a referral service to its 470 full members, all of whom have at least 500 hours training and have passed the association exam. This association is a member of the Canadian Massage Therapists Alliance (CMTA). It has a complaints system.

✦ Alberta Massage Therapists

NOTE: Check the credentials of your practitioner (see above, "Questions to Ask"). This publication cannot and does not certify or represent the qualifications of practitioners, or the quality of care available from them.

BANFF

Tunnel Mountain Massage
Lecour, Patricia
PO Box 403 403-762-6450

CALGARY

Croza, Helen
Eau Claine - YMCA
101 3rd St SW 403-269-6701

Foothills Massage Therapy Clinic
Skidmore, Glen Russel
130-7220 Fisher St SE 403-255-4445

CANMORE

Witmer, Michelle (Shelley)
General Delivery
204-703 8th Ave 403-678-1811

EDMONTON

Body Balance Therapeutic Massage
Hein, Natalie Ann
10244 123rd St 403-455-1764

Holly, Megan
9813 154 St 403-481-4306

Massage Link
Blatz, Peter W.
10837 127th St 403-488-5924

Safehaven Massage Therapy
Chute, Robert C.
202-10518 82nd Ave 403-433-4948

GIBBONS

Bask, J. Lynne
Box 81 403-923-2349

MEDICINE HAT

Bonagofsky, Gerard
1755 17th St E 403-527-2409

Joan Massage Therapy Centre
Graham, Joan
954 S Railway St SE 403-528-2000

ST ALBERT

Solis Massage Therapy
Blain, Collette
28 Grosvenor Blvd 403-459-7553

✦ British Columbia

Massage therapists are regulated in B.C., meaning that a governing body has been established with the responsibility of setting qualification standards and disciplining practitioners.

Legislation

Massage therapists in B.C. are regulated under the *Health Professions Act*, and the Massage Therapists Regulation. This Regulation designates massage therapy as a health profession and names the College of Massage Therapists of B.C. as the governing body under the Act. The College has the duty of regulating the profession of massage therapy in the public interest, including the discipline of practitioners.

In the regulation, "massage therapy" is defined as the kneading, rubbing or massaging of the human body, whether with or without steam baths, vapour baths, fume baths, electric light baths or other appliances, and hydrotherapy. The methods do not include any form of medical electricity.

Restricted Titles and Reserved Acts

Only persons registered with the College may use the titles "massage therapist," "registered massage therapist," "massage practitioner," or "registered massage practitioner." Subject to the rights of other professions and emergency situations, only persons registered with the College may practise massage therapy.

Limitation on Practice

No registered massage therapist may prescribe or administer drugs or anaesthetics, or treat a recent fracture of a bone.

Government Health Care Funding

User fees

Coverage is available under the Medical Services Plan of B.C. for those referred to a massage therapist by a physician. There is a user fee for massage therapist services (set out below), unless you are a member of an exempt group, including those holding a native status card, persons receiving premium assistance, refugees, and those whose premiums are covered by the Ministry of Social Services and Housing. For medicare information, call 1-800-663-7100.

Physician Referral Required for Coverage

If you wish to have your massage therapy covered by the Medical Services Plan, you must be referred by a physician.

Maximum Number of Annual Visits

The maximum number of visits to a massage therapist partially covered by the Medical Services Plan of B.C. is 12 per calendar year for those less than 65 years old, and 15 visits per calendar year for those 65 or over.

Massage therapists who have "Opted In" to the Medical Services Plan

First Office Visit:
Patient pays $7.50 user fee, and the Plan pays $13.48 for a total of $20.98. If the patient is exempt from user fees (see above), the government pays the entire $20.98.

Subsequent Office Visits:
Patient pays $7.50 user fee, with the Plan paying the balance of $7.96, for a total of $15.46. If the patient is

exempt from user fees, medicare covers the entire $15.46.

Massage therapists who have "Opted Out" of the Medical Services Plan

First visit:

The massage therapist sets the fee, but no matter how high the bill, the government pays no more than $13.48. If the patient is exempt from user fees, the most the government will pay is $20.98, and the patient pays the balance.

Subsequent visits:

The government pays no more than $7.96, and the patient pays the balance. If the patient is exempt from user fees, the government would pay a maximum $15.46.

British Columbia Governing Body

College Of Massage Therapists of British Columbia
103-1089 W Broadway
Vancouver, B.C. V6H 1E5
Tel: 604-736-3404
Fax: 604-736-6500

This is the governing body to call to confirm that your massage therapist is registered and has therefore met required qualification standards, or to make a complaint.

British Columbia Association

Massage Therapists' Association of B.C. (MTA of B.C.)
3rd Fl, 34 E 12th Ave
Vancouver, B.C. V5T 2G5
Tel: 604-873-4467
Fax: 604-873-6211

This professional association refers callers to its 940 members, all of whom are registered massage therapists in B.C.

✦ British Columbia Massage Therapists

NOTE: Check the credentials of your practitioner (see above, "Questions to Ask"). This publication cannot and does not certify or represent the qualifications of practitioners, or the quality of care available from them. We cannot and do not confirm that those listed are registered as required by law.

100 MILE HOUSE

Cariboo Therapy Centre
Reid, Marianne RMT
108-272 5th St, Box 1813 . .604-395-2185

BURNABY

West Coast College of Massage Therapy Public Clinic
402-4603 Kingsway 604-437-5801

CAMPBELL RIVER

Discovery Passage Therapeutic Massage
Hebb, S. RMT
120-1260 Shoppers Row . . .604-286-6063

LLA Massage Therapy
Atkinson, Linda L. RMT
450 Harrogate Rd 604-923-4423

CLEARBROOK

Bunker, Edward J. RMT
8-32700 Dahlstrom Ave 604-855-0439

COQUITLAM

Kristie Lee Barton Massage Therapy
Dalman, Siobhan M. RMT
5555 Clarke Rd 604-936-6555

COURTENAY

Worsnop, Lorraine J. RMT
Site 465, Box 32, RR 4 604-334-4228

DELTA

Ladner Massage Therapy
Smithson, Katherine Anne RMT
101-5405 Ladner Trunk Rd . .604-940-1774

DUNCAN

Brown, Michael Lee RMT
7626 Mays Rd, RR 4 604-748-8502

GABRIOLA ISLAND

Arbutus Soft Tissue Pain Clinic
McGinn, Rickee RMT
By Appointment 604-274-9765

Shaw, Elfi RMT
By Appointment 604-247-9561

GIBSONS

Crowhurst, Judith A. RMT
RR 27 S-7, C-27 604-885-4005

HARRISON HOT SPRINGS

Harrison Hotel RMT
Lee, Laura RMT;
North, D. RMT 604-796-2244

HERIOT BAY

Diamond, Joni RMT
By Appointment 604-287-3134

KAMLOOPS

Biro, Donna
4-440 Victoria St 604-828-1690

Downtown Massage Therapy Clinic
Coelho, J. RMT; Patrick, Anita RMT;
Perrett, A. RMT; deVooght, J. RMT
775 Seymour St 604-372-3863

Family Massage Therapy
Milbers, K. RMT
102-156 Victoria St 604-374-6657

Northshore Massage Clinic
Hendry, Blaine RMT; Wheeler, A. RMT
30A-750 Fortune Dr . .604-376-4121

Rodrigues, R. RMT
332 D Victoria St 604-374-6178

KELOWNA

Anderson Massage Therapy
160 Valleyview Rd. 604-765-6778

Kelowna Clinic of Massage Therapy
208-478 Bernard Ave 604-762-3340

KIMBERLEY

Mather, Joanne RMT
215 Moyle St 604-427-7650

MAPLE RIDGE

Golden Ears Massage Therapy Clinic
Vilker-Birchfield, Marina RMT
7A-20691 Lougheed Hwy . . .604-465-4432

Massage Therapy & Remedial Exercise Centre
Libbey, Robert RMT
11942-223rd St 604-467-2636

NELSON

Medical Arts Massage Clinic
Huston, Ann RMT
207-507 Baker St 640-352-9626

NORTH VANCOUVER

Bachmann, Peter Heinrich RMT
203-267 Esplanade 604-980-4491

Lynn at Mountain Massage Therapy Clinic
Foreman, Lisa RMT
102-1258 Lynn Valley Rd . . .604-980-7474

PORT ALBERNI

Oswald, Maureena Lyn RMT
3074 Kingsway 604-723-1404

POWELL RIVER

Beach Gardens Resort & Fitness Centre
Prokopetz, Rose Anne RMT
7074 Westminster Rd 604-485-6969

PRINCE GEORGE

Whitmer, Pohney L. RMT
435 Quebec St 604-564-6639

RICHMOND

Healing Touch Massage Therapy
Bugden, Boyd RMT
210-8140 Cook Rd 604-270-2257

Richmond Massage Therapy Clinic
Hughes, Gillian RMT
7560 Minoru Gate 604-278-6108

SURREY

Bradford, Karen RMT
106-6840 King George
Hwy 604-594-9880

Therapeutic Massage Clinic
Lemay, Penny Lynn RMT
102-10340 134A St 604-588-1656

TOFINO

McQuay, Susan J. RMT
General Delivery 604-725-2907

VANCOUVER

Bennett, Julie S. RMT
Massage Therapy Clinic
5-1744 W Broadway 604-734-4242

Dressler, David M. RMT
330-2025 W 42nd Ave 604-266-3135

Harbourview Massage Therapy
Barker, R. RMT; Chow, M. RMT; Howes, L. RMT;
Lindal, B. RMT; St-Onge, R. RMT
P1-999 W Hastings St 604-669-3298

Hycroft Wellness Centre
Gibson, Gaelen K. RMT;
Hornell, Nancy L. RMT;
Friedman, R. RMT; Walters, D. RMT;
Johnson, L. RMT
214-3195 Granville St 604-731-8027

Massage Therapy Center
Bodewin, S. RMT; Inaba, S. RMT;
Cormier, E. RMT; Davison, B. RMT
158 11th Ave E 604-873-4160

Pacific Coast Massage Therapy
Ingram, Richard G.RMT;
Robins, G. Christopher RMT
909-736 Granville St 604-687-4078

Pacific Massage Therapy Clinic
301-745 W. Broadway 604-872-1818

Podgajny, Pawel RMT
600-1525 Robson St 604-684-0047

Point Grey Massage & Neuromuscular Centre
Thackwray, Johanna Denise
12-2475 Bayswater 604-732-4665

Quinn, Coleen A. RMT
815-1450 Chestnut St 604-739-9339

Soma Therapy Centre
Humeniuk, Christina RMT
2607 W 16th Ave 604-731-7883

Susan J. Brooks & Associates
Beattie, Brenda C. RMT
6564 Victoria Dr 604-327-8852

Vancouver Central Massage Therapy Clinic
Watson, Susan G. RMT
203A-3540 W 41st Ave 604-266-2757

von der Linde, Tilman RMT
3253 W 22nd Ave 604-731-6783

Webster, Marilyn RMT
301-1949 W 5th Ave 604-738-6718

West Coast College of Massage Therapy Public Clinic
555 W Hastings St 604-685-5801

Westside Massage Therapy
Sage, Julia S. RMT
3724 W Broadway 604-224-1011

Yesnik, Vivian RMT
145 W 17th Ave 604-873-8540

VERNON

Alpine Massage Therapy
Roberts, Melanie J. RMT
Ste. 5, 3105 30th Ave 604-545-6992

VICTORIA

Anodyne Therapeutic Massage
Sperling, Bernadine RMT
224-645 Fort St 604-384-5722

Brooks, Janet RMT
1031 Clare St 604-592-5873

Coy, James RMT
313-3995 Quadra St 604-727-7773

Fairfield Massage Therapy Clinic
Timms, Glen M. RMT
8-750 Pemberton Rd 604-595-7248

James Bay Massage Therapy
Paul, Angelika RMT
B-113 Superior St 604-995-0158

Massage Therapy Group
Rady, Barbara RMT; Scandrett, Margot RMT;
Smith, Lynn RMT
201-821 Burdett Ave 604-383-3011

McVicar, Wendy RMT
1334 Minto St 604-382-0444

Reinelt, Michelle RMT
201-306 Burnside Rd W 604-384-1376

Royal Oak Therapeutic Massage Clinic
Reed, Tracy C. RMT
105-4475 Viewmont Ave . . .604-479-1860

Schredel, Patricia RMT
2364 Manhattan Place 604-477-8065

Tillicum Physiotherapy Clinic
Bagshaw, Lindsay RMT
201-306 Burnside Rd 604-384-1376

Trost, Judith RMT
204-1002 Pakington St 604-381-0480

Victoria Massage Therapy Clinic
Stark, Robert RMT
1139A Yates St 604-385-5681

WHISTLER

All Seasons Spa Ltd.
Byford, Lesley RMT; MacEwan, Carol RMT
PO Box 643 604-938-2086

Blue Highways Shiatsu & Massage
Oswald, Theresa RMT
204-4433 Sundial Place 604-938-0777

WHITE ROCK

Center Point Neuromuscular Therapy Clinic
Collins, Marian G. RMT; Stuart, L RMT
46-1480 Foster St 604-536-0021

 # Manitoba

In Manitoba, massage therapists are not regulated, meaning that there is no legislation establishing a governing body to register and discipline qualified massage therapists.

Manitoba Association

Massage Therapy Association of Manitoba
Riverview PO Box 63030
Winnipeg, Manitoba R3L 2V8
Tel: 204-254-0406

Contact the association for a referrral to a massage therapist in your area.

✦ Manitoba Massage Therapists

NOTE: Check the credentials of your practitioner (see above, "Questions to Ask"). This publication cannot and does not certify or represent the qualifications of practitioners, or the quality of care available from them.

BRANDON

Universal Stress & Therapy Clinic
Derkson, Roxanne M.; Heide, Roxanne
Stach, Andrea E.
242-11th St 204-726-8851

WINNIPEG

Kos-Whicher Massage Therapy
Kos-Whicher, Susan; Whicher, Andrew
166 Kane Ave 204-885-1110
2033 Portage Ave 204-831-8494

✦ New Brunswick

In New Brunswick, massage therapists are not regulated, meaning that there is no legislation establishing a governing body to register and discipline qualified massage therapists.

New Brunswick Association

New Brunswick Massotherapy Association
PO Box 21009
Fredericton, New Brunswick E3B 7C2
Tel: 506-459-5788

Call for a referral to one of the association's 64 members, each with a minimum of 2,200 hours of education.

✦ New Brunswick Massage Therapists

NOTE: Check the credentials of your practitioner (see above, "Questions to Ask"). This publication cannot and does not certify or represent the qualifications of practitioners, or the quality of care available from them.

GONDOLA POINT

McConnery, Nancy
16 Valleyview Dr 506-849-1261

OROMOCTO

Campbell, Alexandria Maria
3 Kembles Ct 506-357-3732

SAINT JOHN

Delta Brunswick Delta Hotels
MacIntyre, T.C.
39 King St 506-672-7333

Fraser, Heather R.
Medical Arts Building
115 Hazen St 506-633-1415

Moores, Naomi Kathleen
97 Manners Sutton Rd 506-652-1462

Sewell, Keith L.
182 Champlain Dr 506-696-2277

✦ Newfoundland

In Newfoundland, massage therapists are not regulated, meaning that there is no legislation establishing a governing body to register and discipline qualified massage therapists.

Newfoundland Association

Newfoundland Massage Therapists' Association (NMTA)
PO Box 5032, Station C
St. John's, Newfoundland A1C 5V3
Tel: 709-726-4006

✦ Newfoundland Massage Therapists

NOTE: Check the credentials of your practitioner (see above, "Questions to Ask"). This publication cannot and does not certify or represent the qualifications of practitioners, or the quality of care available from them.

CORNERBROOK

Physical Rehab Inc.
Furey, Kristi Marie
Goodhouse Mall
93 West St 709-634-3788

ST. JOHN'S

Atlantic Massage Therapy Clinic
Rankin, Shirlee M.
701-220 Lemarchant 709-726-2060

Furlong, Nora Ann
318 Newfoundland Dr 709-753-6001

Harmony Centre
Sexton, Sara
119 Bond St 709-754-2217

Hodgson, Pamela
95 Monkstown Rd 709-754-0443

Hounsell, Susan L.
34 Stirling Cr. 709-753-0479

Human Touch Inc.
Clancy, Janine M.; Felix, Barbara Ann;
Mercer, Stephen
230-430-434 Water St 709-722-2639

Shea, Paula B.; Thoden, Tina
51A Long's Hill 709-726-0236

Turnbull, Wendy Jayne
2 Forest Ave 709-754-0096

✦ Northwest Territories

In the Northwest Territories, massage therapists are not regulated, meaning that there is no legislation establishing a governing body to register and discipline qualified massage therapists.

✦ Northwest Territories Massage Therapists

NOTE: Check the credentials of your practitioner (see above, "Questions to Ask"). This publication cannot and does not certify or represent the qualifications of practitioners, or the quality of care available from them.

HAY RIVER

South Slave Massage Therapy
Soares, Hazel
General Delivery 403-874-2664

YELLOWKNIFE

Athletic & Therapeutic Massage Clinic
Korhonen-Wood, Lena M.
7,5102-50th Ave 403-873-3509

Cramer, Jennifer Stranart
7,5102-50th Ave 403-873-3508

✦ Nova Scotia

In Nova Scotia, massage therapists are not regulated, meaning that there is no legislation establishing a governing body to register and discipline qualified massage therapists.

Nova Scotia Associations

East Coast Massage Therapy Association
2176 Windsor St
Halifax, Nova Scotia B3K 5B6
Tel: 902-422-3760
Contact: Steve McCall

Massage Therapists & Bodyworkers Alliance of the Maritimes
2424 Herenow St
Halifax, Nova Scotia B6T 3E5
Tel: 902-422-2222
Contact: Joseph V. Bloggs
This alliance includes practitioners from the following therapies: Feldenkrais, Jin Shin Jyutsu, Massage Therapy, Reflexology, Shiatsu and Trager.

Massage Therapists' Association of Nova Scotia
6129 North St
Halifax, Nova Scotia B3K 1P2
Tel: 902-866-4021/453-5588/429-2190
Contact: Sandra MacDonald

This association is a member of the Canadian Massage Therapists Alliance (CMTA).

✦ Nova Scotia Massage Therapists

NOTE: Check the credentials of your practitioner (see above, "Questions to Ask"). This publication cannot and does not certify or represent the qualifications of practitioners, or the quality of care available from them.

ANTIGONISH

Galloway, Linda
48 Hawthorne St 902-863-2434

BEDFORD

Metro Massage Therapy Clinic
Moravcik, Susan
1597 Bedford Hwy, Ste 307 .902-835-1932

Starr, Joseph
13 Pleasant St 902-835-1912

BRIDGEWATER

Nova Quest Health Associates
Morrison, Susan
64 Dufferin St 902-543-9376

DARTMOUTH

Morven Cottage Massage Therapy
Quen, Pat
46 Dahlia St 902-461-0018

Physioclinic
Chlopicki, Dariusz
Woodlawn Centre 902-423-6687

Quon, Patricia J.
46 Dahlia St 902-461-0018

HALIFAX

Atlantic Massage Therapy Clinic
Gillis, Nicolle; Gray, Lynn;
Jennings, Barry; MacDonald, Sandra;
Murrin, Denise; Sutcliffe, Brian
6129 North St 902-453-5588

Benson, Douglas
By Appointment 902-457-2226

Eastwind Health Associates
Arisz, Judith; Goodman, Mary;
Goodman, Peter; Stick, Kermit
2176 Windsor St 902-422-3760

Grandy, Theresa
Bayers' Rd
Shopping Centre, Ste 321 ...902-453-1420

In Touch Massage Therapy
Berkowitz, Julie
1569 Dresden Row 902-423-4407

Neuromuscular Therapy
Ship, Heidi
19 Idlewylde Rd 902-477-1409

Opalka, Stacey
5385 Young St 902-423-0155

Pamper Yourself
Hunger, Martha; Lippert-Litven, Tina;
Renner, Christina
1333 South Park St 902-429-2225

Sports Medicine Clinic
Pinel, Wayne
St. Mary's University 902-496-8186

Unwinding Massage Therapy
Bell, Holly
6316 Willow St 902-423-2086

Zweep, Terrie Hilary E.
Halifax Professional Centre
216-5991 Spring
Garden Rd 902-492-0699

KENTVILLE

Woodworth-Norris, Patti Jane
150 Park St 902-678-4548

PORT WILLIAM

Geitzler, Judith E.
PO Box 129 902-542-4550

WEYMOUTH

Barrett-Reid, Christina
4684 Main St 902-837-4636

✦ Ontario

In Ontario, massage therapists are regulated. This means that a governing body has been established with the responsibility of setting qualification standards and disciplining practitioners.

Legislation

The governing legislation is the *Regulated Health Professions Act, 1991,* and the *Massage Therapy Act, 1991* and regulations. The *Massage Therapy Act* defines massage therapy as the assessment of the soft tissue and joints of the body, and the treatment and prevention of physical dysfunction and pain of the soft tissues and joints by manipulation. The Act states that the therapy is meant to develop, maintain, rehabilitate or augment physical function, or relieve pain.

Restricted Titles/Representations of Qualifications

Only members of the governing body may use the title "massage therapist" or any variation. As well, only members may hold themselves out as persons qualified to practise in Ontario as a massage therapist or in a specialty of massage therapy.

Ontario Governing Body

College of Massage Therapists of Ontario
1867 Yonge St, Ste 810
Toronto, Ontario M4S 1Y5
Tel: 416-489-2626 or 1-800-465-1933
Fax: 416-489-2625

This is the governing body to call to confirm that your massage therapist is registered and has therefore met required qualification standards, or to make a complaint. Registered massage therapists have a Certificate Registration, issued by the College, clearly showing the therapist's registration number, and a photo ID card with the registration number, current year and renewal number. The College has a Zero Tolerance policy for sexual abuse in the profession.

Ontario Association

Ontario Massage Therapist Association
365 Bloor E, Ste 1807
Toronto, Ontario
Tel: 416-968-6487 or 1-800-668-2022
Fax: 416-968-6818

This association is the voluntary professional body representing registered massage therapists in Ontario. Call for a referral to a registered massage therapist in your area. The association has about 1,200 members. This is also the office of the Canadian Massage Therapists Alliance.

✦ Ontario Massage Therapists

NOTE: Check the credentials of your practitioner (see above, "Questions to Ask"). This publication cannot and does not certify or represent the qualifications of practitioners, or the quality of care available from them. We cannot and do not confirm that those listed are registered with the governing body.

AJAX

Ajax-Pickering Massage Clinic
Castanheiro, Rolph RMT;
Raedisch, Jessica RMT
596 Kingston Rd W 905-437-3202

Crystals Health and Fitness
Terney, LeeAnn RMT
520 Westney Rd S 905-428-2500

Dumas, Carolyn RMT
15 Field Cr 905-428-0740

Park, Lesley, G. RMT
26 Charlton Cr 905-686-3860

ALBERTON

Lovering, Christine G. RMT
533 Alberton Rd 905-648-3109

ALEXANDRIA

Nyamis Massage Therapy Clinic
Baker, Chloe Ann RMT
195 Main St 613-525-2945

ALLISTON

Alliston Natural Therapy Centre
Archer, Jan RMT
By Appointment 705-435-9142

Dolson, Claudia Anne RMT
By Appointment 705-435-0942

Nottawa Sports & Leisure Dome
Turgeon, Lauren RMT
1110 Hwy 89 705-435-5502

ALMONT

Therapeutic Massage in Motion
Aiken, Janice RMT
By Appointment 613-256-6243

AMHERSTBURG

Personal Health Management
Hopper, Dawn RMT
309 Pickering Dr 519-736-6625

ANCASTER

Ashworth, Nancy Isabelle RMT
73 Wilson St W 905-648-6653

Eleyonich, Elizabeth T. RMT
4-151 McNiven Rd 905-648-7623

Lundy, Carolyn J. RMT
495 Golf Links Rd 905-648-2425

ARTHUR

Lynn's Massage Therapy Clinic
Ashford, Brenda RMT; Goranson, Lynn RMT
330 Smith St 519-848-5606

Masso Therapy Health Clinic
Grasley, Evelyn RMT
By Appointment 519-848-2639

ATHENS

Athenian Touch Massage
Purcell, Marnie L. RMT
By Appointment 613-924-1190

AURORA

Aurora Family Health Clinic
Hunt, Nancy Jane RMT
St. Andrew's Village
35-2 Orchard Heights Blvd ..905-727-0119

Aura Therapeutics
Shaw, Laurie C. RMT
203-15017 Yonge St 905-713-0326

Chant Massage Therapy Clinic
Chant, Nancy Mary C. RMT
11-15213 Yonge St 905-713-1485

Corporate Care
Skillins, Cyndy RMT
14845-6 Yonge St,
Hunters Gate 905-841-0788

Mitchell, Cheryl V. RMT
38 Wellington St E 905-713-2273

R.B. Physio Massage Therapy Clinic
Ball, Susan Margaret RMT;
Boettcher, Riko RMT;
Boettcher, L. Paskel RMT
110-34 Berczy St 905-841-8338

Summers, Catherine RMT
16520 Yonge St, RR #2 905-898-1552

AYR

Bolton, Wilma B. RMT
92 Main St 905-632-8841

Findlater, Robert RMT; Michiels, Jo-Anne M. RMT
203-45 Stanley St 905-632-9041/
623-9748

BANCROFT

Bancroft Massage Therapy Centre
LeClair, Donna RMT
By Appointment 613-332-5667

Healthlines Massage & Natural Therapy
Wilkinson, Arlene RMT
By Appointment 613-332-5015

BARRIE

Barrie Health Spa
Henderson, Kimberley A. RMT;
Pretty, Susanne RMT
S102-151 Essa Rd 705-739-9585

Barrie Holistic H. & M. Centre
Martin, Carol Lynne RMT
20 Poyntz St 705-721-4884

Chahor, Jim RMT
20 McConkey Cr 705-727-1886

Charette, Yves R. RMT
44 McVeigh Dr 705-739-8558

D. Freer & Associates
Beauregard, Paul Andre RMT
121 Cundles Rd E........705-733-0660

Eastview Natural Therapy
Hardie, Alison RMT
123 St. Vincent Sts 705-739-0025

Fieldstone Natural Health Centre
Alexander, Katherine RMT; Perry, Margot RMT
By Appointment 705-434-2724

Grisewood, Scott RMT
By Appointment 705-726-0578

Hatfield, Kimberly C. RMT
190 Minet's Point Rd 705-728-9909

James, Joyce RMT
M-4 Cedar Point Dr 705-721-0350

Lynch, Jennifer RMT
78 Toronto St 705-722-4203

Meyerhoffer, Erik T. RMT
79 High St 705-721-1611

Mitchinson-Bailey, Lori RMT
9 Pinsent St 705-737-5956

Moulton, Kenneth RMT
13 Wellington St W 705-721-8818

Neuwelt, Margo RMT
4-80 Bradford St 705-722-6263

Oasis Neuromuscular Therapy
Smith, David R. RMT
499 Grove St 705-791-0109

Pamir Stress Centre
Mireault, Paul H. RMT
82 Mary St 705-737-4148

Pol Robertson, Arlene RMT
193 Wellington St E 705-727-1545

Quinn Rehab Services (c/o Sunnidale Medical Centre)
Melanson, David J. RMT
2 Friessen Place, RR #2 705-726-2362

Tavares, Dorothy Marie RMT
208-255 Kozlov St 705-728-0259

Van Sinclair, Sandra RMT
2-52 High St 705-737-0558

Walker, Wendy Anne RMT
48 Perry St 705-728-3165

BAYFIELD

Bayfield Massage Therapy
McKee, Darlene L. RMT
By Appointment 519-565-2344

Nivins, Sandra RMT
By Appointment 519-565-2231

BEAVERTON

Evans, Clinton P. RMT
Surette, Mary RMT
304 Victoria Ave 705-426-7849

BEETON

Beeton Therapeutic Massage Clinic
Averell, Carol-Lee RMT
60 Main St W 905-729-0138

BELGRAVE

Hartleib, Marjorie RMT
By Appointment 519-887-9305

BELLEVILLE

Pain Relief Clinic
Gable, Stephen J. RMT; Quinn,
Angela Ann RMT
300 N Front St 613-967-4733

Witley, Michael James RMT
327 Front St 613-962-6646

BETHANY

Christian, Phyllis RMT
By Appointment 705-277-1730

BLACKBURN HAMLET

Blackburn Hamlet Chiropractic Office
Gardiner, Susan J. RMT; Gravel, Ute RMT
21-110 Bearbrook Rd 613-837-6690

BOBCAYGEON

Bobcaygeon Medical Centre
Bird, D. Elaine RMT
85 Bolton St 705-738-6363

BOLTON

Biller, Warren RMT
8156 Castlederg Side Rd ...905-857-9602

Bolton Massage Therapy Clinic (c/o Courtyard Chiropractic Office)
Inman, Sandra G. RMT
18 King St E 905-951-2081

Health Investments
Mortimer, Christine RMT
131 Haines Dr 905-857-2170

Perfect Complexions
McCallum, Gordon RMT
Bolton County Mkt,
301 Queen St S 905-857-7866

BOWMANVILLE

Drysdale, Elizabeth RMT
Rehabilitation Department
47 Liberty St S 905-623-3331

Hands in Motion Massage Therapy & Sports Injury Clinic
Aldworth, Dan RMT; Slemon, Paul RMT
123 King St E 905-697-3111

Optimal Health Chiropractic Centre
Hullachan, Linda RMT
152 Church St 905-697-0355

BRACEBRIDGE

Therapy in Massage
McVittie, Carol RMT
133 Wellington St S 705-645-6811

BRADFORD

Bradford Chiropractic
Huber, Nicole RMT
200-157 Holland St E 905-775-4848

Bradford Massage Therapy Clinic
Dale, Michael RMT
354 Maple Grove Ave 905-775-5539

St. Pierre, Corey RMT
335 Maplegrove Ave 905-898-2230

BRAMALEA

Bramalea Therapeutic Massage
Mair, Aileen E. RTM; Yan, Mark S. RMT
15 Mayfair Cr 905-458-7664

BRAMPTON

Body Care Massage Therapies
Hillier, Leslie RMT
165 Main St N 519-453-8910

City Centre Chiropractic
Spidalieri, Susan RMT
109-169 Queen St E 905-453-1806

Glynn, Michael P. RMT
402-18 Kensington Rd 905-791-7011

Regency Racquet & Fitness
Krieger, Janine RMT
25 Kings Cross Rd 905-792-2232

Sampson, Julie Anne RMT
43 Jessie St 905-450-8291

Susan's Massage Therapy
Mulrooney, Susan RMT
215-341 Main St N 905-453-6759

Wallis & Associates
Adamiak, Barbara RMT; Brakel, Leslie RMT;
Fulton, Cheryl L. RMT; Kothe, Heidi RMT;
Levac, Julie C. RMT
101-118 Queen St W 905-796-7575

Von Zuben, Cheryl RMT
200 County Court Blvd 905-874-9037

Zeijlstra, Tekla RMT
243 Vodden St W 905-796-2740

BRANTFORD

Blackmore, Stephanie L. RMT
4-33 Nelson St 519-756-2608

Brant Massage Therapy Clinic
Martyniuk, Diane L.
189 Brant Ave 519-751-0326

Brantford Chiropractic Associates
Harrington, P. RMT; Langlois, Annette M. RMT
124 Charing Cross St 519-752-3881/
756-1303

Hands in Motion (c/o Family Wellness Clinic)
Mailing, Joan RMT
124 Charing Cross St 519-751-3488

Keresturi, Kimberley M. RMT;
Yates, Shelley RMT
11-330 West St 519-759-5542

Massage Therapy Centre
Hampshire, Allen N. RMT
54 Church St 519-759-3259

Massage Therapy in the Park
Odegaard, Gordon RMT
575 Park Drive N 519-756-3220

Studio Massage
Polowianiuk, Yaroslaw RMT
16 Alma St 519-756-8171

BROCKVILLE

Brockville Therapeutic Massage
Barraclough, Jennifer A. RMT;
McConnell, Cornelia RMT
By Appointment 613-345-0711

BROOKLIN

Lenarduzzi, Lois RMT
20 Shepherd Rd 905-655-4076

BURLINGTON

Appleby Massage Therapy Clinic
Winkler, Ernst RMT
20-511 New St 905-333-1979

BLS Therapy Clinic
Stasevich, Bonnie Lee RMT
438 Bower Ct 905-333-6468

Bodyworks
Law, Susan M. RMT
1463 Ontario St 905-681-3589

Burlington Family Care Clinic
Frances, James D. RMT
700 Guelph Line 905-681-7707

Burlington Therapy Clinic
McCarthy, Sandra M. RMT
45A-760 Brant St 905-333-4601

Follicle Beauty & Therapy Centre
Donec, Julie Taisa RMT; Gair, Kimberley RMT;
Gough, Sara E. RMT
3300 New St 905-681-0277

Gray, Karon D. RMT
2nd Fl, 1078 Botanical Dr ...905-333-4601

Headon Massage Therapy Clinic
Carrasco, Dominic RMT; Fitterer, Annette RMT;
Solanki, Renuka RMT
5-1450 Headon Rd 905-332-8770

Lakeshore Chiropractic Clinic
Rossy, Bozena RMT
2159 Lakeshore Rd 905-333-1104

Sampson-Rivet, Judith A. RMT
280 Plains Rd W 905-527-5573

Therapeutic Massage
Black, Roma RMT; Donelan, June RMT;
MacDonald, Marlene RMT
2025 Caroline St 905-623-7494

CALEDON

McWilliams, Joan RMT
By Appointment 519-927-3243

CALEDONIA

Haldimand Massage Therapy Clinic
Wetherell, Derek RMT;
Zorn-McIntosh, Brenda L. RMT
44 Argyle St N 905-765-8454

CAMBRIDGE

Biesel, Brenda A. RMT
24 George St N 519-623-7800

Brent/Cressman Massage Therapy
Brent, Nancy A. RMT; Cressman,
Lois A. RMT; Shillum, Kelly RMT
111 Westminster Dr N 519-650-4232

Cambridge Massage Therapy Clinic
Jorgenson, James George RMT
9 1/2 Grand Ave S 519-623-0140

Coleman, Virginia Lee RMT
255 Water St N 519-621-0771

Connell, Paul RMT
1172 King St E 519-653-7139

Derma-Tech
Brown, Ian RMT
18 Cambridge St 519-621-2421

Evans, Jo-Ann RMT
42 Parkhill Rd E 519-624-8782

Freeman Massage Therapy Clinic
Freeman, Thomas L. RMT
38 Linndale Rd 519-622-1150

Gardner, Pamela D. RMT
141 Ainslie St N 519-622-1712

Hogan, Deborah Christine RMT
113 Elliot St 519-623-5994

Naturopathic Healthcare Centre
Radatus, Maria Theresa RMT
119 Ainslie St N 519-622-0961

Spa in the City
Schaaf, Valerie RMT
18 Cambridge St 519-621-2421

Sparkes Massage Clinic
Sparkes, Heidi RMT
348 King St E,
Front Lower 519-650-5768

CAMALACHIE

Gardiner, Lorna RMT
3846 Egremont Rd 519-899-2442

CAMPBELLVILLE

McGaffin, Holly RMT
By Appointment 905-854-0406

CANNIFTON

Peake, Peggy Elizabeth RMT
By Appointment 613-962-5833

CANNINGTON

Riddolis, Carolyan RMT
By Appointment 705-437-4107

CARLETON PLACE

Carleton Place Chiropractic Centre
Dixon, Christine M. RMT
9 Emily St 613-257-3632

CARLISLE

Martyn, Jennifer RMT
1462 Centre Rd 519-689-0977

CARP

Carp Chiropractic Clinic
Browne-Tucker, Rosemary RMT
422 Donald B. Munro Dr . . .613-839-5316

CAVAN

Bradley, Douglas L. RMT
By Appointment 705-741-1378

CHATHAM

Nature's Clinic
Brick, Laureen A. RMT
276 Grand Ave W 519-351-3369

CHELTENHAM

Island, Marijane RMT
14452 McLaughlin Rd,
RR #1 905-838-3268

CLARKSBURG

Lanktree, Andrea RMT
46 Russell St 519-599-3237

CLINTON

Cornerston Spa
Garon, Denise RMT
79 Albert St 519-482-1205

COBOURG

Cobourg Therapeutic Massage Clinic
Clarke, Anita RMT; Parsons,
David Michael RMT
326 Division St 905-372-4518

Lalonde, Ian RMT
32A King St W 905-373-0346

Liebregts, P. Dianne RMT
By Appointment 905-342-3391

Natural Therapeutics Body Shop
Vader, Anita M. RMT
499A George St 905-372-4747

Van de Langeryt, Lara RMT
236 Walton St 905-373-9088

COLLINGWOOD

Marsden Massage Therapy
Marsden, John L. RMT
By Appointment 705-445-0231

Massage Therapy Clinic
Przybylski, Eva RMT; Przybylski, John RMT
27 Third St 705-445-2806

McPherson, Susan RMT
By Appointment 705-445-3844

Reckie, Brenda Ann RMT
72 Pine St 705-445-0013

Rueffer, Leanne RMT
524 First St 705-446-0437

Therapeutic Massage
Nave, Douglas R. RMT
2-168 Hurontario St 705-444-6631

COMBER

Suave, Yvonne RMT
By Appointment 519-687-3275

CONCORD

Dufferin-Steeles Chiropractic Health Centre
Campbell, Anne RMT; Trimarchi, Georgio E. RMT
102-1520 Steeles Ave W . .905-738-6303

Royal Rehab
Boczar, Piotr RMT
400-1600 Steeles Ave W . .905-761-0322

COOKSTOWN

Cookstown Health Centre
Smith, Regina RMT
By Appointment 705-458-0400

CORNWALL

Clinton, Joy RMT
120 Ninth St E 613-936-0746

MacGregor, Kathryn J. RMT
1390 Cornwall Centre 613-932-7956

Maximum Fitness
McIntosh, Julie Lalonde RMT
235 Pitt St 613-933-9969

COURTICE

Sherrington, Gail Lilian RMT
39 Hillhurst Cr 905-432-9448

Webster, Jayne RMT
36 Pidduck St 905-404-1427

DELHI

Rapai Jr., Paul RMT
RR #3 519-582-1242

DRAYTON

Helping Hands Massage
Bowman, Roxanne RMT
By Appointment 519-638-3029

DRYDEN

Dryden Massage Therapy Clinic
Latter, Genefer M. RMT
56 King St, Lower Level 807-223-6000

DUNDAS

Dundas Massage Therapy Clinic
Johnston, Michaela RMT; May-Dailman,
Marlene RMT
211 King St W 905-627-3301

Hall, John William RMT
By Appointment 905-627-5154

DUNNVILLE

Isaic, Jill R. RMT
410 Lock St W 905-774-6457

DURHAM

Macgillivray, Don J. RMT
By Appointment 519-369-2334

Walton, Marilyn RMT
By Appointment 519-369-5370

ELMIRA

Davidson, Sonia Lynn RMT
63-1 Arthurs St S 519-669-3840

Massage Therapy Clinic
Roch, Rudolph E. RMT
45 Church St W 519-669-5180

ELMVALE

Leck, Eve Eliz. Ann RMT
4 Queen St E 705-322-0986

ELORA

Elora Holistic Health Centre
Skoggard, Peter W. RMT
204 Geddes St 519-846-2579

Moffatt, Cameron J. RMT
22 Metcalfe St 519-846-9532

Vettor, Sacha RMT
231 Melville St 519-846-0835

ERIN

Back to Normal Inc.
Shields, Mary E. RMT
By Appointment 519-833-7400

Sue's Moves Fitness Centre
Pendry, Jodi L. RMT
2 Guelph Rd 519-833-7271

ESSEX

County Clinic for Massage Therapy
De Vittori, Louisa RMT
10th Con Col N #10867 519-776-6733

Health & Body
Ross, Lori Lynn RMT
39 Maidstone Ave E 519-776-6135

EXETER

Exeter Massage Therapy Clinic
Burt, Lori Jean RMT
2-476 Main St, Upper Level .519-235-3722

Farquhar, Rebecca RMT
502 Main St (Rear) 519-235-4587

Rader, Andrea Karen RMT
By Appointment 519-235-4565

FENLON FALLS

Summit Therapy
Vaare, Jari RMT
61 Juniper St 705-887-1508

FERGUS

North Wellington Massage Therapy Clinic
Barker, Karen S. RMT; Huber,
Georgia Ann RMT
170 Forfar St E 519-787-0098

FLESHERTON

Aquarius Health Resort
Vanry, Cornelia RMT
RR #4 519-924-2157

FONTHILL

Bover, Karen P. RMT
1512 Pelham St 905-892-8920

M. Holmwood Massage Therapy Clinic
Holmwood, Marlene E. RMT
209 Hwy #20 E, Birchley Pl .905-892-4431

Switzer, Dean D. RMT
10 Hwy #20 E 905-892-3003

FOREST

Milne, Elizabeth A. RMT
By Appointment 519-786-2768

GANANOQUE

Manion, Linda Maureen RMT
360 King St E 613-542-3478

GEORGETOWN

Caldwell, H. Ed RMT
12638 Eighth Line, RR #1 . .905-877-2345

Cockton, Sara A.G. RMT
3-80 Guelph St 905-873-7679

De Courcy, Sandra J. RMT
28 Elena Ct 905-873-2777

Georgetown Therapeutic Massage Clinic
Dew, David RMT; Walker, Dale Arthur RMT
31A Main St 905-873-1924

Graham, Rosemary T. RMT
RR #2, 9595 Trafalgar Rd . . .905-877-0531

GLOUCESTER

Blair Estates Massage Therapy
Cybulskie, Arlene A. RMT
4626 Cosmic Pl 613-741-7768

Bouchard, Myriam RMT
2157 Stonehenge Cr 613-744-5255

Ottawa Massage Therapy Clinic & Associates
Rowbottom, Gwendolyn RMT; Russell, Conrad Edward RMT
By Appointment 613-748-5454

Russell, Frances J. RMT
3565 Trappers Rd 613-521-0773

GODERICH

Dickson, Pamela Susanne RMT
201-166 The Square 519-524-6879

MacDonald, Sandra D. RMT
56 Church St 519-524-2365

Natural Image
Schenk-Snell, Katherine RMT
Suncoast Mall,
397 Bayfield Rd 519-524-5641

Sheardown, Maureen RMT
35A West St 519-524-1214

GORMLEY

Alvarez, Mary Lou RMT
By Appointment 905-727-6979

Lainesse, Claude RMT
14649 Woodbine
Ave, RR #1 905-713-6630

GRAFTON

St. Anne's Country Inn & Spa
Ryan, Rebecca RMT
RR #1 905-349-2493

GRAVENHURST

Muskoka Massage Therapy
Mitchell, Lisa RMT
135 Muskoka Rd N 705-687-9004

GRIMSBY

Anita Heins Massage Therapy Clinic
Brown, Scott RMT; Heins, Anita RMT;
Lommen, Frances Ann RMT
18 Ontario St 905-945-0700

Chiropractic Clinic, The
Coke, Shawna Lyn RMT
208-155 Main St E 905-945-6768

GUELPH

Aboud, Patricia Jane RMT
87 Galt St 519-836-5994

Ann St Chiropractic Clinic
Doherty, Robert J. RMT; Martin, Joilyn A. RMT
595 Woolwich St 519-822-4224

Blakely, David H. RMT
58 Lyon Ave 519-824-2766

Caring Hands
Hartwick, Carwin M. RMT
150 Woolwich St 519-836-9193

Changer, Chris RMT
66 Toronto St 519-822-1872

**Cowbrough, Joanne M. RMT;
De Stefano, Frank RMT;
Hobson, Margaret RMT**
363 Woolwich St 519-763-0784

D. & M. Young Enterprises Inc.
Young, Deborah A. RMT
189 Eramosa Rd 519-763-0459

Deborah's Massage Therapy Clinic
Proulx, Deborah E. RMT
36 Forster Dr 519-822-8034

European Aesthetics Spa
Colanardi, Josephine L. RMT
275 Woolwich St 519-837-8636

Family Chiropractic Centre
Breakey, Willa R. RMT
987 Gordon St 519-837-1234

Gayle, Jana RMT
32 Ervin Cr 519-763-3843

Goodden Therapeutic Massage Clinic
Goodden, Anne RMT
23 Lambert Cr 519-767-1626

Guelph Therapeutics
Fabry, Peter Alan RMT;
MacDonald, Karen E. RMT;
Stewart, Virginia RMT
177 Woolwich St 519-767-0594

Hansma, Meintje RMT
11-485 Silvercreek Pkwy N .519-837-1411

Hopkins, Charlene Ann RMT
40 Norwich St E 519-763-7774

Jacobi-Warren, Penny A. RMT
324 W Acres Dr 519-837-3022

Jewell, Susan RMT
175 Renfield St 519-836-1464

Johnston, Shirlene RMT
1453 Gordon St 519-821-7391

Martin, Sarah R. RMT
17 Summit Cr 519-821-9364

Mills, Stephanie RMT
8 Church Ln 519-763-2436

Munro, Susan C. RMT
114 Dovercliffe Rd 519-836-6412

Norfolk Massage Therapy Centre
Forrest, Louise Mary RMT;
MacDonald, Katherine A. RMT
111 Norfolk St 519-763-4363/6988

Overbaugh, Judith K. RMT
168 Paisley St 519-821-0996

Parkinson, Melanie L. RMT
210 Kortright Rd W, Unit 3 . .519-763-8745

Peppard, Sandra L. RMT
214-435 Stone Rd 519-837-0411

Roy, Minette RMT
104-40 Baker St 519-767-0900

Sandra Marie's Massage Therapy
Drummond, Sandra M. RMT
111 Norfolk St 519-763-6988

Scott Therapeutic Massage Clinic
Rennick-Hyde, Renee RMT;
Scott-Goulden, Debra RMT;
Shervington, Catherine RMT
343B Waterloo Ave 519-632-5112

Townsend, Dorothy T. RMT
101-511 Edinburgh Rd S . . .519-837-9711

Wellington Chiropractic Group
Johnston, Joy Shirley RMT;
Van Beek, Michel A. RMT;
Veres, Christine RMT; White, Patricia RMT
12 Waterloo Ave 519-822-4205

Wellington Therapeutic Massage Clinic
Sanders, Bonnie RMT; Sparrow, Noreen RMT
328 Woolwich St 519-763-1835

Woolwich Neuromuscular Therapy
Gordon, Craig S. RMT
279 Woolwich St 519-822-2021

HAMILTON

Advantage Chiropractic Health Centre
Presta, David RMT
3-66 Mall Rd 905-574-1181

Baron, Susznne RMT
845 Fennel Ave E 905-389-3395

Carson Chiropractic Office
Hopkins, Christine RMT 905-528-2494

Cook, Shoona D. RMT
136 Yonge St 905-528-6426

Crosthwaite Massage Therapy Clinic
Attrill, Sheila RMT; MacLeod, Elizabeth RMT
23 Crosthwaite Ave S 905-312-0550

Drieman, Louise RMT
314-1868 Main St W 905-526-7938

Dundas Community Physiotherapy
Lantsouzovski, Edouard RMT
307-1001 Main St W 905-627-2700

Embleton, Peter Andrew RMT
13 Welbourn Dr 905-388-5408

Emerald Therapeutic Massage Clinic
Jaskiw, Yolande M. RMT
122 Emerald St N 905-528-3595

Family Chiropractic Centre
Sobie, Sharon Anne RMT
136 Young St 905-528-6426

Gabriele, Nicholas A. RMT
49 Barons Ave S. 905-549-7752

Great Lakes Therapeutics
Stubbs, David G. RMT
118 George St 905-572-7141

Hazen, Barbara J. RMT
866 Main St E 905-544-5688

Holistic Centre
Zulak, David RMT
500 James St N 905-521-9664

Howatt, Martha Janet RMT
203-104 George St 905-523-8549

International Managed Health Care
Reid, Doug RMT
503-304 Victoria Ave 905-525-5598

Just Dial Mas-sage
Braun, Susan RMT
132-762 Upper James St . . .905-627-7243

Main West Therapeutics
Davis, Steve B. RMT;
Peterson-Langille, R. Ann RMT
17-1685 Main St W 905-521-1262

Mountain Massage Therapy Clinic
Burnett, Marlene R. RMT
231 Solomon Cr 905-575-5100

Natural Health Clinic
Fernandez, Marian RMT;
Macdonald, Kevin RMT
288 Gray's Rd, Unit 1 905-573-1105

Rath Massage Therapy
Rath, Mark A. RMT
18 Juliebeth Dr 905-388-7120

Rosedale Chiropractic Clinic
Firlotte, Shauna RMT
230 Graham Ave S 905-545-7570

Stonechurch Family Health Centre
Pettit, Jennifer RMT; Turnbull, Todd B. RMT
549 Stonechurch Rd E 905-572-8222

Stress Aid
Robinson, Heidi RMT
58 Morgan Rd 905-575-5795

Turnbull & Associates
Blacklock, Candace L. RMT
539 Stonechurch Rd E 905-575-8222

Wellington Wellness Clinic, The
Dartnall, Scott RMT; Turnbull, B. Robert RMT
136-293 Wellington St N . . .905-525-5572

West Hamilton Massage
Kennan, David RMT
17-1685 Main St W 905-523-5844

Young, Christopher RMT
444 Fennell Ave E 905-575-2833

HANOVER

Hanover Neuromuscular Therapy
Younger, John A. RMT
369-9th St 519-364-7866

Misch, Annette R. RMT
550-10th St 519-364-7456

HAWKESBURY

Aalders-Smith, Sibylla W. RMT
40-151 Main St E 613-632-1942

HEARST

Morin-Veilleux, Suzanne RMT
1425 Front St, Hwy 11 705-372-1550

HENSALL

Barker-Millar, Darlene RMT
RR #1 519-263-5382

HOLLAND LANDING

McConnell, Marsha R. RMT
2-19173 Yonge St 905-830-0880

Park Ave Therapy Centre
Belanger, Matthew P. RMT; Kalpin, Lee RMT
9 Park Ave 905-853-0672

HUNTSVILLE

Huntsville Natural Therapy Centre
Hall, Judy RMT
6-29 King William St 705-789-1468

ILDERTON

Burchill, Joan RMT
RR #2 519-666-2038

INGERSOLL

Howlett, Kenneth J.
90 Charles St W 519-485-3000

Oxford Rehab Clinic
Biro, Laura Marie RMT
70 Thames St N 519-425-4545

Underwood, Bradley, W. RMT
Whittaker, Paula D. RMT
B-45 Charles St 519-485-5959

JACKSON'S POINT

Barbara Hinton Therapeutic Massage
Hinton, Barbara RMT 905-722-5796

Isjima, Fujio RMT
By Appointment 905-722-3166

Kary, Allan James RMT
By Appointment 905-772-9762

KANATA

Family Chiropractic Centre
Pickard, James M. RMT
214-99 Kakula Rd 613-529-7660

Kanata Orthopaedic Physiotherapy Clinic
Lincoln, Kathryn Maureen RMT
405-580 Terry Fox Dr 613-599-8132

Terra Health Centre
Pek, Katerina RMT
10 Mowbray St 613-839-2758

KENORA

Thompson, Joanne Patricia RMT
Stone House, 225 Main St S .807-468-5577

KESWICK

Cole, Dawn RMT
198 Garden Ave 905-478-6896

De Vries, John RMT
107 Oakcrest Dr 905-476-2440

Keeler, Brenda Erlene RMT
16-204 Simcoe Ave 905-476-6475

Melling-Coles, Constance RMT
35 Bruce Ave 905-476-1087

Ross, Lorie L. RMT
By Appointment 905-476-4469

KETTLEBY

Ebbs, Sarah RMT
By Appointment 905-939-8809

KILLALOE

Natural Therapy Centre, The
Atkinson, Margaret RMT
153B Queen St 613-757-3638

Tyrell, Brian
RR #4 613-756-5899

KINCARDINE

Julia's Health & Beauty Spa
Langlois, Loraine RMT
335 Durham Market Sq 519-396-8515

Kincardine Massage Therapy Clinic
Harman, Christine RMT
890 Queen St 519-396-4018

KING CITY

Health Kneads
Wilcken, Mark RMT
200-117 Humber Cr 905-833-2684

King Chiropractic Clinic
Poulis, Georgia S. RMT
2-2174 King Rd 905-833-3300

King City Natural Health Centre
Carmichael, Bradley W. RMT
1229 King Rd 905-773-5122

King Massage Therapy Clinic
Newman, Joanne RMT
13067 Keele St 905-833-2310

Sadecki, Barbara S. RMT
251 Kingscross Dr 905-833-4730

Sunrise Therapy
Brown, Dawn-Marie RMT
295 Cavell Ave 905-833-5436

KINGSTON

Bird, Liz RMT
501-128 Elliot Ave 613-549-7188

Dabrowski, Rita B. RMT
Rutter, Jane Hilary RMT
114-645 Gardiner's Rd 613-384-6571

Emery, Meghan RMT
24 Lorne St 613-549-5809

Kingston Health Professionals
Churchill-Start, Amanda Louise RMT;
Fry, Michael C. RMT
163 Brock St 613-549-2877/2817

Kingston Wellness Centre
Black, Robert H. RMT; Garieri, Michelle RMT;
King, Lois RMT; Mason, Diane RMT
5-120 Princess St 613-531-9355

Let Go Wellness Centre
Sinfield, Sahaj Shantam RMT
202 Montreal St 613-549-1391

McNutt, Catherine A. RMT
444 Bagot St 613-549-1783

New Horizons Therapy Centre
Billings-Brammer, Angelica RMT;
Brown, Elizabeth Ann RMT;
Gurnsey, Cheryl RMT
2 Cataraqui St 613-549-5975

Perry, Barbara RMT
420 MacDonnell St 613-546-0360

Providence Centre
Higgins, Sister Jean RMT
1200 Princess St 613-542-8826

KIRKLAND

Soilleux, Robert F. RMT
By Appointment 705-567-2233

KITCHENER

A Natural Alternative: Massage Therapy
Lussa, Ann RMT; Prouty, Shirley RMT
69 Highland Rd E,
Main Level 519-571-7292/8258

Achtemichuk, Barbi RMT
83 Louisa St 519-745-4563

Belmont Centre Physical Medicine
Schmidt, Kimberly RMT
301-564 Belmont Ave W . .519-743-4355

Brendemuehl, Barbara RMT
102 Courtland Ave E 519-743-1914

Brenneman, Deanna M. RMT
20 Westmount Rd W 519-749-2060

Clarke, Ann M. RMT
549 Dunbar Rd 519-749-8430

Cutting Room, The
Blaskavitch, Lori A RMT 519-741-0527

De Caen, Erick RMT
84 Weber St W 519-743-2522

Fairway Massage Therapy
Martin-Diehl, Tracey L. RMT;
Ziegenbein-Reid, Britta S. RMT
6-5 Manitou Dr 519-894-1606

Grey, Olive RMT
209-824 King St W 519-743-5890

Gurney, Darryl RMT
1106 Union St 519-741-9557

Healing Hands Therapeutic Massage Clinic
Kaduc, Michella RMT
756 Victoria St S 519-571-9031

Health & Beauty Institute, The
Ueberschag, Janet RMT
737 Belmont Ave W 519-749-1996

Highland Rehabilitation Centre Ltd.
Nickerson, Lawrence T. RMT
403 Highland Rd W,
2nd Fl 519-578-6720

Hoeft, Ralph RMT
278 Lawrence Ave 519-571-0544

Kabin, Marje RMT
65 Belmont Ave E 519-742-0380

Kanai, Junji RMT
208-824 King St W 519-744-5040

Kosynski, Christiane RMT
165 Mill St 519-579-5919

Lacinger, Helena RMT
Lean, Jan RMT
22 Water St S . . .519-578-9350/570-3484

Lancaster Massage Clinic
Mueller, Dale N. RMT
307 1/2 Lancaster St W 519-743-8822

Massage Therapy Associates
Knarr-Peev, Renee RMT; Pallot, Julie RMT
242 Queen S S 519-742-0426/7128

McLellan, Janet RMT
166 Roberts Cr 519-744-4020

Merkt, Erwin J. RMT
403 Highland Rd W 519-579-4603

Milton, Teresa A. RMT
10 Hillcrest Ln 519-745-8788

Murray, Richard Sashman RMT
11 Geneva Cr 519-743-1756

Nadeau, Marlene RMT
Rovina Diana RMT
6-100 Highland Rd W 519-570-2257/
571-7291

Queen St Massage Therapy Clinic
Schuster, Stefan M. RMT
188 Queen St S 519-576-0806

Relax & Restore Massage Service
Sklar, Brian R. RMT
659 King St W 519-576-8044

Rockway Massage Therapy
Near, Tammy Lee RMT
589 Charles St 519-744-4745

Sanderson Massage Therapy
Eby, Bonita RMT; Sanderson, John D. RMT
301-678 Belmont W 519-570-2257

Scheerer, Jeff RMT
622 Charles St E 519-571-9114

Steel, Vivian RMT
152 Weber St W 519-576-5877

Ward, Hannelore RMT
210 Mill St 519-579-8317

Whitney, Jane RMT
174 Victoria St S 519-570-3510

Wholistic Health Care
Dabski, Michal RMT;
Kavanagh, Patti D. RMT
7 Clarence Pl 519-576-7320

Young, Vanesa RMT
110 Highland Cr 519-745-0567

LAKEFIELD

Doyle, Murray M. RMT
By Appointment 705-652-0632

McLean, Michelle Elaine RMT
By Appointment 705-652-1553

Miller, Anne Marie RMT
By Appointment 705-877-1074

LAMBETH

Essentials Registered Massage Therapy & Aesthetics
Harmos, Felix RMT
10 Main St 519-652-2410

Fayez Beauty Spa
Galbraith, Colleen RMT
6289 Longwoods Rd 519-652-2780

Southwest Wellness Clinic
Case, Janice E. RMT
20 Main St W 519-652-6484

Touch of Tranquility Massage Therapy Clinic
Bennett, Andrew RMT;
Van de Ven, Maureen J. RMT
30 Main St E 519-652-5730

LEAMINGTON

Alternative Health Centre
Johnston-Klemens, Cheryl RMT
407-33 Princess St 519-322-0976

Natural Therapy Clinic
Preyde, Mariette Ann RMT
24 Queens Ave 519-322-1333

Therapeutic Massage Clinic
Darowski, Peter Anthony RMT
100 Talbot St W 519-322-0761

LINDSAY

Ananda Wellness Centre
Neder, John S. RMT; Renaud, Christine RMT
73 William St S 705-324-6530

Ayer, Terry RMT
30 Richard Ave 705-324-0821

Deitch, Rosemary RMT
206 Lindsay St S 705-878-0463

Healing Place, The
Jung, Diane RMT; Ouellet, Kathleen RMT
2 Albert St N 705-328-0393

LISTOWEL

Newman, Christine Anne RMT
102 Main St W 519-291-4050

LITTLE CURRENT

Fowler, Jacqueline RMT
By Appointment 705-368-1094

LONDON

AAMTOL
Gagne, Ray RMT
82 Wharncliffe Rd S 519-663-9068

Abbinett, Donica L. RMT
434 Clarence St 519-433-8280

Ardene, Sylvia RMT
506-587 Talbot St 519-672-0878

Atrium Massage Therapy Associates (YMCA - London Central)
Harvey, Robyn T. RMT; Lillie, Janet RMT
382 Waterloo St 519-667-3300/3306

Avalon Centre
Corry, John W. RMT
121 Oxford E 519-657-2422

Being In Touch
Graham, Bonnie RMT
69 Beaconsfield Ave 519-438-2698

Bludau, Linda RMT
304 Maurice St 519-679-9794

Body Health Massage Therapy
Boniface, Sandra RMT; Major, Karen RMT;
McCrea, Lisa RMT
635 Richmond St 519-432-8711

Brimner, Susan RMT; Sweeney, Rosalind RMT
360 Queens Ave 519-432-5458

Brown, Allison J. RMT
14 St. Neots Dr 519-432-1499

Cameron, Brenda M. RMT
116 Tufton Pl 519-668-0908

Campbell, Donna RMT; O'Malley, Christine RMT
1217 Oxford St W, Unit #3 .519-473-9455

Carol Myers Massage Therapy
Myers, Carol E. RMT
142 Tecumseh Ave E 519-433-4515

Central Massage Therapy Clinic
Groenewegen, Angela J. RMT;
Santala, Elaine RMT
310-450 Central Ave 519-660-0414

Chelsey Park Health Club
MacKenzie, Lori RMT
312 Oxford St W 519-438-9891

Chernick, Yonina RMT
635 Richmond St 519-432-8711

Cheveric, Charlene M. RMT
323 Southcrest Dr 519-474-1647

Chrysler, Sandra RMT
559 Grosvenor St 519-679-0761

Coatsworth, Vickie J. RMT
2-1193 Oxford St E 519-659-2500

Colborne Family Medical Centre
Leis, Sherry RMT; McPherson, Ian D. RMT
203-612 Colborne St 519-432-8522

Commissioners Hill Massage Therapy
Reid, Shawn RMT
182 Commissioners Rd E 519-686-7922

Cordari-Ayres, Silvia RMT
43-90 Chapman Ct 519-471-6549

Davis, Leslie RMT
665 Fanshawe Park Rd 519-438-9805

DiGiuseppe, Donato RMT; DiGiuseppe, Jodi RMT
518 Quebec St 519-452-7313

Downtown Clinic
Wyse, C. Jane RMT
362 Oxford St E 519-434-2795

Doyle, Susan RMT; Loyens, Diane RMT
994 Oxford St E 519-659-8479

Fibison, Ellen E. RMT
187 Sanders St 519-451-5327

Filipowski, Kornel RMT
765 Lady Brook Cr 519-680-1990

Filippini, Wendy RMT
765 Hellmuth Ave 519-851-0069

Fisher, Karen RMT
1-44 Stanley St 519-455-8139

Fitness Forum
Ross, Sheryl RMT
900 Jalna Blvd 519-681-1123

Four Seasons Massage Clinic
Dewbury, Deborah RMT;
Fitzmaurice, Patricia RMT
533 Queens Ave 519-434-9198

Glen, Betty Mae RMT
101-280 Queens Ave 519-443-0006

"Hands On" Massage Therapy Clinic
Allen, Craig D. RMT
8-521 Nottinghill Rd 519-641-2311

Health Network
Arnsby, Angela M. RMT;
Barfoot, Catherine RMT; Curtis, Kristen RMT;
Rubel, Mary Arlyn RMT; Sullivan, Kelly RMT
121 Oxford St E 519-433-7400

Hughes, Ruth RMT
243 Main St 519-733-8111

Huron & Highbury Chiropractic Centre
Locke, Gerald RMT
1315 Highbury Ave 519-451-4000

Kennedy, K. Nicole RMT
540 Queens Ave 519-432-5752

Lane, Rosemary RMT
364 Wortley Rd 519-438-5823

Leblanc, Michael J. RMT
3-92 Cartwright St 519-434-9372

Lewis, Kimberly RMT
310-1233 Huron St 519-433-6720

London Massage Therapy Centre
Denis, Jeffrey David RMT;
Gavin, Claire E. RMT;
Ketersturi, Karen L. RMT; Short, Sheila RMT
582 St. James St 519-673-3007

Lynas, Cindy
Peesker, Julie RMT
167 Oxford St W 519-433-1716

Morales, Blanca RMT
Ponsford, Laurie-Ann RMT
135 Wortley Rd 519-434-3946

Nikodym, Alois RMT
103 Oxford St W 519-438-3966

Peckham, Karen RMT
2-1193 Oxford St E 519-457-1870

Poissant, Susan RMT
196 Central Ave 519-433-6245

Powell, Becky RMT
472 Crumlim Side Rd 519-659-0465

Purres, Melanie E. RMT
897 Lorne Ave 519-642-7177

Robb, Denise RMT
232 Oxford St W 519-858-3068

Rowell, Richard A. RMT
1269 Commissioners Rd W .519-472-1830

Sales, Tanya RMT
666 Wonderland Rd N 519-474-7200

Seaman, Sandra Isobel RMT
402-570 William St 519-434-3946

Stearne, Christine RMT
619-595 Proudfoot Ln 519-472-3169

Stothers, Marta RMT
410-520 Wellington St 519-439-8102

Taron Massage Therapy Clinic
Hodgson, Brian J.W. RMT;
Robson, Catherine L. RMT
225 Colborne St 519-663-9159

Tillane's R & R Massage Therapy Centre
Beaulieu, Tillane RMT
200-217 York St 519-432-9419

Tyr Massage
Stilwell, Michael J. RMT
844 Wonderland Rd S 519-667-5052

Vandenbussche, Ginelle RMT
454 Oxford St E 519-645-1596

Walker, Jeanne Marie RMT
579 Central Ave 519-432-1098

Wass, Holly, RMT
17 Windsor Cr 519-645-8000

Waymouth, Mary Catherine RMT
822 Maitland St 519-672-1657

Wesley, Lorraine RMT
23 Tamarack Cr 519-472-5046

Westmount Chiropractic Clinic
Ryan, Catherine RMT
844 Wonderland Rd S 519-672-2000

MAPLE

Scodeller, Denise I. RMT
2301 Major MacKenzie Dr ..905-832-9272

MARATHON

Hui, Mary H. RMT
By Appointment 807-229-2762

MARKHAM

Ashgrove Therapy Centre for Massage, Shiatsu & Reflexology
Sharifi, Manoocher RMT
301-6633 Hwy #7 East 905-294-8614

DeFinney Chiropractic & Sports Injury Clinic
So, Terri RMT
101-5871 Hwy #7 E 905-294-0454

Healing Hands Massage
Marsig, Krista RMT
46 Sir Gawaine Pl 905-472-8377

H.P.B.C. Rehab
Ursomarzo, Daviano S. RMT
105-675 Cochrane Dr 905-940-2627

Markham Massage
Watts-Ostridge, Lesley RMT
27 Dewitt Ct 905-294-6773

Markham Pain Clinic
Bellinger, June Ann RMT;
Cunningham, Ross E. RMT;
Pretzsch, Margin G. RMT
1-4981 Hwy 7 E 905-470-2626

Mayfair Parkway Massage Therapy Clinic
Campbell-Hosey, Belinda L. RMT
By Appointment 905-475-0350

Med Care
Shortt, Dianne RMT
2900 Steeles Ave E 905-294-8191

MyoRehab Therapy
Schifitto, Gaciano RMT
108 Cairns Dr 905-471-4059

One-to-One Injury & Pain Clinic
Thiessen, Monika RMT;
Wakefield, Simon A. RMT
207-144 Main St N 905-472-6340

Percy, Lorraine RMT
25 Rouge River Circle 905-472-9762

Rehab Wellness
Graham, Sheila RMT;
McDonald, Robert L. RMT
12 Main St N 905-471-9355

Safe Space Therapeutic Massage Clinic
Lee, Ivy Seng-Hun RMT
309-18 Crown Steel Dr 905-513-7939

16th Ave Chiropractic & Sports Injuries Clinic
Djas, Rhonda RMT
203-9275 Hwy 48 N 905-471-8810

Steels, Brenna RMT
8500 Warden Ave 905-470-2400

MEAFORD

Family Chiropractic Centre
Tyhurst, Kenneth RMT
51 Skyes St N 519-538-3747

Meaford Massage Clinic
McCarthy, John F. RMT
RR #4 519-538-1781

MIDLAND

Midland Massage Therapy
Bryant, Marie RMT
288 King St 705-527-0459

Warrilow, Katherine M. RMT
519 Hugel Ave 705-527-1598

MILTON

Baron, Rae RMT
11-250 Satok Cr 905-878-9041

Solanki, Natverlal J. RMT
533 Trafalgar Ct 905-878-3037

Wilson, Karen J. RMT
320 Highside Dr 905-876-1248

MILVERTON

Hasenpflug, Louise T. RMT
3 Main St N 519-599-2212

MINDEN

Of Sound Body
Ziorjen, Jacqueline RMT
By Appointment 705-286-1123

Perry, Monica RMT
By Appointment 705-754-1394

MISSISSAUGA

AIM
Muklewicz, Adam RMT
503-71 King St 905-897-9222

Airport Fitness & Racquet
Pankiw, Dawn J. RMT
3270 Caroga Dr 905-405-0055

Airport Massage Therapy Clinic
Barnes, Chris RMT; Hallson, Sherry RMT;
Term. 2, Pearson
International Airport 905-676-2840

Applewood Centre for Injury Rehabilitation
Eagar, Alison I. RMT
201-1077 N Service Rd ...905-272-2161

Bew-tique Therapeutic
Whitton, Erin B. RMT
516 Chantenay Dr 905-897-1570

Bloor-Dixie Physiotherapy & Rehabilitation Centre
Kolakowska, Anna RMT;
Kolakowski, Slawomir RMT
401-3415 Dixie Rd 905-602-4240

Body Balance Massage Therapy Clinic
Zienkiewicz, Dorota RMT
202-3476 Glen Erin Dr 905-607-9800

Brendel, Wolfgang RMT
2411-45 Kingsbridge
Garden Circle 905-568-2013

Daniel, Helen RMT
1395 Lorne Park Rd 905-278-2051

Dixie Sport & Physiotherapy
Oldnall, David A. RMT
1420 Burnhamthorpe Rd E .905-625-9295

Dunwin Chiropractic Centre
Dale, Sandra RMT
2285, #2 Dunwin Dr 905-828-0236

Erin Mills Chiropractic Clinic
Cook, Rhonda Lynn RMT;
Daciw, Carolyn Stephanie RMT;
O'Malley, Mary T. RMT
5-3105 Glen Erin Dr 905-828-2014

For Your Health
Brooks, Anthea M. RMT
312-2000 Credit Valley Rd ..905-569-2271

Gudaniec, Dariusz RMT
1380 Daniel Creek Dr 905-858-1959

Gullace, Frank D. RMT
5237 Castlefield Dr 905-858-2516

Homewood, Muriel RMT
595 Roselaire Tr 905-712-1949

Injury Management Centre
Eddy, William J. RMT; Enns, Annette R. RMT;
Geen, Sally RMT; Zaranek-Klos, Beata RMT
2124 Hurontario St 905-272-2655

International Managed Health Care
Astrein, Alexey RMT
1A-60 Bristol Rd E 905-890-3700

Inwood, Janet R. RMT
262 Randi Rd 905-272-3970

ITM
Ladret, Lara RMT
2021 Cliff Rd 905-275-0157

Juhasz, Violet RMT
1005-3533 Derry Rd E 905-677-6898

Kenko Alternative Therapy Academy
Kirpal, Paul Parsram RMT;
Lewis, Charlotte RMT
1107 Lorne Park Rd 905-891-8652

Kiasal Consultants Inc.
Salehi, Michele RMT
201-1325 Eglington Ave E ..905-238-0969

Lady Fitness & Beauty Spa
Kelly, Boyd RMT
100-6465 Millcreek Dr 905-812-1902

Lafontaine Massage Therapy Health Centre
Lafontaine, Sylvie RMT
11-3355 Hurontario St 905-566-5300

Lorenc, Paul RMT
Lorne Park Plaza,
1107 Lorne Park Rd 905-891-8652

M.T.M. Centre (c/o Chiropractic Centre)
West, Kendra RMT
100 City Centre Dr 905-848-8900

Massage Therapy at City Centre
Spoz, Dariusz RMT
900 Rathburn Rd W 905-897-5005

McDonald, Lorensa RMT
993 Raintree Ln 905-891-1263

Mississauga Massage Therapy Centre
Janik, Wioletta RMT
503-50 Burnhamthorpe
Rd W 905-896-1151

Mississauga Physical Rehabilitation & Wellness Centre
Xu, Ru Jun RMT
11-3355 Hurontario St 905-566-5300

Mississauga Therapeutic Health Clinic
Edwards, Jean RMT; McCrae, Marie RMT; Savard, Deborah RMT
1295 Burnhamthorpe Rd E .905-206-0525

Mulligan, Carolin J. RMT
5-92 Lakeshore Rd E 905-278-1778

Namaste Health & Wellness Centre
Pounall, Dennis Oswald RMT
3-169 Dundas St E 905-270-5167

Northern Telecon Health Centre
Eckel, Sue RMT
3 Robert Speck Pkwy 905-566-3406

Orc Massage Therapy
Iamarino, Gina D. RMT
884 Southdown Rd 905-822-5240

Potym, Anita RMT
701-45 Kingsbridge
Garden Circle 905-568-2936

Repper, Karl RMT
338 Kingsbridge Garden Circle905-568-3962

Roque Enterprises
Roque, Sofia RMT
4215 Garnetwood Ch 905-571-6292

Schiafone, Tiziana RMT
115-1550 Enterprise Rd 905-564-0512

Seunarine, Karen J. RMT
57-4101 Westminster Pl 905-270-0897

Shafayat Health Clinic
Seegobin, Savitri RMT; Waleski, John RMT
Delta Meadowvale Inn
6750 Mississauga Rd 905-821-0209

Shakti Rehab Centre
Zienkiewicz, Dariusz RMT
17-7895 Tranmere Dr 905-677-7897

Todd, Teresa P.
2205 Cliff Rd 905-277-4202

Ventures In Harmony
Horvath, Christine RMT
105-5805 Whittle Rd 905-712-2979

Wagman, Sandra RMT
43-2145 Sherobee Rd 905-272-2626

Wiley, Richard James RMT
5583 Cosmic Cr 905-507-1497

Wyeld, Brenda RMT
8M-3034 Palston Rd 905-275-3991

MITCHELL

Hunsberger, Kenneth Edward RMT
220 Maple Ct 519-348-8025

MOUNT ALBERT

Blackstopp, Jan RMT
RR #1 905-473-6464

Mount Forest Natural Health Centre
MacDonald-Reeves, Heather C. RMT
248 Main St N 905-323-4148

Navarra, Angeline RMT
21102 McCowan Rd 905-473-5125

MUIRKIRK

Pack, Joanne M. RMT
RR #2 519-678-3204

NAPANEE

Hymson, Timothy John RMT
140 Industrial Blvd 613-354-2696

NEPEAN

Craniosacral Therapy Centre/Massage Therapy Care
Pouliotte, Ronald J. RMT
88 Centrepointe Dr 613-224-0705

Greenbank Massage Therapy Centre
Forsyth, Kimberly A. RMT
143 McClellan Rd 613-726-1797

Nepean Sports Medicine Clinic
Hopper, Sharon RMT
1701 Woodroffe Ave 613-727-8712

Ploughman, Robert RMT
1547 Merivale Rd 613-526-3823

Spilchen-Bicho, Leah RMT
65 Thornbury Cr 613-727-5755

Taylor Therapy
Taylor, Kimberly RMT
513-91 Valleystream Dr ...613-828-2908

NEW HAMBURG

G.W. Baechler Massage Therapy
Baechler, Gerry W. RMT
By Appointment 519-662-2956

New Health Perspectives
Gerber, Sherry RMT
3 Waterloo St 519-662-2123

Wilmont Massage Therapy Centre
Snyder, Bonnie J. RMT
10 Byron St 519-662-1409

NEW LISKEARD

Jepsen, Cynthia Annie RMT
Pinewood Ctr, 221
Whitewood Ave 705-647-7333

NEWMARKET

A.M. O'Neil-Leslie-Davis Chiropractic
O'Neil, Anne-Marie RMT
10-1065 Davis Dr 905-853-4900

Aim Glenway
Sheppard, Tammy RMT
470 Crossland Gate 905-898-2230

Black, Susan P. RMT
543 Timothy St 905-836-4325

Canadian Medical Dental Centre
Morton, Kathryn RMT
Upper Canada Mall,
17600 Yonge St 905-853-4546

Dean, Susan RMT
353 Ontario St 905-898-3661

Gabor, Paul RMT
302-531 Davis Dr 905-836-8742

Hands On Health Care
Henkel, Janet J. RMT
27-17817 Leslie St 905-836-9505

International Managed Health Care
Monaghan, Sarah RMT
615 Davis Dr 905-895-0462

Lumsden, Diana RMT
109 Main St S 905-895-1299

Maduro, Anne-Marie Selina RMT
76 Prospect St 905-953-8088

Micallef, Theresa RMT
16635 Yonge St 905-830-9100

Mulock Chiropractic
Lester, Elizabeth J. RMT; McFarlane, Linda RMT
4-140 Mulock Dr 905-853-9685

Newmarket's Natural Health Centre
Graeme, Laura RMT
1-17665 Leslie St 905-853-0172

Persechini Fitness Centre
MacDonald, Barbara RMT; Richmond, Linda RMT
77 Davis Dr 905-836-9131

Smith, Grant R. RMT
109 Main St S 905-895-1299

Walker, C. Jill RMT
4294 St. John's
Side Rd, RR #3 905-642-8038

Wellspring Common
Levine, Mark L. RMT; Osbourne, Judy RMT
203-637 Davis Dr 905-830-9320

Zacchigna, Lisa RMT
214-16755 Yonge St 905-898-6644

NIAGARA FALLS

Dagmar's
Sindelar, Dagmar RMT
4255 Ellis St 905-356-5372

Hand in Hand
Halle, Carole N. RMT
4465 Drummond Rd 905-357-1944

Hodgkinson, Deborah RMT
6679 O'Neil St 905-354-9440

Niagara Falls Chiropractic Clinic
Zanchetta, Eva RMT
3950 Portage Rd 905-357-5566

Niagara Falls Injury Rehab Centre
Lefebvre, Tim J. RMT
14-4025 Dorchester Rd 905-354-7713

Pelkey, Robert J. RMT
2-6161 Thorold Stone Rd ..905-336-2472

Rathwell Clinic
Anderson, Rosalind RMT
4052 Welland St 905-295-6833

Tanning Salon
Cardwell, Carlee RMT; Cuplo, Jodi C. RMT
4681 Queen St 905-357-9611

Van Dyke, Cynthia M. RMT
8250 Rideau St 905-354-5474

NIAGARA-ON-THE-LAKE

Hack, Irmgard RMT
By Appointment 905-468-5555

Health Dynamics
File-Meyer, Maureen RMT
412 Mississauga St 905-468-5229

Prince of Wales Hotel Health Club
Campbell, Martha A. RMT
Queen & King 905-468-3246

White Oaks Inn & Racquet Club
Black, Susan L. RMT; Ryczko, Simone RMT
RR #4, Taylor Rd 905-688-6800

NORTH BAY

Brinkman, Olga L. RMT
53 Joseph St. 705-497-0998

Brown, Vanessa L. RMT
3-288 Worthington St. W ..705-495-1315

Caring Treatments Massage & Hydrotherapy Clinic
Stricker, Susan L. RMT
3-288 Worthington St W 705-497-0683

Massage Therapy Clinic
Sanders, Cameron RMT
101-269 Main W 705-476-2266

Total Health
Degagne, Lise G. RMT
437 Sherbrooke St 705-472-7547

Total Health Clinic
Moreau, Lilliane RMT
91 Champlain St 705-474-7377

NORVAL

Silva, Janice Gail RMT
9 Green St 905-877-2811

OAKVILLE

Cook, Julie-Anne RMT
2079 Marine Dr 905-825-1391

File, Beata RMT
21-415 River Oaks Blvd W ..519-257-3911

Glen Abbey Recreation & Aquatic Centre
Stewart, P. Terry RMT
1415 Third Line 905-815-5950

Hassard Chiropractic Clinic
Furukawa, Cheryl Lynn RMT
2361 Lakeshore R d W 905-847-2225

Mangan, Michael Shawn RMT
288 Mary St 905-844-0072

Menuha Therapy Centre
Moffatt, Gwen RMT; Ross, Carolyn RMT;
Sanders, Krista RMT
135 Brant St 905-845-3323

Nottinghill Place Chiropractic Clinic
MacEachern, Margaret RMT
205-1131 Nottinghill Gate .905-827-4197

Oakville Massage Therapy/Rehab Centre
Simpson, Janet RMT; Szekeres, Csaba RMT
145 Dunn St 905-849-2291

Oakville Shiatsu & Massage Therapy Centre Ltd.
Bailey, Bonnie RMT; Flanagan, Paul RMT;
Prack, Frederick RMT;
Prydz, Ingegerd Rut RMT;
Sweetman, Thomas RMT; Young, Tori RMT
304-125 Lakeshore Rd E ..905-845-3137

Pieronne-Knight, Zorana RMT
1116 Windbrush Dr 905-847-0188

Roe Massage Therapy
Boutari, H. Maureen RMT; Roe, Karen RMT
208 Wyecroft St 905-339-2139

Schumann, Laureen RMT
1201 Glen Valley Rd 905-847-5860

Weeks, Carol RMT
C85-1500 Tansley Dr 905-827-5892

OMEMEE

Gallagher, Deborah RMT
7 Sarah Cr 705-799-6117

ORANGEVILLE

Ashbee, Judy A. RMT
4 Third St 519-940-0522

H.P.C.
Prodoehl, Hedi RMT
RR #5 519-941-3398

Labrash, Elizabeth RMT
RR #1 519-941-9319

Longbottom, N. Lynn RMT
10 Wellington St 519-942-1684

M.F.C. Therapy
Crockett, Michelle F. RMT
2A Church St 519-941-1121

McBurney-Van Trigt, Peggie RMT
20 Faulkner St 519-941-4195

Peace Within
Logan, Cynthia Ann RMT
3 First St 519-941-9316

Pihack, Ann M. RMT
15-15 Sherbourne St 519-942-1711

Scott, Linda K.
By Appointment 519-942-3951

ORILLIA

Healing Touch
Calverley, Rosemary E. RMT
185 Laclie St 705-329-2256

Hill, Kerry J. RMT
390 Laclie St 705-326-2200

Huronia Natural Health Centre
Gdanski, David RMT; Gleason, Deone RMT;
Robinson, Debra RMT
83 Albert St N 705-327-0327

Johnston, Mara RMT
333 Mary St 705-327-0785

Joyce, Laura J. RMT
16B Matchedash St N 705-325-4787

Ledlow, Janice RMT
138 Mississauga St N 705-327-0061

Natural Revival Therapies
Pigeon, Johanna RMT
203-10 Peter St N 705-329-3659

Willow Court Massage Therapy
Bozek, Joanne P. RMT; Cherry, Gayle RMT;
Thompson, Richard RMT
4A-575 West St South 705-327-0457

ORLEANS

Orlean's Physiotherapy
Tattersall, John Arthur RMT
2555 St. Joseph 613-830-3145

Sanders, Marie-Jean RMT
209-1720 Marsala Cr 613-830-7354

ORO STATION

Berry, Jennifer M. RMT
44 Howard Dr 705-487-6186

ORONO

Toal, Cher G. RMT
7571 Oak School Rd 905-983-5733

OSHAWA

Active Recovery Clinic
Mason, Michelle L. RMT
111 King St E 905-571-1729

Busst, Anne RMT
1400 Ritson Rd N,
Suite 202 905-721-0104

Central Health & Chiropractic
Goulding, Deborah B. RMT
2-50 Richmond St E 905-433-1500

Den Hartog, Arigie RMT
1384 Sharbot St 905-728-6617

Deschamps, Annette RTM
801 Gentry Cr 905-723-5140

Garniss, Sheila RMT
292 King St W 905-725-8111

Kineducare Wellness Centre
Friede, Cheryle RMT; Winkler, Lois A. RMT
4-909 Simcoe St N 905-434-5398

La France's Natural Therapy Clinic
La France, Linda Anne RMT
17 Ontario St 905-721-0363

Long, Jo-Anne Malachowski RMT
875 King St E 905-434-6778

Soloform Muscle Therapy
Wilson, NoraLynn N. RMT
308 Wagar St 905-579-0206

Syme, Deanna RMT
133 Tounton Rd W, Unit #4 ..905-436-6666

OTTAWA

Abdelshahid, Onsy RMT
By Appointment 613-828-9915

Acadia Therapeutic Clinic
Kettles, Elaine RTM
203-1719 Bank St 613-737-0000

Alexander, Doug RMT; Alexander, Leona RMT
324 Oakdale Ave 613-722-8588

Aquasphere Centre Inc.
Armitage, Elizabeth RMT;
Ayoubzadeh, Pejman RMT;
Manaigre, Monique RMT;
Noailles, Kathleen RMT
24 Clarence St 613-241-7001

Belyea, Lee RMT
301-267 O'Connor St 613-563-7193

Blundell, Eric F. RMT
By Appointment 613-225-5483

Body-Mind Continuum
Philpott, Wendy RMT; Skerl, Nada RMT;
Wolfe, Paul L. RMT
346 Somerset St W 613-230-3527

Britannia Chiropractic Clinic
McMullin, Kimberly RMT
1315 Richmond Rd 613-736-7271

Cawny's Health & Beauty Clinic Institute
Shambare, Chipocheme R. RMT
206-400 Slater St 613-233-9422

Chiropractic Care Centre
Hood, Sarah A. RMT
210-35 O'Connor St 613-237-3886

Darcy B. Keenan Therapeutic Massage Clinic
Keenan, Darcy B. RMT
303 Harmer Ave S 613-722-9798

Dolmage, Ian RMT
161 Mulvihill Ave 613-728-8800

Erickson, April Dawn RMT
212-330 Metcalfe St 613-236-9492

Fernandes, Blanche RMT
204-260 St. Patrick St 613-562-2657

Fuoco, Mary-Louis RMT
2357 Sheldon Ave 613-828-2380

Furlong, Claire RMT
4-501 Athlone Ave 613-728-2152

Glass, Susan RMT
464 Somerset St W 613-233-1410

Graham, Alison RMT
49-286 Wilbrod St 613-567-0948

Groleau, Suzanne RMT
310-294 Albert St 613-235-5186

Hampton Holistic Chiropractic Clinic
Hamilton, Mary RMT
209-1419 Carling Ave 613-761-1600

Health Clinic, The
Despres, Rita RMT
4-335 Cooper St 613-236-2651

Hebert, Maurice RMT
Chateau Laurier Hotel,
1 Rideau St 613-241-1414

Herron-Di Gangi, Sheila RMT
204 Switzer Ave 613-722-3268

Holistic Clinic
Ruptash, Laura RMT
2211 Riverside Dr 613-521-5355

Hunt Club Chiropractic Clinic
Staudinger, Isabel M. RMT
1179 Hunt Club Road

Ireland, Diane RMT
7-104 Queen Elizabeth Dr ..613-232-9045

Khalsa, Siri Bandh Kaur RMT
204 Flora St 613-563-4399

Laurijssen, Antonius RMT
119 Pretoria Ave 613-230-2324

Lavalee, Jean Luc RMT
By Appointment 613-560-7337

Lemmon, Marion RMT
908-110 Boteler St 613-241-8518

Long, Hugette RMT
3-313 Irene Cr 613-729-8643

MacNeil, Patricia RMT
1561 Clover St 613-523-4962

Masso Therapy Clinic
Schneider, Dieter A. RMT
19 Fairmont Ave 613-722-3815

Maya, Sunny RMT
1110-400 Slater St 613-860-0362

McLaughlin, Deborah RMT
814 Holt Cr 613-731-9640

Metcalfe Massage Therapy Clinic
Bourque-Sirrs, Diane G. RMT;
Dikland, Brenda RMT; Fitch, Pamela RMT;
Gravel, Sue D. RMT; Lafleur, Paul RMT;
Snow, Christine Y. RMT
607-180 Metcalfe St 613-235-2377

Multi-Modal Pain Institute
Gilbert, Nancy RMT
480 Somerset St W 613-230-3028

Mystic Crystal, The
Macies, Dana M. RMT
1 Bassano St 613-727-0092

Nancy Blake Enterprise
Blake, Nancy J. RMT
901 Rob Roy Ave 613-829-1326

Ottawa Athletic Club
Bradden, Karen RMT
2525 Lancaster Rd 613-523-1540

Ottawa General Massage Clinic
Holownia, A. Kim RMT
501 Smyth Rd 613-737-8350

Ottawa Massage Therapy Clinic & Associates
Knight, Michelle Yvette RMT
Elgin Medical Centre,
270 Elgin St 613-237-2121

Ottawa South Chiropractic Clinic
Kerr, Stacey L. RMT
204-2430 Bank St 613-738-2443

Parkway Orthopedic & Sports Medicine Clinic
Grodin, Madeleine RMT
410-1730 St. Laurent Blvd ..613-738-8800

Patel, Alpha D. RMT
204-260 St. Patrick St 613-562-2657

Puddister, Catherine Jane RMT
4-277 Irene Cr 613-722-4850

R.A. Physiotherapy & Massage Therapy Clinic
Hourdebaigt, Jean-Pierre RMT;
Villeneuve, Florent RMT
2451 Riverside Dr 613-523-8145

Rideau Chiropractic Centre
Zaluski, James David RMT
445 Cumberland St 613-241-8043

Rideau Clinic
Podwysocki, Christyna M. RMT
406-45 Rideau St 613-241-8800

St-Onge, Julie RMT
78 Hinton Ave N 613-724-1141

Scott, Jan RMT
55 Boyce Ave 613-829-5178

Therapeutic Institute
Zacharewicz, Helga RMT
105-261 Cooper St 613-233-2870

Wellness House
Bernis, Elfriede Jeller RMT
148 Richmond Rd 613-722-7799

Westboro Clinic
Lui, Richard RMT
371 Churchill 613-728-1247

Westin Hotel Health Club
Hay, Stacey L. RMT
11 Colonel By Dr 613-560-7337

Williams, Roger V. RMT
303 Riverdale Ave 613-730-2016

YMCA/YWCA
Oddie, Maren RMT
180 Argyle Ave 613-788-5020

OWEN SOUND

Fraser, Lisa Dianne RMT
804-2nd Ave W 519-376-4868

Massage Therapy Centre, The
Hoffman, Sandra M. RMT;
MacDonald, William RMT;
Wilkinson, Don RMT
860-2nd Ave W 519-371-4999

Myatt, Edward RMT
1-469 Eighth St E 519-371-9883

PALGRAVE

Remedial Massage Therapy
Hall, Pamela M. RMT
By Appointment 905-880-1056

PARIS

Paris Massage Therapy
Williamson, Lucretia RMT
120 Grand River St N 519-442-5562

Van Sickle, Elizabeth RMT
55 William St 519-442-2128

PARRY SOUND

Land, Janice RMT
By Appointment 705-746-7665

PEMBROKE

Pembroke Massage Therapy Centre
Delnicke-Templeton, Margit RMT
563 Mackay St 613-732-2758

PENETANGUISHENE

Thomas, Cindy RMT
By Appointment 705-533-2985

PERTH

Hladun, Trudy A. RMT
By Appointment 613-264-2872

PETERBOROUGH

Anderson, Valerie RMT
614 River Rd S 705-743-3780

Anderson Clinic
Crowe, Daniel D. RMT
80 Hunter St E 705-742-3822

Bach/Karooch
Christopher, Karen RMT
572 Neal Dr, RR #6 705-749-1894

CARE - Rehabilitation & Lifestyle Centre
Dirycz, Barbara RMT
181 Simcoe St 705-741-6171

Gardiner, Frances RMT
445 Arndon Ave 705-745-3190

Germain, Anita RMT
487 Purnell St 705-745-2070

Gray, Carrie Lynne RMT
817 Milford Dr 705-742-0162

Harris, Betty Ann RMT
2153 Springwood Rd 705-743-9570

Holme, Catherine
1-340 Charlotte St 705-740-9693

McKague, Robert D. RMT
430 McDonnel St 705-743-1085

McPherson, Patricia RMT
637 Spillsbury Dr 705-740-0120

Moncrief, Smyth & Associates Massage & Hydrotherapy Clinic Inc.
Moncrief, Chris RMT; Nicoletti, Lori RMT;
Smyth, Jim RMT; Spradbrow, Nicole RMT
308 Charlotte St 705-742-8244

Peterborough Chiropractic Group
Rayner, Robert Jay RMT;
Seltitz, Johanne S. RMT
166 McDonnel St 705-748-6611

Peterborough Healing Arts Centre
Kane, Joyce RMT; March, Debra RMT;
Riddell, Mark RMT; Soligo, Ravi-Inder RMT
314 Rubidge St 705-743-2600

Pettigrew, Blaine RMT
403 McDonnel St 705-743-1085

Shupka, Lorraine RMT
403 McDonnel St 705-743-1085

Simmonds, Janice RMT
123 Tivey St 705-876-8561

Tougas, Kim RMT
1095 Whitefield Dr 705-748-0771

Towns, Charlotte Dianne RMT
By Appointment 705-652-0632

White, Patricia Diane RMT
1300 Hudson St 705-749-2473

Winn, Margaret RMT
403 McDonald St 705-743-1085

PETERSBURG

Bernier, Monique Anne RMT
By Appointment 519-634-5181

PETROLIA

Crescent Park Therapy Clinic
Barney, Norman R. RMT; Bregman, Louise RMT
4233 Emma St 519-882-0339

PICKERING

Amberlea Chiropractic & Sports Injury Clinic
Sheldon, Renee RMT
1822 Whites Rd 905-831-8531

Boylan & Associates
Boylan, Lynn Ann
21-1794 Liverpool Rd 905-420-1443

Brown, Alvin
1117 Ridgewood Ct 905-420-1142

Fletcher Chiropractic Clinic
Haromy, F. Michael RMT; Katz, Jeff RMT
7-1450 Kingston Rd 905-831-9696

Hughes, Maureen RMT
107-1885 Glenanna Rd 905-831-3939

Joints 'n' Things Sports Rehab Clinic
Cook, Donald C. RMT
314-1550 Kingston Rd 905-837-6613

Keogh, Tracy RMT
1545 Willowside Ct 905-839-3425

Mollins-MacKay, Leanne B. RMt
926 Krosno Blvd 905-831-5946

Persaud, Nadera RMT
553 Downland Dr 905-831-2558

POINT EDWARD

Johnston, Tracey RMT
704 Mara St 519-332-1847

Meridan Hair, Skin & Wellness Spa
Massa, Delia RMT
704 Mara St 519-332-0021

PORT CARLING

Curry's
Curry, Elise RMT
25 Todholm Dr 705-765-5586

PORT COLBORNE

Ontario Rehabilitation Institute Inc.
Furry, Tracey A. RMT
258 Killaly St W 905-835-6590

O'Shea, Colleen
52 Clarence St 905-835-6689

PORT ELGIN

Preston, Brien RMT
569 Mill St 519-389-2466

PORT HOPE

Country House Massage Therapy
Medd, Caroline RMT
RR #1, 7311 Mill St 905-797-1079

Graham, Kelly Scott RMT
23 Alfred St 905-885-4618

Massage for Health
Scrimgeour, Virginia M. RMT
40 Martha St 905-885-4282

Port Hope Medical Centre
Dunne, Marilyn RMT
249 Ontario St 905-885-1976

PORT PERRY

Bathie, Robina L. RMT
186 Casimir St 905-985-3702

Remler, Linda RMT
13225 Mast Rd, RR #4 905-985-2782

PUSHLINCH

Massage Therapy Clinic
Brown, Beverley G. RMT;
Kinzie, Katherine RMT
RR #2 519-651-0401

QUEENSVILLE

Thorne, Merrill David RMT
1289 Ravenshope Rd, RR #1 905-478-1221

RENFREW

Aikenhead, Ruth RMT
330 Queen St S 613-432-3218

Hass-Slavin, Louise A. RMT
By Appointment 613-432-7898

RICHMOND HILL

Bathurst-Elgin Chiropractic Clinic
Astbury, Terry RMT
24-10815 Bathurst St 905-737-7463

Betts, Tania Marie RMT
10039 Yonge St 905-727-2333

Elder, C. Gavin RMT
141 King Rd, Unit 2 905-773-2225

Gail's Therapeutic Massage
Sheehan, Gail RMT
12919 Yonge St 905-773-9624

Hall, Jon T. RMT
91 Church St S 905-780-0151

Hillsview Massage & Therapy Centre
Akiwenzie, L. Kim RMT; Koch, Jeanne RMT; Kruger, Karen RMT
4-9640 Bayview Ave 905-508-7103

Jussila, Eija RMT
21 Willowbank AVe 905-773-8096

Michele Mihalik Massage Therapy
Mihalik, Michelle RMT
105 Wright St 905-737-4945

New Directions in Health
Boulton, Nicholas J. RMT; Churchill, Susan A. RMT; Stonebridge, Geroge W. RMT
102-9955 Yonge St 905-737-0810

Richmond Hill Natural Therapies
Degano, Belinda RMT; Ross, Linda M. RMT
1116 Church St S 905-883-9355

Richmond Hill Therapeutic Massage
Muncie, Martha RMT; Slivaric, P. Nick RMT; Vidoczy, Peggy RMT; Wilson, Alexandra RMT
2 Merrylynne Dr 905-883-0673

Serenity Spa, The
Persad, Randal S. RMT
110-9011 Leslie St 905-881-7915

Turman, Virginia RMT
30 Elizabeth St S 905-508-0936

Unionville Massage & Therapy Clinic
Fendelet, Audrey RMT; Smith, Patty J. RMT
4-9640 Bayview Ave 905-508-7103

ROCKWOOD

Gibson-Smye, Teressa Ann RMT
By Appointment 519-856-9626

RUTHVEN

Martens, Barbara RMT
RR #2 519-839-4347

SARNIA

Foster, Christopher S. RMT
239 Ontario St 519-344-4003

Ross-Marshall, Margaret RMT
307 Wellington St 519-383-6655

Soininen, Lee-Ann RMT
230 Vidal St N 519-332-4810

SAULT STE. MARIE

Beauty of It
Clark, Mary D. RMT
80 March St, 2nd Floor 705-942-6603

Chiropractic Clinic
Knuuttila, Terri RMT
373 McNabb St 705-759-3771

Drigan, Leslie RMT
3-730 Pine St 705-254-5603

Hafonen, Eva-Marie RMT
18-123 March St 705-759-4704

Maione, Giancarlo RMT
391 Pim St 705-759-1353

Natural Health Clinic
Wilkinson, J.D. Denis RMT
509 Wellington St E 705-759-7900

YMCA
Puusep, Heinrich RMT
235 McNabb St 705-949-3133

SCHOMBERG

Anodyne Massage
Forbes, Donald Floyd RMT
232 Main St 905-939-2213

SEAFORTH

Preszcator, Kimberly D. RMT
77 Main St 519-527-1242

SHALLOW LAKE

Rimmer, Denise RMT
154 Sir Air John's Cr 519-935-2812

SHANTY BAY

Lifemates Therapy
Kaczanowski, Janet RMT
32 Patterson Rd 705-722-5098

SIMCOE

Cygan, Christine RMT
25 Water St 519-426-1980

Simcoe Massage Therapy Clinic
Fros, Darlene J. RMT; Lechner, Karina RMT; Thomson-Richer, Kathleen RMT
92 Norfolk St S 519-428-4294

SIOUX LOOKOUT

Hansen, Monique RMT
90 Front St 807-737-4258

Williams, Sue RMT
By Appointment 807-737-4258

SMITHS FALLS

Get Pampered
Cullen, Jodie Elizabeth RMT
20 Main St E 613-284-8141

Ouellette, Catherine RMT
7 Grovenor St 613-283-0218

SOUTH RIVER

Harmon, Tausha C. RMT
By Appointment 705-386-0834

SPARTA

Bejcek, Katrina RMT
By Appointment 519-775-0184

SPRINGFIELD

Dance, Trisha Marie RMT
By Appointment 519-765-4122

ST. AGATHA

Heimpel, Patricia
106 Clarence Ave 519-747-3117

ST. CATHERINES

Bach Massage Clinic
Doctor, Fariya RMT; Strohback, Tracy RMT
278 Welland Ave 905-688-5211

Back & Neck Health Centre
Harrison, Carol RMT; Katzman, Debbie Lynn RMT
310 Lake St 905-646-2888

Berard, Charlene M. RMT
20 Welland Vale Rd 905-988-6460

Bodymax Fitness Centre
Dillon, Donald Quinn RMT
Royal Ct Plaza,
300 Bunting Rd 905-938-0233

Cooper, Elizabeth E. RMT
85 Maple St 905-704-0564

Cowherd Chiropractic
Mackie, Tracy L. RMT
30-100 Fourth St 905-682-5500

Drynan & Associates
Carbonara, Orazio RMT; Neumann, Kristine RMT; Wiens, Heidi E. RMT
3 Geneva St 905-641-3000

Fast, Jacqueline RMT
236 Glenridge Ave 905-688-4949

Funk, Jennifer RMT
17 Bolger Dr 905-937-7035

Gittings, Caren Jeanette RMT
5 Shepherds Circle 905-988-1270

Hands On Treatments
Leivonen, Kristine RMT
162 Geneva St 905-704-1067

Hern, Kevin RMT
320 Vine St 905-646-6768

Kennedy, Renate RMT
52 Albert St 905-988-6458

Massage for Health Inc.
Durksen Leach, Lucy RMT; Dyck, Kimberly RMT; Hawkins-Curtis, Molly RMT; Lougheed, Fiona RMT
21-235 Martindale Rd 905-685-4597

McKellar, Wendy
33 Lakeshore Rd, Unit 3 & 4 905-935-1400

Medi-Massage Inc.
Enns-chin, Frieda RMT; Head, Karen RMT; Wiens, Darlene RMT
23-100 Fourth Ave 905-984-8494

M/T Massage & Hydrotherapy Clinic
Janzen, Margaret RMT; Janzen, Timothy G. RMT
9 Beecher St 905-984-8841

Niagara Health Centre
Leblanc-Turton, Ramona RMT
180 Vine St 905-682-5411

Pelham Health Centre Massage Therapy Clinic
Baltus, David P. RMT; Iler, Andrew A. RMT
117-245 Pelham Rd 905-687-7290

Thompson-Howse, Heidi RMT
408 Niagara St 905-646-2631

Versluis, Nellie RMT
196 Dorothy St 905-938-0640

Westlake Sq Chiropractic Centre
Friesen, Margaret A. RMT
353 Lake St 905-934-4357

ST. JACOB'S

Brueckman, Scott RMT;
Jonas, Julie Anne RMT
10 Parkside Dr 519-664-1222

ST. MARY'S

Wildwood Care Centre
Siegner, Rebecca J. RMT
By Appointment 519-284-0123

ST. THOMAS

High St Recreational Complex
Bentley, Cynthia RMT
20 High St 519-631-2418

Lush, Dean Rodney RMT
Priddle, Wendy RMT
18 Metcalfe St 519-631-2829

Natural Health Therapy Centre (YMCA)
De Bolt, Margaret M. RMT;
Taylor, Carrie Ann RMT;
White, Karen RMT
672 Talbot St 519-631-6300

St. Thomas Psychiatric Hospital
Litman, Larry C. RMT
By Appointment 519-631-8510

STIRLING

Downstream Massage Therapy Clinic
Rucinski, Jo-Ann B. RMT;
Troy, Deborah Diane RMT
By Appointment 613-395-0486

STITTSVILLE

Main St Family Health Centre
Trebble, Stacy RMT
1250 Main St 613-831-7372

Stittsville Chiropractic Clinic
Sabourin, Christopher RMT
By Appointment 613-836-1711

STONEY CREEK

Bodden, Daniel RMT
102 King St E 905-622-8358

Boyce, Catherine Lynn RMT
121 Cove Cr 905-643-8114

Lantz, Todd RMT
Hlth Sciences Bldg,
15 Mountain Ave S 905-662-2011

Paramount Family Clinic & Massage Therapy
Jeffrey, Mary Anne RMT
1050 Paramount Dr 905-573-6468

Stoney Creek Chiropractic Clinic
Jugloff, Michael RMT
70 King St E 905-662-1637

Thacker, Candace RMT
26 King St E 905-662-2735

STOUFFVILLE

On Site Therapeutic Massage Inc
Bolton, Wendy E. RMT
By Appointment 905-642-5904

Stouffville Chiropractic Centre
Hoover, Harold RMT
6-96 Main St 905-640-3562

Stouffville Therapeutic Centre for Massage, Shiatsu & Reflexology
Concil, Marita R. RMT
Imperial Centre,
303-37 Sandiford Dr 905-642-4237

STRATFORD

Albert St Massage Therapy Clinic
Mummery, Dianne Theresa RMT;
Usher, Nicola RMT
42 Albert St 519-272-0079

Benton, Anthony RMT
348 Ontario St 519-272-1141

Cole, Sherry M. RMT
91 Brunswick St 519-273-6906

Perth Massage Therapy Clinic
Roach, W. Peter RMT
4-15 Downie St 519-273-2042

Rhodes Massage Therapy Clinic
Rhodes, Paul J. RMT
30 Rebecca St 510-272-2747

Stratford Massage Clinic
Anderson, Neil RMT; Jackson, Ann RMT
Rudolph, Donald RMT
288 Ontario St 519-237-5298

Trachsel, Betty Margery RMT
245 Downie St 519-273-3107

Tribick, Jane E. RMT
228 Erie St 519-271-7116

STRATHROY

Tyhurst Associates
Ternoey, Terri Lynn RMT
117 Thomas St 519-245-2580

Verheyen, Karen F. RMT
By Appointment 519-245-6255

STREETSVILLE

Couves, Dianne RMT
17 Main St 905-567-9200

SUDBURY

A Ta Sante
Larose-Doyon, Helene RMT
269 Colonila Ct 705-525-5967

Alliance Massage Therapy
Kivi, Kari T. RMT
1375 Regent St S 705-523-1365

Biasucci, Maria L. RMT
1-44 Kathleen St 705-671-9973

Gravelle, Gerri-Lee RMT
260 Walnut St 705-670-9477

McConnell, Karen C. RMT
208 Loach's Rd 705-522-1509

Registered Massage Therapy Clinic
Ramsay, Nancy-Jo RMT; Rumball, Peggy RMT
105-845 Regent St S 705-673-7682

Sudbury Natural Therapy Clinic
Chevrette, Mark RMT; Kivi, Kai Mikael RMT;
Robinson-Bornn, Irene RMT
77 Davidson St 705-675-1014

Teale, Jason J. RMT
374 Antwerp Ave 705-674-1376

SUNDERLAND

Hug, Priska RMT
S2080 Durham Rd 13, RR #4 705-357-1889

SUTTON WEST

Canadian College of Massage & Hydroptherapy
Anderson, David RMT; Gibbons, Paul R. RMT
By Appointment 905-722-6557/8682

Corkum, Natash RMT
1-122 High St 905-722-3599

Frick, Susan M. RMT
By Appointment 905-722-6140

Toninger, Eva Christina RMT
By Appointment 705-437-4997

TARA

Massage & Hydrotherapy
Herron, Leanne E. RMT
RR #2 519-934-2768

TAVISTOCK

Country Clinic for Therapeutic Massage
Witmer, Crystal A. RMT
32 Homewood Ave 519-655-3999

TECUMSEH

"Hands On" Massage Therapy Clinic
Banfill, Karen RMT; McIntyre, Sidonia RMT;
Medd, Kimberley RMT;
Motychka, Jeanette Lynn RMT;
Motychka, Jennifer Ann RMT
1041 Lesperance Rd 519-969-0393/
979-2672

Health Touch Therapeutic Massage Clinic
Hammer, Kelly Frances RMT;
Sandre-Levy, Susy RMT
Santia, Riccardo Antonio RMT;
Yako, Freda RMT
269 Lesperance Rd 519-969-4880

Natural Health Unlimited
Kennedy, Linda RMT
2470 St. Alphonse St 519-735-8764

Tecumseh Massage Therapy Clinic
Astles, Geoffrey Warren RMT;
Stewart, Susan E. RMT
106-11811 Tecumseh Rd E ..519-969-9388

TERRA COTTA

Campbell, Abigail J. RMT
16012 Shaws Creek Rd 905-838-1683

THORNHILL

ABACUS
Johnston, James L. RMT
169 Crestwood Rd 905-889-7971

Bis, Darek RMT
303-7131 Bathurst St 905-731-5554

Ellis, Una RMT
2-6790 Yonge St 905-886-9778

Farcas, Alex RMT
800 Steeles Ave W 905-660-4484

Glickman, Jodi Rayne RMT
320-300 John St 905-882-7688

Hesperus Therapy Centre
Aide, Haide H.A. RMT
5-9100 Bathurst St 905-882-4949

Integrated Health Recovery
Simkhovitch, Zachary RMT ..905-731-2606

Kieran, Jane RMT
7-9100 Bathurst St 905-886-1003

Kroll, Rejanne B. RMT
41 McKelvey Dr 905-731-0828

Levy, Sandy J. RMT
66 Tanjo Ct 905-707-5522

Mannion, Thomas RMT
102-900 Steeles Ave W 905-660-9543

North-Med Chiropractic & Massage
Murphy, Sean RMT
LL1-7131 Bathurst St 905-882-4476

Novick, Linda RMT
206-390 Steeles Ave W 905-881-0214

Nucci, Lou RMT
320-300 John St 905-882-7688

Physical Medicine Clinic, The
Trives, Cristina RMT
207-340 Steeles Ave W 905-764-8858

Skyrise Medical Centre
Manzo, Francesco A. RMT
217-7330 Yonge St 905-881-6922

Street, Linda RMT
8-100 Henderson Ave 905-882-8039

THOROLD

Froese, Guenther RMT
92 Pine St N 905-227-5341

THUNDER BAY

Confederation College Exercise Therapy Centre
Stouffer, Kerry Lee RMT
By Appointment 807-622-9529

Gleeson Massage Therapy Clinic
Gleeson, Lorne C. RMT;
Loftus, Kathryn Susanne RMT
707-1265 Arthur St E 905-622-3112

Healing Touch
Faulkner, Karen RMT
2055 Ridgeway St E 807-623-0812

Holland, Sita Jo-Ann RMT
430 Elliot St 807-683-3829

Jerome, William P. RMT
402 Ray Blvd 807-343-7926

Mersereau, Jo-Ann RMT
379 Oliver Rd 807-346-4050

Mohring, Marvin RMT
497 E Mary St 807-622-4979

Natural Health & Healing Centre
Raycevich, Melanie RMT
817 Victoria Ave E 807-622-4325

Sosnowski, Karen RMT
1111 Victoria Ave E 807-623-4033

Thunder Bay Massage Therapy Clinic
Hrabowy, David B. RMT; Merits, Arundel RMT
6-4A S Court St 807-346-8417

Triangle of Health
Bivins, Marlene A. RMT
600 Victoria Ave 807-625-6536

Tuomi, Jeannie RMT
16 Regent St 807-346-8975

TILBURY

Chretien, Agathe T. RMT
4 Ella St 519-682-2279

TILLSONBURG

Active Health Care Centre
De Groote, Dora RMT
9 Woodcock Dr 519-688-3901

Baldwin St Chiropractic Clinic
Walcarius, Kelly K. RMT
40 Baldwin St 519-688-7777

Burwell, Leanne RMT
RR #2 519-688-1271

Pettinger, Cathleen E. RMT
45 Hardy Ave 519-688-9011

Sanders, Joseph David RMT
264 Tillson Ave 519-688-0285

TIMMONS

Martin Chiropractic Clinic
Martin, Antonio RMT
404-690 Riverpark Rd 705-268-8411

Massage by Holly Boychuck
Boychuck, Holly RMT
129-The 101 Mall 705-268-6477

Massotherapy Centre
Brillon, Francine RMT
By Appointment 705-267-3033

Melodies Massage
Caron, Lizane Melodie RMT
440 Brousseau Ave 705-360-1550

TOBERMORY

Northcott, Michael RMT
By Appointment 519-596-8193

TORONTO

Accident Assessment & Treatment Centre Inc.
Bergman, Ilana RMT
205A-1670 Dufferin St 416-652-5944

Accident Injury Management Clinic
Southall, John P. RMT
B02-3030 Lawrence Ave E ..416-438-2222

Adams, Lawrence RMT
11 Cudia Cr 416-261-8618

Adelaide Club
Kuppek, Monika RMT
1 First Canadian Place 416-367-9957

Advanced Bodywork Systems
Brown, Eric RMT;
Fishman, Stacey T. RMT;
Katz, Stewart Geoffrey RMT;
Meikle, Alison RMT
306-2 Gloucester St 416-962-3791

Advanced Therapeutics
Willson, Susan F. RMT; Oates, Kevin D. RMT
1398 Queen St E, Main Floor 416-466-8267

Aitken, Starr A. RMT
17 Chester Hill Rd 416-425-5978

Alaminos, Martina RMT
74 Lawrence Ave W 416-486-0083

Alger, Christopher J. RMT
100 Granby St 416-596-1522

Allen, Andrea RMT
77 Tudor Glen Cr 416-282-6508

Alliance Health & Rehabilitation
Yakymchuk, Ola RMT
203-741 Broadview Ave 416-406-2790

Alternative Health Care Services
Greig, Dennis Ross RMT
102-1 Gloucester St 416-967-6891

Anita Lorelli Physiotherapy Clinic Inc.
Bingham, Milton RMT
712-2 Carleton St E 416-971-7947

APEX Consulting & Training Inc.
Camilleri, Mariel RMT
503-245 Roehampton Ave .416-322-7617

Attica
Woodford, Katie RMT
2279 Queen St E 416-690-9199

Aurora Massage Therapy Clinic
Crilly, Kathleen RMT;
Fiore, Lina RMT;
Hodgson, Lisa RMT;
Saraiva, Fatima RMT;
Widdis, Lynn Louise RMT
123 Queen St W, 3rd Floor .416-365-0674

Baker, Paul J. RMT
1010-100 Gloucester St 416-967-5108

Basic Beauty Spa
Holmes, Cynthia J. RMT
50 Cumberland St 416-923-9664

Bathurst Jewish Centre
Hew, Roy RMT
4588 Bathurst St 416-636-0965

Bathurst-Steeles Chiropractic Centre
6257 Bathurst St,
Second Floor 416-222-7900

Bazydlo, Thomas RMT
48 Glenlake Ave 416-763-3706

Beaches Body Care Centre
Poirier, Arthur J. RMT
1007A Kingston Rd 416-698-8097

Beaches Therapeutics
Deschenes, Cindy M. RMT;
Lacroix, Richard C. RMT;
Mann, Margaret L. RMT; Watson, Carol RMT
1908 Queen St E 416-690-7082

Beaches Wellness Centre
English, Sydney RMT; Underhill, Caroline RMT
2276 Queen St E 416-698-7070

Beatty, Kara RMT
89 Amelia St 416-926-0328

Bellwood Health Services Inc.
Shin, Derek K. RMT
1020 McNicholl Ave 416-495-0926

Bennett, Esther RMT
By Appointment 416-949-3347

Berton, Patricia RMT
80 Hogarth Ave 416-465-4184

Birks, Wendy M. RMT
121 Harcourt Ave 416-778-9573

Blacklock, Mary Alison RMT
404-1010 Broadview Ave ..416-423-3147

Blade, Hilda Viola RMT
311-2 Milepost Pl 416-425-4519

Blake, Andrew M. RMT
52 Arundel Ave 416-463-9813

Bloor Park Club
Beck, Lynn J. RMT; Howe, Sally Anne RMT
80 Bloor St E 416-922-1262

Bloor Park Medical
Kopec, Leszek RMT
208-726 Bloor St W 416-533-6000

Bloor Valley Club
Tonus, Edward J. RMT
555 Sherbourne St 416-961-4695

Bloor-West Massage Therapy
Kondrak, Angela RMT
2378A Bloor St W 416-762-8220

Bloordale Massage Therapy Clinic
Drysdale, Harry RMT
4209 Bloor St W 416-626-2406

Boardwalk Massage Therapy
Elliott, Alexis S. RMT; Sayliss Sharron RMT
2279 Queen St E,
2nd Floor 416-693-7308

Body & Soul
Fisher, Douglas Kent RMT
1443 Bathurst St 416-533-1034

Body Harmony Therapeutic Massage
Caswell-Aitken, Heather RMT
459 Concord Ave 416-538-8119

Body Health
Puchta, Andrezej RMT
201-1482 Bathurst 416-651-0060

Body Mechanix
Busillo, Pat RMT
120 Overbrook Pl 416-633-4269

Bodylogic Therapeutic Massage Treatments
Ranalli, Nancy RMT
209-2126 1/2 Queen St E ..416-693-9922

Boon, Larissa J. RMT
844 Davenport Rd 416-656-9420

Bosich, Sandra G. RMT
56 Glen Agar Dr 416-622-3707

Bouchard, Cheryl RMT
515-1756 Victoria Park Ave .416-757-2561

Bouzanne, Carmel RMT
56 Glendale Ave 416-516-1255

Bray, Wendy S. RMT; Dubreuil, Denise RMT
401-170 St. George St 416-921-3160

Briede, Charlotte Ariadne RMT
500 Clinton St 416-535-7991

Bucci, Remo RMT
55 St. George's Blvd 416-247-1241

C. Robson Therapeutic Centre Ltd.
Robson, Cynthia RMT
2390 Eglinton Ave E 416-751-4368

Cabbagetown Chiropractic Health Centre
Sharkey, Janet RMT
214 Carlton St 416-922-3020

Cambridge Club, The (Sheraton Centre)
D'Aguanao, John RMT
100 Richmond St W,
11th Floor 416-862-1077

Canadian Natural Health & Healing Centre, The
Borsenko, Alec P. RMT
971A Bloor St W 416-537-9653

Carlaw Therapy Centre
Hoyland-Young, Michael RMT;
Magraw, Kristi RMT
312-245 Carlaw Ave 416-462-9340

Carter, Lindsey J. RMT
15 Simpson Ave 416-466-7972

Castlefield Chiropractic & Massage
Yearwood, Glenn Arthur RMT
2497A Yonge St 416-487-6331

CCMH - North York Campus
Skog, Carina B. RMT
5150 Yonge St 416-250-7776

Central Chiropractic Group
Plant, Susan RMT
16 York Mills Rd 416-512-2225

Centre for Massage & Psychotherapy
Medley, Lorin RMT
409-99 Atlantic Ave 416-538-2969

Chapman, Nadra RMT
27 Belmont St 416-923-3030

Chariot, The
Camacho, Keith RMT
1069 Bathurst St 416-534-1140

Chertov, Maria RMT
1512-6030 Bathurst St 416-663-1207

Chiropractic Clinic
Galmstrup, Elisa RMT
1 Valentine Dr 416-447-7600

Chiropractic Clinic
Wilsher, Lynn RMT; Tirabassi, Elena RMT
700-208 Bloor St W 416-920-3231

Chiropractic Clinic, The
Abel, Cathy RMT; Giesbrecht, Dennis B. RMT;
Godson, Barry RMT
400-1407 Yonge St 416-924-0777

Chiropractic Rehab Wellness Centre
Young, Eileen RMT
505-4430 Bathurst St 416-633-3000

Chiu, Diana Li-Chu RMT
206-110 Maitland St 416-929-1381

Chmelova, Martina RMT
809-150 Longboat Ave 416-360-5797

Chow, Janet RMT
31 Glenelia Ave 416-222-6016

Christoff, Daryl RMT
404-344 Bloor St W 416-928-9650

Chu, C. Anne RMT
19 Craig Cr 416-483-6380

Ciglen, Philip S. RMT
5016-3080 Yonge St 416-767-7575

City Centre Therapeutic Massage Clinic
Madej, Robert RMT
130-5 Park Home Avenue ..416-250-0823

Civello Spa
MacIsaac, Neil RMT; Moore, Arlene RMT
887 Yonge St 416-924-9244

Clark, Donna RMT
75 Browning Ave 416-406-0184

Classic Nails & Aesthetics
Gentili, Luciana RMT
290 The West Mall 416-620-0432

Claudia Salzmann & Associates
Hewlett, Karen RMT; Salzmann, Claudia RMT;
Schneider, Kathryn RMT
78 Amelia St 416-923-0494

Clifford, Paul RMT
4-1601 Bathurst St 416-656-6273

Cline, Rick RMT
681 Brock Ave 416-538-0268

Colborne Therapy Centre
Colborne, E. Margaret RMT;
Doyle, Jacqueline RMT;
Haigh, Larry RMT; Misener, Jocelyn E. RMT;
Tse, Wendy RMT; Villeneuve, Barbara F. RMT
202-32 Berwick Ave 416-487-7216

Columbus Centre, The
Chinn, Raymond A. RMT; Ricci, Nadia RMT
901 Lawrence Ave W 416-789-7011

Connacher, Sandra RMT
183 Bessborough Dr 416-481-8804

Connolly, Cheryl RMT
309-19 Lascelles Blvd 416-483-6623

Constand, Andrew RMT
216 Lawrence Ave E 416-486-6085

Copeland Sports Injury Management
Copeland, Lori Jean RMt
344 Riverdale Ave 416-469-2145

Cornelius-Kirkpatrick, Sue RMT
717 Bloor St W, Room F 416-466-8430

Cornfield, David RMT
556 Delaware Ave N 416-535-2859

Coulter Clinic
Coulter, Jacalyn A. RMT
Yonge-Eglinton Centre 416-322-6506

Cox, Jennifer A. RMT
307-2161 Yonge St 416-322-3619

Cranial Therapy Centre, The
Harris, Robert F. RMT; McLaughlin, Alix RMT
205-110 Richmond St E 416-368-6855

Creative Health Services
Symonds, Adrian P. RMT
40 Ritchie Ave 416-531-3924

Crosby, Darby RMT
301-85 Lowther Ave 416-324-8693

Crossley, C. Leanne RMT
20 Bessarion Rd 416-226-6454

Cuaresma Associates
Cuaresma, Melanio U. RMT
51 Woody Vineway 416-490-0415

D'Bonnabel Esthetics
de Barros, Philip RMT
602 Yonge St 416-924-9716

Danforth Massage Therapy Clinic
Barraclough, H. Wray RMT;
Corman, Anne Marie RMT;
Hegge, Gillian R. RMT
456 Danforth Ave, 2nd Floor 416-406-6171

David L. MacIntosh Sport Medicine Clinic
Ratz, Edward RMT
55 Harbord St 416-978-4678

Davidson, Pamela Joan RMT
24 Moore Ave 416-488-0701

Davis, Gloria R. RMT
6-116 Glen Manor Dr 416-691-1715

De Caro, Omiliano RMT
880 Broadview Ave 416-536-1392

De Goeij, Jacqueline RMT
3-153 Walmer Rd 416-921-4500

Dellandrea, Edith M. RMT
17 Criscoe St 416-769-6262

Dillon, M. Kathleen RMT
176 St. George St,
Ground Floor 416-787-1070

Donvale Massage Therapy Clinic
Burnham, Kimberly RMT;
Gradzik, Andrew RMT
204-597 Parliament St 416-966-2410

Dorothy Madgett Relaxation & Physiotherapy Clinic
Dolan, Kathryn RMT
1124-123 Edward St1 416-340-7070

Downsview Chiropractic
Krongold, John Y. RMT
552 Sheppard Ave W 416-787-5193

Downsview Rehab Centre
Ge, Sunping RMT
15-1126 Finch Ave W 416-739-6507

Dryden, Patricia J. RMT
470 Delaware Ave 416-537-7051

Duke, Shelley RMT
604-190 St. George St 416-961-8123

Dundas Chiropractic Office
Schmanda, Walter R. RMT
203-3416 Dundas St W 416-767-2225

Dundas-University Chiropractic Clinic
Fine, Janet R. RMT; Joneikies, Ralf RMT
200-438 University Ave 416-598-4999

Dunfield Club, The
Heron-Gransaull, Mary Margaret RMT
110 Eglinton Ave E 416-485-0200

Dylan, Arielle RMT
209-30 Walmer Rd 416-966-9462

East End Health Services
Wong, Laura RMT
343 Coxwell Ave 416-778-5858

East Scarborough Physiotherapy Clinic
Zander, Karolyn RMT
5550 Lawrence Ave E 416-283-6893

Eglinton Chiropractic Clinic
Martin, Lynne B. RMT
12-2221 Yonge St 416-488-3660

Elizabeth's Health Studio
Mezes, Elizabeth RMT
1006 Eglinton Ave W 416-787-9411

Energy Harmonics
Caron, Margi RMT
90A Hogarth Ave 416-463-9360

Enersis
Levere, Roger Lee RMT
607-2 Carlton St 416-966-9936

Engel, Robert L. RMT
2780 Jane St 416-745-2162

Epps, Douglas V. RMT
11 Willow Ave (Ward's Island)416-203-9928

Essence Skin Care & Massage Therapy
Ludwig, Linda M. RMT; Woottom,
Delores RMT; Rattray, Fiona S. RMT
206-1986 Queen St E .416-694-4090/4060

Eszter's Foot & Bodycare Ltd.
Sabijan, Mary RMT
4136 Dundas St W 416-232-0244

Etobicoke Massage Therapy
Hoeijenbos, Afina C. RMT
43 Turnvale Rd 416-746-5900

Etobicoke Wellness Centre
Korpershoek, Jurian RMT
43 Turnvale Rd 416-633-9420

European Massage Centre Inc.
Goralski, Tomasz RMT
108-2238 Dundas St W 416-532-6137

Featherston, Joan A. RMT
400 Dupont St 416-924-8402

Feldenkrais Centre, The
Neill, Judith E. RMT
201-390 Dupont 416-967-1220

Feres Manual Therapy
Feres, Yvonne C. RMT
401-2828 Bathurst St 416-785-3314

Ferguson, Mary E. RMT
681 Brock Ave 416-923-3330

Figure & Face
Barczak, Carola S. RMT
24 Bellair St 416-960-6200

Fin, Bella Spektor RMT
4922 Yonge St 416-225-7457

Finlay-Young Jane RMT
103 Barton Ave 416-531-4851

First Canadian Medical Centre
Porter, Karen RMT
By Appointment 416-368-9675

First Chiropractic Care Centre
Amaron, Brian RMT
102-700 Lawrence Ave W . . .416-787-1127

Foster, Andrew RMT
113 Glebmount Ave 416-696-0089

Fournier, Cathy L. RMT
Frewin, Lynda RMT
42 Douglas Ave 416-322-6506

Frazer, Audrey RMT
110-500 Scarlett Rd 416-242-8171

Fuke-Wilson, Vera RMT
217 Glen Lake Ave 416-766-5503

Fulop, Mary RMT
774 1/2 Yonge St 416-921-2669

Fung, Tom RMT
2656 Midland Ave 416-292-3641

Furgiuele, Nick RMT
165 Montrose Ave 416-534-7809

Ganymede
Bootland, Leslie Edward RMT
101-25 Wood St 416-979-8801

Gardner, Craig RMT
77 Gates Ave 416-699-7064

Generations Massage Therapy
Bryce, Heather RMT
1050 Avenue Rd 416-487-2098

Gerrard, Debra A. RMT
73-541 Steeles Ave W 416-733-7829

Gibvey Massage Clinic
Burket, Simone RMT; Gibbon, Bonnie RMT;
Gibbon, Richard RMT; Olson, LInda RMT
1272A The Queensway 416-503-2569

Girdauskas, Ramona RMT
20 High Park Blvd 416-536-5437

Glawdan, Jan RMT
734 Spadina Ae 416-925-5754

Glen Echo Therapies
Blayways, Sheila RMT; Latendorf, Julia RMT
3471B Yonge St 416-489-9564

Godi, Christina RMT
30 Queen Victoria St 416-466-2083

Granite Club Ltd.
Rezner, Susan RMT;
Wesolowski, Marek R. RMT
2385 Bayview Ave 416-510-6668

Graves, Alan W. RMT
409-1801 O'Connor Dr . . .416-288-8117

Green, Janice RMT
802-284 Bloor St W 416-924-8882

Green Unicorn, The
Sinclair, Nancy Jane RMT
515 Concord Ave 416-535-0426

Gregory, Suzanne RMT
176 St. George St,
Main Fl, Rm 7 416-921-8366

Griffin, Diana M. RMT
170 Howland Ave 416-538-0271

Hachigian, Catherine RMT
22 Valleyview Gardens 416-769-1037

Hamilton, Leigh RMT
1410-3559 Eglinton Ave W . .416-766-7735

Hands on for Health
Black, Lorea Anne RMT; Chana, Rosie M. RMT;
McCarthy, P. Lynne RMT
12-2 Thorncliffe Park Dr 416-467-7843

Hands on for Health
Cai, Lin RMT
915 Bathurst St 416-588-1362

Hansen, Mimi RMT
142 Park Home Ave 416-250-5443

Hawaiian Isle Health Club
Omori, Keiko RMT
1649 Bloor St W 416-537-3281

Hazelton Spa
Moeller, Norman R. RMT
87 Avenue Rd 416-922-9226

He, Hui RMT
402-40 Teesdale Pl 416-698-9827

**Healing Hands Massage Therapy
Clinic**
Stebbing, Teresa L. RMT
59 Adelaide St E, 2nd Floor .416-365-1016

**Health Bound Therapeutic
Massage Clinic**
Saari, Tuula RMT
275 Greenfield Ave 416-221-5046

Health Focus
Moore, Paula-Jane RMT; Sharland, Mary RMT
355A College St 416-922-4909

Health Recovery Clinic
Chipman, Kimberley RMT
200-10 Milner Business Ct . .416-754-8459

Health Spectrum
Kluczynski, Vlodek RMT
18 Charnwood Rd 416-445-2200

Healthwinds Spa
Gadsby, Alison RMT; Kline, Kailee RMT;
Szuty, Robert RMT; Town, Heather A. RMT
LL01-2401 Yonge St 416-488-9545

Heaslip, Gail RMT
22 Follis Ave 416-537-9206

Heller-Goldberg, Sheila RMT
6 Lauder Ave 416-656-5421

Henkel, Karen RMT
704-125 Lawton Blvd 416-483-4914

Henley Gardens Massage Therapy
Naulls, Derek RMT
1089 Kingston Rd 416-698-1844

**HER Therapeutic Massage &
Hydrotherapy Clinic**
Rimer, Helga E. RMT
87-14 London Green Cr 416-633-6683

Hirji, Rishma RMT
37 Bellwoods Ave 416-603-9187

Hoad, Jonathan RMT
203-245 Roehampton Ave . .416-656-8248

Hoff-Szabo, Susan RMT
3805-88 Bloor St E 416-962-9933

Holistic Rehabilitation Centre
Krol, Konrad Marek RMT
407-3443 Finch Ave E 416-490-9400

Hsu, Mindy RMT
922-170 St. George St 416-944-1312

Hulton, Andrea M. RMT
505-2200 Ave Rd 416-381-5665

**Human Touch Centre Therapeutic
Massage**
Verzuu, Theresia RMT
303-2238 Dundas St W . . .4167-588-9773

Humbertown Plaza - South Office
Eustace, Roberta RMT
1-270 The Kingsway 416-233-7505

Hunt, David RMT
501-1650 Sheppard Ave E . .416-502-9400

Hunter, Wendy C. RMT
321 Woodmount Ave 416-424-3493

Hurst, Christopher RMT
100 Bain Ave, #8 The Oaks .416-469-2817

Hyschuk, Laurence Grant RMT
2 Glenwood Ave 416-767-2825

Inhairent Solutions
Pepper, Tracy RMT
2066 Avenue Rd 416-322-9292

Institute for Advanced Skincare
Ruork, Liz RMT
66 Avenue Rd 416-962-0001

**Institute of Sports Medicine and
Human Performance**
Carscadden, Cindy RMT;
Kosobucki, Michael RMT
110-185 The West Mall 416-620-6861

**International Managed Health
Care**
Martinen, Eric Walter RMT
340 College St 416-922-8154

**International Managed Health
Care**
McCartney, David RMT
425 Bloor St E, Ground Floor 416-928-2130

Intuitive Touch Therapies
Rhodes, Patricia RMT
1938 Queen St E 416-693-4777

**J. Mardarowicz Therapeutic
Massage**
Mardarowicz, Jack RMT
105-2299 Dundas St W . . .416-353-4113

Jackman, Marie RMT
608-66 Isabella St 416-967-0752

Jacobson, Miriam D. RMT
429 Eglinton Ave W,
2nd Floor 416-487-6175

James, Heather RMT
36 Madison Ave 416-929-9160

Janet Croken Enterprises
Croken, Janet E. RMT
71 Douglas Cr 416-926-3737

Jinnah Chiropractic
Lynn, Marlene RMT
200-2171 Queen St E 416-690-9777

Jo-elle Studio
Brazier-Hagarty, Nicki RMT
179A Danforth Ave 416-463-8839

Jones, Julie Elizabeth RMT
304-11 Anglesley Blvd 416-239-6085

Jones, Monika RMT
65-100 Burrows Hall Blvd . .416-298-7109

Jong, Sylvia S. RMT
403-73 Coe Hill Dr 416-762-8500

Keep in Touch Therapies
Clark, Jo-Anne A. RMT;
Markham, Margaret J. RMT;
Westney, F. Jean RMT
208-348 Danforth Ave 416-465-7594

**Kennedy-Sheppard Chiropractic
Centre**
Dobek, Beata RMT
2235 Kennedy Rd 416-281-0070

Kikkawa College
Kikkawa, Mitsuki RMT; Patel, Nancy RMT
1 Riverview Gardens 416-762-4857

Kilpatrick, Bartholome RMT
252 Wright Ave 416-516-9376

Kimlen Therapies
Lim, Linda Kimlen Cuan RMT
By Appointment 416-461-2470

King Rehabilitation Centre
Adamowicz, Alexsander RMT
748 King St W 416-504-6712

**Kingston Rd Massage Therapy
Clinic**
Coughlan, Angela D. RMT;
Dabek, Danuta RMT
927 Kingston Rd 416-694-6767

Know Your Body Best
Bearss, Lorelei RMT;
Brown, Susan Ellen RMT;
Hartford, Kim RMT;
Hines, Alison RMT;
Michael, Marsha RMT;
Nabozniak, Evelyn RMT;
Rennett, Constance RMT
Carrot Common Mall,
14-348 Danforth Ave 416-466-1515

Kole, Mary RMT
50A Borden St 416-967-7466

Kossobudzki, Izabella RMT
15 Bentley Dr 416-252-3433

Kothe, Max O. RMT
94 MacPherson Ave 416-962-9992

Kowalski, Marianne RMT
1104-111 Lawton Blvd 416-485-0399

Kulhay Chiropractic Clinic & Wellness Centre
Thompson, Susan Elizabeth RMT
607-2 St. Clair Ave W 416-961-1900

L. & B. Body Care Inc.
Torrens, Mary Judy RMT
1172 Weston Rd 416-242-4998

Labrie, Suzanne L. RMT
33-72 Isabelle St 416-922-7253

Lacroix, Joan RMT
1-344 Roselawn Ave 416-484-0897

Lam, David RMT
368 Dupont St 416-925-6752

Lam School Advanced Esthetics
Lam, Hubert RMT
916 Markham Rd 416-439-3350

Laszlo, Hajnal RMT
311-15 Eva Rd 416-695-0332

Laviola, Anthony RMT
13 1/2 Perth Ave 416-531-8897

Lebold, Cynthia Eileen RMT
103 Madison Ave 416-515-8655

Lee, Coranna S. RMT
166B Niagara St 416-806-6675

Leili Terts Massage Therapy
Terts, Leili RMT
37 Donora Dr 416-757-8679

Lewis, Timothy Elliot RMT
98 Hogarth Ave 416-466-9075

Life Chiropractic Health Centre
Bowden, Treneta RMT
98 Syminston Ave 416-534-7927

Lifeline Therapeutics
McGregor, Anne D. RMT
217-40 Orchard View Blvd ..416-440-0398

Listro Chiropractic
McDonald, Rob RMT; Roberge, Anne RMT
111 Redpath Ave 416-481-3378

Litnovetsky Hydrotherapy & Massage
Litnovetsky, Rita RMT
111-5460 Yonge St 416-221-2728

Litoch, Sergei RMT
30 Althea St 416-767-4062

Lombardi, Marylou RMT
88 Rosewell Ave 416-484-6717

Loo, May RMT
219 Yarmouth Rd 416-531-3297

Lorentzen, Monika RMT
6C Park Ave 416-694-2586

Lowe, Virginia RMT
71 West Ave 416-469-4248

Lower Village Chiropractic Clinic
Bohez, Anita RMT; Lee, Christina RMT;
McRae, Campbell RMT
245 St. Clair Ave W 416-323-1077

Lucas, Susan M. RMT
176 St. George St, 2nd Floor .416-922-6354

Luck Chiropractic Clinic
Clapperton, Anderw
1848 Bloor St W 416-766-3812

Lupuliak, Judy RMT
618 Shaw St 416-537-2284

M.C. Aesthetic Studios
White, Ian Gordon RMT
2200 Yonge St 416-481-0357

MacDonald, Jane Allison RMT
3-3685 Keele St 416-630-2225

MacInnis, Pamela RMT
213-4155 Bathurst St 416-235-9788

MacPherson, Hugh RMT
417-45 Carlton St 416-979-5611

Maloney, Kathleen RMT
817-200 Roehampton Ave ..416-488-3363

Manea, Stella RMT
1612-7 St. Dennis St 416-467-8447

Manulife Centre Club, The
Roy, Wanda RMT
55 Bloor St W, 2nd Floor ...416-694-0412

Marks, Marlaina Lynne RMT
28 Wineva Ave 416-699-6165

Marosvary, Irene RMT
21B Vaughan Rd, Unit 117 ..416-657-8268

Massage & Hydrotherapy Centre
Brendle, Eckbert J. RMT
2350 Bayview Ave 416-512-0052

Massage Therapy Clinic
Campbell, Kenneth C. RMT
71 Ninth St 416-255-2041

Massotherapy
Leoni, Enrico RMT
306-960 Lawrence Ave W ...416-784-0180

Matrix Interactive Health Care
Davidson, Andie RMT
3164 Yonge St 416-484-6161

Maxabilitation
Drexler, Marion RMT
101-255 Yorkland Blvd 416-492-9355

McCloskey, Jason M. RMT
12 Shortland Cr 416-245-9987

McCord, Janice RMT
310-1920 Ellesmere Rd ...416-439-9542

McCowan Chiropractic
Carson, Sharlene RMT
By Appointment 416-292-4100

McDougall, Nugent RMT
192 Giltspur Dr 416-746-3510

McEachern, Scott P. RMT
844 Davenport Rd 416-953-2991

McGuire, Diane J. RMT
316-19 Carr St 416-365-9801

McKinnon, Bruce A. RMT
508-170 St. George St 416-929-9350

McNeely, Cindy RMT
26 Webster Ave 416-920-7092

McWilliams, Laurel RMT
By Appointment 416-487-6717

Meehan, Maria E. RMT
202-7 Walmsley Blvd 416-480-2569

Mekis, Marjan Mario RMT
246A Jane St 416-766-6872

Melillo, Antoinette RMT
51 Coquette Rd 416-743-1934

Melkonian, Ara RMT
680 Bathurst St 416-516-0537

Melrose Physio Fitness
Smith, Beryl RMT
368 Melrose Ave 416-789-3043

Mikoczy, Veronika K. RMT; Mikoczy, Imre Emery RMT
542 Indian Rd 416-537-7554

Miller, Scott RMT
By Appointment 416-925-7514

Mills, Susan RMT
463 Dovercourt Rd 416-535-4625

Minkkinen, Marita RMT
2-206 Galley Ave 416-535-2482

Modilevsky, Igor RMT
1410-5900 Yonge St 416-226-6735

Morris, Barbara RMT
156 Bartlett Ave 416-535-6764

Morrison, Michelle RMT
2 Gormley Ave 416-482-0027

Morrow, Fiona L. RMT
3B Wendover Rd 416-236-9919

Murphy, Deborah A. RMT & Aromatherapist
17 Ross Ave 416-754-4830

Muscle Up Therapy Centre
Segal, Amira RMT
1670 Dufferin St 416-652-9862

Naglis, Ria RMT
368 Balliol St 416-486-0049

Naturopath Clinic
Dubrowsky, Jessica L. RMT
93 Harbord St 416-961-2225

Neighbourhood Wellness Clinic
Girard, Nicole RMT; McLarnon, Gail E. RMT
1320 Yonge St 416-923-3330

90 Medical Group
Zauva, Anita RMT
90 Eglinton Ave E 416-489-5818

Nordenson, Berit RMT
20 N Glen Ave 416-622-4651

Noronha, Moira RMT
32B Greenlaw Ave 416-651-0817

North York Therapeutic Massage & Shiatsu
Ikeda, Marilyn RMT
199 Sheppard Ave W 416-222-0363

Nostbakken, Grace RMT
316 Dupont St 416-964-7919

Nouvelle Maria Spa & Salon
Brooks, Kaaren RMT; Changoo, Dale RMT;
Monaghan, Dinah RMT; Pyka, Bogdan RMT
37 King St E 416-363-4333

Novick, Julie RMT
209-161 St. George St 416-929-6410

O'Keefe, Michele Mitzi RMT
3-148 Hilton Ave 416-532-2321

Opaalite Massage Clinic
Moore, Marion F. RMT
370 King St W 416-595-2520

Ordell, Lisa D. RMT
102-25 Bedford Rd 416-961-0800

Orthopaedic Therapy Clinic, The
Tyner, Mary G. RMT
70 Yorkville Ave 416-925-4687

Oswald Chiropractic Offices
Adams, Peter RMT
410-200 St. Clair Ave W 416-972-6279

Oszust, Ewa Marta RMT
63 Constance St 416-767-1494

Otani Shiatsu Centre
Ebata, Noriko RMT
24 Roncesvalles Ave 416-533-9964

Outtrim, Norma RMT
304-2181 Queen St E 416-698-2977

Overzet, Jerry G. RMT
2201-131 Beecroft Rd 416-226-3816

Pain Management Consultants
Burgemann, Gerhard RMT
410-3420 Finch Ave E 416-495-7729

Painter, Shirley M. RMT
808-141 Erskine Ave 416-322-3837

Palmer, Lidia L. RMT
1004-580 Christie St 416-651-9491

PCR
Belnavis, Clive RMT
2100 Finch Ave W 416-665-7783

Pek, Lucy RMT
658 Sheppard Ave W 416-231-5343

Perera, Anne E. RMT
581 Huron St 416-929-9759

Peters, Marilyn RMT
208 Glenwood Cr 416-759-5562

Phillips, Diana RMT
8-69 Leacrest Rd 416-425-3821

Phippard, Haley RMT
215 Glen Rd 416-967-3696

Physiosport Therapy Clinic
Wu, Yujing RMT
4040 Finch Ave East, L1 ...416-754-3893

Physiotherapy on Bay
Coady, Candice Lynn RMT
1401-60 Bloor St W 416-921-7318

Pieczynski, Leszek RMT
903-345 Merton St 416-932-3281

Pilates Downtown
Goodwin, Gwendolin RMT
457 Richmond St W 416-769-9747

Piper, Lois C. RMT
501-161 Eglinton Ave E 416-932-3889

Platt, Nancy RMT
19 Kensington Ave 416-599-7403

Plattel, Sonja RMT
1806-10 Martha Eaton Way .416-245-2591

Pleasantview Chiropractic Centre
Brunetti, Laurie RMT
205-2772
Victoria Park Ave 416-497-2772

Practicable Therapies
De Pinto, Raffaelle David RMT
29 Talbot Rd 416-223-5169

Pro Massage
Giesel, Peter RMT
340-4544 Sheppard Ave E ..416-291-0617

Procka, Milan RMT
77 Highcroft Rd 416-778-8921

Proctor, Cheryl RMT
45 Langley Ave 416-466-4102

Professional Therapeutic Massage Clinic
Olabode, Isaac RMT
101-a235 Sheppard Ave E ..416-297-1145

Prose, Ellen RMT
325 Salem Ave 416-533-0418

Proulx, Suzanne RMT
911-666 Spadina Ave 416-920-0691

Raha, Ly RMT
23 Ballyronan Rd 416-444-8938

Raymond, Sandra RMT
50 St. Clair Ave E, 4th Floor .416-920-0239

Redfren, Cheryl RMT
24 Densgrove Rd 416-439-0999

Rehabilitation & Therapeutic Massage
Bezmozgis, Mendel RMT
403-333 Wilson Ave 416-638-5359

Rehabilitative & Performance Therapies
Koziej, Walter RMT
2 Queen St W, 5th Floor 416-599-0430

Reimer, Lois RMT
75 Byng Ave 416-223-8785

Rellinger, James RMT
233 Glendonwynne Rd 416-763-4382

Remedial Massage Therapy
Stasyk, Josephine RMT
507 Broadview Ave 416-463-4361

Repo-Davis, Laura Elina RMT
463 Dovercourt Rd 416-534-1512

Rosedale Chiropractic Centre
Brawley, Kimberley RMT; Munro, Marina RMT
O'Connor, Colleen RMT
365 Bloor St E 416-975-0499

Roth, Gera J. RMT
155 Dell Park Ave 416-789-2567

Rouge Valley Therapeutics
Stiles, Christine RMT
91 Rylander Rd 416-283-3666

Royal York Chiropractic Centre
Rockliffe, Margaret RMT
4237 Dundas St W 416-233-5413

Ruddy, Bradley RMT
190-2356 Gerrard St E 416-750-8556

Ruhrmann, Ingrid RMT
54 Torbrick Rd 416-463-0764

Rutherford Massage Therapy Clinic
Grosse, Kelly Anne RMT;
Rutherford, Jo-Ann RMT;
Shulman, Jan M. RMT
666 Burnhamthorpe Rd 416-626-8849

Saganski, Michael RMT
451 Parkside Dr 416-762-5538

Sagara, Leslie RMT
200-394 Bloor St W 416-968-0815

Saunders, Desmond RMT
1806-730 Dovercourt Rd ..416-536-8785

Scarborough General Hospital
Lilley, Cynthia Lorraine RMT
310-3030 Lawrence Ave E ..416-438-7277

Schell, Pauli RMT
259 Chisholm Ave 416-698-7367

Schenk, Kenneth W. RMT
10-39 Leduc Dr 416-742-7410

Schilf, Lothar RMT
By Appointment 416-482-6373

Schmucker, Stephen RMT
604 Lauder Ave 416-651-4858

Schneid, Tzila, RMT
210 Cockfield Ave 416-630-5270

Schnurr, Corrine RMT
14 Russett Ave 416-538-7426

Seerveld, Anya R. RMT
162 Bastedo Ave 416-698-9008

Seto Massage Therapy
Seto, Robert RMT
59 Marjory Ave 416-466-5286

Shakespeare, Shelley B. RMT
121 Browning Ave 416-778-4514

Sheppard Rehabilitation Centre
Locke, Kim RMT
307-4002 Sheppard Ave E .416-321-8321

Shiatsu Acupuncture Clinic
Samadi, Leon RMT; Tanaka, Tim H. RMT
1100-80 Bloor St W 416-929-6958

Shiatsu Centre
Harris, Anne RMT
205-110 Richmond St E ..416-368-6855

Shiatsu Centre Ltd.
Saito, Tetsuro RMT
1069 Bathurst St 416-534-1149

Shiatsu Clinic West
Makino, Nobuko RMT
3101 Bloor St W 416-236-2583

Shiatsu Dohjoh
Saito, Ken RMT
206-320 Danforth Ave 416-466-8780

Shiatsu Institue
Clarke, Dawn RMT; Goldman, Heather RMT
2578A Yonge St 416-322-0439

Shiatsu School of Canada
Kamiya, Kanunobu RMT
547 College St 416-323-1818

Skorupko, Lily RMT
809-60 Mountview Ave 416-769-7784

Slabotsky, David RMT
802-50 Prince Arthur Ave ..416-964-1860

Slusar, Annie RMT
714-111 Pacific Ave 416-604-9321

Smith, Allan RMT
198 Quebec Ave 416-766-6863

Soft Tissue Therapy Centre Inc.
Iskander, Nagi Naguib RMT
14 Summerglade Dr 416-321-8036

Spa at the Elmwood
Banning, Stephanie A. RMT;
Cragg, Wendy RMT;
Fontana, Louise A. RMT; Rossi, Cynthia RMT;
Sutton, Tamara Joy RMT
18 Elm St 416-977-6751

Spadina-Bloor Massage Therapy Clinic
Billung-Meyer, Michele RMT;
Goring, Stephen RMT;
Scarcello, Lorelia RMT
404-344 Bloor St W 416-928-9650

Spavaganza Salon & Spa
Staples, Brendan Michael RMT
36-20 Bloor St E 416-922-7727

Spectrum Healing Naturopathic Clinic
Eng-Khalsa, Eileen RMT
130 Hallam St 416-534-0002

Sports & Injury Rehab Clinic
Whelpley, Christine Ann RMT
310-3030 Lawrence Ave E .416-438-7277

Spruce Haven
Aaron, Susan RMT
47 Spruce Hill 416-699-3211

Squires, Rodney RMT
1605-81 Dalhousie St 416-214-0220

St. Clair Club
Rodger, Patricia RMT
12 St. Clair Ave E 416-927-8042

St. Clair Health Centre
Bourgeois, Mary Lou RMT
201-15 St. Clair Ave W 416-944-1600

Steinberg, Andrea RMT
301-525 Chaplin Cr 416-781-7740

Steinebach, Elizabeth RMT
111 Woodbine Ave 416-694-0158

Stevens, Agnes RMT
115 Glen Park Ave 416-785-3622

Stott Studio
Simmons, Wendy RMT
456 Danforth Ave, 3rd Floor .416-461-1347

Supportive Touch
Sato, Jeanette Kazuko RMT
19 Kensington Ave 416-581-1210

Sutherland-Chan Clinic
Berg, Sharon J. RMT; Bishop, Peggy RMT;
Hancock, Gail RMT; Smookler, David S. RMT;
Assman, Sabine C. RMT
Royal Bank Plaza 416-364-6561

Sutherland-Chan Clinic
Chan, Grace K. RMT; Curties, Debra RMT;
O'Neil, Erlan RMT
330 Dupont St,
4th Floor 416-924-1107/747-9762

Sutherland-Chan Clinic
Corradini, Cristina RMT; Harford, Terry RMT;
Ishikawa, Frances RMT; Martens, Sean RMT;
McKerracher Ronald RMT;
Seniscal, Caryn RMT; Steel, R. Harry RMT
732 Spadina Ave 416-960-4769

Sutherland-Chan Clinic
Loy, Lindsey R.A. RMT
First Canadian Place 416-368-6787

Sutherland-Chan Clinic Inc.
Brzozowska, Jadwiga RMT;
Wilson, Lorraine RMT
200-105 Gordon Baker Rd ..416-492-1615

Szadziuk, Jacek
1715-65 High Park Ave 416-767-2167

Szarek, Anna RMT
102-3273 Bloor St W 416-233-0907

Talley, Diana RMT
28 Hillside Dr 416-429-5083

Tam, Jimmy RMT
54 Kenfin Ave 416-321-5951

Tension Clinic, The
Thouard, Michael RMT
19 Cowan Ave 416-539-9895

Thain, Diane RMT
2200 Yonge St 416-481-4184

Therapeutic Insight Services
Bruce, Donna Ann RMT
1408-75 The Don Way
West 416-499-7141

Therapeutic Massage
Dorey, Wendy RMT
43 Elm St 416-520-7553

Therapeutic Massage Clinic
Pieczula, Wojciech RMT
LL06-4190 Finch Ave E 416-299-3506

Therapeutic Massage Institute
Berezowski, Bob RMT
79 Wellington St 416-865-0900

Therapeutic Massage Registry Ltd.
Henriksen, Jette RMT; Schwarz,
Leona Reimer RMT;
St. Laurent, Claire RMT;
von Boetticher, Sabine RMT
212A St. Clair Ave W 416-926-0099

Therapeutic Skin Care Centre
Toscano, Maria Del Carmen RMT
6012A Yonge St 416-733-7638

Therapeutically Yours
Kelly-Lawrence, Marie RMT
23 Golfwood Heights Dr 416-246-0067

Thrasher Duch, Rene I. RMT
402-350 The East Mall 416-233-0094

Time Out On-Site-Massage
Hastings, Fjola RMT
101-1 Spencer Ave 416-588-0815

Timofte, Simion RMT
76 Elise Terrace 416-733-8804

Todhunter, Richard RMT
181 Harbord St 416-535-9305

Tomlinson, David RMT
129 Colin AVe 416-485-0904

Tops Health Studio
Angelic, Anita RMT 416-398-7426

Toronto Cricket, Skating & Curling Club
141 Wilson Ave 416-487-4581

Toronto General Hospital
Culp, Dianne RMT
B1-90 Gerrard St W 416-340-4377

Toronto Pain & Headache Clinic
206-9 Bloor St E 416-925-2579

Toronto West Therapeutic Massage
North, Christine RMT
2822 Dundas St W 416-766-9108

Townshend Massage Therapy
Townshend, Kurt RMT
245 St. Clair Ave W 416-323-1077

Travers, Monique A. RMT
8 Muirdale Ave 416-249-9310

Tschudi, Indranie RMT
544A Yonge St 416-972-6182

Unwinding Sports Massage & Stress Clinic
Ruebottom, Ann RMT
290 St. Clair Ave W 416-323-1671

van der Rassel, Susan M. RMT
903-48 Isabella St 416-922-0472

Vidovich, Franziska RMT
595 Coldstream Ave 416-787-2223

Village Spa
Fornasier, Cristine M. RMT;
Kozen, Deborah Rose RMT
Bayview Village,
2901 Bayview Ave 416-224-1101

Vlatkovic, Ivan RMT
715-63 Widdicombe
Hill Blvd 416-241-5028

Walker, Alfred RMT
108 Grenadier Rd 416-533-9618

Walker, Roderick James RMT
1-313 Brunswick Ave 416-960-5088

Walsh, Karen RMT
501-1650 Sheppard Ave E . .416-502-9400

Walton, Candace RMT
1104-66 Oakmount Rd 416-604-9825

Warburton, Laura RMT
202 Broadway Ave 416-487-5537

Ward, Susan L. RMT
By Appointment 416-256-1170

Wass, Mary RMT
193 College St 416-408-0702

West End Holistic Health Centre
McKenzie, Bonnie RMT
2826 Dundas St W 416-763-3211

West End Massage Therapy
Aiken, Nita RMT;
Heaney, Daniel G. RMT;
Potvin, Marcel RMT;
Reznyak, Kenneth RMT
14 Heintzman St 416-766-4202

WestPoint Therapeutic Centre
Music, Lutfija RMT
213-2 Dunbloor Rd 416-233-6077

Wilder, Steven RMT
517A St. Clair Ave W 416-533-3864

Wilkie, Norma J. RMT
1017 Logan Ave 416-463-0528

Willetts, Marah RMT
62 Nipigon Ave 416-512-0843

Williams, James RMT
103 Barton Ave 416-531-4851

Williamson, Gina Sheila RMT
10-2483 Lakeshore Blvd W .416-251-0469

Willow Therapy Centre
Hill-Hammond, Pamela RMT;
MacPherson, Anita RMT;
Kempel, Deborah RMT;
Porter, Mary-Jane RMT
2560 Gerrard St E 416-690-1161

Wilson, Heather V. RMT
272 Winona Dr 416-652-0826

Windt, Dana RMT
1657 Bathurst St 416-485-1751

Winicki, Elizabeth RMT
1074 Wilson Ave 416-247-3291

Winter Clinical Massage Associates
Winter, P. Anne RMT
528-170 St. George St 416-928-1723

Wintercorn, Lynn RMT
65 Overlea Blvd 416-467-5748

Woburn Chiropractic Clinic
Dobrzanski, Witold RMT
836 Markham Rd 416-439-3710

Wong, Sharon RMT
12 Hurlingham Cr 416-444-0194

Yap, Cecil RMT
1603-2550 Pharmacy Ave . .416-495-0711

YMCA - Scarborough
Hann, Julie L. RMT
230 Town Center Court 416-296-9622

York Medical Centre
Mleczek, Agnieszka RMT
4700 Keele St 416-661-7015

Yorkdale Massage Therapy
McPhee, Andrea RMT; Strathdee, Lori RMT;
Tudor, Jo-Ann (Mary) RMT
3401 Dufferin St 416-783-7712

Yorkville Chiropractic Centre
Frasson, Gabriel RMT; Peacock, Rosalin S. RMT
805-94 Cumberland St 416-928-0003

You Need A Massage
Puddephatt, Lisa RMT
7451 Kingston Rd 416-284-4846

Young, Barbara RMT
347 Clinton St 416-537-7998

Zador, Helen RMT
811-130 Rosedale Valley Rd .416-961-6721

Zambonelli, Mark RMT
310-4800 Leslie St 416-492-0021

Zhong's Therapeutic Massage Clinic
Zhang, Zhong-Quan RMT
2006-716 The West Mall . . .416-695-2565

Ziegenhagen, Doris RMT
14 Tofield Cr 416-748-0665

Zorzos, Robert G. RMT
482 Pape Ave 416-406-0696

TOTTENHAM

Living Unlimited
Weston, Ronald RMT
RR #2 905-236-6268

Shaw, Stacey RMT
83 Queen St S 905-841-3372

TRENTON

LeBel, Lise Yvette RMT
10 Stewart St 613-394-6601

UNIONVILLE

Trines, Edward RMT
52 Northolt Cr 905-475-7263

Unionville Massage Therapy Centre
Low-Keen, Georgia RMT;
Polley, Pamela J. RMT;
Topol, Jaroslava RMT
210-4591 Hwy 7E 905-477-1707

UXBRIDGE

Begg Chiropractic Centre
deBlicquy, Elain D. RMT
290 Hwy 47 S, RR #1 905-852-9700

Nature's Accolade
Marshall, Robert W. RMT
201 Main St N 905-852-7733

Uxbridge-Brock Therapeutic Massage Clinic
Hawkins, Edith Boyce RMT
Testa Professional Bldg,
2 Campbell Dr 905-852-9771

Uxbridge Massage Therapy Station
Blyth, Norine RMT
91 Franklin St 905-852-5422

VANIER

Fairhall, Carol RMT
129 Deschamps St 613-746-4923

VINELAND

Lopes, Lorraine RMT
3937 Vineyard Cr 905-562-3893

VIRGIL

Janzen, Mary Ann RMT
By Appointment 905-682-7012

Tiessen, Janice RMT
By Appointment 905-468-3053

WARKWORTH

Boardman, Rinchen RMT
RR #1 705-924-3380

Plathan, Helen RMT
RR #4 705-924-3437

WATERDOWN

Flamborough Massage & Accupuncture Clinic
Dienstadt, Diane RMT; Tonizzo, Nadia RMT
11 Mill St S 905-689-1454/7175

WATERLOO

Accent on Health
Voisin, Colleen RMT
221 Baker St 519-743-9843

Beechwood Chiropractic & Massage Centre
Sheridan, Verna RMT; Williston, Wendy C. RMT
450 Erb St W 519-888-6030

Beechwood Massage Therapy
Reinhardt, Michael RMT
625A Pinerow Cr 519-747-0372

Bender, Susan M. RMT
152 Albert St 519-885-2797

Birgit Stoll's Massage Therapy Clinic
Fulop, Tara RMT; Walch, Birgit RMT
262 King St N, 2nd Floor . .519-747-9091

Catt, Lyle D. RMT
RR #1 519-567-0361

Cooke, Cara E. RMT
69 Bridgeport Rd E 519-747-9520

Dolan, April RMT
261 Bowman St 519-744-4721

Dupuis, Jody E. RMT
4-279 Weber St N 519-747-2225

Edgar, Christopher A. RMT
85 Alexandra Ave 519-579-6721

European Institute of Massage Therapy
Lewandowski, Krzysztof RMT
Westmount Rd N 519-886-8834

Gascon/Stoll Massage Therapy Clinic
Gascon, Sharon RMT; Mantzios, Lambrini RMT
262 King St N 519-747-9091

Heeney, Kevin William RMT
106-445 Beechwood Pl 519-886-0750

Helping Hands Massage Therapy
Kleinknecht, Lindsay RMT
64 Union St E 519-579-0086

Hutchinson, Viniita Susan RMT
13 Dunbar Rd S, 1st Floor . .519-886-6724

ITM - The Centre for Soft Tissue Therapy & Rehabilitation
Meldazy, Richard RMT; Pryce, Muriel RMT
69 Bridgeport Rd E 519-747-9520

Kayser Massage Therapy
Kayser, Annemarie RMT
399 Lakeview Dr 519-725-3027

Kennedy-Sirrs Massage Therapy Clinic
Arsenault, Ann Marie RMT;
Kennedy, Maureen RMT
124 King St N 519-746-8230

Kiraly Jr., Imrich
419-605 Davenport Rd 519-747-0022

MacGregor, Jeannie RMT
341 Browning Place 519-746-0498

Martin, Marjorie Dawn RMT
129 Park St 519-744-7139

Massage & Sports Therapy Centre
Acorn, David RMT; McCrea, Ann RMT;
Scroggins, Susan C. RMT
1-168 Lexington Ct 519-746-6764

Massage Therapy Clinic
Mader, Richard J. RMT; Mader, Richelle RMT
392 Albert St 519-885-0721

Northfield Family "Health Centre"
Veiledal, K.C. RMT
202-99 Northfield Dr E 519-746-1350

Northfield Massage Clinic
Barless, Larry Michael RMT
380 King St N 519-725-3638

Park Place Therapeutics
Epp, Jane RMT; Ertel, Lauren J. RMT
129 Park St 519-743-8199/1444

Patton, Ann E. RMT
140 Columbia St 519-747-1044

Professional Touch
Martin, Lissa RMT
181 Park St, Upper Level . . .519-578-6168

Rennie Wholistic Therapy
Rennie, Kathleen RMT
360 Regina St N 519-886-4045

Rotermann, Monika RMT
40-693 Beechwood Dr 519-725-4436

Sheila Grange Massage Therapy Clinic
Grange, Sheila M. RMT; Kennedy, Sheryl RMT
121 Park St 519-570-1900

Sykes, Elizabeth Anne RMT
86 Weber St S 519-744-8717

T. Hebert Massage & Craniosacral Therapy
Hebert, Tracy RMT
102 White Oak Place 519-886-4572

Taylor Loriann RMT
17 Bismark Ave 519-579-0960

True Natures
Ingall, Amanda RMT; Thomas, Jennyfer RMT
76 Regina St N 519-884-4525

Union St Therapeutic Massage Clinic
Hughes-Krenze, Joy L. RMT
10 Union St E 519-576-1013

Verbaegen, Andy RMT
124 King St N 519-746-8230

Waterloo/Northfield Massage Therapy
Sawyer, Deborah RMT; Trotter, Alice RMT;
Tuerk, Rita-Marie RMT
421 King St N 519-725-3638

Weber, Lynne A. RMT
G115-155 Frobisher Dr 519-888-6133

Weigel, Julie Ann RMT
10 Spring St E 519-886-2450

WELLAND

Adams, Eden L. RMT
31 Royal Oak Dr 905-788-3063

Goupil, Frank J. RMT
Perrotto, Michelle E. RMT
233 Division St 905-735-3098

Pierrette's
Ranieri-Kean, Eva RMT
14 Douglas Ave 905-788-9119

Zamora, Audra Marie RMT
2 Donna Marie Dr 905-735-9703

WELLESLEY

Jacobs, Michele RMT
RR #2 519-656-3331

WESTPORT

Morris, Evelyn R. RMT
RR #1 613-273-4590

WHITBY

Accident Injury Management
Bruni, Selena RMT
420 Green St 905-668-8222

Brock Therapeutics
Linkvist, Kristina RMT
501 Brock St S 905-665-7111

Durham Massage & Hydrotherapy
Blucher, Lisa C. RMT
731 Hyland St 905-666-0406

Durham Muscular Therapy Clinic
Bowen, Johanna H. RMT
861 Dundas St W 905-666-0046

Family Wellness Clinic
Josephs, Timothy RMT; Kennedy, Barbara
Jayne RMT
1631 Dundas St E 905-728-7121

Hands on Health Care
Palamar, Anna H. RMT;
Schembri-Diskey, Martez RMT
LL-209 Dundas St E,
Executive Ste 905-666-1393

Johnson, Patricia R. RMT
Moffat, Lesley H. RMT
420 Crawforth St 905-430-7986

Rayman-Stormes, Sonia RMT
134-10 Bassett Blvd 905-666-8971

Rossland Chiropractic Associates
Struna, Erica RMT
204-701 Rossland Rd 905-430-6787

Szymanowski, Paul RMT
17 Springsyde St 905-721-2132

Whitby Massage Therapy Clinic
Clifton, Leeson RMT; Elste, Christine RMT;
Pascoe, Shannon RMT;
St. John, Lisa Marie RMT
7-519 Dundas St E 905-430-2183

WHITEVALE

Corporate Health Services
Beare, L. Gail RMT
3226 Gladstone St 905-294-3904

WINDSOR

Bioenergy Health Centre
Veselka, Jan RMT
2224 Walker Rd 519-252-2199

Eaves, Cecil RMT
1836 East Gate Estates 519-948-4512

Enkin, Kate RMT
2793 Longfellow St 519-250-8195

Gaudario, Manuel RMT
1225 Cottage Pl 519-945-9441

Genesis Health Centre
Way, Kelly-Ann RMT
79 Giles Blvd E 519-258-5269

Gonda, Deborah RMT
Fitzpatrick, Deborah BHK RMT
9280 Disputed Rd, RR #3 . .519-978-2630

Hardie, Ruth M. RMT
1502-150 Park St W 519-252-7616

Helping Hands Massage Therapy
Diemer, Brian John RMT
9833 Tecumseh Rd E 519-979-1427

Kuglin, Piotr RMT
1455-21 Polonia Park Pl . . .519-974-3493

Lefaive-Prsa, Julie Lynn RMT
431 St. John 519-948-3384

Ottawa Mall Chiropractic
Keddie, Brian A. RMT
1471 Ottawa St 519-977-5928

Reaume, Monique M. RMT
3143 Church St 519-966-8298

Robinet, Theresa C. RMT
4-575 Assumption St 519-258-5203

Smye, S. Meredith RMT
50-2224 Walker Rd 519-971-2737

Studio Scruples
Fiedler-Marmus, Gisela RMT
20 Chatham St E 519-973-5598

Walkerville Chiropractic
Charette, Suzanne RMT
1275 Walker Rd 519-258-7979

Windsor Chiropractic Centre
Fizzell, Ross RMT
458-1720 Howard Ave 519-258-9833

Windsor Massage Therapy Clinic
Beaulieu-Van Vlack, Dawn M. RMT;
McQueen, Michelle RMT
105-630 Tecumseh Rd E 905-258-0603

WOODBRIDGE

Mueller, Susan M. RMT
401-5308 Hwy 7 905-856-7038

Pine Valley & Hwy 7 Chiropractic Clinic
DiLuca, Elsa RMT
202-7700 Pine Valley Dr ...905-856-8611

Thistlewood Medical Building
Deza, Heather RMT
103-8077 Islington Ave N ..905-850-3285

Woodbridge Physiotherapy Centre
Maloney, Barry S. RMT; McCrank, Colleen RMT
100-4500 Hwy 7 905-856-3777

WOODSTOCK

Almas, Susan RMT
787 St. Albans Cr 519-539-9715

Chen, Fu RMT
379 Hunter St 519-421-1011

Gdanski Massage Therapy Clinic
Gdanski, Glen RMT
45 Wellington St S 519-539-2555

Natural Health Care Centre
Leffler, Lyle RMT; Leffler, Tammy RMT
312 Dundas St 519-539-4752

Olive Branch Natural Health Clinic
Burns, Thomas C. RMT
62 Wellington St S 519-539-7781

Oxford Massage Therapy Office
Gdanski, Paul RMT
312 Dundas St 519-539-3310

Tesolat, Walter RMT
183 Victoria St 519-421-0680

Prince Edward Island Massage Therapists

NOTE: Check the credentials of your practitioner (see above, "Questions to Ask"). This publication cannot and does not certify or represent the qualifications of practitioners, or the quality of care available from them.

CHARLOTTETOWN

Island Massage Therapy
Scales, Heather
18 Garfield St, Upper Level ..902-368-7033

Québec

In Québec, massage therapists are not regulated, meaning that there is no legislation establishing a governing body to register and discipline qualified massage therapists. This also means that no minimum educational standards exist for those calling themselves massage therapists. However, the association listed below sets standards for its members.

Québec Association

La Fédération Québécoise des Masseurs et Massothérapeutes
1265 Mont Royal E, Ste 204
Montréal, Québec H2J 1Y4
Tel: 1-800-363-9609 or 514-597-0505

Contact the Federation, founded in 1979, for a referral to one of its 1,500 professional members. Masseurs have at least 400 hours training, and the massothérapeutes have at least 1,000 hours, including more training in the therapeutic aspects of massage.

✦ Québec Massage Therapists

NOTE: Check the credentials of your practitioner (see above, "Questions to Ask"). This publication cannot and does not certify or represent the qualifications of practitioners, or the quality of care available from them.

GATINEAU

Labonte, Lise
2-257 Essiambre St 819-663-5692

HULL

Hardy, Lisette
104-232 Alexandre Tache ...819-776-0660

MONTREAL

Reynaud, Florence
4901 Hutchison St 514-272-8738

✦ Saskatchewan

In Saskatchewan, massage therapists are not regulated, meaning that there is no legislation establishing a governing body to register and discipline qualified massage therapists. This also means that no minimum education standards exist for those calling themselves massage therapists.

Saskatchewan Association

Saskatchewan Massage Therapists Association
33 Columbia Dr
Saskatoon, Saskatchewan S7K 1E6
Tel: 306-653-5650

✦ Saskatchewan Massage Therapists

NOTE: Check the credentials of your practitioner (see above, "Questions to Ask"). This publication cannot and does not certify or represent the qualifications of practitioners, or the quality of care available from them.

OUTLOOK

Hanson Massage Therapy
Hanson, Arleigh
318 Saskatchewan Ave W,
Box 965 306-867-8715

REGINA

Professional Therapeutic Massage Services
Giles, Susan
118 Michener Dr 306-789-9752

SASKATOON

8th Street Chiropractic Health & Wellness Clinic
Grabowski, Patty L.
1269 8th St 306-955-1561

Cantrill Muscle Therapy
614 10th St E 306-374-6000

SHELLBROOK

Folden, Twila M.
PO Box 126 306-747-3106

✦ Yukon Territory

In the Yukon, massage therapists are not regulated, meaning that there is no legislation establishing a governing body to register and discipline qualified massage therapists.

✦ Yukon Territory Massage Therapists

NOTE: Check the credentials of your practitioner (see above, "Questions to Ask"). This publication cannot and does not certify or represent the qualifications of practitioners, or the quality of care available from them.

WHITEHORSE

High Level Centre Inc
Verrier, Shawn
Box 4483 403-668-7029

✦ Midwifery

WHAT IS MIDWIFERY

Midwifery is the art and science of giving supervision, care and advice to women during pregnancy, birth and the period following. "Midwife" in Old English means "with woman." In French, "sage femme," means "wise woman." This age-old tradition is now being revived in Canada. The care given by a midwife usually includes preventive measures, the detection of any abnormal conditions in mother and child, and the referral to physicians when appropriate. Prenatal visits to midwives often include counselling on nutrition and health, as well as preparation for birth and child-care. At the time of birth, midwifery philosophy generally emphasizes pregnancy and delivery as a natural event with medical intervention used only when necessary. Following birth, midwives assist with care of the newborn. Depending upon the jurisdiction, midwives may practise in hospitals, clinics, birth centres or private homes.

The College of Midwives of B.C., the governing body, notes that midwifery is holistic by nature, combining an understanding of the social, emotional, cultural, spiritual, psychological and physical ramifications of a woman's reproductive experience. Similarly, the College of Midwives of Ontario notes in its philosophy statement that care is "based on a respect for pregnancy as a state of health and childbirth as a normal physiologic process and a profound event in a woman's life." The same statement describes midwifery care as personalized and non-authoritarian. These values are also reflected in the approach of the Alberta Association of Midwives.

Resurgence of Midwifery

In the past several years, renewed interest in midwifery and the type of care it represents has led to demands from consumers and midwifery associations for its legal recognition. Midwives are now regulated in Ontario, and they are in the process of becoming regulated in Alberta and British Columbia. Other provinces are expected to follow. In announcing in 1996 that B.C. would regulate midwives, Health Minister Andrew Petter stated: "The recognition of midwifery as a health profession is consistent with policies in every other industrialized Western country." He added: "Midwives are the primary caregivers in 80 per cent of births worldwide." In response to requests from Québec women and couples, the province's National Assembly unanimously adopted an Act in 1990 authorizing the practice of midwifery on an experimental basis in eight pilot projects managed by a health care institution.

In recognition of the value of midwifery services, the World Health Organization (WHO) in 1985 recommended that the training of professional midwives be encouraged, adding that care during normal pregnancy, birth, and post-partum should be the duty of this profession. Public opinion in Canada would seem to support the practice of midwifery. A 1993 Québec survey, conducted by the Fédération des CLSC and the Conseil du statut de la femme, found that 80% of the Québec population was in favour of the pilot project birth centres now operating. And the popularity of midwifery in Ontario is such that demand in 1996 was more than double the capacity of the province's midwifery program.

Routine Hospital Procedures Questioned

The revival of midwifery - and with it the choice of home births - coincides with a growing number of concerns being raised about the approach to childbirth in many hospitals. The loss of control experienced by women during labour in hospitals was cited as one of the reasons for the demand for home births in Canada in a 1994 report by the Newfoundland Provincial Advisory Committee on Midwifery. Similarly, a survey of routine maternity care published in 1995 by Health Canada and the Canadian Institute of Child Health, a non-profit organization based in Ottawa, found that several hospital procedures were routinely followed, despite questionable benefits. For example, the survey found that about half the women admitted to hospital to give birth received routine intravenous fusion (I.V.s). The report noted that evidence shows that having women eat and drink during labour would serve the same purpose as I.V.s, which may have potentially serious unwanted effects on the baby. As well, the report stated that the routine or liberal use of episiotomies (surgical enlargement of the vagina for delivery) in Canadian hospitals should be abandoned, with this surgery performed only when there are indications, such as the inability to give birth without intervention.

QUESTIONS TO ASK

✦ Is your midwife registered? You can check by contacting your provincial governing body (College of Midwives). See addresses and telephone numbers below, "Midwifery in Your Province - Governing Body" (in Alberta, "Registry of Midwives - Professional & Technical Service"). This question applies only if you live in a province where mid-wifery is regulated - Ontario, and soon, Alberta and B.C. In Québec, midwives serving at the pilot project birth centres are regulated as part of the province's pilot project.

✦ Is your midwife a member of a professional association? This is particularly important if you live in a jurisdiction where midwifery is unregulated (outside Ontario, and soon Alberta and B.C.)

NOTE: Contact the association to discuss the qualifications and background of your prospective midwife (see below, "Midwifery in Your Province - Association"). Also note the law in your jurisdiction (see below, "Government Regulation").

✦ What is the extent of your midwife's training and experience, and what is the background of the back-up midwife, if any?

NOTE: As a benchmark, to qualify as a midwife in B.C. and Ontario, a person must have attended at least 60 births, at which the student was a primary caregiver for at least 40. Similar clinical experience is recommended in Alberta.

✦ What complications has your midwife seen and handled, and what is the procedure in emergency situations? Under what circumstances will your midwife refer you to a physician?

✦ How frequently will you see the midwife during your pregnancy, how long will the visits be, and what will they involve? What is the procedure during the period after birth?

✦ Does your midwife have privileges at a hospital in case you wish, or require, a hospital birth? At what stage in labour does your midwife suggest leaving for hospital?

✦ If you wish a hospital instead of a home birth, what are the hospital's policies regarding childbirth?

NOTE: Alberta's Association for Safe Alternatives in Childbirth suggests the following questions regarding hospital care: May the woman choose the birth position? Are any medical procedures routinely performed such as intravenous drips or episiotomies (surgical enlargement of the vagina for delivery)? After birth, is the baby required to immediately leave the mother to go to a nursery for observation, or may you hold your newborn? Are women allowed to eat or drink during delivery if they wish?

✦ What is the total cost of the midwife's service? Are there additional charges for water births, first visits or out-of-town births? Make inquiries regarding the total cost before your first appointment.

NOTE: Midwifery services are fully covered by government health funding in Ontario. Full or partial funding will also be available under the programs being developed in Alberta and B.C. In the meantime, the cost of home births ranges from $800 to $1,200 in Alberta.

GOVERNMENT REGULATION

Regulation means that there is provincial legislation establishing a professional governing body. This body, usually called a "College," is given a duty in law to protect the public. Governing bodies are established to ensure that regulated practitioners meet specific standards before they practise, to investigate complaints, and to take disciplinary action against practitioners where appropriate.

Provinces that Regulate Midwifery

Ontario became the first province in Canada to regulate midwives in 1993, with a governing body established to register qualified midwives. Alberta and B.C. have also begun to regulate midwifery, and are in the process of registering midwives. And in Québec, a pilot project is in progress under legislation passed in 1990. The Québec government is to decide in 1998 whether to legalize midwifery, based on an evaluation of the project. This would allow for home births, which are not part of the pilot project.

For details regarding legal regulation of midwives in Alberta, B.C. and Ontario, and the pilot project in Québec, see below "Midwifery in Your Province."

Provinces that Do Not Regulate Midwifery

Midwifery is not regulated outside Alberta, B.C., Ontario and Québec. However, Manitoba is developing legislation to regulate midwives. The possibility of introducing similar legislation is being considered in the Northwest Territories, Saskatchewan, and the Yukon Territory. In these jurisdictions, as well as in New Brunswick, Newfoundland, Nova Scotia and Prince Edward Island, legislation is in place restricting the practice of medicine. In certain provinces, midwifery is specifically cited as a prohibited practice unless a person is registered as a physician, as in Saskatchewan's *Medical Profession Act, 1981* (sections 2(k), 80) and Manitoba's *Medical Act*, sections 2(1)(d), 15). In other provinces, obstetrics or obstetrical procedures are cited as prohibited without a licence to practise medicine, as in the *Medical Acts* of New Brunswick, Newfoundland, Nova Scotia, and Prince Edward Island, and the *Medical Profession Acts* of the Yukon and Northwest Territories. In Newfoundland, where limited midwifery practice is available from nurse-midwives under legislation governing nurses, a 1994 final report of a Provincial Advisory Committee on Midwifery called for a new Midwifery Act to cover the full scope of midwifery care and license midwives. This Committee called for repeal of a 1920 piece of legislation, *An Act Respecting the Practice of Midwifery*. This legislation allows for the establishment of a Midwifery Board, but the Act is not in use, and no Midwifery Board is in place (see below, "Midwifery in Your Province - Newfoundland").

GOVERNMENT HEALTH CARE FUNDING

Partial or full government health care funding for midwifery services is provided only in the provinces where midwives are regulated, have a pilot project or are becoming regulated: Alberta, B.C., Ontario and Québec. In Alberta, government funding of midwifery services will be determined by each of the province's 17 regional health authorities. As a result, such funding may therefore not be available in all parts of the province. There is also concern about the adequacy of funding in Alberta. (see below, "Midwifery in Your Province - Government Health Care Funding").

NATIONAL ASSOCIATION

NOTE: Provincial associations are listed under each province (see below, "Midwifery in Your Province").

Canadian Confederation of Midwives
Confederation Canadienne des Sage-Femmes
132 Cumberland Cr
St. John's, Newfoundland A1B 3M5
Tel: 709-739-6319
e-mail: pherbert@morgan.ucs.mun.ca
Coordinator: Pearl Herbert

Founded in 1967, this is a non-profit national confederation of midwives' associations. The confederation promotes the right of every woman to midwifery care, and seeks the implementation of midwivery legislation in each province and territory. The confederation also coordinates communications among professional midwives' associations across Canada, and represents Canadian midwives. The Confederation has adopted policy statements of the International Confederation of Midwives, 1993.

MIDWIFERY EDUCATION

Those seeking a career in midwifery should be aware that midwives are regulated, or in the process of becoming regulated in Alberta, B.C. and Ontario, with Manitoba expected to follow. In Newfoundland, limited midwifery practice is permitted by nurse-midwives under legislation governing nurses. In provinces where midwifery is not regulated, there is legislation restricting the practice of medicine.

Alberta

Alberta's Midwifery Regulation requires midwives to complete an educational program and to pass exami-

nations, as well as to have a minimum level of experience. The recommendations include attendance at 60 births within the past five years, including 40 births for which the midwife was the primary caregiver, 30 births which involved continuity of care, 10 births in hospital and 10 out of hospital. A bachelor's degree in midwifery is recommended, and a program for such a degree is being developed for Alberta universities. Experienced midwives without formal training may be registered if they can demonstrate competence in key areas. Contact the Professional and Technical Services office for more details (see below, "Midwifery in Your Province - Alberta - Registry of Midwives - Professional and Technical Services"). Contact the Alberta Association of Midwives for information on recommended training programs, including a program in New Zealand. The Association has published a list of recommended courses that may be taken in preparation for midwifery school. This list is available from the Alberta Association and is also reprinted in material prepared by College of Midwives of B.C. (see addresses below, "Midwifery in Your Province").

British Columbia

The College of Midwives of British Columbia refers aspiring midwives to the Ontario university program (see below), as well as the programs in Washington State and in Britain (see below, "Training Programs Outside Canada"). An Education Committee has been struck to establish the approval process for midwifery education in B.C. Initial registration requirements include clinical experience with attendance at a minimum of 60 births, including 40 at which the applicant was the principal midwife . The College of Midwives of B.C. recommends the following reading for those considering a midwifery career: *Helping Hands* by Carla Hartley; *Heart & Hands* by Elizabeth Davis and *Becoming a Midwife* by Caroline Steiger. For details on registration requirements contact the College (see below, "Midwifery in Your Province - British Columbia - Governing Body").

Ontario

In Ontario, a midwifery program recognized by the College of Midwives of Ontario and leading to the degree Bachelor of Health Sciences (B.H.Sc.) in Midwifery is jointly offered by Laurentian University, McMaster University and Ryerson Polytechnic University (see addresses below). The program is completed in three years (with 11 months of schooling in each year) for the equivalent of a four-year program. At Ryerson, a part-time program that may be completed in four to seven years is also available, and at Laurentian University, the program is offered in either French or English. Students may enrol in the program at any one of the three universities. The curriculum includes courses from basic sciences, social sciences, health sciences, and women's studies, in addition to clinical practice. The admission process normally involves three steps: i) assessment of academic eligibility; ii) review of personal submissions regarding background experience; and iii) personal interview. Mature candidates and those with prior midwifery education will be considered.

Before a graduate or person with equivalent training may register as a midwife in Ontario, she or he must meet additional requirements, including the attendance at a minimum of 60 births, of which the student must be the primary caregiver for 40. For details on requirements for registration, contact the College of Midwives of Ontario (see below, "Midwifery in Your Province - Ontario - Governing Body"). Midwives' salaries range from $55,000 to $70,000 a year in Ontario.

Ontario Universities' Application Centre
650 Woodlawn Rd W
Box 1328
Guelph, Ontario N1H 7P4
Tel: 519-823-1940 or 1-800-265-8341 (Ontario only)
Fax: 519-823-5232

Requests may be made to this Centre for application forms for the Ontario University midwifery program at one of the universities. The deadline date for completed applications to be received by the Centre is normally February 1 for the school year starting in September.

Laurentian University
Midwifery Education Programme Office
935 Ramsey Lake Rd
Sudbury, Ontario P3E 2C6
Tel: 705-675-4842/1151, ext 3951

McMaster University
Midwifery Education Programme Office
St. Joseph's Hospital
Fontbonne Building, 6th Floor
50 Charlton Ave E
Hamilton, Ontario L8N 4A6
Tel: 905-521-6015

Midwifery Programme Admissions Office: 905-522-1155, ext 5273

Ryerson Polytechnic University
Office of Admissions
350 Victoria St
Toronto, Ontario M5B 2K3
Tel: 416-979-5027/5036

Midwifery Education programme: 416-979-5104

Québec

Québec midwives wishing to practise midwifery within the framework of the pilot projects must have college or university training or the equivalent in a specific set of subjects as set out in a regulation made under the midwifery legislation. The required subjects include basic anatomy and physiology, pathology, pediatrics, anatomy and physiology of reproduction. Also included are practical and clinical components, such as obstetrical care procedures. Many trainee midwives upgrade their skills at the University of Québec, Trois-Rivieres. For more information, contact:

Unité de Coordination des Projets Sages-Femmes
Ministère de la Santé et des Services sociaux
1075, chemin Sainte-Foy, 2-ième étage
Québec, Québec G1S 2M1
Tel: 418-643-1117
Fax: 418-643-1118.

Training Programs Outside Canada

Contact the College of Midwives or Registry in your province to ensure that any training program you choose meets registration requirements. Contact the Alberta Association of Midwives for information regarding the training program in New Zealand.

Seattle Midwifery School
2524 - 16th Ave S, #300
Seattle, Washington USA
98144
Tel: 206-322-8834

English National Board for Nursing, Midwifery & Health Visiting
PO Box 2EN
London W1A 2EN
England
Tel: 011-44-171-391-6200

✦ Midwifery in Your Province

Each province is listed alphabetically below, with the following information:

Legislation

✦ procedures that your midwife is permitted to perform under law, where such laws exists

✦ circumstances where the law requires you to consult with another medical professional

NOTE: The information given regarding legislation is by way of interest, and does not purport to offer legal advice or comprise a complete account of the legislation or regulations. If legal advice is required, consult a lawyer qualified to practise in your jurisdiction.

Government Health Care Funding

✦ information on government health care funding in Alberta, British Columbia, Ontario and Québec

Governing Bodies

✦ addresses and telephone numbers of governing bodies, where they exist

✦ these are the offices you may contact to make a complaint or to check if your midwife is registered

Midwifery Associations

✦ addresses and telephone numbers of provincial midwifery associations, which often provide referrals, or whose representatives may discuss the qualifications of practitioners

Midwives

✦ names, addresses and telephone numbers of midwives, listed alphabetically by city or region

NOTE: This publication cannot and does not certify or represent the qualifications of midwives, or the quality of care available from them. In jurisdictions where midwives are required to be registered, we cannot and do not confirm that those listed are registered as required by law.

✦ Alberta

Alberta midwives are in the process of becoming regulated, meaning that there is legislation governing the practice of midwifery, with a governing body being established to register midwives.

Legislation

Midwifery is a designated health discipline under Alberta's *Health Disciplines Act*. Midwives are in the process of becoming regulated under a new Midwifery Regulation, and government officials expect to have a register of midwives by early 1997. Once the register is in place, ensure that your midwife is registered by contacting the Professional & Technical Services office or the Alberta Association of Midwives (see addresses and telephone numbers below).

The Midwifery Regulation requires midwives to complete a program of studies and to pass examinations, as well as to have a minimum level of experience. Experienced midwives without formal training

may be registered if they can demonstrate competence in key areas.

Use of Title

A person registered pursuant to the Regulation will be entitled to use the name "midwife"(section 7).

Scope of Practice

Section 8 of the Regulation provides that a midwife may:

(a) provide counselling and education related to childbearing,

(b) carry out assessments necessary to confirm and monitor pregnancies,

(c) advise on and secure further assessments for the earliest possible identification of pregnancies at risk,

(d) identify conditions in the woman, fetus or newborn that necessitate consultation with or referral to a physician or other health professional,

(e) care for the woman and monitor the condition of the fetus during labour,

(f) conduct spontaneous vaginal births,

(g) examine and care for the newborn in the immediate postpartum period,

(h) care for the woman in the postpartum period and advise her and her family on newborn and infant care and family planning,

(i) take emergency measures when necessary,

(j) perform, order or interpret screening and diagnostic tests in accordance with Schedule 1(Schedule 1 of the Regulation lists the types of tests that may be taken and the data that may be interpreted)

(k) perform episiotomies and amniotomies and repair episiotomies and lacerations not involving the anus, anal sphincter, rectum and urethra,

(l) prescribe and administer drugs in accordance with Schedule 2 (Schedule 2 of the Regulation lists the substances), and

(m) on the order of a physician relating to a particular client, administer any drugs by the route and in the dosage specified by the physician.

Primary Health Care Provider/Requirement for Medical Consultation

In regard to a normal pregnancy, a midwife may, in accordance with guidelines approved by the Board of the College, engage in the practice of midwifery as a primary health care provider. If medical conditions exist or arise during pregnancy that may require management by physician, a midwife must consult with a physician in accordance with Board guidelines. If such management is required, the midwife must transfer primary responsibility for care, or aspects of care, to a physician, and may engage in the practice of midwifery in collaboration with the physician, to the extent agreed to by the client, physician and midwife (Regulation, section 9(1),(2),(3)).

Standards of Conduct

A midwife is required to execute all duties in accordance with generally accepted standards of practice and be guided by the welfare and best interests of the client. The midwife must also inform clients regarding the midwife's scope of practice and individual ability, and stay informed of new developments in the field. The midwife must also maintain client confidentiality unless required by legislation or court order to disclose information.

Practice Review Committee

The Regulation establishes a Practice Review Committee consisting of midwives, consumer representatives and a physician to conduct reviews of the practice of a midwife in accordance with College guidelines.

Liability Insurance

Midwives are required to carry professional liability insurance with an insurer acceptable to the Board.

Place of Birth

A midwife may provide services in a variety of settings.

NOTE: For those living in southern Alberta, women may also give birth at the Briar Hill Birthing Center in Calgary, with assistance from any midwife who has applied for registration, until the registration process is complete. The address is: 1616 20A Street NW, Calgary, Alberta T2N 2L5; Tel: 403-284-5950.

Government Health Care Funding

As of 1996, midwifery was not covered under Alberta Health. The cost for pre-natal and post-partum care, including about 10 months of visits with two midwives in attendance at birth, is $800-1,200. Some midwives charge additional costs for water births, or out-of-town births. As midwives become registered, decisions on government funding and hospital privileges will be made by each of Alberta's 17 Regional Health Authorities. As a result, funding may not be uniformly available throughout the province. This is a cause for concern among midwives and their supporters in Alberta, who are actively lobbying for uniform coverage.

Registry of Midwives

Professional & Technical Services
Alberta Ministry of Labour
8th Floor, 10808 - 99th Ave
Edmonton, Alberta T5K 0G5
Tel: 403-422-5685 (outside Edmonton, call toll-free 310-0000)
Fax: 403-427-8686

Contact this office of the provincial government for referrals once the register of midwives is in place. Officials expect the register to be complete by early 1997. This office will also provide information on the formation of a governing committee to handle disciplinary matters until a College of Midwives is established.

Alberta Associations & Organizations

Alberta Association of Midwives
PO Box 1705
Main Post Office
Edmonton, Alberta T5J 2P1
Tel: 403-437-5579

The association is the professional body representing Alberta's midwives. The association will provide assistance in choosing a midwife, as well as information for those seeking a career in midwifery.

Association for Safe Alternatives in Childbirth (ASAC)
Box 1197, Main Post Office
Edmonton, Alberta T5J 2M4
Tel: 403-425-7993

This non-profit association was formed in 1979 as a consumer group representing parents and health care professionals concerned with choices in childbirth. The association recommends that you interview any potential caregiver, including the midwife, at least once before engaging services. If you need help in preparing for an interview, contact the association. The association provides listings of midwives in your area, and has available a 16-page booklet entitled "Preparing for Birth: What every pregnant woman should know".

Calgary Association of Parents and Professionals for Safe Alternatives in Childbirth (CAPSAC)
300-223 12th Ave SW
Calgary, Alberta T2R 0G9
Tel: 403-237-8839

This association, founded in 1975, is dedicated to the recognition and implementation of midwifery, and safe family-centred maternity care. It holds meetings on the third Wednesday of every second month at 7:30 p.m.

Midwifery Regulation Advisory Committee
Alberta Ministry of Labour
8th Floor, 10808 - 99th Ave
Edmonton, Alberta T5K 0G5
Tel: 403-422-5685 (outside Edmonton, call toll-free 310-0000)
Fax: 403-427-8686

Alberta Midwives

NOTE: Check the credentials of your midwife (see above, "Questions to Ask"). This publication cannot and does not certify or represent the qualifications of midwives, or the quality of care available from them.

CALGARY AND AREA

Birth Partnership
Allyjan, Arlette; Fraser, Bobbie;
Harvey, Sheila
By Appointment 403-246-8845

Birth Wise Midwifery Care
Day, Sara; Robb, Karen;
Fraser, Sharyne (Innisfail)
By Appointment 403-276-2355

Briar Hill Birth Centre
1616 20A St NW 403-284-5950

Calgary & District Midwifery Associates
Lenstra, Patty; Moulton, Meryl;
Salkeld, Penny; West, Joy
1616 20A St NW 403-289-8334

Calgary Midwifery Collective
Dowell, Susan; Smulders, Evonne
By Appointment 403-270-0440

Foothills Nurse Midwifery Program
Allyjan, Arlette; Fraser, Bobbie;
Harvey, Sheila; Lenstra, Patty;
Moulton, Meryl; Salkald, Penny;
West, Joy
By Appointment 403-670-1341

Galbraith, Kathy (Lethbridge)
By Appointment 403-756-3879

MacLagan, Cherry (Rolling Hills)
By Appointment 964-2010

Pettersson, Jo
Canmore 403-678-6009

EDMONTON AND AREA

Classic Health Care
Ellis, Maureen
10576-113 St 403-421-4372

Gibbons, Donna
By Appointment 403-426-3936

Greenlagh, Joanna
By Appointment 403-922-5593

Harness, Cathy
By Appointment 403-464-2893

Natural Birth
Gostkowski, Marthe
By Appointment 403-439-3200

Passages
Flanagan, Kerstin; Lester, Wendy;
Moore, Linda; Scriver, Barbara;
Walker, Noreen
202-10518-82nd Ave 403-431-0181

Tutt, Marie
By Appointment 403-426-3936

With Woman
Damsma, Annita; James, Susan;
Pullin, Sandy
By Appointment 403-425-0916

RED DEER AND CENTRAL ALBERTA

The Birth Place
Sharyne Fraser; Cheri Purpur
By Appointment 403-342-4661

✦ British Columbia

B.C. midwives are in the process of becoming regulated, meaning that legislation and a regulation is in place to allow for the registration of qualified midwives. The College of Midwives of British Columbia is the governing body, established to register midwives. In the Fall of 1996, the College is scheduled to begin licensing midwives who meet registration requirements.

Legislation

Midwifery is designated as a health profession under the provincial *Health Professions Act*, and midwives are regulated under the *Midwives Regulation*. Following are highlights of this regulation.

Reserved Title

Only persons registered as midwives with the College of Midwives of B.C. may use the title "midwife." (section 3)

Scope of Practice

Subject to any bylaws made by the College board, registered midwives may:
(a) assess, monitor and care for women during normal pregnancy, labour, delivery and the post-partum period,
(b) counsel, support and advise women during pregnancy, labour, delivery and the post-partum period,
(c) manage spontaneous normal vaginal deliveries,
(d) care for, assess and monitor the healthy newborn, and
(e) provide advice and information regarding care for newborns and young infants and deliver contraceptive services during the 3 months following birth.

Reserved Acts

Subject to section 14 of the *Health Professions Act* (which exempts other professions and voluntary emergency first aid), section 5(1) of the regulation permits only registered midwives to:
(a) conduct internal examinations of women during pregnancy, labour, delivery and the post-partum period,
(b) manage spontaneous normal vaginal deliveries, and
(c) perform episiotomies and amniotomies during established labour and repair episiotomies and simple lacerations.

The above section does not apply on a reserve to an aboriginal person who practised aboriginal midwifery prior to the coming into force of this regulation.

Limitations on Practice

Registered midwives must advise clients to consult a medical practitioner for a medical examination during the first three months of pregnancy. The midwife must consult with a medical practitioner regarding any deviations from the normal course of pregnancy, labour, delivery and the post-partum period that indicate pathology, and transfer responsibility when necessary.

While home births are permitted only as part of the province's home birth demonstration project until December 31, 1998, this does not apply on a reserve to an aboriginal person who practised aboriginal midwifery prior to the coming into force of the regulation.

Government Health Care Funding

As of printing, the B.C. government had committed to funding of midwifery in principle, but had not determined the amount. For information on funding, contact the B.C. Ministry of Health, Communication & Public Affairs, 604-952-1881.

B.C. Model of Midwifery Practice

The midwifery model of practice in B.C. is a community-based primary care system, incorporating the principles of continuity of care, informed consumer choice, and choice of birth setting.

Governing Body

College of Midwives of B.C.
F-502-4500 Oak Street
Vancouver, B.C. V6H 3N1
Tel: 604-875-3580
Fax: 604-875-3581

Call for information about the registration or education of midwives. The College regulates the profession of midwifery, including the registration of qualified midwives.

British Columbia Associations

Midwives Association of B.C.
Box 55, 2147 Commercial Dr
Vancouver, B.C. V5N 4B3
Tel: 604-736-5976

This is the professional association of midwives in B.C. Contact the association for information, or to hear a recorded message giving the names of midwives in B.C.

Midwifery Task Force
1108 Rose Street
Vancouver, B.C. V5L 4K8
Tel: 604-251-5976

This group is the consumer body of the midwifery movement of B.C.

Aboriginal Midwifery

A Committee on Aboriginal Midwifery is in the process of being established. Under the Midwives Regulation, aboriginal midwifery means traditional aboriginal midwifery practices, including the use of traditional herbs, medicines and other cultural and spiritual practices. It also includes contemporary aboriginal midwifery practices. Under the Midwifery Regulation, and subject to the bylaws of the College board, aboriginal registrants may practise aboriginal midwifery. An aboriginal person who practised aboriginal midwifery prior to the coming into force of the Regulation may, on a reserve, perform acts otherwise reserved for registered midwives. This includes internal examinations, management of normal vaginal delivers and performance of episiotomies and amniotomies during established labour, and their repair.

✦ British Columbia Midwives

NOTE: Check the credentials of your midwife (see above, "Questions to Ask"). This publication cannot and does not certify or represent the qualifications of midwives, or the quality of care available from them.

LANGLEY

Barkham, A.
23048-64th Ave 604-533-7101

Spence, Sandra
By Appointment 604-533-1705

MAPLE RIDGE

Cooper, Jean
11294 Burnett St 604-467-0531

SALT SPRING ISLAND

Lyons, Jeanne
189 Walkers Hook
Ganges 604-537-5930

Martin, Heather
184 Hillcrest Dr
Fulford Harbour 604-653-9729

Ramsey, Maggie, RN
115 King Rd
Fulford Harbour 604-653-4561

VANCOUVER & LOWER MAINLAND

**The Midwifery Group
(3 locations):**
Main Street Clinic
Vancouver 604-877-7766
8th Avenue Clinic
Vancouver 604-731-4733
White Rock Clinic 604-536-6315

Thompson, Patti
3-3051 W 8th Ave
Vancouver 604-733-0675

Women's Hospital Midwifery Program
Little, Debra (Director)
By Appointment 604-875-3095

VICTORIA

Lyons, Luba
35 Cambridge St 604-381-1977

Maguson, Caroline
By Appointment 604-383-7438

Millar Lewis, K.
2823 Dysart Rd 604-384-8460

Ray, Barbara
3042 Albany St 604-384-9062

SECHELT AND THE SUNSHINE COAST

Clemens, Wendy
3312 Beach
Roberts Creek 604-885-2950

Olsson, D.
459 Central
Granthams Landing 604-886-8847

COURTENAY/MERVILLE

Kozlick, D.
By Appointment 604-338-1993

Minard, F.
6973 Farnham Rd
Merville 604-337-5891

✦ Manitoba

The government has made a commitment to regulate midwifery in Manitoba. Currently, a person who acts as a midwife is deemed to be practising medicine, which is prohibited without a licence under the province's *Medical Act*, sections 2(1)(d), 15.

Manitoba Associations

Association of Manitoba Midwives
Norwood, PO Box 83
Winnipeg, Manitoba R2H 3B8

Manitoba Traditional Midwives' Collective
2-487 Telfer St S
Winnipeg, Manitoba R3G 2Y4
Tel: 204-775-3862

✦ Newfoundland

Currently, the practice of midwifery is not regulated in Newfoundland. Newfoundland's *Medical Act* restricts the practice of medicine to registered medical practitioners. The Act's definition of the practice of medicine includes obstetrics. There is legislation, *An Act Respecting the Practice of Midwifery, 1920*, which would allow for the establishment of a Midwifery Board, but the Act is not in use. The 1994 final report of the Provincial Advisory Committee on Midwifery, presented to the Deputy Minister of Health, called for the replacement of this Act with a new Midwifery Act to cover the full scope of midwifery care and to license midwives.

The government has not acted on this recommendation. However, the government does recognize the practice of midwifery by nurse-midwives at the Grenfell Regional Health Services in St. Anthony and Goose Bay.

Newfoundland and Labrador Association

Newfoundland and Labrador Midwives Association
132 Cumberland Cr
St. John's, Newfoundland A1B 3M5
Tel: 709-739-6319
e-mail: pherbert@morgan.ucs.mun.ca

✦ Newfoundland Midwives

NOTE: Check the credentials of your midwife (see above, "Questions to Ask"). This publication cannot and does not certify or represent the qualifications of midwives, or the quality of care available from them.

ST. ANTHONY/GOOSE BAY

Grenfell Regional Health Services (GRHS)
West St 709-454-0347/3333

✦ Northwest Territory

Midwifery is currently not regulated in the Northwest Territories, but such regulation is under consideration as part of a review of the province's *Medical Profession Act*. The Act prohibits the practice of medicine without a licence. The practice of medicine is defined in the Act to include obstetrics.

✦ Nova Scotia

Midwifery is not currently regulated in Nova Scotia. The new *Medical Act* (1996) creates an offence of practising medicine without a licence. The definition of the practice of medicine includes offering or undertaking to perform any obstetrical procedure or surgical operation. Midwives in this province practise a more restricted form of midwifery.

Nova Scotia Association

Association of Nova Scotia Midwives
Box 968
Wolfville, Nova Scotia B0P 1X0
Tel: 902-678-5446

✦ Ontario

Ontario midwives are regulated, meaning that there is a governing body established under provincial law to register and discipline midwives. Midwifery is a fully-funded health care service (see below, "Government Health Care Funding").

Legislation

Midwives are regulated under the Ontario *Midwifery Act, 1991*, and the regulations made under the Act. The Act defines the practice of midwifery as "the assessment and monitoring of women during pregnancy, labour and the post-partum period and of their newborn babies, the provision of care during normal pregnancy, labour and post-partum period and the conducting of spontaneous normal vaginal deliveries" (section 3).

Midwives are a self-governing health profession under the *Regulated Health Professions Act, 1991*. Aboriginal midwives providing traditional midwifery services to aboriginal persons or members of an aboriginal community are exempt from the Act. The Act sets out the duties of the governing body (in this case, the College of Midwives of Ontario) in governing the practice of the profession and protecting the public interest (Schedule 2, *Health Professions Procedural Code*). This includes procedures for investigating complaints and disciplining members (to make a complaint, see below, "Governing Body - College of Midwives").

Restricted Title

No person other than a member of the College of Midwives may use the title "midwife" or a variation, or hold himself or herself out as a person qualified to practise midwifery. However, an aboriginal person who provides traditional midwifery services may use the title "aboriginal midwife", or a variation or abbreviation.

Authorized Acts

Under section 4 of the Act, Midwives registered with the College are authorized, subject to the terms, conditions and limitations on his or her certificate of registration, in:

1. Managing labour and conducting spontaneous normal vaginal deliveries.

2. Performing episiotomies and amniotomies and repairing episiotomies and lacerations, not involving the anus, anal sphincter, rectum, urethra and periurethral area.

3. Administering, by injection or inhalation, a substance designated in the regulations.

4. Putting an instrument, hand or finger beyond the labia majora during pregnancy, labour and the post-partum period.

5. Taking blood samples from newborns by skin pricking or from women from veins or by skin pricking.

6. Inserting urinary catheters into women.

7. Prescribing drugs designated in the regulations.

Government Health Care Funding

Midwifery services are completely funded through the Ontario Ministry of Health. Show your Ontario Health Card at your midwifery clinic for coverage. If you require an Ontario Health Card, call 416-482-1111 within Metro Toronto. Outside Toronto, check your Blue Pages under Ministry of Health, Health Insurance, Customer Service.

Ontario Midwifery Program

The Ministry of Health organizes and funds the Ontario Midwifery Program. The Ontario midwifery practice is based on three principles: continuity of care during pregnancy, labour and the six weeks following birth; informed choice; and choice of birthplace. Ontario midwives must have either a baccalaureate degree in health sciences (midwifery) from a university in Ontario or equivalent qualifications. They must also have current clinical experience and professional liability insurance. In Ontario, a woman may choose a home birth or hospital birth, provided the midwife has hospital privileges. A midwife with such privileges may admit and discharge their own clients and attend at hospital deliveries as the primary caregiver. Midwives are also entitled to order tests during pregnancy, such as blood and urine tests, and ultrasound as needed. They also have access to certain medications, such as analgesics for control of labour pain.

For questions related to government policies on midwifery, funding and integration of midwifery services into health care settings, contact Bonnie Heath, Coordinator, Ontario Midwifery Program, Ontario Ministry of Health, at 416-327-7540. The funding body is Lebel Midwifery Care at 416-585-7709.

Ontario Governing Body

The College of Midwives of Ontario
2195 Yonge St, 4th Fl
Toronto, Ontario M4S 2B2
416-327-0874

Call the College to ensure that your midwife is registered, or to request an updated list of registered midwives (see below "Listings"). The College regulates the practice of the profession, sets the standards of practice and governs the members in accordance with Ontario law.

Ontario Associations & Organizations

Association of Ontario Midwives
2050 Sheppard Ave E, Ste 205
North York, Ontario M2J 5B3
Tel: 416-494-4819

This is the professional body for Ontario midwives. The association will provide information about midwifery and provide the name of a midwifery practice in your area. Activities include promoting midwifery as an integral part of the health care system. Membership is open to professionals and interested members of the public

The Ontario Midwifery Consumer Network
Tel: 905-648-0698 (Barb Guran)

This is a voluntary consumer group working to ensure accessible midwifery care for Ontario women. Its role includes government lobbying and public education. Information brochures are available in 6 languages.

Aboriginal Midwifery
As noted, an aboriginal person who provides traditional midwifery services is exempt from regulation by the College. For more information, contact the Aboriginal Health Office at 416-314-5513.

Ontario Midwives

NOTE: For the names of 1996 graduates of the Ontario Midwifery Education Programme, who will be registered as midwives in the Fall of 1996, contact the College of Midwives of Ontario (see above, "Governing Body"). Check the credentials of your midwife (see above, "Questions to Ask"). This publication cannot and does not certify or represent the qualifications of midwives, or the quality of care available from them. We cannot and do not confirm that those listed are registered as required by law.

ALLISTON

Caring Hands Midwifery Services
Laverty, Dianne
103 Victoria St W 705-435-2406

ELMSDALE

Birth Options Resource Network Midwifery Services
Columbia-Rains, Susan
R.R.#1, Box 7, Site 3C 705-636-0685

HAMILTON AREA

Hamilton Midwifery Care
Kaufman, Karyn; McDonald, Helen; Penczak, Kathy; McNiven,Patty; Naik,Mina; Porteous, Rena; Ristok, Jennifer; Shaver, Dianne; Wylie, Mary
40 Forest Ave, Hamilton 905-524-5833

KINGSTON AREA

Community Midwives of Kingston
Hunking,Mary; Rose, Susan; Sexsmith, Kelly
303 Bagot St, #106 613-546-5912

KITCHENER-WATERLOO AREA

Community Midwifery Services
Molnar, Mary
23 Dill St, Kitchener 519-578-3292

New Life Midwifery Associates
Honey, Carol
174 Victoria St, Kitchener . . .519-576-3067

Waterloo-Oxford-Wellington Midwives
St. Jacobs Family Birthing Home
Cressman, Elsie; Cressman, Evelyn
Entwistle,Royce; Fioravanti, Maggie
General Delivery, St. Jacobs .519-664-1680

LONDON AREA

Womancare Associates
Johnson, Elana
458 Queens Ave, #2, London 519-645-0316

MARKDALE

Midwives' Cooperative (2 clinics - also see Stayner)
Keffer, Heather; Kryzanauskas, Michelle; Morrow, Mary; Nichols, Luci; Seddon, Freda
20 Toronto St 519-986-4296

MILLBANK AREA

Countryside Midwifery Services
Ropp, Violet
PO Box 70 519-595-4815

MISSISSAUGA (NORTH AND WEST SUBURBAN TORONTO)

Midwifery Care Associates
Duncan, Kathi; Hutton, Eileen; Leslie, Mary Ann; Meltzer, Shirley; Pemberton, Ellen; Rogers, Judy
120 Traders Blvd E, #208 . . .905-890-4914

OTTAWA AREA

Midwifery Collective
Daviss, Betty Anne
36 Glen Ave, Ottawa 613-730-0282

Midwifery Group of Ottawa
Bandrowska-Maloney, Teresa; Parkin, Diane; Soderstrom,Bobbi; Teevan, Jan
11 Rosemont Ave, #408 613-729-9957

PETERBOROUGH AREA

Community Midwives of Peterborough
Kilroy, Katrina
312 Rubidge St, Unit A 705-743-9032

Kawartha Community Midwives
Mews, Charlotte; Howlett, Susan; Mory, Jaylene
190 Charlotte St, Unit C 705-745-7640

POWASSAN (NORTH BAY AREA)

Birth Care
Wheeler, Ava
238 King St N 705-724-2229

SARNIA/LAMBTON COUNTY

Midwifery Services of Sarnia/Lambton
Smith, Debbie
420 East St N, #12
Sarnia 519-337-2229

SEAFORTH AREA

Huron Community Midwifery Services
Wilts, Susan
R.R. #1, Auburn 519-523-4295

STAYNER

Midwives' Cooperative (2 clinics - also see Markdale)
Keffer, Heather; Kryzanauskas,Michelle; Morrow,Mary; Nichols, Lucie; Seddon, Freda
235 Main St W, Box 190 . . .705-428-6903

STRATFORD AREA

Stratford Midwifery Clinic
Tanner, Louise
206-386 Cambria St 519-272-2640

SUDBURY AREA

Sudbury Community Midwifery Practice
Pratique communautaire de sage-femme de Sudbury
Brechin, Heather; Nixon, Anne;
Rose, Christine; Tyson,Holliday;
Vandersloot, Arlene
124 Cedar St, #209 705-670-2763

THUNDER BAY AREA

Thunder Bay Community Midwifery Practice
Kemeny, Barbara
215 Van Norman St,
rear office 807-344-6754

TORONTO

Community Midwives of Toronto
Lynch, Bridget; MacGillivray, Jay;
Roch, Barbara; Ruskin, Catherine
344 Bloor St W, #201 416-944-9366

Midwife Alliance
Bradley, Anna Jean; Burton, Heather;
Gallagher, Shawn
2238 Dundas St W, #204 ...416-534-9161

Midwives Collective of Toronto
Allemang, Elizabeth; Katherine, Wendy;
Tate, Merryn; Van Wagner, Vicki
344 Dupont St, #403 416-963-8842

Riverdale Community Midwives
Moscovitch, Linda; Sharpe, Mary;
Sternberg, Chris
457A Danforth Ave 416-461-7334

UNIONVILLE (YORK REGION)

Midwifery Services of York
Kilthei,Jane; Lenske, Larry
4581 Highway 7
E, #103-F 905-470-9885

WHITBY

Midwifery Services of Durham
Cameron, Carol; Cannon, Peggy;
Smith, Christine
103-1/2 Mary St W 905-430-9581

✦ Prince Edward Island

Midwifery is currently not regulated in Prince Edward Island. The province's *Medical Act* prohibits the practice of medicine without a licence, with obstetrics included in the definition of the 'practice of medicine' (sections 1,56).

Prince Edward Island Association

Prince Edward Island Midwives' Association
PO Box 756
Cornwall, PEI C0A 1H0

✦ Québec

A midwifery pilot project is currently under way and the government is to decide in 1998 whether to legalize midwifery. In 1990, the National Assembly adopted an act authorizing the practice of midwifery on an experimental basis in eight pilot projects managed by a health care institution such as a hospital. At each birth centre, the Consel multidisciplinaire de la pratique des sage-femmes (consisting of midwives, physicians, a nurse and a user) supervise the practice and handle any complaints. There are currrently seven projects in operation.

Legislation

The *Act respecting the Practice of Midwifery within the framework of the Pilot Projects* authorizes midwives working in the birth centres to "provide the required care and services to a woman during pregnancy, labour, delivery and the postnatal period" (section 2). Birth centres are also subject to a regulation, adopted by order in council of the Québec Cabinet, which stipulates the circumstances in which a physician must be consulted during the pregnancy and the mother or baby transferred during the birthing process. The regulation defines the obstetrical and neonatal risks. A second regulation outlines the general standards of competence and training of midwives.

Scope of Practice

The practice of midwifery includes, but is not limited to, prenatal and postnatal counselling of the parents,

preventive care, detection of abnormal conditions in the woman or newborn child, the delivery, the provision of care to the woman and the newborn child, and family planning.

Government Health Care Funding

Complete government health funding is available for midwifery services through Quebec's Pilot Project.

Certification of Midwives

The midwives in the pilot project have been certified by the Comité d'admission à la pratique des sages-femmes. The committee is composed of a physician, nurse, midwives and representatives from educational institutes and the general population appointed by the government after consultation. Midwives must first complete an examination process and participate in a program to update their skills and knowledge.

Birth Centres

A maximum of 350 women give birth annually at a birth centre. Clients visit the centre frequently during pregnancy to become familiar with all the midwives and other pregnant women and their partners. If a hospital transfer is required, the midwife accompanies the client. The Comité d'admission à pratique des sage-femmes has determined that, because midwives specialize in normal pregnancies and births, the birth centre may be used by healthy women whose pregnancies and births are expected to be free of complications.

Pilot Project Information

Marie Leclerc
Coordonnatrice des projets-pilotes sages-femmes
Ministère de la Santé et des Services sociaux
1075, chemin Sainte-Foy, 2-ième étage
Québec, Québec G1S 2M1
Tel: 418-643-1117
Fax: 418-643-1118

Québec Associations & Organizations

Association des Sages-Femmes du Québec
54 Boul Chambord
Lorraine, Québec J6Z 1P5

Les Sages-Femmes du Québec
BP 354
Station CDN
Montréal, Québec H3S 2S6
Tel: 514-738-8090

✦ Québec Midwives (Maison de Naissances/Birth Centres)

NOTE: Check the qualifications of your midwife (see above, "Questions to Ask"). This publication cannot and does not certify or represent the qualifications of midwives, or the quality of care available from them.

GATINEAU

Madame Céline Dufour, coordonnatrice
Maison de Naissance de l'Outaouais
175, rue Maple 819-669-2323

MONT-JOLI

Madame Johanne Gagnon, coordonnatrice
Maison de Naissances Collette-Julien
40, rue Saint-Paul 418-775-3636

MONTREAL-CENTRE

Madame Christiane Brunelle, coordinnatrice
Maison de Naissances Côte-des-Neiges
6560, Côte-des-Neiges 514-736-2323

POINTE-CLAIRE

Madame Michèle Champagne, coordonnatrice
Maison de naissance
CLSC Lac Saint-Louis
180, avenue Cartier,
3-ième étage 514-697-1199

POVUNGNITUK

Madame Colleen Crosby, coordonnatrice
Centre de
Santé Innulitsivik 819-988-2957

SAINT-ROMUALD

Madame Raymonde Gagnon, coordonnatrice
Maison de Naissances Mimosa
182, rue de l'Eglise 418-839-0205

SHERBROOKE

Madame Hélène Cornellier, coordonnatrice
Centre de Maternité de l'Estrie
205, rue Murray 819-564-0588

✦ Saskatchewan

The introduction of legislation to regulate midwifery is being considered in Saskatchewan. In the meantime, midwives are not regulated, and engaging in the practice of midwifery is an offence under Saskatchewan's *Medical Profession Act, 1981* (sections 2, 80).

Saskatchewan Association

Midwives' Association of Saskatchewan
2836 Angus St
Regina, Saskatchewan S4S 1N8
Tel: 306-586-2241

✦ Yukon Territory

Legislation to regulate midwifery is currently being developed. In the meantime, midwifery is not regulated. Under the *Medical Profession Act*, a person not registered under the Act who practises or professes to practise medicine is liable on summary conviction to fine or imprisonment, or both. The practice of medicine is defined in the act to include the practice of obstetrics.

Naturopathic Medicine

WHAT IS NATUROPATHIC MEDICINE

Naturopathic medicine is a system of diagnosing, treating and preventing disease without the use of drugs or surgery. The philosophy is founded on the healing power of nature, and naturopathic doctors use a variety of natural methods and substances to support and stimulate the body's inherent self-healing ability. The Ontario Naturopathic Association states that the naturopathic physician views the individual as an integral whole, and symptoms of disease as "warning signals of improper functioning of the body and unfavourable lifestyle habits." The goal of Naturopathic Medicine is to treat the underlying causes of illness, rather than suppress symptoms, and to educate patients toward preventive lifestyles.

Naturopathic medicine, as a distinct profession, was established in North America by Benedict Lust, a German immigrant, who incorporated the first school of naturopathic medicine in 1905 in New York state. Naturopaths who are qualified naturopathic doctors (N.D.s) in provinces where they are regulated (British Columbia, Manitoba, Ontario, and Saskatchewan) may act as primary care providers, trained to work in cooperation with all other health care practitioners. They have received four years of training from a college recognized by the province's governing body, and have passed licensing examinations. Many naturopathic physicians are also licensed chiropractors.

As well, there are practitioners who are not regulated and who also use the titles of naturopath, or other titles such as natural healer, natural health consultant, or holistic practitioner. The amount of education received by these practitioners varies widely, and it is often less than the four years required of naturopaths where they are regulated. These educational programs may not include medical training in diagnosis or clinical training. In Québec, for example, naturopthic medicine is practised by two groups - naturopaths and naturothérapeutes. While the terms are sometimes used interchangeably, members of the first group are often considered general practitioners trained to offer a range of holistic health care services, while the consultants (naturothérapeutes) are specialists in a particular technique, such as massage. However, neither group receives the four years of training required in provinces where naturopaths are regulated and neither is trained to diagnose medical problems, according to L'Association des Diplômes en Naturopathie du Québec. The initials N.D. are sometimes used to refer to naturopaths with a diploma in Québec, but these initials do not signify that the practitioners are naturopathic doctors (see below, "Naturopathic Medicine Education").

BENEFITS OF NATUROPATHIC MEDICINE

Qualified naturopathic physicians, in provinces where they are regulated, are primary care providers trained to diagnose and treat acute and chronic illnesses, and to recognize conditions which require conventional medical treatment. Naturopaths treat colds, flus, ear infections, food sensitivities, chronic fatigue, depression, anorexia and addiction, muscle aches, diabetes, and immune deficiency disease. Many naturopathic doctors work with medical doctors, dentists and chiropractors to complement their treatments.

Naturopathic doctors commonly provide the following treatments: acupuncture, botanical medicine, clinical nutrition (use of diets, vitamins and supplements), homeopathic medicine (use of highly diluted natural substances to stimulate the body's self-healing abilities), lifestyle counselling, hydrotherapy (therapeutic use of water to affect circulation and healing), soft tissue and bone techniques to restore muscle and posture alignment, ultra-sound, sinewave therapy (muscle stimulation) and magneto therapy (regeneration for fractures and nerve damage).

Diagnosis

Diagnosis is a critical issue in health care. Qualified naturopathic physicians, in provinces where they are regulated, take your medical history and perform physical examinations, using standard diagnostic instruments and laboratory tests. Naturopathic doctors emphasize the importance of patients being diagnosed as well by conventional medical doctors, particularly in cases of serious illness, although opinions may vary on this issue. In Ontario, naturopathic physicians currently may not order certain diagnostic tests, and instead they must arrange for their patients to obtain X-rays and CAT-scans from medical physicians or chiropractors.

QUESTIONS TO ASK

✦ Is your naturopathic doctor registered? This question applies only if you live in a province where naturopathic physicians are regulated (B.C., Manitoba, Ontario and Saskatchewan). You can check by contacting the governing body in your province (see addresses and telephone numbers below, "Naturopathic Medicine in Your Province - Governing Body").

✦ How much training has your naturopathic doctor received, and from which college? This question is particularly important if you live in a province where naturopathy is not regulated (Alberta, New Brunswick, Newfoundland, Nova Scotia, Prince Edward Island, Québec and the Territories).

NOTE: The names of colleges in Canada and the U.S. are are listed below, along with a notation as to whether they are recognized by the governing bodies in provinces where naturopathic doctors are regulated (see below, "Naturopathic Medicine Education"). If your naturopathic doctor has been trained elsewhere, you may wish to ask about the extent of the training in diagnosis and treatment.

✦ Is your naturopathic doctor a member of a professional association? You may wish to contact the association to discuss your practitioner's qualifications. Again, this question is particularly important if you live in a province where naturopathic doctors are not regulated. Many associations also give referrals (see below "National Association" and "Naturopathic Medicine in Your Province - Association")

NOTE: Bear in mind that associations do not necessarily check the qualifications of their members. Also note that these associations are not governing bodies established by legislation to register and discipline practitioners.

✦ How much experience does your practitioner have, and does it include treatment of your particular condition? What were the results?

✦ Does your practitioner emphasize a particular form of treatment, such as homeopathic medicine, or specialize in pediatrics, women's health, sports medicine or palliative care? Some naturopathic doctors are also registered chiropractors.

✦ Does your practitoner have professional and patient references?

NOTE: While reputable practitioners respect their patients' confidentiality, they may arrange for a patient to contact you.

✦ Is naturopathic treatment appropriate for you? Under what circumstances will your naturopath refer you to a medical physician or other health professional?

✦ What is the estimated number of treatments required for your condition, and what are the fees for consultations and visits?

NOTE: Only residents of B.C. have partial government health funding. If you live in B.C., ask if your practitioner is 'opted in'. If not, your share of the fee is higher (see below, "Naturopathic Medicine in Your Province - B.C.").

GOVERNMENT REGULATION

Regulation means that there is provincial legislation establishing a professional governing body. This governing body, usually called a College, is given a duty in

law to protect the public. Governing bodies are established to ensure that regulated practitioners meet specific standards before they practise, to investigate complaints, and to take disciplinary action against practitioners where appropriate.

Provinces That Regulate Naturopathic Doctors

In Canada, naturopathic physicians are regulated and licensed in British Columbia, Manitoba, Ontario and Saskatchewan, with legislation in these provinces establishing governing bodies responsible for registering qualified practitioners and disciplining them. Call the governing body in your province to ensure that your naturopathic doctor is registered and therefore has met specified educational standards, or to make a complaint (see below, "Naturopathic Medicine in Your Province - Governing Body").

For more information regarding regulation of naturopathic medicine in British Columbia, Manitoba, Ontario, and Saskatchewan see below, "Naturopathic Medicine in Your Province".

Provinces That Do Not Regulate Naturopathic Doctors

In all other provinces and territories, naturopaths are not regulated as practitioners (Alberta, New Brunswick, Newfoundland, Northwest Territories, Nova Scotia, Prince Edward Island, Québec and the Yukon). This means that there is no legislation establishing a governing body responsible for registering qualified naturopaths and disciplining them. This also means that there are no minimum educational standards for those calling themselves naturopaths or naturopathic doctors, although some associations set professional standards for their members. Each of these provinces and territories has legislation restricting medical practice, with varying definitions of what constitutes the practice of medicine.

GOVERNMENT HEALTH CARE FUNDING

B.C. is the only province that provides government health care funding for treatments by a registered naturopathic physician (see below "Naturopathic Medicine in Your Province - B.C. - Government Health Care Funding").

WORKERS' COMPENSATION BOARDS

Contact the board in your province to determine if naturopathic treatment is covered and considered appropriate to your case.

PRIVATE HEALTH INSURANCE COVERAGE

Many private health insurance companies cover naturopathic treatment under their extended health care plans. Consult your policy or speak with your agent.

NATIONAL ASSOCIATION

The Canadian Naturopathic Association
4174 Dundas St W, Ste 304
Etobicoke, Ontario M8X 1X3
Tel: 416-233-1043
Fax: 416-233-2924

This association provides general information on naturopathic medicine, and refers callers to naturopathic physicians across Canada. It also provides general education information for those interested in becoming naturopathic physicians. The Association represents the interests of naturopathic physicians and promotes naturopathic medicine across Canada. The Alberta Association of Naturopathic Practitioners, British Columbia Naturopathic Association, Manitoba Association of Naturopathic Practitioners, Nova Scotia Naturopathic Association, Ontario Naturopathic Association and the Saskatchewan Association of Naturopathic Physicians are constituent members of the Canadian Naturopathic Association. Its membership includes suppliers of naturopathic products.

For a referral to a naturopathic physician close to you, you may also contact your provincial association.

NATUROPATHIC MEDICINE EDUCATION

For those interested in a career in naturopathic medicine, the Canadian College of Naturopathic Medicine (listed below) is the only college in Canada recognized by the governing bodies of naturopathic physicians in all provinces where they are regulated. Also listed are three colleges in the United States offering programs in naturopathic education. Refer to the notes under each of these U.S. colleges for information on the regulatory bodies that recognize them. The Canadian College of Naturopathic Medicine and the three U.S. colleges each offers a full-time, four-year program in naturopathic medicine.

In provinces where naturopathic doctors are regulated - British Columbia, Manitoba, Ontario and Saskatchewan - they must complete four years of professional training at a recognized college of naturopathic medicine, as well as pass licensing exams. For details on the licensing requirements in these provinces, contact the governing body (see below, "Naturopathic Medicine in Your Province").

In all other provinces - Alberta, New Brunswick, Newfoundland, Nova Scotia, Prince Edward Island, Saskatchewan, Québec, and the Territories - naturopathic doctors are not regulated, and there are no legislated minimum standards for education and training. However, several provincial professional associations set standards comparable to those established in provinces where naturopathic practitioners are regulated. If you are seeking a career in an unregulated province, you should be aware that legislation exists, usually in the form of a *Medical Act* or *Medical Profession Act*, restricting the practice of medicine in these provinces.

In Québec, there are a number of training schools offering a diploma in naturopathy (diplôme de naturopathie), with graduates using the initials N.D. to signify Naturopathe Diplômé. These training programs are frequently offered on a part-time basis over three years. A number of colleges also offer training for natural health consultants ("naturothérapeutes). Many such programs are about three months in length. Contact one of the Québec associations for their lists of recognized schools (see below, "Naturopathic Medicine in Your Province - Québec).

In choosing a training program, one may wish to compare the qualifications of faculty (their education and experience), student-teacher ratios, admission requirements, program content and length, number of clinical hours, and all fees and contract terms, including refund policies. Most provinces have legislation requiring private vocational schools to meet certain minimum standards, often related to financial stability, for the protection of consumers. These requirements vary from province to province, and certain health care training programs are not covered by such legislation. Contact the Ministry of Education or Advanced Education in your province for more information on their policies regarding registration of private vocational schools.

Canadian College of Naturopathic Medicine
2300 Yonge St, Box 2431
18th Floor
Toronto, Ontario M4P 1E4
Tel: 416-486-8584
Fax: 416-484-6821

This is Canada's only four-year, full-time program in naturopathic medicine, awarding the graduating student a Doctor of Naturopathic Medicine (N.D.) diploma. The college, founded in 1978, is recognized by all four provinces that regulate naturopathy, and has gained status as a candidate for accreditation by the Council on Naturopathic Medical Education, a U.S. national accrediting agency. This Council is recognized by the U.S. Secretary of Education. (The status indicates that the College complies with the standards of the Council and will be considered for accreditation). Applicants to the College must have three years of full-time university studies at an accredited institution, including one year of general biology, one year of general chemistry, and one term of organic chemistry, biochemistry and psychology. However, a Bachelor of Science degree is recommended. The curriculum includes studies in homeopathic medicine, nutritional biochemistry, botanical medicine, clinical nutrition, soft tissue manipulation, acupuncture and Oriental medicine, naturopathic assessment, hydrotherapy, radiology, physiology, anatomy, pathology, and physical and clinical diagnosis. The teaching clinic of the

College, open to the public, is the Naturopathc College Clinic in Toronto.

National College of Naturopathic Medicine
11231 S.E. Market St
Portland, Oregon 97216
USA
Tel: 503-255-4860
Fax: 503-257-5929

This college offers a four-year graduate program leading to the granting of the title "Doctor of Naturopathic Medicine" (N.D.) by the Oregon Office of Educational Policy and Planning. The College, founded in 1956, is recognized by all four provinces regulating naturopathic doctors in Canada, and is accredited by the U.S. national accrediting agency, the Council on Naturopathic Medical Education. Admission requirements include a bachelor's degree from a recognized university, with certain required courses. The curriculum includes homeopathy, Chinese medicine, botanical studies, hydrotherapy, nutrition, obstetrics, environmental medicine, anatomy, physiology and pathology. The college offers a Certificate of Homeopathic Therapeutics to candidates who wish to develop a high level of expertise in homeopathic prescribing. The college also offers additional training for students who wish to practise naturopathic obstetrics.

Bastyr University
Naturopathic Medicine Program
144 N.E. 54th St
Seattle, Washington 98105
USA
Tel: 206-523-9585 (ext 110 for admissions)

This university, founded in 1978, offers a four-year program, leading to the Doctor of Naturopathic Medicine (N.D.) degree. It is recognized by all four provinces regulating naturopathic doctors in Canada and is accredited by the U.S. national accrediting body, the Council on

Naturopathic Medical Education. Admission requirements include a minimum of three years of undergraduate study, with certain required courses. The curriculum includes homeopathy, clinical nutrition, Oriental medicine, manipulation, hydrotherapy, obstetrics and basic medical sciences. A joint program with the Oriental Medicine Department leads to the N.D. degree and a degree in acupuncture. Students may also earn degrees in clinical nutrition and naturopathic obstetrics.

Southwest College of Naturopathic Medicine and Health Sciences
6535 E. Osborn Rd, Ste 703
Scottsdale, Arizona 85251
USA
Tel: 602-990-7424
Fax 602-990-0337

This college has so far been officially recognized by the regulating bodies in B.C. and Manitoba, two of Canada's four provinces where naturopathic physicians are regulated. Those living in Saskatchewan or Ontario wishing to attend Southwest should check current policy regarding recognition by contacting the provincial governing body (see below, "Naturopathic Medicine in Your Province - Governing Body"). The college was granted status in 1994 as a candidate for accreditation by the Council on Naturopathic Medical Education, the U.S. national accrediting body. The status indicates that the College complies with the standards of the Council and will be considered for accreditation. The College admission requirements include a minimum of three years course work at an accredited university, with minimum grades in particular courses. The curriculum includes anatomy, physiology, pathology, hydrotherapy, homeopathy, botanical medicine, natural childbirth, radiology and clinical diagnosis.

✦ Naturopathic Medicine in Your Province

Each province is listed alphabetically below, with the following information:

Legislation

✦ procedures that your naturopath is permitted to perform under law, where such laws exists

✦ other legal requirements, where they exist, such as prohibitions on unregistered persons from practising naturopathic medicine

NOTE: The information given regarding legislation is by way of interest, and does not purport to offer legal advice or comprise a complete account of the legislation or regulations. If legal advice is required, consult a lawyer qualified to practise in your jurisdiction.

Government Health Care Funding

✦ details on government health care funding for naturopathic medicine in B.C., the only province where it is available

Governing Bodies

✦ addresses and telephone numbers of regulatory bodies, where they exist

✦ these are the bodies to contact to make a complaint or to check if your naturopath is registered

Provincial Associations

✦ addresses and telephone numbers of naturopathic practitioners' associations, which often provide referrals, or with whom you may discuss the qualifications of practitioners

Naturopaths

✦ names, addresses and telephone numbers of naturopaths, listed alphabetically by city

NOTE: Check the credentials of your practitioner (see above, "Questions to Ask"). This publication cannot and does not certify or represent the qualifications of practitioners, or the quality of care available from them. In jurisdictions where practitioners are required to be registered, we cannot and do not confirm that those listed are registered as required by law.

✦ Alberta

Naturopaths are not regulated as practitioners in Alberta. This means that there is no provincial legislation establishing a governing body responsible for registering qualified naturopaths and disciplining them. However, there is an association that sets professional standards for members.

Alberta does have legislation restricting medical practice, which is in the process of being revised to create a system of restricted acts, similar to the concept of the 'controlled act' in Ontario legislation. Only those authorized under the new legislation would be permitted to perform any of the restricted acts.

Alberta Association

Alberta Association of Naturopathic Practitioners
921-17th Ave SW
Calgary, Alberta T2T 0A4
Tel: 403-244-4920

Call the association for a referral or to ensure that your naturopath has been educated to the association's standards. The association recognizes the four-year training programs at the colleges in Portland, Etobicoke, Seattle and Scottsdale (for details regarding these colleges, see above, "Naturopathic Medicine Education").

✦ Alberta Naturopaths

NOTE: The following names were provided by the Alberta Association of Naturopathic Practitioners as registered members who have graduated from schools recognized by the association. However, this publication cannot and does not certify or represent the qualifications of practitioners, or the quality of care available from them.

CALGARY

Arrata, Dr. Eric, ND
#400, 1228 Kensington
Rd NW 403-270-0891

Jensen, Dr. Karen, ND
#4, 1230A-17th Ave SW 403-228-1907

Lofting, Dr. Bruce, ND
3708-54th Ave SW 403-270-3372

Rakhra, Dr. Raj, ND
#304, 1235-17th Ave SW . . .403-244-4941

Scott, Dr. Susan, ND
6620 Huntridge Hill NE 403-295-8547

Skaken, Dr. Ross, ND; Skaken, Dr. Sinnoi, ND
921-17th Ave SW 403-244-4920

EDMONTON

Garner, Dr. Kevin, ND
#106, 9942-82nd Ave 403-439-2522

Pearman, Dr. Robert, ND
10326-81st Ave 403-433-9669

RED DEER

Roy-Poulsen, Dr. Jytte, ND
4907-48th St 403-347-1103

✦ British Columbia

Naturopathic physicians are regulated in B.C., meaning that there is legislation establishing a governing body responsible for registering practitioners who meet its educational standards (see below, "British Columbia Governing Body"). There is government health care coverage under the B.C. Medical Services Plan (see below, "Government Health Care Funding").

Legislation

Naturopaths are regulated under the province's *Naturopaths Act*, which defines naturopathy as the art of healing by natural methods or therapeutics and, "without limiting the generality of the foregoing, for the purposes of this Act, shall be deemed to include the first aid treatment of minor cuts, abrasions and contusions, bandaging and the taking of blood samples" (section 1).

Following are other highlights of the legislation:

Duties and Objects of Governing Body

The legislation establishes the duties and objects of The Association of Naturopathic Physicians of British Columbia. These include serving and protecting the public, superintending the practice of naturopathy, and establishing and enforcing standards of education and professional ethics. The Association also has the object of requiring naturopathic physicians to provide an individual with access to the his or her health care records in appropriate circumstances.

Protection of Title

No person is entitled to practice as a naturopathic physician, drugless physician, sanipractic physician, drugless healer or to convey in any manner that the person is entitled to practise as such unless the person is registered under the Act.

Prohibition of Unregistered Persons to Practise

Unregistered persons who practice naturopathy for hire, gain, reward, remuneration, or the expectation of it, commit an offence.

Prohibition Re Drugs and Surgery

The Act states that nothing in it authorizes a person to prescribe or administer drugs except those defined in regulations, to use or administer anaesthetics, or to practise surgery.

Inspections

Inspectors may investigate the premises of naturopaths without a court order. Court-authorized searches and seizures are also provided for in the Act.

Penalties

Every person who commits an offence under the Act is liable to fines on first and second offences, and imprisonment for third or subsequent offence.

Impact of other Legislation

Nothing in another Act or law of the province prohibits registered naturopathic physicians from practising in accordance with the Act, the rules and regulations. However, naturopathic physicians must abide by the provisions of the province's health legislation imposing duties on physicians regarding contagious or infectious diseases.

Government Health Care Funding

Naturopathic doctors may be "opted in" to the Medical Services Plan of B.C., or "opted out". User fees apply, as set out below, but certain groups are exempt, including those holding a native status card, persons receiving premium assistance, those whose premiums are covered by the Ministry of Social Services and Housing, and refugees. There is also coverage in certain circumstances for house treatments, emergency and prolonged visits. For Plan information, call 1-800-663-7100.

Maximum Number of Annual Visits

The maximum number of visits to a naturopathic physician is 12 per calendar year for those less than 65 years old, and 15 visits per calendar year for those 65 or over.

Naturopathic Physicians who have "Opted In" to the Medical Services Plan

First Office Visit:
Patients pay a $7.50 user fee, and the Plan pays $12.50. If the patient is exempt from user fees (see above), the government pays the entire $20.

Subsequent Office Visit:
Patient pays a $7.50 user fee, and the Plan pays balance of $7.20, for a total of $14.70. If the patient is exempt from user fees, the government pays the entire $14.70.

Naturopathic Physicians who have "Opted Out" of the Medical Services Plan of B.C.

First Office Visit:
The naturopath may charge more than $20. But the government will still pay a maximum $12.50. For example, on a bill of $35, the patient pays $22.50, and the government $12.50. For patients exempt from user fees, the government will pay up to $20, and the patients pay the balance.

Subsequent Office Visits:
The government pays a maximum $7.20, and the patient pays the balance. If the patient is exempt from user fees, the government would pay $14.70 toward subsequent visits.

British Columbia Governing Body

Association of Naturopathic Physicians of B.C.
218-409 Granville St
Vancouver, B.C. V6C 1T2
Tel: 604-688-8236
Fax: 604-688-8476

Call to ensure that your naturopathic physician is registered or to make a complaint. On request, the association will send information on naturopathic education to prospective students.

British Columbia Association

British Columbia Naturopathic Association
204-2786 W 16th Ave
Vancouver, B.C. V6K 3C4
Tel: 604-736-6646
Tel: 604-736-6048

Call for a referral to a naturopathic physician in your area.

✦ British Columbia Naturopaths

NOTE: Check the credentials of your practitioner (see above, "Questions to Ask"). This publication cannot and does not certify or represent the qualifications of practitioners, or the quality of care available from them. We cannot and do not confirm that those listed are registered as required by law.

ABBOTSFORD

Taams, Dr. Pieter C.
30061 Township Line 604-856-5687

Vallee Acupunture Clinic
Vallee, Dr. Brian, ND
3-2664 Gladys Ave 604-859-3311

BURNABY

Burnaby Natural Health Clinic
By Appointment 604-435-6980

COQUITLAM

Johnson, Dr. Marguerite L., ND
126-3030 Lincoln Ave 604-942-0294

Olsen, Dr. Steven, ND
211-3030 Lincoln Ave 604-942-9925

COURTNEY

Braidwood Naturopathic Clinic
Marinaccio, Dr. Heather, ND;
Phillips, Dr. C.G., ND
2-204 N Island Hwy 604-334-0655

CRANBROOK

Kozak, Dr. Loren T., ND
122-11th Ave S 604-426-5228

CUMBERLAND

Kind, Dr. Christopher, ND
3738 Minto 604-336-8349

DUNCAN

Bennett, Dr. Peter, ND
416 Jubilee St 604-748-4217

Dodds, Dr. Cam, ND
109 Kenneth St 604-746-9509

KALEDEN

South Okanagan Naturopathic Clinic
Ure, Dr. Audrey Shanley, ND
100 Dogwood 604-497-6060

KELOWNA

Back & Body Health Centre
Russell, Dr. William, ND
206-2365 Gordon Dr 604-868-8578

Lobay, Dr. Douglas, ND
210-1980 Cooper Rd 604-860-7622

Salloum, Trevor K.
557 Bernard Ave 604-763-5445

Swetlikoff, Dr. Garrett, ND
160-1855 Kirschner Rd 604-868-2205

LADNER

Ladner Natural Health Clinic
Keyzer, Dr. Jacob, ND
4861 Delta 604-946-1424

LANGLEY

Brown, Dr. Timothy, ND
20609 Douglas Cr 604-530-1626

Langley Naturopathic Clinic
Tyler, Dr. Scott, ND
5521-208th St 604-530-3130

Sleigh, Dr. E.R.
20787 Fraser Hwy 604-534-9121

MAPLE RIDGE

Chapell, Dr. Sheree, ND
230-22529 Lougheed Hwy . .604-467-0506

MISSION

Ewing, Dr. Robert J.
8045 Clegg 604-820-8161

NANAIMO

Pacific Holistic Centre
Kuramoto, Dr. Doug, ND
202-55 Victoria Rd 604-753-0280

Yim, Dr. John, ND
450 Juniper 604-755-1930

NANOOSE BAY

Eco-Med Wellness Centre
Kuprowsky, Dr. Stefan, ND
515-1655 Stroulger 604-468-7133

NELSON

Kozak, Dr. Loren T., ND
612 Front St 604-352-1991

Put, Dr. Richard, ND
812 Vernon 604-354-4433

NEW WESTMINSTER

New Westminster Naturopathic Clinic
Isles, Dr. Cynthia, ND
207-800 McBride Blvd 604-522-4204

NORTH VANCOUVER

Delbrook Naturopathic Medical Centre
Bayley, Dr. D., ND; Naesgaard, Dr. Heather
100-3711 Delbrook Ave 604-968-9191

North Shore Naturopathic Clinic Ltd.
Cousins, Dr. Mark, ND; Matsen, Dr. Jonn, ND
156 W 3rd 604-986-7774

PENTICTON

Penticton Naturopathic Clinic
Mazurin, Dr. Alex, ND
106-3310 Skaha Lk Rd 604-492-3181

South Okanagan Naturopathic Clinic
Ure, Dr. Audrey Shanley, ND;
Ure, Dr. Sherry, ND
105 Vancouver Ave 604-493-6060

PORT COQUITLAM

Cashion, Dr. Ken, ND
130-1465 Salisbury 604-941-0744

PORT MOODY

Johnson, Dr. Marguerite
2226 St John's 604-931-1146

RICHMOND

Richmond Naturopathic Medical Clinic
Jheeta, Dr. Raj, ND
230-8211 Ackroyd 604-273-7753

SAANICHTON

Connoly, Dr. Lisa M., ND
6711 Mark Ln 604-652-3770

SALT SPRING

Bennett, Peter, ND
130 McPhilips Ave 604-537-4419

Salt Spring Island Health Clinic
Alsberg, Charles E., ND; Puhky, R.
2551 Fulford-Ganges 604-653-4216

SECHELT

Rochon, Denise, ND
By Appointment 604-885-3150

SIDNEY

Sidney Naturopathic Health Centre
Yam, Dr. C. Peter, ND
2321 James White Blvd . . .604-656-7178

SILVERTON

Azzopardi, Dr. Lisa Ann, ND
613-6th St 604-358-2562

SURREY

Olson, Dr. Scott B., ND
14957-108 Ave 604-588-8706

TRAIL

Hunt, Dr. Jeffrey, ND
1338a Cedar Ave 604-368-6999

VANCOUVER

Ajina, Dr. Nabeel, ND
202-2786 W 16th 604-737-3600

Burrard Intergrated Health Clinic
Wang, Dr. David, ND; Naim, Dr. J;
Szymanski, Dr. Geoff
604-1200 Burrard 604-687-0119

Chan, Dr. Jim, ND
100-3380 Maquinna 604-435-3786

Chow, Dr. Phoebe, ND
2298 Newport 604-327-0021

Dack, L.O.; Feldman, Murray; Gimbel, Susan; South, Dr. L.
2246 Spruce St 604-732-7276

Glew, Dr. Tom, ND; Weiss, Dr. Sid, ND
207-2678 W Broadway 604-738-4085

Herington, Dr. Heather, ND
104-966 W 14th 604-732-4325

Integrative Healing Arts Centre
Brown, Dr. Harold S., ND;
Chan, Dr. Lawrence, ND
958 W 8th Ave 604-738-1012

McGuinness, Dr. Kerry, ND
203-2786 W 16th 604-737-7776

NaturoMed Health Clinic
Dalen, Dr. C.; Martin, Dr. B
200-44D W. Hastings St. . . .604-681-8380

Pacific Coast Naturopathic Centre
Louie, Dr. Laura; Fainstat, Dr. Paula
312-2083 Alma 604-222-2433

Pincott, Dr. Ingrid, ND; Roscoe, Dr. Paulette, ND
108-3195 Granville 604-731-4183

Posen, Dr. Eric, ND
301-958 W 8th 604-738-1019

Reichert, Dr. Ronald, ND
1964 W Broadway 604-737-2611

Soma Therapy Centre
2607 W 16th 604-731-7883

Vancouver Centre For Homeopathy
Klein, Louis H.; South, Dr. Lianne, ND
2246 Spruce St 604-732-7276

Vancouver Naturopathic Clinic
Swetlikoff, Dr. Lorne; Louie, Dr. Laura
105-2786 W 16th Ave 604-738-2111

VERNON

McKinney, Neil, ND
206, 2910-30th Ave 604-549-1400

Okanagan Naturopathic Clinic
Miller, Dr. J. Douglas, ND
3004-33rd St 604-549-3302

Vernon Naturopathic Clinic
Adamson, Dr. Bruce, ND
103, 3401-33rd St 604-542-1040

VICTORIA

Fairfield Naturopathic & Acupuncture Clinic
O'Halloran, Dr. Jane, ND; Rohon, Dr. Juan F.
1255 Fairfield Rd 604-384-9694

Ihara, Dr. Bruce, ND
1075 Matheson Lk Pk 604-478-1333

Maplewood Naturopathic Centre
Durward, Dr. Dorthea; Ringdahl, Dr. Sally
3540 Maplewood 604-480-0650

Victoria Naturopathic Clinic
Kempling, Dr. Philip H., ND; Rode, Dr. Albert M., ND; Cooper, D.; Seth-Smith, P.
206-1175 Cook St 604-382-1223

WEST VANCOUVER

West Vancouver Clinic of Naturopathic Medicine
Farnsworth, Dr. Kelly, ND; Morello, Dr. Gaetano, ND; Vanderlinden, K., ND
101, 585-16th 604-925-3037

WESTBANK

Skaken, Dr. Luci, ND
3012 Glenrosa Rd 604-768-4766

WHITE ROCK

Coastal Naturopathic Clinic
Fleming, Dr. Robert, ND;
Seliski, Dr. Lawrence, ND;
Torrance, Dr. Patricia, ND
1187 Johnston Rd 604-531-0252

Tonskamper, Dr. Gudrun, ND
304-1493 Johnston 604-536-1400

White Rock Homeopathic Clinic
Levendusky, Dr. Paul, ND; Tessler, Dr. Neil, ND
202-15210 North Bluff604-535-1454/8600

WINFIELD

Wagstaff, Dr. S. Craig, ND
11270 Robinson 604-766-3633

✦ Manitoba

Naturopathic physicians are regulated in Manitoba, meaning that there is legislation establishing a governing body responsible for registering practitioners who meet its educational standards (see below, "Governing Body"). There is no government health care coverage.

Legislation

Manitoba's Naturopathic doctors are regulated under *The Naturopathic Act*, which defines naturopathy as "a drugless system of therapy that treats human injuries, ailments, or diseases, by natural methods, including any one or more of the physical, mechanical, or material, forces or agencies of nature, and employs as auxiliaries for such purposes the use of electro-therapy, hydrotherapy, body manipulations, or dietetics" (section 1).

Establishment of Governing Body

The Act establishes the powers and duties of the governing body, The Manitoba Naturopathic Association, allowing it to make regulations concerning such matters as the qualifications of registered members, disciplinary procedures, and complaint investigation.

Practice by Unregistered Naturopaths An Offence

The board of the Association issues licenses under the Act to qualified naturopaths, and no person other than a registered naturopath may engage in the practice of naturopathy, or use the title "naturopath" or any word, title or designation implying that the person is engaged in such practice.

A person who is not registered and who practises naturopathy, either by itself or in conjunction with any other method of treatment of the body for disease and the causes of disease, for gain or the hope of gain, commits an offence under the Act. There is a separate offence for unregistered persons who hold themselves out as naturopaths, or who advertise as such. Offences carry penalties of fines for first and second offences, and

imprisonment for third offences. No prosecution under the Act may be commenced after two years from the date of the alleged offence.

Limitations on lawsuits for Malpractice

No registered naturopath is liable for any action for negligence or malpractice for professional services unless the action is commenced within two years from the date professional services terminated regarding the complaint.

Notice of Contagious Disease

Any naturopath who has reason to believe that a patient has any contagious or infectious disease or other disease dangerous to public health must give notice in writing to the health officer in the municipality where the patient resides.

Medical Act Not to Apply

Nothing in the province's *Medical Act* prohibits a registered naturopath from practising naturopathy for hire, gain or hope of reward.

Certain Practices Prohibited

The Act states that nothing in it authorizes any person to prescribe or administer drugs for use internally or externally, or to use or direct or prescribe the use of anaesthetic for any purpose, or to practise surgery or midwifery.

Governing Body/Professional Association

Manitoba Naturopathic Association/
Manitoba Association of Naturopathic Practitioners
179 Mossdale Ave
Winnipeg, Manitoba R2K 0H7
Tel: 204-661-2437

Call to ensure that your naturopath is registered, to make a complaint, or to ask for a referral.

✦ Manitoba Naturopaths

NOTE: The following list was provided by the Manitoba Association of Naturopathic Practitioners. However, this publication cannot and does not certify or represent the qualifications of practitioners, or the quality of care available from them. We cannot and do not confirm that those listed are registered as required by law.

BRANDON

Conyette, Paul
709A-10th St 204-727-3524

WINNIPEG

C & M Holistic Centre
Lendvai, Ray
100-912 Portage Ave 204-774-3266

Kroeker, George
179 Mossdale Ave 204-661-2437

Steinkamp, Paula
301 Nassau St N, Lwr Level .204-475-0764

Turner, Chris
459 William Ave 204-956-1555

✦ New Brunswick

Naturopaths are not regulated as practitioners in New Brunswick. This means that there is no provincial legislation establishing a governing body responsible for registering qualified naturopaths and disciplining them. This also means that there are no minimum educational standards for those calling themselves naturopaths. New Brunswick has legislation restricting medical practice to licensed physicians.

✦ New Brunswick Naturopaths

NOTE: Check the credentials of your practitioner (see above, "Questions to Ask"). This publication cannot and does not certify or represent the qualifications of practitioners, or the quality of care available from them.

CARAQUET

Landry, M., ND
By Appointment 506-727-2173

DALHOUSIE

**Clinique Naturotherapeutique
D'Acupuncture & Herbology**
111 Brunswick 506-684-5144

SHIPPAGAN

**Infirmiere Medicine Douce-
Naturopathes**
Madelaine, Jacques, ND; Podvin, Dominique
146 Premiere 506-336-4857

✦ Nova Scotia

Naturopaths are not regulated as practitioners in Nova Scotia. This means that there is no provincial legislation establishing a governing body responsible for registering qualified naturopaths and disciplining them. This also means that there are no minimum educational standards for those calling themselves naturopaths. However, the Nova Scotia Naturopathic Association, listed below, has adopted educational standards for its members. Note that Nova Scotia has legislation restricting medical practice.

Nova Scotia Association

Nova Scotia Naturopathic Association
Box 825, 139 Union Street
Berwick, Nova Scotia B0P 1E0
Tel: 902-538-8733

Call if you wish to ensure that your naturopath is a member, and therefore has met the association's educational standards and has passed its exam. The Association has adopted membership standards similar to those of regulatory bodies in other provinces. For example, naturopath members must be trained at the Etobicoke (Toronto), Portland, Seattle, or equivalent schools, and an entrance exam must be passed. The Association is seeking legislation to regulate naturopathic physicians.

✦ Nova Scotia Naturopaths

NOTE: Check the credentials of your practitioner (see above, "Questions to Ask"). This publication cannot and does not certify or represent the qualifications of practitioners, or the quality of care available from them.

BERWICK

Valley Naturopathic Clinic
Hare, Lois M., ND
139 Union 902-538-8733

BRIDGETOWN

Bolliger, Dr. Manon
2078 Highway 201 902-665-5216

HALIFAX

L-C Acupuncture & Natural Therapy Clinic
6165 Quinpool Rd 902-492-8839

YARMOUTH

Harbourfront Naturopathic Clinic
Schmid, H.J.
Harbourfront Pl
99 Water St 902-742-0082

✦ Ontario

Naturopathic physicians are regulated in Ontario, meaning that there is legislation establishing a governing body responsible for registering and disciplining practitioners (see below, "Governing Body"). There is no government health care funding.

Legislation

Naturopaths have been regulated since 1925 under the *Drugless Practitioners Act*. They are exempt from the restrictions regarding controlled acts contained in s.27(1) of the *Regulated Health Professions Act, 1991* for the purpose of carrying on activities within the scope of the practice of naturopathy under the *Drugless Practitioners Act* (Ontario Reg. 887/93, section 3). Naturopathic physicians have applied for status as a self-governing health profession under the more modern and comprehensive *Regulated Health Professions Act, 1991*.

In the meantime, Regulation 278 under the *Drugless Practitioners Act* defines a "drugless therapist" as any person who "practises or advertises or holds themself out in any way as practising the treatment by diagnosis, including all diagnostic methods...of any ailment, disease, defect or disability of the human body by methods taught in colleges of drugless therapy or naturopathy and approved by the Board (of Directors of Drugless Therapy).

The regulation states that every drugless practitioner must register with the Board. The Board may appoint an inspector to investigate complaints, and the regulation also allows for the suspension or cancellation of the certificate of registration of any drugless practitioner for incompetence or misconduct.

Governing Body

Board of Directors of Drugless Therapy - Naturopathy
4195 Dundas St W
Toronto, Ontario M8X 1Y4
Tel: 416-236-4593
Fax: 416-236-4387

Call to ensure that your naturopath is registered. You may also ask for a referral in your area, but this is normally handled by the Ontario Naturopathic Association.

Ontario Association

Ontario Naturopathic Association
4174 Dundas St W, Suite 304
Etobicoke, Ontario M8X 1X3
Tel: 416-233-2001
Fax: 416-233-2924

The Association will provide information on naturopathic medicine or refer you to a naturopathic doctor. Office hours are Monday-Friday 8 a.m. to 12 noon, but there is an answering service. If you wish a referral, let the association know what area you live in and the closest intersection.

✦ Ontario Naturopaths

NOTE: Check the credentials of your practitioner (see above, "Questions to Ask"). This publication cannot and does not certify or represent the qualifications of practitioners, or the quality of care available from them. We cannot and do not confirm that those listed are registered.

ANCASTER

Milroy, Pamela, ND
393 Wilson St E 905-648-5200

AURORA

Aurora Naturopathic Clinic
15213 Yonge St 905-727-1206

AYR

Farquharson Naturopathic Clinic
RR #1 519-632-8581

BARRIE

Clark, Glenda J., ND
24 Poyntz St 705-721-5776

BEAMSVILLE

Patel, Mukesh M., ND
5026 King St 905-563-5444

BELLEVILLE

Valchar, Dr. Jan, DC & ND
218 College St W 613-968-9626

BLACKSTOCK

Bowmanville Chiropractic & Naturopathic Clinic
168 Church St 905-623-4004

BOBCAYGEON

Total Life Care
Grant, Dr. Muriel, ND
129 Main St 705-738-4451

BOLTON

Total Life Care
Grant, Dr. Muriel M., ND
25 Queen St N 905-857-4341

BRAMPTON

Levine, Dr. Howard, DC & ND
Bramalea City Centre 905-793-0332

BRANTFORD

Hauk, Alfred, ND
134 Charing Cross St 519-759-7896

BRIGHT'S GROVE

Vanderheyden, Dr. Terry, ND
2695 Hamilton Rd 519-869-4309

BURLINGTON

Ataner, Dr. Chiler
By Appointment 905-632-4485

CARNARVON

Carnarvon Naturopathic Centre
By Appointment 705-489-2763

CHATHAM

Nature's Clinic
276 Grand Ave W 519-351-3369

CONSTANCE BAY

Wellspring, Schad, ND
109 Shady Lane 613-832-0987

DUNDAS

Dundas Naturopathic Centre
May, Marilyn A., ND; Spring, J.D., DC & ND;
Saunders, Paul R., ND
211 King St W 905-627-9434

ELMIRA

Roth, Patricia ND
45 Church St W 519-669-5180

GALT

Naturopathic Healthcare Centre
119 Ainslie St N 519-622-0961

GEORGETOWN

Kuindersma, Cathy
10 Mountainview Rd S 905-873-2361

GUELPH

Guelph Community Health Centre
Armour, Dr. Pauline; MacIntosh, Terry, ND
89 Wyndham St N 519-821-6638

McKinstry Natural Health Clinic
McKinstry, Barbara, ND
115 Norfolk St 519-821-2240

Thut, Albert, ND
32 Yorkshire St N 519-822-6551

HAMILTON

Healthcare Alternatives
By Appointment 905-540-1802

Naturopath Clinic
Seibert, Horst
226 Locke St S 905-523-8816

Presta David; Rivet, Dr. Quinn
3-66 Mall Rd 905-574-1181

HESPELER

Morton Homeopathic & Naturopathic Health Care
200 Glenforest Rd 519-658-9079

INGERSOLL

The Health Centre
Johnson, Dr. W. Rod, DC & ND
90 Charles St W 519-485-3000

KITCHENER

Dronyk Clinic
2880 King St E 519-894-0024

Durant, Dr. Susan, ND
460 Frederick St 519-578-7595

Meissner Natural Health Care
Fuke, Ellie, ND
174 Victoria St S 519-579-6150

Natural Balance For Life
1084 Weber St E 519-894-6989

KLEINBURG

Pragnell, Dr. Richard, DC & ND
855 Nashville Rd 905-893-2771

LONDON

Czeranko, Susanna, ND
1288 Highbury Ave 519-451-3252

Eisenstein, Michael, ND; Vanderheyden, Terry, ND
111 Waterloo St 519-434-6342

London West Health Centre
Dronyk, Dr. Robert, DC & ND
307 Commissioners Rd W . . .519-471-1917

Naturopathic Medicine & Health Clinic
Grabreck, Reiner, ND
208-746 Base Line E 519-433-3060

MARKHAM

Budo Life Centre
3-200 Steelcase Rd E 905-940-9447

Markham Homeopathic Centre
Hardy, Dr. Gary
5762 Hwy 7 905-472-2186

MILTON

Summerfield, Charlene L.
225 Main St E 905-878-5200

MISSISSAUGA

Blaszczyk, Dr. Anna
102 Surbray Grove 905-949-9958

Brunton, Dr. Carolyn
5805 Whittle Rd 905-712-4251

Credit Landing Medical Centre
Goodman, Dr. Jess; Heinen, Shirley, ND
224 Lakeshore Rd W 905-278-3868

Kaganovsky, Alexey, ND
5805 Whittle Rd 905-890-4946

Meridian Naturopathic Clinic
2087 Dundas St E 905-238-9001

Omar, Fareed, ND
4141 Dixie Rd 905-238-2917

MOUNT FOREST

Aletris Natural Health Clinic
Main St & Birmingham St E . .519-323-1116

Mount Forest Natural Health Centre
McKibbin, Blaine; Rappard, Dr. Daphne, DC & ND
248 Main St N 519-323-4148

NEPEAN

Toplak, Dr. A., DC & ND
60 Larkspur Dr 613-726-9547

NEW HAMBURG

New Hamburg Natural Health Care Center
Gerber, Sherry
3 Waterloo St 519-662-2123

NEWMARKET

Equinox Naturopathic Centre
Deres, Marlene;
Roke, Dorothy, ND; Zimmermann, Anke, ND
431 Timothy St 905-895-8285

Newmarket Natural Health Centre
Gatis, Robert L., ND
17817 Leslie St 905-853-0172

NIAGARA FALLS

Prytula, Dr. Michael, ND
6117 Biamonte Pkwy 905-374-1332

NORTH BAY

Wolf, John, ND
723 Bloem St 705-497-9402

OAKVILLE

Bronte Natural Health Clinic
Gustin, Darlene; Schumann, Laureen
2368 Lakeshore Rd W 905-825-8787

Meridian Naturopathic Clinic
113 Jones St 905-847-2470

Oakville Natural Health Clinic
Cheng, Bill; Cheng, Steve
77 Lakeshore Rd W 905-842-0226

Oakville Naturopathic Clinic
127 Trafalgar Rd 905-844-7718

ORILLIA

Ingard, Dr. R. Anton
West St N 705-325-7311

OSHAWA

Kellerstein, Dr. J., DC & ND
111 Simcoe St N 905-433-8666

Oshawa Naturopathic Clinic
122 Simcoe St N 905-433-7066

Rohn, Suzanne, ND
18 Gibbons St 905-728-5512

OTTAWA

Ayoubzadeh, S., ND
505-381 Kent St 613-235-0003

Clinique de Medecine Naturopathique et Homeopathique
Lafond, Michele, ND
206-195 boul Greber 613-246-5082

Lortie, Louise, ND
By appointment 613-243-7951

Optihealth Centre
Clark, Shawna, ND; Villeneuve, Joel, ND
320-2249 Carling Ave 613-829-7100

Total Health Naturopathic Clinic
88 Centrepointe Dr 613-225-3774

Your Natural Health Centre
2660 Southvale Cr 613-737-1177

PALMERSTON

Palmerston Chiropractic and Naturopathic
336 Main St W 519-343-2264

PETERBOROUGH

Anderson Naturopathic Clinic
80 Hunter St E 705-742-0213

Millar, John, ND
403 McDonnel St 705-743-2008

PICKERING

Erry, Dr. Rajeery;
Lubczynski, Celina; Mehta, Dr. A.K
1450 Kingston Rd 905-420-6025

POINT EDWARD

Reid, Donna, ND
704 Mara St 519-332-1847

RICHMOND HILL

Centre For The Ways & Natural Healing Arts
10265 Yonge St, 2nd Fl ...905-737-6875

Martalog, Anca, BSc, ND
124 Major McKenzie E 905-884-7965

ST. CATHARINES

Lauermeier, Jane
162 Geneva St 905-682-3362

SARNIA

Natural Healing Clinic
Wanner, Louis
1282 Andrew Ct 519-542-6019

SAULT STE. MARIE

Natural Health Clinic
509 Wellington St E 705-759-7900

SHELBURNE

Wood Naturopathic Clinic
242 Main St E 519-925-0122

STONEY CREEK

Natural Therapies
Patel, Mukesh M.
72 Centennial Pkwy S .905-662-6199/6566

SUNDRIDGE

Davidson, Alan L.
By appointment 705-384-7244

THORNHILL

Centre For Self Directed Wellness
Sussman, Dr. Averam, DC & ND
390 Steeles Ave W 905-881-0214

THUNDER BAY

Holistic-Cranton Wellness Centre
379 Oliver Rd 807-343-7932

TILLSONBURG

Active Health Care Centre
Bureau, Dr. J.L.
9 Woodcock Dr 519-688-3901

TIMMINS

Geddes Naturopathic Clinic
Geddes, Kelly
255 Algonquin Blvd E 705-268-9711

Timmins Naturopathic Clinic
Rivard, Darcelle, ND
96 Maple St S 705-267-6699

TORONTO

Acupuncture, Chiropractic & Naturopathic Medicine
Cheng, Dr. Bill
778 Gerrard St E 416-469-2709

Adirim, Dr. Herbert, DC & ND
600 Sherbourne St 416-922-6866

Amodeo, Frank
105 Granby 416-340-1973

Ania, Fernando, ND
3255 Yonge St 416-481-8816

B.N. Natural Health Clinic
Beserminji, Dr. Nada
2555 Eglinton Ave E 416-265-3309

Beaches Naturopathic Clinic
2279 Queen St E 416-699-2865

Begin, Marty
715 Bloor St W 416-533-2078

Bloor Naturopathic Clinic
2333 Dundas St W 416-534-0510

Bortnick, Dr. A., DC & ND
1126 Eglinton Ave W 416-782-2113

Da Costa Rees, Jose
108 Yorkville Ave 416-968-0300

Davis, Paul J.
2390-A Bloor St W 416-761-9722

Deer Park Naturopathic Clinic
Timothy, Bryan
200 St. Clair Ave W 416-921-3837

Dobosz, Dr. Lidia, ND
2150 Bloor St W 416-604-9144

Dunk, Dr. Kenneth, DC & ND
Zambri, Saveria A., ND
1042 Coxwell Ave 416-423-5996

Elan Vital Naturopathic Clinic
Adams, Dr. Michael, ND;
Armengol, Dr. Hania, ND
69 Yorkville Ave 416-972-6470

Goreshnik, Dr. Zilia, ND
1315 Finch Ave W 416-638-9933

Hartnett-Starkovski, Lydia, ND
16 Bimbrok Rd 416-269-8979

Healthstyles Naturopathic Clinic
Boghossian, Marina, ND; Moore, Angela, ND;
Wales, Patricia, ND
23 Florence Ave 416-226-4478

Helen Cohen Naturopathic Doctor & Associates
1245 Dupont St 416-538-7839

Hunt, Dr. Verna, DC & ND;
Roth, Dr. George, DC & ND
2826 Dundas St W 416-763-3211

Institute For the Advancement of Natural Therapy
Dadamo, James, ND; Medrek, Robert, ND
186 St. George St 416-968-0496

Heritage Holistic Centre
100 Harbord St 416-924-3764

Kew Beach Naturopathic Clinic
1986 Queen St E 416-690-6168

Kura, Dr. Martin, DC & ND
4218 Lawrence Ave E 416-282-7937

Lam, David
368 Dupont St 416-925-6752

Lawrence-Yonge Naturopathic Clinic
Baron, Dr. R.
3080 Yonge 416-486-9797

Leca, R.
458 Eglinton Ave W 416-485-0600

Love, Daria
14 Prince Arthur Ave 416-961-0208

Luby, Kenneth, ND
235 Danforth Ave 416-461-2200

McKenzie, Kim
2826 Dundas St W 604-736-3211

McLean, John F.
2477 Bloor St W 416-767-9245

Medrek, Robert
186 St George St 416-968-0496

Meridan naturopathic Clinic
93 Harbord St 416-961-2225

Milne, Dr. George, DC & ND
989 Eglinton Ave W 416-785-0111

The Naturopathic College Clinic
2300 Yonge St,
18th Floor 416-486-8260

Naturopathic Medicine on Bay Wellness Clinic
330 Bay St 416-363-6135

Naturopathic Medicine Therapies Institute
Srajeldin, Dr. Fateh
5468 Dundas St W 416-207-0207

Nelson, Dr. Brian, DC & ND
120 Carlton St 416-964-1318

Okabe, Dale
100 Granby 416-340-7688

Ovens, Helena
1986 Queen St E 416-690-6168

Renaissance Naturopathic Centre
85 Buttonwood Ave 416-242-9371

Rozbicka, Danuta, ND
3269 Bloor St W 416-234-8133

Scheer, Jacob
2100 Finch Ave W 416-739-7766

Seena Naturopathic Clinic
19 Varna Dr 416-787-3096

Shrubb, Dr. Eric, DC, ND
816 Kennedy Rd 416-751-6998

Smith, Michael
365 Bloor St 416-975-0499

Soares Health Service Ltd.
1620 Dupont St 416-767-4554

Spectrum Healing Naturopathic Clinic
130 Hallam 416-534-0002

Stedmann, Neal
100 Harbord St 416-924-3764

Thuna's Wholistic Centre
298-A Danforth Ave 416-461-8191

Toronto Naturopathic Clinic
180 Bloor St W 416-944-3526

Toronto Wellness Centre
22 Wellesley W 416-920-2722

Total Life Care
Grant, M., DC, ND
106-2588A Yonge St 416-485-3013

Wellness Institute
Roth, Dr. George, DC & ND
954 Royal York Rd 416-234-1888

West End Holistic Health Centre
Godfrey, Anthony, ND;
McKenzie, Dr. Kim, DC & ND
2826 Dundas St W 416-763-3211

WATERLOO

Anousaya, C.; Bender, John, ND; Tunstall, Richard, ND
22 McDougall Rd 519-885-3720

WHITBY

Northumberland Naturopathic Clinic
Adams, Mikhael, ND; Armengol, Hania, ND
287 Division St 905-377-0298

WINDSOR

Campbell, Dr. Lauri
203-2525 Rose Ville
Garden Dr 519-944-6000

WOODBRIDGE

Scott Health Centre
Scott, Dr. W; Scott, Dr. L.; Weir, Dr. J.
5220 Hwy 7 905-851-2216

WOODSTOCK

Quantum Health Centre
513 Admiral St 519-539-1992

✦ Québec

Naturopaths are not regulated as practitioners in Québec. This means that there is no provincial legislation establishing a governing body responsible for registering qualified naturopaths and disciplining them. This also means that there are no minimum educational standards for those calling themselves naturopaths. Québec has legislation restricting medical practice to licensed physicians.

Québec Associations

Academy of Naturopaths and Naturotherapists (ANN)
64 De Pontiac
Bromont, Québec J0E 1L0
Tel: 514-534-5304

The Academy is a multidisciplinary group whose members include naturopaths, homeopaths, acupuncturists and other practitioners. The Academy has a code of ethics for members and offers professional liability insurance.

L'Association des Diplômes en Naturopathie du Québec
1250, rue Rudolphe Forjet, # 300
Sillery, Québec G1S 3Y7
Tel: 514-385-4269

This association of about 100 members represents naturopaths with a diploma in naturopathic medicine. Call for a referral.

L'Association Nationale des Naturothérapeutes
222 Dominion, Ste. 85
Montréal, Québec H3J 2X1
Tel: 514-939-1457

The Association states that many extended health care plans cover the cost of seeing a naturopath belonging to the organization. The association recognizes the CENAB and Ecole Supérieure de Naturopathie.

Association Professionnelle Des Naturothérapeutes Du Québec
6731 rue St-Denis
Montreal, Québec H2S 2S3
Tel: 514-279-6641

This association will provide referrals to its professional members.

✦ Québec Naturopaths

NOTE: Check the credentials of your practitioner (see above, "Questions to Ask"). This publication cannot and does not certify or represent the qualifications of practitioners, or the quality of care available from them.

ALMA

Plaza I, Les Naturistes
500, Sacre Coeur O 418-662-7893

ALYMER

Acupuncture Auriculomedecine Homeopathie Nat.
7, Front 819-684-5257

BELOEIL

Institut Canadien de Sante Holistique
640, rue Parkview 514-464-0805

Trudeau Paradis Gisele Naturpotherapeute
605, Vaquelin 514-467-4459

BLACK LAKE

Sante Harmonie Enr
1472, Laliberte 418-423-5182

BOUCHERVILLE

Bureau, C.E.O.
306, Monseigneur
Lafleche 514-655-6249

BROSSARD

Prevention Jeunesse Rive-Sud Brossard Inc.
3105, Rome 514-445-1322

CAP-DE-LA-MADELEINE

Sillon, Claudine
203-980, Thibeau 819-372-9625

CHAMBLY

Au Tournesol Enr
Centre da Chats Place 514-658-0218

CHATEAUGUAY

Goyer, Marc, ND
25 rue Principale 514-699-9769

Lamontagne, Lise & Daniel, ND
255, Danjou 514-691-7591

Le Panier Vert
25, rue Principale 514-699-9769

CONTRECOEUR

Blanchard, Francois
8610, Alanic 514-743-2008

FERME NEUVE

Centre Alternatif
94, rue 12 819-587-4026

GATINEAU

Lavoie, Dr. Claude, ND
1134, boul Maloney E 819-663-0516

Lortie, Louis, ND
34, de Turin 819-243-7951

Naturopaths & Homeopaths Medecine Clinic
Lafond, Michele, ND
206-195, boul Greber 819-246-5082

Sante-Bonheur
1134, boul Maloney E 819-663-0516

GRANBY

Bergeron, Marco
463, Mountain 514-378-6783

Labbe, Nelson
297, St-Jacques 514-375-1745

Maison Sante Granby Enr
Duval, Johanne; Rainville, Christiane
33, Guy 514-375-2696

HULL

Brunette, Madeleine, ND
6, de la Gravite 819-776-4495

Clinique de la Croix d'Or
398, boul
Alexandre Tache 819-778-1574

De Grace-Raymond, Joanne, ND
221, ch Freeman 819-595-4940

Marquis, Dr. Jacques, ND
4, Ste-Marie 819-777-1319

JOLIETTE

Energie Sante
Forand, Francoise; Macameau, Gerald; Rigaudie, Alain
533, boul Manseau 514-755-6150

LA BAIE

Bouchard, Isabelle, ND
473, des Pins 418-544-2784

LABELLE

Raynault, Suzanne, ND
7151, boul
du Cure Labelle 819-686-5559

LAC MEGANTIC

Salon Cheveux Dor Enr
5368, Frontenac 819-583-1167

LONGUEUIL

Allium
1568, ch de Chambly 514-677-3057

Larose, Ronald, ND
359, St-Charles O 514-646-5230

Meunier, Nicole, ND
195, ch de Chambly 514-928-9695

LOUISEVILLE

Aliments Naturels Fleur de Sarrasin
Benoit, Pierre, ND
10, St-Aime 819-228-9994

MCMASTERVILLE

Bussieres Tessier, Claudette
155, Normandie 514-464-9580

MONT-JOLI

Centre de Naturotherapie
Dufour, Helene, ND
1564, Jacques-Cartier 418-775-3040

MONTREAL

Centre Naturopathique
5726, Sherbrooke O 514-482-0549

Centre Naturopathique Verdon Labelle
Labelle, Yvan, ND; Verdon, Johanne, ND
1274, rue Jean-Talon E 514-272-0018

Centre Regeneration F. Bergeron
1012, Mont Royal E 514-524-1487

Chalifoux, Anne-Marie, ND
738, Bloomfield 514-277-1498

Clinique Bine-Etre
6830, du Parc 514-273-6263

Clinique Naturopathique Lesage
Lesage, Jacques, ND
6671, rue St-Denis 514-273-1844

Clinique Passena Inc.
Hamel, Claude, ND; Limoge, Christian, ND
369, Gounod 514-389-3026

College Canadien des Naturopathes
6830, du Parc 514-273-6263

Cote, Jean Jacques, ND
6655, rue St-Denis 514-271-1807

Dawson, Dr. Douglas J., ND
5255, Henri Bourassa O 514-333-7324

Foisy, Roger, ND
603, Louvain E 514-388-1402

Goyer, Marc, ND
8687, St-Denis 514-385-1801

Savard, Georges, ND
815, Henri Bourassa E 514-389-2393

Sentiers de la Nature
4058, Monselet 514-955-5617

MONTREAL NORD

Moutte, Dr. Lea
5309, Damos 514-329-0599

OKA

Dion-Blouin, Lorraine, ND
1985, ch Oka 514-479-8074

PINCOURT

Boivin, C.
177 Northcote Dr 514-425-3811

QUEBEC

Beliveau, Celine, ND
779, av 2 418-525-9300

Gagnon, Andree, ND
1305, boul Lebourgneuf 418-626-5454

RIMOUSKI

Centre de Sante Holistique & de Naturotherapie
Dufour, Helene, ND
145, Lepage 418-724-2001

Centre de Therapies Naturelles de Rimouski Inc.
158, Ste-Therese 418-722-0303

Duchesne, Gabrielle, ND
10-140, St-Germain O 418-725-3331

RIVIERE-DU-LOUP

Landry, Jacynthe, ND
500, La Fontaine 418-867-8159

ROSEMONT

Harmonia
6662, av 28 514-722-0422

SHERBROOKE

Aux Sources Conseil Magas Alim Naturels
699, Conseil 819-346-9900

Belanger, Bernard, ND
806, Langlois 819-562-6979

Centre de Sante Eintergrale Leveil Enr
63, Alexandre 819-823-1477

Centre de Therapies Holistiques
806, Langlois 819-562-6979

Gosselin Marie-Anne Naturotherapeute
63, Alexandre 819-823-1477

Parent, Gilles, ND
778, rue McManamy 819-821-3998

ST-ALEXIS-DE MONTCALM

Naturotherapeute de Lanaudiere
Bernier, Sylvie; St-Amour, Jocelyn
16, Liard St 514-839-7526

ST-BASILE LE GRAN

Bellemare, Raymond, ND
4, Laporte 514-653-9906

ST-CHARLES BORROMEE

Croteau, Josee, ND
247, Visitation 514-755-6349

ST-DAMIEN DE BRANDON

Clinique Sante-Soleil
7704, ch Montauban 514-835-2616

ST-HYACINTHE

Institut Deesse Beaute Enr
1740, Girouard O 514-773-0083

Naturiste Marche de Sante
1772, des Cascades O 514-773-4243

ST-JEROME

Menard, Sylvie, ND
757, rue 9 514-436-3393

ST-JOVITE

Centre Nature Etre-Plus Enr Naturotherapie
Bilodeau, Yolande, ND
865, Ouimet 819-425-3811

ST-LAMBERT

Centronature
434, Victoria 514-923-5720

ST-LAURENT

Parent, Gilles, ND
1505, Decelles 514-747-2259

ST-PIE

Naturo Sante Plus
158, Lacasse 514-772-5448

ST-THERESE

Vita Sante Naturelle
58, St-Joseph 514-434-9799

STE-AGATHE-DES MONTS

Visa Sante Naturelle
94-A, Principale E 819-326-3896

STE-DOROTHEE

Ouellet, Katerie, ND
645, pl Publique 514-969-1374

STE-JULIE

Blouin, Marc
1643, Principale 514-922-9909

Clinique de Medecine Chinoise Naturopathie
2000, ch du Fer a Cheval . . .514-922-9306

THETFORD MINES

Dostie, Clement & Lisette
707, av 8 418-338-1989

TROIS-RIVIERES

Concept Action Sante
3920, Louis Pinard 819-691-1077

TROIS-RIVIERES-OUEST

Clinique Naturiste Trois-Rivieres-Ouest
Lemieuxn, Ferdinand, ND
173, Bellevue 819-377-3610

VAL MORIN

Clinique Asana Medecine Douce
366, des Merisiers 819-322-3444

VICTORIAVILLE

Papillon, Huguette
39, boul Gregoire 819-357-2651

WARWICK

Sentier du Mieux-Etre
7, rt 2 819-358-5464

Saskatchewan

Naturopathic physicians are regulated in Saskatchewan, meaning that there is legislation establishing a governing body responsible for registering practitioners who meet educational standards (see below, "Governing Body"). There is no government health care coverage.

Legislation

Saskatchewan naturopaths are regulated under *The Naturopathy Act*. The Act defines naturopathy as the art of healing by natural methods as taught in recognized schools of naturopathy.

Practice by Unregistered Naturopaths An Offence

The Act prohibits anyone other than a naturopathic practitioner registered under the act to either engage in the practice of naturopathy or to use titles such as Naturopathic Practitioner, Naturopath, or Doctor of Naturopathy. The Act also explicitly states that is an offence to practise naturopathy without being registered under the Act, with penalties providing for fines on first and second offences and imprisonment on subsequent offences. No prosecution may be commenced for an offence against the Act after two years from the date of the alleged offence.

Duties of Regulatory (Governing) Body

The Act establishes the authority of the Saskatchewan Association of Naturopathic Practitioners and its council. The council is required to maintain a register of naturopathic practitioners, establish disciplinary procedures and investigate complaints.

Limitations on Lawsuits for Malpractice

The Act also states that no registered naturopathic practitioner shall be liable in an action for negligence or malpractice unless the lawsuit is commenced within twelve months of the date the professional services regarding the complaint were terminated.

Certain Practices Prohibited

The Act states that nothing in it or in the bylaws made by the Council shall authorize any person to prescribe or administer drugs for use internally or externally, to use or direct or prescribe the use of anaesthetics for any purpose whatsoever, to treat venereal disease or a communicable disease as defined in the province's public health legislation, or to practise medicine, surgery, midwifery or any method of treatment other than naturopathy.

Notice of Contagious Disease

A naturopathic practitioner who has reason to believe that a patient has a contagious or infectious disease must give immediate notice in writing of the fact to the medical health officer in the municipality where the patient resides.

Medical Profession Act Not to Apply

The Act states that nothing in the province's *Medical Profession Act* regarding the licensing of medical doctors prohibits the practice of naturopathy by practitioners under the Act.

Governing Body

Saskatchewan Association of Naturopathic Physicians
Registrar: William McGill, N.D.
R.R. #2, Stn Main
Saskatoon, Saskatchewan S7K 3J5
Tel: 306-384-1580
Fax: 306-384-1548

Contact the Association to ensure that your naturopath is properly registered, or to make a complaint. The Association recognizes degrees in naturopathy awarded after 4,500 academic hours of study.

Saskatchewan Association

Saskatchewan Association of Naturopathic Physicians
1945 McKercher Dr, #6
Saskatoon, Saskatchewan S7K 4M4
Tel: 306-955-2555

This is the professional association of naturopathic physicians. Call for a referral to a naturopathic physician near you.

✦ Saskatchewan Naturopaths

NOTE: The following list was provided by the Canadian Naturopathic Association, on behalf of the Saskatchewan Association of Naturopathic Physicians. However, this publication cannot and does not certify or represent the qualifications of practitioners, or the quality of care available from them. We cannot and do not confirm that those listed are registered as required by law.

BATTLEFORD

Gleisberg, Peter
Box 716, 17 Chemin Bellevue 306-937-2204

FT. QU'APPELLE

Present Jahn, Wendy
Box 1991 306-332-1881

SASKATOON

Mahan, Edward
1945 McKercher Drive #6 . . .306-955-2555

McGill, William
R.R. #2, Stn Main 306-384-1580

Wallace, Norman
410-105 21st St E 306-664-3244

UNITY

Schafer, Garry
201 Main St 306-228-2512

Nutritional Consulting

WHAT IS NUTRITIONAL CONSULTING

Nutritional consultants assess nutritional imbalances and offer suggestions for improvement. A nutritional assessment takes into account an individual's intolerances, allergies, degree of exposure to environmental poisons, lifestyle, eating habits, and symptoms of nutritional imbalance, such as discomfort in bright light. On the basis of this assessment, the nutritional consultant makes suggestions regarding a balanced approach to food, the eating of whole foods (unprocessed and without additives), and the use of vitamin and nutritional supplements. The nutritional consultant takes a holistic approach, focusing on the body's ability to heal itself. Those who specialize as nutritional consultants usually have about 1,000 hours of training (one year). Nutritional counselling is also an integral part of Ayurvedic medicine (see "Ayurveda"), naturopathic medicine (see "Naturopathic Medicine") and traditional Chinese medicine (see "Acupuncture and Traditional Chinese Medicine"). As in many areas of alternative health, there are nutritional self-help books and natural nutrition courses available.

Not the Same as Dieticians

Registered or certified nutritional consultants are not dieticians. Dieticians are government-regulated practitioners registered with a governing body, such as the College of Dietitians of Ontario. Members use protected titles such as 'Registered Dietician.' Dieticians in Québec are members of the Ordre professionnel des Diététistes du Québec. Depending upon the province, dieticians have a university degree specializing in food and nutrition, followed by a hospital internship or higher university degree. Dieticians work in hospitals, public health departments, research laboratories, corporate product development and recipe analysis departments, or as consultants in private practice.

BENEFITS OF PROPER NUTRITION

Proper nutrition assists the body in maintaining and building physical strength and good health. A well-functioning body is less susceptible to a wide range of conditions, including insomnia, diabetes, arthritis, fatigue, digestive problems such as diarrhea or constipation, skin problems, circulation problems, heart and kidney disease, and cancer. Importantly, nutritional consultants do not make claims to replace physicians, and those seeking assistance for health problems are advised to consult a physician or other regulated health professional, such as a chiropractor or naturopathic doc-

tor (naturopathic doctors are regulated in British Columbia, Manitoba, Ontario and Saskatchewan).

QUESTIONS TO ASK

✦ How much training does your nutritional consultant have, and from which school? Did the training include courses in anatomy and physiology? Did it lead to a diploma or designation such as Registered Nutritional Consultant?

NOTE: Training programs for nutritional consultants range from about six months to one year, and are offered through correspondence courses or in classroom settings. The non-profit Nutritional Consultants Organization of Canada (NCOC) sets standards for Registered Nutritional Consultants (see below, "National Association").

✦ Does your nutritional consultant have a working relationship with other health care professionals? Under what circumstances will your nutritional consultant refer you to a physician or other regulated health professional? Is your nutritional consultant trained to recognize conditions that require a physician's care?

✦ How much experience does your nutritional consultant have? Can your consultant give examples of nutritional imbalances that he or she has been able to identify and redress in clients?

✦ What is your nutritional consultant's background, and does it include training in other areas of health care? If so, what is the extent of the training?

✦ What is the price of a consultation? Is your practitioner affiliated with a particular company's line of vitamin or food supplement products?

GOVERNMENT REGULATION

Regulation of Practitioners

Unlike dieticians, nutritional consultants are not regulated or licensed in any province of Canada, except insofar as practitioners, such as naturopathic doctors trained in nutrition are regulated (see "Naturopathic Medicine - Government Regulation"). This means that there is no legislation establishing a regulatory body to register practitioners who meet specific educational standards. This also means that there is no minimum educational requirement for persons calling themselves nutritional consultants. However, private organizations or schools set their own standards for titles such as

'Registered Nutritional Consultant' or 'Certified Nutritional Counsellors.' Every province has legislation restricting the practice of medicine, or limiting certain medical acts to authorized practitioners. Schools offering diplomas or certificates in nutritional consulting often include courses on offering nutritional advice without offending provisions of such legislation.

Regulation of Food Products

The federal government regulates food through the *Food and Drugs Act* and regulations. There are restrictions on claims that may be made in advertising to the general public and on product labels. The Act prohibits claims as to a product being a treatment, preventative or cure of any of the 40 diseases, disorders or abnormal physical states listed in Schedule A to the Act.

NATIONAL ASSOCIATION

Nutritional Consultants Organization of Canada (NCOC)
1201 Division St
Kingston, Ontario K7K 6X4
Tel: 613-544-4297 or 1-800-406-2703
Fax: 613-544-9256

This independent, non-profit corporation was founded in 1983 to raise public awareness of nutritional consulting and to establish standards of practice for nutritional consultants. Professional members of the organization who meet its educational and ethical standards receive the designation "Registered Nutritional Consultant." Registered Nutritional Consultants sign a 10-point pledge covering aspects of the practice of consulting. For example, the consultant makes a commitment in the pledge to assess nutritional imbalances and weaknesses to help clients support their unique nutritional requirements. The consultant also makes a commitment not to diagnose illness, nor provide therapy to relieve illness. As well, the consultant promises to recommend that a person consult with a licensed physician for the treatment of disease. If you would like to find a Registered Nutritional Consultant in your area, contact the organization, or contact a Registered Nutritional Consultant listed in this directory (see below, "Nutritional Consultants in Your Province"). Those wishing to become an RNC may write to the organization for an application form. The two schools of nutrition recognized by the NCOC are the Edison Institute of Nutrition and the Canadian School of Natural Nutrition (see below, "Nutritional Consulting Education").

NUTRITIONAL CONSULTING EDUCATION

Some of the well-known programs in natural nutrition are listed below. If you wish to become a nutritional consultant, it is advisable to contact several schools before making a choice. Compare the program content and length, admission requirements, and fees and contract terms, including refund policies. In addition, it is useful to request to speak with students and graduates of the various programs.

Most provinces have legislation requiring private vocational schools to meet certain minimum standards, often related to financial stability, for the protection of consumers. These requirements vary from province to province, and certain health care training programs are not covered by such legislation. Contact the Ministry of Education or Advanced Education in your province for more information on their policies regarding registration of private vocational schools.

alive Academy of Nutrition
7436 Fraser Park Dr
Burnaby, B.C. V5J 5B9
Tel: 604-435-1919
Fax: 604-435-4888

This Academy offers a variety of certificate and diploma nutritional consulting home study courses. Required courses for a Diploma in Nutritional Consulting (DNC) include applied nutrition, nutritional consulting, anatomy, physiology and nutrition. Two elective courses must be selected from a list including courses in vegetarianism, herbs and healing, homeopathy, and sports nutrition. The Academy was established in 1992 as the educational department of *alive* Magazine.

Canadian School of Natural Nutrition
10720 Yonge St, Unit 220
Richmond Hill, Ontario L4C 3C9
Tel: 905-737-0284 or 1-800-328-0743
Fax: 905-737-7830

This school offers classroom studies leading to a diploma recognized by the Nutritional Consultants Organization of Canada, and the designation of Registered Nutritional Consultant. Classes are offered either as a one- year, full-time day program, or a two-year, part-time, night program. The curriculum includes courses on the fundamentals of nutrition, anatomy and physiology, symptomatology (analysis of symptoms of nutritional deficiencies), environmental influences, pediatric nutrition, preventive nutrition, allergies, alternative diets such as vegetarian and Ayurvedic, and legal considerations of practice. A correspondence course program is also available.

Edison Institute of Nutrition
2 Bloor St W, Ste 100
Toronto, Ontario M4W 3E2
Tel/Fax: 1-800-456-9313

The Institute offers several home study programs. Those interested in applying to the Nutritional Consultants Organization of Canada for the designation of Registered Nutritional Consultant must complete the Certificate Program and the Practitioner Program. These programs includes courses on holistic nutrition, nutritional assessment, jurisprudence, vitamins and minerals, herbalism and homeopathy, vegetarianism, pediatric nutrition, environmental poisons, sports nutrition, anatomy and physiology, biochemistry, allergies, preventive nutrition, and nutritional cardiology. High school graduation is not an admission requirement, but candidates must demonstrate maturity, sound moral character, academic aptitude and commitment to the study of nutrition. Applicants must write a 200-word essay on the reasons for pursuing studies, and submit two professional references. The school also offers a Bachelor's program, for which high school graduation or its equivalency must be demonstrated, and a Master's program, for which a bachelor's degree or professional degree is required.

The Packard School of Nutrition
586 Alexander St
Sudbury, Ontario P3A 1R3
Tel/Fax: 705-560-5275

This school offers diploma correspondence nutrition courses in English or French, leading to the designation 'Certified Nutrition Consultant.' The course takes about six months to complete.

Sutton Institute
Main St S
Exeter, Ontario M0M 1S1
Tel: 519-235-4014

This Institute offers classroom courses in nutrition, herbology, and iridology.

✦ Nutritional Consulting in Your Province

Provinces are listed alphabetically below, with the following information:

✦ names, addresses and telephone numbers of nutritional consultants, listed alphabetically by city

NOTE: Names listed with the notation 'RNC' are Registered Nutritional Consultants with the non-profit Nutritional Consultants Organization of Canada (NCOC). Contact NCOC to confirm a practitioner's registration or to obtain updated membership information.

✦ Alberta Nutritional Consultants

NOTE: Check the credentials of your practitioner (see above, "Questions to Ask"). This publication cannot and does not certify or represent the qualifications of practitioners, or the quality of care available from them.

CALGARY

Andras, Sophia, RNC
#415, 906-8th Ave SW 403-264-1515

Cobblestone Health Ltd.
Cobb, Judith, RNC
#202, 1039-17th Ave Sw ...403-228-2668

Fisher, Terri, RNC
By Appointment 403-938-8370

Health & Sport Nutrition Centre
Smith, Barry, RNC
1112-220
Woodview Dr SW 403-281-3825

Nakai, Sheridan, RNC
#210, 3715-51st St SW 403-242-1700

Philipps, Maureen, RNC
4947 Marian Rd NE 403-250-3024

Powell, Judith, RNC
By Appointment 403-931-3285

van Heerden, Merv, RNC, MA, B.Ed., CHT
By Appointment 403-218-0334

Woods, Rosanne, RNC
1924-12th St SW 403-541-1107

COCHRANE

Ashlie, Riun, RNC
By Appointment 403-815-6446

EDMONTON

Mitchell, Wylma, RNC
15610-78th St 403-472-6052

Zurchuk, Stella, RNC
1116-49th St 403-450-1799

RED DEER

Carlson, Carolyn L., RNC
202-37543 England Way,
Waskasoo Estates 403-343-9197

ST. ALBERT

Unger, Helene, RNC
30 Spruce Cr 403-466-9267

Vincent, Dianne, RNC
44 Sturgeon Rd 403-459-5328

ROCKY MOUNTAIN HOUSE

Eagle's Nest Holistic Centre Ltd
Lawrence, George W., PhD, M.H.
4923 50th St 403-845-6625

STONY PLAIN

Harlington, Laara T., RNC
10 High Park Rd 403-963-3421

✦ British Columbia Nutritional Consultants

NOTE: Check the credentials of your practitioner (see above, "Questions to Ask"). This publication cannot and does not certify or represent the qualifications of practitioners, or the quality of care available from them.

CHILLIWACK

Yamamoto, Mariko, RNC
7455 Leary Cr 604-858-9111

DELTA

Davies, Lesley, RNC
8782 Delcrest Dr 604-583-3911

GOLD RIVER

Myers, Denise, RNC
By Appointment 604-283-7338

HEFFLEY CREEK

Mayas, Diana, RNC
RR #2, Bedard Rd, C-30 604-578-7874

LANGLEY

Gawne, Lynn, RNC
1966-196th St 604-538-2247

LUMBY

Dew, Joan M., RNC
By Appointment 604-547-9631

MILL BAY

Delorey, Herbert, RNC
754 Butterfield Rd, RR #1 ..604-743-7164

NANAIMO

Streu, Ramona, RNC
6881 Philip Rd 604-751-2919

Van De Water, Marijke, RNC
6530 Doumont Rd 604-741-8289

NEW WESTMINSTER

Goddard, Dean, RNC
615G-8th St 604-542-0040

PARKSVILLE

Schmitt, Helga, RNC
By Appointment 604-248-6088

POWELL RIVER

Davis, Valerie, RNC
7320 Field St 604-485-2855

SALT SPRING

The Inner Road to Wellness
Harris, Juanita 604-656-4856

SECHELT

Bergen, Nika, RNC
By Appointment 604-885-2046

SOOKE

Phillips, Jo Anne, RNC
7237 Ella Rd 604-642-6635

SUMMERLAND

Leslie, Lea, RNC
11010 Giant's Head Rd 604-442-5959

VANCOUVER

Ahau Wholistic Centre
4775 Granville 604-738-8584

Balanced Body Health Consultants
208-1748 E Pender St 604-253-2298

VICTORIA

Durkin, Pamela, RNC
403-845 Burdett Ave 604-360-1092

Hedley, Sandra, RNC
Carmanah Pt, 25 Huron St ..604-727-7716

Hiscock, Brenda, RNC
204-920 Hillside Ave 604-388-6322

Irwin, Patricia A., RNC
1451 Bay St 604-727-2474

Prusa, Rosana, RNC
214-500 Rithet St 604-386-7320

Manitoba Nutritional Consultants

NOTE: Check the credentials of your practitioner (see above, "Questions to Ask"). This publication cannot and does not certify or represent the qualifications of practitioners, or the quality of care available from them.

BOISSEVAIN

Hemingway, Don C., RNC
By Appointment 204-534-6288

WINNIPEG

Keith, David, RNC
148 Machray Ave 204-586-6400

Labelle, Marie, RNC
26 George Suttie Bay 204-669-7412

New Brunswick Nutritional Consultants

NOTE: Check the credentials of your practitioner (see above, "Questions to Ask"). This publication cannot and does not certify or represent the qualifications of practitioners, or the quality of care available from them.

BERESFORD

Young, Gisele, RNC, RN
By Appointment 506-783-3085

FREDERICTON

Daigle, Michel, RNC
118 Case St 506-453-3992

NEWCASTLE

Luke, Kumar, RNC
261 King George Hwy 506-622-1156

RENFORTH

Ferguson, Deborah, RNC
22 Elizabeth Parkway 506-847-7049

SIEGAS

Desjardins, Serge, RNC
RR #1 ....506-735-2500 (ext. 2584)

✦ Nova Scotia Consultants

NOTE: Check the credentials of your practitioner (see above, "Questions to Ask"). This publication cannot and does not certify or represent the qualifications of practitioners, or the quality of care available from them.

ANNAPOLIS COUNTY

Parsons, Steve
By Appointment 902-825-6656

DARTMOUTH

Bourque, Maureen, RNC
79 Lakecrest Dr, #102 902-462-5791

Rajhathy, Judit, RNC
12 Richards Dr 902-466-5000

Smith, Rosemary, RNC
6A Somerset St 902-464-9676

DIGBY

Pidutti, Nella, RNC
By Appointment 902-245-6720

HALIFAX

Quinn, Rosemary, RNC & RN
80 Camelot Ln, #122 902-445-2484

MILFORD

McDonald, Michelle, RNC
By Appointment 902-758-3200

NEW GLASGOW

Devane, Marie, RNC
497 Washington St 902-752-6333

✦ Ontario Nutritional Consultants

NOTE: Check the credentials of your practitioner (see above, "Questions to Ask"). This publication cannot and does not certify or represent the qualifications of practitioners, or the quality of care available from them.

BEAMSVILLE

Glessen-Settler, Christa, RNC
4770 Lincoln Ave 905-563-5539

BEAVERTON

Stabback, Nancy, RNC
By Appointment 705-426-5148

BELLE RIVER

Reaume, Lorraine, RNC
237 Bayberry Cr, RR #3 519-727-6461

BOBCAYGEON

McConnell, Lorrie, RNC
31 Main St 705-738-1616

BOLTON

Marasco-Natale, Polyana
274 Allan Dr 905-857-9285

Millson, Marlene, RNC
By Appointment 905-880-2018

Patterson, Sharon, RNC
29 Birchview Cr 905-857-0279

BRACEBRIDGE

Edwards, Jennifer, RNC
By Appointment 705-645-5337

Johnston, Kathyann, RNC
By Appointment 705-645-3991

BRAMALEA

Saffar, Amal, RNC
14 Mayberry Ct 905-793-8243

BRAMPTON

Bakogianni, Marsha, RNC
110 Sheldrake Ct 905-455-9109

Riley, Geoff, RNC
7700 Hurontario St, Ste 408 .905-451-4475

BRANTFORD

Janzen, Rolf P., RNC
205 Brant Ave 519-752-7010

BROCKVILLE

Cossitt, Jennifer, RNC
By Appointment 613-345-5078

BURLINGTON

Loves, Helena, RNC
2404 Prospect St 519-333-9598

CALLANDER

Vlasaty, Christine, RNC
393 King St 705-752-4125

CAMBRIDGE

Hutton, Terilyn, RNC
751 Hamilton St 519-653-3083

CAPREOL

Fawcett, Ken, RNC
By Appointment 705-858-1440

COCHRANE

Palmer, Paul, RNC
By Appointment 705-272-3819

CORBEIL

Lochhead, Margaret, RNC
By Appointment 705-752-4601

COURTICE

McArthur, Elaine, RNC
96 Hemmingway Dr 905-434-2342

DELHI

Jay, Agnes, RNC
450 Delcrest Ave 519-582-2103

ELMIRA

**Ursu, Michael, RNC;
Ursu, Peter, RNC**
By Appointment 519-883-5132

FENWICK

Tucker, Judy, RNC
1581 Maple St N, RR #4 905-892-5610

FISHERVILLE

Sherk, Judith, RNC
By Appointment 905-776-2243

FORT ERIE

Johnson, Rachel Irene, RNC
By Appointment 905-871-9650

GARSON

Racette, Monique, RNC
441 Goodwill Rd 705-693-9394

GUELPH

Cavanagh, Sue, RNC
510-55 Yarmouth St 519-822-6722

HAMILTON

Basham, Kathryn, RNC
133 E 17th S 905-383-7693

Henderson, Paul, RNC
58 Everton Pl 905-574-7365

Lee, Michelle, RNC
21 Rebecca St 905-524-5434

Peacock, Dianne, RNC & RN
68 Broadway Ave 905-525-9140
(ext. 24441)

Simon, Chris, RNC
141 Winchester Blvd 905-574-7996

Simpson, Sharon, RNC
584 Concession St 905-318-8518

INWOOD

Mater, Janet, RNC
By Appointment 519-844-2344

KETTLEBY

Hale, Hugh, RNC
By Appointment 905-618-0275

KINGSTON

Gabourie, Maureen, RNC
256 Collingwood St 613-548-0646

Raymond, Patricia, RNC
1201 Division St 613-544-8535

KITCHENER

Winkler, Steve, RNC
2-26 Blucher St 519-576-2601

LEAMINGTON

Dick, Janet, RNC
RR #2, 137 Concession 3 . . .519-326-5830

LONDON

Caro, Ria, RNC
180 Old Post Rd 519-434-0341

Carwana, Deborah, RNC
830 Princess Ave 519-672-7997

Lok, Peter, RNC
897 Adelaide St N 519-642-2096

Pugh, Dr. Ruth, DC &, RNC
38 Carmen Cr 519-227-1363

Scott, Allene, RNC
120 Cherryhill Dr, Apt 1108 .519-472-0060

MARKHAM

Carleton-Fitchett, Catherine, RNC
110 Markville Rd 905-513-1135

Josephs, Timothy A., RNC
16 Wootten Way N 905-472-0403

MIDLAND

Martin, John, RNC
69 Mary Elizabeth Cr 905-477-7249

Pratt, Rosalie, RNC
By Appointment 705-538-1438

MILTON

Pollack, Nova, RNC
306-80 Ontario St N 905-875-1741

Pyette, Peggy, RNC
5550 Appleby Line,
RR #6 416-335-1766

MILVERTON

Colley, Lise, RNC
46 Main St 519-884-1811

MISSISSAUGA

Ali, Elvis, RNC & ND
45-3460 S Millway 416-964-8572/
537-2273

McLaren, Diane, RNC
6892 Gracefield Dr 905-824-4811

Pyke, Gail, RNC
50 Eglinton Ave W,
Ste 1906 905-890-9099

To Your Health
Borchenko, Lilya, RNC
154 Queen St S, Unit #104 .905-821-3758

NEW HAMBURG

Germann, Kathy, RNC
By Appointment 519-662-2520

NEWMARKET

Cole-Hamilton, Jane, RNC
355 Park Ave 905-895-2040

Poncelet, Dr. Darren, DC & RNC
16,775 Yonge St, Ste 214 . . .905-898-6644

NIAGARA FALLS

Kerr, Deborah C., RNC
6110 Strohan St 905-354-9198

OAKVILLE

Dean, Ellen, RNC
1512 Pilgrim's Way, #622 . .905-585-8861

McKnight, June, RNC
2170 Marine Dr, Ste 703 . . .905-469-0059

Soucie, Cecile, RNC
140-1 Ripley Ct 905-338-5878

ORANGEVILLE

Harris, Carol, RNC
50 Third St, #E2 519-941-7361

McKinney, Peter, RNC
52 Lakeview Ct 519-942-2446

Swann, Carmelyn, RNC
61 Eastview Cr 519-941-3567

ORILLIA

Williams, Lynn, RNC
1 Olive Cr, Unit #3 705-327-0327

OSHAWA

Brown, Carla-Lynn, RNC
By Appointment 905-655-8148

Friede, Cheryle, RNC
909 Simcoe St N, #4 905-434-9398

Head, Kate, RNC
860 Simcoe St N 905-655-5767

OTTAWA

**Shambare, Chipochemeso,
RNC & RN**
206-400 Slater St 613-233-9422

Watson, Ruth, RNC
255 Lincoln Hts Rd 613-721-0071

OWEN SOUND

U-Ming, Peggy-Ann, RNC
571-2nd Ave E 519-376-4251

PEMBROKE

Haring, Jo-Anne I., RNC
By Appointment 613-638-3597

PERTH

Vanderpost, Jennine, RNC
98 North St 613-267-1831

PETERBOROUGH

Bradner, Jean, RNC
2052 Moncrief Rd 705-743-4371

PICKERING

McCarthy, Mary-Jo, RNC
2501 Parkdale St 905-576-6655

PICKERING VILLAGE

Morgan, Audrey, RNC
22 Duffin St 905-420-1443

PONTYPOOL

White, Earl, RNC
By Appointment 705-277-1310

PORT PERRY

Blackburn, Gerald, RNC
21 Fralick's Beach Rd 905-985-7941

RICHMOND HILL

Cameron, Cristina, RNC
9 Timber Valley Ave 905-773-9532

Cheung, Norman, RNC
75 Weldrick Rd E,
TH#1017 416-421-7526

Distin, Julie, RNC
148 Spadina Rd 905-770-4400

**Richmond Hill Natural Health
Centre**
Miscampbell, Danielle, RNC
10720 Yonge St, Ste 220 . . .905-737-0284

RIDGEWAY

McKenzie, Donald, RNC
978 Burleigh Rd 905-894-1657

ST. CATHARINES

Andrew, Keith L., RNC
18 Frontenac Dr 905-646-7335

Boyle, Gail, RNC
808-35 Towering Heights . . .905-988-9185

ST. GEORGE

Yaychuk-Arabel, Irene, RNC
By Appointment 519-448-4381

SAULT STE. MARIE

Soltya, Karen, RNC
1329 Leigh's Bay Rd 705-949-9629

SMITH'S FALLS

Van Ulden, Heather, RNC
By Appointment 613-283-3940

STONEY CREEK

Patel, Daksha, RNC
72 Centennial Parkway S . . .905-662-6566

STRATFORD

Strawbridge, Joyce, RNC & RN
By Appointment 519-271-0822

THORNBURY

McCall, Nancy, RNC
By Appointment 519-599-2640

THORNHILL

Nishihama, Vicki, RNC
170 Dudley Ave, Apt 411 . . .905-773-9532

Olive, Carolyn, RNC
97 Confederation Way 905-709-3261

TORONTO

Barker, Teresa, RNC
5315A Yonge St 416-590-0297

Coulson, David, RNC
47 Thorncliffe Park Dr,
#2104 416-467-7000

Day, Charlene, RNC
161 Franklin Ave 416-512-1168

Dey, Josefina, RNC
207 Dewhurst Blvd 416-325-6750

Eldridge, Thomas, RNC
3 Graham Gardens 416-653-2774

Fejes, Eva, RNC
48-110 George Henry
Blvd 416-223-6574

Healy, Marion, RNC
588 Durie St 416-960-6200

Imbert, Lorrie, RNC
80 Courcelette Rd 416-690-8954

Laberge, Cecile, RNC
102-268 Poplar Plains Rd ...416-967-4928

Lamoureaux-Magro, Diane, RNC
108 Beresford Ave 416-762-9147

Larade, Monica, RNC
1901 Bayview Ave, Apt 304 .416-932-9850

Leung, Anna, RNC
140 Langford Ave 416-469-1727

Lewocz, Karen, RNC
195 Cranbrooke Ave 416-322-5496

Mikhail, Marguerite, RNC
1239 Kipling Ave 416-394-7650

Morin, Sylvie, RNC
104 Pintail Cr 416-325-0980

Natural Health Institute
Levin, Jeff, RNC
258 Dupont St 416-926-1200

Neil, Lynda, RNC
1300 Islington Ave,
#2201 416-668-5828

Putt, Melissa, RNC
4 Sandstone Ln 416-461-2668

Radojcic, Aleks, RNC
5 Carscadden Dr 416-636-8444

Rawlings, Gerri, RNC
1102-40 Pleasant Blvd 416-927-0207

Shmoil, Yoliya, RNC
72 Orpington Cr 416-742-5676

Soehner, Lynn, RNC
1315-55 Harbour Sq 416-594-9823

Vanderstoop, Audrey, RNC
255 Shaw St 416-960-6200

TROY

Barker, Heather, RNC
By Appointment 519-647-2603

UXBRIDGE

Adams, Lisa, RNC
By Appointment 905-852-6412

WATERFORD

Sloan, David, RNC
RR #5, Conc 10,
Cherry Valley Rd 519-443-4747

WATERLOO

Forwell, Margaret Anne, RNC
22 King St S, Ste 403 519-885-4120

Heritage Health Centre
Bricker, Trudy R., RNC
151 Frobisher Dr,
Ste D-113 519-746-4004

Schaner, Joan, RNC
376 Northlake Dr 519-746-2691

Skafte, Kirsten B., RNC
203-445 Beechwood Pl ...519-886-1861

Stokes, Vicki, RNC
84 Marshall St, #10 519-747-4255

Wehi, Diann, RNC
517-M Weber St N 519-746-8937

Wirth, Nena, RNC
610 Bridge St W 519-747-9453

WELLAND

Sharpe-Pietras, Linda, RNC
92 Sumbler Rd 905-732-6608

WHITBY

Crouch, Louise, RNC
57 Regency Cr 905-430-1750

WIARTON

Whitcroft, Thomas C., RNC
By Appointment 519-534-4012

WINDSOR

Faubert, Wendy, RNC
3065 Askin Blvd 519-944-0107

Gadzala, Mira, RNC
10540 Palms Cr 519-979-0176

WOODSTOCK

Reeve, Scott, RNC
275 St. Andrew's Rd 519-539-9234

WROXETER

Legge, Philip J., RNC
16 Main St 519-335-6799

 # Québec Nutritional Consultants

NOTE: Check the credentials of your practitioner (see above, "Questions to Ask"). This publication cannot and does not certify or represent the qualifications of practitioners, or the quality of care available from them.

DOLLARD

Parent, Claude, RNC
84, Lamarche 514-421-0475

LA SALLE

Jew, Steve Y., RNC
1390 Bernie St 514-365-6358

LAVAL

Lamarche, Louise, RNC
272, Rollin, Pont-Viau 514-345-4772

MONTREAL

Baldassarre, Vince, RNC
2655 Springland St 514-761-7414

Gimena, Santiago, RNC & ND
11020, Drouart 514-331-7164

Rochester, Jessica, RNC
5687, Cote St-Antoine 514-488-5177

Thomas, Anne, RNC
2445 Sunset Rd, Apt 410 ...514-731-5231

✦ Saskatchewan Nutritional Consultants

NOTE: Check the credentials of your practitioner (see above, "Questions to Ask"). This publication cannot and does not certify or represent the qualifications of practitioners, or the quality of care available from them.

MOOSE JAW

Adami, Andrew John, RNC
937 James St 306-692-3533

PRAIRIE RIVER

Waskowic, Lorraine, RNC
By Appointment 306-889-4248

PRINCE ALBERT

Anderson, Susan, RNC
630-10th Ave E 306-922-4372

REGINA

Kumar, Vincent, RNC
By Appointment 306-522-2416

Liggett, Ivaleen, RNC
1158 Fleet St 306-789-4443

Stecyk, Cindy, RNC
218 Michener Dr 306-584-2260

SASKATOON

Christie, Rose-Marie, RNC
143 Perreault Cr 306-931-2115

McClare, Glen, RNC
205 Ave G, N 306-244-2606

Pahwa, Ranvir, RNC
331 Keeley Cr 306-664-3873

Osteopathy

WHAT IS OSTEOPATHY

Osteopathy is a form of holistic health care often practised together with conventional medicine by Doctors of Osteopathy (DOs). Osteopathy involves a hands-on diagnostic and treatment technique, called osteopathic manual therapy, to alleviate problems mainly related to the musculo-skeletal system. While the focus on musculo-skeletal disorders is similar to that of chiropractic, there are differences in techniques and training. Osteopathic physicians work extensively with the body's soft tissue, muscles and ligaments to improve joint movement. As well, Doctors of Osteopathy practising in Canada are also physicians, having been trained in the U.S., where Doctors of Osteopathy are licensed as physicians in all 50 states. In Canada, Doctors of Osteopathy with the same training are recognized as medical doctors in certain provinces, but are limited to manual practice of osteopathy in others. By contrast, in Britain, where the profession has recently become regulated, practitioners are trained in the manual techniques of osteopathy, but are not medical doctors.

The philosophy of osteopathic medicine is based on the concept that the body constitutes a biological unit. The body's systems are considered to be interrelated, and dependent upon one another for good health. Osteopathy was founded in 1874 in the United States by Dr. Andrew Taylor Still, who theorized that when the body was properly adjusted, the muscles and joints would be subject to less strain and the body better able to heal itself. In other words, correction of structural problems helps the body to function better. Osteopathic physicians interview patients about their medical history, lifestyle and general health, and diagnose by observing the body framework, testing reflexes and muscles, possibly arranging for X-rays, and using their hands to detect problems in body tissues. If a diagnosis indicates that osteopathic manual therapy may assist, treatment usually involves massage techniques, rhythmic movements and stretching to improve joint mobility, and possibly a thrusting manoeuvre to open a joint (a high velocity, low amplitude thrust). Certain branches of osteopathy involve palpating (examining by feeling with the hands) and gently massaging the body to affect the cerebro-spinal fluid.

Potential in Canada

In contrast to Britain, where the number of osteopathic practitioners has grown from 567 in 1982 to 1,606 in 1992, and the U.S., where the number of Doctors of Osteopathy has increased by about 50% in the last decade to more than 37,000, the number of osteopathic physicians practising in Canada has been declining (Sources: British Medical Association; American Association of Colleges of Osteopathic Medicine). There are now only a handful of practising osteopathic physicians in Canada with training from one of the recognized U.S. colleges (see below "Osteopathic Education"). These Doctors of Osteopathy are located in Alberta, B.C. and Ontario. The reasons for this decline may include the lack of recognition by the medical licensing authorities in certain provinces and the lack of a training program comparable to those offered in the U.S. However, the liberalization of such licensing requirements for U.S.-trained doctors of osteopathy was the subject of a special report entitled "Canada Opens its Doors" in the June 1996 issue of *The DO*, the journal of the American Osteopathic Association. The magazine noted that "Canada has plenty of room for more DO's." Dr. Ted Findlay, a practising Doctor of Osteopathy in Alberta, reports that he has been extremely busy since opening his Calgary practice in 1993.

BENEFITS OF OSTEOPATHY

Once your doctor of osteopathy has ruled out non-medical causes for your illness or injury, he or she may use manipulation. Osteopathy may relieve musculo-skeletal problems, including back pain, spinal and joint problems, and arthritis. The technique is also an adjunctive treatment (supplementary to medical treatment) for asthma, carpal tunnel syndrome, menstrual pain, migraines, sciatica, respiratory disorders, chronic fatigue, allergies, digestive disorders, high blood pressure, cardiac diseases, and disorders of the nervous system.

QUESTIONS TO ASK

✦ Is your osteopathic physician a Doctor of Osteopathy, with training at an institution recognized by the Canadian Osteopathic Association or the American Osteopathic Association? This signifies that they have received training to the standards required for licensure as a physician in Alberta, B.C., New Brunswick, Québec, and all states of the U.S.

NOTE: There are colleges in Canada offering diploma training in manual osteopathy. These are not recognized by the Canadian Osteopathic Association as they do not offer programs equivalent to those of the recognized U.S. colleges. If your practitioner has a diploma, but is not a Doctor of Osteopathy, you may wish to ask about his or her other qualifications as a health practitioner.

✦ Is your osteopathic physician a member of the College of Physicians and Surgeons? This question applies only to those living in Alberta, B.C., New Brunswick and Québec, where Doctors of Osteopathy are members of the Colleges.

NOTE: At the present time, there are no Doctors of Osteopathy practising in New Brunswick and Québec.

✦ Does your osteopathic physician believe that you have any conditions that would make osteopathic treatment inappropriate?

NOTE: A number of conditions have been identified as contra-indicated (to be avoided) for specific areas of the body, such as primary bone tumours and fractures. A qualified osteopathic physician is trained in contra-indications.

✦ If osteopathy is appropriate for your condition, how many treatments will be required and at what cost?

NOTE: There is government medical coverage for treatment by a Doctor of Osteopathy in Alberta and B.C., and partial coverage in Ontario (see below, "Osteopathy in Your Province).

GOVERNMENT REGULATION

Regulation means that there is provincial legislation establishing a professional governing body. This body, usually called a "College," is given a duty in law to protect the public. Governing bodies are established to ensure that regulated practitioners meet specific standards before they practise, to investigate complaints, and to take disciplinary action against practitioners where appropriate.

Doctors of Osteopathy with medical training from a recognized U.S. college are regulated and licensed to practise as physicians in Alberta and British Columbia. In these provinces, practising Doctors of Osteopathy are members of the College of Physicians and Surgeons, the governing body that establishes standards and disciplines physicians. In B.C., where the College of Physicians and Surgeons eased licensing requirements in 1995, Doctors of Osteopathy can choose to be licensed either as full physicans, or as practitioners limited to osteopathic manual therapy.

Other provinces also allow for licensing of osteopathic practitioners as physicians, but no osteopathic physicians are currently practising in these provinces. For example, New Brunswick's *Medical Act* provides for an osteopathic register. In Québec, licensure may be possible under the province's *Medical Act* if certain criteria are met, including fluency in French. Anyone interested in pursuing a career in osteopathic medicine in Québec should first contact the Collège des Médecins du Québec.

In Saskatchewan, *The Osteopathic Practice Act* is in place to establish a regulatory body to regulate the profession. Under this legislation, Doctors of Osteopathy would be governed by their own regulatory body. However, there are presently no Doctors of Osteopathy practising in Saskatchewan.

In Ontario, most practising Doctors of Osteopathy with the same credentials as those licensed as physicians in Alberta, B.C. and the U.S., have been left in a legal grey zone, with no governing body in place. This was to be rectified with a provision in Ontario's *Regulated Health Professions Act, 1991*, to allow for full practice rights for Doctors of Osteopathy. This provisison would allow for their membership in the College of Physicians and Surgeons of Ontario, classed as an osteopath. However, the provision has not yet been proclaimed into force. As an exception, two of Ontario's practising Doctors of Osteopathy are classed as physicians and are members of the College of Physicians and Surgeons (see below, "Osteopathy in Your Province - Ontario").

Currently, in all other provinces and the territories, there are no practising Doctors of Osteopathy and there is no legislation to regulate the profession. This also means that no minimum educational standards exist for those calling themselves osteopathic physicians. There is legislation in every province restricting either the practice of medicine or the practice of specific medical acts, such as diagnosis.

There is no regulatory body in place in any province to govern or discipline those earning diplomas after part-time study in the manual practice of osteopathy.

GOVERNMENT HEALTH CARE FUNDING

Government health care funding for treatment from a Doctor of Osteopathy is available in Alberta, B.C. and Ontario, the three provinces where Doctors of Osteopathy are currently practising (see below "Osteopathy in Your Province"). There are no osteopathic phsyicians practising in Newfoundland, but if a patient consults a registered U.S. osteopathic physician who would otherwise be eligible for licensure as a physician in Newfoundland, the patient will be fully covered by the province's Medical Care Plan.

PRIVATE HEALTH INSURANCE

Some private health insurance companies cover osteopathy as part of their extended health care plans. Check with your insurance agent as to the conditions of coverage.

CANADIAN & U.S. ASSOCIATIONS

The Canadian Osteopathic Aid Society (COAS)
575 Waterloo St
London, Ontario N6B 2R2.
Tel: 519-439-5521

Financial assistance has been available in the past to Canadian students who wish to pursue the study of Osteopathic Medicine at one of the 16 colleges in the United States. Those seriously interested should write to the Canadian Osteopathic Aid Society. In 1996, funds were not available, but the Society states that they may become available in the future.

Canadian Osteopathic Association
575 Waterloo St
London, Ontario N6B 2R2
Tel: 519-439-5521

Call for information about osteopathy, or to discuss the credentials of a practitioner. The Association's Administrative Secretary is Marguerite Torney. This office is also the practice of D.F. Lauder, D.O.

American Association of Colleges of Osteopathic Medicine
6110 Executive Blvd, Ste 405
Rockville, Maryland 20852
Tel: 301-468-0990/2037

This association offers prospective students a centralized application service for all schools.

American Osteopathic Association
142 E Ontario St
Chicago, Illinois 60611
Tel: 312-280-5800

This is the professional body for U.S. osteopathic physicians. Write for information on osteopathic medicine and education.

American Osteopathic Healthcare Association
5301 Wisconsin Ave NW, #630
Washington, D.C. 20015

Write for information on osteopathic medicine.

OSTEOPATHIC EDUCATION

Those interested in a career as a Doctor of Osteopathy must complete four years of medical training at one of 16 accredited colleges of osteopathic medicine in the U.S. (see below). Admission requirements normally include a bachelor's degree with good academic performance in basic sciences. Applicants are also expected to present scores from the Medical College Admission Test (MCAT).

The curriculum includes required subjects in the basic sciences such as anatomy, physiology, biochemistry, pathology, microbiology and pharmacology. Required clinical subjects include medicine, pediatrics, obstetrics, gynecology, surgery, radiology, and preventive medicine. Following graduation and a 12-month rotating internship at an approved hospital, osteopathic physicians wishing to become specialists must serve an additional three to five years of residency or fellowship training to become certified in such specialties as surgery, internal medicine or pediatrics.

The article, "Canada Opens Its Doors" contains a detailed review of the varying requirements for licensure among Canada's provinces. Those interested in pursuing a career may obtain a copy by contacting John Sprovieri, Managing Editor, The DO, at the American Osteopathic Association (Tel: 312-280-5800; Fax: 312-280-3860; the address of the Association is listed above, under the heading "Canadian & U.S. Associations"). Before making a decision as to the province where they wish to practise, students are advised to obtain up-to-date information from the licensing authority (governing body) of the province. In making a career choice, it is also advisable to consult with the Canadian Osteopathic Association, as well as the practising Doctors of Osteopathy listed in this directory.

Listed below are the 16 Colleges of Osteopathic Medicine in the U.S. recognized for licensure in provinces that regulate the practice of osteopathy. In choosing a training program, one may wish to compare the qualifications of faculty (their education and experience), student-teacher ratios, admission requirements, program content and length, number of clinical hours, and all fees and contract terms, including refund policies. In addition, it is useful to speak with students and graduates of the various programs about their standards.

Part-time diploma training is offered in manual osteopathy at colleges in Toronto and Montréal, also listed below. These are not recognized by the Canadian Osteopathic Association, which requires training schools to meet the U.S. standards required for licensure in provinces where Doctors of Osteopathy are regulated. Most provinces have legislation requiring private vocational schools to meet certain minimum standards, often related to financial stability, for the protection of consumers. These requirements vary from province to province, and certain health care training programs are not covered by such legislation. Contact the Ministry of Education in your province for more information on their policies regarding registration of private vocational schools.

Chicago College of Osteopathic Medicine of Midwestern University
555 31st St
Downers Grove, Illinois 60515-1235
Tel: 708-515-6472

College of Osteopathic Medicine of the Pacific
College Plaza
Pomona, California 91766-1889
Tel: 909-623-6116

Kirksville College of Osteopathic Medicine
800 W Jefferson St
Kirksville, Missouri 63501
Tel: 816-626-2121

Lake Erie College of Osteopathic Medicine
1858 West Grandview Blvd
Erie, Pennsylvania 16509
Tel: 814-866-6441

Michigan State University College of Osteopathic Medicine
East Fee Hall
East Lansing, Michigan 48824
Tel: 517-355-9611

New York College of Osteopathic Medicine of New York Institute of Technology
Wheatley Rd, Box 170
Old Westbury, New York 11568
Tel: 516-626-6900

Nova Southeastern University College of Osteopathic Medicine
1750 NE 167th St
North Miami Beach, Florida 33162-3097
Tel: 305-949-4000

Ohio University College of Osteopathic Medicine
Grosvenor and Irvine Halls
Athens, Ohio 45701
Tel: 614-593-2500

Oklahoma State University College of Osteopathic Medicine
1111 W 17th St
Tulsa, Oklahoma 74107
Tel: 918-582-1972

Philadelphia College of Osteopathic Medicine
4170 City Ave
Philadelphia, Pennsylvania 19131
Tel: 215-871-6100

The University of Health Sciences College of Osteopathic Medicine
2105 Independence Blvd
Kansas City, Missouri 64124
Tel: 816-283-2000

University of Medicine and Dentistry of New Jersey - School of Osteopathic Medicine
One Medical Center Dr, Ste 312
Stratford, New Jersey 08084
Tel: 609-566-6990

University of New England College of Osteopathic Medicine
11 Hills Beach Rd
Biddeford, Maine 04005
Tel: 207-283-0171

University of North Texas Health Science Center at Fort Worth - Texas College of Osteopathic Medicine
3500 Camp Bowie Blvd
Fort Worth, Texas 76107
Tel: 817-735-2000

University of Osteopathic Medicine and Health Sciences/College of Osteopathic Medicine and Surgery
3200 Grand Ave
Des Moines, Iowa 50312
Tel: 515-271-1400

West Virginia School of Osteopathic Medicine
400 North Lee St
Lewisburg, West Virginia 24901
Tel: 304-645-6270

Canadian Colleges

Listed below are two Canadian colleges offering diplomas in osteopathy.

Canadian College of Osteopathy
39 Alvin Ave
Toronto, Ontario M4T 2A7
Tel: 416-323-1465

The four-year-old Canadian College of Osteopathy grants a Diploma of Osteopathy - Manual Practice, DOMP. The college, which opened in 1992, is affiliated with the Collège d'Etudes Ostéopathie de Montréal. Admission requirements include a Bachelor of Science degree and licensure as a health professional, such as a registered massage therapist. The college offers a five-year part-time program, followed by a thesis. The program is not equivalent to those offered by the U.S. colleges.

La Collège d'Etudes Ostéopathique de Montréal
5637, Avenue Stirling
Montréal, Québec H3T 1R7
Tel: 1-800-263-2816 or 514-342-2816

This college, founded in 1981, grants a diploma in osteopathy, or diplôme d'ostéopathie. Training is offered in French or English, with a minimum of 12 students required for a class in either language. The college offers a five-year, part-time program, followed by a thesis. The college does not offer training equivalent to that of the U.S. colleges.

✦ Osteopathy in Your Province

Only those provinces with practising Doctors of Osteopathy are listed (Alberta, B.C. and Ontario). The following information is provided:

Legislation

✦ provincial laws governing osteopathic physicians

Government Health Care Funding

✦ details on government health care funding, where it exists

Governing Bodies

✦ addresses and telephone numbers of governing bodies

✦ these are the offices you may contact to check if your practitioner is registered or to lodge a complaint

Provincial Association

✦ address and telephone number of the one provincial osteopathic professional association, located in B.C.

Doctors of Osteopathy

✦ names, addresses and telephone numbers of practitioners, listed alphabetically by city

NOTE: Most of the names of Doctors of Osteopathy listed here were provided by the Canadian Osteopathic Association. Nonetheless, it is wise to check the credentials of your practitioner. This publication cannot and does not certify or represent the qualifications of practitioners, or the quality of care available from them. We cannot and do not confirm that those listed are registered as required by law.

✦ Alberta

Legislation

Osteopathic physicians are regulated under the *Medical Profession Act*, the same legislation governing medical doctors in the province. Under the Act it is an offence to practise osteopathy unless the practitioner is registered as a member of the College of Physicians and Surgeons of Alberta.

Government Health Care Funding

Visits to Doctors of Osteopathy are covered under Alberta Health. Billing is paid as per an office visit to general practitioners for any other medical complaint. For information on Alberta Health coverage, call 403-427-0259 or toll-free 310-0000, and ask for Alberta Health.

Alberta Governing Body

College of Physicians & Surgeons of Alberta
10180-101st St
Edmonton, Alberta T5J 3S4
Tel: 403-423-4764

Call the College to ensure that your osteopathic physician is registered, or to make a complaint.

✦ Alberta Doctors of Osteopathy

NOTE: Check the credentials of your practitioner (see above, "Questions to Ask"). This publication cannot and does not certify or represent the qualifications of practitioners, or the quality of care available from them. We cannot and do not confirm that those listed are registered as required by law.

CALGARY

Findlay, C.E., DO
1603-20th Ave NW 403-282-7165

✦ British Columbia

Legislation

Osteopathic physicians in B.C. are regulated under the provincial *Medical Practitioners Act*. Under the Act, a person who is a graduate of a school or college of osteopathy approved by the American Osteopathic Association and who has passed an examination is entitled on payment of fees to be entered in the register of the College of Physicians and Surgeons of B.C. Doctors of Osteopathy may be licensed either as full physicians or as practitioners limited to osteopathic manipulative medicine.

Government Health Care Funding

Treatment by Osteopathic Doctors is fully covered under the Medical Services Plan of B.C., with no user fees.

British Columbia Governing Body

College of Physicians & Surgeons of B.C.
1807 W 10th Ave
Vancouver, B.C. V6J 2A9
Tel: 604-733-3503/7758

Call to ensure that your osteopathic physician is registered, or to make a complaint.

British Columbia Association

B.C. Osteopathic Association
1105 Pandora Ave
Victoria, B.C. V8V 3P9
Tel: 604-389-1959

✦ British Columbia Doctors of Osteopathy

NOTE: Check the credentials of your practitioner (see above, "Questions to Ask"). This publication cannot and does not certify or represent the qualifications of practitioners, or the quality of care available from them. We cannot and do not confirm that those listed are registered as required by law.

PENTICTON

Barr, Hugh, DO
304-965 King .604-492-2919 (Wednesdays)

VICTORIA

Church, James, DO
Medical Arts Building #270
1105 Pandora Ave 604-389-1959

✦ Ontario

Legislation

Doctors of Osteopathy, with credentials allowing for licensure as fully-trained physicians in all 50 states, Alberta, B.C. and Québec, are not recognized by the College of Physicians and Surgeons in Ontario. The *Regulated Health Professions Act, 1991*, has a provision in its Table providing for membership in the College of Physicians and Surgeons of Ontario, classed as an osteopath. However, this provision has not been proclaimed in force.

Another piece of legislation, the *Drugless Practitioners Act*, and Regulation 280, allows for the regulation of osteopathic physicians, but there is currently no governing body, due to the small number of practitioners. Those previously registered under this Act have therefore had no means of renewing their registration. It is for this reason that the government originally made moves to allow osteopathic physicians to become members of the College of Physicians and Surgeons.

As a result, there is currently no regulatory body for Doctors of Osteopathy and they are technically unregistered health practitioners precluded from the practice of surgery or the prescription of pharmaceuticals.

Members of the public wishing to check the credentials of a Doctor of Osteopathy may contact the Canadian Osteopathic Association (see above, "Canadian & U.S. Associations"). You may wish to confirm that the Doctor has received training from one of the 16 colleges recognized in the United States (see above, "Osteopathic Education").

Government Health Care Funding

The Ontario Health Insurance Plan (OHIP) provides partial coverage for treatment from a Doctor of Osteopathy. The Plan pays a maximum of $12 toward the fee for an initial visit. For example, if the fee for the first visit is $27, the patient pays $15 and OHIP pays $12.

For subsequent visits, OHIP pays a maximum of $9.50, to a maximum of $155 per year. This maximum includes $25 in X-rays per year.

For OHIP information, in Toronto call 416-482-1111; in Ottawa, call 613-783-4400; in Mississauga call 905-275-2730; for other areas, check your telephone book Blue Pages under Health.

✦ Ontario Doctors of Osteopathy

NOTE: Check the credentials of your practitioner (see above, "Questions to Ask"). This publication cannot and does not certify or represent the qualifications of practitioners, or the quality of care available from them. We cannot and do not confirm that those listed are registered as required by law.

BARRIE

Fiddler, Douglas, DO
(Not in private practice)
Emergency -
Royal Victoria Hospital 705-728-9802

LINDSAY

Fiddler David, DO
832 Monarch Rd 705-328-1663

LONDON

Lauder D. F., DO
575 Waterloo St 519-439-5521

ORILLIA

Church, William K, DO
93 Neywash 705-326-9551

TORONTO

Mayen, Oscar L. (U.K.)
100 Granby St 416-340-7688

Pocock R.M., DO
40 Alexander 416-922-4491

✦ Reflexology

WHAT IS REFLEXOLOGY

Reflexology is a natural healing therapy based on the principle that there are 'reflex' points on the feet and hands that correspond to every part of your body. The reflexologist applies finger, thumb and hand pressure to these areas on the feet or hands to influence the health of the corresponding organ or body part. Usually, the client is made comfortable, often in a reclining position, with the reflexologist working on the bare feet. If this is not possible, the session can be given on the hands. The sessions usually last 45-60 minutes. No oils, creams or lotions are used. The Reflexology Association of Canada notes that reflexology was practised thousands of years ago in India, China and Egypt. Reflexology was brought to the West in the early 1900s by Dr. William Fitzgerald, Connecticut laryngologist, and was developed further by American physiotherapist Eunice Ingham.

BENEFITS OF REFLEXOLOGY

The Reflexology Association of Canada notes that reflexologists do not diagnose, prescribe for, or treat any specific illness. The Association also states that its members do not work in opposition to or as a replacement for medical, chiropractic or other healing arts. Rather, reflexology complements and enhances them.

Reflexology reduces stress and tension, and is considered an effective relaxation technique. It is said to improve circulation, help the body to eliminate toxins more efficiently, revitalize the body and bring about balance in the body's systems. Reflexology may help you with: stress, headaches, migraines, constipation, indigestion, congestion, menstrual/pre-menstrual/menopause concerns, tired achy feet, neck/shoulder/back/leg/foot pain, allergies, asthma, sciatica, bladder concerns, insomnia, arthritis, sinusitis, fatigue, anaemia, diabetes or hypoglycemia, edema (excessive accumulation of fluid in the body tissues), fatigue, high or low blood pressure, and prostate problems. Reflexology may also relieve pain from foot problems, such as bunions, hammer-toes, flat feet, or high arches.

QUESTIONS TO ASK

✦ Is your reflexologist certified by the Reflexology Association of Canada? You may check by contacting the association (see below, "National Association").
NOTE: Such certification means that the practitioner has met the standards set by the association, but this does not constitute a licence, such as that required by health practitioners regulated under provincial law.

✦ How much experience does your reflexologist have? Has your reflexologist had experience with a person with your condition, and what were the results?

✦ Is your reflexologist trained in any other form of health care? If so, what is the extent of the training?

✦ Can your reflexologist provide professional references?

✦ What is the price of a session, and how long does it last?

GOVERNMENT REGULATION

There is no government regulation of the practitioners of reflexology in Canada, meaning that there is no legislation establishing regulatory bodies to register and discipline qualified practitioners. This also means that there are no minimum educational standards for those calling themselves practitioners.

However, there is a non-profit organization (see below, "National Association") that accredits training programs and certifies practitioners.

NATIONAL ASSOCIATION

Reflexology Association of Canada
Box 110, 451 Turnberry St
Brussels, Ontario N0G 1M0
Tel: 519-887-9991
Fax: 519-887-9792

This federally-chartered non-profit association, formed in 1976, provides referrals to its certified reflexologists across Canada. The association sets standards for practitioners and teachers of reflexology.

REFLEXOLOGY EDUCATION

Those wishing to become certified reflexologists with the Reflexology Association of Canada must complete 30 hours of classroom training and 60 hours practical training, for a total of 90 hours. This is followed by a written and practical exam and submission of the case histories recorded during practical training.

Training in the theory and practice of reflexology is available from teachers who have been certified by the Reflexology Association of Canada. Various types of programs are offered, each totalling the required 30 hours of classroom training. Training programs are available on weekends, evenings or days.

To locate a qualified teacher in your area, contact the Reflexology Association of Canada, listed above, or call one of the following telephone numbers.

Alberta: 403-944-2576
British Columbia: 604-859-3338
Ontario 519-887-9991
Manitoba: 204-586-4448
Québec: 819-474-3351
Saskatchewan: 306-789-9685

✦ Reflexology in Your Province

Provinces are listed alphabetically below, with the following information:

✦ names, addresses and telephone numbers of Reflexologists, listed alphabetically by city

NOTE: Confirm the certification of your practitioner or obtain the names of newly certified practitioners in your area by contacting the Reflexology Association of Canada (see above, "National Association").

✦ Alberta Reflexologists

NOTE: Check the credentials of your practitioner (see above, "Questions to Ask"). This publication cannot and does not certify or represent the qualifications of practitioners, or the quality of care available from them.

BEAVERLODGE

South Peace Reflexology
Wieliczko, Cicely
By Appointment 403-356-2119

CALGARY

Horrick, John A.
Glenmore Tr & 37th St SW .403-249-0321

DIXONVILLE

Chambers, Kathleen
Chambers, Patty
By Appointment 403-971-2245

EDMONTON

The Helios Centre
Slade, Lauren
10136 - 122nd St 403-444-3668

Robinson, Elsa Y.
111th St & 51st Ave 403-438-1061

Varey, Donna M.
137th Ave & 66th St 403-456-8823

EVANSBURG (EDMONTON)

Fisher, Katherine E.
Wildwood & #16 Hwy
Yellowhead 403-325-2061

GRANDE PRAIRIE

Roch, Marlene P.
124th Ave 403-532-1537

LONGVIEW

Robert, Lise
Highwood Dr 403-558-3663

RED DEER

Webster, Ann M.
Reichley St 403-347-8153

ST. ALBERT

Grandin Health & Healing Centre
Coughlan, Lorraine, MH
367 Rivercrest Plaza 403-459-7796

✦ British Columbia Reflexologists

NOTE: Check the credentials of your practitioner (see above, "Questions to Ask"). This publication cannot and does not certify or represent the qualifications of practitioners, or the quality of care available from them.

CRANBROOK

Hunter, Barb
20th St S 604-426-7287

DUNCAN

Morgan, Dave
By Appointment 604-246-5899

FALKLAND

Talbot, Linda M.
By Appointment 604-379-2678

HOPE

Haynes, Ken W.G.
Box 1881, 430 Hemlock Ave 604-869-2118

KAMLOOPS

Il'mun'rei, Ashana N.
Hugh Allan Dr & Howe 604-374-3135

KELOWNA

Kehler, Peter
Hwy 97 S 604-769-3091

Lauer, Mark
Clifton Rd S & High Rd 604-762-3616

McCarthy, Kim
Bernard & Ellis 604-766-2948

Petersen, Dee
206-290 Mills Rd 604-862-8640

Pittet, Lucille
Ethel & Harvie 604-860-0146

KEREMEOS

Freeman, David F.
Morrison Dr 604-499-2354

LADNER

Service, John
#211, 4738-53rd St 604-738-2156

LANGLEY

Huff, Jane Elizabeth
By Appointment
(mobile service) 604-532-0598

Neudorf, Kate
200th St & 40th Ave 604-533-4414

MISSION

Loch, Liz
12th Ave & Grand St 604-826-5852

Pater, Neeltje
32165-7th Ave 604-820-0541

Reynett, Maureen J.
Hurd St & 7th Ave 604-826-0128

Walters, Catherine
Dewey Trunk Rd 604-730-5513

NAKUSP

Van Houten, Ieneke
119 Broadway 604-265-3242

NANAIMO

Kaminski, Andrea
Howden Dr 604-265-3242

NELSON

Harrison, Carmen
Stanley St 604-361-4593

SOOKE

Leroux, Gabriella C.
West Coast Rd &
Murray Rd 604- 642-2206

Meek, Lori
Kaltasin Rd, RR #1 604-642-4509

SUMMERLAND

Blystone, Anabela
Sinclair & Barclay St 604-494-9053

Woods, Wayne
Lakeshore &
Shaughnessy Ave 604-494-1945

SURREY

Khan, M. Mobeen
King George Hwy &
92nd Ave 604-582-5406

Tan, Cyril C.N.
128th St & 96th Ave 604-680-3668

SYDNEY

Brackenridge, Marianne
Wallace & West Saanich 604-652-2199

VANCOUVER

Cyr, Bonita
Burrard & Broadway 604-734-0851

Hsi, Yen-Ping Chen
E 21st Ave 604-438-7097

Lam, Ling Fei
328 E 19th Ave 604-874-3901

Mah, Benny
E 4th Ave & Rupert St 604-873-7717

Phillips, Gillian
Beach Ave 604-682-6008

Pousette, Erika
Angus Dr 604-266-7407

Sato, Sonoe (Sonya)
12th & Granville 604-732-7265

Shirley, Christopher
W Broadway & Cambie 604-875-8818

Shmitsman, Vladimir
North Grandview Hwy 604-251-9748

Wallace, Frank James
Allison Rd 604-228-9113

VICTORIA

Chickoski, Larry
Grafton St 604-383-6670

Church, Penny
Hwy 1 & Admiral Rd 604-380-2723

Everett, Norville
Fernwood & Denman 604-595-7108

Finegan, Bernadette
Beach & Cavendish 604-360-5858

Harvey-Dawe, Suzanne
Foul Bay Rd 604-592-7499

Kamper, Sandra
St David St 604-598-5890

Koniczek, Susan
Nicholson St 604-727-6780

McAllister, Norma
Bushby St 604-480-4814

McMurray, Josephine
Rowley Rd 604-389-1234

Rippin, Alison I.W.
Royal Oak Dr 604-658-0802

✦ Manitoba Reflexologists

NOTE: Check the credentials of your practitioner (see above, "Questions to Ask"). This publication cannot and does not certify or represent the qualifications of practitioners, or the quality of care available from them.

SHOAL LAKE

Stewart, David M.
South Chestnut St 204-759-2066

ST. BONIFACE

Elmond, Marcien
Provencher & Aulneau 204-237-7238

STONEWALL

Thompson, Lynne
Fourth St W 204-467-2438

WINNIPEG

Clubb, Carole
Arlington St & Portage Ave . .204-775-9810

Drolet, Georgina
Roberta Ave 204-663-1404

Eska, Elaine
Cambridge St 204-475-9808

Foy, Margaret
Renfrew St 204-489-7793

Harrison, Marjorie
Burrows Ave 204-694-8794

Irek, Gordon
Portage Ave & Wall St 204-774-7490

Janzen, Mary
Portage & Rougold 204-888-5989

Jonasson, Candace F.
Riverton 204-669-9418

Lavack, Raymond J.
Winterton 204-667-6760

Loschiavo, Dalyce
Renfrew St 204-489-1609

Melnyk, Irene
Cathedral & Main 204-586-4448

Morin, Doris Lynne
St. Annes & Hull 204-237-7153

Richardson, Susan
Berwick Place 204-942-7541

Rogers, Gail
Stewart St & Portage Ave . . .204-837-2140

Sosa, Teresa
Larsen 204-668-5214

Straczynski, Mira
Sturgen Rd & Ness Ave 204-831-7940

Tuchak, Mary Agnes
Portage & Telfer St 204-762-5770

Varga, Ginzella Gy
Charleswood
(suburb of Winnipeg) 204-832-4291

Vialoux, Robert M.
Roblin Blvd 204-832-4291

Williams, Betty
Dominion St 204-783-9778

Winston, Belle
Ormiston Rd 204-256-9454

Wirz, Werner
Charing Cross Cr 204-256-9874

✦ Nova Scotia Reflexologists

NOTE: Check the credentials of your practitioner (see above, "Questions to Ask"). This publication cannot and does not certify or represent the qualifications of practitioners, or the quality of care available from them.

BROOKLYN/QUEEN'S COUNTY

Dexter, Penelope
By Appointment 902-354-3500

NEW GLASGOW

Blackmore, Barbara
109 Goodman Pl 902-752-7727

✦ Ontario Reflexologists

NOTE: Check the credentials of your practitioner (see above, "Questions to Ask"). This publication cannot and does not certify or represent the qualifications of practitioners, or the quality of care available from them.

AJAX

Wright, C. Suzanne
Westney & Hwy 401 905-686-4325

ALMONTE

Inglis, Natalie
Upper Dwyer Hill
(between #7 & #44) 613-265-3746

AMHERSTBURG

Thrasher, Elise
McCurdy Dr 519-736-8300

ATWOOD/NEWRY/ LISTOWEL

Kuepfer, Madelene J.
Hwy 23 & 10th
Concession 519-356-2661

AURORA

Leiper, Darlene
Yonge St & Wellington 905-727-2776

McCaffrey, Margaret
Yonge & Wellington 905-727-0476

AYTON

Grein, Mary E.
Augusta St 519-665-7581

BANCROFT

Tinney, Noreen E.
By Appointment 613-332-0150

BARRIE

Hewitt, Alana
Bayview Dr & Little Ave . . .705-737-4028

McOuat, Kym
Colleen Ave 705-733-7777

Nedergaard, Connie
Livingstone & Anne St 705-728-9742

Stewart, Joy M.P.
College Cr 705-734-1159

BELFOUNTAIN

Edward, Virginia
Mississauga Rd & Bush St . . .519-927-5559

BLENHEIM

McCorkell, Nancy
By Appointment 519-436-0724

BLUEVALE

Van Den Heuvel, Rikie
By Appointment 519-887-9136

BLYTH

Casey, Carol
Dinsley St 519-523-4933

BOWMANVILLE

Bos, Renee
Optimal Health Centre,
152 Church 905-697-0355

Bragg, Anna
Liberty St N & Conc. Rd #3 . .905-623-9198

Johnston, Sheran
Melores Dr 905-634-2149

BRAMPTON

Carpenter, Naomi
By Appointment 905-455-7338

BURLINGTON

Latulippe, Denise
By Appointment 905-639-1759

CALEDON

Slavica, Maria Bacic
Hwy 10 & Hwy 24 519-942-0887

CAMBRIDGE

Biesel, Brenda
George St N 519-623-7800

Kovak, Valeria
Hawthorne Rd 519-621-1805

Medeiros, Natalia
Rego, Natalie
Grand Ave S 519-621-7390

Quinn, Stacey
West River Rd &
Footbridge Rd 519-623-8685

CAMLACHIE

Andrews, Denise
Mockingbird Ln 519-869-6684

CHATHAM

Kopriva, Barbara J.
Blenheim & Wallaceburg 519-676-4891

CLARKSBURG

Corti, Adrienne
Clarksburg 519-599-6170

Vamplew, Mary E.
Hillcrest Dr & Fulton 519-599-2717

CLIFFORD

Douglas, Sharon
By Appointment 519-327-8558

Metcalfe, Allison
Metcalfe, Debbie
By Appointment 519-367-2447

CLINTON

Bartliff, Rhonda
High St 519-482-5719

Cantelon, J. Irene
Rattenbury St W 519-482-7779

De Groot, Els
Hwy 4 & Hospital 519-482-3488

Feltz, Joyce
Hwy 8 & Conc. 15/16
Goderich Twp 519-482-7276

Marsh, Mary L.
Hwy 4 & Hwy 8 -
331 High St 519-482-9623

McNally, Jeanette J.
Osborne St 519-482-3271

COBALT

Males, Linda
Gillies Lake Rd 705-679-5548

COBOURG

Stillwell, Gail
Division St & Park 905-372-1749

COLBORNE

Clarke, Pamela May
Percy & Hwy #2 905-355-3980

DURHAM

Dove, Jean
By Appointment 519-369-6218

EARLTON

Gravel, Jean-Paul
By Appointment 705-647-7336

GLOUCESTER

Fairbrass, Jacqueline
Rondel St 613-834-7519

GODERICH

Sleightholm, Eileen
Bruce St E 519-524-5641

GODFREY

Whiten-Etheridge, Diane
RR #1 613-374-1445

GRAND BEND

Turnbull, Joanne
By Appointment 519-238-8576

GRAND VALLEY

Smith, M. Joan
Grier St 519-928-2943

GRAVENHURST

Tiikkainen, Ritva K.
Winhara Rd 705-687-2046

GUELPH

Bragg, Cynthia D.
Edinburgh Rd N 519-763-6944

Murphy, Julianna
Eramosa (Hwy 24) &
Woolwich St 519-822-1967

Pettifer, Cheryl
Durham St 519-763-3806

Richards, Evelene Jean
Woolwich & Speedvale 519-836-3526

Vlasman, Ann
Beverly St 519-824-7427

HAILEYBURY

Gillier, Catherine
Amwell 705-672-2840

Laferriere-Hacquard, Aline
Georgina 705-672-5359

HALIBURTON

Holland, Sylvia J.
By Appointment 705-457-1838

HALTON HILLS

Vuksinic, Anne
Trafalgar Rd & Hwy 401 905-877-0355

HAMILTON

Bowen, Bruce Elgin
Gage Ave S 905-544-9634

Brooker, Michael C.
By Appointment 905-547-5131

Damore, Jane
Greencedar Dr 905-385-1016

Dubois, Denise
Stone Church &
Upper Horning 905-574-7117

Goddard, Mary-Ann
King & Quigley Rd 905-573-9104

Labelle, Denny
Upper Wentworth 905-385-3417

Simon, Carolyn
Mohawk Rd E &
Upper Wellington 905-383-7521

Sinai, Larry
Main St W 905-522-3405

Warrener, Tracy
Barton & Sherman 905-547-6993

KINGSTON

Gordon, Diane
By Appointment 613-549-7402

KITCHENER

Atkinson, Ruth
Glasgow St &
Fischer-Hallman 519-742-7678

Constant, David
Blackhorne Cr 519-749-8651

Esmail, Mahmood
Highland Rd W 519-749-1360

Klemetsch, Lisa
Krug & Weber 519-743-4625

McLellan, Janet L.
West Ave &
Highland Rd W 519-744-4020

Moores, Joseph W.
Westmount & Victoria 519-742-8404

Schlonies, Janet
Greenfield Ave 519-893-5381

Stevens, Jolene S.
Daytona St 519-578-9473

LEAMINGTON

Hui, Tai
By Appointment 519-322-5931

Roach, Sonja
By Appointment 519-326-0791

LINDSAY

Buckley, Heather
By Appointment 705-328-0821

Ewart, Jacqueline Ann
Pottinger St 705-324-0097

Ferguson, Anna-Maria
Lindsay St S 705-328-3834

Gaynor, Donna
St. David St 705-878-5539

Kidd, Deborah
By Appointment 705-953-9655

LISTOWEL

**Giesbrecht, Sandra;
Slater, Karen**
Davidson Ave N 519-291-5654

McCutcheon, Jean
Wallace 519-291-2104

LONDON

Allen, Joyce
Springfield Ct 905-822-3174

Brown, Alison
By Appointment 519-588-9420

Caldwell, Lynda
Glenrose Dr 519-641-5049

Danton, Thecla
Dixie & Burnhamthorpe ...905-275-7444

Davey, Barb
Millbank & Southdale 519-649-2093

Getty, Peter
Huron St & Highbury Ave ...519-457-2730

Huffman, Wilma
Winston Churchill &
Burnhamthorpe 905-820-2990

Johns, Priscilla
Keynes Cr 905-824-1635

Klaric, Mirta
Pine Ridge Dr 519-660-8350

Laya, Denise
Adelaide St & Dundas St 519-552-8652

Little, Betty Ann M.
Hamilton Rd & Rectory 519-434-3351

Malec, Jitka
By Appointment 519-453-8327

McMullen, Effie
Dundas & Second St 519-455-1707

McPhee, Sherry
Wellington & Baseline 519-433-3872

Rombough, Heather
Bonaventure Dr 519-452-0379

Salmon, Dorothy
Wonderland &
Southdale Rd 519-641-2761

Samson, Cheryl
Colborne St 519-433-2909

Stawowczyk, Natalia
Moonstream 905-567-4797

Stirling, Victoria
Wonderland &
Springbank 519-472-9254

Szin, Agatha
Burnhamthorpe Ave &
Cawthra Rd 905-848-0338

Turcon, Kathleen
Waterloo & Oxford 519-434-0594

Van-Daele, Joris P.
Wellington & Baseline Rd ...519-433-2929

MILTON

Shannon, Elinore
By Appointment 905-878-1876

MISSISSAUGA

Athey, Isobel
By Appointment 905-822-0645

Castle, Patricia
By Appointment 905-824-0433

Egan, Janet
By Appointment 905-274-6345

Haslam, Sheila
By Appointment 905-624-1245

Macedo, Teresa
By Appointment 905-567-4187

Schmid, Maria
By Appointment 905-848-8997

Wyzlic, Jeanne
By Appointment 905-569-3256

NEPEAN

Paris, Joan
Craig Henry Dr 613-225-0789

Wright, Denise
Sullivan Ave 613-225-9293

NEW HAMBURG

White, Loretta
Waterloo St 519-579-3850

NEW LISKEARD

Benoit, Claire
By Appointment 705-647-6388

Bisson, Ruby
Twin Lakes 705-647-9333

Gibson, Mary
Whitewood Ave 705-647-8599

Jordison, Jerry
By Appointment 705-569-3450

NEWCASTLE

Partington, Ginette
King & Mill St (Hwy #2) 905-987-0510

NEWMARKET

Bisson, Donald
Leslie St 905-478-1710

Hubley, Russell G.
Mt Albert & Woodbine 905-473-9938

Lindsay, Jim
By Appointment/House Calls .905-841-7392

NEWTON

Faber, Janny
Hwy 19 & Hwy 86 519-595-4865

NIAGARA-ON-THE-LAKE

Byl, Margaret
Hwy 55 & Line 3 905-682-2942

File-Meyer, Mora
Mississauga & Mary St 905-468-5229

NIPIGON

Sutton, Cathie
By Appointment 807-887-3319

NORTH BAY

Desjardins, Huguette
Hwy 11 & Hwy 17 705-494-7395

Thompson, Velda E.
Stockdale Rd 705-494-1635

NORTH COBALT

Grant, Wanda
Hwy #11B & Stewart St ...705-672-5417

OAKVILLE

Duarte, Antonio
By Appointment 905-516-4509

Larsson, Kaisa
By Appointment 905-874-8172

ORANGEVILLE

Burnell, Terry
By Appointment 519-941-9004

ORILLIA

Bowers, Joan
By Appointment 705-725-3632

OSHAWA

Eshpeter, Josephine
By Appointment 905-436-9230

Popovic, Joan
By Appointment 905-432-2488

OTTAWA

Dube, Jean Louis
By Appointment 613-990-7182

Zeviar, Eroca
By Appointment 613-233-5155

OWEN SOUND

Brewer, Jim
By Appointment 519-747-9882

Keane, Patricia R.
14th St W 519-371-1232

Visser, Pauline
By Appointment 519-371-4548

PALMERSTON

Campbell, Femmy
By Appointment 519-343-5882

PETERBOROUGH

Brown, Debra J.
Park St S 705-741-1308

Himpfen, Robert
Towerhill Rd 705-740-1091

Smith, Claudia
Concession Rd #16 705-741-0065

PICKERING

Thorpe, Clare
Glenanna Rd 905-839-6914

PORT ELGIN

Waytowich, Nora
Ashwell Cr (Hwy 21 &
David St) 519-832-9575

White, Rachel J.
Waterloo & Frontenac 519-389-2402

PORT PERRY

Froats, Judy
Castle Harbour Dr 905-985-9042

PORT STANLEY

White, J. Suzanne
Front St 519-782-5118

PROTON STATION

Garwood, Lois
Hwy 10 & Hwy 4 519-923-2676

Keramaris, George
15 Vicora Linkway 416-429-5658

RICHMOND HILL

Dietrich, W.
Bayview Ave &
Elgin Mills Rd 905-889-5900

Hare, Faith F.
Yonge St 905-737-6340

Leskiw, Olga
Hwy 7 & Yonge St 905-773-7114

Parkin, Merlyn M.
Major Mackenzie & Yonge ..905-508-6184

Pigeon, Gilles
Baif Ave 905-883-9355

Staub, Michaela (Micki)
King City Side Rd &
Yonge St 905-773-7114

Stewart, Judith
Cooperage Cr 905-884-2290

SARNIA

Ascroft, Janis Lee
Rosewood Manor,
711 Indian Rd 519-542-4528

Moloy, Marion L.
Indian Rd & Michigan Ave ...519-542-4608

Siraco, Lois Jane
Exmouth St 519-332-1781

McNeill, Mickie
North Russell St 519-344-2642

STONEY CREEK

Martin, D. John
By Appointment 905-664-6248

STOUFFVILLE

Hakonson, Heidi
By Appointment 519-642-1010

STOUFFVILLE/ GOODWOOD/ UXBRIDGE

Ceney, Cynthia
By Appointment 905-642-4243

STRATFORD

Coulthard, Sandra
245 Downie St 519-272-2265

Gladding, Jane E.
Redford Cr & St. Vincent St S .519-273-1915

Hueck, Carol Anne
By Appointment 519-273-7319

Walch, Nadia
By Appointment 519-271-5322

STRATHROY

Bernier, Dana
By Appointment 519-847-5579

SUNDERLAND

Bromley, Arlene
Albert St & River St 705-357-1810

SUTTON WEST

Lemon, Ros-Lynne
Hwy #48 & Sutton turn off ..905-722-3631

TECUMSEH

Robenson, Judith
Tecumseh Rd E 519-979-1399

TERRACE BAY

Gosselin, Evelyn R.
East Grove Cr 807-825-9317

THAMESVILLE

Smids, Anita
By Appointment 519-692-4924

THORNHILL

Goldberger, Andrea
Janesville Rd 905-889-8238

Hack, Valerie
Yonge & Hwy 7 905-764-7053

Olive, Carolyn
Yonge St & John St 905-709-3261

THUNDER BAY

Langer, Sue
Kerega Ave 807-939-2984

O'Neill, Lillian
Arichibald St 807-623-4237

Rowson, Lorraine
By Appointment 807-473-3773

TILLSONBURG

Wall, Janis R.
Courtland 519-875-2215

TIVERTON

Coulombe, Marcel R.
By Appointment 519-368-7620

TOBERMORY

Pettifer, Alice E.
By Appointment 519-596-2034

TORONTO

Arieli, Paula
By Appointment 416-636-1880

Arnet, Janaki
By Appointment 416-493-3948

Barczak, Carola
By Appointment 416-964-6400

Bedford, Anne Marie
By Appointment 416-963-5988

Bell, Diana
By Appointment 416-744-7130

Feet For Life
Sandig, Deborah, M.
19 Yorkville Ave, Ste 200 . . .416-920-6271

Gault, Danielle
By Appointment 416-766-5520

Hastbacka, Margot
By Appointment 416-864-2358

Keramaris, George
15 Vicora Linkway 416-429-5658

McGaw, Anna G.
By Appointment 416-923-1394

Perris, Mary-Kay
By Appointment 416-690-8374

Sundar-Singh, Victor
By Appointment 416-424-4360

Woldemichael, Yemane T.
By Appointment 416-966-4035

TOTTENHAM

Eindhoven, Margaret
Hwy 9 & Simcoe Rd, #10 . . .905-936-3031

TRENTON

Semmler, Trudy
English Settlement Rd 613-475-2550

TROY

Bolyea, Barbara
Hwy 5 & Lynden Side Rd . . .519-647-3941

UNIONVILLE

Cameron, Marilyn E.
Barlow Rd 905-474-0219

Polley, Pamela
Hwy 7 & Kennedy Rd 905-477-1707

UNIONVILLE/ MARKHAM

Matchett, Mavis
Kennedy Rd & 14th Ave 905-479-5966

UXBRIDGE

Catherwood, Patricia
Breech St N 905-852-7969

VANDORF (GORMLEY)

Lalonde, Vivian
Bloomington Side Rd &
Woodbine 905-841-3886

WALKERTON

Lang, Ann
By Appointment 519-366-2725

Von Hatten-Baer, Wayne
Elgin St 519-987-2433

WASAGA BEACH

Gawlytta, Marianne
12th St 705-429-6529

WATERLOO

Bell, Margaret
By Appointment 519-664-3698

Gibson, Daisy Joan
Mt Anne Dr 519-884-8014

Harper, Martina
King & William Sts 519-895-1938

Hartman, Abby
King & Columbia 519-571-7700

Hueck, Carol Anne
Beechwood Dr 519-884-4821

WELLAND

Quigley, Brian W.
Le Mirage, 397 Thorold Rd . .905-732-5258

WEST HILL

Celestin, Lawrence
Lawson Rd 905-724-0026

WESTON

Baker, James G.
Rosemount & Church 416-249-6484

Perkin, Margaret
Kipling & 401 Only 416-247-7625

Smolinger, Elizabeth
Finch Ave & Weston 416-747-8327

WINDSOR

Hebert, Madelein
By Appointment 519-944-3053

WOODSTOCK

Wilkins, Margi
By Appointment 519-421-9223

✦ Québec Reflexologists

NOTE: Check the credentials of your practitioner (see above, "Questions to Ask"). This publication cannot and does not certify or represent the qualifications of practitioners, or the quality of care available from them.

AMOS

Caouette, Diane
4e Ave E 819-727-2020

Lambert, Genevieve Ropy
1er Rue E 819-732-7052

ANCIENNE LORETTE

Fortin-Gagnon, Jacqueline
rue du Moulen 418-871-7183

Jobin, Roger
des Metairies 418-682-5114

ANJOU

Vinnac, Yolande
Baldwin 514-356-1760

ARMAGH

Brochu, Sylvie
rue Cadrin 418-466-2144

AUTEUIL

Jette, Madeleine
Salois 514-625-9707

AYLMER

Buteau, Jeannine
des Foudateurs 819-684-2251

Ethier, Marie-Johanne
Talon 819-684-9927

BAIE D'URFE

Sukosd, Corinne
Hwy 20 & Apple Hill Rd 514-457-4679

BARRAUTE

Thiboutot, Real
rte 397 819-734-6733

BEAUCEVILLE

St-Pierre, Gisele
By Appointment 418-774-9259

BEAUPORT

Cloutier, Johanne
Tronquet 418-667-4861

Cote, Suzanne
2336, St-Georges, #1 418-667-9513

Grenier, Sylvie
Bochart 418-667-2500

Tremblay, Gisele Beaumont
rue St-Yves 418-667-4030

Varin, Jocelyne
Monseigneur Gauthier 418-663-3058

BOISCHATEL

Cauchon, Marcel
av Royale 418-822-0609

CYRENNE, GILLES

Cyrenne, Gilles
Ste-Frederic 819-478-5961

Dubois, Suzanne
Larocque 819-477-1840

DUBUISSON

Duval, Denise
Domaine des Feuillus 819-738-7045

FABREVILLE

Malenfant, Sylvie
45 Ave 514-340-8222

FERMONT

Bourassa, Denise
By Appointment 418-287-5375

FORTIERVILLE

Lachance, Yvonne
de la Gare 819-287-4686

FOSTER

Pacquin, Guy
ch Bondville 514-242-0279

FRANKLIN

Bourdeau, Rodrigue
3393, rte 209 514-826-3779

GATINEAU

Allain, Josee
Rouen 819-246-8177

Charlebois-Morin, Line
Asselin 819-771-7620

Dalpe, Rejeanne
rue Hilltop 891-663-0436

Franche, Odette
Fenelon 819-956-3186

**Lafrance, Gerard;
Romain, Germaine**
Lorrain Blvd 819-568-6943

Lyrette, Yvan
Maple 819-776-4181

Pilote, Isabelle
de St-Emilion 819-456-2232

Vigeant, Jeanne
av de Picardie 819-595-4793

GRAND MERE

Bellerive, Suzanne
8th Ave 819-538-1942

HAUTE-MAURICIE

Letourneau, Fernande R.
des Aubepines 819-523-8461

HEBERTVILLE

Munger, Marguerite
Rang St-Andre 418-344-1227

HERVEY JUNCTION (L.A.S.)

Cloutier, Gaetane
St-Charles 418-289-3091

HULL

Bolduc, Rita
Pelletier 819-771-4092

Benoit, Marie-Andree
By Appointment 819-778-4012

LAC ST-CHARLES

Emond, Jacinthe
rue Manick 418-525-4347

Fournier, Francoise
des Pres 418-529-2097

LACHINE

Roy, Georgette
Provost 514-634-8589

LAFONTAINE

Briere, Francois
117, Santa 514-432-7411

Brisson, Normand
Durocher 514-438-2825

LAMBTON

Boulanger, Celine
Principale 418-486-7417

LANCIENNE-LORETTE

Rivard, Luce
rue Notre Dame 418-877-9234

LAVAL

Durocher, Rejean
Lac de Mai Fabreville 514-625-9598

LAWRENCEVILLE

Desharnais, Rachel
Principale N 514-535-6758

LES SAULES

Turgeon, Madeleine
3565, Laurin 418-871-0935

LONGUEUIL

Meunier, Stephane
pl de la Louisiane 814-646-9244

Pellerin, France
725, de Roussillon, apt 210 .514-679-1150

Tardif, Jeannine
Pratt 514-670-4614

LORETTEVILLE

Villeneuve, Yolande
boul, Valcartier 481-842-9598

LORRAINE

Leclerc, Lucille
boul, d'Orleans 514-621-8540

LOUISEVILLE

Masse, Danielle
By Appointment 819-228-2731

MAGOG

Roy, France
Valiquette, RR #5 819-847-0418

MANIWOKI

Saumure, Huguette
Nault 819-449-2768

MATANE

Soucy, Henriette
rue Champlain 418-566-2696

MONTREAL

Beaulieu, Denise
Honore Beaugrand 519-253-0600

Bessette, Carle
7538 St-Denis 518-843-4708

Carroll, Joy
5830 Monkland Ave 514-487-7236

Ethier, Raymonde
rue Guy 514-937-0503

Gamache, Marguerite
9-2565 Davidson 514-421-3287

McKittrick, Patricia
5555 Salaberry St 514-331-4810

Ornstein, Eytan
Clanranald 514-735-8272

Senecal, Carole
Henri Bourassa ouest 514-336-1936

NEUFCHATEL

Claveau, Michelle
Carre Prevel 418-847-0218

NICOLET

Bourassa, Jacqueline
St Jean-Baptista 819-293-2011

Jeanne D'Arc, Allyson
Nourry 819-293-4950

Rheault, Lise Martin
Chemin Fleuve Est 819-293-5357

NORMANDIN LAC-ST-JEAN

St-Pierre, Claudette
St-Cyrille 418-274-4151

PINCOURT

Fox, Denise
6th Avenue 514-453-7330

PARISVILLE

Auger, Josette
Principale 819-263-2323

PINTENDRE

Carrier, Geatane
des Tulipes 418-837-5675

PIOPOLIS

Beaudry, Louise
Rang des Grenier 819-583-2061

POINTE-DU-LAC

Brunelle, Danielle E.
Julien Proulx 819-377-5243

PONT-ROUGE

**Beaumont-Rochette,
Marine**
rue Petite Fossembault 418-873-2467

PORT CARTIER

Beuce, Danielle
Vallea 418-766-7188

Desrosiers, Magelee V.
rue Bijould 418-766-2433

Gagnon, Solange
Trudel 418-766-2715

Gagnon, Ghislain J.
Trudel 418-766-5730

QUEBEC

Arsenault, Madeleine
d'Aubigny Levis 418-649-7271

Blanchard, Madeleine
rue Verrat 418-842-0599

Boily, Monique
rte Penney 418-842-4022

Corriveau, Huguette
du Mousquest 418-628-0336

Daniel, Yolande
Latraille 418-627-3936

Hughan, L.C.
Limoilou 418-529-0548

Jobin, Valerie
ch St-Foy 418-681-9129

St-Onge, Pierre
des Peupliers O 418-624-3164

RIMOUSKI

Caron, Myriam
du Reposs 418-724-2799

Dufour, Lisette
Melanson 418-724-9070

Simard, Adrienne
By Appointment 418-723-6695

RIMOUSKI EST

Lavoie, Marthe
490, St-Germain 418-724-6336

RIVIERE-DU-LOUP

Deschenes, Johanne
rue des Veterans 418-867-8636

ROBERTSONVILLE

Jacques, Celine Gagne
Lassard 418-338-4145

ST-ALEXIS

Chouinard, Claire
St-Louis 418-865-2221

ST-ALPHONSE-DE-GRANBY

Baillageon, Angele
108, Klondike 514-777-1677

ST-ANDRE-AVELLIN

Adeodat, Bernard
939, Ste-Madeleine 819-983-7773

ST-ANTOINE-DE-TILLY

St-Jean, Lise Meilleur
By Appointment 418-886-2902

ST-BENOIT-LABRE

Giroux, Raymonde
Range 6 418-228-5037

ST-CELESTIN

Camirand, Chantal
Cote St-Pierre 819-229-3388

Roux-Cloutier, Carmen
Marquis 819-229-3395

ST-CESAIRE

Pacquette, Sylvie
Norte Dame 514-469-5120

ST-CYPRIEN BEAUCE

Baillargon, Vicky
av Hormidas 418-383-3802

ST-EMILE

Joannette, Danielle
Dom Perignon 418-843-3351

Beaugrand-Joliceour, France
des Feuillus 418-847-6318

ST-ETIENNE DE-LAUZON

Dumont, Nicole
42 Belair 418-836-5108

Gagne, Ginette
des Pommiers 418-831-2647

ST-EUSTACHE

Duval, Raymonde
Globensky 514-974-0588

ST-FRANCOIS

Rheaume, Cecile
Principale 819-845-3661

ST-GEORGES

Paquet, Raymond
162nd Rue 418-228-8400

ST-GEORGES EST

Bureau, Danielle
13450, 58 Ave, RR #3 418-228-5422

Lariviere, Noella
46eme Ave 418-227-0976

Rencourt, Nicole
162 Ave 418-228-9400

ST-GERARD-MAJELLA

Quinn, Suzanne
L'Assomption & Repentigny . .514-589-3457

ST-GERMAIN

Levasseur, Monique
Baillargeon 819-395-4081

STE-BRIGITTE-DE-LAVAL

Labonte, Sylvie
du Calvaire 418-825-3866

STE-CROIX LOTBINIERE

Boisvert, Louise
rue Desrochers 418-926-3766

STE-FOY

Abel-Method, Claire
2359, Chateaubriand 418-872-6610

LaRoche, Claire
rue Gingras 418-659-2718

Neron, Diane
rue Ontario 418-658-2653

STE-GERTRUDE

Gelinas, Jeanne
rte 395 819-732-2214

ST-JUSTICE DE NEWTON

Cote, Carole Caza
3th Rang 514-764-3152

VAL-DES-MONTS

Roy, Lise G.
397 boul du Carrefour 819-671-2064

VAL BELAIR

Cloutier, Johanne
boul Plexinord 418-842-8404

VALLEYFIELD

Le Bel, Jeannine
St-Phillippe 514-333-5513

VASSAN

Jacques, Rene
Vassan 819-824-2817

VAUDREUIL

De Montigny, Rejeanne
Raymond 514-455-0018

Desrosiers, Jeannine
Evangeline 514-455-9311

Julien, Diane
426A, Esther Blondin 514-455-3828

Mailly, Rene
Pinault 514-455-6646

VILLAGE-DES-HURONS

Sioui, Marjolaine
50, Maurice Bastien, Ste 440 418-842-0467

✦ Saskatchewan Reflexologists

NOTE: Check the credentials of your practitioner (see above, "Questions to Ask"). This publication cannot and does not certify or represent the qualifications of practitioners, or the quality of care available from them.

PRINCE ALBERT

Smith, Wayne
By Appointment 306-764-3282

SASKATOON

Smith, Wayne
By Appointment 306-373-9873

SOCONO

Muirhead, Judith
Bromhead 306-456-2268

TISDALE

Reese, Janis C.
Near Leacross (1.5 km) 306-873-5610

WEYBURN

Donald, Willa-Mae
Estevan & Regina 306-842-6052

✦ Rolfing

WHAT IS ROLFING

Rolfing® is a technique of manipulating the muscles and connective tissue to shift the body into alignment. The technique, a form of bodywork, is based on the principle that proper alignment of the body improves its function. Rolfing was developed by U.S. biochemist Ida Rolf in the 1940s. It is performed in a series of 10 standard sessions, during which pressure is applied with the fingers, knuckles, and elbows to bring the body into balance. The Rolf Institute notes that persons with slouched bodies, flat feet, bowed legs or excessive spinal curvature all display complex patterns of strain, tightness and thickening in the muscles and connective tissue. Through the Rolfing technique, the connective tissue is said to be softened and lengthened, allowing the body to fall naturally into alignment.

Rolfing Movement Integration

Over the years, a second form of Rolfing, called Rolfing® Movement Integration, has developed. It focuses on teaching a person how to move with greater grace, ease, and efficiency. This is said to relieve physical stress caused by improper habits of body posture and movement. In a series of sessions, the client and Rolfer discover the client's movement patterns and explore possibilities for freer, more balanced movement in everyday activities, such as desk work, housework, exercise, yoga, and even breathing. Over time, the client learns a simple series of centering movements. This usually involves a series of eight private weekly sessions. The Rolf Institute notes that Rolfing Movement can be undertaken by itself or in conjunction with Rolfing sessions, and states: "Rolfing Movement Integration and Rolfing combined enhance each other: Rolfing frees and integrates the body's structure so the client has more movement options, and Rolfing Movement teaches the client how to use these possibilities in everyday life."

BENEFITS OF ROLFING

The Rolf Institute states that athletes, dancers, students of yoga and meditation, musicians, and people suffering from chronic pain and stress come for Rolfing not only for relief from pain, but for improved performance in their professions and daily activities. The Institute states that Rolfing may also benefit those in psychotherapy by facilitating a deeper connection to their emotional conflicts.

The Rolf Institute has sponsored research at the University of California, Los Angeles, (UCLA) into the effects of Rolfing. Contact the Institute for details.

QUESTIONS TO ASK

✦ Is Rolfing or Rolfing Movement more likely to benefit you?

✦ Is your teacher a Certified Rolfer or certified Rolfing Movement Teacher? Confirm by contacting the Rolf Institute (see below "U.S. Institute").
  NOTE: Such certification means that the practitioner has met the standards set by the Rolf Institute, but this does not constitute a licence, such as that required by health practitioners regulated under provincial law.

✦ How much experience does your practitioner have, and does it include experience with someone with your condition? What were the results?

✦ Can your practitioner provide professional references?

✦ What is the background of your practitioner, and does it include training in other forms of health care?

✦ How many sessions are recommended, and how much will each cost?

GOVERNMENT REGULATION

There is no government regulation of Rolfing practitioners in Canada, meaning that there is no legislation establishing regulatory bodies to register and discipline qualified practitioners. However, there is a private U.S. institute, the Rolf Institute, which has registered Rolfing® as a service mark. The Institute certifies practitioners who meet its standards.

U.S. INSTITUTE

Rolf Institute
PO Box 1868
Boulder, Colorado 80306
Tel: 303-449-5903 or 1-800-530-8875
Fax: 303-449-5978

This is the Institute founded by Ida Rolf. Rolfing Practitioners and Rolfing Movement Teachers are trained and certified only by this Institute.

ROLFING EDUCATION

Those wishing to become a Certified Rolfer or certified Rolfing Movement Teacher must first complete a ten-session Rolfing series and eight Rolfing Movement Integration sessions. Students then complete a five-week Foundations of Bodywork course on anatomy, kinesiology and physiology, as these relate to Rolfing. Those with documented training in massage or bodywork may be exempt from this course.

This is followed by the completion of an admission application and an entrance exam in anatomy, physiology and kinesiology. The principles of Rolfing are then taught as a five-day course, followed by six weeks of Rolfing study and practical training. Students are also assigned a written paper, and work with clients for 10 sessions over an eight-week period. At this point, the student is eligible to be certified as a Rolfer. The total tuition cost, as of 1996, was $12,000 US ($9,800 US for those who had documented training in massage or bodywork). The training program lasts one to two years. An additional four-week course is available for those wishing to be certified as Rolfing Movement Teachers. The tuition fee is $2,700 US.

Training to become a Certified Rolfer is held in the United States, Brazil, Australia and Germany. For more information contact:

The Rolf™ Institute of Structural Integration
205 Canyon Blvd
Boulder, Colorado 80302
Tel: 303-449-5903 or 1-800-530-8875
Fax: 303-449-5978
Email: RolfInst@aol.com

✦ Rolfing in Your Province

Provinces are alphabetically listed below, with the following information:

✦ names, addresses and telephone numbers of Rolfers and Rolfing Movement Teachers, listed alphabetically by city

NOTE: The names in this list were provided by the Rolf Institute. According to the Institute, all members have met requirements for certification. Confirm the certification of your practitioner or obtain the names of newly certified practitioners in your area by contacting the Institute (see above, "U.S. Institute").

✦ Alberta Rolfers

NOTE: Check the credentials of your practitioner (see above, "Questions to Ask"). This publication cannot and does not certify or represent the qualifications of practitioners, or the quality of care available from them.

CALGARY

Rolfing by Joe Bally
Apex Massage Therapy
Ste 314,
1167 Kensington Cr NW 403-269-2200

McGregor, Kathryn Jayne
2505-21st St SW 403-228-2785

EDMONTON

Elements Wholistic Centre
LoCicero, Cheryl
9865-85th Ave 403-433-6390

Grimble, Susan
(limited practice)
1203-9923 103rd St 403-428-7792

LoCicero, Gerard
8420 109th St 403-439-0254

McCarty, Tim
11523 100th Ave, Ste 212 ..403-482-5015

Mysko, Sally Anne
14507-20th St 403-473-7973

British Columbia Rolfers

NOTE: Check the credentials of your practitioner (see above, "Questions to Ask"). This publication cannot and does not certify or represent the qualifications of practitioners, or the quality of care available from them.

COBBLE HILL

Institute for Embodiment Training
(also Victoria & Nanaimo)
Johnson, Will
RR 2 604-743-5971

DELTA

Gabriel, Marten
(limited practice)
PO Box 344 604-946-9475

GROUNDBIRCH

Wetherill, Judee
PO Box 195 604-780-2245

KAMLOOPS

Schneider, Gary; Wellby, Simon
605 Pinewynd Pl 604-554-1189

VANCOUVER

Davison, Barry
158 E 11th Ave 604-873-4150

Inaba, Steve
300-2245 W Broadway 604-730-9778

Nir, Amos
104-750 E 7th Ave 604-875-6568

VICTORIA

Ohlmacher, Ann Rosamond
(limited practice)
996 Green Ridge Cr 604-744-2476

WEST VANCOUVER

Stickel, Phyllise H.
#206-1571 Bellevue Ave . . .604-979-4354

Ontario Rolfers

NOTE: Check the credentials of your practitioner (see above, "Questions to Ask"). This publication cannot and does not certify or represent the qualifications of practitioners, or the quality of care available from them.

OTTAWA

Dayvis, Miranda
448 Brendan 613-729-3990

TORONTO

Owen, James
29 Grange Ave 416-598-3331

The Rolfing Studio
Detwiler, Tara; Hayes, Jennifer
470 Grace St 416-588-4989

Strauch, Kathleen
(Ontario Appointments)
Southfield, Michigan 810-354-3484

Zimmerman, Paul
(Ontario Appointments)
Waterport, New York 716-682-9720

Québec Rolfers

NOTE: Check the credentials of your practitioner (see above, "Questions to Ask"). This publication cannot and does not certify or represent the qualifications of practitioners, or the quality of care available from them.

MONTREAL

Leclerc, Marie-Jose
(limited practice)
By Appointment 514-526-9491

Lewis, Jim
4161 Drolet 514-281-8492

Sauvageau, Louise
405 Prince-Arthur Ouest #17 514-281-0600

✦ Yukon Rolfers

NOTE: Check the credentials of your practitioner (see above, "Questions to Ask"). This publication cannot and does not certify or represent the qualifications of practitioners, or the quality of care available from them.

WHITEHORSE

Holler, Norman
PO Box 5902 403-667-4311

✦ Shiatsu

WHAT IS SHIATSU

Shiatsu is an Oriental therapy in which the practitioner applies pressure to points on the body, using fingers, palms, knees, or cushioned elbows, to relax the body and promote its natural ability to heal. In Japanese, the word "shi" means finger and "atsu" means pressure, and the practice is often described as acupuncture without needles. This is an appropriate description, as shiatsu has its roots in traditional Chinese medicine. As in acupuncture, shiatsu stimulates the flow of energy ("ki" or "chi", pronounced "chee") along the body's network of energy channels, called meridian lines. The practitioner focuses on specific points, called "tsubo," using pressure and massage to clear energy blockages and promote health. Shiatsu is considered an excellent relaxation technique and a method of relieving minor health problems before they become chronic. The client should wear loose clothing. No oils are used.

Two Styles

There are two main styles of shiatsu. Zen-Masunaga is a flowing approach involving pressure to many areas of the body, with the client usually lying on a futon or low table. The second style, Namikoshi, focuses on specific areas and points of the body, with the client often lying on a thick floor mat or a low table. In both styles, the client is encouraged to wear loose, comfortable clothing. In B.C., the Zen-Masunaga style is more frequently practised, and the Namikoshi style is more prevalent in Ontario.

BENEFITS OF SHIATSU

The Shiatsu Therapy Association of Ontario advises that shiatsu is effective in the management of the following conditions: headaches/migraines, back, neck and shoulder pain, sciatica, whiplash, carpal tunnel syndrome, thoracic outlet syndrome, repetitive strain injuries, insomnia, constipation, digestive problems, menstrual difficulties, chronic fatigue syndrome, fibromylagia, multiple sclerosis, arthritis, asthma, and depression. It is also useful for relieving muscular pain due to tension, athletic or dance injuries. The Shiatsu Therapy Association of British Columbia notes that shiatsu may also help promote healthy pregnancies, strengthen the immune system, and improve stamina.

In general, shiatsu is viewed by its proponents as an important part of a preventive and rehabilitative health care program. However, shiatsu therapists do not replace physicians, and do not diagnose disease.

QUESTIONS TO ASK

✦ How much training does your shiatsu therapist have, and from which school? Did the training include supervised practise of shiatsu?

NOTE: The minimum level of education required for beginner practitioners with the Shiatsu Therapy Association of British Columbia is 300 hours. Many members have 1000 hours of training or more. The Shiatsu Therapy Association of Ontario requires 2,200 hours of training, the same number of hours as is required for registered massage therapists in Ontario. (For information regarding recognized shiatsu training schools see below, "Shiatsu Education").

✦ Is your shiatsu therapist trained in anatomy and physiology, CPR First Aid, and contra-indications (areas to avoid, and health conditions requiring particular caution)?

✦ Is your shiatsu therapist a certified practitioner with an association? This question applies primarily if you live in B.C. or Ontario, although associations accept members from other provinces (see below, "Shiatsu in Your Province - Association"). You may wish to contact the association to discuss the qualifications of your shiatsu practitioner, or to locate one in your area.

NOTE: Associations may set standards for their certified members. However, associations are not governing bodies established under provincial law to register and discipline practitioners.

✦ Does your shiatsu therapist have references from other health care practitioners?

✦ How much experience does your shiatsu therapist have, and does it include experience with your condition? Is shiatsu appropriate for you?

✦ What is the background of your shiatsu therapist, and does it include training in other forms of health care? If so, what is the extent of the training?

✦ How long will a session last, and what is the cost?

GOVERNMENT REGULATION

Shiatsu therapists are not regulated by any provincial government and there are no governing bodies to establish qualification standards and to discipline practitioners. However, there are provincial associations that set educational standards for practitioners and certify them. Every province has legislation restricting the practice of medicine, or the performance of specific medical acts, such as diagnosis.

NATIONAL ASSOCIATION

Currently, there are no national associations of shiatsu therapists. However, there are associations in B.C. and Ontario, with members in others provinces. There is also a massage therapist and bodyworkers alliance in Nova Scotia, whose membership includes shiatsu therapists (see below, "Shiatsu in Your Province").

SHIATSU EDUCATION

If you wish to become a practitioner, some of the well-known colleges and programs are listed below. The Shiatsu Therapy Association of British Columbia recognizes the Canadian Acupressure Institute in Victoria, the Sourcepoint Shiatsu Center in Vancouver, and the Shiatsu School of Canada in Toronto. The Shiatsu Therapy Association of Ontario recognizes only the Shiatsu School of Canada for those wishing to become Certified Shiatsu Therapists.

In choosing among schools, it is advisable to compare the qualifications of faculty (their education and professional experience), program content and length, any admission requirements and all fees and contract terms, including refund policies. It is also useful to speak with students and graduates of the various programs about their standards, and to consult with representatives of associations.

Most provinces have legislation requiring private vocational schools to meet certain minimum standards, often related to financial stability, for the protection of consumers. These requirements vary from province to province, and certain health care training programs are not in all cases covered by such legislation. Contact the Ministry of Education or Advanced Education in your province for more information on their policies regarding registration of private vocational schools.

Canadian Acupressure Institute
301-733 Johnson St
Victoria, B.C. V8W 3C7
604-388-7475

The Institute, established in 1994, offers an eight-month, 725-hour certification training program in shiatsu. The curriculum includes: 270 hours of shiatsu training; 170 hours of shiatsu's application to common conditions such as headache, insomnia, and back pain; 115 hours of legal and ethical considerations; 100 hours of anatomy and physiology; 70 hours of CPR First Aid, business management, bodymind counselling skills, ethics, sales, marketing and promotions. Minimum admission requirements include Grade 12 graduation and minimum age of 18.

Mature students will also be considered who are 19 years or older with life experience demonstrating responsibility, fluency in written and spoken English, and good health. The Institute's Calendar contains details on the credentials of the faculty. The Institute also offers a program in acupressure (see "Acupressure"). The school is recognized by the Shiatsu Therapy Association of British Columbia.

Shiatsu Academy of Tokyo
320 Danforth Ave, Ste 206
Toronto, Ontario M4K 1N8
Tel: 416-466-8780
Fax: 416-466-8719

A private vocational school, the Academy offers a two-year, part-time professional Shiatsu Practitioner course.

The Shiatsu Centre
1069 Bathurst St
Toronto, Ontario M5R 3G8
Tel: 416-534-1140

This Centre offers certificate courses in shiatsu.

The Shiatsu School of Canada
547 College St
Toronto, Ontario M6G 1A9
Tel: 416-323-1818 or 1-800-263-1703
Fax: 416-343-1681

This private vocational school, established in 1986, offers a diploma program for those interested in professional career training, as well as a certificate program for those wishing to learning shiatsu to help friends and family. The 2,200-hour diploma program is offered on a full-time (1 1/2 years) or part-time basis (2 1/2 years). The certificate program is 100 hours, taught in two levels. Kaz Kamiya is the founder, director and main instructor. He has studied shiatsu and acupuncture in Japan, and has been in private practice and teaching since 1978. This school is recognized by the professional associations of both B.C. and Ontario.

Sourcepoint Shiatsu Centre
3261 Heather (at 16th Ave)
Vancouver, B.C. V5Z 3K4
Tel: 604-876-0042

This Centre, opened in 1987, offers certificate and diploma professional training for those wishing to become practitioners, as well as training for those who wish to offer treatment to family and friends. The certificate program is a six-month, 300-hour program beginning in January. The diploma program is a 10-month, 700-hour program beginning every September. Co-founder Ted Thomas' credentials include a diploma from the International College of Traditional Chinese Medicine. He is also certified as an instructor by the non-profit American Oriental Bodywork Therapy Association (AOBTA). For information on the AOBTA, see "Acupressure." The school is recognized by Shiatsu Therapy Association of British Columbia.

Zen Shiatsu Institute
358 Dupont St
Toronto, Ontario M5R 1V9
Tel: 416-925-5722

This institute offers a diploma program and introductory workshop, as well as a course on anatomy.

✦ Shiatsu in Your Province

Provinces ares listed alphabetically below, with the following information:

Provincial Associations

✦ addresses and telephone numbers of provincial shiatsu associations, where they exist; such associations often provide referrals

Shiatsu Therapists

✦ names, addresses and telephone numbers of shiatsu practitioners, listed alphabetically by city

NOTE: Those therapists known to offer house call service are indicated by an (H).

✦ Alberta Shiatsu Therapists

NOTE: Check the credentials of your shiatsu therapist (see above, "Questions to Ask"). This publication cannot and does not certify or represent the qualifications of any practitioners, or the quality of care available from them.

CALGARY

Japan Shiatsu Clinic
108-429 14th St NW 403-270-3168

✦ British Columbia

British Columbia Association

Shiatsu Therapy Association (S.T.A.) of British Columbia
PO Box 52084
231 Mountain Highway
North Vancouver, B.C. V7J 2C0
President: Marc Carpentier
Tel: 604-433-9495
Fax: 604-984-7405

Formerly the Shiatsu and Oriental Therapies Education Society (S.O.T.E.S.), this non-profit professional association will provide referrals to shiatsu therapists with a minimum of 300 hours of training. Many professional members have 1,000 hours of training, or more. The purpose of the Association is to encourage public awareness of shiatsu, and to act as a network for therapists.

✦ British Columbia Shiatsu Therapists

NOTE: Listed below are names of shiatsu therapists provided by the Shiatsu Therapy Association (S.T.A.) of B.C. (formerly S.O.T.E.S), signified by the initials 'STA'. Contact the association to confirm the membership of your shiatsu therapist or to obtain updated membership information. Also listed below are names of shiatsu therapists in B.C. who are members of the Shiatsu Therapy Association of Ontario, designated by the initials (CST). Practitioners listed below who are members of neither of these associations are designated by the initial (O), signifying 'other qualifications.' Check the qualifications of your practitioner. This publication cannot and does not certify or represent the qualifications of any practitioners, or the quality of care available from them.

BURNABY

Gentle Winds
Mah, Nora (STA)
322 Gilmore Ave 604-291-2322

CORTES ISLAND

West, Dianne (STA)
By Appointment 604-935-6440

MISSION

Pare, Patricia (STA)
By Appointment 604-820-3435

NANAIMO

Island Shiatsu Therapy
Storey, Elizabeth (CST)(H)
1 Chapel St, #1402 604-753-1646

NORTH VANCOUVER

Carpentier, Marc (STA)
305-235 E 13th St 604-988-5676

Conkin, Mary-Lou (STA)
By Appointment 604-985-5764

Freedhoff, Marla Joy (CST)
1861 Philip Ave 604-986-9535

Lynn at Mountain Massage Therapy
Waddingham, Jacqui (STA)
102-1258 Lynn Valley Rd . . . 604-980-7474

Redfern, Joan (STA)
By Appointment 604-990-0326

Vancouver Namikoshi Shiatso Centre
Chiang, C.L.
347 E 22nd St 604-985-9391

PENDER ISLAND

Easthope, Shelley (STA)
5823 Schooner, RR #1 . . 604-629-3036

RICHMOND

Ageless Traditional Chinese Herbal Centre
Lilam, Dr. David (STA)
3320 Jacombs Rd,
Unit 110 604-433-2847

Berg, Anne-Carine (Anke) (STA)
9800 Elkmond Rd 604-274-3790

SALT SPRING ISLAND

Jacobson, Rachel (O)
By Appointment 604-537-1091

Salty Springs Resort
Snidal, Liz (CST)
1460 N Beach Rd 604-537-4111

SMITHERS

Graham, Bill (CST)
By Appointment 604-847-0144

VANCOUVER

Baker, Ray (STA)
2320 St. Catherines 604-876-9999

Body Alive
Sands, Astarte (STA)
311-825 Granville St 604-669-4031

Bouvier, Diana (STA)
1850 Charles St 604-251-4583

Cabrera, Ferando (STA)
2735 W 10th Ave 604-732-0496

Dixon, Kendall (STA)
1430 West 7th Ave 604-738-2503

Have Thumbs Will Travel
Whyte, Robert (STA)
10-2277 Wall St 604-255-6854

Mangunatmodjo, Yanti (STA)
2565 W 4th Ave . . 604-977-3997 (pager)

Mizutani, Junji (STA)
896 W King Edward Ave . . . 604-874-8537

Ostermann, M. Gyano (STA)
3005 W King Edward Ave . . .604-737-8494

Quest Clinic
Crowe, Lesley (STA)
257-4255 Arbutus St 604-731-1374

Rea, Lesley (STA)
By Appointment 604-876-2206

Sawkins, Allen (STA)
1807-1150 Jervis St 604-202-1473

Shiatsu Therapy Housecalls
Rosenbaum, Saul (STA) (H)
By Appointment . . . . 604-641-5481 (pager)

Sourcepoint Shiatsu & Stress Management
MacKenzie, Annabel (STA); Thomas, Ted (STA);
Van Keith, Colin (STA)
3261 Heather St 604-876-0042

Tetreault, Christine (STA)
903-1010 Burnaby St 604-684-1010

Van Keith, Colin (STA)
406-1238 Seymour St 604-682-7339

VICTORIA

Chrysalis Shiatsu
Kirk, Lynn (STA)
128-645 Fort St 604-384-2001

Coull, Cheryl (CST)
1454 Begbie St 604-595-4960

Gabaglia, Sandra Raja (CST)
2658 Mount Stephen Rd . . . 604-480-4126

Van Orden, Majorie (STA)
15-1240 Balmoral 604-384-6276

Wagner, LiDona (STA)
3-1070 Joan Cr 604-370-1812

WEST VANCOUVER

Fockler, Sylvia K.F. (STA)
1124 Lawson Ave 604-926-0857

Japanese Shiatsu at the Secret Garden
Nakano, Yoshimi (STA); Jacobson, Karen (STA)
2-1718 Marine Dr 604-926-7589

West Bay Clinic
Pulvermacher, Brenda (STA)
3396 Marine Dr 604-922-7242

WHISTLER

Adhara Shiatsu Therapy
Angco, Mariesa (CST)(H)
By Appointment 604-938-9172

Blue Highway's Shiatsu & Massage
Lynch, Randy (STA);
Oswald, Theresa (STA)(H)
Shimizu, Janet (STA)(H)
4433 Sundial Pl, #204 604-938-0777

Chateau Whistler All Seasons Spa
Mangunatmodjo, Yanti (STA)
By Appointment 604-938-2086

Hayter, Geoff (CST)(H)
17-2020 Watson Way 604-932-9532

Shaw, Judy (STA)
B1-2230 Eva Lake Rd 604-932-6867

Whistler Therapeutic Centre
Mangunatmodjo, Yanti (STA)
101 Blackcombe
Professional Bldg 604-938-4943

WHITE ROCK

Johnson, Joan P. (STA)
202-1561 George St 604-541-0838

✦ Manitoba Shiatsu Therapists

NOTE: Check the credentials of your shiatsu therapist (see above, "Questions to Ask"). This publication cannot and does not certify or represent the qualifications of any practitioners, or the quality of care available from them.

WINNIPEG

Shiatsu Clinic of Manitoba
318 Aubrey St 204-783-0974

Vital Care Shiatsu Clinic
Hanes, Angela
726-367 Ellice Ave 204-943-7867

Winnipeg Shiatsu Therapy Centre
Unit 2, 222 Osborne St 204-228-9164

✦ Northwest Territories Shiatsu Therapists

NOTE: Check the credentials of your shiatsu therapist (see above, "Questions to Ask"). This publication cannot and does not certify or represent the qualifications of any practitioners, or the quality of care available from them.

IQUALUIT

Northern Lights Shatsu Therapy
Wilke, Markus (CST)
By Appointment 819-979-0320

✦ Nova Scotia

Nova Scotia Association

Massage Therapist and Bodyworkers' Alliance of
the Maritimes
2424 Herenow St
Halifax B6T 3E5
Tel: 902-422-2222
Contact: Joseph V. Bloggs

This alliance includes practitioners from the following therapies: Aromatherapy, Feldenkrais, Jin Shin Jyutsu, Massage Therapy, Reflexology, Shiatsu and Trager

✦ Nova Scotia Shiatsu Therapists

NOTE: Check the credentials of your shiatsu therapist (see above, "Questions to Ask"). This publication cannot and does not certify or represent the qualifications of any practitioners, or the quality of care available from them.

DARTMOUTH

Breijer, Lena
By Appointment 902-469-5764

HALIFAX

Himmelman, Don
By Appointment 902-429-1253

Masterson, Anne
5520 Victoria Rd 902-422-8135

McCrindle, Robert, DC
1257 Queen St 902-429-3659

✦ Ontario

Ontario Association

Shiatsu Therapy Association of Ontario
PO Box 695, Station P
Toronto, Ontario M5S 2Y4
Tel: 416-762-2260

This non-profit association, with 120 members across Canada, will assist you in finding a Certified Shiatsu Therapist (CST) in your area. The CST designation is the trademark of practising members of the Association. Certified Shiatsu Therapists have 2,200 hours (two years, full-time) education, including course work in anatomy, physiology, pathology and 272 hours of supervised practice in a public clinic setting. Members must now also pass written and practical association entrance exams. The association is a self-regulating, non-profit organization, with its own complaints and disciplines committee, practice guidelines and code of ethics.

✦ Ontario Shiatsu Therapists

NOTE: Names with the designation (CST) are Certified Shiatsu Therapists with the Shiatsu Therapy Association of Ontario (see above). Check the credentials of your shiatsu therapist (see above, "Questions to Ask"). This publication cannot and does not certify or represent the qualifications of any practitioners, or the quality of care available from them.

ACTON

Schvallbe, Evita (CST)
RR #1 519-853-3085

ALMONTE

Almonte Chiropractic Centre
Freeman, Louise (CST)
118 Water St 613-256-2813

AURORA

Irrcher, Eva (CST)(H)
24 Cossar Dr 905-841-0902

BARRIE

Corkett, Darlene (CST)
RR #1 705-722-7288

Tavares, Dorothy Marie (CST)
208-255 Kozlov St 705-728-0259

BOULTER

Groeneveld, Vern (CST)
By Appointment 613-332-2188

BRAMPTON

Ballantine, Tom (CST)(H)
By Appointment 416-322-0439

Frasson, Daniela (CST)
47 Jasper Cr 905-792-3083

Gannon-Baird, Janice (CST)(H)
By Appointment 416-742-1689

Virag, Imre (CST)(H)
By Appointment 905-713-3385

BROCKVILLE

Cameron, Anne C. (CST)
1-265 King St E 613-342-0916

BURLINGTON

Caroline Massage Therapy & Shiatsu Therapy
Slaczka, Donna (CST)(H)
2025 Caroline St 905-333-5222/
637-9832

Olynyk, Natalie (CST) (H)
By Appointment 416-787-3010

CAMBRIDGE

Naturopathic Healthcare Centre
Stever, Kevin (CST)
119 Ainslie St N 519-622-0961

CARP

Carp Chiropractic
Freeman, Louise (CST)(H)
422 Donald B. Munroe Dr . .613-839-5316

DUNDAS/GRIMSBY

Bove, Sandro (CST)
26 Moss Blvd, #38 905-628-3331

Crawford, Ann (CST)
182 King St W 905-526-9252

ESPANOLA

O'Reilly, Patricia (CST)(H)
193 Tudhope St 705-869-5287

FENELON FALLS

Sadiwynk, Paul (CST)
21-5th St, Sturgeon Point
(RR #2) 705-887-6294

GEORGETOWN

Georgetown Therapeutic Massage Clinic
Holmes, Beverley (CST)
31A Main St S 905-873-1924

GUELPH

Canning, Janice (CST)(H)
62 Hayes Ave 519-763-3959

Homewood Health Centre
Schvallbe, Evita (CST)
By Appointment . . .519-824-1762, ext. 172

HAMILTON

Foss, Katrine (CST)
256 Duke St, #404 905-523-6764

Healing Link
Stever, Kevin (CST)
565 Sanatorium Rd 905-574-5445

KINGSTON

Morris, Beth (CST)(H)
328 King St E, 2nd Floor . . .613-547-4736

KITCHENER

Howley, Mary (CST)
622 Charles St E 519-743-3405

LINDSAY

Feldman, Norman (CST)
128 Durham St W 705-878-0829

LONDON

Donald, Leslie (CST)
784 Colborne St, #2 519-858-1834

Shiatsu Healing Centre
McLeod, Leo (CST)(H);
Tsukahara, George (CST)
465 Ridout St S 519-649-6617

Shiatsu Holistic Therapy Clinic
Heckendorn, Kevin (CST) (H)
19 Marley Place
(Wortley Village) 519-434-5544

MISSISSAUGA

Colomby, Joanne (CST)
2383 Basswood Cr 905-607-1880

Kenko Alternative Therapy Academy
Slaczka, Donna (CST)
1107 Lorne Park Rd 905-891-8652

Macauley, Robert (CST)(H)
3493 Ponytrail Dr 905-625-2399

Mississauga Therapeutic Health Centre
Kinnersly, Kelene (CST)
1295 Burnhamthorpe Rd E . .905-206-0525

Pergad-Copoc, Rohana (CST)
971 Zante Cr 905-855-8203

Pickles, Shannin (CST)
2300 S Millway, #105 905-820-9485

Shaw, Linda E.(CST)
1865 Bickford Dr 905-822-0241

Shiatsu Acupuncture Centre
30 Eglinton Ave W at Hwy 10 905-712-3706

Shiatsu for You
Reich, Anna (CST)
94 Lakeshore Rd E, #205 . . .905-891-9523

Sunarth, Natalie (CST)
5194 Sundial Ct 905-273-7113

Turning Point Shiatsu & Acupuncture Clinic
Heath, Esther (CST)(H)
1459 Flaminia Ct 905-822-4504

MOUNT ALBERT

Cowie, Elizabeth (CST) (H)
19081 Centre St 905-473-7060

NEWMARKET

Baggaley, Francia (CST)
663 Red Deer St 905-898-2433

Peressotti, Hugh (CST)(H)
16633 Warden Ave 905-836-2674

OAKVILLE

Batt, Carrie (CST)
1378 Hastings Rd 905-408-4594

Colbeck, Lisa (CST)
2457 Stefi Trail 905-257-2110

Heath, Esther (CST)(H)
By Appointment 905-822-4504

Oakville Shiatsu & Massage Therapy Centre
Krechowicz, Eva (CST)(H)
125 Lakeshore Rd E, #304 . .905-845-3137

Slaczka, Donna (CST)(H)
By Appointment 905-333-5222/
637-9832

OSHAWA

Chernushenko, Raissa (CST) (H)
By Appointment 905-728-9192
(905-686-3100 - access # for Toronto)

Margaret's Health & Beauty
Noseworth, Craig (CST)
909 Simcoe St 905-576-5898

Olynyk, Natalie (CST)(H)
By Appointment 416-787-3010

OTTAWA

Body-Mind Continuum
Simpson, Claire (CST)
346 Somerset St W, #201 . .613-230-3527

Freeman, Louise (CST)(H)
By Appointment 613-839-5316

PARRY SOUND

Stewart, Elizabeth (CST)
12 Bay St 705-746-4410

PETROLIA

Phillips, Lorilee (CST)
By Appointment 519-882-1949

PICKERING

Blais, Jeanette (CST)
400 Kingston Rd, #212 905-509-5816

RICHMOND HILL

Centre of the Emerald Heart
Gouffray, Michelle (CST);
Sild, Peter (CST)
8763 Bayview Ave, #208 . . .905-707-0604

Hillsview Massage & Therapy Centre
Baggaley, Francia (CST)(H)
9640 Bayview Ave, #4 905-508-7103

Richmond Hill Natural Therapies
Chen, Karen (CST)
116 Church St S 905-883-9355

STOUFFVILLE

Alpha Health Care Clinic
Wright, Rosemarie (CST)
34 Civic Ave 905-642-2878

STREETSVILLE

Kinnersly, Kelene (CST)
30 Pearl St 905-812-0244

THORNHILL

Dowd, Charlene (CST)(H)
By Appointment 416-966-4405

Gacser, Marlene (CST)
10 Royal Orchard Blvd 905-889-5188

TORONTO

Anma, Do (CST)
Ishizuka, Tamotsu
177 Major St 416-588-0362

Backovska, Valeria (CST)(H)
2561 Bloor St W, #109 416-760-7658

Beaches Wellness Centre
Neyedly, Elizabeth (CST)
2276 Queen St E 416-698-7070

Becktel, Christine (CST)
392 Woodsworth Rd, #37 . .416-444-0176

Bone, Helen (CST)
53 Claxton Blvd 416-652-9363

Boone, Frances (CST) (H)
3152A Dundas St W 416-769-9477

Buxton, Rosemary (CST); De Moy, Lucy (CST)
472 Palmerston Blvd 416-537-2077/
534-3251

Campbell, Guiomar, P.(CST) (H)
44 Shanly St 416-588-3762

Chen, Karen (CST)
By Appointment 416-299-5465

Chiropractic & Shiatsu Centre
Thornton, Kevin (CST)
2020 Bathurst St 416-783-2333

Classical Chines Medicine Clinic
Neyedly, Elizabeth (CST)
411 Parliament St, #206 . . .416-928-1335

Clearstream Natural Health Clinic
Carbone, Leny;
Sun, Lee Sheng
980 Bathurst 416-530-6959

Coady, Heather (CST)
90 Adelaide St E, #406 416-777-0403

Dixon, Paul (CST)
1654 Bathurst St, #2 416-787-5131

Dorman, Chris (CST)(H)
By Appointment 416-531-5134

Dowd, Charlotte (CST) (H)
70 Charles St E, #14 416-966-4405

Essential Healthworks Therapy
Roecker, Richard (CST)(H)
261 Davenport Rd, #201 . . .416-929-2718

Fardoe, Alison (CST)(H)
By Appointment 416-463-7733

Gacser, Marlene (CST)(H)
By Appointment 416-444-5414/
296-9883

Gannon-Baird, Janice (CST)(H)
83 Avening Dr 416-742-1689

Goldstein, Martin (CST)(H)
54 Lawrence Ave W 416-489-1661

Gonder, Meg (CST)
1029 Logan Ave 416-466-4105

Gut-Omen, Florence (CST)
39 Wedge Court 416-635-6157

Gyaltsen, Tashi (CST)
644 Runnymede Rd,
Floor 2 416-766-2245

Holistic Medical Centre
Thomsen, Andrea (CST)
27 Roncesvalles Ave,
#405 416-604-4810

Intuitive Touch Therapies
Phillips, Timothy L.(CST)(H)
1938 Queen St E 416-693-4777

Keator, Meredith (CST)
681 Markham St 416-532-9742

Keates, Carol (CST)(H)
108 Palmerston Ave 416-603-2069

Khalsa, Hari Darshan Singh (CST)(H)
415 Dovercourt Rd 416-538-6799

Khan, Amanda (CST)
4 Richmond Park Blvd 416-299-6650

Kikkawa College
Kerslake, Simon H.(CST);
Kikkawa, Mitsuki (CST)
1 Riverview Gardens 416-762-4857

Kimlen Therapies
Lim, Linda Kimlen Cuan (CST)(H)
By Appointment 416-461-2470

Kinlough, Louise (CST)(H)
37 Cecil St 416-351-0550

Knox, Jennifer (CST)(H)
1845 Albany Ave 416-538-6577

Krechowicz, Eva (CST)(H)
By Appointment -
High Park 416-766-7127

Kulhay Wellness Centre
Knox, Jennifer (CST)
2 St. Clair Ave W, #607 416-961-1900

Lewis, Majorie (CST)
200 Balliol St, #1601 416-483-1319

Li, Chun (CST)
11 Walmer Rd 416-966-8519

Loney, Jane (CST)(H)
46 Sparkhall Ave 416-778-4489

McPherson, Melodee (CST)
69 Crawford St, 2nd Floor . .416-504-8565

Mizzi, Theresa (CST)
55 Lombard St, #204 416-367-2022

Mu Mei Do Shiatsu & Acupuncture Clinic
Tatsuko, Taminori (CST) (H)
44 Millwood Rd 416-322-7229

Neighbourhood Wellness Clinic
Dempster, Chris (CST)(H);
Eade, Mirella (CST)(H)
1320 Yonge St 416-489-9793/
487-3041

Noseworthy, Craig (CST)(H)
12 Walpole Ave 416-462-9984

Olynyk, Natalie (CST)(H)
By Appointment 416-787-3010

Only Human Shiatsu Therapy
Kremko, Mark (CST)
19 Yorkville Ave, #200 416-962-6275

Otani Shiatsu Centre
24 Roncesvalles Ave 416-533-9964

Phillips, Timothy L.(CST)(H)
22 Rainsford Rd 416-694-6962

Rogers, Joanne (CST)
23 Lascelles Blvd, #1105 . . .416-932-9556

Rostant, Vicki (CST)
95 Braemar Ave 416-484-7219

Shiatsu Acupuncture Centre
30 Eglinton Ave W
(at Hwy 10) 905-712-3706

Shiatsu Acupuncture Clinic
Tanaka, Tim H.(CST); Toyama, Yoshio (CST)
80 Bloor St W, #1100 416-929-6958

Shiatsu & Acupuncture of Tsurusaki
Tsurusaki, Takamasa (CST)
2409 Yonge St, #200 416-488-8414

Shiatsu Centre Ltd
Harris, Tanya (CST) (H);
Praniauskas, J. Carlos (CST);
Saito, Ted (Tetsuro)(CST)(H)
1069 Bathurst St 416-534-1140/1149

Shiatsu Centre
205-110 Richmond St E 416-368-6855

Shiatsu Clinic
Kamiya, Kaz (CST); Strzelecka, Anna (CST);
van der Poorten, Nancy (CST)
517 College St #207 416-323-3700

Shiatsu Clinic West
Heinrichs, Svinda (CST)
3101 Bloor St W., #206 . . .416-236-2583/
922-5758

Shiatsu Dohjoh
206-320 Danforth Ave 416-466-8780

Shiatsu Institute Inc.
Ballantine, Tom (CST)(H);
Eade, Mirella (CST)(H);
Kerslake, Simon (CST); Lewis, Majorie (CST)
2578A Yonge St 416-322-0439

Shiatsu School of Canada Clinic
Kamiya, Kaz (CST)
547 College St 416-323-1818

Shiatsu Therapy
Russell, Diane (CST)
112 Cowan Ave, Unit 34 416-534-6841

Shiatsu Therapy Clinic
Kantarjian, Roxanna (CST)
1315 Lawrence Ave E,
#520 416-510-0019

Sild, Peter (CST)(H)
By Appointment 416-747-8714

Slater, Barbara R. (CST)(H)
35 Canyon Ave, #406 416-398-7017

Steiner, Gregory (CST)
4910 Yonge St, 2nd Floor . . .416-222-9005

Stephenson, Marilyn (CST)
52 Alhambra Ave 416-537-8883

Teevens, Laurie (CST)
449 Lansdowne Ave 416-588-8211

Thompson, Chris (CST)(H)
By Appointment 416-494-8489

Thornton, Kevin (CST)
660 Eglington Ave W,
#102 416-781-1643

Toronto Pain & Headache Clinic
Scott, Gillian (CST)
9 Bloor St E, #206 416-925-2579

Traicus, Daniel (CST)(H)
By Appointment 416-694-1262

Turpin, Robert (CST)
38 Gradewell Dr 416-269-6057

Tyckyi, Julian (CST)
9 Sheffley Cr 416-247-2771

Virag, Imre (CST)(H)
By Appointment 905-713-3385

Ward, Laurie (CST)
529 Euclid Ave, #2 416-535-6182

Windt, Dana (CST)
1657 Bathurst St,
Upper Duplex 416-485-1751

UNIONVILLE

Ashgrove Therapy Centre
Yee, Jeanne (CST)(H)
6633 Hwy 7, #301 905-294-8614

VANDORF

Virag, Imre (CST)(H) - Central Toronto & Brampton
5483 Slater Rd 905-713-3385

WATERLOO

I.T.M. Limited
Pryce, Muriel (CST)
69 Bridgeport Rd E 519-747-9520

Stever, Kevin (CST)(H)
By Appointment 519-698-2877

WHITBY

Whitby Massage Therapy Clinic Inc.
Chernushenko, Raissa (CST)(H)
519 Dundas St E, #7 905-430-2183

✦ Québec Shiatsu Therapists

NOTE: Check the credentials of your Shiatsu therapist (see above, "Questions to Ask"). This publication cannot and does not certify or represent the qualifications of any practitioner, or the quality of care available from them.

BELOEIL

Centre Shiatsu-Energie
675 Sir Wilfrid Laurier 514-464-8383

LA VERNIERE

Shiatsu Miousse Marjolanine Massage
By Appointment 418-986-4279

SALABERRY-DE-VALLEYFIELD

Trudel, Hugo
57 Du Marche 514-377-1164

VICTORIAVILLE

Boutin, Josesh
87 Des Hospitalieres 819-357-1616

✦ Saskatchewan Shiatsu Therapists

NOTE: Check the credentials of your shiatsu therapist (see above, "Questions to Ask"). This publication cannot and does not certify or represent the qualifications of any practitioners, or the quality of care available from them.

REGINA

Shiatsu-Acupressure Centre
Cook, Susan
2474 Atkinson 306-757-9400

Therapeutic Touch

WHAT IS THERAPEUTIC TOUCH

Therapeutic Touch is a method of working with a person's energy flow as a means of inducing relaxation and speeding the healing process. It is usually performed without hands-on contact by the practitioner. The technique was developed in the 1970s by New York nurse Dolores Krieger, PhD, and her mentor Dora Kunz. It is based on the assumption that energy flows freely in and through a healthy person's body, and that the flow of energy is obstructed or depleted during illness or as a result of injury. Therapeutic Touch practitioners attempt to alleviate this energy imbalance by moving their hands around a person's body in a flowing motion, a few inches away from the body, with the intention to help or heal. The approach is presented as a contemporary interpretation of several ancient healing practices and is based on a consciously directed process of energy exchange. The patient remains clothed and relaxed during sessions that do not usually exceed 20 minutes. The Therapeutic Touch Network (Ontario) believes that the technique fits into what it describes as a major paradigm shift that extends across the sciences from physics to medicine and biology: "It involves a transition from the mechanistic Newtonian model to the acceptance of the Einstein paradigm of a complex, yet interconnected, energetic field-like universe." Therapeutic Touch is offered by nurses to patients in many hospitals, as well as to members of the public by practitioners in private practice.

Gaining Rapid Acceptance

Therapeutic Touch is rapidly gaining acceptance, and is being approved for use in growing numbers of hospitals across the country. In 1993, the Toronto East General and Orthopaedic Hospital became the first Canadian hospital to admit Therapeutic Touch into its policy and procedures manual, acknowledging that nurses could use the technique. Shirley Dalglish, coordinator of palliative care, said that the feedback has been positive from patients from the first day: "Cancer patients found increased comfort and a decrease in pain, as well as reduced side effects - less fatigue, less nausea. They say: 'I just feel better.'" Ms. Dalglish said that the hospital offers training for all staff on a voluntary basis. Therapeutic Touch has also been approved by the Victorian Order of Nurses (VON). Maureen Goodram, a nursing supervisor with VON in Ontario, notes that, according to the Health Care Manual for VON (Canada), any nurse may use Therapeutic if a patient wishes, provided that the nurse meets the criteria for training. Other Ontario hospitals which have approved the technique include Pembroke Civic Hospital and St. Joseph's Health Centre in Toronto. As well, the Vancouver Hospital, B.C. Cancer Agency and St. Paul's Hospital in Vancouver, have approved the use of Therapeutic Touch.

BENEFITS OF THERAPEUTIC TOUCH

Therapeutic Touch is considered beneficial for persons of all ages, including newborns, and for those suffering from any illness, injury, chronic or terminal disease, as well as for mothers during and after childbirth. The Therapeutic Touch Network (Ontario) states that research and experience have shown the technique's effectiveness in promoting relaxation, reducing anxiety, changing the patient's perception of pain, and facilitating the body's natural restorative processes.

Therapeutic Touch practitioners do not diagnose or treat disease, nor do they suggest that it is a substitute for medical treatment that may be required. Rather, the technique is presented as a complement to conventional care.

QUESTIONS TO ASK

✦ How much experience does your practitioner have?
NOTE: The Therapeutic Touch Network (Ontario) states that the number of years a person has been actively practising Therapeutic Touch is a good indicator of his or her competence. One year is considered to be the minimum acceptable level of experience.

✦ Has your practitioner been trained by a qualified teacher?
NOTE: If you are seeking Therapeutic Touch, your practitioner should be trained in a program based on the Krieger-Kunz curriculum. There is no formal certification of practitioners, but some networks set standards for recognition of practitioners. For example, the Ontario Network recognizes practitioners who have completed a particular number of courses, have practised for a minimum of one year and have signed a code of ethics. Practitioners may receive a certificate of attendance.

✦ What is your practitioner's background, and does it include training in other forms of health care, such as nursing? A background in health care is useful.

✦ Does your practitioner specialize? For example, some practitioners work extensively with cancer patients.

✦ Does your practitioner have references from other health care practitioners? There is often an formal or informal network of Therapeutic Touch and other health care practitioners.

✦ How many sessions are recommended, how long will they last and how much will they cost?

GOVERNMENT REGULATION

There is no provincial regulation of Therapeutic Touch practitioners in Canada, except to the extent that nurses or other regulated practitioners are trained in the technique. There are no provincial laws establishing governing bodies responsible for registering qualified practitioners of Therapeutic Touch. This also means that there are no minimum educational standards for those calling themselves Therapeutic Touch practitioners. However, some networks have established their own standards for recognition.

CANADIAN & U.S. ASSOCIATIONS

There is no national Canadian association, but there are networks in Alberta and Ontario (see below, "Therapeutic Touch in Your Province). As well, networks are in the process of organizing in B.C. and the Atlantic provinces. There are also informal networks that you may contact through practitioners in other provinces.

Nurse Healers - Professional Associates Inc.
PO Box 444
Allison Park, Pennsylvania 15101-0444
USA
Tel: 412-355-8476

This is a non-profit co-operative of health care professionals for the promotion of healing. The organization supports many healing modalities, one of which is Therapeutic Touch. The organization was founded by Dolores Krieger, PhD, founder of Therapeutic Touch and Professor Emerita, New York University, Department of Nursing.

THERAPEUTIC TOUCH EDUCATION

Therapeutic Touch is a skill that requires sensitivity and must be initially practised with supervision and feedback. Courses are available from individual teachers, community colleges, and hospitals. Introductory courses usually involve 8 to 10 hours of theory and supervised practice. They can be held in a single day or over a period of several weeks. Beginners are encouraged to practise on themselves, family and friends for several months before taking further intermediate and advanced level courses. Year-long programs are available from some advanced teachers.

Due to its nature, and the lack of criteria for objectively measuring a practitioner's effectiveness, Therapeutic Touch does not carry certification at any level of expertise. Depending upon the program, students may receive a certificate of attendance after completing a program.

It is important to learn the technique from a recognized teacher, who has practised Therapeutic Touch intensively for several years. Guidelines for teachers based on the curriculum approved by Dolores Krieger, PhD, are available from established networks. As well, the names of teachers of the Krieger-Kunz method who have met the criteria for recognition by the Ontario Network are listed in full below (see "Therapeutic Touch in Your Province - Ontario"). Recognized teachers are also recognized practitioners, and must meet certain other criteria, including participation in yearly updates through retreats and conferences.

In B.C., where a network has not yet formed, Janie Brown, R.N., teaches in the Lower Mainland and throughout the province. She will also refer prospective students to teachers in their area (604-732-1012). Phyllis Coleman, R.N., (604-537-2378) of Salt Spring Island also teaches in many areas of the province. In Manitoba, Llyn Wren, R.N., is a teacher and practitioner, at 204-775-4620.

In choosing among programs, it is advisable to compare the qualifications of teachers (their education and professional experience), course content and length, all fees and contract terms, including refund policies. It is also useful to speak with students and graduates.

✦ Therapeutic Touch in Your Province

Each province is listed alphabetically below, with the following information:

Therapeutic Touch Associations

✦ addresses and telephone numbers of provincial Therapeutic Touch Networks, where they exist; such networks provide referrals

Therapeutic Touch Practitioners

✦ names, addresses and telephone numbers of Therapeutic Touch practitioners, listed alphabetically by city

NOTE: The Ontario list includes only recognized Therapeutic Touch teachers, who are also recognized practitioners. Teachers of Therapeutic Touch are identified by the letter '(T)'.

✦ Alberta

Alberta Association

Therapeutic Touch Network Alberta
Box 146, 9768 170th St
Edmonton, Alberta T5T 5L4
Tel/Fax: 403-444-4541
Contact: Beverley Snaychuk

This association has about 20 practitioner members from Alberta, B.C., Saskatchewan and the Northwest Territories. Practitioners must have a minimum of one year of experience and sign a code of ethics.

✦ Alberta Therapeutic Touch Practitioners

NOTE: Check the credentials of your practitioner (see above, "Questions to Ask"). This publication cannot and does not certify or represent the qualifications of practitioners, or the quality of care available from them.

CALGARY

Armitage, Marney (T)
By Appointment 403-242-5599

Graham, Melanie (T)
By Appointment 403-249-9489

Terra, Linda (T)
908 Canaveral Cr SW 403-238-3734

EDMONTON

Dundin, Maureen (T)
By Appointment 403-476-8860

Snaychuk, Beverley (T)
By Appointment 403-444-4541

Wakeford, Brenda (T)
By Appointment 403-462-1504

Winton, Shelley (T)
By Appointment 403-454-3279

FORT MCMURRAY

Gigliotti, Louise
By Appointment 430-743-9084

MEDICINE HAT

Spencer, Arlette (T)
By Appointment 403-528-3252

SHERWOOD PARK

Field, Joanne (T)
By Appointment 403-464-4466

✦ British Columbia

British Columbia Association

Victoria Therapeutic Touch Practitioners' Group
c/o Nora Walker
402-707 Esquimalt Rd
Victoria, B.C. V9A 3L7
Tel: 604-388-4562

The group will refer you to a therapeutic touch practitioner in the southern Vancouver Island area. The group offers a free monthly healing circle for members of the public at the Capital Region District (CRD) Health Clinic at 1947 Cook St, Victoria. Call for details.

✦ British Columbia Therapeutic Touch Practitioners

NOTE: Check the credentials of your practitioner (see above, "Questions to Ask"). This publication cannot and does not certify or represent the qualifications of practitioners, or the quality of care available from them.

ALDERGROVE

Lehmann, Ina
#50-27272 32nd Ave 604-856-1978

GOLDEN

Patterson-Robinson, Marijke (T)
By Appointment 604-344-5325

NORTH VANCOUVER

Edmonds, Janice
By Appointment 604-929-1996

Williams, Jane
By Appointment 604-984-0121

SAANICHTON

Adams, Denise
By Appointment 604-652-4372

SALT SPRING ISLAND

Coleman, Phyllis, RN (T)
By Appointment 604-537-2378

Spencer, Carol
By Appointment (Ganges) . . .604-537-2154

SOOKE

Adams, Rosemary
By Appointment 604-642-2660

SURREY

Morrison, Lynette
#113-13900 Hyland Rd 604-591-5755

Patterson, Kim
16698 Fraser Hwy 604-574-7744

TOFINO

Lockwood, Patricia
By Appointment 604-725-3303

VANCOUVER

Brown, Janie (T)
314-2902 W Broadway 604-732-1012

Smith, Lis
1361 W 7th Ave 604-736-4118

Tidball, Janine
204-1665 Arbutus St 604-733-8730

Woods, Lynn
303 E 44th Ave 604-325-7022

VICTORIA

Gilchrest, Kathy
2252 Tinto St 604-595-3284

Merryfield, Jeanette
2819 Inlet 604-383-5517

Roberts, Camille
1280 Vista Heights 604-383-4589

Sadler, Elizabeth
1312 Balmoral Rd 604-592-1673

Walker, Nora
402-707 Esquimalt Rd 604-388-4562

✦ Manitoba Therapeutic Touch Practitioners

NOTE: Check the credentials of your practitioner (see above, "Questions to Ask"). This publication cannot and does not certify or represent the qualifications of practitioners, or the quality of care available from them.

WINNIPEG

Wren, Llyn RN (T)
By Appointment 204-775-4620

✦ New Brunswick Therapeutic Touch Practitioners

NOTE: Check the credentials of your practitioner (see above, "Questions to Ask"). This publication cannot and does not certify or represent the qualifications of practitioners, or the quality of care available from them.

CLIFTON ROYAL

Boyce, Mary Jo
RR #1 506-763-3630

SAINT JOHN

Davidson, Marianne
By Appointment 506-738-2367

✦ Northwest Territories Therapeutic Touch Practitioners

NOTE: Check the credentials of your practitioner (see above, "Questions to Ask"). This publication cannot and does not certify or represent the qualifications of practitioners, or the quality of care available from them.

YELLOWKNIFE

Mercredi, Dianne (T)
By Appointment 403-920-1024/
920-3252

Simons, Martina
By Appointment 403-873-8036

✦ Nova Scotia

Nova Scotia Association

Atlantic Therapeutic Touch Network (ATTN)
Box 156, 1469 Brenton St
Halifax, Nova Scotia B3J 3W7
Tel: 902-423-9085
Fax: 902-425-6731

This group of practitioners is in the process of forming an Atlantic Canada network, and is assembling a list of practitioners.

✦ Nova Scotia Therapeutic Touch Practitioners

NOTE: Check the credentials of your practitioner (see above, "Questions to Ask"). This publication cannot and does not certify or represent the qualifications of practitioners, or the quality of care available from them.

GRAND PRE

Green, Dora
By Appointment 902-542-2690

HALIFAX

Berkowitz, Julie
By Appointment 902-423-4407

Dubreuil, Katherine
By Appointment 902-829-2410

Holden, Jane, RN
By Appointment 902-455-7402

McLaughlin, Shirley
By Appointment 902-423-9085

METEGHAN RIVER

Comeau, Lorna
By Appointment 902-769-2540

YARMOUTH COUNTY

Robicheau, Shirley
Box 32, Port Maitland 902-649-2721

✦ Ontario

Ontario Association

Therapeutic Touch Network (Ontario)
P.O. Box 85551
875 Eglinton Ave W
Toronto, Ontario M6C 4A8
Tel: 416-658-6824 (658-65-TOUCH)

This network of Therapeutic Touch practitioners was formed in 1986 and became incorporated as a non-profit organization in 1994. It promotes the practice and acceptance of Therapeutic Touch as developed by Dolores Krieger, PhD, and her mentor, Dora Kunz.

Call for information on Therapeutic Touch, the name of a recognized practitioner, and for information on education. Recognized practitioners must meet a set of criteria. For example, they must have completed a particular number of courses with recognized teachers, have practised for a minimum of one year and have signed a code of ethics.

✦ Ontario Recognized Therapeutic Touch Practitioners

NOTE: Following are the names of recognized teachers, who are also practitioners. This list was provided by the Therapeutic Touch Network (Ontario). For the names of additional recognized practitioners of Therapeutic Touch, contact the Network. Check the credentials of your practitioners (see above, "Questions to Ask"). This publication cannot and does not certify or represent the qualifications of practitioners, or the quality of care available from them.

AURORA

Hughes-Mann, Dianne (T)
7 Pittypat Ct 905-841-5689

BARRIE

Cugelman, Arlene (T)
16 Maple Cr, RR #3 705-721-1850

Cugelman, Evy (T)
85 Daphne Cr 705-734-0412

BOWMANVILLE

Walker, Barb (T)
2668 Concession 7,
RR #5 905-263-4041

BRAMPTON

Hall, Nancy (T)
6 Hastings Sq 905-793-5476

George, Marlene (T)
34 Norfolk Ave 905-796-0101

Simpson, Mary (T)
123 Queen St W 905-453-7799

CARRYING PLACE

Logan Van Vliet, Donna (T)
By Appointment 613-962-1004

HALIBURTON

Mighton, Marilyn (T)
By Appointment 705-457-9560

LAMBETH

Houseman, V.J. (T)
6564 Decker Dr, RR #3 519-652-2233

LEAMINGTON

McVeigh, Irma (T)
By Appointment 519-326-4741

LONDON

Davis, Heather (T)
1500 Ryersie Rd 519-434-6926

Janelle, Barbara (T)
169 Duchess Ave 519-672-5057

MISSISSAUGA

Birrell, Penny (T)
1051 Cedar Glen Gate,
#43 905-276-8062

May, Diane (T)
115 Hillcrest Ave 905-276-1781

Will, Helen (T)
1392 Hurontario St 905-274-2678

Wyzlic, Jeanne (T)
3196 Dovetail Mews 905-569-3256

NEWBURGH

Pope, Barbara (T)
By Appointment 613-378-6184

OAKVILLE

Burns, Doris (T)
268 Richmond Rd 905-842-3296

PEMBROKE

Watt, Sheila (T)
496 Esther St 613-735-6651

PERTH

Olson, Jane (T)
By Appointment 613-267-7184

PETERBOROUGH

Nelson, Linda (T)
1598 Treetop Rd 705-745-2849

ROCKWOOD

Smith MacKay, Evelyn (T)
RR #5 519-822-4174

ST. CATHERINES

Deane, Margaret (T)
388 Linwell Rd 905-646-4948

Sampson, Linda (T)
36 Church St 905-646-2274

STOUFFVILLE

Beach, Pamela (T)
By Appointment 905-852-6440

THORNBURY

Norman, Mary Ellen (T)
69 Bay St E 519-599-2695

THORNHILL

Cole, Jodi (T)
8 Tamarack Dr 905-731-4713

Hallman, Grant (T)
51 King's College Rd 905-886-3320

TORONTO

Baker, Ellen (T)
79 Shallmar Blvd 416-782-3558

Dalglish, Shirley (T)
43 Pitcairn Cr 416-751-2072

Hawk, Crystal (T)
145 Strathearn Rd 416-656-0991

Homer, Merlin (T)
11 Havelock St 416-536-4206

Johnson, Sandra (T)
60 Kingswood Rd 416-699-4856

Langley, Marguerite (T)
337 Leslie St 416-466-4008

Mayer, Susan (T)
59 Balsam Ave, #18 416-694-2359

Rossiter-Thornton, Maria (T)
By Appointment 416-926-8944

Rykov, Mary (T)
By Appointment 416-538-2271

UXBRIDGE

Forsythe, Donnalee (T)
By Appointment 905-852-7642

VICKER'S HEIGHTS

Langer, Sue (T)
By Appointment 807-939-2984

WATERLOO

Buchanan, Carolyn (T)
526 Thorndale Dr 519-886-4574

Frid, Susan (T)
313 Glenridge Dr 519-885-3764

WINDSOR

Del Bianco, Lee Ann (T)
240 Prado Pl 519-974-6122

✦ Québec Therapeutic Touch Practitioners

NOTE: Check the credentials of your practitioner (see above, "Questions to Ask"). This publication cannot and does not certify or represent the qualifications of practitioners, or the quality of care available from them.

LAVAL

Giasson, Marie (T)
733 rue Luc 514-689-3112

✦ Saskatchewan Therapeutic Touch Practitioners

NOTE: Check the credentials of your practitioner (see above, "Questions to Ask"). This publication cannot and does not certify or represent the qualifications of practitioners, or the quality of care available from them.

PRINCE ALBERT

Pillipow, Della
By Appointment 306-764-7853

SASKATOON

Ljunggren, Laurel (T)
151 Skeena Cr 306-242-0536

Trager

Trager® is a form of bodywork developed by U.S. physician Milton Trager to teach individuals to move their bodies with greater ease. The approach combines light rhythmic movements and exercises to facilitate relaxation and increase physical mobility. Trager does not involve tissue manipulation or any heavy pressure. During a session, the practitioner moves the client's trunk and limbs gently and rhythmically to allow the client to experience effortless and graceful movement. The practitioner is taught to work in a relaxed, meditative state of consciousness. A session typically lasts 1 to 1 and 1/2 hours. No oils or lotions are used. After the session, the client is instructed in the use of a system of simple free-flowing movement sequences to practise at home. This system, called Mentastics®, or mental gymnastics, is meant to help clients recreate the sensory feelings produced during the session with the practitioner.

BENEFITS OF TRAGER

The Trager Approach is considered a learning experience for those wishing to move their bodies more freely and lightly. The approach attracts athletes, as well as people suffering from neuromuscular disorders such as polio, muscular dystrophy and multiple sclerosis.

The Trager Institute notes that the approach does not involve the diagnosis or treatment of disease, nor is it a substitute for medical treatment when such attention is required or desired. The Institute states: "Whenever there is a suspicion of physical or mental disorder, we recommend a physician be consulted before the Trager Approach is initiated."

QUESTIONS TO ASK

✦ Is your practitioner certified? Confirm by contacting the Trager Institute (see below "Institute").

NOTE: Such certification means that the practitioner has met the standards set by the Institute, but this does not constitute a licence, such as that required by health practitioners regulated under provincial law.

✦ How much experience does your practitioner have? Does your practitioner specialize in a particular area? Can your practitioner provide professional references?

✦ What is your practitioner's background, and does it include training in other forms of health care?

✦ How many sessions are recommended, and how much will each cost?

NOTE: The Trager Institute states that sessions with certified practitioners generally range from $35 to $75 US. Fees should be confirmed with individual practitioners.

GOVERNMENT REGULATION

There is no government regulation of Trager practitioners in Canada, meaning that there is no legislation establishing regulatory bodies to register and discipline qualified practitioners. However, the Institute listed below has set standards for certification, and has registered the name "Trager" and "Mentastics" as service marks.

INSTITUTE

The Trager® Institute
21 Locust Ave
Mill Valley, California 94941
Tel: 415-388-2688
Fax: 415-388-2710
Internet: tragerd@aol.com

This is the Institute founded by Milton Trager. Contact the Institute for referrals to certified practitioners near you, or for information on training and certification (also see below, "Trager Education").

TRAGER EDUCATION

For those interested in pursuing a career in Trager, the Trager Institute offers training in Canada when there is sufficient demand for the program.

Prior to applying for the beginner training, which is the first step toward certification, applicants must have received a minimum of two sessions from a certified Trager Practitioner, or they must have received one session and attended either a workshop or 6 hours of classes. The practitioner giving the session or the workshop leader must recommend that the applicant be accepted, and the application must include a deposit of $150 US.

The Trager Institute's professional certification program takes a minimum of six months to complete. It consists of six days of beginner training and five days of intermediate training, with periods of fieldwork and evaluations. This is followed by a six-day anatomy and physiology training session. The fieldwork consists of giving and documenting at least 60 Trager sessions without charge and receiving at least 20 sessions. In 1996, the total approximate program cost to meet minimum requirements was $2,515 US for 269 hours.

Once certified, the Trager practitioner is required to take at least one 3-day practitioner training session a year for the first three years. Starting with the fourth year, one training every three years is required. The Institute oversees the quality of Trager work, and reserves the right to grant or revoke the use of its internationally registered service marks.

Trager in Your Province

Each province is listed alphabetically below, with the following information:

Provincial Associations
✦ addresses and telephone numbers of the provincial associations in Ontario and Nova Scotia

Trager Practitioners
✦ names, addresses and telephone numbers of Trager practitioners, listed alphabetically by city

NOTE: The names in this list were provided by the Trager Institute. Confirm the certification of your practitioner or obtain the names of newly certified practitioners in your area by contacting the Trager Institute. (see above, "Institute").

Alberta Trager Practitioners

NOTE: Check the credentials of your practitioner (see above, "Questions to Ask"). This publication cannot and does not certify or represent the qualifications of practitioners, or the quality of care available from them.

BRETON

Polischuk, Kathy
PO Box 667 403-696-2348

CALGARY

Beckett, Kim
1444 Remington Rd NE 403-230-3423

EDMONTON

Aiudi, Gerry
9912 86th Ave 403-439-6705

Aris, Linda
9648 80th Ave 403-433-4758

Cole, Nancy
15707, 106th St 403-456-2789

Reid, Robert
11224-23B Ave NW 403-438-4130

EDSON

Bowman-Ruck, Patricia
PO Box 8010 403-723-3399

SHERWOOD PARK

Hoffmeyer, Chery Ann
473 Viscount Cr 403-467-2179

✦ British Columbia Trager Practitioners

NOTE: Check the credentials of your practitioner (see above, "Questions to Ask"). This publication cannot and does not certify or represent the qualifications of practitioners, or the quality of care available from them.

SALMON ARM

Lazzarotto, Joanna
1540-60th St SE 614-832-8407

VANCOUVER

Benedict, Leslie
102-2252 W 5th Ave 604-733-4607

Madrone, Michael
102-2252 W 5th Ave 604-736-2700

Vindberg, Inge
1701 Wallace St 604-222-4017

VICTORIA

Dodwell, Elizabeth
3759 Waring Place 604-472-1657

WINLAW

Avis, Larry
PO Box 76 604-226-7849

Nova Scotia

Nova Scotia Association

Massage Therapist and Bodyworkers' Alliance of the Maritimes
2424 Herenow St
Halifax B6T 3E5
Tel: 902-422-2222
Contact: Joseph V. Bloggs

This alliance includes practitioners from the following therapies: Feldenkrais, Jin Shin Jyutsu, Massage Therapy, Reflexology, Shiatsu and Trager.

✦ Nova Scotia Trager Practitioners

NOTE: Check the credentials of your practitioner (see above, "Questions to Ask"). This publication cannot and does not certify or represent the qualifications of practitioners, or the quality of care available from them.

HALIFAX

Starr, Joseph
13 Pleasant St 902-835-1912

Ontario

Ontario Association

The Trager® Practitioners of South Central Ontario
48 Glen Echo Rd
Toronto, Ontario M4N 3E3
Tel: 416-322-3962

Leave your name and address on the association's recording service to receive information on Trager and a list of the Toronto area certified practitioners belonging to the association. Indicate if you are interested in training, which is offered through the Trager association in Toronto by the U.S. Trager Institute.

✦ Ontario Trager Practitioners

NOTE: Check the credentials of your practitioner (see above, "Questions to Ask"). This publication cannot and does not certify or represent the qualifications of practitioners, or the quality of care available from them.

BRAMPTON

Cain, Mary
44 Mary St 905-452-7239

ELMWOOD

Thomas, Frank
RR 3 519-894-1176

Van Manen, Cecilia
RR 3 519-369-2141

KANATA

Cheeseman, Audrey / Rick
65 Bernier Terrace 613-591-5230

KINGSTON

Hardcastle, Anne
487 Bagot St 613-531-0566

Kaufman, Malka
110 Montreal St 613-542-8166

Perry, Barb
12 Raglan Rd 613-546-0360

Van Luven, Polly
36 York St 613-542-5426

LONDON

Ferguson, Debbie
1105 Richmond St, #201 . . .519-645-8810

Gorodzinsky, Adela
10 Thirlmere Rd 519-642-1966

Harris, John
1069 Lombardo Ave 519-432-7314

Kreowska, Helena
66 Guildwood Walk 519-474-1028

Long, Janet
16 Mohegan Cr 519-659-7054

McGrail, Jaime
401-140 Oxford E 519-438-2753

Peirce-Totten, Beverley
43 Glenview Cr 519-432-1274

Sellery, Helene
18 Hunt Club Dr 519-471-1711

Stevens, Vicky
1619 Alderbrook Rd 519-657-9986

Swan, Bonnie
591 Talbot St, #11 519-434-1332

Thomas, Anjali
426 Ridout St S 519-680-1719

Van Daele, Joris
745 Rowntree Ave 519-433-2929

NEWMARKET

Raouf, Wafik
526 Sandford St 905-853-2743

OTTAWA

Henri, Christine
100 Marlowe Cr 613-230-0914

Yanover, Sandra
206 Carleton Ave 613-729-2294

PARRY SOUND

Stewart, Elizabeth
By Appointment 705-389-3738

PETERBOROUGH

Wakeford, Dorothy (Thea)
1228 Bathurst St 705-743-4909

PETROLIA

Bradley, Janet / Richard
4438 Discovery Lane 519-882-2475

SARNIA

Tait, Janet
#1-263 Vidal St N 519-337-7841

STIRLING

Svoboda, Patricia
131 Church, PO Box 212 . . .613-395-2533

STRATHROY

Johnson-Lingard, Alice
291 Adelaide St 519-245-2627

TAMWORTH

Harrison, Jeannie
PO Box 143 613-379-5595

TORONTO

Abraham, Elizabeth
By Appointment
(Bloor/St George) 416-599-9202

Booth, Yvonne
By Appointment
(Greenwood/Queen) 416-778-5098

Goldstein, Bayla
By Appointment
(Eglinton/Avenue Rd) 416-489-8090

Levinson, Charlotte
By Appointment
(Yonge/St Clair) 416-967-3489

Markham, Margaret
45 Elvina Gardens 416-481-2713

Overy, Paul
By Appointment
(Dupont/Spadina) 416-966-1582

Pinto, David
By Appointment
(Yonge/Lawrence) 416-488-2024

Shaddick, Anne
198 Rusholme Rd 416-532-5079

Warren, Hal
By Apppointment
(Shepperd/Bayview) 416-255-1747

Westney, Jean
By Appointment
(Chester/Danforth) 416-465-7594

WOODSTOCK

McBurney, Lois Ann
RR 3 519-539-5914

 # Québec Trager Practitioners

NOTE: Check the credentials of your practitioner (see above, "Questions to Ask"). This publication cannot and does not certify or represent the qualifications of practitioners, or the quality of care available from them.

CAP-ROUGE

Jean, Pauline
4066 Pierre Gallet 418-652-9202

CHELSEA

Martin, Ginette
PO Box 708 819-827-1734

GATINEAU

Lariviere-Clairoux, Jacqueline
591 Hurd 819-643-1047

HULL

Perras, Ghislaine
18 St-Louis, #6 819-771-0177

ILE-BIZARD

Brisebois, Micheline
10 Roussin 514-620-4888

JOLIETTE

Michaud, Gisele
1346 Lepine 514-756-0950

LA PRAIRIE

Tougas, Yvette
175 Houde 514-659-5036

MONTREAL

Beaule, Manon
1713 rue Galt 514-766-3331

Bourbeau, Claire
8820 Berri St 514-381-0297

de Montigny, Louise
4139 Drolet 514-843-8382

Fournier, Yvette
10729 av Vianney 514-387-4864

Gervais, Nathalie
6612 Marquette 514-270-3660

Lafontaine, Denis
4139, rue Drolet 514-843-8382

Lorrain, Raymonde
6913 Wiseman, #4 514-272-4586

Paquin, Elise
1232, est Mont-Royal 514-525-4126

Tsampalieros, Peter
7768 Bodinier 514-493-4796

Turcotte, Isabelle
6571 av Christophe-Colomb . .514-495-2403

NEUVILLE

Daigle, Amritra
175 Du Poitou 418-876-3568

NOTRE-DAME-DES-PRAIRIES

Beauparlant, Guy
118 1er av 514-752-1086

Durand, Monique
14 av des Sapins 514-759-2227

OUTREMONT

Voisard, Louise
853 Stuart 514-277-9786

QUEBEC

Garneau, Carole
1057 Les Erables, #5 418-529-9779

Lord, Sarto
425 Burton 418-649-9310

RIMOUSKI

Cote, Aline
466 Ernest Lapointe, #4 . . .418-724-2506

RIMOUSKI-EST

Chouinard-Gagnon, Diane
9, 8e Av 418-723-1586

ST-LAMBERT

Payette, Yolande
415, Brixtons, #3 514-465-2153

ST-LAMBERT-DE-LEVIS

Leblanc, Suzanne
507, ch des Eperviers 418-889-8220

ST-MARC-DES-CARRIERES

Vohl, Helene
568 av Principale 418-268-5206

TROIS-RIVIERES

Trudeau, Diane
857 St-Pierre 819-375-3237

VAL-DAVID

3050 Doncaster 819-322-2889

✦ Yukon Trager Practitioners

NOTE: Check the credentials of your practitioner (see above, "Questions to Ask"). This publication cannot and does not certify or represent the qualifications of practitioners, or the quality of care available from them.

WHITEHORSE

Buchan, Cheryl
9 Cedar Cr 403-667-6951

✦ Government Regulation at a Glance

This table shows where alternative health care practitioners are regulated across Canada. Regulation means that there is legislation (a provincial statute) establishing a governing body to register or license practitioners who meet professional standards. The Northwest Territories are not listed as none of the practitioners is regulated in that jurisdiction.

NOTE: The federal government regulates products such as homeopathic remedies, herbal remedies, and food products through the *Food and Drugs Act* and regulations.

	Alberta	British Columbia	Manitoba	New Brunswick	Newfoundland	Nova Scotia	Ontario	Prince Edward Island	Québec	Saskatchewan	Yukon
ACUPUNCTURISTS	*Health Disciplines Act & Regulation,* p. 14 (Governing Body, p. 15)	*Health Professions Act & Acupuncturists Regulation,* p. 17 (Governing Body, p. 17)					See note 1 below		*Professional Code, An Act Respecting Acupuncture & Regulations* p. 27 (Governing Body, p. 28)		See note 2 below
CHIROPRACTORS	*Chiropractic Profession Act & Regulations,* p. 58 (Governing Body, p. 58)	*Chiropractors Act,* p. 64 (Governing Body, p. 64)	*The Chiropractic Act & Regulation,* p. 71 (Governing Body, p. 71)	*The Chiropractic Act,* p. 74 (Governing Body, p. 74)	*Chiropractors Act & Regulation,* p. 75 (Governing Body, p. 75)	*Chiropractic Act & Regulations,* p. 76 (Governing Body, p. 77)	*Regulated Health Professions Act, 1991 Chiropractic Act, 1991 & Regulations,* p. 78 (Governing Body, p. 78)	*Chiropractic Act,* p. 93 (Governing Body, p. 93)	*Professional Code & Chiropractic Act,* p. 94 (Governing Body, p. 94)	*The Chiropractic Act, 1994,* p. 103 (Governing Body, p. 103)	*Chiropractors Act,* p. 105 (Licensing Body, p. 105)
MASSAGE THERAPISTS		*Health Professions Act Massage Therapists Regulation,* p. 133 (Governing Body, p. 134)					*Regulated Health Professions Act, 1991 Massage Therapy Act, 1991 & Regulations,* p. 138 (Governing Body, p. 138)				

1. Acupuncturists are not regulated in Ontario, meaning that there is no governing body to ensure that practitioners meet certain standards. However, acupuncture is permitted under the *Regulated Health Act Professions, 1991* (see p. 23).
2. Acupuncturists are not regulated in the Yukon, but guidelines exist (see p. 36).

	Alberta	British Columbia	Manitoba	New Brunswick	Newfoundland	Nova Scotia	Ontario	Prince Edward Island	Québec	Saskatchewan	Yukon
MIDWIVES	Health Disciplines Act & Midwifery Regulation, p. 164 (Registry of Midwives, p. 165)	Health Professions Act & Midwives Regulation, p. 167 (Governing Body, p. 167)			(See note 3 below)		Regulated Health Professions Act, 1991 Midwifery Act, 1991 & Regulations, p. 170 (Governing Body, p. 170)		(See note 5 below)		
NATUROPATHIC PHYSICIANS		Naturopaths Act, p. 180 (Governing Body, p. 181)	The Naturopathic Act, p. 183 (Governing Body, p. 183)				Drugless Practitioners Act & Regulation 278, p. 185 (Governing Body p. 185)			The Naturopathy Act, p. 190 (Governing Body p. 191)	
OSTEOPATHIC PHYSICIANS	Medical Profession Act, p. 204 (Governing Body, p. 204)	Medical Practitioners Act, p. 205 (Governing Body, p. 205)		Medical Act, p. 201 (See note 6 below)			(See note 4 below)		Medical Act, p. 201 (See note 6 below)	The Osteopathic Practice Act, p. 201 (See note 6 below)	

3. Midwives are not regulated. Newfoundland's *Act Respecting the Practice of Midwifery, 1920* is not in use (see p. 169).
4. Osteopathic physicians in Ontario have been left in a legal grey zone. The section of *Regulated Health Professions Act, 1991* that would regulate the profession has not been proclaimed (see pp. 201, 206).
5. Midwives are not regulated in Québec, but midwifery services are available through a government pilot project (see p. 172).
6. No osteopathic physicians are currently practising.

✦ Other Organizations and Clinics

Chelation Therapy

Chelation therapy is a method of using the drug, EDTA, for removing toxins and metabolic wastes from the bloodstream, as a means of preventing heart attacks and as an alternative to heart bypass surgery. Its proponents say that the therapy is painless and effective, and that many patients have successfully used it as a cost efficient alternative to heart bypass surgery. However, the Heart & Stroke Foundation of Canada states that, because "there is no scientific evidence that chelation therapy is beneficial, and there is evidence that it may cause harmful side effects, the Heart and Stroke Foundation of Canada does not recommend this therapy." The Foundation refers to evidence that chelation therapy may cause significant kidney damage. Supporters of the therapy say that this risk is minimal if chelation is performed properly by a physician experienced in the practice. Supporters suggest patients choose a doctor with years of experience in the therapy, who is aware of the protocol of the American Board of Chelation Therapy or the American College of Advancement in Medicine (ACAM). Chelation is performed by about 24 medical doctors in Canada. Contact the associations listed below for information from supporters of chelation therapy, and for referrals.

EDTA Chelation Association of Alberta
349-9768 - 170th St
Edmonton, Alberta T5L 4Y5
Tel: 403-430-8093 or 403-449-4610

The association is in the process of changing its name and broadening its mandate to include advocacy for choice in health care

Chelation Association of Manitoba
307-234 Ronald St
Winnipeg, Manitoba R3J 3J4

Chelation Association of Nova Scotia
Margaree Valley, General Delivery
Nova Scotia B0E 2C0
Tel: 902-248-2009

The EDTA Chelation Association of B.C.
6262A Fraser St
Vancouver, B.C. V5W 3A1
Tel: 604-327-3889

The EDTA Chelation Association of Saskatchewan
1850 Victoria Ave E
Regina, Saskatchewan S4N 7K3
Tel: 306-789-0111

Consumer & Advocacy Organizations

Canadian Natural Health Association
439 Wellington St W, Ste 5
Toronto, Ontario M5V 1E7
Tel: 416-977-2642; 24-hour-info-line: 416-322-4225
Fax: 416-977-1536

This non-profit association, founded in 1960 as the Canadian Natural Hygiene Society, provides information on healthful living through public lectures and social events. It also provides referrals to alternative or complementary health care practitioners. The association has about 1,200 members across Canada and North America. An annual membership fee is $35, and includes discounts on alternative health care services and products, as well as a subscription to a bi-monthly newsletter, *Living Naturally*.

Citizens for Choice in Health Care - B.C.
PO Box 30136
Saanich Centre Postal Outlet
Victoria, BC V8X 5E1
Tel: 604-655-4868
Fax: 604-655-4879
email: cchc@get-info.net
http: //get-info.net/vnet/cchc.htm
Contact: Judy Kubrak

This group is organizing a petition campaign for changes to B.C.'s *Medical Practitioners Act* similar to those passed in Alberta (Bill 209, the *Medical Profession Amendment Act*) to protect physicians who practise alternative medicine from charges of unprofessional conduct.

Citizens for Choice in Health Care - Manitoba
PO Box 51046, RPO Tyndall
Winnipeg, Manitoba R2R 2S6
Tel: 204-633-7724 or 204-489-0207

This new organization is campaigning for freedom of choice in health care.

Citizens for Choice in Health Care - Nova Scotia
c/o Shirley Atwood
RR #2
S. Ohio, Nova Scotia B0W 3E0
Tel: 902-761-2884

This group actively lobbies for the rights of individuals to choose the most appropriate form of health care. It is seeking changes in legislation, including protection in law for physicians who practise complementary medicine. The group publishes the quarterly *Self-Health* newsletter, edited by Yarmouth herbalist Mark Taylor.

Citizens for Choice in Health Care - Ontario
128 Queen St S, Box 42264
Mississauga, Ontario L5M 4Z0
Tel: 905-826-9384
Fax: 1-905-895-5621

This group is seeking legislation to protect consumer access to complementary or alternative health care when conventional medicine does not meet health needs. It is in favour of the Ontario legislature passing a law similar to that passed in Alberta (Bill 209, the *Medical Profession Amendment Act*), which protects medical doctors who practise alternative or complementary medicine.

Consumer Health Organization of Canada
250 Sheppard Ave E, Ste 205
Willowdale, Ontario M2N 6M9
Contact: Libby Gardon
Tel: 416-222-6517
Fax: 416-225-1243

This non-profit organization was founded in 1975 to promote a "wholistic" approach to health, which encompasses a person's physical, mental, emotional, spiritual, social and economic well-being. The group provides information on alternative therapies, organizes conferences and conventions, and distributes a monthly newsletter, as well as the *Health Freedom News* magazine. You may also contact the organization for information about dentists practising alternative dentistry in your area. The organization encourages groups to form local chapters. It has about 1,500 members across Canada.

Health Action Network Society (HANS)
202-5262 Rumble St
Burnaby, B.C. V5J 2B6
Tel: 604-435-0512
Fax: 604-435-1561

This is an independent, charitable organization dedicated to disseminating information on alternative health care to members across Canada.

My Health/My Rights
2309 Horton Street
Ottawa, Ontario K1G 3E7
Tel: 819-684-3060
Fax: 819-684-6351

This organization lobbies government for legislative changes to protect consumers' freedom of choice in health care products. It is working toward the establishment of a Canadian dietary supplement act similar to existing legislation in the United States.

National Coalition for Health Freedom
3 Fermanagh Ave
Toronto, Ontario M6R 1M1
Tel: 416-537-7437
Contact: Miriam Hawkins

This coalition focuses on public education and advocacy. It has collected thousands of names on a petition to object to proposed changes to the federal *Food and Drugs Act* and other legislation that may restrict the availability of herbal remedies.

Dentistry - Alternative

Some dentists are taking an alternative approach to dentistry that takes into account the health of the entire body. Many of these dentists, for example, use dental fillings that contain no mercury. Health Canada acknowledged in a release dated August 21, 1996 that many Canadians are concerned over the risk of mercury toxicity from silver amalgam fillings, partly as a result of recent proposals by some countries to severely restrict its use, or to ban it. Health Canada states that there is insufficient evidence to justify a ban, but recommends that non-mercury fillings be considered for children, pregnanat women, patients with impaired kidney function, and individuals with allergic hypersensitivity to mercury. The Canadian Dental Association (CDA) and Health Canada suggests that patients discuss their circumstances with their dentist to choose the most appropriate fillings.

If you are seeking a dentist practising alternative dentistry, you may wish to contact the Consumer Health Organization of Canada, listed above. As well, the Foundation for Toxic-Free Dentistry will provide the names of dentists practising mercury-free dentistry in Canada. However, as with any health care practitioner, you are urged to check the qualifications of your dentist, and to ensure that he or she is registered with the governing body in your province.

Foundation for Toxic-Free Dentistry
PO Box 608010
Orlando, Florida 32860-8010
USA

Write to the Foundation for names of dentists practising mercury-free dentistry in Canada. The Foundation cautions that it has no personal knowledge of any dentist's qualifications.

Environmental Health Organizations & Clinics

Environmental medicine practitioners assess the effects of foods, chemicals, water, and indoor and outdoor air quality on health. Environmental medicine treatment often includes environmental controls, dietary changes, and nutritional supplements. Contact the organizations and clinics listed below for more information.

Allergy and Environmental Health Association - Toronto Branch
PO Box 2311, Station C
Downsview, Ontario M3N 2V8

Canadian Society of Environmental Medicine
6901 Second Line West
RR 6, Mississauga, Ontario L5M 2B5

This society is seeking to establish standards of practice for physicians practising environmental medicine.

Environmental Health Clinic
Women's College Hospital
76 Grenville St
Toronto, Ontario M5S 1B2
Tel: 416-351-3764

This clinic opened in March 1996, and is staffed by a health care team of physicians and nurses with a special interest in the care and investigation of persons with Environmental Sensitivity Disorders. A written referral from your primary care physician is necessary. If you have difficulty finding a primary care physician, contact the clinic for help.

Environmental Health Clinics - Nova Scotia
Victoria General Hospital
519 Bethune Building
Halifax, Nova Scotia B3H 2Y9
902-860-0057
Second Location:
Dalhousie University
PO Box 2130
Fall River, Nova Scotia B2T 1K6
Tel: 902-860-0551
Fax: 902-861-1914

These clinics serve patients suffering from illnesses related to the environment. A new specially designed research and treatment clinic is under construction at Dalhousie University that will replace both existing locations. These clinics treat only residents of Nova Scotia, as the services are provincially funded.

Environmental Health Group
275 King St E, Ste 223
Toronto, Ontario M5A 1K2

This group publishes a newsletter, and is involved in seeking public support for Dr. Krop, an Ontario physician who practises environmental medicine. The College of Physicians and Surgeons of Ontario has brought charges of professional misconduct against Dr. Krop.

Environmental Hypersensitivity Association of Ontario
Box 27545 Yorkdale Postal Outlet
Toronto, Ontario M6A 3B8
Tel: 905-826-9384

This non-profit association provides information and networking for those with environmental hypersensitivities, or multiple chemical sensitivities. The association publishes a quarterly newsletter, *Positive Reaction*.

Nova Scotia Allergy & Environmental Health Association
PO Box 31323
Halifax, Nova Scotia B3K 5Y5
Tel: 902-866-1002

This is a non-profit organization for those with concerns about the relationship between the environment and health.

Medical Doctors - Complementary Medical Associations

Listed below in alphabetical order by city across Canada are medical doctors with a special interest in complementary medicine. Inclusion of the names of physicians is not intended to imply an endorsement on their part of any material contained in this publication. A new national complementary medical association is currently being formed. For information, contact Dr. W. LaValley, President, Chester, Nova Scotia or Dr. Wiancko, Vice-President, Edmonton, Alberta (see their telephone numbers and addresses below). Doctors in B.C. have recently formed an Association of Complementary Physicians. For information, call Dr. R. Rogers in Vancouver (listed below).

Physicians with a special interest in complementary medicine are invited to add their names to this list in future editions at no charge. Contact the publisher at the address noted in the "Important Notice to Our Readers" at the front of this book.

Hajela, Raju, MD (ayurveda)
PO Box 1873
Amherstview, Ontario K7L 5J7
Tel: 613-634-4105

Soriano, Jeanette, MD (chelation)
Clinic #5, 1330-15 Ave SW
Calgary, Alberta T3C 3N6
Tel: 403-229-0040

LaValley, William, MD
Box 2020, 227 Central St.
Chester, Nova Scotia B0J 1J0
Tel: 902-275-4555

Aung, Stephen, MD (acupuncture)
9904-106th St
Edmonton, Alberta T5K 1C4
Tel: 403-426-2760

Okolo, Godwin, MD (chelation)
9535-135 Ave
Edmonton, Alberta T5E 1N8
Tel: 403-476-3344

Sereda, Andrew, MD (chelation)
10413-51 Ave
Edmonton, Alberta T6H 0K4
Tel: 403-435-1991

Trethart, Tris, MD
8621-104 St
Edmonton, Alberta T6E 4G6
Tel: 403-433-7401

Wiancko, K.B., MD
The Phoenix Chelation Clinic
205-9509-156th St
Edmonton, Alberta T58 4J5
Tel: 403-483-3900

Cooper, A., MD (chelation)
Box 283
Fairview, Alberta T0H 1L0
Tel: 403-539-5348

Fargas-Babjak, A., MD (acupuncture)
McMaster University Medical Centre
Hamilton, Ontario L8N 3Z5
Tel: 905-521-2100

Bouchard, Jean-Guy, MD
Case Postale 387
Kedgwick, New Brunswick E0K 1C0
Tel: 506-284-2032

Leyton, Edward, MD
420 McDonnell St
Kingston, Ontario K7L 4E4
Tel: 613-542-5663

Krop, Joseph J.
6901 Second Line West
Mississaugua, Ontario L5M 2B5
Tel: 905-564-0122

Gall, Jim, MD (ayurveda)
7 Frances St
Mitchell, Ontario N0K 1N0
Tel: 519-348-8402

Molot, John, MD
309-185 Somerset W
Ottawa, Ontario K2P 0J2
Tel: 613-235-6734

Jaconello, Paul, MD
Jaconello Health Centre
751 Pape Ave., Ste 201
Toronto, Ontario M4K 3T1
Tel: 416-463-2911

Rapson, Linda (acupuncture)
Rapson Pain Clinic
600 Sherbourne St, Ste 207
Toronto, Ontario M4X 1W4
Tel: 416-968-1366

Rona, Zoltan, MD (nutritional medicine; herbal medicine)
1466 Bathurst St., Ste 305
Toronto, Ontario M5R 3J3
Tel: 416-534-8880
Fax: 416-534-6723
http://www.wwonline.com/rona/zpr.htm

Nolan, Kevin, MD
205-2786 W 16th Ave
Vancouver, B.C. V6K 4M1
Tel: 604-736-8338

Rogers, Roger, MD
206-2786 W 16th Ave
Vancouver, B.C. V6K 4M1
Tel: 604-734-7125

Houston, James, MD (ayurveda)
203-1711 Cook St
Victoria, B.C. V8T 3P2
Tel: 604-382-3456

Lam, Christopher, MD (medical acupuncture)
135-1555 McKenzie Ave
Victoria, B.C. V8N 1A4
Tel: 250-472-3338
Fax: 250-472-3290

Malthouse, Stephen, MD (homeopathy)
141 Turner St S
Victoria, B.C. V5V 2J9
Tel: 604-383-0454

Nunn, Peter, MD
3775 Cadboro Bay
Victoria, B.C. V8P 5E2
Tel: 604-384-4313

Vancouver Hospital Research & Treatment Centre

Tzu Chi Institute for Complementary and Alternative Medicine
c/o Vancouver Hospital & Health Sciences Centre
855 W 12th Ave
Vancouver, B.C. V5Z 1M9
Tel: 604-875-4111
Fax: 604-875-4035

This Institute, scheduled to open in the fall of 1996, will be a research, education, information centre and treatment facility for alternative and complementary medicine. The Institute is a partnership between Vancouver Hospital and the Tzu Chi Buddhist Compassion Relief Foundation, an international organization founded in 1966. The Foundation is contributing $6 million over five years. Dr. Wah Jun Tze, MD, will serve as president of the Institute. Dr. Tze is a professor in the Department of Pediatrics at the University of British Columbia.

Alternative Health Care: The Canadian Directory

Do you know someone who could benefit from *Alternative Health Care: The Canadian Directory*? It's a great gift, offering vital information on the Canadian alternative health care scene. The directory is designed to help consumers check the qualifications of practitioners, and includes thousands of listings of practitioners and associations in 20 major alternative health care fields. The directory is also a valuable resource for students seeking career information on educational institutes, and for professionals interested in networking.

Please send me _____ copies of Alternative Health Care: The Canadian Directory at $19.95, plus $3.50 for GST and shipping for each copy. I have enclosed a cheque or money order made payable to Noble Ages Publishing Ltd. in the amount of $ (Cdn). _____

Full Name: _____

Street Address: _____ Apt#: _____

City: _____ Province:_____

Postal Code: _____

Telephone #:_____

Please send this completed form with your cheque or money order to:

Noble Ages Publishing Ltd.
1543 Bayview Ave, Unit 530
Toronto, Ontario
Canada M4G 3B5

Please allow three to five weeks for delivery.
For an order of ten or more books, we offer a discount. Please write to us for details.